Understanding and Managing People at Work

An Introduction to Organisational Behaviour and Human Resource Management

We work with leading authors to develop the strongest
educational materials bringing cutting-edge thinking and best
learning practice to a global market.

Under a range of well-known imprints, including Financial
Times/Prentice Hall, Addison Wesley and Longman, we craft
high quality print and electronic publications which help
readers to understand and apply their content, whether
studying or at work.

Pearson Custom Publishing enables our customers to access a
wide and expanding range of market-leading content from
world-renowned authors and develop their own tailor-made
book. You choose the content that meets your needs and
Pearson Custom Publishing produces a high-quality printed
book.

To find out more about custom publishing, visit
www.pearsoncustom.co.uk

Understanding and Managing People at Work

An Introduction to Organisational Behaviour and Human Resource Management

Compiled from:

Organising and Managing Work:
Organisational, Managerial and Strategic Behaviour
in Theory and Practice
by Tony J. Watson

Management and Organisational Behaviour 6th Edition
by Laurie J. Mullins

Human Resource Management 5th Edition
by Derek Torrington, Laura Hall and Stephen Taylor

Contemporary Human Resource Management:
Text and Cases
by Tom Redman and Adrian Wilkinson

People Resourcing: HRM in Practice 2nd Edition
by Stephen Pilbeam and Marjorie Corbridge

PEARSON
Custom
Publishing

Pearson Education Limited
Edinburgh Gate
Harlow
Essex CM20 2JE

And associated companies throughout the world

Visit us on the World Wide Web at:
www.pearsoned.co.uk

First published 2004

This Custom Book Edition © 2004 Published by Pearson Education Limited

Taken from:

Organising and Managing Work:
Organisational, Managerial and Strategic Behaviour in Theory and Practice
by Tony J. Watson
ISBN 0 273 63005 9
Copyright © Pearson Education Limited 2002

Management and Organisational Behaviour 6th Edition
by Laurie J. Mullins
ISBN 0 273 65147 1
Copyright © Laurie J. Mullins 1985, 1989, 1993, 1996, 1999, 2002
Chapter 9 Copyright © Linda Hicks 1993, 1996, 1999, 2002
Chapter 10 Copyright © Linda Hicks 1999, 2002
Chapter 17 Copyright © David Preece 1999, 2002

Human Resource Management 5th Edition
by Derek Torrington, Laura Hall and Stephen Taylor
ISBN 0 273 64639 7
Copyright © Prentice Hall Europe 1987, 1991, 1995, 1998
Copyright © Pearson Education Limited 2002

Contemporary Human Resource Management: Text and Cases
by Tom Redman and Adrian Wilkinson
ISBN 0 201 59613 X
Copyright © Tom Redman, Adrian Wilkinson
and Pearson Education Limited 2001

People Resourcing: HRM in Practice 2nd Edition
by Stephen Pilbeam and Marjorie Corbridge
ISBN 0 273 65580 9
Copyright © M. Corbridge and S. Pilbeam 1998
Copyright © S. Pilbeam and M. Corbridge 2002

ISBN 1 84479 014 2

Printed and bound by Antony Rowe

Contents

Introduction

Welcome to *Perspectives on People at Work.* We are delighted to introduce you to the module.

Workplaces today are as complex as they are dynamic. So understanding people at work has never been more important. This module is designed to help you understand people at work from a range of perspectives: the individual, groups, employers/organisations, trade unions and societal. In taking these *Perspectives on People at Work,* the module spans the subject areas of organisational behaviour and human resource management. Both subject areas are essential elements in the knowledge and skill sets of managers in all types of organisations. Whether you are studying for a general business degree or specialising in a functional degree, such as risk management, or a contextual degree, like hospitality management, the module has relevance to your prospective working life and career development.

To support *your* learning in and from the *Perspectives on People at Work* module, we have commissioned Pearson Education to produce this customised textbook. An added benefit is that it will be a resource for you in the future if you continue to study HRM & D modules such as *Learning at Work* (Level 2), *Human Resource Processes and Practices* (Level 3), *Work Relations in a Changing Society* (Level 3), *Resourcing and Reward* (Level 3), *Human Resource Strategies* (Level 4), *People and Change Management* (Level 4) and *International and Comparative Employment Relations* (Level 4).

We very much hope you will enjoy and succeed in this module.

The Division of Human Resource Management and Development
Caledonian Business School

Acknowledgement

The Division of Human Resource Management and Development would like to thank Pearson Education for donating book prizes for student performance on this module.

CHAPTER 1

Organising and managing work: study and practice

Objectives   Having read this chapter and completed its associated activites, readers should be able to:

- Appreciate the value of a focus on the management of work as a starting point for thinking about work organisations and their management.

- Recognise the advantage of a *management of work* focus over both a 'people management' or a 'structures and procedures' way of talking and thinking about management and work organisation.

- See how the style of *Work Organisation and Management Studies* adopted in the present book builds upon and goes beyond the traditional business school subject of *Organisational Behaviour*.

- Note the contribution which various social science disciplines make to Work Organisation and Management Studies.

- Recognise a continuity between social-science thinking and a critical form of common sense.

- Understand the importance and value of developing Work Organisation and Management Studies as a critical study.

- Discriminate between perspectives, theories and research findings in terms of how useful (or 'true') they are when it comes to relating theory and practice.

1

Managing work

To create the goods, services and quality of life people look for in the modern world some rather complex patterns of cooperative human behaviour have to be orchestrated or 'managed'. The academic study of the organising and managing of work involves taking a step back from our day-to-day involvement in these patterns of behaviour and trying systematically to understand how they come about. Such a study also has the potential to help us achieve a better quality of productive cooperation than we typically manage in contemporary work organisations.

We study work organisation and its management because we are interested in the various individual human motivations, interests, values and meanings which play a part in bringing about the patterns of behaviour we see in workplaces ranging from shops, offices and factories to schools, hospitals and universities. But the study also has to concern itself with the ways in which these patterns of human activity and meaning themselves come to be an influence on what occurs in the world. Once human beings create groups, societies, cultures, classes, governing institutions and organisations, what they do in their lives becomes significantly shaped by them. One of the things which makes the study of the organising and managing of work so challenging is that it has to understand how individual choices and initiatives, on the one hand, and already existing and *emerging* structures and patterns on the other hand, both play their parts in social life. And these two influences – of human initiative and structural context – do not work separately. They are inextricably intertwined.

To understand these complexities is not simply an exciting intellectual challenge. It is not just something one might do as an alternative to getting practically involved in work organisation and management. The complexities are ones with which we have to come to terms if we are to be more than direction-less and muddled practitioners in the world of work organisation. In this first chapter of *Organising and Managing Work* we will be looking carefully at ways in which we can take up these challenges. A further key aim of the chapter, however, is to establish, from the start, a critical frame of mind and to challenge some of the over simplifications which we tend to make in our ordinary or 'everyday' thinking about work and its management. Let us consider one of these tendencies now – and look at how we can usefully challenge such apparently reasonable ways of looking at work management.

Activity 1.1

Look carefully at what Mark Merryton has to say about the most difficult aspects of his job, in Cases and Conversations 1.1. Ask yourself what you think his notion of being a manager is – beyond the obvious role of applying the market research skills that he has 'at his fingertips' and being 'creative' about customers.

2

Understanding and Managing People at Work

4

Managing people and herding cats

What would you say is the most difficult aspect of your job as marketing director for the company, then?

Oh, without doubt it's the people side, if you know what I mean.

Trying to work out what the customers are going to want next – that sort of thing?

Good heavens, no. That's the straightforward side. I think I know what I'm doing on that one. I've got the market research techniques at my fingertips and I'm sharp enough to keep on top of things customer-wise and product-wise. But since my last promotion I find that managing the department has almost wholly become a matter of managing the people in it.

So the problem is . . . ?

It's the people management thing. It's handling the people who work for me. They are a constant headache. I've tried to read the books and I've been on people management courses. I didn't miss one of the OB classes on my MBA course. But I still despair at the difficulty I have with managing the people in my function: sorting out who is going to do what, getting them to do the things I want, getting them to finish things on time, even getting them to be where I want them. And that's before I get into all the recruiting, training, appraising and all that stuff.

Why is this do you think?

Perhaps it's because they are marketing people. We often say that managing marketing people is like herding cats. Can you imagine trying to herd cats? It's a powerful image, isn't it?

Indeed it is. And I've heard it numerous times. Only the other day I heard it applied to university lecturers by a faculty dean. And I've heard it applied to engineers, shop workers, hospital staff, secretaries . . .

Yes, I'm sure. And just look at my secretary. I'm meant to be her boss. She can be quite good but I often feel that she is managing me more than I am managing her.

So it's not just marketing people then?

Understanding and Managing People at Work

No, I suppose it's not.

And what about your fellow managers, how do you get on with them?

Some good and some bad. But there are some really difficult people in the business I have to deal with. And this includes several people that I don't myself manage – you know, people in other functions. They can make life difficult. I think it's down to their not being properly managed. The managing director himself is not very good at managing his top team. And my finance director friend is utterly hopeless at managing the people who work for him.

This conversation will surprise no one who has been involved in managerial work. As you read this you may be puzzled at why your attention is being drawn to language that is utterly normal in many workplaces – to wording that you hear every day and take for granted. But, as has already been implied, a key purpose of this book is to encourage you to stop short from time to time and think about just what is going on beneath the 'taken-for-granted' surface of everyday organisational life. To pause and reflect critically from time to time on what one is saying, how one is framing reality, and what is happening as a consequence of this, is a valuable habit for any organisational practitioner. Mark Merryton appears to subscribe to a popular notion of what 'management' is about. Let us examine his arguments carefully.

One of the key themes to be developed and applied throughout the book is the idea that the way we talk and think about the world is closely implicated in how we act in the world. We will be considering the idea that the language and concepts we apply to the world around us can be seen as a *framing of reality* that, to a certain extent, brings about that reality. This is similar to an insight which people often draw upon when explaining how a particular 'mindset' shaped the way someone behaved in a certain situation. Without going into a detailed explanation of this idea at this stage, we can helpfully apply the 'framing' idea to the above conversation. Mark Merryton is in effect telling the interviewer about how difficult people are to relate to or 'deal with' at work. This is a fairly straightforward point to make. We all know that our fellow human beings are quirky, unpredictable and not readily amenable to doing what anyone else tells them to do. But Mark is more specific in the way he frames this general argument. He adopts as a key framing idea the notion of *managing people*. He sees part of his job as one of 'managing the people in my department' and he mentions the courses on 'people management' that he has attended. He tells us that he believes he should be 'managing' his secretary and that the managing director should be 'managing' the directors in his 'top team'. Not only does he refer to the finance director as being bad at 'managing the people' in the finance function, he speaks of the people in that department *working for* the finance director as opposed to working for the organisation which is their actual employer.

The idea of people management and the concept of employees working for a particular 'boss', as opposed to working for the employing organisation is probably a widely accepted notion in modern culture. One of the leading British

Understanding and Managing People at Work

6

management magazines, for example, is called *People Management*. But is this title one that can easily be accepted as a realistic and helpful way of thinking about or 'framing' managerial work? Let us think hard about this often taken-for-granted notion.

Each reader will have answered the first question according to his or her own personal feelings about work and authority. It is not the place of an academic text to lay down or prescribe one particular moral position rather than another. However, it is one of the key arguments of this book that moral issues and choices run through every aspect of organisational and managerial work. It is therefore important to note that Mark Merryton was taking a particular ethical position about work and employment generally and his managerial role specifically when he spoke in the way he did. He may or may not have fully thought out his personal ethical view of the relationship between managers and the people working in the area for which they have responsibility. But such a position is implicit in the words he uses. To help us reflect on what this might be, let us set out a contrary view to the one Mark expresses.

It can be argued that a manager does not have the moral right to direct, manage or 'boss' any individual in their area of responsibility *as a whole person* or in *the totality of their workplace behaviour*. Instead, they have a limited authority to give instructions to employees in tightly prescribed and limited areas of activity. The moral basis of that authority lies in its purpose – to fulfil those work tasks in which the employees have contractually agreed to participate. Employees in modern democratic societies do not sign a contract of employment on the assumption that managers appointed by their employer will have the right to manage them as a person. The manager is appointed to manage the work tasks – and as part of this has limited rights to instruct people. But these rights only exist as means to specific organisational ends and not because of any 'right to command' over the person as a whole. It is thus morally improper to encourage a view of managerial and organisational work based on a principle of 'managing people'.

Is this ethical view simply an alternative to the one implicit in Mark Merryton's words, one that we can adopt or reject solely in terms of our personal ethical position? It is not. It is much more than this. While accepting that it has

5

Understanding and Managing People at Work

been expressed in words that might not be fully acceptable to everyone, this ethical position is one implicit in the cultures of modern democratic societies. Moving out of an ethical mode of discussion, then, back into a social-science analytical mode, one can argue that there is a conflict between the 'managing people' view of managerial authority that some managers take and the values or the morality of the wider society of which they are a part. And this suggests that to adopt a focus on people management when one is looking at the 'human aspects' of work organisation is unrealistic – as well as morally dubious.

To recognise a clash between a 'people management' ethic and the ethical assumptions of the wider society, then, is already to accept one significant way in which such a framing of managerial activity is unrealistic. And further grounds readily suggest themselves if we go on to think generally about the people who are allegedly to 'be managed'. While there may be people in the labour markets of modern societies who are happy to subjugate themselves to the wills of 'bosses' at work, such individuals are surely very rare. We will be looking more closely at the complex issue of just what a human being is in Chapter 4. For present purposes, however, it is sufficient to note that one of the key ways that members of the human species differ from other animals is that they are active agents in the shaping of their lives. However meek or submissive particular individuals might be, each human being is nevertheless always the owner and shaper of their own identity, to some degree. As far as the historical record can tell us, no human group in the history of the human species has yet found another group over which it could exert complete control. And this applies even in the extreme conditions of slave societies or extermination camps, where human beings have still demonstrated what looks like an inherent tendency of the species – to resist being managed. We might say that it is not just that cats are inherently 'un-herdable' but that human beings are inherently 'unmanageable'. Which, of course, is not to say that work tasks, involving human beings, cannot be managed.

What is to be concluded from all this reflection? It is to suggest that the widespread tendency to frame – to think about and understand – managerial and organisational work in terms of the management of people is unwise and misleading. It is unrealistic and impracticable, therefore, to focus on the 'management of people' when studying organisational and managerial behaviour. The focus, instead, needs to be on the management of work. The starting point for any consideration of organisational and managerial behaviour is more usefully taken to be the work tasks that are to be carried out. It is these which are organised and 'managed', not the people who carry out the tasks. To understand the behaviours that arise when work tasks are to be done, it is necessary to recognise that work tasks are always *to an extent managed by everyone involved in those tasks*. Work management is not simply what people formally designated as 'managers' do. The nature of the work done by people holding managerial posts will be a concern of Chapter 3. However, there is another common and over simplified idea about management that we need to address at this stage of our thinking – one that perhaps needs even more critical attention than the 'people management' conception that we have looked at.

Understanding and Managing People at Work

Activity 1.3

The manager we are about to meet in Cases and Conversations 1.2, 'The madness of Hands-off Harry', has a conception of his job which seems to have little of the 'people management' con- cerns which were expressed by Mark Merryton. Compare Harry's way of 'framing' managerial work with that of Mark. How would you characterise his view of how work should be managed?

The madness of Hands-off Harry

Cases and Conversations 1.2

You've heard what the team leaders call me, haven't you?

What is that, Harry?

Come on, I'm sure they've told you that they call me Hands-off Harry.

Well yes, now that you mention it. Do you mind?

Not at all. Well, I did at first because I thought they weren't taking me seriously. I thought they might be laughing at the way I talk about running the department in a 'hands-off' manner. I think they understand my philosophy though, really.

And that philosophy is?

That the manager's job is to lay down all the procedures, the schedules, the targets and the monitoring systems and to keep an eye on all the reports that come up from the shopfloor and all that. You ensure that everyone's been trained in the training school in exactly how to do the job and that they value the job they've got in such a modern facility. They know they will get the pay they want if they meet the targets. Nothing should go wrong if I, as the manager, have got all these systems running properly.

7

Understanding and Managing People at Work

And have you?

More or less – I recognise that things have to be tweaked as you go along. But the team leaders can do that. You just don't need the manager to go out there and, well, sort of get in the way.

But surely people don't simply go along with all the rules and procedures coming from an invisible figure in this office at the end of this long corridor.

Oh, so you've heard the 'invisible man' quip from Joe, have you? He's never been happy with the team leader role but, as I have said to him, modern factories should not need overseer types watching over them. But I do respect what you are saying. And you are right, that all my brilliant paperwork procedures are not enough. There is also the set of values that everyone has absorbed – they've all been through the total quality scheme. All those cultural things are in place. Maybe it doesn't all work like clockwork. But it does work, as long as I do my bit here with my charts and things – and do all the business at the management meetings – I can be Hands-off Harry in the department.

What it appeared that Harry Carse did not know was that the machine operators in his department treated their invisible manager with contempt. They would joke that he stayed in his office (which was indeed at the end of a long corridor off the shopfloor) because he was a madman. They did, however, more or less meet all the targets that Harry set – albeit working in a generally sullen manner. So perhaps it did not 'matter' that Harry remained remote. The three team leaders in the department argued, however, that if Harry 'managed in a more hands-on manner' and 'got to know' the machinists, that there was a strong possibility that much higher output and quality targets could be set.

It is impossible for us to know whether these team leaders are right about whether the department might increase its output if Harry managed it in a different way. However, his case is useful because he talks about managing in a way which helpfully contrasts with Mark Merryton's. He frames managerial work very much as a matter of setting up formal arrangements, procedures, structures and so on. These are not entirely mechanistic notions. His concept of formal arrangements includes cultural matters like 'values' and the idea of people being influenced by principles such as those of total quality management. This means that we cannot argue that he necessarily rejects the idea of 'managing people' – he might argue that he does this but does it remotely – as his nickname of Hands-off Harry implies. However, in the terms preferred here, we can say that his conception of managing work is one that prioritises the structural arrangements side of things rather than the human initiatives side of things.

As we implied earlier we must not go too far in separating out the two aspects of work organisation and management – the direct human initiative aspect, and the structural arrangements aspect. The two are intertwined. Harry Carse may appear simply to run his department through systems, rules and values rather than through direct 'human' interventions. But those procedures and principles were devised by human initiatives taken by Harry and by other managers. Rules, structures and procedures – as much as they sometimes seem to take on a life of their own – do not exist separately from either the human initiatives that are behind them or from the human interpretations of those whose actions at first sight are shaped by them. And it is important to remember that part of the justification for focusing on the 'management of work' in a broad sense was to recognise that the formal managerial work

Understanding and Managing People at Work
10

done by 'the manager' – whether it takes the form of setting up procedures or directly attempting to influence people – is only one part of the overall way in which the organisation and management of work is achieved. This is something which appears to be recognised in what Sadie Rait has to say about the case of hospital Ward 17.

Activity 1.4

Read what Sadie Rait has to say in Cases and Conversations 1.3 about her job as a hospital ward manager. Ask yourself:

- What is Sadie's idea of being a manager?
- How does her concept of managerial work differ from that of Mark Merryton or Harry

Managing Ward 17
Cases and Conversations 1.3

Although I am called the Ward Manager, the job is not very different from when my predecessor did it. She was called the Ward Sister though.

Does the new title mean you are a 'manager' in any sense that she was not, would you say?

No, I wouldn't – except strangely that she was much more a manager type than I am. Strange perhaps, but she managed things much more than I do. It was much more, 'You do this, you do that'. She was the one you might want to call a manager rather than me.

In what sense are you less a manager than she was, then?

Thinking about it, I wouldn't actually. We are both managers, but I see management in a different way. You would see Mary Ann obviously 'managing', if you know what I mean. But I work differently. The way I see it is that there is a great deal on the ward that has to be managed – and that I cannot take all of that on. So every nurse, porter, ancillary and clerk is managing the place.

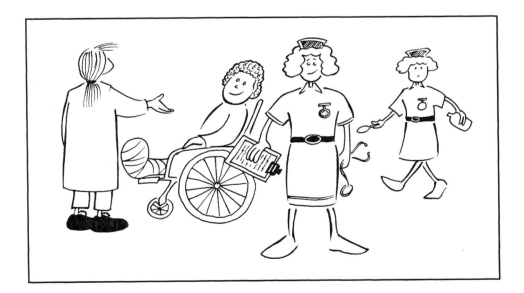

9

Understanding and Managing People at Work

11

And the doctors?

Whoops, sorry. I suppose them too. Well what I was going to say – and perhaps it's why I forgot the doctors – but perhaps not [laughing], was that the nurses as a team manage this ward. I don't manage the nurses. I wouldn't even try. What I say to them is that I am just the first among equals. I say we manage it together and that I just have watch how it all adds up – and, of course, be accountable to Hospital Trust management.

So you don't find yourself giving people instructions or even disciplining nurses who fall short?

Oh yes I do. I draw up work rosters for example and I've had to do formal disciplines on several occasions. I frequently have to chase people up. But, you see, that is all within the whole set of rules that the Trust sets. The hospital is managed by people but also through rules, systems, procedures, protocols, professional knowledge we all bring with us – all that.

By The Trust, you mean . . .?

Well, the management board have done a lot to change how the hospital's work is managed – through the mission and key values statements they've developed and the new culture that everybody has had a say in.

From this account of her approach to hospital ward management we can identify something of Sadie Rait's style of relating to the people who work on the ward. But what is most interesting to us at this stage is not so much how she manages relationships in her job. It is that she appears to 'frame' the managerial task in the hospital as one that many people contribute to, in addition to the not insignificant directing role undertaken by herself as the official 'manager' – including 'chasing people up'. And without taking on a Hands-off Harry type of faith in the power of structures and procedures, she clearly frames the management of work as something going well beyond managerial *behaviours* as such. Work is managed through structures, procedures and meanings (the hospital is 'managed through rules, systems, procedures, protocols, professional knowledge . . . mission and key value statements . . . the new culture') as well as by specific actions of human actors – managerial and non-managerial. The work of Ward 17 is managed by the day-to-day actions and initiatives of Sadie and her staff but it is also in part managed by the structures and procedures of the hospital. Not only this but the factors which might impede or undermine the effective managing of the ward include both these types of factor. Members of staff choosing for personal reasons not to work cooperatively with others would be an example of the human choice and initiative type of factor. And a set of financial circumstances which meant that the ward was always short of the necessary number of nurses would be an example of the more structural type of factor.

We have then identified three ways of talking about management or 'framing' it, as we see in Figure 1.1. The preference here is clearly for Sadie Rait's notion of what management is – her way of 'framing' her managerial role. It is preferred because it is a much more realistic way of talking about the activity, not least in its recognition that the management of work is only partly done by 'managers'. It also implies that what occurs in workplaces is not just an outcome – or sum – of direct human actions. It also involves structures or arrangements which stand in some sense outside specific actions as such. This

Understanding and Managing People at Work

12

Managing people

Managing structures and procedures

Managing work through relationships and procedures

FIGURE 1.1 Three ways of talking about organising and managing

latter facet of work organisation is given primacy of attention by Harry Carse while, it would seem, Mark Merryton lays emphasis on the direct action side of things. The relationship between these two facets of work management and organisations – the direct action and the structural – is an important matter for understanding the organising and managing of work. However, the importance of looking at how relatively direct and individualistic actions like 'leading' or 'motivating' are related to more structural phenomena like bureaucratic structures or cultural patterns is rarely acknowledged in the 'subject' of Organisational Behaviour (OB) as it is taught in business and management courses. It is in giving a fuller consideration to such matters that we go beyond orthodox organisational behaviour thinking.

Building on the Organisational Behaviour tradition

The latter part of the twentieth century has seen enormous growth in institutions engaged in educating people for careers in business and management. Increasingly these activities have been concentrated in the departments of management or the 'business schools' of universities and colleges. A fairly standard type of curriculum has developed in the business schools of the USA and other English speaking countries that have followed the American lead in this style of education. This has involved dividing up the knowledge and teaching relevant to the directing of complex work enterprises into different 'subjects'. Some of that packaging follows an immediately obvious logic. Knowledge related to dealing with customers, for example, has been gathered into the subject area of *marketing* while issues of finance and accounting control form another subject and techniques of planning and coordinating production and service activities a further one of *operations management*. Other parts of the curriculum deal with areas which similarly reflect the way businesses tend to be functionally divided – purchasing, personnel or human resource management for example. But how much attention is given to the issue of how the enterprise as a whole is to be managed?

11

Understanding and Managing People at Work

13

Activity 1.5

Look at the basic curriculum of a business school you know about or a general management programme within the school and ask yourself (or even a tutor!):

■ Is there a section of the programme or a 'subject' called 'management' available for study?

■ If there is not, where in the curriculum are all the specialist or functional elements brought together into an overview of how the enterprise or *the organisation as whole* is managed or directed?

Quite often there is no such subject as 'management', even within those university or college departments which name themselves 'school of management' or where there are individuals with the title, 'Professor of Management'. This might seem strange. This does not mean, however, that there is no attempt to provide an integrative subject. And the area where one will typically be told the curriculum provides the kind of integrative study we have in mind is in a subject called 'Strategy' or, sometimes, 'Strategic Management'. This gets students to study the way organisations – and predominately commercial business organisations – behave or 'perform' as entities in their economic and societal environment. It is here one might therefore expect to see the social sciences used to analyse how such complex patterns of human activity and structural dynamics come about and are *managed*. But generally, and with the exception of the use of a limited amount of material from economics, there is only a marginal use of theoretical or research insights in strategy teaching into how human behaviours and meanings are shaped into the complex patterns of activity which enable them to relate to their customers, clients, markets or environments. A large part of the time spent studying 'strategy' involves students reading, talking and writing about descriptive case studies of relationships between corporations and their efforts to compete with other corporations. Strangely perhaps, issues of human patterning of behaviour and cooperation and the task of demonstrating the potential of social science analysis are handed over to another subject: organisational behaviour or 'OB' as generations of business students have come to know it.

One might expect a subject with the title of 'Organisational Behaviour' to study the managing and organising of cooperative activities in the context of how the organisation relates to all those external bodies upon which its future is dependent. OB only does part of this job however. It intends to look 'inward', leaving much of the 'outward' focus of the study of organisational performance to the subject of strategy. Its emphasis tends to be on the 'means' through which organising is brought about, with little reference to the 'ends' that it serves. And in doing this, it seriously risks its analytical integrity since these 'ends' – in practice if not in the classroom – fundamentally influence the organisational 'means'. Issues of profitability, market share or government policy, for example, lie in the realm of the strategists while the OB people look at the

Understanding and Managing People at Work
14

individual human behaviours, the group formations, the job designs and the organisation structures *in their own terms*, isolating them from their vital strategic context. But even attention to these internal processes is limited in the typical OB curriculum – restricted in large part to the more formal or official aspects of management. It gives only limited attention to the ambiguities, confusions and conflicts which are as much a part of work management activities as all the motivational and leadership efforts, the job and organisation designing, the culture and organisational change initiatives which form the bulk of the curriculum. Even at the level of formal managerial processes, a proportion of these is left to another area of the curriculum. Where are the processes of selecting, recruiting and dispensing with organisational members or the relationships with organised labour dealt with? By and large, these are left to the subject of 'human resource management'.

Organisational Behaviour is a thriving area of teaching and study activity and, indeed, of book publishing. It is developing in sophistication. There are attempts to develop the curriculum in places by bringing into the story the politics of managerial relationships or devoting chapters to conflict more generally. And some attention is given to contextual influences on certain aspects of organisational choice in the guise of 'contingencies' (covered below in Chapter 8). But the tendency for books and courses to run through unlinked accounts of matters of individual behaviour in one section, group behaviours in another and structural and change issues in others is dominant. At a theoretical level, this means that a fault line runs beneath the whole OB landscape. There is a deep hole beneath the surface created by the neglect of what is perhaps the most fundamental challenge which social science has grappled with over the years. This is the issue, referred to earlier, of understanding how the aspects of human choice and initiative in social life, on the one hand, relate to structural and cultural aspects on the other. Leadership, for example, has to be seen as related to wider cultural patterns and not just to the characteristics and actions of particular individuals. What happens at the level of group behaviour must be seen in the context of the overall structural pattern of the organisation, if not of the whole society, in which the group is located. We need to have some understanding of these matters if, for example, we are going to recognise where as human actors in organisational contexts we have choices and where we are structurally constrained. It has to be understood if we want to recognise where we can influence matters by direct actions and where we have to influence them by devising structures and procedures and encouraging shared understandings. These are surely vital things for us to understand if we are interested in how work is managed or might be managed differently. To do this we have both to build upon and 'go beyond' OB.

One of the first things that has to be done to go beyond OB is to abandon the popular device used in many texts or presenting a whole series of different theoretical approaches (the classical approach, the human relations approach, the systems approach and so on) and, after some limited indication of the strengths and weaknesses of each of these, leaving the reader to make up his or her own mind. This might sound fair-minded and liberal, but it is an opting out of the

Understanding and Managing People at Work
15

social science writer's responsibility to provide the reader or student with some general criteria by which they might judge what is a useful or a misleading model, a good theory or a bad theory. The failure to develop an integrative theoretical framework makes it very difficult for any connections to be drawn between, say, the 'motivations' of individual organisational members and the prevailing culture of the organisation or, say, between the principles of job design adopted in an organisation and the values and beliefs of the senior managers. OB books fail badly in this respect by, for example, discussing individual 'motivation' in one section of the book and 'organisational culture' in another, without seriously examining how these relate to each other.

Organising and Managing Work, while trying to overcome this problem, is not turning its back on the organisational behaviour tradition. While dealing with many of the issues traditionally tackled in OB and looking at much of the work normally covered in the subject, it attempts both to overcome some of the existing weaknesses and to build upon the firmer base thus laid down. It will do this by:

● organising and integrating the various areas and levels of analysis within a single unifying theoretical perspective – one which has at its heart a recognition of the constant interplay between individual initiatives and structural circumstances;

● explaining and then applying a commitment to a particular style of critical management studies;

● providing the reader with a criterion for judging how some perspectives and theories are 'better' than others;

● connecting the concerns normally associated with the 'subject' of Organisational Behaviour with some of those generally tackled in the separate subjects of Strategic Management and Human Resource Management, as represented in Figure 1.2.

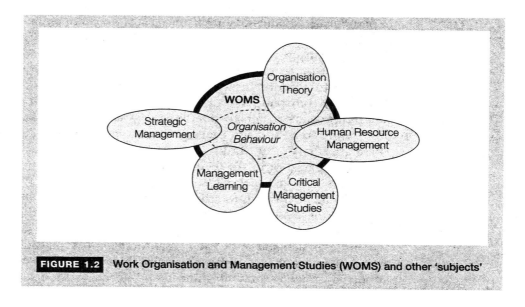

FIGURE 1.2 Work Organisation and Management Studies (WOMS) and other 'subjects'

14

Understanding and Managing People at Work

16

Figure 1.2 includes three further 'subjects' alongside the fairly standard business school subjects of Strategic Management and HRM. These are Organisation Theory/Organisation Studies, Management Learning, and Critical Management Studies. The first of these looks at many of the same issues as OB but does it with a primarily academic focus – concerning itself first and foremost with scholarly understanding rather than with the implications of such understandings for practice. The materials to be found in journals such as *Organisation Studies* or many of the books listed in Reading Guide 1 are nevertheless invaluable for the more practice-oriented *Work Organisation and Management Studies*. This is especially so because the subject has been much more attentive to the question of relating individual level activities to bigger 'structural' patterns. It has also been more concerned with taking a critical stance than OB, something which has also informed the emergence of Critical Management Studies (Reading Guide 13) – in effect an application of the more critical ideas of Organisation Theory directly to issues of managerial activity. Management Learning is another emergent field of specialist study with its own academic journal, *Management Learning*, and a concern to bring together theoretical developments in the understanding of human learning processes with issues of both educating and 'developing' managerial practitioners (see Reading Guide 11). *Organising and Managing Work* is informed by this development in its recognition of the central importance of issues of learning to all aspects of the organisation and management of work.

All of these developments in the study of the organisation and management of work in modern societies can be understood, perhaps ironically, as aspects of work organisation themselves. This is to say that these different 'subjects' have not 'come about' straightforwardly to reflect different aspects of human activity which exist 'out there' in the world of work and its management. There is no chunk of work activity going on in the world which is 'strategic management' and which can be separated from another chunk of reality which is 'management learning'. In part, the academic subjects reflect a division of labour among managerial practitioners. Some managers, for instance, are paid to operate more 'strategically' than others are. However, the pattern of academic subjects we tend to see in business schools are probably more an outcome of the ways in which teachers, researchers, writers and publishers have chosen to carve up their territories than a straightforward reflection of the 'realities' of organisational practice. This carving up involves all the career building interests, interpersonal conflicts, market pressures, confusions and ambiguities which characterise all work organisations and the people who work in them. We cannot expect those working in academic organisations to be immune to any of this.

These comments inevitably apply to the writing of *Organising and Managing Work* itself, of course. We will shortly consider the justification that can be offered for such a departure and what it involves. First, however, it is time to clarify formally where we have got to with our notion of Work Organisation and Management Studies.

Understanding and Managing People at Work

Work Organisation and Management Studies

Work Organisation and Management Studies, as a subject which both incorporates and goes beyond existing ways of looking at work organisation and management, can be formally defined.

Work Organisation and Management Studies   *Concept*

The analysis of the human aspects of work organisation and its management which draws on the social sciences to develop insights, theories and research findings with a view to informing the choices, decisions and actions of people who have a practical involvement with organisations.

We need to note several things about this concept of Work Organisation and Management Studies.

- What is studied is the 'human aspects of work organisation and its management'. This language is not meant to imply that attention is only paid to 'human aspects' at the level of the human individual. The focus is on work *organisation* and management, which means that patterns of human activity and thinking going beyond the level of the individual are as important as thinking about the human individual. As has already been explained, the concern is with the interplay of factors at the level of human initiative and choice and factors at the level of social, political and economic context, or structure.

- The subject *informs* the choices, decisions and actions of people involved in practices in organisations. There is no question of developing an academic subject which can tell people what they should do in the complex area of work management. The area is far too complex for there to be any basic rules or even sets of guidelines about 'how to do management'. Not only this but, given the moral factors which must come into every human situation where power and authority are involved, it would be quite wrong for a textbook to attempt to provide guidance in this way. What it can do, however, is to provide insights into the range of factors and issues which are relevant to any particular choice (of, say, job design or planning an organisational change programme). The actual choice or decision that is made is a matter for those involved in the particular organisational situation – with all the political, moral and specific local considerations coming into play alongside the insights which can be derived from academic study of the managing and organisation of work.

- Reference is made to 'organisational practitioners' rather than 'managers' as the potential 'users' of the subject. This is done in recognition of the fact that people other than those formally designated as managers are closely involved in the way work tasks are managed. If there are ideas in Work Organisation and Management Studies which would be helpful to a manager in an organisational situation wishing to have his or her understanding enhanced by academic thinking then surely those ideas are going to be equally relevant to

16

anyone else concerned with that situation. This would be the case regardless of the person's formal authority in the organisation or, for that matter, their degree of commitment to official organisational policies.

- The social sciences are 'drawn on' by Work Organisation and Management Studies. The subject is not seen as a social science in its own right. A variety of social science disciplines can be turned to provide research findings, theoretical resources or insights that might be helpful in understanding organisational issues. This does not mean, however, that we simply turn in a random or *promiscuous* manner to the vast bank of social science materials every time they wish to analyse a particular situation. Each individual is likely to build up their set of preferred social science concepts as their learning proceeds. They then turn to the books and journals for further insight, as the need arises, and incorporate the new learning into their ever-developing personal framework of understanding.

Organisational behaviour has tended to draw primarily on the social science disciplines of sociology, psychology and social psychology. Work Organisation and Management Studies, as conceived of here, follows this and similarly supports the contributions of the main disciplines with insights from economics, political science and anthropology. The key concerns of each of these are outlined in Table 1.1.

All of these disciplines can be seen as providing resources which can be drawn upon when wishing to understand the organising and managing of work in general or any particular organisational situation or problem in particular. Many of the human issues that can arise in the organisational context do not fall into any one obvious disciplinary territory and many of them might use ideas from more than one discipline. Bearing this in mind, see how you get on with Activity 1.6.

TABLE 1.1 Focal and supporting social science disciplines for Work Organisation and Management Studies	
Focal social science disciplines	**Supporting social science disciplines**
Psychology focuses on individual characteristics and behaviour and on such matters as learning, motivation and individual ('personality') differences	**Economics** supports the sociological concern with the economic context and, also, the psychological concern with decision-making (through its attention to 'rational' decisions made by economic actors)
Social psychology focuses on group characteristics and behaviour, on roles, attitudes, values, communication, decision-making and so on	**Political science** supports the sociological concern with power and conflict and the social–psychological concern with decision-making (through its concern with the state and other institutions handling matters of power and difference of interest)
Sociology focuses on structures, arrangements or patterns and how these both influence and are influenced by individual and group behaviour. It is concerned with the structure of the social and economic system as well as with the organisational structure and issues of technology, conflict, power and culture	**Anthropology** supports the social-psychological concern with norms, values and attitudes and the sociological concern with cultures (both organisational and societal) with insights taken from the study of non-industrial or 'less advanced' societies about such things as rites, rituals, customs and symbols

Understanding and Managing People at Work

Activity 1.6

Read the story about Rose Markey taking over as the manager of The Canalazzo restaurant (Cases and Conversations 1.4), thinking about the issues which Rose is going to have to deal with to satisfy her employers. Following the characterisations of the six social sciences set out in Table 1.1, note the factors or issues that you think might be identified as, respectively, psychological, social–psychological, sociological, economic, political and anthropological.

Rose takes over The Canalazzo

Cases and Conversations 1.4

Rose Markey had been working for a national chain of restaurants for only a couple of years when they asked her to take over a restaurant which they had recently acquired. They had bought The Canalazzo restaurant from the Italian family which had established the business some twenty or so years previously. The family had decided to return to Italy and to warmer summers. The company had originally put in one of their older managers to run the newly acquired restaurant. However, they were very disappointed with what was being achieved. Their director of finance argued that the turnover of the business simply did not justify the investment that had been made in the purchase of the business and in the redecoration of the premises. When they challenged the first manager they had put in, he talked of his resentment at being asked to move to a new part of the country at the age of 55. He persuaded the company to give him an early retirement settlement so that he could return to the part of the country he had lived in for most of his life. They were pleased to do this because it was clear, the human resources manager told Rose, that this man's poor motivation and attitude to customers was increasingly being reflected in the way the staff of the restaurant went about their work.

When Rose arrived at the restaurant she soon learned that her predecessor had clashed on several occasions with local police officers about serving late drinks. This was likely to get back to the magistrates and the

Understanding and Managing People at Work

20

restaurant would be in danger of failing to have its drinks licence renewed when it was next due for review. The manager's defence was that he was simply following local customs in the town whereby customers would have a night out that would bring them into the restaurant only after spending most of the evening in a public house. It was not his fault, he said, that the police officers and the magistrates all lived outside of the town and didn't know about this.

When it came to the problems with the staff, Rose found that her predecessor had set up a strongly hierarchical set of relationships among them. This seemed to be accepted, albeit grudgingly, by the people who worked in the kitchen. But it was resented by the waiting staff who were largely part-time workers studying at the local university. Not only this, but the group of waiters – who all knew each other from the university – and the kitchen workers, all of whom had left school at 16, tended only to speak to members of their own group. The chef, who was a middle-aged Italian, regularly fell out with the headwaiter – a woman a dozen years younger than him. Their respective ideas about how young female staff should be treated were poles apart and these differences led to frequent arguments. Overall there was very little coordination between the kitchen and the restaurant. All of this, Rose decided, seriously affected the quality of service the customers received.

Perhaps psychological factors are the first to suggest themselves here, ranging from issues of differences of personality and temperament among different employees of the restaurant to ones of motivation and personal commitment. The varying sets of attitude in the restaurant are clearly a matter of social–psychological interest as are the problematic patterns of communication and the way the two groups of kitchen and restaurant staff have developed to create a division among the junior staff as a whole. All of this feeds into the sociological factors and issues. There is a power structure within the restaurant and this has elements which relate to sociological variables such as age, gender and ethnicity – all of which relate to the way society as a whole is organised. But there are also sociological factors about the way the restaurant fits into the local economy and community, both as a provider of services and a source of labour. Here there is a clear overlap with economic issues of market organisation and this, in turn, relates to the most obvious economic issues of financial performance, turnover (and, by implication, profitability) and investment. Issues of a formal political nature (i.e. relating to issues of the role of the state) are present with regard to the police and magistrates, and there are obvious informal 'political' issues running right through the whole set of relationships in the restaurant. This is in addition to whatever the 'informal' politics of the relationship between local police officers and restaurant managers might be. Anthropological issues of informal customs might also be involved but, more obviously, the anthropological notions of custom and ritual are highly relevant to the patterns of restaurant use which influence the pattern of work which has to be managed by Rose Markey and the rest of the staff of The Canalazzo.

19

Understanding and Managing People at Work

Common sense and social science

One of the first thoughts occurring to anyone trying to make sense of the problems of The Canalazzo restaurant might be that 'common sense' is likely to be just as helpful as ideas from psychology, sociology or anthropology. It has, nevertheless, been a tradition of social science teachers to contrast social science thinking with common-sense thinking and, not surprisingly, to argue that social science analysis is to be preferred to common sense. But an alternative response might be to say, 'It all depends on what you mean by common sense'. This is necessary, in fact, because there are two quite different usages of the term 'common sense' that often get muddled up. It is useful to distinguish between *everyday common sense* and *critical common sense*.

Everyday common sense
Concept

Analysis based on unthought-out, taken-for-granted, immediately 'obvious', everyday assumptions about the world and human activity within it.

Everyday common sense is necessary for 'getting by' in our daily lives. We all make quick assumptions about what is going on around us, drawing on all kinds of stereotypes, half-remembered experiences and simplistic cause–effect connections. This is necessary to cope with our daily lives. We would not cope with life if we stopped, sat back and deeply pondered on every eventuality that faced us between getting up in the morning and going to bed at night. But perhaps we can see why social scientists claim that their more analytical style of thinking has advantages over this. In the work context, for example, individuals frequently offer woefully simplistic generalisations such as 'People only go to work for the money' – typically adding, 'It stands to reason' or, 'It's obvious' or, 'It's common sense isn't it?' This is a good example of everyday common sense, based as it is on easy, unthought-out, taken-for-granted assumptions. Assumptions like these make life simpler – at first sight, anyway. But such assumptions are often dangerous guides to action on matters of any importance or complexity such as designing a pay system or 'reward structure', for example.

We therefore turn to critical common sense as a style of thinking which involves being essentially logical or rational about things in the way which is common to all human beings when they are alertly and critically putting their mind to whatever matter is in hand.

Critical common sense
Concept

Analysis based on the basic logic, rationality, hard-headedness to be found in human beings whenever they step back from the immediate situation and critically put their minds to an issue or problem.

This is the kind of common sense that we can more reliably use as a guide to action when more complex matters of work organisation and management arise. It is an activity of the same order as that in which the scientist engages. Science,

TABLE 1.2 Two types of common sense in practice	
Everyday common sense and pay	**Critical common sense and pay**
If you pay employees in proportion to their output they will produce more than if they get the same wage whatever they turn out	Pay for output might work. But employees might prefer the comfort of a steady work rate and the security of a steady wage. They might resent the pressures of a bonus system on group relations
They will clearly work better under a performance-related pay system	It would be wise to find out what the particular employees' requirements are before deciding for or against a performance-related pay system

in this view, is essentially a formalised version of critical common sense. Scientific thinking – in principle if not always in practice – is the more formal, systematic and painstakingly analytical application of critical common sense.

Critical common sense analysis tends to start from a consideration of the most obvious or likely explanation of what is going on; the everyday common sense explanation in fact. But it then goes on to ask whether things are really as they seem at first. Alternative explanations are considered and attention is paid to available evidence in judging the various rival explanations. We can see the two types of common sense compared in Table 1.2 and the managerial implications of applying each of them, in this case in deciding for or against a performance-related pay system.

The considerations about performance related pay connected in Table 1.2 to a critical common sense way of thinking about work behaviour are indeed similar to ones which have emerged from social science research and theorising about the relationship between pay and behaviour.

 **Link**   See, in particular, the 'expectancy' theory of work motivation explained in Chapter 9, p. 300. Similar arguments to these critical common sense ones were developed in the light of one of the famous Hawthorne experiments – The Bank Wiring Observation Room experiment – by Roethlisberger and Dickson (1939, Reading Guide 1).

The critical study of organising and managing

A critical common sense frame of mind is obviously relevant to any kind of practical human endeavour. But it has particular relevance to academic work – and especially to studies that claim to be scientific. Scientific analysis, as has already been suggested, can be understood as an especially rigorous or systematic application of critical common sense. And this would suggest that we could not do social science at all without being critical in the sense of constantly questioning taken-for-granted ideas and practices. However, there has been a growing trend of questioning the extent to which social-science study of work behaviour and managerial practice has been sufficiently critical.

21

Understanding and Managing People at Work

The crux of the problem that all writers and researchers interested in managerial issues have to face up to is the fact that managerial activities are always and inevitably implicated in issues of power and relative advantage and disadvantage between human groups and human individuals. Everyone engaged in management research and management education is therefore faced with a dilemma. How do they reconcile providing knowledge that might help improve the effectiveness of work activities with the fact that in doing so might help some people ('managers' and the employers of managers, say) more than others ('the managed', for example)? Helping make work organisations more efficient or more effective is not a politically neutral matter.

In a world where valued resources tend to be scarce and there is continuous competition for the goods, services and rewards provided by work organisations, any intervention can involve one in taking sides between the relatively advantaged and the relatively disadvantaged. The social scientist is in danger of becoming a 'servant of power', as an early polemic on such matters put it (Baritz, 1960, p. 39, Reading Guide 13). One way of handling this dilemma is suggested by some members of the emergent 'critical management studies' movement. Their strategy amounts, in effect, to 'going on the attack' against managerial ideologies and activities that are felt by the critical scholar to be 'wrong' or 'harmful'. Critical research and writing would, for example, offer its students 'an appreciation of the pressures that lead managerial work to become so deeply implicated in the unremitting exploitation of nature and human beings, national and international extremes of wealth and poverty, the creation of global pollution, the promotion of "needs" for consumer products etc.' (Alvesson and Willmott, 1996, p. 39, Reading Guide 13). Such a critical management study is committed to exposing the political implications of managerial work with an ambition of helping achieve 'emancipatory transformation' – the transformation of both people and society. And, in the workplace itself, a 'critical' version of the concept of empowerment is called for, 'empowering employees to make more choices and to act more effectively to transform workplace relations' (Thompson and McHugh, 1995, p. 22, Reading Guide 13).

These advocates of critical management studies, critical management education and critical organisation studies want their work to help change the balance of power in the worlds of work and employment. But they are not just critical of the existing patterns of power prevailing in organisations and society at large. They also aim their critical fire at the type of writing and teaching which constitutes the orthodoxy in contemporary business and management schools. And the main thrust of this critique is against the assumption behind much of this orthodoxy that success in managerial and organisational work comes from acquiring, developing and applying *skills* and *techniques* – skills and techniques which are neutral and 'innocent' in a political sense. Issues of power, inequality, conflict (at interpersonal, group and class levels), gender and ethnicity are either ignored or treated as peripheral matters which, from time to time, get in the way of smooth organisational functioning. Sympathy with this latter criticism has been an important inspiration for the writing of the present text and it informs the critique of what is called the *systems-control* orthodoxy and its displacement

22

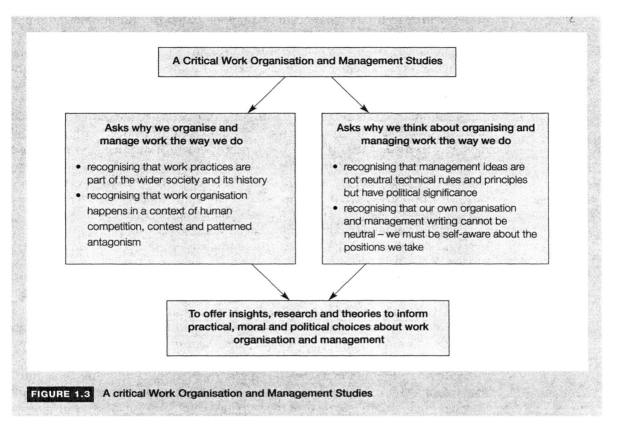

FIGURE 1.3 A critical Work Organisation and Management Studies

by a more realistic and politically sensitive *process-relational* perspective. But the whole text is underpinned by a particular notion of a critical organisation and management study, which is summarised in Figure 1.3. It is a notion that shares much ground with the work being produced under the flag of 'critical management studies' but its overlap is only partial, as the earlier Figure 1.2 suggested.

The conception of a critical organisation and management study adopted in *Organising and Managing Work* differs from that taken by some of the critical thinkers whose ideas were looked at above. This is primarily with regard to the issue of arguing for 'transformation', at both the personal and the social levels. It is felt that the choices that these transformations would entail are a matter for political and moral debate in society generally and for contestation within organisations themselves. They are not transformations which social science can or should push people towards. What the social sciences can do is to illuminate or inform those debates with information and insights derived from both research investigations and theoretical reflections. And if these insights, research contributions and theories are going to have any real potential to *make a difference* to practices in the world outside the classroom and library, there has to be an openness about the fact that all social science analysis is itself value-laden. To contribute to either societal or organisational debates about how work tasks are to be organised and managed as if this were simply a matter of deciding which

Understanding and Managing People at Work
25

power-neutral technique or procedure to adopt would be dishonest at the moral level and misleading at the level of informing practice.

This means that no study of organisations and management can claim to be objective or in some sense 'value-free'. A critical study of organisation and management must keep asking questions of itself – as the words on the right-hand side of Figure 1.3 suggest. This entails recognising that the management and organisational ideas that are dealt with are not matters of technique or neutral principles, devoid of political significance. It also requires a degree of self-awareness in writing and teaching and a commitment to judiciously revealing our own biases and moral inclinations where this is necessary to help the reader or student take one's inevitable partiality into account. This principle was followed early in the present chapter where the notion of 'people management' was *engaged with* as a matter of morality as well as pragmatic realism.

The writing of the early part of this chapter was also relevant to the words on the left-hand side of Figure 1.3. The essence of critique is *questioning* and a critical study has to ask questions about the organisational activities that it is studying as well as constantly questioning what it is producing itself in its 'literature'. We looked critically at the way several practising managers speak about managerial work and raised questions about the practice of speaking of management in terms of 'managing people' or 'managing structures and procedures' rather than 'managing work'. This argument will be built upon as *Organising and Managing Work* develops. And as we ask questions about how and why work organisation practices are as they are we will constantly bear in mind that work organisations are only in an extremely limited way a separate phenomenon from the economy and society of which they are part. They did not historically 'evolve' in the working out of some divine or abstract principle of increasing organisational efficiency. The hierarchy of jobs in today's organisations, for example, is both an outcome of and a contributor to the hierarchy of class and status which has developed in society as individuals and groups have competed with each other for advantage over the years. By the same token, markets do not exist 'out there' as part of the 'economic context' of business organisations. They are *made* by organisational initiatives as much as they are served by organisations. A critical perspective also requires us constantly to observe that differences of interest – and the frequent alignment and re-alignment of interests – are inherent in organisations. They permeate the managerial strata of organisations as well as underlying the basic tensions between employees and employers.

Activity 1.7

Quickly re-read Cases and Conversations 1.4 and how Rose Markey 'took over' at The Canalazzo restaurant. Then read the sequel to that story (Cases and Conversations 1.5), 'Rose and The Canalazzo under threat'. Make a note of all the ways in which an understanding of both parts of The Canalazzo story would require attention to factors to which, it is argued above, a critical study of organisation and management draws attention. The wording on the left-hand side of Figure 1.3 is a starting point for your analysis.

Understanding and Managing People at Work

After six months' managing The Canalazzo restaurant, Rose Markey prepared for her annual performance appraisal at the headquarters of the company which owned the restaurant. She was still finding her job quite a struggle. She had begun to adjust to living in the north of the country, having only ever lived in the south previously. She had established good relationships with the local police and the worry about losing the drinks licence had disappeared. However, she was having difficulties with the chef, who resented a woman being in charge of the restaurant. The problems with the chef were exacerbated by the fact that the kitchen staff seemed pleased to see her discomforted whenever she got into an argument with him. And the kitchen staff's uncooperative attitude towards the waiters had got worse. They knew that Rose was a university graduate and frequently mocked her southern middle-class accent in the same way they regularly mimicked what they called the 'posh' accents of the largely-student waiting staff. They saw Rose and the waiters as people who were only in their present jobs as a means towards something better later on.

In spite of these difficulties, Rose felt sure she could succeed in improving the restaurant's popularity. She believed she could win over the chef in the long run, by encouraging him to develop some more adventurous menus and attracting a new clientele. This, she thought, would encourage him to discipline his kitchen staff more effectively – especially with regard to their relationships with the waiters.

Rose was excited about explaining all of this to the manager who was to do her appraisal. However, before she could even begin to talk about what she was doing, he told her that the company was considering closing the restaurant. A rival had ousted the chief executive of the company. The new managing director wanted, she said, to take the whole business 'up-market'. A restaurant in a northern town with a declining local economy did not 'fit into the new scheme of things'. Rose was to be offered redundancy – the terms of which she was invited to go and discuss with the Human Resources manager.

When Rose found the HR manager, he immediately invited her to go to a nearby wine bar for a drink. He explained that as an old friend of the former managing director he had felt it wise to seek a job with another

25

business. He had been successful in this and therefore felt able, he said, to let Rose know that he believed she had been badly treated. He said that the possibility of closing the restaurant had arisen before Rose had been moved there. Rose had been chosen to take the Canalazzo job because one or two of the headquarter's managers felt that her 'face did not fit'. She was not only the one graduate trainee manager they employed. She was the only one with a black face.

The story of Rose and The Canalazzo involves many of the normal problems that someone is likely to face when trying to manage work – in a struggling restaurant or anywhere else. Alongside the obvious problems about the nature of the market for the particular services offered, and the need to achieve better coordination of the restaurant's division of labour, are a whole series of interpersonal and intergroup relationship problems. But most of these relate in some way to the patterns of conflict, inequality and discrimination existing in the wider culture and society. A critical organisation and management study would take all of this into account in an analysis of what was occurring. This would take it well beyond attention to orthodox issues of motivation, leadership and group relations. But it would also recognise the wider pattern of economic ownership which was relevant to issues in The Canalazzo and observe the way in which boardroom politics can affect what happens at a local workplace level in an organisation. There are politics at every level – workplace, organisation and society. A critical Work Organisation and Management Studies would see these as centrally important matters, not merely as ones providing the 'context' in which the basic day-to-day application of managerial techniques and motivational skills have to be applied.

By now, after two visits to The Canalazzo restaurant, two things should be apparent about analysing all the complexities of organisational and managerial behaviour as it occurs in 'real life' (as opposed to how it appears in the idealised world of standard management texts). First, as we saw in Activity 1.7, we have to look critically at facets of social, cultural, political and economic life that go way beyond a simple search for efficient management techniques. A whole series of moral issues arise in the Canalazzo story. Second, as we saw in Activity 1.6, we have to turn to a range of social-science sources for help in analysing these matters. But each of these social sciences itself has a range of perspectives, models, concepts, theories and research studies on which we might draw when analysing whatever organisational or managerial issues interest or concern us. How do we choose between these?

Knowledge and the informing of practice

One of the ways in which we said that we needed to 'go beyond' Organisational Behaviour was to avoid the very popular OB textbook device of organising material according to a variety of different 'schools' or theoretical approaches or perspectives (the 'classical', 'human relations' or 'systems', for example). Although some texts point out the merits and demerits of each of these, readers are more or less left to decide for themselves which way of looking at organisa-

26

tions they prefer. However fair and reasonable this may seem at first, it avoids the issue of advising students of work organisation and management about what broad criteria they might apply to any piece of research or theorising they come across when trying to understand organisational or managerial practices. And this militates against taking a critical stance with regard to the study of work organisation and management itself. How do we make judgements about the relative value of one piece of analysis or knowledge compared with another?

To deal with this question we have to get involved with issues of *epistemology*. This is the branch of philosophy that deals with the relationship between the way the world is and the knowledge we have of that world. And it has a specific concern with the sort of truth claims that can be made for particular propositions or pieces of knowledge. This might seem a rather complex issue for us to get involved in here, something we can leave to philosophers while we get on with looking directly at organisations and their management. However, we really cannot duck the matter. It is vital to any understanding of how we relate 'theory and practice'.

Whether we like it or not, we all make epistemological judgements every day of our lives. We may have to decide, for example, 'how much truth there is' in the story we just read in our newspaper about an imminent business takeover. We might be concerned with 'how much truth there is' in the picture of society painted by the politician whose speech we have just listened to. Or we might be anxious about 'how much truth there is' in stories we have heard about a local school 'failing' and being closed down. Broadly speaking there are three approaches or 'theories' we can apply to such matters – approaches we can also take to the sort of accounts and analyses we come across when studying organisations and management. These are shown in Table 1.3.

TABLE 1.3 Three ways of deciding the 'truth' of knowledge	
Three ways of deciding the 'truth' of an item of knowledge	For example . . .
Correspondence theories of truth judge an item of knowledge in terms of how accurately it paints a picture or gives a report of what actually happened or 'is the case'	A jury is asked to apply this principle (qualified by the notion of 'beyond reasonable doubt') when deciding between the accounts given by the prosecution and the defence. A judgement has to be made as to whether 'x' actually did or did not kill 'y'
Coherence/plausibility theories of truth judge an item of knowledge in terms of how well it 'fits in with' everything else we have learned about this matter previously	We might apply this principle when deciding whether a piece of gossip about somebody we know is true or false. We ask whether or not it fits with everything else we have seen of them and heard about them
Pragmatist theories of truth judge knowledge in terms of how effectively one would fulfil whatever projects one was pursuing in the area of activity covered by the knowledge, if we based our actions on the understanding of those activities which it offers	We might apply this principle when comparing what a promotional tourist brochure says about a foreign city we are going to visit and what is said in a book by an independent author drawing on their first-hand experiences. We have to decide which account of that city we are going to heed when deciding what to wear, how to address local people, how to find food that we like, or avoid being robbed

27

In everyday life we apply all three ways of deciding the validity of a piece of knowledge. We do this in organisational contexts as much as we do in the other areas of life used in the examples in Table 1.3. But the pragmatist approach to making judgements is obviously the most relevant to deciding what practices we are going to follow in any situation, in the light of the knowledge about that situation which is available to us. In the case of deciding which of the two tourist guides to trust, we would clearly be wise to apply the pragmatist 'theory of truth'. We would similarly be wise to apply this principle if we were considering taking a job with a particular organisation and had available to us, say, both the organisation's recruitment brochure and an article written by a researcher who had carried out participant observation research in that organisation. Which of these two 'pieces of knowledge' is the 'truer' one, we would tend to ask. And we would ask ourselves this question because we would be concerned to decide the most appropriate way to behave when entering the organisation. We would, in this respect, be applying a pragmatist theory of truth claims in the same way that we do when we compare the account of a product given in the manufacturer's advertisement and a report on the product published by an independent consumer association.

In the light of these examples, it is clear that a pragmatist approach to judging the sorts of material one comes across in studying organisations and management is invaluable. The wisdom of such an approach derives from its pragmatically realistic acceptance to two things:

- It is impossible when looking at organisational issues to have enough information – free of interpretation, free of biased reporting, free of the tricks of human memory and free of ambiguity – to apply the correspondence theory of truth. This applies to social life in general as well as to organisations specifically. Because everything we are told about the world is mediated by language and interpretation, we can never receive an account which accurately reports or 'mirrors' that world.

- There are no absolute truths or 'final laws' which social scientific analysis can offer with regard to organisations or any other aspect of social life. One proposition, theory or research study can be judged to be truer than another, however. But this is only to the extent that it will tend to be a *more trustworthy, broad guide to practice* in the aspect of life it covers than the other. It cannot be wholly correct, totally true, or completely objective. One piece of knowledge is simply more useful than the other as an account of 'how things work' which we can use to inform our practices.

This pragmatist approach to judging the validity of the sorts of material we are going to study derives from a particular school of philosophy, the pragmatist philosophy of Charles Pierce, William James and James Dewey as well as, in part, the neo-pragmatist thinking of Richard Rorty (see Reading Guide 4). But it also fully accords with the relatively straightforward notion of *critical common sense* looked at earlier. It leads us to the eminently sensible critical common sense practice of reading management and social science books (or considering any other kind of knowledge for that matter) and asking ourselves, 'To what extent should I take into account this knowledge when deciding what to do in practice?'. If one

Understanding and Managing People at Work
30

theory, one research study, or even one piece of fictional writing, is thought to be more helpful in informing our practical projects than another, then it is a *better* theory, article or book. It is 'truer' in the pragmatist sense of 'true'.

To emphasise the relevance of pragmatist criteria for evaluating pieces of organisational and management knowledge is not to argue for completely turning our backs on the other criteria for judging truth. The concept of justice applied in many societies requires us to work with the correspondence theory of truth, for example, in courts of law or other types of judicial or bureaucratic enquiry. Yet, even here, as we noted earlier, the ultimate impossibility of this is recognised in the acceptance that a judgement can only achieve a reliability which is 'beyond *reasonable* doubt'. We are therefore much safer, for most purposes, applying the more modest pragmatist criterion for judging truth claims. And we are certainly much safer applying this approach than making too much use of coherence or plausibility theories of truth. We apply these all the time – when, for example, we ask how one statement on some issue 'stacks up against' everything else we have heard on that matter. At the level of ordinary or everyday common sense we have to do this. But it is not good enough when we are engaged in the more rigorous and critical common sense type of thinking which we frequently have to do in the complex area of organising and managing work. Too many poor theories in the organisational and management sphere have an immediate plausibility, one that soon disappears when rigorous and critical common sense is applied to them.

 Link The endlessly taught and cited 'hierarchy of needs' theory of work motivation is subjected to this kind of analysis in Chapter 9, pp. 291–7, and shown to fall down badly in pragmatist terms.

The reader of *Organising and Managing Work* is invited to apply the pragmatist criterion of validity to everything that is offered in the forthcoming chapters. It is the criterion that has been applied to the arguments developed throughout the book. It informs the recommendation of a *process-relational* perspective for looking at organising and managing work, instead of the orthodox *systems-control* perspective which is critically examined in Chapter 2, for example. Also, it can be applied to the different ways of talking about managerial work that we have considered in the present chapter. Activity 1.8 can help demonstrate this.

Activity 1.8

Apply the 'pragmatist theory of truth' to the view of managerial work expressed in Cases and Conversations 1.1, 1.2 and 1.3, respectively, by Mark Merryton, Harry Carse and Sadie Rait (summarised in Figure 1.1). You can do this by assuming that you are planning to take up a managerial career and are wondering which of these informal 'theories of management' is likely to be most useful to you when deciding how you will act once in a managerial post.

Understanding and Managing People at Work
31

This activity should help you see why Sadie Rait's account of 'what management is all about' was identified earlier as a 'more realistic way' of talking about that activity than the way Mark and Harry 'framed' managerial work. Pragmatist thinking suggests that anyone doing managerial work is likely to be more effective at whatever they are trying to do in that job if they recognise that:

- 'management' is done by non-managers as well as managers;
- that managerial work involves *both* dealing directly with 'people' and setting up structures and procedures.

Mark and Harry's 'theories of management' were much more simplistic than this and would tend to be less helpful when it came to informing practice. They are less 'true' than Sadie's account in the sense that they would be less useful as indicators of 'how things work' in managerial activities and would thus be less useful when it comes to informing practice.

One way in which this broad principle of utility applies to all scientific thinking is in science's use of concepts.

Concepts   *Concept*

Concepts are the working definitions that are chosen or devised to make possible a particular piece of scientific analysis. They are the way scientists define their terms for the purpose of a specific investigation. They therefore differ from dictionary definitions which tend to have a much more general applicability.

In our everyday lives, we are used to looking for *correct definitions* of phenomena, ones that will be generally helpful to us when communicating within a broad public language. If we wish to analyse phenomena with the greater degree of rigour and focus that distinguishes scientific analysis, however, we find ourselves having more carefully to *conceptualise* phenomena. This means devising working definitions which are helpful to us in trying to analyse and understand some aspect of the world. Thus an economist will conceptualise money more rigorously than the person in the street will 'define' it. Psychologists will do similarly with regard to 'intelligence' – working with different concepts of intelligence at different times. What this means is that in engaging in an enterprise like writing *Organising and Managing Work*, one develops concepts that are useful to one's purposes. One does not turn to a dictionary for the universally 'correct' definition. Thus, every time there is a 'defining of terms' in this book (usually using the device of a 'concept box'), it is done to be *helpful* to the purposes of the book – and *useful* to the readers who are interested in improving their understanding of how work is organised and managed. The whole enterprise of the book is based on the notion that some ways of conceptualising, 'management' or 'organisation', say, are more useful than others. The intent is not to find a 'correct' definition of what 'management' or 'organisation' is but to use concepts that help us critically engage with the world.

The pragmatist style of thinking is also relevant, in a very basic way, to the arguments set out earlier for the *critical analysis* of Work Organisation and Management Studies. Doing this, it was argued, involved appreciating that work organisation

Understanding and Managing People at Work
32

happens in a context of contest, inequality and conflict and that management ideas are more than neutral rules, principles or guides to action; they always have political significance. Knowledge of organisations and management which gives full recognition to these matters, according to the pragmatist principles, would be better – as a set of resources for informing practice – than knowledge which ignored them. This is because an organisational practitioner, managerial or non-managerial, would be better placed to succeed in whatever their purposes might be if they were informed in this way. We might go as far as to say that an individual who tried to undertake any kind of organisational task without a strong awareness of the political dimension of organisational life would be a fool! It follows from this that critical thinking is equally relevant to a manager, a non-managerial worker or someone wishing to challenge and undermine the whole enterprise. To put this another way, there cannot be 'managerially biased' knowledge – other than inadequate or misleading knowledge. If there is work organisation knowledge which helpfully informs the practices, projects and purposes of managers, then it is likely to be equally helpful to anyone else operating in that context – including someone wishing to oppose 'managerial' initiatives. The same principle applies to other spheres of human activity: knowledge which helps a government rule can also help an opposition to bring it down; knowledge which helps a police force fight crime can equally help criminals carry out crimes more successfully, for example.

As far as *Organising and Managing Work* is concerned, everything in the book is intended to inform people involved in the management of work – whatever the nature of that involvement might be. The book should be helpful to those designated as 'managers'. But it should be equally relevant to someone whose 'project' is to have a quiet life at work, make an investment or customer decision about a work organisation or set out in some way to oppose the managers of an organisation. In this spirit, we now move forward in Chapters 2 and 3 to look at some of the major ways in which our understanding of organisations and managerial work is changing – and changing in a direction which can make it more effective than previously as a resource for informing our practices in the management of work.

Summary

In this chapter, the following key points have been made:

- The most helpful way to think about issues of work organisation and management is to focus on all those activities which contribute to the management of work tasks, only then considering how such activities are divided up between people who have the title of 'manager' and those which do not.

- There are both moral and practical problems with the notion of 'managing people'.

- Approaches to managerial work that focus on the 'management of structures and procedures' are equally inadequate.

- There are both 'people' elements and 'structure-procedure' aspects to managerial work, and both have to be taken into account both in thinking about management and engaging in it. Managerial work needs to be recognised as something which entails both

31

Understanding and Managing People at Work

directly relating to people and establishing working structures or procedures. The interplay between these two aspects of management – and between the choices that are possible and the factors which influence those choices – is complex and will be a theme of much of what is to follow in later chapters.

- Although the academic subject of Organisational Behaviour has been the main vehicle for bringing social science thinking into the study of management and organisation, it has a number of inadequacies. The present book attempts to overcome many of these.

- Work Organisation and Management Studies, as a subject attempting to build upon and go beyond Organisational Behaviour, is linked with several other established and developing academic subjects, including management learning, critical management studies, strategic management and human resource management.

- Work Organisation and Management Studies is the study of the human aspects of work organisation and its management which draws on the social sciences to develop insights, theories and research findings with a view to informing the choices, decisions and actions of organisational practitioners.

- The social science disciplines drawn upon by *Organising and Managing Work*, and their analytical styles, are not essentially different from 'common sense' thinking. In fact, they have a close continuity with what can be called 'critical common sense'.

- In the spirit of 'critical common sense', the style of *Work Organisation and Management Studies* adopted here can be identified with certain aspects of the emergent tradition of 'critical management studies'. This entails continually asking, first, why work is organised and managed in the way it is and, second, why we think about and study work and its management in the ways we do. It also involves continuous recognition of the extent to which work organisation happens in a context of human competition, context and patterned antagonism as well as recognising that management ideas are not neutral technical rules and principles but always have political significance.

- To be able to relate what we study to issues of practice in the organisational and managerial world we need some criteria for judging the relative merits of the theories, research studies and other materials that are available to us. The most useful criterion we can apply to judging theories, and the rest, is one derived from pragmatist philosophy. There is no way of judging absolute truth or validity. But some accounts can be seen as 'truer' than others. It is suggested that one piece of material may be judged to be 'truer' than another to the extent to which it better informs human practices or 'projects' in the aspect of human activity with which it deals.

Reading

Reading Guides 1, 2, 4 and 13 contain material that supports and takes further much of what is covered in Chapter 1.

Understanding and Managing People at Work
34

Chapter 9

INDIVIDUAL DIFFERENCES

Linda Hicks

Organisations consist of people working together. Individuals have different abilities, personalities, learning experiences and attitudes. It is not surprising that they perceive work in different ways. Emphasising individual differences and valuing diversity is a key driver in the search for equality at work. Differences between individuals can be a source of developing creativity or the root of conflict and frustration. It is one of the tasks of management to recognise and harness potential talent and achieve individual and organisational goals.

Learning objectives

To:

➤ focus on the changing relationships at work and the significance of valuing difference and diversity;

➤ outline the importance of the individual's contribution to the organisation and factors affecting behaviour and performance;

➤ examine the major difficulties of studying personality and apply the key issues of personality studies to the work organisation with particular reference to personality assessment;

➤ explain how differences in ability are identified and measured, and how psychological tests are used in the workplace;

➤ detail the significance of attitudes, their functions, change and measurement, with particular reference to the culture of organisations;

➤ apply the principles of attitude change to the workplace;

➤ examine the importance of gender research and organisational behaviour, and women's position and status;

➤ consider ways to achieve equality at work and a work–life balance.

The changing nature and scope of managing individuals at work

Managing relationships in the twenty-first century

Are organisations moving into a mature multi-cultural phase? Is there sensitivity within organisations to tackle issues of racism, sexism, and ageism? Are managers able to cope with the changes in structure, culture, work attitudes and expectations?

Managing relationships at work has always been a key skill, but in the twenty-first century there are new demands for an unpredictable future. The speed at which organisations are undergoing change places continuous pressure on individuals at work. The paradox that 'change is now a constant feature' in organisational life has become a key feature in academic journals. Being able to manage the process of change is a necessity for all managers regardless of the type and nature of the organisation.

Although hierarchy and bureaucracy still exist in many organisations, the trend towards flatter, matrix-based structures has grown. It is commonplace for employees to work in project teams, to work at home, to communicate informally to colleagues and to cope with the juggling of family demands and work. Managers require skills that facilitate achievement through working with colleagues rather than dictating to subordinates. They need sensitivity to the work climate and they require skills, which will enable them to effect changes that foster well being and satisfaction.

The changes have been triggered by a number of factors:

- increase in the number of graduates in the work place;[1]
- increase in the number of teleworkers;[2]
- increase in the proportion of women working;[3]
- increase in the number of employees with family responsibilities;[4]
- changes to the nature and scope of skills required in the workplace;[5]
- move to more informal patterns of communication via e-mail and internet;
- increase in global business patterns and cross-cultural relationships;
- increase in pressures to communicate instantly.

Equal opportunities to managing diversity

Managers need to be aware of future demographic trends; for instance, Equality Direct[6] predicts that by the year 2010, 40 per cent of the labour force will be over 45 years of age. Alterations to the identity that individuals hold have also been apparent over the last decade. Devolution and regionalisation have increased and paradoxically so too has the trend towards greater integration into multi-national groupings (in terms of both company mergers and political agendas). A complex range of possible identities and affiliations results. Consider a Scottish national living in the United States, working for a Japanese company and directing European markets: such a manager will have a diverse set of allegiances which may in turn affect motivation and morale. The growth of the portfolio worker and contract worker results in an employment relationship, which is short-term, instrumental and driven by outcomes and performance. Loyalty to the organisation and commitment to mission statements does not enter into such a partnership. The rise of consumerism in and out of the workplace has led to greater understanding and expectations of 'rights' and redress of perceived injustice. It is not only morally and socially acceptable to treat all people fairly in the workplace; legislation insists that managers do so.

It is 25 years since the Sex Discrimination Act in the UK and although there have been some important victories there is considerable work to be done. The Race Relations (Amendment) Act will have a significant impact on public sector organisations. A code of practice, to be released in the summer of 2001, will provide the mandatory set of guidelines for the public sector. The reluctant employer is having its hand forced by statutory obligations. The Disability Rights Commission is also seeking 'Actions'[7] and commitment from organisations rather than kind words and wishes.

Understanding and Managing People at Work

36

The business case

All these changes amount to a picture in which the white males will no longer dominate. Instead, we can anticipate a complex pattern where, ideally, individual differences will be valued and celebrated and at the very least, equal opportunities practice will be observed. Personal qualities and characteristics that may have been downgraded, ignored or regarded as nuisance factors, will be perceived in this new situation as adding value. Organisations which embrace difference and diversity as opposed to those which are merely compliant will, it is claimed, succeed in a fiercely competitive climate. As J. M. Barry Gibson, Chief Executive of Littlewoods, has stated:

> *The fact is that if we effectively exclude women, ethnic minorities and disabled people we are fishing in a smaller pool for the best possible talent. As a service organisation, we ought to reflect the style, taste and opinions of our consumers, who of course represent sexes, all colours and creeds, all ages and disabilities. The main point is that cultural diversity will strengthen the quality of the company and will make us much more outward-looking.*[8]

However, *Kirton and Greene*[9] argue that the 'business case' should be broadened to include wider issues of social justice and social responsibility. *Liff and Cameron*[10] argue that organisational culture needs to radically shift to win the 'hearts and minds rather than just achieve reluctant compliance'. In their article, which uses women as their illustration, they assert that there are real dangers in conventional equality measures which underlie the failure of some organisations to implement equal opportunity policies. Focusing on women as having special problems requiring special treatment results in resentment and defensive attitudes from managers. They believe that one of the first essential stages to enact change is to consider the organisational culture and the way in which it could move to an equality culture. Further examination of equality practices will be discussed at the end of this chapter.

Defining diversity

Valuing differences in people is easy to write about but not necessarily easy to do in practice. It means relating and working with people who hold different perspectives and views, bring different qualities to the workplace, have different aspirations and have different customs and traditions. It means that we need to recognise the prejudices we hold and question them before we act. Differences are challenging; they challenge our views, our perceptions and attitudes and require us to see things from a different frame of reference. Managing diversity does not mean that we champion our own values and try and shift other people's values to conform and match our own. For *Kandola and Fullerton* diversity is defined as:

> *The basic concept of managing diversity accepts that the workforce consists of a diverse population of people. The diversity consists of visible and non-visible differences, which will include sex, age, background, race, disability, personality and workstyle. It is founded on the premise that harnessing these differences will create a productive environment in which everybody feels valued, where their talents are being fully utilised, and in which organisational goals are met.*[11]

It is possible to argue, therefore, that greater reserves of emotional intelligence are required of managers if they are to be successful managers of diversity. Encouraging individuality and at the same time expecting group cooperation and teamwork are potential triggers for tension. Creativity and independence are desired characteristics but so too are conformity to organisational goals and standards of performance.

Recruiting and selecting committed company-staff who offer valuable individuality is a key to an organisation's health and effectiveness. The criteria used to reject or accept applicants are a major indicator of an organisation's values and beliefs. The selection process has been described as a 'cultural sieve'[12] and as an important method of control.[13] Indeed Tom Peters[14] has suggested that organisations need to review their selection requirements and, instead of checking that every minute of every day is accounted for when appointing applicants, they should consider applicants who have 'broken out' from the mould, rebelled from the system and thus demonstrated original thought. Peters regards such personal qualities as key attributes for leading-edge organisations.

However, this individualistic approach contrasts with the notion that organisations need team players who will be co-operative. As soon as the new recruits begin their employment a 'psychological contract' is struck which forms the basis for obedience and conformity expected of the employees by the company. The manager's responsibility is to ensure that the socialisation process enables the new recruits to quickly learn the rules of the system. Rewards, if given at this stage, for correct behaviour and attitudes, will promote conformity and provide further incentives for the individuals to match the organisation's needs. (The recruitment and selection of staff is discussed in Chapter 20.)

Recognition of individuality

Recognition of good performers and performance is an essential part of the process of management. Managing people in organisations requires not only an understanding of the employees, but also a recognition of the culture of the organisation; for some organisations, creativity and individuality may be the last thing they would want to see between 9 and 5, but for others these characteristics are essential.

A discussion of individual behaviour in organisations is therefore riddled with complexity and contradictions! Managers are required to be competent at selecting the individuals who will be valuable to the organisation. They need to be observant about the individuals who are performing well and have the potential to develop within the organisation. They also need to be able to value difference and be sensitive to contrasting needs. Finally managers need to know themselves and understand their own uniqueness and the impact their personality has on others.

Organisation change and individual differences

Knowledge of some of the fundamental issues relating to individual differences is essential for managers during periods of change. Managing some areas of change may be relatively straightforward, e.g. the transfer of computer skills when learning a new software package, but other change may be 'messy' and more complex. When organisations merge or are taken over, the management of people takes on a different dimension in terms of sensitivity required. In this situation there is an implicit requirement of changes in attitudes and beliefs. Such changes may lead to new mind-sets, new attitudes and new perceptions which enable people to cope and adjust to the different world. At these times effective management is vital; managers will be expected to understand the strains that their employees feel during times of change, but at the same time be able to deal with their own stress levels.

This part of the book addresses the ways in which it is possible to differentiate between individuals. Personality, the heart of individual differences, is explored first in this chapter. The emotional demands required by organisations of their employees are identified and discussed. There then follows an examination of the importance and functions of attitudes. This leads to a discussion where we focus on the gender dimension in organisations. In addition to analysing the historical, psychological and societal context we will also consider issues related to the implementation of equality practices. An understanding of the ways in which people learn is fundamental to an appreciation of individual differences and is considered in Chapter 10. The process of perception and the impact of gender differences are examined in Chapter 11.

Motivation is also included within this part of the book, as individuals differ significantly with regard to their needs, their ambitions and the ways in which they satisfy their goals (*see* Chapter 12).

Personality

It is possible to differentiate between individuals in terms of the following criteria:

- types/traits;
- gender;
- abilities;
- physique;
- development aspects;
- motivation;
- attitudes;
- perception;
- social and cultural aspects;
- ethnic origin.

All of these characteristics shape our sense of self, and so in one way we all share the same 'human-ness'. Some of us share the same gender type or the same personality dimensions; we may have the same ability levels or share similar socio-economic backgrounds, but our uniqueness stems from the dynamic ways in which these features combine.

Dynamics – the key to understanding personality

Psychologists tend to specialise and focus on one of the features listed above. Clearly, this is essential for the dedicated research required but, when applying theories to people at work, it is important to remember that a holistic view should be taken which takes into account the dynamic processes. If we consider the interaction of a person with a high intelligence score and a strong sense of honesty, the dynamics will result in a completely different set of behaviour patterns to someone with high intelligence and a tendency towards dishonesty. We could predict a very different set of attitudes too. To have a 'whole' understanding of the individual at work, we must take into account the ways in which an individual's traits interact. We must go beyond the study of pure psychology and evaluate the extent to which their studies can be applied in practice.

The application of theory to the world of work is not always easy and some students find the process confusing when the theory does not match with their own experiences. Psychological investigations emphasise the complexity and variety of individual behaviour and insist that simple answers and explanations are generally inadequate. Students may therefore have to adjust their attitudes and perceptions about the world and for some students this experience may be uncomfortable. The study of personality provides an excellent example of some of the complexities involved in applying psychological theory in practice.

Let us consider two individuals who share similar characteristics. They are both 24 years old, and have lived in the same area; both have a first class honours degree in engineering and they have identical personality assessment profiles. However, we would still predict differences with regard to their attitude and performance in the workplace. In addition, differences would be predicted in the ways that they interacted with others and in the ways that others interacted with them. If one of the engineers was female and/or Asian, a further set of assumptions might start to appear. It is not only the features themselves which identify individuals as being different but it is also their interaction which leads to a unique pattern of behaviour. The complexities of the process pose a number of interesting questions which psychologists have tried to solve and in this context it is not surprising perhaps that differing theories and ideas have evolved. (*See* Tables 9.1 and 9.2.)

Table 9.1 Dilemma 1 – The role of early experiences

To what extent is our personality constant throughout life?

Solution (a) – Adaptable
If we consider the two young engineers described above, it could be argued that the personality of each is a culmination of experiences. Their personalities have been shaped by the people around them from their very earliest years. Early family life – the relationship between family members, the size of the family, the rewards and punishments exercised by parents – would have had an influence on the type of person each is now. In other words, the environment and early learning experiences have contributed to their personality development.

Solution (b) – Constant
Perhaps the young engineers have a core-inherited part of their personality which has remained resistant to change. The way in which they have responded to the world has remained consistent with their true 'self'.

Table 9.2 Dilemma 2 – Assessment of personality

Is it possible to 'measure' an individual's personality?

Solution (a) Yes, there are identifiable traits.
Identifying an individual's personality typically refers to distinguishing traits or types. For instance, Joe is an introvert (type); he is placid, quiet and reflective. John, however, is an extrovert (type); he is excitable, sociable and loud. Personality traits are usually identified by what people do, the behaviour they exhibit. This is the way that all of us would normally describe another's personality. Some psychologists, instead of watching behaviour, ask questions about behaviour which the individual answers on a paper questionnaire. They would assert that asking a person to report on the way they feel or behave is a legitimate way of assessing personality. These self-reporting questionnaires would then be subject to quantitative methods. Thus, psychologists have made it possible to quantify the strength of a person's trait and to enable comparisons to be made with others. Such information then becomes a basis for prediction. For example, if a person has a high score on extroversion, it would be possible to predict the way in which the individual might behave in a given situation. These measuring techniques are subject to some controversy.

Solution (b) No, personality is unique.
Do people always reveal their true 'self'? Is it possible that circumstances may force them to behave in a way that is unlike their 'typical' behaviour? Or do people choose to act in a certain way because they think it is appropriate? Is it possible to measure the 'strength' of a trait? Can people reliably report on their own behaviour or is there a real difference between what people say and what people do? Instead of requiring individuals to respond to set questions, it may be more appropriate to use open-ended techniques. This ensures that individuals use their own definitions, and allows for greater understanding about their motivations and causes of behaviour.

Figure 9.1 identifies the links between the dynamics of **personality** and life's experiences.

Understanding and Managing People at Work

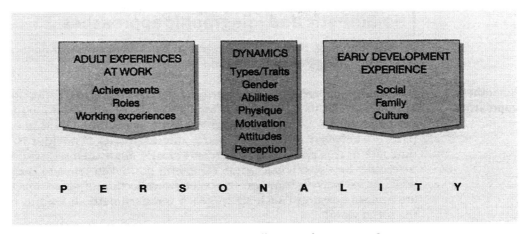

Figure 9.1 To what extent does our personality remain constant?

Uniqueness and similarities

The dilemmas described in Tables 9.1 and 9.2 focus on two major issues of prime importance in the study of personality. First, is personality a constant throughout our lifetime, which remains resistant to change and circumstances? Second, to what extent can we measure and compare individuals on the basis of their personality? This second question assumes that it is possible to distinguish personality characteristics in the first place. Psychologists have produced various theories to solve both these dilemmas and one of the ways of making sense of these theories is to see them working at different levels. (*See* Table 9.3.)

Studying individual differences therefore presents a set of interesting problems for psychologists. A review of the theories in the next section will show that they often work at one of the levels shown in Table 9.3, resulting in differing approaches and emphasis.

This section will discuss two major approaches to the study of personality and their handling of the dilemmas of constancy and assessment. Applications of personality studies to organisations and their management will be discussed at the end of the section.

Table 9.3 Different levels of personality research

Level	Psychologists' research interests
LEVEL 3 ☺ ☺ ☺ ☺ ☺ ☺ ☺ ☺ ☺ ☺ ☺ ☺ Universal human features	Common human aspirations
LEVEL 2 ☺ ☺ ☺ ☺ ☺ ☺ ☺ ☺ ☺ Some shared features – gender; ability	Identification, measurements, comparison (nomothetic)
LEVEL 1 ☺ Unique combination of features	'Self' – Unique interaction with the world (idiographic)

Nomothetic and idiographic approaches

Broadly speaking, personality studies can be divided into two main approaches which have been labelled nomothetic and idiographic.

Nomothetic approaches

Nomothetic approaches are primarily concerned with the collection of group data. This means that such theorists accumulate evidence with regard to the identification of personality traits; producing effective measurements of the traits in order to draw comparisons between individuals. Being able to predict behaviour is a major aim and outcome of this approach. Researchers closely align themselves to studies which are 'scientific' in a positivistic sense. (The term positivism refers to the branch of science which is exclusively based on the objective collection of observable data – data which are beyond question.) Such an approach transfers methods used in natural sciences to the social world.

Nomothetic approaches tend to view environmental and social influences as minimal and view personality as consistent, largely inherited and resistant to change. Although they would not diminish the difficulties that measuring personality brings, nomothetic approaches would claim that it is possible to measure and predict the ways in which personality types would behave given certain circumstances.[15]

Nomothetic approaches would:

- solve dilemma 1 with solution (b) in Table 9.1;
- solve dilemma 2 with solution (a) in Table 9.2; and
- focus on level 2 as described in Table 9.3.

Idiographic approaches

Idiographic approaches are concerned with understanding the uniqueness of individuals and the development of the self concept. They regard personality development as a process which is open to change. They regard individuals as responding to the environment and people around them, and see the dynamics of the interactions as playing a critical part in shaping personality. The measurement of traits is seen as largely inappropriate in that one person's responses may not be comparable to another's. They suggest that personality assessment is not a valid method of understanding the unique ways in which a person understands and responds to the world. The depth and richness of a person's personality can not be revealed in superficial paper-and-pencil questionnaires. Furthermore, the categories defined by psychologists are too narrow in scope and depth.

Idiographic approaches would:

- solve dilemma 1 with solution (a) in Table 9.1;
- solve dilemma 2 with solution (b) in Table 9.2; and
- focus on level 1 as described in Table 9.3.

Complementary approaches

Some researchers do not fit easily into either of these two broad approaches. *Freud*, for instance, is idiographic in the sense that he is interested in the self and its development, but his theory does not allow for personality growth and change after childhood.[16] *Kelly's* Personal Construct Theory also bridges the two approaches.[17] His theory will be explored later in this chapter.

The approaches can be seen as complementary; indeed, it could be argued that different foci are important in understanding the many complicated facets of personality.

Theoretical approaches: nomothetic

The two main theories discussed under this approach are:

- Eysenck's theory of main personality types; and
- Cattell's identification of personality traits.

Eysenck

Hans Eysenck followed a tradition of writers by applying the four basic types introduced by Hippocrates: melancholic; sanguine; phlegmatic; and choleric. Eysenck's approach was influenced by the positivistic tradition; his aim was to produce objective evidence of personality differences using large samples of the population. By investigating 700 servicemen, he was able to use rigorous statistical data to test his hypotheses.[18] His findings supported the notion that there were two major differences which could be measured: extroversion and stability (*see* Figure 9.2).

Individuals in Eysenck's theory could, therefore, be one of four main personality types. The type would lead to a predisposition of traits which would, itself, lead to the likelihood of certain behaviours. For instance, a person typed as an extrovert would be responsive and outgoing and in a new social situation s/he would predictably initiate conversation among a group of strangers.

Eysenck's theory and his subsequent Personality Inventory allowed identification of a personality type. From this description, it was possible to predict likely behaviours. Eysenck had a clear view about the constancy of personality. He believed that personality was largely inherited and that introverts and extroverts are born with differing physiological tendencies. Furthermore, he argued that the personality we are born with is largely unalterable by environmental influences.

Supporting research evidence

Although it could be argued that Eysenck's theory is too simplistic in terms of the number and range of types proposed, his theory has an impressive amount of supporting research evidence. His approach has immediate appeal to managers in organisations who are concerned with predicting the future behaviour of their employees, either for selection or promotion.

One of his earlier studies indicated that stable introverts were generally found among the most successful businessmen. Collecting data from 1504 managers he found that finance, research and development and consultants were the most introverted and, perhaps unsurprisingly, that sales managers the most extroverted.[19] Stability seemed to be manifest regardless of the type of work the managers did but their degree of extroversion seemed to vary, depending on the nature of their work. It certainly seems plausible that personality determines both preferences for occupations and goes some way towards predicting performance at work. *Furnham* surmises whether personality changes if an individual is in a job that is ill-suited to his/her personality. He cites research, which indicates that personality scores change as a result of being exposed to a different and challenging environment. [20] Given the evidence that personality is a useful predictor of behaviour it is not surprising that the use of psychometric tests has grown substantially over the past decade and that the majority of large companies use occupational tests.[21] (Further information about testing is given on page 323.)

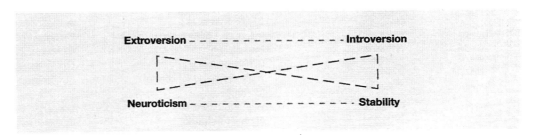

Figure 9.2 Eysenck's personality types

Cattell

Cattell's work resembles Eysenck's in the methods used to study personality. He used quantitative, objective techniques in order to analyse his data (although he used a different factor analytic measure), and followed traditional scientific procedures in order to understand the basic dimensions of personality.[22] Cattell used three main sources for the collection of personality data.

1 **L-data** (life record data) – ratings by trained observers.
2 **Q-data** (self-rating questionnaire) – responses to a questionnaire which measured personality traits (Cattell 16PF Questionnaire).
3 **T-data** (test data) – observations collected in specific situation tests.

Personality factors

The data collected were factor-analysed by Cattell resulting in the identification of two main types of personality traits:

● **surface traits** – which seem to cluster together consistently; and
● **source traits** – which seem to underlie and determine the traits which are likely to 'surface' into behaviour.

Cattell identified 16 personality factors (or source traits). (*See* Table 9.4.)[23]

Unlike Eysenck, he did not 'type' individuals but used 'traits' as his main personality descriptor (although there is much similarity between Cattell's second-order factors and Eysenck's 'types'). They also differed with regard to the determinants of personality: Eysenck viewed the inherited physiological basis as the main determinant, whereas Cattell was more interested in taking social factors into account when understanding an individual's personality. Both theorists have contributed to a lively debate about personality structure and its measurement, and in doing so have advanced the selection techniques available to managers.[24]

Table 9.4 Cattell's personality factors

Factor	High score	Low score
A	Outgoing	Reserved
B	More intelligent (abstract thinker)	Less intelligent (concrete thinker)
C	Higher ego strength (Emotionally stable)	Lower ego strength (Emotionally unstable)
E	Dominant	Submissive
F	Surgency (optimistic)	Desurgency (pessimistic)
G	Stronger superego strength (conscientious)	Weaker superego strength (expedient)
H	Parmia (adventurous)	Threctia (timid)
I	Presmia (tender-minded)	Harria (tough-minded)
L	Protension (suspicious)	Alaxia (trusting)
M	Autia (imaginative)	Praxernia (practical)
N	Shrewdness	Artlessness (unpretentious)
O	Insecure – guilt-proneness	Self-assured
Q1	Radicalism	Conservatism
Q2	Self-sufficiency	Group dependence
Q3	High self-concept control (controlled)	Low self-concept control (casual)
Q4	High ergic tension (tense, frustrated)	Low ergic tension (relaxed, tranquil)

(Adapted and reproduced with permission from Cattell, R. B. and Kline, P., *The Scientific Analysis of Personality and Motivation*, Academic Press (1977) Table 4.1, pp. 44–5.)

Understanding and Managing People at Work

The Big Five

Identifying the personality traits, which seem to be particularly dominant in distinguishing individuals, has been the dominant subject of research personality research in UK and USA. There is now a body of evidence, which suggests that five dimensions capture distinct differences between people. These traits, known as the Big Five,[25] are:

- extroversion/introversion
- agreeableness/hostility
- conscientiousness/heedlessness
- emotional stability/instability
- openness or intellect/closed-mindedness

Results from a wide number of studies have shown that these factors can be identified as being significant in measuring the variation between people.[26] Of these, conscientiousness is linked to high levels of job knowledge and performance across a range of different occupations. However, some researchers are critical of the descriptors used.[27] *Bentall*[28] suggests they are 'tainted by the investigators' values' and continues: 'I suspect that most people will have a pretty clear idea of where they would like to find themselves on the dimensions of neuroticism, extraversion, openness, agreeableness and conscientiousness.' He questions the ethical and political nature of the scales.

Theoretical approaches: idiographic

Idiographic approaches emphasise the development of the individual and of individuals' views of themselves – their self concept. Supporters of idiographic approaches are critical of the nomothetic approach which attempts to categorise individuals on the basis of group data. They argue that the techniques used to collate the group data are questionable and the outcome inappropriate to an understanding of personality. For the idiographic researchers, personality is expressed through the experiences and development of the individual. It cannot be understood outside a social context and has to be studied in the light of individuals' own perceptions of their world. Idiographic researchers would always take into account the social circumstances of the person and in particular the relationships with others, family life and social conditions. The following theories are typical examples of the idiographic approach.

- *Carl Rogers'* theory claims that personality is embedded within personal relationships. He emphasised the importance of fulfilment and psychological growth, placing at the centre people's knowledge of their own feelings. For Rogers, the expression of emotion was critical in freeing up people's autonomy and creativity in the quest for self-actualisation. The process of becoming a person requires the ability to give and receive unconditional regard – the warmth and respect for the *person*, who they *are*, regardless of how they behave.[29]
- *G. H. Mead* was unable to separate the notion of an individual's personality from the concept of society. He claimed that:

  A person is a personality because he belongs to a community, because he takes over the institutions of that community into his own conduct.[30]

  As individuals we can only have a sense of self in relation to others. He proposed the idea that the self has two components: one which is spontaneous and unique (I), and the other which is learnt through exposure to society (me).
- *C. Cooley*, like Mead, emphasised the importance of early development and socialisation. He believed the emotion and sensation that we hold of 'self' was instinctive but was developed by experience. His phrase 'the looking-glass self' suggests that we come to know ourselves through our relationship with others and their reactions to us.[31]

Understanding and Managing People at Work

Erikson

Erik Erikson's theory is a good example of the idiographic approach. He viewed personality development as continuing throughout life. He was interested in the effect of experiences on the development of the self concept and how different individuals resolved personal conflicts.[32]

Although he recognised the importance of early childhood in establishing certain basic concepts of trust, autonomy and initiative, he disagreed with *Freud's* emphasis on the effects of early development. (*See* section below.)

Tensions and conflicts

For Erikson, all eight stages of life produce different tensions and conflicts which have to be resolved. (*See* Table 9.5.)

Successful resolution produces a healthy personality, whereas difficulties in earlier stages may produce problems later on. Erikson's theory not only makes considerable sense in terms of face validity (i.e., 'it feels right' factor) but also links with other research indicating that managers' motivations and goals change with age. *Hunt*, for instance, identified nine different career/life stages.[33]

Table 9.5 Erikson's eight stages of personality development

Stage 1	Trust	v	Mistrust	1st year
Stage 2	Autonomy	v	Doubt	2–3 years
Stage 3	Initiative	v	Guilt	4–5 years
Stage 4	Industry	v	Inferiority	6–11 years
Stage 5	Identity	v	Role confusion	12–18 years
Stage 6	Intimacy	v	Isolation	Young adult
Stage 7	Generativity	v	Self-absorption	Middle age
Stage 8	Integrity	v	Despair	Old age

(*Source*: Adapted from Erikson, E. H. *Identity and The Life Cycle*, Norton (1980) Worksheet Table Appendix. © 1980 by W.W. Norton & Company, Inc. © 1959 by International Universities Press, Inc. Used by permission of W.W. Norton & Company Inc.)

Other theoretical approaches

Other significant theoretical approaches include:

● **Psychoanalytic approaches** – *Sigmund Freud* and neo-Freudians; and
● **Cognitive approaches** – *George Kelly*.

Freud

A discussion on personality would not be complete without a mention of *Sigmund Freud* (1856–1939). His psychoanalytic approach emphasised the importance of:

● early childhood experiences, particularly parental relationships and dealing with trauma;
● different levels of consciousness and the influence of the unconscious mind on behaviour;
● understanding the 'whole' person in relation to their past.[34]

Early childhood experiences were seen by Freud as paramount in understanding the adult personality. He described the development of all individuals as one which progressed through a number of stages: (i) oral; (ii) anal; and (iii) phallic (*see* Figure 9.3).

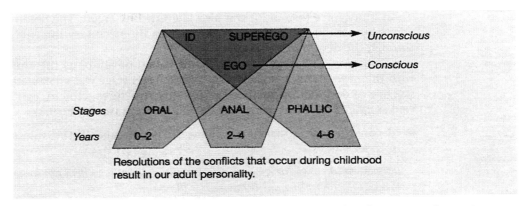

Resolutions of the conflicts that occur during childhood result in our adult personality.

Figure 9.3 Representation of Freud's personality theory, development and structure

These changes are, for Freud, significant in that if the child finds the stage too difficult and the conflicts too hard and traumatic, an arrested development or 'fixation' could result. This means that the problems associated with the stage may be relived at a later time in adult life.

As an example, if we consider the oral stage of development (*see* Table 9.6), the young child enjoys sucking from his or her mother's breast or bottle but food is now being presented on a spoon. This requires not only a different feeding position (a chair rather than a soft comfortable lap), but a different, less pleasurable action than sucking. For some children this may be very traumatic and tears may result, whereas others may find this change easy and enjoyable. Of course, much depends on the way in which the change is tackled by the parent and the extent to which the parent will choose the moment to introduce food on a spoon. For some parents the change may seem significant, and may signify a welcome step towards independence; for others it may be the end of the 'baby' stage and they may feel a sense of sorrow and conflict.

Freud's stages highlight the importance of the parent–child relationship. If the child finds the stage too problematic and the change results in a 'battle' between parent and child, the likelihood of the stage becoming fixated is higher. A fixation at the oral stage of development may result in the adult gratifying his/her oral needs in stressful situations as an adult. They may resort to cigarettes, chocolate, drink or they may be verbally aggressive or sarcastic to others.

Table 9.6 Freud's three stages of development

Freud's stages of development	Critical change
Oral stage Pleasures associated with the mouth and lips.	Child weaned from breast or bottle to food on a spoon.
Anal stage Pleasures associated with expelling (or withholding) faeces.	Child able to control bowel movements and use a potty.
Phallic stage Pleasures associated with genital area.	Child recognises difference between male and female.

An inner force (or libido) was also identified by Freud. The libido was seen as a universal human characteristic which provides the necessary life energy for progression through the developmental stages.

The personality structure of the individual develops as the child comes to terms with the new changes at each stage of life. Each stage was characterised by an internal struggle of domination by three personality structures – the **id**, **ego** and **superego** – as well as external conflict with outside relationships (*see* Figure 9.3).

- **Id** consists of the instinctive, hedonistic part of self. *Gross* described the baby at birth as:

  bundles of id ... whenever we act on impulse, selfishly, or demand something here and now, it is our id controlling our behaviour at those times.[35]

  It is governed by the pleasure principle.

- **Superego** is the conscience of the self, the part of our personality which is influenced by significant others in our life.

  The id and superego are in conflict with each other, with the id desiring certain behaviours and the superego attempting to discipline and control behaviour.

- **Ego** has to make sense of the internal conflict in our mind between the id and superego and the external world. The ego is the decision-making part of our personality and is engaged in rational and logical thinking. It is governed by the reality principle.

These conflicts and tensions, rooted in the past and repressed within the unconscious, were seen by Freud as the key to an understanding of adult personality.

Freud's theory has been heavily criticised on the grounds that:

- it is not replicable and his arguments were circular;
- samples used were atypical;
- it is subjective and unscientific;
- a heavy emphasis on early childhood makes it highly deterministic; and
- it disregards later development and changes.

His theory should, however, be seen in its historical context and in terms of its impact upon the development of later theories and ideas. In a recent review of Freudian theory *Andrews and Brewin*[36] cite research supporting oral and anal tendencies and offer support for some of his ideas on depression and paranoia. Freud was also given positive review concerning 'slips of the tongue'. These incidents occur when what was actually said was not intended. For Freud 'slips of the tongue' illustrate the conflict that can exist between our mental forces and the struggle we have in suppressing our desires. In this review, *Reason* suggests that slips do indeed represent 'minor eruptions of unconscious processing' but would caution the idea that all slips were in some way intentional.[37]

Applications to organisational behaviour

With regard to organisational behaviour, Freud's theory still has much to offer with respect to understanding stress at work. When the going gets tough it is easy to slip into habitual ways of responding that have been learned as children. Within the working context, such behaviour may be seen as inappropriate and yet bring immediate relief or comfort to the individual. Instances include regressing into temper tantrums or gaining relief by excessive eating or drinking and can be seen to protect the ego from a painful memory or unwanted impulse. Freud labelled these **defence mechanisms**. The most readily observable ones in the workplace include:

- **Regression** – adopting childhood patterns of behaviour;
- **Fixation** – inflexible and rigid behaviour or attitudes;

- **Rationalisation** – elaborate 'covering-up' of ideas/motives;
- **Projection** – attributing feelings and motives to others.

(*See* also the discussion on frustrated behaviour in Chapter 12.)

In summary, Freud saw adult personality as being largely determined by the strength of inner drives and impulses and the resolutions of these tensions within early childhood experiences. Freud's overwhelming interest lay in understanding the conflicts that exist for the person and how people come to terms with their anxieties and tensions. His interest therefore lay in understanding the whole person and not in identifying traits or types.

Neo-Freudians   Freud produced a generation of scholars who developed his ideas to produce their own theories and models of personality development. Although of course rooted in Freudian thinking, the neo-Freudians have deviated from Freud in important respects. Two of the most significant are *Karen Horney* and *Melanie Klein*.

- Although *Karen Horney* accepted certain principles of Freud's theory with regard to unconscious motivation, she disagreed with the predominance of sexual forces and her theory suggests far more optimism than Freud's.[38]
- *Melanie Klein* encouraged the study of the sources of anxiety. She suggested that the principal source of anxiety was the fear of the death instinct. She posited that early childhood is a critical time for the formulation and development of lifelong mental attitudes.

Jung

Carl Jung's theory is of particular significance in that it bridges Freudian ideas with modern approaches of personality test design. His theory identifies life energy as concerned with hopes and goals of the future and not just of the past. Unlike Freud, Jung describes three levels of personality:

- a conscious level (daily reality);
- an unconscious level (contains our own unique complexes); and
- a collective unconscious level (store of universal and evolutionary experiences).

Jung identified four universal aspects of our personality which he referred to as archetypes which we all share. For instance, according to Jung, we all strive for self-actualisation; have a darker self; have both masculine and feminine qualities; and have a persona – a role we can play.[39]

Personality functions and attitudes   However, it was Jung's identification of personality functions and attitudes which was applied to the rigours of systematic testing by *Isabel Briggs-Myers and Katherine Briggs*.[40] Jung identified differences between individuals in terms of their libidinal energy which could flow outwards to the external world (extrovert) or inwards to their inner world (introvert). Personality differences would also be manifest through differing cognitive functions of thinking, feeling, sensation and intuition. The **Myers–Briggs Type Indicator (MBTI)** is based on these theoretical constructs with the additional dimension of style of living. The personality types are shown in Figure 9.4.

The MBTI has promoted considerable research interest, particularly with regard to the correlation between personality type, occupations and management style.

Sensing types		Intuitive types	
ISTJ Quiet, serious, earn success by thoroughness and dependability. Practical, matter-of-fact, realistic and responsible. Decide logically what should be done and work towards it steadily, regardless of distractions. Take pleasure in making everything orderly and organised – their work, their home, their life. Value traditions and loyalty.	**ISFJ** Quiet, friendly, responsible, and conscientious. Committed and steady in meeting their obligations. Thorough, painstaking and accurate. Loyal, considerate, notice and remember details about people who are important to them, concerned with how others feel. Strive to create an orderly and harmonious environment at work and at home.	**INFJ** Seek meaning and connection in ideas, relationships and material possessions. Want to understand what motivates people and are insightful about others. Conscientious and committed to their firm values. Develop a clear vision about how best to serve the common good. Organised and decisive in implementing their vision.	**INTJ** Have original minds and great drive for implementing their ideas and achieving their goals. Quickly see patterns in external events and develop long-range explanatory perspectives. When committed, organise a job and carry it through. Sceptical and independent, have high standards of competence and performance – for themselves and others.
ISTP Tolerant and flexible, quiet observers until a problem appears, then act quickly to find workable solutions. Analyse what makes things work and readily get through large amounts of data to isolate the core of practical problems. Interested in cause and effect, organise facts using logical principles, value efficiency.	**ISFP** Quiet, friendly, sensitive and kind. Enjoy the here-and-now, what's going on around them. Like to have their own space and to work within their own time frame. Loyal and committed to their values and to people who are important to them. Dislike disagreements and conflicts, do not force their opinions or values on others.	**INFP** Idealistic, loyal to their values and to people who are important to them. Want an external life that is congruent with their values. Curious, quick to see possibilities, can be catalysts for implementing ideas. Seek to understand people and to help them fulfil their potential. Adaptable, flexible and accepting unless a value is threatened.	**INTP** Seek to develop logical explanations for everything that interests them. Theoretical and abstract, interested more in ideas than in social interaction. Quiet, contained, flexible and adaptable. Have unusual ability to focus in depth to solve problems in their area of interest. Sceptical, sometimes critical, always analytical.
ESTP Flexible and tolerant, they take a pragmatic approach focused on immediate results. Theories and conceptual explanations bore them – they want to act energetically to solve the problem. Focus on the here-and-now, spontaneous, enjoy each moment that they can be active with others. Enjoy material comforts and style. Learn best through doing.	**ESFP** Outgoing, friendly and accepting. Exuberant lovers of life, people and material comforts. Enjoy working with others to make things happen. Bring common sense and a realistic approach to their work, and make work fun. Flexible and spontaneous, adapt readily to new people and environments. Learn best by trying a new skill with other people.	**ENFP** Warmly enthusiastic and imaginative. See life as full of possibilities. Make connections between events and information very quickly, and confidently proceed based on the patterns they see. Want a lot of affirmation from others, and readily give appreciation and support. Spontaneous and flexible, often rely on their ability to improvise and their verbal fluency.	**ENTP** Quick, ingenious, stimulating, alert and outspoken. Resourceful in solving new and challenging problems. Adept at generating conceptual possibilities and then analysing them strategically. Good at reading other people. Bored by routine, will seldom do the same thing the same way, apt to turn to one new interest after another.
ESTJ Practical, realistic, matter-of-fact. Decisive, quickly move to implement decisions. Organise projects and people to get things done, focus on getting results in the most efficient way possible. Take care of routine details. Have a clear set of logical standards, systematically follow them and want others to also. Forceful in implementing their plans.	**ESFJ** Warm-hearted, conscientious and cooperative. Want harmony in their environment, work with determination to establish it. Like to work with others to complete tasks accurately and on time. Loyal, follow through even in small matters. Notice what others need in their day-to-day lives and try to provide it. Want to be appreciated for who they are and for what they contribute.	**ENFJ** Warm, empathetic, responsive and responsible. Highly attuned to the emotions, needs and motivations of others. Find potential in everyone, want to help others fulfil their potential. May act as catalysts for individual and group growth. Loyal, responsive to praise and criticism. Sociable, facilitate others in a group, and provides inspiring leadership.	**ENTJ** Frank, decisive, assume leadership readily. Quickly see illogical and inefficient procedures and policies, develop and implement comprehensive systems to solve organisational problems. Enjoy long-term planning and goal setting. Usually well informed, well read, enjoy expanding their knowledge and passing it on to others. Forceful in presenting their ideas.
Introverts		**Extroverts**	

Figure 9.4 The Myers–Briggs Type Indicator showing characteristics frequently associated with particular personality types

(Modified and reproduced by special permission of the Publisher, Consulting Psychologists Press, Inc., Palo Alto, CA 94303 from *Myers–Briggs Type Indicator Report Form* by Isabel Briggs-Myers. Copyright © 1976 by Consulting Psychologists Press, Inc. All rights reserved. Further reproduction is prohibited without the Publisher's written consent. 'Myers–Briggs Type Indicator' and 'MBTI' are registered trademarks of Consulting Psychologists Press, Inc.)

Cognitive theory: Kelly's personal construct theory

Kelly's theory of personal constructs does not just consider personality development; it considers the whole person in terms of their perceptions, attitudes and goals. For Kelly, personality is the individual's way of construing and experimenting with their world. Kelly was critical of separating the study of personality apart from the 'whole' person:

> *The castrating effect of separating personality off as a mini-psychology in its own right is perhaps best seen in the curiously named study of 'individual differences', which in fact turns out to be the study of group sameness. As a result we have focused on the establishment of general dimensions, at some point along which all individuals can be placed, rather than on a study of the dimensions which each individual develops in order to organise his own world.*[41]

For Kelly it was critical to take data from one individual person (idiography) and to employ a technique which could cope with the qualitative nature of the data to be collected. He developed the Repertory Grid which was able to measure an individual's construct of the world. Kelly was thus able to employ a clear and valid measure within an idiographic approach. This was an important advance in idiographic techniques and the repertory technique has become increasingly important as a research tool. It enables the person to use his/her own constructions of the world but in such a way that they are comparable and measurable.

Illustration of Kelly's repertory grid technique

An example of the repertory grid technique is provided from a case study by *Fiona Wilson*. The research examined the impact of computer numerical control (CNC) technology in the engineering industry. Its main objective was to explore the effect of new technology on the responses of both craftsmen and managers in two differing companies. One of the research measures used to explore the subjective experiences of the workers was Kelly's Repertory Grid. Wilson describes it as a 'formalised conversation' and says that 'It is an attempt to stand in others' shoes, to see their world as they see it, to understand their situation, their concerns'.[42]

Using this technique, Wilson was able to measure the workers' own feelings and motivations, and to understand the impact that technology had on their job, their skills and sense of self worth. She noted in her conclusion that the strategic decisions made by the two companies in their utilisation of the new technology made a direct and measurable impact on the perception and attitudes of the craftsmen. An example of the repertory grid is given in Table 9.7. (*See* Assignment 1 at the end of this chapter for an application of the repertory grid.)

Table 9.7 An example of a first repertory grid

1	CNC job	Skilled turner's job	Ideal job (professional footballer)	Job I would enjoy (electrician, own business)	Job I would not enjoy (a job on an oil rig)	Job I would hate (miner)	7
Boring	3	4	7	7	2	1	Interesting
Unskilled	2	5	7	6	2	2	Skilled
Not physically demanding	4	5	7	2	7	7	Physically demanding
Gives no job satisfaction	2	5	7	6	2	2	Gives job satisfaction

Table 9.7 continued

1	CNC job	Skilled turner's job	Ideal job (professional footballer)	Job I would enjoy (electrician, own business)	Job I would not enjoy (a job on an oil rig)	Job I would hate (miner)	7
Unsafe working conditions	5	3	5	6	2	1	Safe working conditions
Dirty work conditions	4	2	6	7	2	1	Clean work conditions
A job in which I am not respected	2	5	7	7	2	2	A job in which I am respected
A job with no challenge	3	6	7	7	3	3	A challenging job
A job in which I do not reap the gains	2	2	7	7	2	2	A job in which I reap the gains
A job where I am tied to one place	2	3	7	7	1	2	A job where I am free to move about

(Reprinted with permission of Fiona Wilson from Case 4, 'Deskilling of work?' The Case of Computer Numerical Control in the Engineering Industry', first published in Jim McGoldrick (ed.) *Business Case File in Behavioural Science*, Van Nostrand Reinhold (1987).)

Applications within the work organisation

Organisations regard personality as being of key significance in their decision-making and it would be rare for organisations not to take the personality of a candidate into consideration at a selection interview. For some organisations, personality is the major criterion for selection or rejection. The hospitality industry, for example, is replete with research studies demonstrating the potency of personality.[43] So, how do organisations assess a candidate's personality?

The interview remains the most usual method of selection, but there is an increasing use of objective psychometric measures. Such growth in psychometric testing is significant and a number of studies have demonstrated its growing popularity.[44] Concern has been expressed about the use and misuse of psychological instruments and there is a continuing debate within psychological circles with regard to the validity of these measures.[45] Psychological measures can be distinguished between tests of:

- typical performance (of which personality assessment is one example); and
- maximum performance (including ability and intelligence tests).

These differences are discussed in detail in the next section. There are controversies and sensitivities surrounding the use of any psychological test, but tests of typical performance are especially problematic in certain circumstances. As *Anastasi* has stated:

> *The construction and use of personality inventories are beset with special difficulties over and above common problems encountered in all psychological testing. The question of faking and malingering is far more acute in personality measurement than in aptitude testing.*[46]

Recent critics have accused consultants and practitioners of inappropriate use of personality assessments and claim low validity between non-work-related personality assessments and work performance.[47] *Goss* suggests that the use of personality assessments not only is an infringement of the individual's privacy but also leads to unfortunate organisational consequences with 'cloning' as an outcome. Such techniques can be perceived as a form of social engineering and an insidious form of organisational control.[48]

Aware of these problems, the British Psychological Society has produced guidelines and codes of practice for users of psychometric tests. A number of studies positively support the use of personality assessments as an aid to selection decisions.[49] Furthermore, evidence is emerging to show that where personality questionnaires have been specifically designed and related to work characteristics, prediction and validity scores are much higher.[50]

Despite reservations concerning personality questionnaires, they can be particularly valuable if individuals complete them for their own benefit and development. As an introduction in a self-awareness programme, personality questionnaires can initiate discussion about individual differences. In these situations there is no judgement about better or worse characteristics or matching of individuals to personnel specifications; rather, the discussion centres on the value of individual differences and the strengths which each personality type can bring to the working situation.

Producing a good team of people requires understanding of the team's strengths and weaknesses. A balanced team with complementary personalities, skills and abilities is ideal. Personality questionnaires can therefore be the first part of this process – an audit of strengths and weaknesses. This could be followed by group training exercises designed to develop strengths and balance the weaknesses of the team. An effective team at work should be aware of the division of their strengths and weaknesses.

> *None of us is perfect; but a group of people, whose strengths and talents complement each other, can be.*[51]

Early leadership studies attempted to identify the personality traits in an effort to establish differences between the leaders and the followers. These studies were unsuccessful in finding recurring personality traits among leaders. More recent approaches have established ways of analysing the dynamics of the situation/leader/group. (*See* Chapter 8 for further details.) The interaction between personality and expected role behaviour is certainly an interesting area of study.

Although personality is a powerful determinant of a manager's effectiveness, account must also be taken of the social rules and expectations within the workplace. There is no doubt that in some organisations these expectations are very forceful and insist upon behaviour which conforms to cultural demands. In some roles the individual's personality is in danger of being undermined. For instance, it would be a surprise to meet an introverted, quiet and reflective Head Chef in a major hotel or a paramedic who was frantic, nervy and hysterical.

Stress and the individual

Personality is a contributing factor in the understanding of stress. Individuals who have a personality classified as Type A are more likely to suffer from heart disease under severe stress than individuals with a Type B personality.[52] Stress is a complex topic. It is individually defined and is intrinsically tied into an individual's perceptual system. Everyone has a range of comfort within which they can feel steady and safe. Stress occurs when the individual feels that they are working outside of that comfort zone. Individuals will differ when they feel discomfort. The effects of stress will differ too; for some, the incidence of stress may energise and activate but for others it may immobilise. Headaches, muscular tension, fatigue and hypertension have all been cited as effects of stress.[53] The physiological effects of stress wear down the body making it more vulnerable to illness.

The costs of stress at individual, organisational and national levels are well known. *Cooper* has indicated the high incidence of stress throughout organisations irrespective of job seniority. He suggests that every job has its own stress fingerprint.[54] Stress is a term, which is commonly used and misused; being 'stressed out' may be said by some individuals at the slightest amount of pressure and tension. It also contains a perverse sense of status; for instance a librarian complained bitterly that her role was regarded as having low stress, implying that jobs given a 'high stress' position also ranked high in prestige.

What causes stress?

Cooper and others[55] have identified six major sources of stress at work:

- intrinsic to the job – working conditions, shift work, etc.;
- role in the organisation – overload; underload;
- relationships at work – particularly with the boss;
- career development – mid-life being a critical stage;
- organisational structure and climate – the extent of rules and regulations;
- home–work interface – particularly the growth of dual-career families.

Conflicts at work are another undeniable cause of stress and a sub-category of Cooper's model. Evidence of bullying at work has recently been uncovered in research completed by *Edelmann and Woodall*[56] in schools. Bullies in their study were typically over the age of 40 (85.3%), in positions of authority, marginally more likely to be female (52.9%) and were described by their victims as being insecure about themselves because of the stress and workload pressures (33.7%). The cost of being bullied was high and resulted in a number of ailments, both physiological and psychological. The researchers reported that the incidence of bullying was on the increase, and to prevent a worsening situation appropriate steps need to be taken. Such actions included proper management training and clear procedures to deal with bullying acts. (Stress at work is also discussed in Chapter 18.)

Harassment not only puts strains on working life but also can transfer to impact upon relationships at home. Victims may lose their commitment to work and, depending on how the incident(s) is dealt with, may lose their motivation to work, their respect of their line manager and work colleagues. *Equality Direct* lists the following list of behaviours amounting to harassment:

- any physical contact which is unwanted;
- the display of offensive material;
- shouting at colleagues or personal insults;
- coercion, isolation or freezing out;
- persistent criticism;
- unwelcome remarks about a person's dress, appearance or marital status;
- setting impossible deadlines.[57]

Because the nature of human stress is complex and socially and culturally bound, it is interesting to reflect on its possible developments. Is it the case that stress predominates nowadays because our expectations are still bound within the bureaucratic organisations of earlier decades of work? Personal life commitments are significantly tied into full employment and a career for life (with a 25-year mortgage and easier credit arrangements) and yet evidence is growing of organisations' requirements for shorter and more flexible working patterns. Perhaps, with an increasing awareness of the changing nature of work patterns and a reorganisation of the interface between work and home, stress may be reduced or at the very least may be perceived in new ways. Are we currently at the cusp of new changes where a new generation may have differing expectations and may adapt their lives to suit a new order and style?

Ability

It is self-evident that different occupations require different skills, competencies and abilities. It is also the case that individuals vary with regard to their mental abilities and the extent to which they apply them at work. The 'happy' scenario is that a match should occur between the individual's abilities and their occupation, but reality suggests that this is not always the case. The extremes include employees bored rigid with a simple task who become slipshod in their attitude and make a succession of mistakes, and the employees who have been promoted beyond their capability. The result could be stress either for the individuals unable to cope or their work colleagues who are picking up the debris left behind. It can be assumed that a person's ability is dependent upon his or her intelligence, but the study of intelligence has revealed a number of controversies and sensitivities.

In a similar vein to the studies of personality, different schools of thought have emerged with regard to the study of abilities. Similar debates to the ones that surround the study of personality have also swirled around the research on intelligence.

- Is intelligence inherited? Is it constant throughout life? Is it dependent upon our life's experiences, our culture, our education, etc.?
- What is the nature of intelligence? Can it be measured and how?

Is intelligence inherited? The **nativists** believe that intelligence is mostly inherited (nature), while the **empiricists** believe that our environment shapes our behaviour and mental abilities (nurture). *Galton's*[58] thesis suggested that genius seemed to run in families and proposed that intelligence must be inherited. He studied eminent families and noted that sons of famous fathers also showed special talents and abilities. The notion that such sons may have 'rich' and stimulating environments with the opportunity to learn and develop talents did not enter into Galton's argument.

Cyril Burt's influential work in the 1930s not only lent support to the genetic argument but also influenced educational policy. However, in the 1980s, fraudulent practice was uncovered with the discovery that the data and the research assistants had been invented by Burt.[59]

Other sources of evidence about inherited intelligence have come from studies completed on twins. Identical twins who were separated at birth and reared in different homes were considered as ideal subjects for investigating whether intelligence was inherited. If it was found that the intelligence tests revealed similar results at the end of their childhood, this would be compelling support for the inherited argument. However, many critics argued that there were in fact great similarities in the class background of different families. Rather than comparing twins who experienced substantial differences in their upbringing, the twins had often been placed in homes which came from a similar community – thus the strength of the genetic argument was diluted.

Howe[60] summarises recent convincing evidence to show that intervention can have an impact on IQ. He cites evidence from early intervention programmes such as Head Start initiatives and other schooling effects, from studies of child adoption and from nutritional studies. Howe concludes that: 'The empirical findings provide no support for the pessimistic conclusion that low intelligence and the problems associated with it are inevitable and unalterable.'

The political implications of research into the nature of intelligence are striking. Some of the earliest theories influenced the educational philosophy of England and Wales, including how children were selected for different types of secondary education and the kind of help that should be given to children with special needs.

Can intelligence be measured and how?

Binet and Simon,[61] working in France, were the first psychologists to measure ability in a systematic and structured way. They were responsible for identifying children with special educational needs and they developed a battery of exercises for children to perform at specific ages. They established a mental age for each task based on the 'normal' ability of children and were therefore able to identify those children whose mental age was not the same as their chronological (actual) age.

Terman[62] working at Stanford University in the United States advanced the ideas of Binet and developed an intelligence test known as the Stanford–Binet Test which was designed to measure intelligence across a wide scale. The tests were able to provide a 'score' of the child's intelligence. The Intelligence Quotient (or IQ) was the calculation of the:

$$\frac{\text{Mental age}}{\text{Chronological (Actual) age}} \times 100 = \text{Intelligence Quotient}$$

Hence a child who is 10 years and has a mental age of 10 will have an IQ score of 100; a child of 10 years with a mental age of 12 will have an IQ score of 120; and a child of 10 years with a mental age of 8 will have an IQ score of 80.

What is the nature of intelligence?

Arguments have raged within psychologists' circles as to the nature of intelligence. Is it dependent on a general overall factor which will have an overarching effect on specific activities? Or are specific activities independent of each other?

In other words, if a child shows a high level of ability at mathematics is this dependent on an overall high general ability? General ability can be seen as a kind of powerhouse which releases some of its energy into the child's ability at mathematics. (For other children it may act as a limiting factor.)

Spearman[63] proposed a two-factor theory of intelligence and suggested that every intellectual task involves a level of mental agility – a general factor (g) – plus specific abilities (s). This idea, developed by *Vernon*,[64] resulted in a model which placed abilities in a hierarchy (*see* Figure 9.5).

Abilities at the lower end of the hierarchy in Figure 9.5 are more likely to correlate, so hence if a child has a good vocabulary, she is more likely to have abilities in reading and comprehension too.

Crystallised and fluid intelligence

Cattell suggests that the g factor could be constructed as having one dimension which is independent of any direct learning or experience. He called this **fluid intelligence** which he suggested was the type of abstract reasoning ability which is free of any cultural influences. The second dimension, called the **crystallised intelligence**, is dependent upon learning, cultural experiences and is part of our general understanding of the world around us. *Bartram and Lindley*[65] suggested that the two abilities should not be seen as distinct but that:

> ... in effect, there is a continuum from fluid ability at one end to crystallised ability at the other. In practice we do not have tests of 'pure ability' as there will always be some impact, however slight, of our culture and background. But the distinction is a useful one.

Other psychologists have argued that the presence of 'g' – this powerhouse – is an unnecessary artefact. What is important in understanding abilities is the way in which

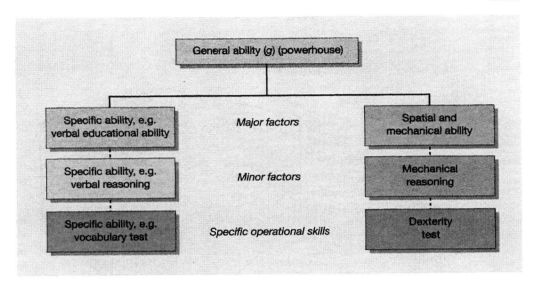

Figure 9.5 A hierarchy of abilities

(*Source*: Adapted from P. E. Vernon, 'The hierarchy of abilities', in Wiseman, S. (ed.) *Intelligence and Ability*,) Penguin (1959.)

the different abilities can be identified and measured. *Thurstone*[66] claimed seven primary mental abilities which can be separately measured resulting in a profile of scores:

- spatial ability
- perceptual speed
- numerical reasoning
- verbal reasoning
- memory
- verbal fluency
- inductive reasoning.

Other models of intelligence

Guilford[67] criticised theories which aimed to simplify intelligence into a small number of factors. He devised a model which identified 120 different abilities and suggested that intellectual ability requires individuals to think in one of three dimensions.

- **Content.** What must the individual think about (for example, meaning of words or numbers)?
- **Operations.** What kind of thinking is the individual required to do (for example, recognising items, solving a problem, evaluating an outcome)?
- **Products.** What kind of outcome or answer is required (for example, classifying or reordering items)?

(*See* Figure 9.6.)

Guilford also expressed concern about the convergent nature of tests that required a single solution or answer. He suggested that tests should also be looking at an individual's ability to produce divergent answers.

Intelligence – one or many?

Gardner[68] regarded the simplification of intelligence in terms of an IQ measure as unrealistic in the light of different intelligent behaviour that could be observed in everyday life. Although intelligence tests may offer one explanation of why an individual performs better in an academic institution, and may be a legitimate measure of such behaviour, it failed to take into account the full range of intelligent activity. He

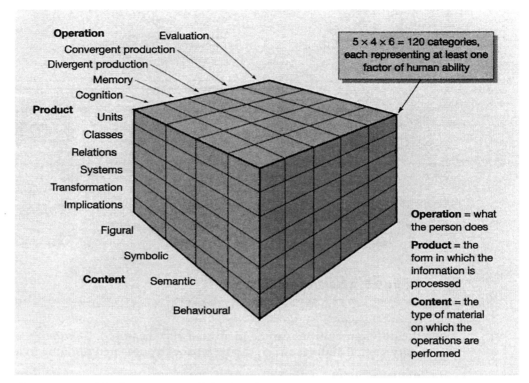

Figure 9.6 Guilford's structure of the intellect model
(*Source*: J. P. Guilford, 'Three faces of intellect', in Wiseman, S. (ed.) *Intelligence and Ability*, Penguin (1959).)

suggested that there was a multiple of intelligences and categorised them into seven varieties (all of which could be further divided):

Verbal	Akin to the factors described in earlier theories
Mathematical	
Spatial capacity	Ability shown by artists and architects
Kinaesthetic	Abilities of a physical nature
Musical	Abilities of musicianship
	Interpersonal – skills with other people
Personal intelligences	Intrapersonal – knowing oneself

Agreement from other psychologists concerning the multiple dimensional aspect of intelligence has further developed the idea of a 'practical intelligence',[69] which describes the kind of problem-solving strategies individuals use in their work situation. The work situation may allow a range of flexible solutions to problems, enabling divergent and creative thinking to take place. (See Chapter 10 for further development of creative thinking.)

An elaboration of some of Gardner's ideas was made by *Goleman*[70] who agreed that the classic view of intelligence was too narrow. He felt that the emotional qualities of individuals should be considered as these, he felt, played a vital role in the application of intelligence in everyday life. He identified the key characteristics as:

abilities such as being able to motivate oneself and persist in the face of frustrations; to control impulse and delay gratification; to regulate one's moods and keep distress from swamping the ability to think; to emphasise and to hope.

Understanding and Managing People at Work

Emotional intelligence has received considerable attention over the last few years as the concept has been identified as a key aspect of managing people effectively. *Goleman* suggests that emotional intelligence or EI predicts top performance and accounts for more than 85 per cent of outstanding performance in top leaders[71] The Hay Group working with Goleman have identified 20 specific competencies that make up the four components of emotional intelligence and have produced an inventory designed to measure Emotional Competence (*see* Figure 9.7). The Emotional Competence Inventory defines EI as: 'The capacity for recognising our own feelings and those of others, for motivating ourselves and for managing emotions within ourselves and with others.'[72]

Testing

The early tests of intelligence have evolved into a large psychological business. Most people will have taken a **psychological test** of one kind or another by the time they are an adult in employment. Tests may be administered at school, college or as part of the selection assessment process at work. The use of tests is widespread and growing.[73] They are perceived to be useful as an objective discriminating tool, but they are not without some controversies and sensitivities.

Tests are broadly divided by the British Psychological Society into:

1 *Tests of typical performance.* These assess an individual's typical responses to given situations. Here answers indicate an individual's choices and strength of feelings. Answers are not right or wrong as such, but identify preferences. Personality assessments and interest inventories are examples of such tests. Although valuable in certain circumstances, tests of typical performance have certain limitations, as discussed in the previous section.

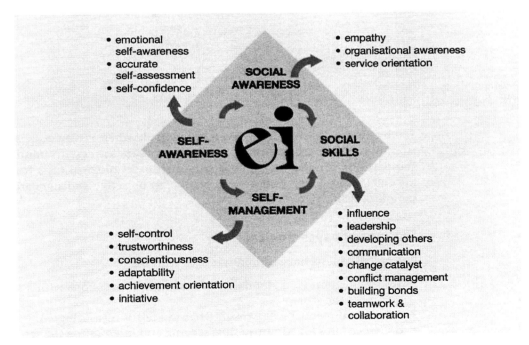

Figure 9.7 Emotional competence

(Reproduced with permission from Hay Group © 1999 Hay Group Limited. All rights reserved.)

Understanding and Managing People at Work

2 *Tests of maximum performance.* These assess an individual's ability to perform effectively under standard conditions. Performance on these tests, which include ability and aptitude tests, can be judged as right or wrong. Ability tests come in many different forms and may test a **general intellectual functioning** or a **specific ability** (such as verbal reasoning, numerical reasoning, etc.).

Alice Heim developed a series of general ability tests – AH series – which are widely used to assess general ability. They test three key areas: verbal, numerical and diagrammatical reasoning. For example, an individual would be asked questions similar to the following:

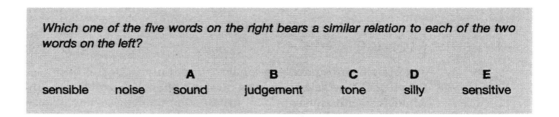

Modern Occupational Skills Tests are an example of specific ability tests and measure a range of clerical and administrative skills: verbal checking; technical checking, numerical estimation, etc. They claim to be an aid in the selection of administrative staff. Their tests are short and can be used singly or together as a battery of tests. The individual would be asked questions similar to the following:

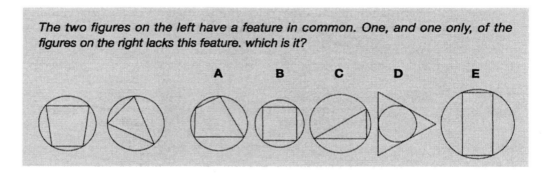

Some tests are designed to be given individually whereas others are suitable for administering within a group situation. However, there are certain minimum features and standards of conditions which distinguish psychological tests from other forms of informal assessments; tests are essentially 'an objective and standardised measure of a sample of behaviour'.[74]

Features of psychological tests

Psychological tests have certain standard features:

1 Tests will comprise a standard task, or a set of questions with a standard means of obtaining the score.
2 A technical manual will explain what the test is measuring, how it was constructed, the procedures for administering, scoring and interpreting the test.

3 Details of the test's validity (what the test claims to be measuring – and what it is not measuring) and reliability (the test's ability to measure consistently) will also be shown in the manual along with the inferences that can be drawn from the data.

For a test to be considered as a psychological instrument it must be **objective, standardised, reliable, valid** and **discriminating** (*but not discriminatory*).

The selection and choice of the test should be based on a number of other key features such as its acceptability, practicality, time, costs and perceived and actual added value. Reviews of general ability tests are generally positive. One paper indicated that general mental ability tests show 'impressive criterion-related validity across all job types'.[75] While another in the US claimed that:

Measures of ability, achievement and knowledge (especially general mental ability) are probably the most valid and useful predictors of performance in most jobs.[76]

Limitations of tests

All tests have limitations. Tests can only sample behaviour at one particular moment in time. The information they provide is dependent upon good testing practice and will only add further evidence to the decision-making process. Tests will not provide *the* answer. Some individuals are very nervous and may not perform at their best and indeed some may feel indignant that they are obliged to take a test at all.

Jackson[77] identifies a central area of concern in his discussion of fairness in testing. He distinguishes between fairness of outcome and fairness of process. In the selection process he suggests that **fairness of outcome** implies 'choosing the best person for the job'. This is dependent upon measures of later performance to confirm the predictive validity of the test. Such processes are essential if organisations are to be certain of the value of tests and are not merely using tests as an administrative convenience to keep the shortlist shorter!

By **fairness of process**, Jackson refers to errors and bias that can occur during the testing process. Some problems can be limited by good testing practice, but other sources of bias are more complex. Certain tests have been found to show differences in average performance levels between men and women or between different racial or ethnic groups. *Feltham et al.* suggests that the test may not in itself be unfair but using the test will lead to different outcomes and different proportions of people being selected.[78] Some tests have been found to have an adverse impact. Psychologists need to work with personnel professionals to be certain that all parts of the testing process are fair and objective.

Tests should be kept under review. Were they useful? Did they enable a confident prediction of future work behaviour and performance? Unfortunately, many organisations may spend considerable time and money on training and in choosing a test, but then do not perform adequate research and set up suitable evaluation procedures for testing the test.

If organisations do not treat the candidate fairly – that is, provide them with feedback of results – a damaging impact on the reputation of the organisation can result. The testing process means that candidates spend a considerable amount of their own personal time on a process which is demanding and potentially intimidating. If they feel they have been treated with respect they maintain a positive image of the organisation even if it has rejected them.[79] The personal, intrusive and threatening nature of the psychological tests should not be forgotten.

Exhibit 9.1 illustrates the main arguments for and against the use of psychological tests.

The use of psychological tests as part of the staff selection process is discussed in Chapter 20.

Exhibit 9.1

Why use psychological tests?

1 They make decisions about people
  - more systematic
  - more precise.

2 They predict future performance and reduce uncertainty.

3 They provide more accurate descriptions of people and their behaviour. Precise definitions and measured variables lead to further studies and improve understanding of the relationship between tests and performance.

But

  - Tests should be seen as an additional source of information only.
  - Tests may be expensive and time-consuming.
  - Without proper professional practice, they can be misused and results abused.
  - They may be seen as an intrusion.
  - They may be regarded as inappropriate.
  - Practice may have an effect on test results.

Attitudes

There are no limits to the attitudes people hold. Attitudes are learned throughout life and are embodied within our socialisation process. Some attitudes (such as religious beliefs) may be central to us – a core construct – and may be highly resistant to any change, whereas other, more peripheral attitudes may change with new information or personal experiences. Specific events, particularly traumatic ones such as redundancy, may have a dramatic effect on our attitudes.

What are attitudes?

So what are **attitudes** and how can they be distinguished from beliefs and values?

- **Attitudes** can be defined as providing a state of 'readiness' or tendency to respond in a particular way.[80]
- **Beliefs** are concerned with what is known about the world; they centre on what 'is', on reality as it is understood.
- **Values** are concerned with what 'should' be and what is desirable.

Gross suggests that

> *to convert a belief into an attitude, a 'value' ingredient is needed which, by definition, is to do with an individual's sense of what is desirable, good, valuable, worthwhile and so on.*

It has been suggested by Gross that whereas 'adults may have thousands of beliefs, they may have only hundreds of attitudes and a few dozen values'.[81] *Hofstede* defines values as 'broad tendency to prefer certain states of affairs over others'.[82]

The functions of attitudes

Katz has suggested that attitudes and motives are interlinked and, depending on an individual's motives, attitudes can serve four main functions.

- **Knowledge.** One of the major functions is to provide a basis for the interpretation and classification of new information. Attitudes provide a knowledge base and framework within which new information can be placed.

- **Expressive.** Attitudes become a means of expression. They enable individuals to indicate to others the values that they hold and thus to express their self-concept and adopt or internalise the values of a group.
- **Instrumental.** Held attitudes maximise rewards and minimise sanctions. Hence, attitudes towards other people (or objects) might be held because of past positive (or negative) experiences. Behaviour or knowledge which has resulted in the satisfaction of needs is thus more likely to result in a favourable attitude.
- **Ego-defensive.** Attitudes may be held in order to protect the ego from an undesirable truth or reality.[83]

Prediction of behaviour

Is it possible to predict behaviour, if we know an individual's attitude?

Research suggests the answer is 'No'. It seems that we do not always behave in a way that is true to our beliefs; what we say and what we do may be very different. Such evidence indicates that attitudes can be revealed not only in behaviour but also by the individual's thoughts (although these may not be revealed in public) and by feelings, the strength of which demonstrates the extent to which the attitude is a core or peripheral construct.

A classic study by *La Piere* illustrates this point. Visiting American hotels and restaurants with a Chinese couple, *La Piere* found no sign of prejudiced attitudes in the face-to-face situation, but there were marked racist attitudes in the follow-up attitude survey. He found complete contradictions between public and private attitudes.[84]

These findings have important implications for the study of attitudes and reveal two important issues for the psychologist and manager.

1 Attitudes cannot be seen; they can only be inferred.

Given that the attitudes employees hold are important for morale and the effectiveness of organisations, it is important that there is confidence in the measurement techniques used to assess the strength of attitudes. As attitudes are inferred, heavy reliance is placed therefore on the accuracy of assessment. Although there are a number of different techniques which could be used to measure attitudes, the two most common techniques are **direct observation** and **self-reporting techniques**.

All of us observe others and assess attitudes on the basis of communication style (both verbal and non-verbal) and behaviour. This is an example of an in-formal approach – unsystematic, spontaneous and based on our understanding of social cues. We may be wrong in our judgement. Students who turn up late for classes, slouch on their seat and do not ask questions may still hold very positive attitudes towards organisational behaviour. Managers may also be erroneous in their assumptions and beliefs about their colleagues (both subordinates and superiors). Their beliefs may never have been tested out – merely assumed to be correct.

Organisations which assess their employees' attitudes by using attitude questionnaires (self-reporting techniques) are attempting to systematically gauge and measure these assumptions. Attitude questionnaires are time-consuming to design and administer. The questions asked, their relevance, style and length are all important variables in the validity of the questionnaire. So, too, is the honest completion of questionnaires.

Making public people's private attitudes may also have its dangers as expectations of change may be envisaged. If these do not occur, disappointment and low morale may be the result.[85] (*See also* the discussion on the Johari window in Chapter 14.)

Attitude questionnaires are used by many companies as a barometer for the attitudinal climate of organisations and as such enable managers to be in touch with employees' views and feelings.

2 Attitudes are often shared within organisations and as such are embodied in the culture of organisations.

This does not imply that attitudes are constructed just within the organisations. Classic research has shown the influence of the wider community in the formation of orientations towards work. Differences in class/orientation may elicit a range of loyalties and possibly produce opposing perceptions of commitment, loyalty and co-operation.

For example, *Salaman* states that 'the commitment and co-operation of worker members of the organisation is frequently regarded by senior management as problematic and uncertain' and suggests that consensus and control has to be achieved by the selection and manipulation of attitudes, values and knowledge.[86] Thus, counter-cultures are recognised as having a powerful influence on the maintenance of an organisation's integrity. *Kanter* suggests that people within counter-cultures who change their orientation and identify with organisational values face criticism and hostility from their peer group.[87]

Thus research suggests that attitudes are not just individually formed but arise out of interaction with others. They are often 'locked-in', often regarded as obvious, mere common sense, and are so much taken for granted that they may be overlooked. Sharing the belief system of others also has affective outcomes. If people feel that they belong and are included, it enables them to feel good about working in an organisation. If, on the other hand, people do not feel part of the organisation – if they feel that they do not share the dominant attitudes and beliefs – negative emotional consequences are likely to result. Studies of token women in management support these ideas.

Attitudes, managers and culture

Although the role, power and responsibility of managers vary from organisation to organisation, all managers regardless of status contribute to the maintenance of the organisation's culture. In one sense the position of manager is a formal recognition of success and as such managers play a key role in personifying the culture. It has been suggested that managers and their culture are inseparable from each other and that managers consistently influence and affect the perceptions and attitudes of their subordinates.[88] Organisations may initiate rituals and ceremonies to encourage and maintain certain attitudes and beliefs.[89] Many attitudes and ideas become permanent and unchallengeable, making them highly resistant to change.[90]

A shared understanding
Research by *Hicks* in the hotel industry revealed that irrespective of personal circumstances (age, gender, education, social class) managers had been exposed to a process which had 'encultured' them to a shared understanding of the industry, resulting in common attitudes on a range of topics. Attitudes towards their management trainees were found to be significant with regard to the trainees' development; high expectation of their trainees ensured broad training opportunities and the use of their own personal network of contacts to ensure their protégés' success. The significance of positive attitudes of managers towards their trainees cannot therefore be over-emphasised.[91]

Attitude change

The permanency of attitudes clearly has implications for attitudinal change. At the beginning of this section it was pointed out that whereas peripheral attitudes may easily change with new information or experiences, central attitudes tied into other cognitive systems may be much more difficult to shift.

Theories on attitude change stress the importance of **balance** and **consistency** in our psyche.

- *Heider*, for example, suggests that not only would we find it uncomfortable to hold two conflicting attitudes, but to do so would motivate us to change one of the attitudes in order to reach a balanced state.[92]
- Cognitive dissonance is the term given to the discomfort felt when we act in a way that is inconsistent with our true beliefs. Like balance theory, it suggests that we are motivated to reduce its impact.[93]

The process of attitude change is dependent on a number of key factors, the most important being:

- why an attitude is held in the first place;
- why it should change;
- what the benefits are and to whom;
- what the outcomes are if it does not change.

Considerable research has demonstrated the importance of the following variables in a programme of attitude change:

- the persuader's characteristics;
- presentation of issues;
- audience characteristics;
- group influences;
- outcome of attitude change (reward or punishment).

The implementation of change

The last decade has produced tumultuous change for employees and their managers. It would be rare indeed to find an organisation which has not experienced some degree of change in structure, product, processes, philosophy, culture or ownership. The way in which these changes are implemented can have a dramatic impact on the attitudes of staff. Research has shown that when organisations merge, even when they appear to be compatible in terms of their style and philosophy, stress and negative attitudes can result.[94] The affective component of attitudes therefore should not be underestimated; neither should its relationship with a host of other variables concerned with the motivation and morale of individuals at work. The ways that organisations can promote a positive climate to change will be examined in Chapter 10.

Morgan suggests that managers require increasing skill and competence in dealing with the 'emerging waves and challenges'. He believes that organisations and their managers need to 'develop the attitudes and skills that facilitate proactive management' and that special attention will need to be devoted to 'mobilise the energies and commitments of people through the creation of shared values and shared understandings'.[95]

Gender and organisations

This section examines the participation of men and women in the workforce, and in particular reviews the position and status of women.

One of our initial perceptions and classifications of another individual is the identification of his or her gender.

- How does this perception affect our behaviour?
- What difference does it make if our work group is predominantly male or female?
- Do women and men have different experiences at work?
- Are not organisations rational and neutral institutions – so why should gender make a difference?

- Does it matter that many classic theories have been carried out on men, by male researchers?
- What has been the influence of equal opportunity policies on work behaviour and on the position of women in organisations?

This section will explore the ways in which organisational behaviour can be more clearly understood by looking at the gender dimension. Traditionally, this area has been ignored and the result of this neglect has only recently been raised as an issue for concern. *Alvesson and due Billing* suggest that:

> *A gender perspective implies analysing the importance, meaning and consequences of what is culturally defined as male or masculine as well as female or feminine ways of thinking (knowing), feeling, valuing and acting. A gender perspective also implies an analysis of the organisational practices that maintain the division of labour between the sexes.*[96]

They claim that knowing and understanding these perspectives is important in a full analysis of organisational behaviour. Organisations may reinforce thinking patterns and behaviour, and individuals may in their turn maintain and encourage such patterns. The relationships between individuals and organisations are dynamic and may be reaffirmed in a number of subtle as well as explicit and overt ways. For example, a waitress attending tables may earn tips by being effective **and** feminine. The service and caring aspects of the role are reinforced and she may learn to focus on certain behaviours that attract more tips. For example, she may be particularly attentive to men.

However, gender research is replete with contradictions and confusions. Although there is a body of evidence to confirm the position, status and (lack of) power of women in organisations – aspects that can be measured and quantified – such clarity is blurred when it comes to understanding the subjective and qualitative aspects of working life.

It is not helpful to view all men and all women as homogeneous. There may be as many differences within each gender as between the two genders. Social class, race and age will affect attitudes, beliefs and values and may impinge upon different understandings of gender. Although earlier organisational research could be criticised as having been conducted by men largely investigating male behaviour, so too much of the research on women has been dominated by white middle-class women assuming their values are those ones which should be upheld.

Emotions, politics and gender

Emotions and politics surround the issue of gender. *Alvesson and due Billing*[97] suggest that some people may be over-sensitive to gender and interpret any negative comment as if it is symbolic of an act of discrimination. Likewise under-sensitivity may also occur and organisations may remain gender blind to everyday instances of bias and distortion. Although not easy, achieving the right balance (neither overwhelming nor rejecting the pervasiveness of gender) is an important skill in managing men and women at work.

Gender research illustrates the often contradictory nature of thinking and behaviour. Although stereotyped views attempt to bring some simple consistency and predictabilities into our worlds, the reality of behaviour confounds the issues. For instance, is the stereotype that women are more emotional and caring than men valid?

- Are men and women really so different in the expression of their emotions? Emotions of pleasure, stress and aggression are not just dominated by the one gender; observation of men and women at work reveals the spread of emotional responses.
- Are women really more caring than men? Cannot some men be as empathetic as some women, but is such behaviour similarly interpreted?

Women and men can be seen as both weak and strong, rational and emotional; but the interpretation and judgement may be different depending on the gender of the individual. An aggressive response by a man may be seen to be powerful, but by a woman may be seen as unfeminine and bossy.[98]

Glass ceiling and other practices

A view of the position and status of women at work does produce consistency of evidence in respect of where women work. Male domination of privilege and power within organisations is still an identifiable feature in organisations.

A review of statistical evidence reveals that the places where women work have not changed substantially and remain different in kind from male occupations. In essence, women are working in occupations which reflect their perceived role in society, and they are generally found servicing and caring for others. It is recognised that many organisations have adopted equal opportunity policies and are seriously examining whether they are fulfilling the potential of all their staff. However, statistics reveal that progress is slow and the number of women holding senior managerial positions is still insignificant (from 2 per cent in 1974 to 22 per cent in 2000).[99]

A '**glass ceiling**' still exists in many organisations, preventing women from rising to the top. Although changes were suggested by the Hansard Society Commission in 1990,[100] concerning working structures and practices and 'outmoded attitudes about the roles of women', the impact of such measures has been limited. The Report suggested ways in which the domestic role of women could be tackled more successfully in tandem with a managerial career. It did not challenge societal expectations of the dual role of women. Reported changes were ones of improvement rather than redress of women's position. Given the difficulties in changing attitudes, and the pervasiveness of organisational culture in maintaining beliefs, such an optimistic approach can now be seen as unrealistic. Other reports also reveal slow progress and conclude that the glass ceiling is being penetrated, but at a very slow pace. Women executives are still a rare sight in the city and in business generally.[101]

This slow pace is mirrored in a diverse range of occupational settings including institutions of Higher Education. In 1990, universities were criticised by the Hansard Society Commission as 'bastions of male power and privilege.[102] In 1995 statistics revealed that only 7.3 per cent of professors are women, and women make up just 25 per cent of junior lecturers. Women tending to be located within the lower points of the lecturer grades and *Helen Brown* noted that:

> the 19 per cent of full-time academic staff who are women are disproportionately located in lower grades and (where data are available) paid less than men in comparable positions through all grades.[103]

Some universities have embraced the notion that structural and cultural factors are major contributors in inhibiting women's career progression and are actively implementing equal opportunities policies. Brown notes that the success of a programme will be dependent upon 'clear leadership, accurate information about the composition of the workforce and practical supportive measures'.

Equal pay was the subject of a research programme initiated by the Equal Opportunities Commission.[104] The campaign called 'Valuing Women' was launched in October 1999 when data revealed that full-time working women earn only 81 per cent of the average hourly earnings of men. In addition to encouraging greater awareness of pay issues it also urged employers to audit their pay systems to identify any potential pay discrimination. A task force was set up to suggest workable solutions to the gender pay gap. Three studies were also commissioned to assess attitudes and awareness of equal pay. Line managers, sixth-form students were targeted as well as a National Survey implemented. The findings indicated there was low awareness of the gender pay gap. Amongst students 60 per cent considered that men and women with the same qualifications and doing the same jobs would earn the same pay (69 per cent male; 53 per cent female) and they were shocked that this was not the case. Both male and female line managers agreed that men were generally paid more than women, and that female employees sometimes receive less pay than their male counterparts even when doing the same job. It was felt that men are more aggressive than women in negotiating promotion and women are more likely to accept their current pay and position. It was agreed that salaries were rarely discussed openly in the workplace and employees are not generally aware of what their colleagues earn.

The survey indicates that the positive attitude held by young women is potentially misplaced. It would appear that equality issues should still be on the agenda of many organisations. Successful women executives receive good publicity and this can be perceived as 'women's issues' being a relic of the past.[105] Although there are more women now in middle management positions there are dangers that the reality is masked.

Equal Opportunities Policy

Equal Opportunity polices have been under scrutiny by researchers to establish whether such policies make a difference to behaviour. The increasing number of organisations joining Opportunity 2000[106] gave some credence to the notion that equal opportunities policies were becoming common practice in business. *Liff and Cameron*[107] argue that such policies have two elements:

● measures to ensure that women are treated in the same way as men;
● measures to address the distinctive characteristics of women which seem to disadvantage them in the workplace.

For Liff and Cameron measures which fall in the second category expose women to be perceived as different/deficient and requiring 'help'. By benefiting from such special treatment leads to potential hostility and resentment from men; a backlash could result. *Blakemore and Drake*[108] also point out the controversies that surround equal opportunities policies. They suggest that one of two images are portrayed: one which suggests that policies are concerned too much with power, influence and political correctness; the other image suggests that they are trying to mask real and continuing discrimination behaviour.

In their conclusion, Blakemore and Drake believe there is some room for optimism and quote examples from legislation which identify some progress and achievement. In particular, they note that best practice has occurred where attention has been focused on practical steps and actions rather than trying to change hearts and minds. Although they suggest changes have been rather of a 'ratchet' variety than an engine of change, change has occurred nonetheless. Such positive steps should be tempered by the prevalence of sexual harassment in the workplace and the unchanging roles of men and women. Men are unwilling to take on more domestic work or child care which leads Blakemore and Drake to propose that:

a 'role' related model of equality policy in the future will perhaps have to address the question of how to resocialise men for domestic work rather than women for paid work.

The message that these writers are advocating is one of partnership. It is of little value to focus on just 'women's issues' without taking a view on the changing role of men. The part that organisations can play is to look at the encouragement they are giving to men as well as women in balancing their lives. We will consider some of these work-life balance initiatives at the end of this section, but first a consideration of the changing nature of men and women's contribution to work.

Historical context

Historical context

What is the historical context of men and women at work? Where have the changes occurred?

It is commonly felt that women's participation in the labour force has been increasing steadily. The increase in the number of married women working since the Second World War has been identified as a significant change and *Lewis* asserts that the older married woman is the typical female worker.[109] Historians have identified that going to work changed the notion of work as something that was public, paid and therefore seen to be valuable.

Interestingly, in the nineteenth century, occupations that women were engaged upon were very similar to their household tasks: 35 per cent of working women were servants; 19.5 per cent textile workers; 15.6 per cent dressmakers. For men at that time work was not only more variable but generally higher paid. The textile industries, for example, provided certain lower paid jobs for women and there were few opportunities for training for higher paid work.

The social class of women

Many craft guilds excluded women except for the wives of master craftsmen. The social class of the women had a determining effect on whether they would work or not. 'A lady must be a real lady and nothing else' was typical of the attitudes held. The government's publicity encouraging women to work for the 'War Effort' was focused particularly on the middle classes who had not been employed and the First World War marked the beginning of their inclusion into the labour force.

However, these work opportunities were short-lived as men returning to work demanded their jobs and women were encouraged to retreat into their previous domestic positions. *Lewenhak* reports that women who refused to take domestic work offered to them at the Labour Exchange had their benefits stopped and the marriage bar, relaxed during the war years, was once more re-established.[110]

Women's participation in the labour market was transformed once more as a result of the Second World War. This provided women with greater occupational opportunities which had been positively discouraged at other times. However, many employers de-skilled jobs, divided the labour and offered lower wages to women.

Pattern of women's employment

Although there have been noticeable changes in the pattern of women's employment and a substantial change in the number of women working, little has changed in the structure of their employment. There are four main recurrent themes.

- Women have occupied different positions from men not only in content (horizontal segregation) but also in power and responsibility (vertical segregation). This pattern has been constant over time.
- The jobs that women have occupied (and are still occupying) mirror the domestic/servicing, caring functions. This pattern has been encouraged by both government and employers in the policies that have been enacted over the century.
- The value and status placed on these occupations have been low: occupations concerned with domestic work are usually unpaid (housework) or low paid.
- Women's role outside the workplace is inextricably bound with their life in the domestic sphere.

One theme of variation is evident, however: the number of women in occupations has fluctuated over the century with an upsurge of numbers during wartime. A pattern of working has been established, defined as 'bi-modal', whereby women enter the labour force, leave and re-enter at an older age.[111] The time spent not working has shrunk considerably in recent years.

Understanding women's position and status

Why should men's and women's working experiences be so different? Five explanations are presented. These should not be seen as competitive but as all contributing to the understanding of women's position and status in the organisational world. The explanations are:

- economic theories;
- psychological sex differences;
- the socialisation process;
- orientations and motivations towards work; and
- working practices.

Economic theories

Two major economic theories seek to explain and predict labour patterns of women's employment:

- human capital theory; and
- dual labour market theory.

Human capital theory

The main tenet of human capital theory is that to have the benefit of choices in the workplace, individuals are required to make a substantial investment – for example, in education and training.[112] Human capital theory predicts that women will acquire less schooling and training than men, and will have less time to reap rewards of investment. Whatever skills they had learned will be outdated during their period at home.

The interrupted pattern of women's employment therefore decreases the incentives for both women and employers to engage in their training. Although this may explain the position for some it does not explain the position of women who *do* invest their time in education and training. Neither does it explain the disparities in earnings which exist between men and women where *neither* have committed themselves to education and training.

Dual labour market theory

Dual labour market theory argues that the labour market is divided into two separate markets: the primary market consisting of jobs with career prospects, high wages and stable employment; and the secondary market whose jobs are dead-end, low paid and with poor prospects. Research evidence shows that women, and ethnic groups, are over-represented in the secondary market.[113] *Loveridge and Mok* suggest that women comprise an 'outgroup' and are treated as such, and form the basis of an industrial reserve providing the source of additional labour when society requires it.[114]

Although these explanations are rich in detail they leave unexplored the origin of women's roles as looked at by psychologists and sociologists.

Psychological sex differences

Is it the case that men and women follow different occupational routes because these match their particular sex type? Significantly, it has been found that the male species are far more vulnerable physically. For example, *Gross* comments that 'there is no doubt that males are, biologically, the weaker sex!'.[115]

In their classic review of this subject, *Maccoby and Jacklin* claimed support for differences between males and females in terms of visuo-spatial ability, mathematical ability and aggressiveness (male scores higher); and verbal ability (female scores higher). But they also explored a number of myths which surround sex differences and concluded there were more similarities than differences between the sexes.[116]

Biological differences

Studies focusing on biological differences remain unsupported without the inclusion of inter-relational factors. The reciprocal effect that babies and parents have on each other provides fascinating data on the preferential treatment that parents give their babies depending on their sex. It has been found that mothers are less responsive to boys crying than girls, even at the age of three weeks.[117] Studies have also shown the different interpretative connotations placed on behaviour which fits the stereotype of active, energetic boy, and passive, nurturing girl.[118]

One conclusion to draw is that biology alone cannot explain differences in women's position. Attention must be focused on social issues, and the influence and impact of the socialisation process.

The socialisation process

The family consists of a number of psychologically intense and powerful social relationships in which it is possible to see how little girls and little boys learn their gender, identity and role. The definition of gender, what it is and what it means to family members, is reinforced from external agencies (for example, the media and school) so that messages concerning gender are continuously being processed and reaffirmed. As *Barrett* has said:

> *gender identity is not created once and for all at a certain point in the child's life but is continually recreated and endorsed, modified or even altered, substantially through a process of ideological representation.*[119]

One study demonstrated the overriding effect of societal influences on a child's gender role learning. The trivia, tiny events and language all created a particular picture and image which established a gender consciousness. Many studies support the notion that everyday language and events identify, acknowledge and maintain the dependent, subordinate position of women.[120]

Gender shaping

Gender shaping occurs in education in overt forms of schooling, for example curriculum; and in the 'hidden' patterns of behaviour such as teachers' values and expectations. Evidence indicates that girls traditionally prefer to study humanities rather than science and achieve a higher number of passes in these preferred subjects. Even in newer subjects such as computing, boys dominate.[121]

It is more likely that a child starting school will be taught by a woman. Indeed the number of men choosing to teach in nursery/primary schools is falling (from 18.1 per cent in 1994 to 16.6 per cent in 1998).[122] However, just under half of all head teachers are male (42.7 per cent) whilst the majority of staff in peripheral roles such as cleaners, cooks, administrative staff are women. Staffing in secondary schools is more gender-balanced in terms of the proportion of male and female teachers (male: 46.9 per cent and women 53.1 per cent) but male head teachers outrank the number of female head teachers by almost 3:1. This cultural backcloth or 'hidden curriculum' would seem to reaffirm the notion of male dominance in education.

Young women of all ages taking examinations in GCSE and A level had, overall, higher success rates than young men in 1999.[123] However, there were certain subject successes for boys and these were in the subjects of geography, physics, chemistry biology, IT and physical education. Although more boys chose to study mathematics, physics and technology women had higher success rates than men. Choice led by gender stereotypes still exists in the States. A recent research study indicated that the choice of majors by US undergraduates showed that there was little movement over time in the arts, science and engineering fields. The number of women choosing business had increased whilst education saw a loss in numbers.[124]

An interesting and potentially linked issue is the difference that has been found between boys and girls in their self-evaluation of intelligence and ability. Girls are more likely to underestimate their own ability whereas boys overestimate and exaggerate theirs.[125] *Furnham*[126] cites work by Beloff in which she found a six-point difference by males who estimated their intelligence significantly higher than females. She suggests that 'women see themselves as intellectually inferior compared to the young men'.[127] Furnham also reports on studies, which show consistent sex differences in self-estimates of mathematical and spatial intelligence, but not for verbal intelligence. Three explanations are suggested for these self-estimates: sociological variables, biological reasons and data interpretation, and he concludes:

> *For some researchers this remains a shocking finding explicable only by sociological processes; for others it represents a reasonable grasp of reality. (p. 15)*

Orientations and motivations towards work

It is perhaps salutary to recognise that women workers have tended to be overlooked within many of the classical studies on orientation and motivation. Early studies tended to focus entirely on men (for example, the work of *F. W. Taylor*); or avoid an interpretation of gender divisions (recall, for example, the discussion in Chapter 3 on sex power differential in the Hawthorne experiments).

There is also a common, underlying suggestion that for 'he' one may also assume 'she'. For example, *Alban-Metcalfe* commented that anyone reading the management literature may well:

> *gain the impression that the managerial population is hermaphrodite since the vast majority of studies (which transpire when examined) have been based upon exclusively male samples which are interpreted as if the findings apply equally to females and males.*[128]

Decisions about working
Early studies by *Hunt* revealed that decisions about working revolved around women's primary responsibility for home care. Differences in motivations among the sampled women depended on the life stage which they had reached. Hunt claimed it was not possible to discuss motivation without taking into account the social context of work and home.[129]

There may also be pressure upon women to give 'legitimate' reasons for wanting to work. *Marshall* discusses the double bind for women.[130] Although it is seen to be acceptable for women to say they need the money (and therefore have little choice but to work) such a reason suggests that women do not desire to satisfy their own personal developmental needs. Thus, women may be seen as not holding work values concerning a high level of organisational commitment. However, if women are seen to be overly ambitious then they must be neglecting their primary role in society as a woman.

Of course, there are dangers inherent in gender research, which studies of motivation highlight. It is self-evident that not all women (or all men) share similar motives. There will be differences within each gender as well as between the genders. A study carried out in Australia illustrated this problem. They focused attention on the grouping traditionally considered to be the most homogeneous, that of the female part-time worker. Although the majority were content with their working hours and the freedom it gave them to look after dependent children, not all the sample had family responsibilities and some (20 per cent of the sample) would have preferred to work full-time. The study drew attention to the diverse range of motivations and reasons for part-time working.[131]

Working practices

Is it the case that men and women experience different working practices? This idea contradicts the view that organisations are neutral and objective entities but suggests that work itself has a masculine blue print. Recent research has suggested that the following practices seem to have gendered bias:

- recruitment and selection;
- informal communication;
- career development; and
- attitudes.

Recruitment and selection

Investigations into (supposedly) neutral personnel procedures have found that informal criteria based on gendered stereotypes are maintained in selection decisions.[132] It has been suggested that there is a gap between the rational procedures of specifying scientifically the job, and the informal evaluation of recruiting candidates and evaluating their suitability.[133]

Informal communication

Informal communication within organisations has also been studied and it has been shown that advice from 'gatekeepers' affect women's opportunities and their perceptions of themselves. For example, one study reported that males and females received different career advice.[134] In another study, young female lawyers were subjected to greater scrutiny than male applicants in terms of their motivation and attitude.[135]

Career development

The socialisation period has been found to have a marked effect on subsequent performance and work-related values. The formation of appropriate bonds between individuals and the group are crucial in order that the new member feels involved and accepted by the organisation. Exclusion from a group has far-reaching effects for information transmission, decision-making and eventual career progression.[136]

Training opportunities are vital for personal development and career success. Studies in various industries indicate that women are frequently not encouraged to study; or they are encouraged to study in functional specialisms (such as personnel management or public relations) rather than in mainstream managerial activities.[137]

The under-representation of women in one study was blamed at the male bias in professional development. They urged a rethink of the content of senior management courses and a move towards more mentoring.[138]

Training and development programmes at the start of the employment career have also been examined for gender bias. Barriers and problems in choice and selection of training were examined in a study conducted by the DfEE and the Local Government National Training Organisation. They were concerned at the gender imbalance of the Modern Apprenticeship scheme. (The work-based training scheme was introduced in the UK in the early 1990s.) Barriers included peer group and parental pressure as well as poor careers advice.[139]

Despite legislation there is still evidence of bias in personnel processes and there is considerable dissatisfaction among women that they are not having a fair chance of promotion.[140]

A study concluded in the USA that white and black women and black men all suffer from a glass ceiling, whereas white men enjoy the benefits of a glass escalator. They found that white men were more likely to have a speedy promotion if the percentage of women in the firm rises.[141]

Evetts[142] identifies three issues which present difficulties for women in their careers and suggests a new way of constructing and perceiving the 'successful' career.

- **The combining of paid and unpaid work responsibilities.** Evetts regards the notion of a successful career as the one-dimensional, hierarchical, vertical upward movement as having negative effects for both men and women. Although she recognises the changes that have taken place in organisations with respect to family-friendly policies, there is still a need for the recognition of a multi-dimensional career which takes a positive view of 'family' work outside the organisation.
- **Conceptions of management.** Does management need to be aggressive, competitive, ambitious? Evetts suggests that if management is seen in a stereotypical masculine way that women's progress in managerial careers will always be stifled. She suggests that:

  By changing our conception of management to include an ability to express feelings, and form empathic relations with others, we might also begin to change our understanding of the good manager as well as of the good career.

- **The language of careers.** It is suggested that the language used to describe merit, promotion and appraisals are likely to apply more readily to male occupations. Although there is the assumption that language is free of gender, there are inbuilt assumptions about experiences which are valued (sport, community positions) and other activities which are not (raising children, caring for the elderly).

Evetts proposes that the 'successful career is ready for redefinition' and suggests that it should have a multi-dimensional nature. In a recent paper by Evetts further research is encouraged into women's career paths which should take into account three major dimensions: cultural (family and feminine ideologies); structural issues (organisational processes) and action (women's strategies and preferences).[143] Such a view is also in keeping with other research on careers which promotes a portfolio approach for careers in the twenty-first century.[144, 145]

Attitudes

Paternalistic attitudes also reveal that male managers frequently think it 'best' not to send a woman on an assignment or ask her to attend late meetings. Although intentions might be well-meaning, the lack of opportunities for women to be placed in challenging or risky situations places them at a disadvantage *vis-à-vis* men.

Kanter illustrates the pervasiveness of status levelling whereby women's status is levelled down and men's levelled up.[146] Thus a woman answering the telephone will usually be assumed to be the secretary, whereas a man will be assumed to be the boss. Token women have particular difficulties in that they are forced to play a role which is constrained by male rules and strategies. They are often excluded from informal relations, and thus from important informal networks and communication.[147]

The term 'homosociability', coined by Kanter, labels the process whereby members of the same sex are preferred, promoted and developed. Inevitably in most organisations this equates with male development. It is often a pleasure for senior managers to mentor and develop a younger person with whom they can identify. Given that informal relations and networks within organisations play a powerful part in determining career opportunities, then young men are placed in an advantaged position.

Leadership, management and women

Changes in the way organisations are structured and managed may be good news for a more feminine style of leadership. (*See* Chapter 10 on learning.) If the effectiveness of organisations requires a style which is facilitative and participatory, this should augur well for women who prefer the more social, less hierarchical modes of management. That is, if there are real differences in managerial styles between men and women. Certainly there is support for this argument.[148]

Alimo-Metcalfe[149] promotes the view that women prefer to use a transformational style, prefer to share information and have a more inclusive approach, but she also expresses concern that as techniques of assessment become more sophisticated, sources of bias may become less obvious and hence less likely to be challenged.

Other researchers quote evidence to show there is little or no difference between men and women leaders.[150] Such conflicting findings have led *Alvesson and Due Billing* to produce a model which aims to make sense of differing perspectives (*see* Figure 9.8[151]). In addition to the arguments on gender similarity (or not), they also consider the impact of differing organisational approaches.

Due Billing and Alvesson argue that the notion of feminine leadership may not be especially valid or useful. Workplaces, which are organised without the stereotyping of gender, might evolve new and more effective models of leadership [152]

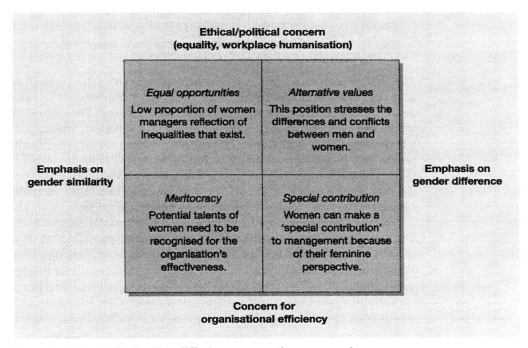

Figure 9.8 Matrix indicating differing perspectives on gender

(*Source*: Adapted from 'Approaches to the Understanding of Women and Leadership' in *Understanding Gender and Organisations* by Alvesson, M. and Due Billing, Y. Reproduced with permission from Sage Publications Ltd, 1997.)

Positive approaches

Reviews and articles explaining the position and status of women typically conclude with exhortations to organisations to introduce and promote schemes which would positively help and support women. The logic of introducing such schemes is based on good business sense in that women represent an untapped human resource. There has been considerable media hype about the progress of women at work and yet this is not revealed in the latest statistics. Improving the 'lot' of women can also provoke resentment from men.

Perhaps the most positive approach to take is for an organisation to acknowledge the changing working pattern of all employees and to consider the best working practices for managing a diverse workforce. This should not be done mechanically but by analysis of the organisation and its workforce. Organisations need to analyse, consciously debate and question their unwritten assumptions and expectations in order to reveal prejudices inherent in the culture of their organisations. Analysis of the way in which culture is expressed in all its trivial detail would lead to an understanding of perceptions and attitudes. Until a full analysis is completed it remains doubtful if more egalitarian practices will develop.

Employees should go through a three-stage process of auditing existing policies, setting measurable goals and making a public commitment from top management to achieving them. A number of agencies see work-life balance as key to equality for women and men.[153] Equality Direct's appeal is to the 'bottom-line':

Businesses prosper if they make the best use of their most valuable resource: the ability and skills of their people. And these people, in turn, will flourish if they can strike a proper balance between work and the rest of their lives.[154]

The first of a series of guides[155] has been produced with practical advice, case studies, and suggested benefits by the Government, supported by research evidence. The assumptions are that if employees are given greater control and choice over where, when and how much time is worked, a more satisfied, valued, committed and less stressed workforce will result. The notion is that everybody, regardless of age, race or gender will prefer to work to a rhythm of work that suits his or her lifestyle. The focus has moved from one that is only focusing on women's needs to one of inclusiveness. It is a compelling idea as it avoids the difficulties of hostility and resentment potentially caused by the selective focus on women's needs. (*See* Figure 9.9.)

However, only time will tell whether the exhortations will work. Will there be stigma attached to employees who choose to work part-time? Will people who choose to work at home miss out on potential promotion opportunities? Are there preferred career tracks, which exclude routes other than the traditional linear paths? So, even if the opportunities are open to all, in reality the political and cultural nature of the organisation prevents career-hungry individuals from choosing such options. (*Please see* Chapter 22 for more detail on the working of cultural processes in organisations.)

Synopsis

■ The individual member is the first point of study and analysis in organisational behaviour. One of the essential requirements of organisations is the development and encouragement of individuality within a work atmosphere in which common goals and aims are achieved. Emphasising individual differences and valuing diversity is a recent catalyst for helping the equality agenda in business. However, organisations

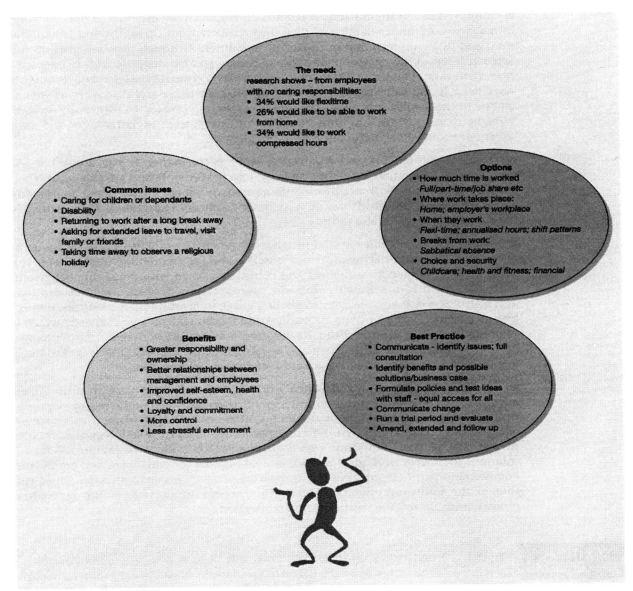

Figure 9.9 Finding an appropriate work-life balance[155]

may require evidence that promoting diversity issues will lead to a greater competitive edge. One of the distinguishing factors of successful managers in any organisation is their ability to manage relationships and really bring out the best in the people that work with and report to them. Managing relationships well depends on an understanding and awareness of the staff and of their talents, abilities, interests and motives. It is also dependent upon effective social skills and emotional intelligence.

■ Encouraging and developing each member at work is essential for individual and organisational health and is a major task of management. Recognising and improving individual talent and potential is critical to ensure that the many roles and functions of an organisation are achieved effectively. However, differences between individuals can also be the source of problems and conflict. Personality clashes may occur; differences of attitudes and values may lead to polarisation and discrimination:

■ Improved self-awareness and accelerated development are essential to the education of managers. An understanding of their own characteristics, strengths and weaknesses may lead to an appreciation of others' personalities. Although psychologists do not agree in terms of the relative importance of certain factors, there is much to be gained from both nomothetic and idiographic approaches. Personality assessment techniques have been found to be helpful in terms of self-knowledge and discovery as well as adding to the rapidly enlarging repertoire of assessment centres. In mentoring an individual's development, an understanding of the causes of behaviour and past experiences can be helpful in terms of future planning.

■ A major influencing factor affecting work performance is the ability of the employee. Ensuring that the right people are selected for work and are able to use their intelligence effectively is a critical personnel process, now helped by the appropriate use of psychological tests. However, tests are not a panacea and can, if inappropriately used, lead to a sense of false security.

■ Assessment of attitudes is vital in selecting potential employees and future managers, and yet informal measures of observation are frequently used. Given the difficulties of attitude measurement and doubts associated with predicting behaviour, such assessment is fraught with problems. Managers may hold incorrect assumptions and beliefs about their colleagues. Without a gauge to measure these attitudes, ineffective management decisions may be made. Attitudes can take on a permanency which is maintained by the culture of the organisation and thus be very resistant to change. Moreover, the power of attitudes should be recognised particularly with regard to influencing newer members of the organisation and their development.

■ Understanding the ways in which working practices may have an unintended adverse impact on women is a critical area of research to be conducted by organisations. Until practices are free of gender bias it is unlikely that women will have an equal role in organisations. The differing approaches taken by psychologists offer complementary perspectives from which to analyse individual behaviour. Practical solutions to flexible work may produce mutual benefits for employees and employers, but evaluation of these practices is a necessary outcome. This analysis is developed further in the following chapters which examine the importance of the perceptual process, learning and the nature of work motivation.

CRITICAL REFLECTIONS

'OK, so it is important to understand that managing is all about people, and every person is an individual in his or her own right. But many theories and models about behaviour appear to apply to people in general. Surely we should be more concerned with a study of differences among individuals rather than similarities among people?'

What are your own views?

Among the factors that exert pressures on our personality formation are the culture in which we are raised, our early conditioning, the norms among our family, friends, and social groups, and other influences that we experience. The environment to which we are exposed plays a substantial role in shaping our personalities.
Robbins, S. P. *Organizational Behavior*, Ninth edition, Prentice Hall International (2001), p. 93.

How would you describe the environmental factors which have helped shape your personality and how is this manifested in the work situation?

'Freud's personality theories have no practical use or value to the organisation.'

Debate.

Understanding and Managing People at Work

1 Identify the major ways in which individual differences are demonstrated at work. Discuss strengths and limitations to the employer and employee of
   a people of the same age and/or race working together;
   b people working different hours (flexi-time, part-time).

2 You are required to interview one person from your work or study group. You need to produce an assessment of their personality. What questions will you ask and how accurate do you feel your assessment will be? What are some of the problems of using this method?

3 What are psychometric tests and when should they not be used?

4 Why are attitudes difficult to measure and change? How would you promote awareness of the needs of students (or work colleagues) with disabilities? What would you do? What reactions might you encounter?

5 Design a simple questionnaire to administer to your work/college colleagues on attitudes towards reducing stress at work.

6 Hold a debate: 'This house believes that low intelligence cannot be improved.' Draw up evidence for and against this statement. At the end of the debate, reflect on the strength of emotional responses and consider the political arguments that have been addressed.

7 Analyse the evidence which suggests that men's and women's attitudes and motivations to work are different.

8 List recommendations you would make to a young Asian women about to embark on a management career. Consider the differences you would make if you were to advise young white men. Compare your list with others in the group.

9 'Work-life balance is all about good management practice and sound business sense'. Is it? Critically evaluate this statement.

10 Men and women need to work in partnership to establish equality in the workplace. Critically discuss.

Assignment 1

Using Kelly's repertory grid technique and Wilson's framework (Table 9.7 in the text), complete your own **personal construct grid**.

The repertory grid is a method for exploring personal construct systems. A grid is made up of three components: the elements; the constructs (which are the ways in which the person differentiates between the elements); and an assessment value (or score).

a Produce the elements

Answer the following:

1 the job I do now;
2 the job I used to do (where appropriate);
3 an ideal job;
4 a job I would enjoy;
5 a job I would not enjoy; and
6 a job I would hate.

Understanding and Managing People at Work

b Develop the constructs

Write your answer at the top of each column. Now, select two elements (for example, 1 and 2) and compare with a third (for example, 6). State the way in which the two elements are alike, and different from the third. Write your answer in the rows. These are your constructs.

For example, I am now a lecturer (element 1) and I used to be a personnel officer (element 2), and a job I would hate would be a factory operative (element 6). The ways in which I see elements 1 and 2 as alike, and different from 6, are in the intellectual demands of the jobs.

Select different triads until you have exhausted all possible constructs.

c Score the constructs

Examine each construct in relation to the elements (jobs) you have described. Score between 7 (high) and 1 (low).

d Now compare:

(i)   Your pattern of scores for element 1 and element 3. What does this tell you about your current career and motivation?

(ii) Your pattern of scores with the grid completed by an engineering craftsman as shown in the section in the text on personality. (*See* Table 9.7.)

(iii) Your constructs and elements with other colleagues.

e *Assess* the strengths and weaknesses of using the repertory grid technique.

Assignment 2

Role play the following situations:

SITUATION 1

Mumtaz has just completed her fast-track graduate programme and is now looking forward to a Development Centre which will determine the next promotion step. She is anticipating an international assignment.

She is already gaining a reputation for hard work and creative ideas and exudes confidence. She is acutely aware that she has been the only female Asian on the programme. The organisation's dominant culture is white and male. A letter arrives from the HR Department with the news that the Development Centre falls in the middle of Ramadan, a time when she needs to fast and partake in regular prayer. She knows that the socialising aspects of the Development Centres are important and that a formal lunch is prepared for each of the three days.

She is unsure whether she should inform her line manager of her anxieties, but she decides to arrange a meeting.

Role-play the meeting in triads: one playing the part of Momtaz, the manager and the observer. Take turns playing different roles, with different outcomes. Discuss the feelings, attitudes and behaviours that were being portrayed.

SITUATION 2

Jordan is a highly successful salesman who works for an international IT organisation. As part of the rewards package for sales staff, exotic prizes are offered to the best sales teams. Jordan is part of the North West team, which has exceeded its targets over the last quarter. The team is currently in the lead to win a trip on the Orient Express and a weekend in Venice.

The announcement is made and the team has won the prize. There is great joy and celebration in the office, especially as each team member can take their partner on the trip. Jordan is gay but has not 'come out' at work. He wants to include his partner, but is uncertain of the reaction of his colleagues. At the pub that evening he broaches the subject to two of his work colleagues ...

Role play the meeting with one observer. Take turns playing different roles, with different outcomes. Discuss the feelings, attitudes and behaviours that were being portrayed.

 Visit our website www.booksites.net/mullins for further questions, annotated weblinks, case material and internet research material.

Notes and references

1 http://www.hesa.ac.uk/press/sfr38/sfr38 [accessed 26.02.01]. Statistical first release, *Student enrolments on Higher Education Courses at Publicly Funded Higher Education Institutions in the United Kingdom for the Academic Year 1999/2000* (the total number of enrolments at UK HEIs increased by 1% to 1,757,200 from the previous year and by 8% from the years 1995/96).

2 http://www.ukonlineforebusiness.gove.uk/advice/publications/teleworking/statistics Teleworkers 5.8% of all workforce (7.3% men; 4.0% women) accessed 11.02.01. In the US 9% of US workers telework (41% believe their jobs are teleworkable).

3 EOC (Equal Opportunities Commission) Series Briefings: Women and Men in Britain: The Labour Market [accessed 10.2.01].

4 EOC(Equal Opportunities Commission) Series briefings: The Work-Life Balance [accessed 10.2.01].

5 EOC (Equal Opportunities Commission) Series Briefings: Women and Men in Britain: The Labour Market [accessed 10.2.01].

6 Equality Direct to be found at *http://* www.equalitydirect.org.uk.

7 The campaign for the Disability Rights Commission has been launched with the slogan 'Actions speak louder than words' (2001).

8 'Littlewoods: Increasing diversity, Increasing profits' *Equal Opportunities Review* no. 81, September/October 1998, pp. 20–7.

9 Kirton, G. and Greene, A-M. *The Dynamics of Managing Diversity*, Butterworth Heinemann (2000).

10 Liff, S. and Cameron, I. 'Changing Equality Cultures to Move Beyond Women's Problems' *Gender, Work and Organization* vol. 4 no. 1, January 1997, pp 35–46.

11 Kandola, R. and Fullerton, J. *Managing the Mosaic Diversity in Action*, IPD (1994), p. 19.

12 Turner, B. *Exploring the Industrial Sub-culture*, Macmillan (1977).

13 Salaman, G. 'Organisations as Constructions of Social Reality', in Salaman, G. and Thompson, K. (eds) *Control and Ideology in Organisations*, MIT Press (1983).

14 Video 'Management Revolution and Corporate Reinvention', BBC for Business (1993).

15 Eysenck, H. J. *The Structure of Human Personality*, Methuen (1960).

16 Freud, S. *New Introductory Lectures on Psychoanalysis*, Penguin (1973).

17 Kelly's theory as described by Bannister, D. and Fansella, F., in *Inquiring Mind: The Theory of Personal Constructs*, Penguin (1971).

18 Eysenck, H. J. *Eysenck on Extroversion*, Crosby, Lockwood Staples (1973).

19 Eysenck, H. 'Personality Patterns in Various Groups of Businessmen', *Occupational Psychology*, vol. 41, 1967, pp. 249–50.

20 Furnham, A. *Personality at Work*, Routledge, London (1992).

21 Mabey, B. 'The Majority of Large Companies Use Occupational Tests', *Guidance and Assessment Review*, vol. 5, no. 3, 1989.

22 Personality tests have been debated by: Bartram, D. 'Addressing The Abuse of Personality Tests', *Personnel Management*, April 1991, pp. 34–9; and Fletcher, C. 'Personality Tests: The Great Debate', *Personnel Management*, September 1991, pp. 38–42.

23 Cattell, R. B. and Kline, P. *The Scientific Analysis of Personality and Motivation*, Academic Press (1977).

24 Howarth, E. 'A Source of Independent Variation: Convergence and Divergence in the Work of Cattell and Eysenck', in Dreger, R. M. (ed.) *Multivariate Personality Research*, Claiton (1972).

25 McCrae, R. R. and Costa, P. T. 'More Reasons to Adopt the Five-Factor Model', *American Psychologist*, vol. 44, no. 2, 1989, pp. 451–2.

26 Bayne, R. 'The Big Five versus the Myers-Briggs', *The Psychologist*, January 1994, pp. 14–17.

27 Mount, M. K., Barrick, M. R. and Strauss, J. P. 'Validity of Observer Ratings of the Big Five Personality factors', *Journal of Applied Psychology*, April 1994, p. 272.

28 Bentall, R. P. 'Personality Traits May Be Alive, They May Even Be Well, but Are They Really Useful?', *The Psychologist*, July 1993, p. 307.

29 Rogers, C. *A Way of Being*, Houghton Mifflin (1980).

30 Mead, G. H. *Mind, Self and Society*, University of Chicago Press (1934), pp. 152–64.

31 Cooley, C. 'The Social Self' in *Theories of Society*, ed. Parsons, T., Shils, E., Naegele, K. D. and Pitts, J. R., The Free Press, New York (1965).

32 Erikson, E. H. *Identity and Life Cycle*, Norton (1980).

33 Hunt, J. W. *Managing People at Work: A Manager's Guide to Behaviour in Organisations*, Third edition, McGraw-Hill (1992).

34 Freud, S. *New Introductory Lectures on Psychoanalysis*, Penguin (1973).

35 Gross, R. D. *Psychology – The Science of Mind and Behaviour*, Arnold (1987), p. 658.

36 Andrews, B. and Brewin, C. R. 'What Did Freud Get Right? *The Psychologist* Vol. 13, no. 12, December 2000, pp. 605–7.

37 Reason, J. 'The Freudian Slip Revisited'. *The Psychologist* vol. 13, no. 12, December 2000, pp. 610–11.

38 Horney, K. *The Collected Works of Karen Horney*, Norton (1963).

39 Jung, C. G. *Analytical Psychology: Its Theory and Practice*, Routledge and Kegan Paul (1968). See also: Jacobi, J. *Psychology of C. G. Jung*, Seventh edition, Routledge and Kegan Paul (1968).

40 Briggs-Myers, I. *Introduction to Type*, Oxford Psychologists Press (1987); and Hirsch, S. K. and Kummerow, J. *Introduction to Type in Organisations*, Oxford Psychologists Press (1990).

41 Kelly's theory as described by Bannister, D. and Fansella, F., in *Inquiring Mind: The Theory of Personal Constructs*, Penguin (1971), pp. 50–1.

42 Wilson, F. 'Deskilling of Work? The Case of Computer Numerical Control in the Engineering Industry, Case 4', in McGoldrick, J. (ed.) *Business Case File in Behavioural Science*, Van Nostrand Reinhold (1987).

43 Stone, G. 'Personality and Effective Hospitality Management', Paper presented at the International Association of Hotel Management Schools Symposium, Leeds Polytechnic, Autumn 1988; and Worsfold, P. A. 'Personality Profile of the Hotel Manager', *International Journal of Hospitality Management*, vol. 8, no. 1, 1989, pp. 55–62.

44 Bartram, D. 'Addressing the Abuse of Psychological Tests', *Personnel Management*, April 1991, pp. 34–9; Newell, S. and Shackleton, V. 'Management Selection: A Comparative Survey of Methods Used in Top British and French Companies', *Journal of Occupational Psychology*, vol. 64, 1991, p. 23.

45 Kline, P. 'The Big Five and Beyond', Conference Paper given at the British Psychological Society Occupational Psychology Conference, University of Warwick, January 1995.

46 Anastasi, A. *Psychological Testing*, Macmillan (1988), p. 560.

47 Blinkhorn, S. and Johnson, C. 'The Insignificance of Personality Testing', *Nature*, 348, 1990, pp. 671–2.

48 Goss, D. *Principles of Human Resource Management*, Routledge (1994).

49 Rice, G. H., Jnr and Lindecamp, D. P. 'Personality Types and Business Success of Small Retailers' *Journal of Occupational Psychology*, 62, 1989, pp. 177–82.

50 Gibbons, P., Baron, H., Nyfield, G. and Robertson, I. 'The Managerial Performance and Competences', Conference Paper given at the British Psychological Society Occupational Psychology Conference, University of Warwick, January 1995.

51 Platt, S. with Piepe, R. and Smythe, J. *'Teams': A Game to Develop Group Skills*, Gower (1988).

52 Rosenmann, R., Friedman, F. and Straus, R. 'A Predictive Study of CHD', *Journal of the American Medical Association*, vol. 89, 1964, pp. 15–22 and in Warr, P. and Wall, T. *Work and Well Being*, Penguin (1975).

53 Melhuish, A. *Executive Health*, Business Books (1978).

54 Cooper, C. 'Papering over the cracks: individual strategies or organizational intervention in dealing with stress at work'. Conference paper given at the British Psychological Society Occupational Psychology conference, University of Warwick, January 1995.

55 Cooper, C., Cooper, R. D. and Eaker, L. H. *Living with Stress*, Penguin (1988); Cartwright, S. and Cooper, C. L. *No Hassle! Taking the Stress out of Work*, Century (1994).

56 Edelmann, R. J. and Woodall, L. J. 'Bullying at work', *The Occupational Psychologist*, no. 32, August 1997, pp. 28–31.

57 http://equalitydirect.org.uk [accessed 11.02.01]

58 Galton, F. *Psychometric Experiments* Brain 2 (1879), pp. 149–62.

59 Haynes, N. and Orrell, S. *Psychology: An Introduction*, Longman (1987).

60 Howe, M. J. A. 'Can IQ Change?' *The Psychologist*, February 1998, pp. 69–72.

61 Binet, A. and Simon, Th. 'Méthodes Nouvelles pour le Diagnostic du Niveau Intellectuel des Anormaux', *Année Psychologique* 11, 1905, pp. 191–244.

62 Terman, L. M. *The Measurement of Intelligence*, Houghton Mifflin (1916).

63 Spearman, C. *The Abilities of Man*, Macmillan (1927).

64 Vernon, P. E. 'The Hierarchy of Abilities' in Wiseman, S. (ed.) *Intelligence and Ability*, Second edition, Penguin (1973).

65 Bartram, D. and Lindley, P. A. *Psychological Testing an Introduction*, BPS Open Learning Programme on Psychological Testing (Level A) (1994), p. 25.

66 Thurstone, L. L. 'Primary Mental Abilities' *Psychometric Monographs*, no. 1, 1938.

67 Guilford, J. P. 'Three Faces of Intellect' in Wiseman, S. (ed.) *Intelligence and Ability*, Penguin (1959).

68 Gardner, H. *Frames of Mind*, Second edition, Fontana (1993).

69 Sternberg, R. J. and Wagner, R. K. *Practical Intelligence*, Cambridge University Press (1986).

70 Goleman, D. *Emotional Intelligence*, Bloomsbury (1996), p. 34.

71 Goleman, D. *Working with Emotional Intelligence*, Bantam Books, New York (1998).

72 Boyatzis, R., Goleman, D and Hay/McBer, *Emotional Competence Inventory Feedback Report*, Hay Group (1999).

73 Williams, R. S. 'Occupational Testing; Contemporary British Practice', *The Psychologist*, January 1994, pp. 11–13.

Understanding and Managing People at Work

74 Anastasia, A. *Psychological Testing*, Macmillan Publishing (1988), p. 23.

75 Robertson, I. 'Personnel Selection Research: Where are We Now?' *The Psychologist*, January 1994, pp. 17–21.

76 Schmitt, N., Ones, D. S. and Hunter, J. E. 'Personnel Selection', *Annual Review of Psychology* 43 (1992), pp. 627–70.

77 Jackson, C. *Understanding Psychological Testing*, BPS Books (1996).

78 Feltham, R., Baron, H. and Smith, P. 'Developing Fair Tests', *The Psychologist*, January 1994, pp. 23–5.

79 Inman, M. *Participants' Perceptions of Assessment Centres*, Unpublished MSc Personnel Management dissertation, University of Portsmouth (1996).

80 Ribeaux, P. and Poppleton, S. E. *Psychology and Work*, Macmillan (1978).

81 Gross, R. D. *Psychology: The Science of Mind and Behaviour*, Edward Arnold (1987).

82 Hofstede, G. *Culture's Consequences: International Differences in Work-Related Values*, Sage (1980).

83 Katz, D. 'The Functional Approach to the Study of Attitudes', *Public Opinion Quarterly*, 21, 1960, pp. 163–204.

84 La Piere, R. T. 'Attitudes versus Action', *Social Forces*, 13, 1934, pp. 230–7.

85 Sykes, A. J. M. 'The Effect of a Supervisory Training Course in Changing Supervisors' Perceptions and Expectations of the Role of Management', *Human Relations*, 15, 1962, pp. 227–43.

86 Salaman, G. 'Organisations as Constructions of Social Reality', in Salaman, G. and Thompson, K. (eds) *Control and Ideology in Organisations*, MIT Press (1983).

87 Kanter, R. M. *Men and Women of the Corporation*, Basic Books (1977).

88 Schein, E. H. *Organisational Culture and Leadership*, Jossey-Bass (1985).

89 Peters, J. and Waterman, R. H. *In Search of Excellence*, Harper & Row (1982).

90 Hofstede, G. *Culture's Consequences: International Differences in Work-Related Values*, Sage (1980).

91 Hicks, L. *Gender and Culture: A Study of the Attitudes Displayed by Managers in the Hotel Industry*, Unpublished doctoral thesis, University of Surrey, 1991.

92 Heider, F. 'Attitudes and Cognitive Organization', *Journal of Psychology*, 21, 1946, pp. 107–12.

93 Festinger, L. A. *A Theory of Cognitive Dissonance*, Row, Peterson and Co. (1957); Reissued by Stanford University Press and Tavistock Publications (1962).

94 Cartwright, S. and Cooper, C. L. 'The Psychological Impact of Merger and Acquisitions on the Individual', Paper presented at The British Psychological Society Occupational Psychology Conference, Liverpool, January 1992.

95 Morgan, G. 'Emerging Waves and Challenges: The Need for New Competencies and Mindsets', in Henry, J. (ed.) *Creative Management*, Sage (1991), pp. 283–93.

96 Alvesson, M. and due Billing, Y. *Understanding Gender and Organizations*, Sage Publications (1997), p. 7.

97 *Ibid.*

98 Kanter, R. M. *Men and Women of the Corporation*, Basic Books (1977).

99 Palmer, C. Some still more equal than others The Observer Sunday February 11, 2001.

100 Hansard Society Commission Report, *Women at the Top*, The Hansard Society (1990).

101 Holton, V., Rabberts, J. and Scrives, S. (Ashridge Management Research Group), 'Women on the Boards of Britain's Top 200 Companies: A Progress Report', *The Occupational Psychologist*, no. 24, April 1995.

102 *Hansard Society Commission Report, op. cit.*

103 Brown, H. 'Equal Opportunities Policy' in Heather Eggins (ed.), *Women as Leaders and Managers in Higher Education*, The Society for Research into Higher Education and Open University Press (1997), p. 112.

104 EOC (Equal Opportunities Commission) *Attitudes to Equal Pay: Valuing Women* http://www.eoc.org./valuing women [accessed 02.02.01].

105 Wheatcroft, P. 'Britain's 50 Most Powerful Women', *Management Today*, April 2000, pp. 48–51.

106 Opportunity2000 *3rd Annual Report*, London: Business in the Community (2000).

107 Liff, S. and Cameron, I. 'Changing Equality Cultures to Move Beyond Women's Problems' *Gender, Work and Organization*, vol. 4, no. 1, January 1997, pp. 35–46.

108 Blakemore, K. and Drake, R. *Understanding Equal Opportunity Policies*, Prentice-Hall Harvester Wheatsheaf (1996).

109 Lewis, J. *Women in England 1870–1950*, Wheatsheaf Books (1984).

110 Lewenhak, S. *Women and Work*, Macmillan (1980).

111 Hakim, C. *Occupational Segregation*, Research Paper No. 9, Department of Employment, November 1979.

112 Amsden, A. (ed.) *Papers in the Economics of Women and Work*, Penguin (1980).

113 Smith, J. and Ward, M. *Women's Wages and Work in the Twentieth Century*, Rand (1984).

114 Loveridge, R. and Mok, A. 'Theoretical Approaches to Segmented Labour Markets', *International Journal of Social Economics*, no. 7, 1980.

115 Gross, R. D. *Psychology: The Science of Mind and Behaviour*, Edward Arnold (1987).

116 Maccoby, E. and Jacklin, C. *The Psychology of Sex Differences*, Stanford University Press (1974).

117 Donelson, E. *Sex Differences in Developmental Perspective*, Homewood Learning Systems (1975).

118 Condry, S. and Condry, J. C. 'Sex Differences: A Study of the Eye of the Beholder', *Annual Progress in Child Psychiatry and Child Development*, 1977, pp. 289–301.

119 Barrett, M. *Women's Oppression Today*, Verso (1980), p. 206.

120 Garbucker, M. *There's A Good Girl*, The Women's Press (1988).

121 Newton, P. 'Computing: An Ideal Occupation for Women', in Cozens, J. F. and West, M. (eds) *Women at Work*, Open University Press (1991).

122 DfEE (Department for Education and Employment) *Statistics of Education – Teachers England and Wales*, 1999 edition, http://www.dfee.gov.uk/statistics/DB/VOL/v0113/794-t21 [accessed 17.02.01].

123 DfEE (Department for Education and Employment) *Statistics of Education GCSE/GNVQ and GCS A/AS level and Advanced GNVQ Examination Results* [accessed 17.02.01].

124 Turner, S. E. and Bowen, W. G. 'Choice of Major: the Changing (Unchanging) Gender Gap', *Industrial and Labor Relations Review* (USA) vol. 52, no. 2, January 1999, pp. 289–314.

125 Rosenkrantz, P., Vogel, S., Bee, H. and Broverman, D. 'Sex Role Stereotypes and Self Concepts in College Students', *Journal of Consulting and Clinical Psychology*, vol. 32, 1968, pp. 287–95.

126 Furnham, A. 'Thinking about Intelligence', *The Psychologist*, vol. 13, no. 10, October 2000, pp. 510–15.

127 Beloff, H. 'Mother, Father and Me: Our IQ', *The Psychologist*, vol. 5, 1992, pp. 309–11.

128 Alban-Metcalfe, B. 'Attitudes to Work: Comparison by Gender and Sector of Employment', *The Occupational Psychologist*, no. 3, December 1987, p. 8.

129 Hunt, A. *A Survey of Women's Employment*, HMSO (1968).

130 Marshall, J. *Women Managers: Travellers in a Male World*, Wiley (1984).

131 Walsh, J. 'Myths and counter-myths: an analysis of part-time female employees and their orientation to work and working hours', *Work, Employment and Society*, vol. 3, no. 2, June 1999, pp. 179–204.

132 Collinson, D. *Managing to Discriminate: A Multi-Sector Study of Recruitment Practices*, EOC Research Report (1986).

133 Webb, J. 'The Politics of Equal Opportunity: Job Requirements and the Evaluation of Women's Suitability', Paper presented at The Psychology of Women at Work International Research Conference, London, 1988.

134 Terborg, J. 'Women in Management: A Research Review', *Journal of Applied Psychology*, vol. 62, no. 6, 1977, pp. 647–64.

135 Podmore, D. and Spencer, A. 'Joining the Professionals: Gender Issues in Recruitment and Careers of Solicitors', Case 5, in McGoldrick, J. (ed.) *Business Case File in Behavioural Science*, Van Nostrand Reinhold (1987).

136 Kanter, R. M. *Men and Women of the Corporation*, Basic Books (1977).

137 *Equal Opportunities for Women in the Civil Service*, HMSO (1983).

138 McLay, M. and Brown, M. 'The Under-representation of Women in Senior Management in UK Independent Secondary Schools', *International Journal of Educational Management*, vol. 14, no. 3, 2000, pp. 101–7.

139 Wren, J. 'Challenging Gender Stereotyping in Modern Apprenticeships', *Equal Opportunities Review*, no. 81, Sept/Oct 1998.

140 Bevan, S. and Thompson, M. *Merit Pay, Performance Appraisal and Attitudes to Women's Work*, Institute of Manpower Studies, Sussex (1992).

141 Maume, D. J. 'Glass Ceilings and Glass Escalators: occupational segregation and race and sex differences in managerial promotions', *Work & Occupations*, vol. 26, no. 4, November 1999, pp. 483–510.

142 Evetts, J. 'Career and Gender: The Conceptual Challenge' in Evetts, J. (ed) *Women and Career: Themes and issues in advanced industrial societies*, Longman (1994), pp. 223–33.

143 Evetts, J. 'Analysing Change in Women's Careers: Culture, Structure and Action Dimensions', *Gender, Work and Organizations*, vol. 7, no. 1, January 2000, pp. 57–68.

144 Arnold, J. *Managing Careers into the 21st Century*, Paul Chapman Publishing (1997).

145 Herriot, P. *The Career Management Challenge*, Sage (1992).

146 Kanter, R. M. *Men and Women of the Corporation*, Basic Books (1977).

147 Cooper, C. and Davidson, M. *High Pressure: Working Lives of Women Managers*, Fontana (1982).

148 Loden, M. *Feminine Leadership, or How to Succeed in Business Without Being One of the Boys*, Time Books (1986).

149 Alimo-Metcalfe, B. 'Leadership and Assessment' in Vinnicombe, S. and Colwill, N. L. (eds) *The Essence of Women in Management*, Prentice-Hall (1995), p. 107.

150 Powell, G. N. *Women and Men in Management*, Sage (1988).

151 Alvesson, M. and Due Billing, Y. *Understanding Gender and Organizations*, Sage (1977).

152 Due Billing, Y., and Alvesson, M. 'Questioning the Notion of Feminine Leadership: A critical perspective on the gender labelling of leadership', *Gender, Work and Organization*, vol. 7, no. 3, July 2000.

153 EOC (Equal Opportunities Commission) Briefing series: *The Work-Life Balance*, http://www.eoc.org.uk [accessed 02.02.01].

154 http://www. equalitydirect.org.uk [accessed 11.02.01] p. 1.

155 DfEE (Department of Education and Employment) Creating a Work-Life Balance: A good practice guide for employers, September 2000.

Chapter 11

THE PROCESS OF PERCEPTION

Laurie Mullins and Linda Hicks

We all have our own picture of the world, and the extent to which we share this world with others is a complex and dynamic process. It is vital that managers are aware of their own perceived reality and of perceptual differences between individuals that may cause organisational problems. A particularly important aspect of the perceptual process is the perception of women. Managers need to understand the importance of perception and effective communication, including how this influences dealings and relationships with other people.

Learning objectives

To:

➤ explain the nature of the perceptual process;

➤ detail internal and external factors which provide meaning to the individual;

➤ examine the organisation and arrangement of stimuli, and perceptual illusions;

➤ identify problems, distortions and bias with particular regard to the perception of people;

➤ examine links between perception and communication, and transactional analysis;

➤ provide an understanding of women's position and status in the organisational world;

➤ recognise the importance to managers of the study of perception.

The perceptual process

The significance of individual differences is particularly apparent when focusing on the process of **perception**. This is a characteristic feature of behaviour which has particular importance to the manager. We all see things in different ways. We all have our own, unique picture or image of how we see the 'real' world. We do not passively receive information from the world; we analyse and judge it. We may place significance on some information and regard other information as worthless; and we may be influenced by our expectations so that we 'see' what we expect to see. Although general theories of perception were first proposed many years ago the importance of understanding the perceptual process is arguably even more significant today. Perception is the root of all organisational behaviour; any situation can be analysed in terms of its perceptual connotations. Consider, for instance, the following situation.

> A member of the management team has sent a memorandum to section heads asking them to provide statistics of overtime worked within their section during the past six months and projections for the next six months. Mixed reactions could result:
>
> ● One section head may see it as a reasonable and welcomed request to provide information which will help lead to improved future staffing levels.
> ● Another section head may see it as an unreasonable demand, intended only to enable management to exercise closer supervision and control over the activities of the section.
> ● A third section head may have no objection to providing the information, but be suspicious that it may lead to possible intrusion into the running of the section.
> ● A fourth head may see it as a positive action by management to investigate ways of reducing costs and improving efficiency throughout the organisation.
>
> Each of the section heads perceives the memorandum differently based on their own experiences. Their perceived reality and understanding of the situation provokes differing reactions.

Individuality　We are all unique; there is only one Laurie Mullins, and one Linda Hicks, and there is only one of you. We all have our own 'world', our own way of looking at and understanding our environment and the people within it. A situation may be the same but the interpretation of that situation by two individuals may be vastly different. For instance, a lively wine bar may be seen as a perfect meeting place by one person, but as a noisy uncomfortable environment by another. One person may see a product as user-friendly, but another person may feel that it is far too simplistic and basic. The physical properties may be identical in terms of how they 'are', but they are perceived quite differently because each individual has imposed upon the object/environment their own interpretations, their own judgement and evaluation.

Selectivity in attention and perception

It is not possible to have an understanding of perception without taking into account its sensory basis. We are not able to attend to everything in our environment; our sensory systems have limits. The physical limits therefore insist that we are selective in our attention and perception. Early pioneer work by psychologists has resulted in an understanding of universal laws which underlie the perceptual process. It seems that we cannot help searching for meaning and understanding in our environment. The way in which we categorise and organise this sensory information is based on a range of different factors including the present situation (and our emotional state), and also our past experiences of the same or similar event.

Some information may be considered highly important to us and may result in immediate action or speech; in other instances, the information may be simply 'parked' or assimilated in other ideas and thoughts. The link between perception and memory processes becomes obvious. Some of our 'parked' material may be forgotten or, indeed, changed and reconstructed over time.[1]

We should be aware of the assumptions that are made throughout the perceptual process, below our conscious threshold. We have learnt to take for granted certain constants in our environment. We assume that features of our world will stay the same and thus we do not need to spend our time and energy seeing things afresh and anew. We thus make a number of inferences throughout the entire perceptual process. Although these inferences may save time and speed up the process they may also lead to distortions and inaccuracies.

Perception as information processing

It is common to see the stages of perception described as an information processing system: information (stimuli) (Box A) is selected at one end of the process (Box B), then interpreted (Box C), and translated (Box D), resulting in action or thought patterns (Box E), as shown in Figure 11.1. However, it is important to note that such a model simplifies the process and although it makes it easy to understand (and will be used to structure this chapter) it does not give justice to the complexity and dynamics of the process. In certain circumstances, we may select information out of the environment because of the way we categorise the world. In other words, arrows should also lead back from Box E to Box A.

For instance, if a manager has been advised by colleagues that a particular trainee has managerial potential the manager may be specifically looking for confirmation that those views are correct. This process has been known as 'top-down', because the cognitive processes are influencing the perceptual readiness of the individual to select certain information. This emphasises the active nature of the perceptual process. We do not passively digest the information from our senses, but we actively attend and indeed, at times, seek out certain information.

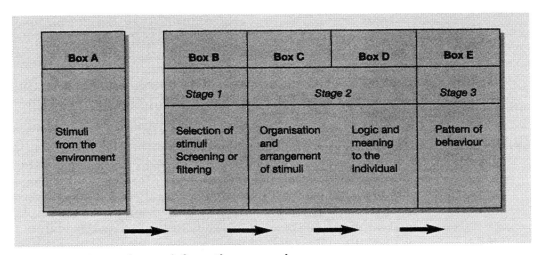

Figure 11.1 Perceptions as information processing

Meaning to the individual

The process of perception explains the manner in which information (stimuli) from the environment around us is selected and organised, to provide meaning for the individual. Perception is the mental function of giving significance to stimuli such as shapes, colours, movement, taste, sounds, touch, smells, pain, pressures and feelings. Perception gives rise to individual behavioural responses to particular situations.

Despite the fact that a group of people may 'physically see' the same thing, they each have their own version of what is seen – their perceived view of reality. Consider, for example, the image (published by W. E. Hill in Puck, 6 November 1915) shown in Figure 11.2. What do you see? Do you see a young, attractive, well-dressed woman? Or do you see an older, poor woman? Or can you now see both? **And who can say with certainty that there is just the one, 'correct' answer?**

Figure 11.2

Internal and external factors

The first stage in the process of perception is selection and attention. Why do we attend to certain stimuli and not to others? There are two important factors to consider in this discussion: first, internal factors relating to the state of the individual; second, the environment and influences external to the individual. The process of perceptual selection is based, therefore, on both internal and external factors.

Internal factors

Our sensory systems have limits, we are not able to see for 'miles and miles' (unlike the classic song by 'The Who'). Neither are we able to hear very low or very high pitched sounds. All our senses have specialist nerves which respond differentially to the forms of energy which are received. For instance, our eyes receive and convert light waves into electrical signals which are transmitted to the visual cortex of the brain and translated into meaning.

Our sensory system is geared to respond to changes in the environment. This has particular implications for the way in which we perceive the world and it explains why we are able to ignore the humming of the central heating system, but notice instantly a telephone ringing. The term used to describe the way in which we disregard the familiar is 'habituation'.

Sensory limits or thresholds

As individuals we may differ in terms of our sensory limits or thresholds. Without eye glasses some people would not be able to read a car's number plate at the distance required for safety. People differ not only in their absolute thresholds, but also in their ability to discriminate between stimuli. For instance, it may not be possible for the untrained to distinguish between different grades of tea but this would be an everyday event for the trained tea taster. This implies that we are able to learn to become more discriminatory and are able to train our senses to recognise small differences between stimuli. It is also possible for us to adapt to unnatural environments and learn to cope.[2]

We may also differ in terms of the amount of sensory information we need to reach our own comfortable equilibrium. Some individuals would find loud music at a party or gig uncomfortable and unpleasant, whereas for others the intensity of the music is part of the total enjoyment. Likewise, if we are deprived of sensory information for too long this can lead to feelings of discomfort and fatigue. Indeed, research has shown that if the brain is deprived of sensory information then it will manufacture its own and subjects will hallucinate.[3] It is possible to conclude therefore that the perceptual process is rooted to the sensory limitations of the individual.

Psychological factors

Psychological factors will also affect what is perceived. These internal factors, such as personality, learning and motives, will give rise to an inclination to perceive certain stimuli with a readiness to respond in certain ways. This has been called an individual's perceptual set. (*See* Figure 11.3.)

Differences in the ways individuals acquire information has been used as one of four scales in the Myers–Briggs Type Indicator (discussed in Chapter 9). They distinguish individuals who 'tend to accept and work with what is given in the here-and-now, and thus become realistic and practical' (sensing types), from others who go beyond the information from the senses and look at the possible patterns, meanings and relationships. These 'intuitive types' 'grow expert at seeing new possibilities and new ways of doing things'. Myers and Briggs stress the value of both types, and emphasise the importance of complementary skills and variety in any successful enterprise or relationship.[4]

Personality and perception have also been examined in the classic experiments by *Witkin et al.* on field dependence/independence. Field dependent individuals were found to be reliant on the context of the stimuli, the cues given in the situation, whereas field independent subjects relied mainly on their own internal bodily cues and less on the environment. These experiments led Witkin to generalise to other settings outside the psychological laboratory and to suggest that individuals use, and need, different information from the environment to make sense of their world.[5]

The needs of an individual
The needs of an individual will affect their perceptions. For example, a manager deeply engrossed in preparing an urgent report may screen out ringing telephones, the sound of computers, people talking and furniture being moved in the next office, but will respond readily to the smell of coffee brewing. The most desirable and urgent needs will almost certainly affect an individual perceptual process.

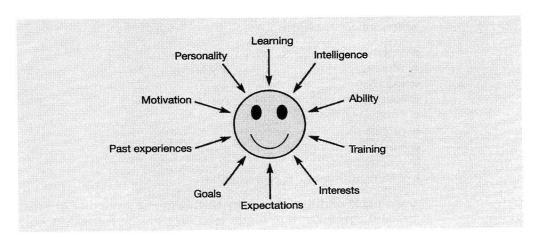

Figure 11.3 Factors affecting an individual's perceptual set

Understanding and Managing People at Work

The 'Pollyanna Principle' claims that pleasant stimuli will be processed more quickly and remembered more precisely than unpleasant stimuli. However, it must be noted that intense internal drives may lead to perceptual distortions of situations (or people) and an unwillingness to absorb certain painful information. This will be considered later in this chapter.

Previous experiences

Learning from previous experiences has a critical effect throughout all the stages of the perceptual process. It will affect the stimuli perceived in the first instance, and then the ways in which those stimuli are understood and processed, and finally the response which is given. For example, it is likely that a maintenance engineer visiting a school for the first time will notice different things about it than a teacher attending an interview or a child arriving on the first day. The learning gained from past experiences colours what is seen and processed.

Our language plays an important role in the way we perceive the world. Our language not only labels and distinguishes the environment for us but also structures and guides our thinking pattern. Even if we are proficient skiers, we do not have many words we can use to describe the different texture of snow; we would be reliant on using layers of adjectives. The Inuit, however, have 13 words for snow in their language. Our language is part of the culture we experience and learn to take for granted. Culture differences are relevant because they emphasise the impact of social learning on the perception of people and their surroundings.

The way in which people interact are also subject to cultural differences and such differences may be misconstrued. The ways in which words are used and the assumptions made about shared understanding are dependent upon an individual's culture and upbringing. For example, in cultures where it is 'normal' to explain all details clearly, explicitly and directly (such as the USA) other cultures may feel the 'spelling out' of all the details unnecessary and embarrassing. In France, for instance, ambiguity and subtlety are expected and much is communicated by what is **not** said. *Hall and Hall* distinguished low context cultures (direct, explicit communication) from high context cultures (meaning assumed and non verbal signs significant).[6]

External factors

The knowledge of, familiarity with or expectations about, a given situation or previous experiences, will influence perception. External factors refer to the nature and characteristics of the stimuli. There is usually a tendency to give more attention to stimuli which are, for example:

- large;
- moving;
- intense;
- loud;
- contrasted;
- bright;
- novel;
- repeated; or
- stand out from the background.

Any number of these factors may be present at a given time or situation. It is therefore the **total pattern** of the stimuli together with the **context** in which they occur that influence perception. For example, it is usually a novel or unfamiliar stimulus that is more noticeable, but a person is more likely to perceive the familiar face of a friend among a group of people all dressed in the same style uniform. The sight of a fork-lift truck on the factory floor of a manufacturing organisation is likely to be perceived quite differently from one in the corridor of a university. The word 'terminal' is likely to be perceived differently in the context of, for example: (i) a hospital, (ii) an airport or (iii) a computer firm. Consumer psychologists and marketing experts apply these perceptual principles with extraordinary success for some of their products.

Organisation and arrangement of stimuli

The Gestalt School of Psychology led by Max Wertheimer claimed that the process of perception is innately organised and patterned. They described the process as one which has built-in field effects. In other words, the brain can act like a dynamic, physical field in which interaction among elements is an intrinsic part. The Gestalt School produced a series of principles, which are still readily applicable today. Some of the most significant principles include the following:

- figure and ground;
- grouping; and
- closure.

Figure and ground

The figure–ground principle states that figures are seen against a background. The figure does not have to be an object; it could be merely a geometrical pattern. Many textiles are perceived as figure–ground relationships. These relationships are often reversible as in the popular example shown in Figure 11.4.

What do you see? Do you see a white chalice (or small stand shape) in the centre of the frame? Or do you see the dark profiles of twins facing each other on the edge of the frame? Now look again. Can you see the other shape?

The figure–ground principle has applications in all occupational situations. It is important that employees know and are able to attend to the significant aspects (the figure), and treat other elements of the job as context (background). Early training sessions aim to identify and focus on the significant aspects of a task. Managerial effectiveness can also be judged in terms of chosen priorities (the figure). Stress could certainly occur for those employees who are uncertain about their priorities, and are unable to distinguish between the significant and less significant tasks. They feel overwhelmed by the 'whole' picture.

Figure 11.4

Understanding and Managing People at Work
91

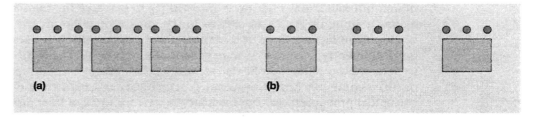

Figure 11.5

Grouping

The grouping principle refers to the tendency to organise shapes and patterns instantly into meaningful groupings or patterns on the basis of their proximity or similarity. Parts that are close in time or space tend to be perceived together. For example, in Figure 11.5(a), the workers are more likely to be perceived as nine independent people; but in Figure 11.5(b), because of the proximity principle, the workers may be perceived as three distinct groups of people.

Taxi firms, for example, often use the idea of grouping to display their telephone number. In the example below which of the following numbers – (a), (b) or (c) – is most likely to be remembered easily?

347 474	347474	34 74 74
(a)	(b)	(c)

Similar parts tend to be seen together as forming a familiar group. In the following example there is a tendency to see alternate lines of characters – crosses and noughts (or circles). This is because the horizontal similarity is usually greater than the vertical similarity. However, if the page is turned sideways the figure may be perceived as alternate noughts and crosses in each line.

$$\times \quad \times \quad \times \quad \times \quad \times \quad \times \quad \times \quad \times$$
$$o \quad o \quad o \quad o \quad o \quad o \quad o \quad o$$
$$\times \quad \times \quad \times \quad \times \quad \times \quad \times \quad \times \quad \times$$
$$o \quad o \quad o \quad o \quad o \quad o \quad o \quad o$$

It is also interesting to note that many people when asked to describe this pattern refer to alternate lines of noughts and crosses – rather than crosses and noughts.

There is also an example here of the impact of cultural differences, mentioned earlier. One of the authors undertook a teaching exchange in the USA and gave this exercise to a class of American students. Almost without exception the students described the horizontal pattern correctly as alternate rows of crosses and noughts (or zeros). The explanation appears to be that Americans do not know the game of 'noughts and crosses' but refer to this as 'tic-tac-toe'.

Closure

There is also a tendency to complete an incomplete figure – to (mentally) fill in the gaps and to perceive the figure as a whole. This creates an overall and meaningful image, rather than an unconnected series of lines or blobs.

In the example in Figure 11.6[7] most people are likely to see the blobs as either the letter B or the number 13, possibly depending on whether at the time they had been more concerned with written material or dealing in numbers. However, for some people, the figure may remain just a series of eleven discrete blobs or be perceived as some other (to them) meaningful pattern/object. According to Gestalt theory, perceptual organisation is instant and spontaneous. We cannot stop ourselves making meaningful assumptions about our environment. The Gestaltists emphasised the ways in which the elements interact and claimed that the new pattern or structure perceived had a character of its own, hence the famous phrase: 'the whole is more than the sum of its parts'.

Figure 11.6
(Reproduced by permission of the author, Professor Richard King, University of South Carolina, from *Introduction to Pschology*, Third edition, 1996, published by the McGraw-Hill Companies Inc.)

Perceptual illusions

Here are some examples to help you judge your own perceptive skills.

In Figure 11.7 try reading aloud the four words.

M – A – C – D – O – N – A – L – D
M – A – C – P – H – E – R – S – O – N
M – A – C – D – O – U – G – A – L – L
M – A – C – H – I – N – E – R – Y

Figure 11.7

It is possible that you find yourself 'caught' in a perceptual set which means that you tend to pronounce 'machinery' as if it too were a Scottish surname.

In Figure 11.8[8] which of the centre, black circles is the larger – A or B?

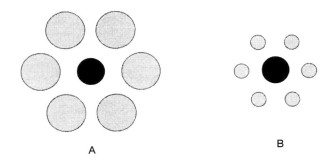

A   B

Figure 11.8
(*Source*: Hellriegel, Don, Slocum, John, W. Jr. and Woodman, Richard, W. *Organisation Behaviour*, Eighth edition, South-Western College Publishing (1998) p. 76.)

Although you may have guessed that the two centre circles are in fact the same size, the circle on the right (B) may well **appear** larger because it is framed by smaller circles. The centre circle on the left (A) may well **appear** smaller because it is framed by larger circles.

Understanding and Managing People at Work

Figure 11.9

(Reproduced with permission from Luthans, F. *Organisational Behaviour*, Seventh edition, McGraw-Hill. Reproduced with permission from the McGraw-Hill Companies Inc. (1995) p. 96.)

Finally, in Figure 11.9[9] which of the three people is the tallest? Although the person on the right may appear the tallest, they are in fact all the same size.

The physiological nature of perception has already been discussed briefly but it is of relevance here in the discussion of illusions. Why does the circle on the right in Figure 11.8 look bigger? Why does the person on the right look taller in Figure 11.9? These examples demonstrate the way our brain can be fooled. Indeed we make assumptions about our world which go beyond the pure sensations our brain receives.[10]

Beyond reality   Perception goes beyond the sensory information and converts these patterns to a three-dimensional reality which we understand. This conversion process, as we can see, is easily tricked! We may not be aware of the inferences we are making as they are part of our conditioning and learning. The Stroop experiment illustrates this perfectly.[11] (*See* Assignment 1 at the end of this chapter.) An illustration of the way in which we react automatically to stimuli is the illusion of the impossible triangle. (*See* Figure 11.10.)

Even when we know the triangle is impossible we still cannot help ourselves from completing the triangle and attempting to make it meaningful. We thus go beyond what is given and make assumptions about the world, which in certain instances are wildly incorrect. Psychologists and designers may make positive use of these assumptions to project positive images of a product or the environment. For instance, colours may be used to induce certain atmospheres in buildings; designs of wallpaper, or texture of curtains, may be used to create feelings of spaciousness or cosiness. Packaging of products may tempt us to see something as bigger or perhaps more precious.

Understanding and Managing People at Work
94

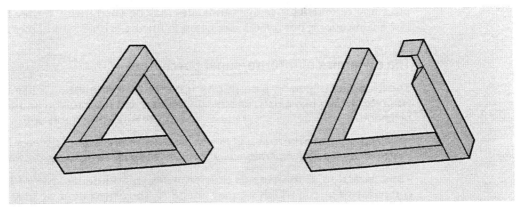

Figure 11.10 The impossible triangle
(*Source:* Gregory, R. L. *Odd Perceptions*, Methuen (1986) p. 71. Reprinted by permission of the publishers, Routledge/ITPS Ltd.)

Person perception

Perceptual distortions and inaccuracies may not only affect our perception of the environment but also affect our perception of people. Although the process of perception is equally applicable in the perception of objects or people, there is more scope for subjectivity, bias, errors and distortions when we are perceiving others. The focus of the following section is to examine the perception of people, and to consider the impact this has on the management and development of people at work.

Perceiving other people

The principles and examples of perceptual differences discussed above reflect the way we perceive other people and are the source of many organisational problems. In the work situation the process of perception and the selection of stimuli can influence a manager's relationship with other staff. Some examples might be as follows.

- the way in which a manager may think of a number of staff: for example, either working in close proximity; or with some common feature such as all clerical workers, all management trainees or all black workers; as a homogeneous group rather than a collection of individuals each with his or her own separate identity and characteristics;
- the extent to which allowance is made for flexibility and tolerance given for personal initiative, imagination or individual action by staff; rather than insistence on continuity, formal regulations or set procedures;
- the degree to which unanimity is perceived, and decisions made or action taken in the belief that there is full agreement with staff when, in fact, a number of staff may be opposed to the decision or action.

A manager's perception of the workforce will influence attitudes in dealing with people and the style of managerial behaviour adopted. The way in which managers approach the performance of their jobs and the behaviour they display towards subordinate staff are likely to be conditioned by predispositions about people, human nature and work. An example of this is the style of management adopted on the basis of McGregor's Theory X and Theory Y suppositions, which is discussed in Chapter 7. In making judgements about other people it is important to try and perceive their underlying intent and motivation, not *just* the resultant behaviour or actions.

The perception of people's performance can be affected by the organisation of stimuli. In employment interviews, for example, interviewers are susceptible to contrast effects and the perception of a candidate is influenced by the rating given to immediately preceding candidates. Average candidates may be rated highly if they follow people with low qualifications, but rated lower when following people with higher qualifications.[12]

The dynamics of interpersonal perception

The dynamics of person perception cannot be overestimated. Unlike the perception of an object which just exists, another individual will react to you and be affected by your behaviour. This interaction is illustrated in the following quotation:

> *You are a pain in the neck and to stop you giving me a pain in the neck I protect my neck by tightening my neck muscles, which gives me the pain in the neck you are.*[13]

The interaction of individuals thus provides an additional layer of interpretation and complexity. The cue which we may attend to, the expectation we may have, the assumptions we may make, the response pattern that occurs, leave more scope for errors and distortions. We are not only perceiving the stimulus (that is, the other person) but we are also processing their reactions to us, and therefore we are only one part of this process.

Thus person perception differs from the perception of objects because:

- it is a continually dynamic and changing process; and
- the perceiver is a part of this process who will influence and be influenced by the other people in the situation.

(*See* Figure 11.11.)[14]

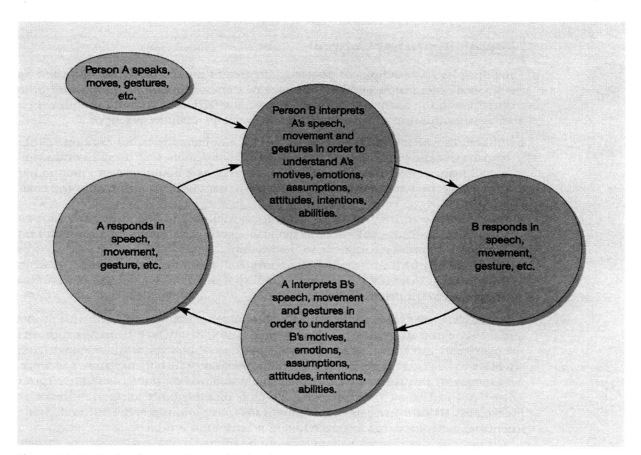

Figure 11.11 Cycle of perception and behaviour

(*Source*: Guirdham, Maureen, *Interpersonal Skills at Work*, Second edition, Prentice-Hall (1995) p. 145.)

Setting and environment

Person perception will also be affected by the setting, and the environment may play a critical part in establishing rapport. For example, next time you are involved in a formal meeting consider the following factors which will all influence the perceptual process.

- **Why?** Purpose of and motives for meeting. Emotional cost to parties.
- **Who?** Status/role/age/gender/ethnic group/appearance/personality/interests/attitudes. Previous encounters.
- **When?** Time of meeting.
- **Where?** Environment/culture.
- **How?** Past experience. Rapport.

Perception and communication

It is difficult to consider the process of interpersonal perception without commenting on how people communicate. Communication and perception are inextricably bound. How we communicate to our colleagues, boss, subordinates, friends and partners will depend on our perception of them, on our 'history' with them, on their emotional state, etc. We may misjudge them and regard our communication as unsuccessful, but unless we have some feedback from the other party we may never know whether what we have said, or done, was received in the way it was intended. Feedback is a vital ingredient of the communication process. The feedback may reaffirm our perceptions of the person or it may force us to review our perceptions. In our dealings with more senior staff the process of communication can be of special significance including non-verbal communication, posture and tone.[15] (The importance of body language is discussed later in this chapter.)

Transactional analysis

Transactional analysis (or TA) is one of the most popular ways of explaining the dynamics of interpersonal communication. Originally developed by *Eric Berne*, it is now a theory which encompasses personality, perception and communication. Although Berne used it initially as a method of psychotherapy, it has been convincingly used by organisations as a training and development programme.[16]

TA has two basic underlying assumptions:

- All the events and feelings that we have ever experienced are stored within us and can be replayed, so we can re-experience the events and the feelings of all our past years.
- Personality is made of three ego states which are revealed in distinct ways of behaving. The ego states manifest themselves in gesture, tone of voice and action, almost as if they are different people within us.

Berne identified and labelled the ego states as follows:

- **Child ego state** – behaviour which demonstrates the feelings we remember as a child. This state may be associated with having fun, playing, impulsiveness, rebelliousness, spontaneous behaviour and emotional responses.
- **Adult ego state** – behaviour which concerns our thought processes and the processing of facts and information. In this state we may be objective, rational, reasonable – seeking information and receiving facts.
- **Parent ego state** – behaviour which concerns the attitudes, feelings and behaviour incorporated from external sources, primarily our parents. This state refers to feelings about right and wrong and how to care for other people.

He claimed that the three ego states were universal, but the content of the ego states would be unique to each person. We may be unaware which ego state we are operating in and may shift from one ego state to another. All people are said to behave in each of these states at different times. The three ego states exist simultaneously within each individual although at any particular time any one state many dominate the other two.

Preferred ego state

We all have a preferred ego state which we may revert to: some individuals may continually advise and criticise others (the constant Parents); some may analyse, live only with facts, and distrust feelings (the constant Adult); some operate with strong feelings all the time, consumed with anger, or constantly clowning (the constant Child). Berne emphasised that the states should not be judged as superior or inferior but as different. Analysis of ego states may reveal why communication breaks down or why individuals may feel manipulated or used.

Berne insists that it is possible to identify the ego state from the words, voice, gestures, and attitude of the person communicating. For example, it would be possible to discern the ego state of a manager if he/she said the following:

'Pass me the file on the latest sales figures.'
'How do you think we could improve our safety record?'
(Adult ego state)

'Let me help you with that – I can see you are struggling.'
'Look, this is the way it should be done; how many more times do I have to tell you...?'
(Parent ego state)

'Great, it's Friday. Who's coming to the pub for a quick half?'
'That's a terrific idea – let's go for it!'
(Child ego state)

A dialogue can be analysed not only in terms of the ego state but also whether the transaction produced a **complementary reaction** or a **crossed reaction**. By complementary it is meant whether the ego state was an expected and preferred response, so for instance if we look at the first statement, 'Pass me the file on the latest sales figures', the subordinate could respond: 'Certainly – I have it here' (Adult ego state), or 'Can't you look for it yourself? I only gave it to you an hour ago' (Parent ego state).

The first response was complementary whereas the second was a crossed transaction. Sometimes it may be important to 'cross' a transaction. Take the example 'Let me help you with that – I can see you are struggling' (Parent ego state). The manager may have a habit of always helping in a condescending way, making the subordinate resentful. If the subordinate meekly accepts the help with a thankful reply this will only reinforce the manager's perception and attitude, whereas if the subordinate were to respond with 'I can manage perfectly well. Why did you think I was struggling?', it might encourage the manager to respond from the Adult ego state and thus move his/her ego position.

Understanding of human behaviour

Knowledge of TA can be of benefit to employees who are dealing with potentially difficult situations.[17] In the majority of work situations the Adult–Adult transactions are likely to be the norm. Where work colleagues perceive and respond by adopting the Adult ego state, such a transaction is more likely to encourage a rational, problem-solving approach and reduce the possibility of emotional conflict.

However, if only the world of work was always of the rational logical kind! Communications at work as elsewhere are sometimes unclear, confused and can leave the individual with 'bad feelings' and uncertainty. Berne describes a further dysfunctional transaction, which can occur when a message is sent to two ego states at the same time. For instance an individual may say 'I passed that article to you last week, have you read it yet?' This appears to be an adult-to-adult transaction and yet the tone of voice, the facial expressions **imply** a second ego state is involved. The underlying message, says 'Haven't you even read that yet ... you know how busy I am and yet I had time to read it!' The critical parent is addressing the Child ego state. In such 'ulterior transactions' the social message is typically Adult to Adult, and the ulterior, psychological message is directed either Parent–Child or Child–Parent.

Given the incidence of stress in the workplace, analysis of communication may be one way of understanding such conflict. By focusing on the interactions occurring within the workplace, TA can aid the understanding of human behaviour. It can help to improve communication skills by assisting in interpreting a person's ego state and which form of state is likely to produce the most appropriate response. This should lead to an improvement in both customer relations and management–subordinate relations. TA can be seen therefore as a valuable tool to aid our understanding of social situations and the games that people play both in and outside work organisations.

TA emphasises the strong links between perception and communication and illustrates the way in which they affect each other. However, it does not answer how we construct our social world in the first place, what we attend to and why, or why we have positive perceptions about some people and not others. To answer these questions we can concentrate on the stages of the perceptual process – both selection and attention, and organisation and judgement – and apply these to the perception of people.

Selection and attention

What information do we select and why? The social situation consists of both verbal and non-verbal signals. The non-verbal signals include:

- bodily contact;
- proximity;
- orientation;
- head nods;
- facial expression;
- gestures;
- posture;
- direction of gaze;
- dress and appearance;
- non-verbal aspects of speech.

Verbal and non-verbal signals are co-ordinated into regular sequences, often without the awareness of the parties. The mirroring of actions has been researched and is called 'postural echoing'.[18] There is considerable evidence to indicate that each person is constantly influencing the other, and being influenced.[19]

Cook has suggested that in any social encounter there are two kinds of information which can be distinguished:

- **static information** – information which will not change during the encounter: for example, colour, gender, height and age; and
- **dynamic information** – information which is subject to change: for example, mood, posture, gestures and expression.[20]

The meanings we ascribed to these non-verbal signals are rooted in our culture and early socialisation. Thus it is no surprise that there are significant differences in the way we perceive such signals. For instance dress codes differ in degrees of formality. *Schneider and Barsoux* summarise some interesting cultural differences:

Northern European managers tend to dress more informally than their Latin counterparts. At conferences, it is not unlikely for the Scandinavian managers to be wearing casual

Understanding and Managing People at Work

clothing, escaping from the office uniform of the tie and jacket. Meanwhile the French counterparts are reluctant to remove their ties and jackets. For the Latin managers, style is important, while Anglo and Asian managers do not want to stand out or attract attention in their dress. French women managers are more likely to be dressed in ways that Anglo women managers might think inappropriate for the office. The French, in turn, think it strange that American businesswomen dress in 'man-like' business suits (sometimes with running shoes).[21]

Impression management

In some situations we all attempt to project our attitudes, personality and competence by paying particular attention to our appearance, and the impact this may have on others. This has been labelled 'impression management'[22] and the selection interview is an obvious illustration. Some information is given more weight than other information when an impression is formed. It would seem that there are central traits which are more important than others in determining our perceptions.

One of these central traits is the degree of warmth or coldness shown by an individual.[23] The timing of information also seems to be critical in the impressions we form. For example, information heard first tends to be resistant to later contradictory information. In other words, the saying 'first impression counts' is supported by research and is called **'the primacy effect'**.[24] It has also been shown that a negative first impression is more resistant to change than a positive one.[25] However, if there is a break in time we are more likely to remember the most recent information – **'the recency effect'**.

Dealings with other people

There are a number of well-documented problems which arise when perceiving other people. Many of these problems occur because of our limitations in selecting and attending to information. This selectivity may occur because:

● we already know what we are looking for and are therefore 'set' to receive only the information which confirms our initial thoughts; or
● previous training and experience have led us to short-cut and only see a certain range of behaviours; or
● we may group features together and make assumptions about their similarities.

The Gestalt principles apply equally well to the perception of people as to the perception of objects. Thus we can see, for example, that if people live in the same geographical area, assumptions may be made about not only their wealth and type of accommodation but also their attitudes, their political views and even their type of personality.

Organisation and judgement

The ways in which we organise and make judgements about what we have perceived is to a large extent based on our previous experiences and learning. It is also important at this point to be aware of the inferences and assumptions we make which go beyond the information given. We may not always be aware of our pre-set assumptions but they will guide the way in which we interpret the behaviour of others. There has been much research into the impact of implicit personality theory.[26] In the same way that we make assumptions about the world of objects, and go beyond the information provided, we also make critical inferences about people's characteristics and possible likely behaviours.

A manager might well know more about the 'type of person' A – a member of staff who has become or was already a good friend, who is seen in a variety of social situations and with whom there is a close relationship – than about B – another member of staff, in the same section as A and undertaking similar duties, but with whom there is only a formal work relationship and a limited social acquaintance. These differences in relationship, information and interaction might well influence the manager's perception if asked, for example, to evaluate the work performance of A and B.

Judgement of other people can also be influenced by perceptions of such stimuli as, for example:

- role or status;
- occupation;
- physical factors and appearance; and
- body language.

Physical characteristics and appearance

In a discussion on managing people and management style, *Green* raises the question of how managers make judgements on those for whom they are responsible including positive and negative messages.

> *In my personal research people have admitted, under pressure, that certain physical characteristics tend to convey a positive or negative message. For example, some people find red hair, earrings for men, certain scents and odours, someone too tall or too short; a disability; a member of a particular ethnic group and countless other items as negative ... Similarly there will be positive factors such as appropriate hairstyle or dress for the occasion ... which may influence in a positive way.*[27]

Related characteristics

A person may tend to organise perception of another person in terms of the 'whole' mental picture of that person. Perceptual judgement is influenced by reference to related characteristics associated with the person and the attempt to place that person in a complete environment. In one example, an unknown visitor was introduced by the course director to 110 American students, divided into five equal groups.[28] The visitor was described differently to each group as:

1 Mr England, a student from Cambridge;
2 Mr England, demonstrator in psychology from Cambridge;
3 Mr England, lecturer in psychology from Cambridge;
4 Dr England, senior lecturer from Cambridge;
5 Professor England from Cambridge.

After being introduced to each group, the visitor left. Each group of students was then asked to estimate his height to the nearest half inch. They were also asked to estimate the height of the course director after he too left the room. The mean estimated height of the course director, who had the same status for all groups, did not change significantly among groups. However, the estimated height of the visitor varied with perceived status: as ascribed academic status increased, so did the estimate of height. (*See* Table 11.1.)

Table 11.1 Estimated height according to ascribed academic status

Group	Ascribed academic status	Average estimated height
1	Student	5' 9.9"
2	Demonstrator	5' 10.14"
3	Lecturer	5' 10.9"
4	Senior lecturer	5' 11.6"
5	Professor	6' 0.3"

(*Source:* Adapted from Wilson, P. R. 'Perceptual Distortion of Height as a Function of Ascribed Academic Status', *Journal of Social Psychology*, no. 74, 1968, pp. 97–102, published by John Wiley & Sons Limited. Reproduced with permission.)

Understanding and Managing People at Work

The importance of body language

We have referred previously in this chapter to the particular significance of body language and non-verbal communication. This includes inferences drawn from posture, invasions of personal space, the extent of eye contact, tone of voice or facial expression. People are the only animals that speak, laugh and weep. Actions are more cogent than speech, and humans rely heavily on body language to convey their true feelings and meanings.[29] It is interesting to note how emotions are woven creatively into e-mail messages. Using keyboard signs in new combinations has led to a new e-language. For example to signal pleasure :), or unhappiness :–c, or send a rose @>---> encapsulate feelings as well as words. The growth of this practice has led to an upsurge of web pages replete with examples.

> According to *Mehrabian*, in our face-to-face communication with other people the message about our feelings and attitudes come only 7 per cent from the words we use, 38 per cent from our voice and 55 per cent from body language, including facial expressions. Significantly, when body language such as gestures and tone of voice conflicts with the words, greater emphasis is likely to be placed on the non-verbal message.[30]
>
> Although actual percentages may vary, there appears to be general support for this contention. For example, according to *Pivcevic*: 'It is commonly agreed that 80 per cent of communication is non-verbal; it is carried in your posture and gestures, and in the tone, pace and energy behind what you say'.[31] And *McGuire* suggests when verbal and non-verbal messages are in conflict: 'Accepted wisdom from the experts is that the non-verbal signals should be the ones to reply on, and that what is not said is frequently louder than what is said, revealing attitudes and feelings in a way words can't express.[32]

In our perceptions and judgement of others it is important therefore to watch and take careful note of their non-verbal communication. However, although body language may be a guide to personality, errors can easily arise if too much is inferred from a single message rather than a related cluster of actions. According to *Fletcher*, for example: 'you won't learn to interpret people's body language accurately, and use your own to maximum effect, without working at it. If you consciously spend half an hour a day analysing people's subconscious movements, you'll soon learn how to do it – almost unconsciously'.[33] However, as *Mann* points out, with a little knowledge about the subject it is all too easy to become body conscious. Posture and gesture can unmask deceivers but it would be dangerous to assume that everyone who avoids eye contact or rubs their nose is a fibber. Nevertheless an understanding of non-verbal communication is essential for managers and other professions where good communication skills are essential.[34]

Cultural differences
There are many cultural variations in non-verbal communications, the extent of physical contact, and differences in the way body language is perceived and interpreted.[35] For example, Italians and South Americans tend to show their feelings through intense body language, while Japanese tend to hide their feelings and have largely eliminated overt body language from interpersonal communication. When talking to another person, the British tend to look away spasmodically, but Norwegians typically look people steadily in the eyes without altering their gaze. When the Dutch point a forefinger at their temples this is likely to be a sign of congratulations for a good idea, but with other cultures the gesture has a less complimentary implication.

In many European countries it is customary to greet people with three or four kisses on the cheek and pulling the head away may be taken as a sign of impoliteness. All cultures have specific values related to personal space and 'comfort zone'. For example, Arabs tend to stand very close when speaking to another person but most Americans when introduced to a new person will, after shaking hands, move backwards a couple of steps to place a comfortable space between themselves and the person they have just met.

Exhibit 11.1

Hospitals set to play it by ethnic book

Staff receive guide to help them tend people from different cultures, writes Tanya Johnson

Touching a patient to comfort them would be one of the most natural gestures for a nurse.

But being touched by a nurse of the opposite sex could offend an orthodox Jew because being comforted like that is not welcome in Judaism.

Similarly, touching or removing a Sikh's turban could also cause offence because it has deep spiritual and moral significance.

Now a book has been produced to help staff at Portsmouth hospitals understand the differences between ethnic minority groups and avoid unwittingly offending them.

Called the *Ethnic Minority Handbook*, it contains all the information doctors and nurses need when dealing with patients of different religious persuasions.

It was completed by Florise Elliott, Portsmouth Hospitals NHS Trust's ethnic health coordinator, who said: 'It's always important for people to be aware of other people's cultures.

'This makes staff aware of other cultures and differences in ways of living.'

The book has sections for Buddhists, Chinese people, Christians, Mormons, Hindus, Jehovah's Witnesses, Jews, Muslims, Sikhs and spiritualism and was compiled with help from representatives from each culture.

As well as guidance on diet, language, cultures, death and post-mortems, each section contains contacts hospital medical staff can ring if they need advice.

One is Jewish spokesman Julius Klein, a member of the Portsmouth and Southsea Hebrew Congregation, who welcomed the book.

He said: 'It's excellent. One of the difficulties when people go into hospital is trying to put over certain things about their culture and life that the hospital needs to know.

'Anything that helps inform the nursing staff about minorities must be a good thing.'

Each ward at Queen Alexandra Hospital, Cosham, and St Mary's Hospital, Milton, will have a copy of the book which was started by the hospital's service planning manager Petronella Mwasandube.

About 1,500 of the 37,500 annual cases the hospitals deal with are people from ethnic minority groups which does not include emergencies.

(Reproduced courtesy of The News, Portsmouth, February 16, 1999.)

Attribution theory

It seems, therefore, that part of the process of perceiving other people is to attribute characteristics to them. We judge their behaviour and their intentions on past knowledge, and in comparison with other people we know. It is our way of making sense of their behaviour. This is known as attribution theory.

Attribution is the process by which people interpret the perceived causes of behaviour. The initiator of **attribution theory** is generally recognised as *Heider*, who suggests that behaviour is determined by a combination of **perceived** internal forces and external forces.[36]

- **Internal forces** relate to personal attributes such as ability, skill, amount of effort or fatigue.
- **External forces** relate to environmental factors such as organisational rules and policies, the manner of superiors, or the weather.

Behaviour at work may be explained by the **locus of control**, that is whether the individual perceives outcomes as controlled by themselves, or by external factors. Judgements made about other people will also be influenced strongly by whether the cause is seen as internal or external.

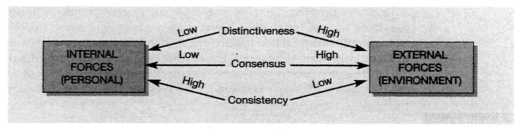

Figure 11.12 Representation of attribution theory

Basic criteria in making attributions

In making attributions and determining whether an internal or external attribution is chosen, Kelley suggests three basic criteria: distinctiveness, consensus and consistency.[37]

- **Distinctiveness.** How distinctive or different was the behaviour or action in this particular task or situation compared with behaviour or action on other tasks or situations?
- **Consensus.** Is the behaviour or action different from, or in keeping with, that displayed by most other people in the same situation?
- **Consistency.** Is the behaviour or action associated with an enduring personality or motivational characteristic over time, or an unusual one-off situation caused by external factors?

Kelley hypothesised that people attribute behaviour to internal forces or personal factors when they perceive **low distinctiveness, low consensus** and **high consistency.** Behaviour is attributed to external forces or environmental factors when people perceived **high distinctiveness, high consensus,** and **low consistency** (*see* Figure 11.12).

An example of these criteria related to a student who fails a mid-sessional examination in a particular subject is given in Table 11.2.[38]

An additional consideration in the evaluation of task performance within an organisational setting is whether the cause of behaviour was due to 'stable' or 'unstable' factors.

- **Stable factors** are ability, or the ease or difficulty of the task.
- **Unstable factors** are the exertion of effort, or luck.[39]

The combination of internal and external attributions, and stable and unstable characteristics, results in four possible interpretations of a person's task performance (*see* Table 11.3).

Table 11.2 Example of criteria in making attributions

	Distinctiveness	**Consensus**	**Consistency**
Internal attribution	Student fails all mid-sessional examinations	Student is the only one to fail	Student also fails final examination
External attribution	Student gains high marks on other mid-sessional examinations	All students in the class get low marks	Student obtains a good mark in final examination

(*Source*: Adapted from Mitchell, Terence R., *People in Organisations*, Second edition, McGraw-Hill (1982) p. 104. Reproduced with permission from The McGraw-Hill Companies Inc.)

Understanding and Managing People at Work

Table 11.3 Classification of possible attributions for performance

	Internal attributions	External attributions
Stable factors	ABILITY	TASK DIFFICULTY
Unstable factors	EFFORT	LUCK

Implications of attribution theory

Employees with an internal control orientation are more likely to believe that they can influence their level of performance through their own abilities, skills or efforts. Employees with an external control orientation are more likely to believe that their level of performance is determined by external factors beyond their influence.

Studies appear to support the idea that staff with an internal control orientation are generally more satisfied with their jobs, are more likely to be in managerial positions, and are more satisfied with a participatory style of management, than staff with an external control orientation.[40] As a generalisation it might be implied that internally controlled managers are more effective than those who are externally controlled. However, this does not appear to be always the case.[41]

People with a high achievement motivation may perceive that successful performance is caused by their own internal forces, and their ability and effort, rather than by the nature of the task or by luck. If members of staff fail to perform well on their tasks they may believe that external factors are the cause, and as a result may reduce the level of future effort. On the other hand, if staff perform well but the manager perceives this as due to an easy task or to luck, the appropriate recognition and reward may not be given. If the staff perceive that good performance was due to ability and/or effort the lack of recognition and reward may well have a demotivating effect.

Perceptual distortions and errors

We have seen that differences in perception result in different people seeing different things and attaching different meanings to the same stimuli. Every person sees things in his or her own way and as perceptions become a person's reality this can lead to misunderstandings. The accuracy of interpersonal perception and the judgements made about other people are influenced by:

- the nature of the relationship between the perceiver and the other person;
- the amount of information available to the perceiver and the order in which information is received;
- the nature and extent of interaction between the two people.[42]

There are four main features which can create particular difficulties and give rise to perceptual problems, bias or distortions, in our dealings with other people. These are:

- stereotyping;
- the halo effect;
- perceptual defence; and
- projection.

The perceptual paradox

These problems with people perception arise because of the selectivity which exists in the perceptual process. We do not enjoy living in a world where uncertainty abounds and our perceptual system works to minimise our energy consumption. We do not have to start every day afresh – we have our store of memories and experiences to guide us.

The paradox is that this process is also our downfall. Errors and bias are inherent in such a system. Although exhortations can be made for us to become more aware of our own biases and to take more time in making judgements we are working against our normal quick-fire perceptual system.

Stereotyping

This is the tendency to ascribe positive or negative characteristics to a person on the basis of a general categorisation and perceived similarities. The perception of that person may be based more on certain expected characteristics than on the recognition of that person as an individual. It is a form of typecasting. **Stereotyping** is a means of simplifying the process of perception and making judgements of other people, instead of dealing with a range of complex and alternative stimuli. It occurs when an individual is judged on the basis of the group to which it is perceived that person belongs. When we see all people belonging to a particular group as having the same characteristics we are stereotyping individuals. Pre-judgements are therefore made about an individual without ever really knowing whether such judgements are accurate; they may be wildly wrong.

Examples of common stereotyping may be based on:

- **nationality**, e.g., all Germans are orderly and industrious;
- **occupation**, e.g., all accountants are boring;
- **age**, e.g., all young people are unreliable, no old person wants to consider new ideas;
- **physical**, e.g., all people with red hair have fiery temperament;
- **education**, e.g., all graduates are clever;
- **social**, e.g., all unemployed people are lazy;
- **politics**, e.g., all Labour voters are in favour of strong trade unions, all Conservative voters support privatisation.

Although stereotyping condenses the amount of information that we need to know and thus enables us to cope with a vast information flow, the consequences of attributing incorrect characteristics are extremely negative.

Figure 11.13
(Reproduced with permission from Viv Quillin.)

Social implications

Stereotyping infers that all people within a particular perceived category are assumed to share the same traits or characteristics. A significant social implication of stereotyping is therefore the perception held about particular groups of people based on, for example:

- gender;
- race;
- disability;
- religious belief;
- age.

(By way of an example, the illustrative case on pp. 408–11 focuses on the effects of stereotyping women.)

A major danger of stereotyping is that it can block out accurate perception of the individual or individual situation.[43] Stereotyping may lead to potential situations of prejudice or discrimination. An example might be the perception of people with HIV or AIDS.[44]

Stereotyping may work either negatively or favourably for a particular group of people. For example, a sizeable number of employers still maintain negative and inaccurate stereotypes about the capabilities and training of older workers.[45] However, B&Q, the UK's largest home-improvement chain, have claimed improved profit figures partly because of the older age profile of their employees: they have a policy of staffing certain stores with people over 50 years of age.

The halo effect

This is the process by which the perception of a person is formulated on the basis of a single favourable or unfavourable trait or impression. The **halo effect** tends to shut out other relevant characteristics of that person. Some examples might be as follows.

- A candidate for employment who arrives punctually, is smart in appearance and friendly may well influence the perception of the selectors, who then place less emphasis on the candidate's technical ability, qualifications or experience for the job.
- A new member of staff who performs well in a first major assignment may be perceived as a likely person for promotion, even though that assignment is not typical of the usual duties the member of staff is expected to undertake.
- A single trait, such as good attendance and time-keeping, may become the main emphasis for judgement of overall competence and performance, rather than other considerations such as the quantity, quality and accuracy of work.

A particular danger with the halo effect is that, where quick judgements are made on the basis of readily available stimuli, the perceiver may become 'perceptually blind' to subsequent stimuli at variance with the original perception, and (often subconsciously) notice only those characteristics which support the original judgement.

The rusty halo effect

The process may also work in reverse: **the rusty halo effect**. This is where general judgements about a person are formulated from the perception of a negative characteristic. For example, a candidate is seen arriving late for an interview. There may be a very good reason for this and it may be completely out of character. But on the basis of that one particular event the person may be perceived as a poor time-keeper and unreliable. Another example may be a new member of staff who performs poorly in a first major assignment. This may have been due to an unusual set of circumstances and not typical behaviour, but the person may still be perceived as a bad appointment.

Perceptual defence

Perceptual defence is the tendency to avoid or screen out certain stimuli that are perceptually disturbing or threatening. People may tend to select information which is supportive of their point of view and choose not to acknowledge contrary information. For example, a manager who has decided recently to promote a member of staff against the advice of colleagues may select only favourable information which supports that decision and ignore less favourable information which questions that decision.

Projection

Attributing, or projecting, one's own feelings, motives or characteristics to other people is a further distortion which can occur in the perception of other people. Judgements of other people may be more favourable when they have characteristics largely in common with, and easily recognised by, the perceiver. Projection may also result in people exaggerating undesirable traits in others that they fail to recognise in themselves.

Perception is distorted by feelings and emotions. For example, a manager who is concerned about possible redundancy may perceive other managers to be even more concerned. People have a tendency to perceive others less favourably by projecting certain of their own feelings or characteristics to them. As another example, supervisors may complain that their manager did not work hard enough to secure additional resources for the department, when in fact the supervisors failed to provide the manager with all the relevant information and statistics.

Discussed by *Freud* in his description of defence mechanisms, projection is a way in which we protect ourselves from acknowledging that we may possess undesirable traits and assign them in exaggerated amounts to other people. For instance, a manager who considers all subordinates as insincere may be projecting one of the manager's own characteristics. Perception of 'self' and how people see and think of themselves, and evaluate themselves, are discussed in Chapter 14.

Illustrative example – perception of women

The perceptual process has been outlined as selective and subjective: we perceive the world in our own terms and expect the world to 'fit' into our constructs. Throughout our development we have learned to distinguish what is important and significant (figure) from information which is additional and contextual (ground). This process is repeated when we join new organisations or have a new job within the same organisation. Fitting into the organisation involves selecting information which is necessary from that which is less significant. At times, the process can be distorted and we can also be 'tricked' into seeing the world in particular ways.

Beliefs about women and their roles

One of the most common stereotypes is to view women in terms of their biology and reproductive abilities. Unlike men, beliefs about women and their roles focus outside the workplace rather than inside. For instance, the prospect of women marrying and having children leads people to question their permanency as employees, and results in organisations viewing their engagement as high risk, with a low return on investment in their training.

In middle years the additional responsibilities of having children are often assumed to be the major role of women. This leads to further beliefs regarding their assumed lack of time and ambition for senior positions. Women, for a period stretching over twenty years, could be perceived as less reliable, less promotable and less ambitious than men.

Judy Owen wins battle against Professional Golfers' Association to wear trousers

Judy Owen who has fought for her right to wear trousers to work has won her battle against the Professional Golfers' Association.

Judy told an Employment Tribunal in Birmingham how she was harassed and bullied by her manager Gerry Paton, because of her sex. She said Mr Paton had 'ordered' her to wear skirts as part of his campaign to undermine her. Eventually, as a result of this treatment she resigned.

Judy joined the PGA in April 1998 as a training manager and was shocked by the constant way in which women were undermined. Mr Paton referred to women golfers as dykes, lesbians, and described women as 'emotional and manipulating'. Ms Owen said that such disrespect for women generally was a clear demonstration of Mr Paton's inability to see professional women as equals.

On Ms Owen's second day at work she was told by Mr Paton's secretary not to wear a smart trouser suit because 'ladies don't wear trousers at the PGA'. Judy Owen had worn trousers to meetings before officially taking up her post and was not advised that this was against the PGA's policy.

She asked for clarification, but because she had not been shown any policies relating to a dress code, several weeks later she again wore a smart trouser suit to work, and was humiliated by Mr Paton sending her home to change into a skirt. Ms Owen said Mr Paton had 'bullied' and 'harassed' her. She was signed off work with stress after several incidents of bullying and harassment and eventually resigned.

The PGA denied its dress code is discriminatory and said Ms Owen had 'provoked' Mr Paton by wearing trousers. They had denied that Judy Owen was treated unfairly and confirmed that they did not have a written policy on dress code.

Ms Owen said she was 'extremely pleased' that the Employment Tribunal had found in her favour and that she hoped it would set an example to other women to stand up for their rights.

Ms Owen said:

Trousers can be a smart, practical and sometimes more professional alternative for women at work. Out of date stereotypes of appropriate dress for women should not prevent women wearing trousers which have considerable practical disadvantages.

Smart trousers are now a widely accepted alternative to skirts for women at work. Even conservative professions like the bar now consider trousers to be acceptable business dress for women. Cheri Blair wears them and no-one has accused her of not being dressed appropriately. Women MPs in Parliament wear them too. The fact that the PGA thought it could inflict these kinds of prejudicial judgements on its female employees is outrageous. I'm extremely pleased that finally I have won this important judgement on behalf of women.

However, I am saddened that after more than 18 months of this battle the PGA still has no written equal opportunities policy in place and that they still ban women from wearing trousers. I would have hoped that in the modern workplace, employers would accept that trousers are acceptable dress for women.

Clare Hockney, the Equal Opportunities Commission solicitor who fought the battle for Judy said:

This is fantastic and now gives women the right to wear smart trousers to work. It has now been deemed unlawful sex discrimination to refuse to allow women to wear a smart trouser suit as an option for work. This issue had not been directly tested since 1977 and standards of what is conventional dress for men and women has moved on.

Julie Mellor, the Chair of the EOC, said:

This is a memorable victory for Judy and for the EOC who backed her claim. We believe that women should be judged on the quality of their work, not on what they wear. Women in all walks of life now wear smart trousers to work, and it's now almost a year since David Beckham wore a sarong! It's right that the law should reflect these changes.

It is no longer acceptable for employers to impose old-fashioned stereotypes about what they think it is appropriate for women or men to wear to work. Judging individuals on how they look is clearly discriminatory to women and can prevent them achieving their potential in the workplace. How can such a situation be good for business? It's a great day for Judy.

Source: www.eoc.org.uk/html/press_releases_2000_1.html. Accessed 10 February 2001. Reproduced with permission.

Instead of stereotyping women and viewing them as a group with identical life patterns, it would clearly be more equitable to judge women individually. This would seem particularly relevant as statistics reveal that nearly two-thirds of women at work who leave to have a baby are economically active within nine months of childbirth.[46]

Stereotypes about women employees

In the workplace, there are many commonplace stereotypes about women employees. Women may be perceived as: an 'earth-mother'; a counsellor figure; a 'pet' brightening up the place; a 'seductress'; a sex object; an 'iron maiden'; a man-hater.[47] In addition, women who have made it to the top have to face other pressures concerned with their visibility and uniqueness. The token woman has to contend with additional interest because of her gender and she may be excluded from social activities and male 'chat'.

Some studies have focused on the behavioural characteristics of men and women, and have noted that women may be caught in a 'double bind'. If they show typical feminine characteristics it is thought they do not have the ambition to go further; whereas if they demonstrate assertiveness and determination they can be considered to be too aggressive, pushy and masculine.

Understanding the organisational process

Although some organisations may discriminate, it is the view of the authors that perceptions of women are not always calculated: they are often made automatically and without conscious thought – in much the same way as we may be tricked by visual illusions. In fact, perceptual illusions are a very appropriate way of understanding the organisational processes affecting women.

The 'Ames Room' is relevant for this purpose.[48] This is a room of an irregular size with one of the far corners at a greater distance than the other, although the room is arranged and decorated so that it gives the appearance of being rectangular. If two people of the same size stand in diagonally opposite corners, one in the furthest corner, and the other in the near corner, a visual illusion occurs whereby our perception of depth is 'tricked' to see the farthest away looking dramatically smaller. (*See* Figure 11.14.)

By analogy it is possible to see the room as representing the culture of the organisation surrounded by beliefs and traditions, rather like pictures on the wall. They seem reasonable, logical and appropriate. The individual standing at the farthest corner of the room could be seen as the female, the nearest the male. Both people are in the room surrounded by the culture; but one, the male, is nearest and most visible. He is perceived differently and advantageously, whereas the woman is perceived in a relatively inconsequential way. If the woman stays at the back of the room in an ancillary position, or leaves the room altogether, she is reinforcing the beliefs around the walls.

Some women, however, do become managers and these exceptional women would then join the male corner and would seem to become larger in size and more visible. However, the perceptual distortion is complete because the lone woman could legitimately be viewed as a 'trick', as an illusion. For the males, their position fits and they have only to prove their merit for a management post, and not that they are different from the norm. Their success will feed back into the system and reaffirm the beliefs that are held.

Applications to the organisational setting

This illusion can be applied to any organisational setting. *Hicks* found, for example, that even in hotels, which mirror the domestic world of women and should suit perfectly the alleged skills of women, a male ethic resides.[49] The female manager is atypical, a deviation from the norm, and women can be seen to be the disadvantaged gender group. Men and women are perceived very differently. Young, male trainees are expected and encouraged to do well, it is considered 'normal'; whereas young women and their assumed needs are less likely to fit into the demands of the industry. Young women are expected to diversify and specialise in roles considered suitable for their gender such as personnel or public relations.

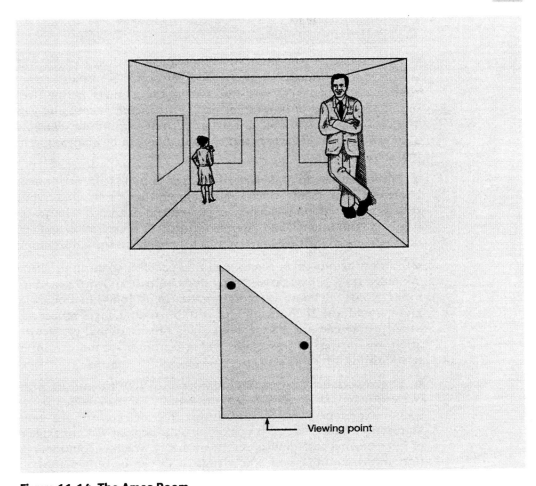

Figure 11.14 The Ames Room

(*Source*: Hicks, L. 'Gender and Culture: A Study of the Attitudes Displayed by Managers in the Hotel World'. Unpublished doctoral thesis, University of Surrey, 1991, p. 303.)

For any organisation to be effective it is imperative that the staff are competent to do their work and satisfy the 'psychological contract' (discussed in Chapter 2). One part of the role of managers is to select and train those people who they predict will perform successfully on the job, and then to monitor and assess their competence for future promotion. Accordingly, it clearly seems important for managers to be aware of their own prejudices and assumptions concerning women. By opening channels and encouraging and developing all staff, trust might be fed back into the system from which equity could begin and stereotypes might end.

Britain's top businesswomen To conclude this discussion it is of interest to note two recent comments from the *Management Today* listing of Britain's most powerful businesswomen:

The top 50 women do no fit any pattern. They wield the kind of power and influence that defies stereotypes.[50]

So, after 20 years of discussion and debate about how the glass ceiling is to be shattered, the proportion of women in the boardroom has grown by just 2% and Marjorie Scardino (Pearson's CEO) is still the only female chief executive of a FTSE-100 company.[51]

Synopsis

■ The process of perception links individuals to their social world. Although we all see the world through our own 'coloured spectacles' we also have the opportunities to share our experiences with others. By learning others' perspectives and by widening our understanding of how others may see the world, depth and variety is encouraged and problems of bias and distortion become minimised. Perception is the root of all organisational behaviour and any situation can be analysed in terms of its perceptual connotations.

■ For managers, an understanding of perception is essential to ensure that they are aware of the problems which can arise from the process of perceptual selectivity. The process of perception is innately organised and patterned. The process of perception is based on both internal and external factors. The organisation and arrangement of stimuli is influenced by three important factors: figure and ground; grouping; and closure.

■ Part of the process of perceiving other people is to attribute characteristics to them. We judge their behaviour and intentions on past knowledge and in comparison with other people we know. Perception gives rise to individual behavioural responses in given situations. The principles of perceptual differences reflect the way we perceive other people and are the source of many organisational problems. In the work situation, the process of perception and selection of stimuli can influence a manager's relationship with other staff.

■ The importance of communication and the way we interact with others cannot be overestimated, as our well-being and morale can be affected by the nature of these social experiences. Communication and perception are inextricably bound. Transactional analysis (TA) is one of the most popular ways of explaining the dynamics of interpersonal communication. It is a theory which encompasses personality, perception and communication. Knowledge of TA can be of benefit to employees dealing with potentially difficult situations.

■ The ways in which we organise and make judgements about what we have perceived is to a large extent based on previous experiences and learning. It is also important to be aware that there are inferences and assumptions which go beyond the information given. Judgements of other people can also be influenced by such stimuli as role or status; occupation; physical factors and appearance; and body language. The social situation consists of both verbal and non-verbal signals. It is necessary to be aware of cultural differences in non-verbal communications.

■ Part of the process of perceiving other people is to attribute characteristics to them. Attribution is the process by which people interpret the perceived causes of behaviour. There are a number of difficulties which arise with interpersonal perception. Four main features which may give rise to perceptual distortions or errors are: stereotyping; the halo effect; perceptual defence; and projection. The perceptual process is selective and subjective. In the work situation perceptual differences reflect the way we perceive other people. One particularly important example is the perception of women.

Understanding and Managing People at Work

CRITICAL REFLECTIONS

'Managers require an understanding of perception in order to help judge the behaviour and intentions of other people'.

'Right, but remember that it is not unreasonable to argue that there is no such thing as reality – only the individual's perception or interpretation of reality.'

'But how then can managers avoid organisational problems which result from perceptual differences?'

What are your own views?

Those organizations that can create a culture that challenges unhelpful perceptual processes (stemming, say, from ignorance, prejudice or arrogance) will, in our view, be more able to absorb new information and respond intelligently to change. Broadening our mind, however, is much easier said than done. To understand why this is so, it is worth looking at influences on our perceptual processes. At the most fundamental level lie our values and beliefs. These also colour what we see and how we interpret events. Given this, it is important we reflect on how our own values influence the decisions we make.

Dainty, P. and Anderson, M. 'Mindset for Managers', in Chowdhury, S. *Management 21C*, Financial Times Prentice Hall (2000), pp. 109–10.

How would you, as a senior manager, attempt to broaden perceptions and challenge unhelpful perceptual processes among your staff?

'There is considerable truth in the commonly held perception that women's motivations and attitudes to work are different to men's.'

Debate.

REVIEW AND DISCUSSION QUESTIONS

1 Explain your understanding of the process of perception. Why is the study of perception important in the study of management and organisational behaviour?

2 Discuss those factors which affect selection and attention in the process of perception. Give examples of how perceptual selectivity is the source of organisational problems.

3 Explain the most significant principles which influence the organisation and arrangement of stimuli. Provide your own example of each of these principles.

4 What factors influence the judgements we make of other people from different cultures? Explain the main distortions or errors in interpersonal perception. Support your answer with practical examples.

5 Explain the principles of attribution theory and its importance to, and implications for, management. Apply the principles to your *own* working life.

6 Transcribe a short dialogue you have had with a colleague, friend, or boss and analyse the responses in Transactional Analysis (TA) terms.

7 Think of a situation where you have felt 'locked' in to a familiar, uncomfortable groove of transactions with someone. Apply TA to the situation and evaluate the extent to which TA helps you to understand the situation.

8 Discuss critically the significance and implications of stereotyping *and* the halo effect. Give practical examples from your own experience.

9 During the period of one week, review the media (television and radio, advertisements, films, newspapers and magazines) for evidence of traditional male and female stereotypes. In a group discussion evaluate the impact and power of these stereotypes.

Understanding and Managing People at Work

Assignment 1

STROOP – ILLUSTRATIVE EXPERIMENT

a Write two vertical lists of 20 colour names in felt tip pen. For the first list use the correct colour pen for the colour word you are writing (for example, blue pen for the word blue). Repeat some of the colours but place them in random order.

b For the second list, use different colour pens for the colour word (for example, use a red pen for the word blue).

c Now ask a colleague to read out loud the colour that the word is written in (not the word itself). Compare the amount of time it takes your colleague to read out the two lists. The second list probably not only took longer, but had more mistakes and more hesitations.

William Stroop, who first conducted this experiment, noted that the task interferes with expected behaviour. It is difficult to stop yourself from reading the word (the result of our early learning) which in this case directly impairs performance.

Assignment 2

INFERENCE – OBSERVATION

a Read the following short story.

b Then read the 15 statements about the story and check each to indicate whether you consider it to be true, false or ?

'T' means that the statement is *definitely true* on the basis of the information presented in the story.

'F' means that it is *definitely false*.

'?' means that it may be either true or false and that you cannot be certain which on the basis of the information presented in the story. If any part of a statement is doubtful, mark it '?'.

c Answer each statement in turn. You may refer to the story as often as needed but do not go back to change any answer later and do not re-read any statements after you have answered them.

d After you have completed checking all 15 statements, work in small groups of three to five and discuss your individual answers. How much agreement is there among members of your group? On what basis did members of your group give different answers and how did their perception of the statements about the story differ?

Do not change any of your first individual answers. However, if as a result of your group discussion you would now give a different answer to any of the statements, note this alongside your original answer.

The story

A businessman had just turned off the lights in the store when a man appeared and demanded money. The owner opened a cash register. The contents of the cash register were scooped up, and the man sped away. A member of the police force was notified promptly.

Statements about the story

1	A man appeared after the owner had turned off his store lights.	T	F	?
2	The robber was a man.	T	F	?
3	The man who appeared did not demand money.	T	F	?
4	The man who opened the cash register was the owner.	T	F	?
5	The store owner scooped up the contents of the cash register and ran away.	T	F	?
6	Someone opened a cash register.	T	F	?
7	After the man who demanded the money scooped up the contents of the cash register, he ran away.	T	F	?
8	While the cash register contained money, the story does *not* state *how much*.	T	F	?
9	The robber demanded money of the owner.	T	F	?
10	A businessman had just turned off the lights when a man appeared in the store.	T	F	?
11	It was broad daylight when the man appeared.	T	F	?
12	The man who appeared opened the cash register.	T	F	?
13	No one demanded money.	T	F	?
14	The story concerns a series of events in which only three persons are referred to: the owner of the store, a man who demanded money, and a member of the police force.	T	F	?
15	The following events occurred: someone demanded money, a cash register was opened, its contents were scooped up, and a man dashed out of the store.	T	F	?

Visit our website **www.booksites.net/mullins** for further questions, annotated weblinks, case material and internet research material.

Notes and references

1 Bartlett, F. C. *Remembering* Cambridge, Cambridge University Press (1932).

2 Kohler, I. 'The Formation and Transformation of the Visual World', *Psychological Issues*, 3, 1964, pp. 28–46, 116–33.

3 Bexton, W., Heron, W. and Scott, T. 'Effects of Decreased Variation in the Sensory Environment', *Canadian Journal of Psychology*, vol. 8, 1954, pp. 70–6.

4 Briggs-Myers, I. *Introduction to Type*, Oxford Psychologists Press (1987).

5 Witkin, H. A., Lewis, H. B., Hertzman, M., Machover, K., Meissner, P. P. and Wapner, S. S. *Personality Through Perception*, Harper & Row (1954).

6 Hall E. T. 'The Silent Language of Overseas Business', *Harvard Business Review*, vol. 38, no. 3, 1960, pp. 85–7.

7 Morgan, C. T. and King, R. A. *Introduction to Psychology*, Third edition, McGraw-Hill (1966), p. 343.

8 Hellriegel, D., Slocum, J. W. and Woodman, R. W. *Organizational Behaviour*, Eighth edition, South-Western College Publishing (1998), p. 76.

9 Luthans, F. *Organizational Behaviour*, Seventh edition, McGraw-Hill (1995), p. 96.

10 For further examples of perceptual teasers, see Tosi, H. L., Rizzo, J. R. and Carroll, S. J. *Managing Organizational Behaviour*, Third edition, Blackwell (1994).

11 Stroop, J. R. 'Studies of Interference in Serial Verbal Reactions', *Journal of Experimental Psychology*, vol. 4, no. 18, 1935, pp. 643–62; and Penrose, L. S. and Penrose, R. 'Impossible Objects: A Special Type of Illusion', *British Journal of Psychology*, part 1, February 1958.

12 Wexley, K. N., Yukl, G. A., Kovacs, S. Z. and Sanders, R. E. 'Importance of Contrast Effects in Employment Interviews', *Journal of Applied Psychology*, 56, 1972, pp. 45–8.

13 Laing, R. D. *Knots*, Penguin (1971), p. 30.

14 Guirdham, M. *Interpersonal Skills at Work*, Second edition, Prentice-Hall (1995), p. 145.

15 See, for example: Pivcevic, P. 'Taming the Boss', *Management Today*, March 1999, pp. 68–72.

Understanding and Managing People at Work

16 Berne, E. *Games People Play*, Penguin (1966).

17 See, for example: Stewart, I. and Jaines, V. *TA today: A New Introduction to Transactional Analysis*, Life Space Publishing (1987).

18 Kendon, A. 'Some Functions of Gaze Direction in Social Interaction', *Acta Psychologica*, 26, 1967, pp. 22–63.

19 Mehrabian, A. *Nonverbal Communication*, Aldine Atherton (1972).

20 Cook, M. *Interpersonal Perception*, Penguin (1971).

21 Schneider, S. C. and Barsoux, J. L. *Managing Across Cultures*, Prentice Hall (1997), p. 26.

22 Goffman, E. *The Presentation of Self in Everyday Life*, Penguin (1971).

23 Asch, S. E. 'Forming Impressions on Personality', *Journal of Abnormal and Social Psychology*, 41, 1946, pp. 258–90.

24 Miller, N. and Campbell, D. T. 'Recency and Primacy in Persuasion as a Function of the Timing of Speeches and Measurements', *Journal of Abnormal and Social Psychology*, 59, 1959, pp. 1–9.

25 Hodges, B. 'Effect of Volume on Relative Weighting in Impression Formation', *Journal of Personality and Social Psychology*, 30, 1974, pp. 378–81.

26 Gahagan, J. *Interpersonal and Group Behaviour*, Methuen (1975).

27 Green, J. 'When Was Your Management Style Last Applauded?', *Chartered Secretary*, December 1998, p. 28.

28 Wilson, P. R. 'Perceptual Distortion of Height as a Function of Ascribed Academic Status', *Journal of Social Psychology*, no. 74, 1968, pp. 97–102.

29 See, for example: Torrington, D. *Face-to-Face in Management*, Prentice-Hall (1982).

30 Mehrabian, A. *Tactics of Social Influence*, Prentice-Hall (1970).

31 Pivcevic, P. 'Taming the boss', *Management Today*, March 1999, p. 70.

32 McGuire, T. 'Don't Just Listen', *Chartered Secretary*, September 1998, p. 24.

33 Fletcher, W. 'Let Your Body Do The Talking', *Management Today*, March 2000, p. 30.

34 Mann, S. 'Message in a Body', *Professional Manager*, November 2000, pp. 32–3; and Ribbens, G. and Thompson, R. *Understanding Body Language in a Week*, Institute of Management and Hodder & Stoughton (2000).

35 See, for example: Green, J. 'Can You Read Other People's Body Talk?' *Administrator*, February 1994, pp. 8–9.

36 Heider, F. *The Psychology of Interpersonal Relations*, John Wiley and Sons (1958).

37 Kelley, H. H. 'The Process of Causal Attribution', *American Psychologist*, February 1973, pp. 107–28.

38 Mitchell, T. R. *People in Organizations: An Introduction to Organizational Behaviour*, Third edition, McGraw-Hill (1987).

39 Bartunek, J. M. 'Why Did You Do That? Attribution Theory in Organizations', *Business Horizons*, September–October 1981, pp. 66–71.

40 Mitchell, T. R., Smyser, C. M. and Weed, S. E. 'Locus of Control: Supervision and Work Satisfaction', *Academy of Management Journal*, September 1975, pp. 623–31.

41 Durand, D. E. and Nord, W. R. 'Perceived Leader Behaviour as a Function of Personality Characteristics of Supervisors and Subordinates', *Academy of Management Journal*, September 1976, pp. 427–38.

42 For a more detailed analysis of the accuracy of interpersonal perception and problems in judgement of others, see: Krech, D., Crutchfield, R. S. and Ballachey, E. L. *Individual in Society*, McGraw-Hill (1962).

43 For a fuller discussion see, for example: McKenna, E. F. *Business Psychology and Organisational Behaviour*, Lawrence Erlbaum (1994).

44 See, for example: Atkin, A. 'Positive HIV and AIDS Policies at Work', *Personnel Management*, December 1994, pp. 34–7.

45 Taylor, P. and Walker, A. 'Employers and Older Workers', *Employment Gazette*, vol. 101, no. 8, August 1993, pp. 371–8.

46 *Equal Opportunities Review*, no. 54, March/April 1994, Industrial Relations Services, London, p. 3.

47 Cooper, C. and Davidson, M. *High Pressure: Working Lives of Women Managers*, Fontana (1982).

48 Ames, A. 'Visual Perception and the Rotating Trapezoidal Window', *Psychological Monographs*, vol. 65, no. 7, 1951.

49 Hicks, L. 'Gender and Culture: A Study of the Attitudes Displayed by Managers in the Hotel World', Unpublished doctoral thesis, University of Surrey, 1991.

50 Hamilton, K. 'The Women Who Move Britain', *Management Today*, March 1999, pp. 39–44.

51 Wheatcroft, P. 'Britain's 50 Most Powerful Women', *Management Today*, April 2000, p. 48.

Chapter 21   Diversity: the legal framework

An important part of employment law in the UK is concerned with deterring employers from discriminating unfairly at any stage in their relationship with an individual worker. It is an area of law which is well established but which is also developing fast in new directions. As we write there are specific statutes making it unlawful to discriminate on the following grounds:

- sex;
- marital status;
- race;
- national origin;
- ethnicity;
- disability;
- union membership or non-membership;
- that individuals are part-time workers;
- that individuals are ex-offenders whose convictions are spent.

Wider protection is in the process of being established, principally as a result of European Union directives. Soon it will also become unlawful to discriminate against workers employed on fixed-term contracts, or on the grounds of their **age** or their **religious or political beliefs**. The position on **sexual orientation** remains unclear. Recent case law (notably *MacDonald* v. *Ministry of Defence* 2000) suggests that discrimination on grounds of sexual orientation is a form of unlawful sex discrimination. However, similar past rulings have subsequently been overturned by the appeal courts, so it cannot yet be stated with certainty that employers are acting unlawfully when discriminating against gays and lesbians.

Discrimination law operates rather differently in the case of each of the above grounds, providing a rather greater degree of protection to those discriminated against on the grounds of sex or race than to union members or ex-offenders. In this chapter we review the legal position in each area, establishing the core principles of discrimination law and using illustrative examples from tribunal cases. In the following chapter we look more generally at employment policy on equality issues and at the practices associated with the effective management of diversity.

Activity 21.1   What other grounds, aside from those currently covered by the law, would you consider should be covered by discrimination law? Are there any that are currently covered that you think should not be?

Discrimination on grounds of sex or marital status

The two major Acts of Parliament that govern sex discrimination matters in the UK are the Equal Pay Act 1970 and the Sex Discrimination Act 1975. Although both came into effect over 25 years ago they have been subsequently amended in important ways. Sex discrimination is an area of law in which there is EU competence, so appeals can be made to the European Court of Justice. UK law can also be challenged in the European courts if it is considered that it fails to comply in some way with Article 141 of the Treaty of Amsterdam (formerly Article 119 of the Treaty of Rome) or with EU directives in the sex discrimination field.

Employer actions are policed to some extent by the Equal Opportunities Commission (EOC) which is required to keep the legislation under review, to conduct formal investigations into employer actions where it has reason to suspect there has been a contravention of the law, to issue codes of practice and to provide legal assistance to employees who consider themselves to be victims of unfair discrimination. On many occasions the EOC has itself represented employees before employment tribunals. It also brings its own test cases in a bid to push back the frontiers of sex discrimination law.

The Equal Pay Act 1970

The Equal Pay Act 1970 was the first legislation promoting equality at work between men and women. Although passed in 1970, it only came into force in December 1975. It was subsequently amended, and its scope extended, by the Equal Pay (Amendment) Regulations 1983 and by the Sex Discrimination Act 1986. The Act is solely concerned with eliminating unjustifiable differences between the treatment of men and women in terms of their rates of pay and other conditions of employment. It is thus the vehicle that is used to bring a case to tribunal when there is inequality between a man's contract of employment and that of a woman. In practice the majority of cases are brought by women and concern discriminatory rates of payment, although there have been some important cases brought by men focusing on aspects of pension provision.

The Act, as amended in 1983, specifies three types of claim that can be brought. These effectively define the circumstances in which pay and other conditions between men and women should be equal:

1 **Like work:** where a woman and a man are doing work which is the same or broadly similar – for example where a woman assembly worker sits next to a male assembly worker, carrying out the same range of duties.
2 **Work rated as equivalent:** where a man and a woman are carrying out work which, while of a different nature, has been rated as equivalent under a job evaluation scheme. We cover this aspect of equal pay in greater detail in Chapter 35.
3 **Work of equal value:** where a man and a woman are performing different tasks but where it can be shown that the two jobs are equal in terms of their demands, for example in terms of skill, effort and type of decision making.

In order to bring a case the applicant must be able to point to a comparator of the opposite gender with whom he or she wishes to be compared. The comparator must be employed by the same employer and at an establishment covered by the same terms and conditions. When an equal value claim is brought which an employment tribunal considers to be well founded, an 'independent expert' is appointed to carry out a job evaluation exercise in order to establish whether or not the two jobs being compared are equal in terms of the demands they make.

Employers can employ two defences when faced with a claim under the Equal Pay Act. First they can seek to show that a job evaluation exercise has been carried out which indicates that the two jobs are not like, rated as equivalent or of equal value. To succeed the job evaluation scheme in use must be both analytical and free of sex bias (see Chapter 35). Second, the employer can claim that the difference in pay is justified by 'a genuine material factor not of sex'. For this to succeed, the employer has to convince the court that there is a good business reason for the unequal treatment and that there has thus been no sex discrimination. Examples of genuine material factors that have proved acceptable to the courts are as follows:

■ different qualifications (e.g. where a man has a degree and a woman does not);
■ performance (e.g. where a man is paid a higher rate than a woman because he works faster or has received a higher appraisal rating);
■ seniority (where the man is paid more because he has been employed for several years longer than the woman);
■ regional allowances (where a man is paid a London weighting, taking his pay to a higher rate than that of a woman performing the same job in the Manchester branch).

The courts have ruled that differences in pay explained by the fact that the man and woman concerned are in separate bargaining groups, by the fact that they asked for different salaries on appointment or because of an administrative error are not acceptable genuine material factor defences. It is possible to argue that a difference in pay is explained by market forces, but evidence has to be produced to satisfy the court that going rates for the types of work concerned are genuinely different and that it is therefore genuinely necessary to pay the comparator at a higher rate.

Where someone wins an equal pay claim they are entitled to receive up to six years' back pay to make up the difference between their salary and that of their comparator. Until 1999 there was a limit of only two years, but this was successfully challenged in the European Court of Justice in the case of *Levez* v. *T.H. Jennings (Harlow Pools) Ltd*. At the time of writing the six-year limit is itself the subject of legal challenge and may thus be removed in the near future.

| WINDOW ON PRACTICE | Ms Smith was taken on to work for a company as a stockroom manager at a salary of £50 a week. After a few months she discovered that her predecessor (a man) had been paid £60 a week for doing the same job. As there was no suitable male comparator currently employed by the firm, she decided to bring an equal pay case using her predecessor as her male comparator. The European Court of Justice decided that this was acceptable under the terms of Article 119 of the Treaty of Rome. Ms Smith thus won her case. |

In a more recent case, a woman who had been employed in a senior role resigned and was subsequently replaced by a man who was paid a considerably higher salary. She brought an equal pay claim against her former employer citing her successor as the male comparator. This too was ruled acceptable under the terms of the European Treaties.

Sources: *Macarthy's Ltd* v. *Smith* (1980), *Diocese of Hallam Trustees* v. *Connaughton* (1995).

The Sex Discrimination Act 1975

The Sex Discrimination Act also came into force in December 1975 and was designed to complement the Equal Pay Act 1970 by dealing primarily with non-contractual forms of sex discrimination such as employee selection, the provision of training opportunities, promotion, access to benefits and facilities and dismissal. It also applies outside the workplace, so case law that relates to events which have nothing at all to do with employment can be the source of important precedents. The Act covers all workers whether or not they serve under contracts of employment or are employed and all job applicants. The only groups excluded are ministers of religion, soldiers who may serve in front-line duties and people employed to work abroad. It thus remains permissible for firms recruiting employees to work in Saudi Arabia exclusively to select men. The Act applies equally to men and women, and also protects people from unfair discrimination on the grounds that they are married.

There are three headings under which claims are brought; direct discrimination, indirect discrimination and victimisation, the way the law works in each case being rather different.

Direct discrimination is straightforward. It occurs simply when an employer treats someone unfavourably and when sex or marital status is an important factor in this decision. In judging claims the courts use the 'but for' test, asking whether the woman would have received the same treatment as a man (or vice versa) but for her sex. Examples of direct sex discrimination include advertising for a man to do a job which could equally well be done by a woman, failing to promote a woman because she is pregnant or dismissing a married woman rather than her single colleague because she is known to have a working husband.

If an employer is found to have discriminated *directly* on grounds of sex or marital status, except in one type of situation, there is no defence. The courts cannot, therefore, take into account any mitigating circumstances or make a judgment based on the view that the employer acted reasonably. Once it has been established that direct discrimination has occurred, proceedings end with a victory for the applicant. The one exception operates in the area of recruitment, where it is possible to argue that certain jobs have to be reserved for either women or men. For this to be acceptable the employer must convince a court that it is a job for which there is a 'genuine occupational qualification'. The main headings under which such claims are made are as follows:

- **authenticity** (e.g. acting or modelling jobs);
- **decency** (e.g. lavatory or changing room attendants);
- **personal services** (e.g. a counsellor engaged to work in a rape crisis centre).

Direct discrimination on grounds of pregnancy or maternity is assumed automatically to constitute unlawful sex discrimination. This means that there is no defence of reasonableness whatever the individual circumstances. It is thus unlawful to turn down a job application from a well-qualified woman who is eight months pregnant, irrespective of her intentions as regards the taking of maternity leave.

Indirect discrimination is harder to grasp, not least because it can quite easily occur unintentionally. It occurs when a 'requirement or condition' is set which has the effect, in practice, of disadvantaging a significantly larger proportion of one sex than the other. In other words, if substantially fewer women than men can comply with the condition, even if it is applied in exactly the same way to both men and women, it is potentially unlawful. A straightforward example is a job advertisement which specifies that applicants should be taller than 5 feet 10 inches. This is indirectly discriminatory because a substantially smaller proportion of women are able to comply than men. The same rule applies in the case of discrimination on grounds of marital status, an example being that of an employer who offers promotion on the basis that the employee must be prepared to be away from home for considerable spells of time, when in reality such absence was never or rarely required.

Indirect discrimination differs from direct discrimination in that there are defences that an employer can deploy. For example, an employer can justify the condition or requirement they have set 'on grounds other than sex', in which case it may be lawful. An example might be a job for which a key requirement is the ability to lift heavy loads. It is reasonable in such circumstances for the employer to restrict recruitment to people who are physically able to comply, for example by including a test of strength in selection procedures. The fact that more men than women will be able to do so does not make the practice unlawful, provided the lifting requirement is wholly genuine.

In the USA the 'four-fifths rule' applies in judging cases of indirect discrimination, meaning that a practice is unlawful where the proportion of one sex that can comply with the condition is fewer than 80 per cent of the other. At present there is no such convention in the UK, meaning that it is for individual tribunals to decide what exactly constitutes 'a substantially smaller proportion' of men or women when judging these cases.

> **WINDOW ON PRACTICE**
>
> A leading case in indirect sex discrimination law is *Price v. Civil Service Commission* (1977). This concerned a requirement set by the Civil Service that applicants for posts of executive officer level should be between the ages of 17 and 28. Mrs Price, who was 36, claimed that an advertisement for an executive officer was indirectly discriminatory against women on the grounds that a substantially greater proportion of men could in practice comply with the age requirement. Her case was based on the contention that many women were outside the labour market during these ages bringing up children. The Employment Appeals Tribunal agreed with her and declared the age limitation to be unreasonable.

In the field of sex discrimination the term 'victimisation' means the same as it does in other areas of employment law. An employer victimises workers if it disadvantages them in any way simply because they have sought to exercise their legal rights or have assisted others in doing so. An employee would thus bring a claim of victimisation to a tribunal if they had been overlooked for promotion having recently successfully settled an equal pay claim. Importantly victimisation covers situations in which someone threatens to bring an action or plans to do so even if no case is ultimately brought.

Positive discrimination

Positive sex discrimination involves directly or indirectly discriminating in favour of women in situations where they are underrepresented – usually at senior levels in an organisation or in occupational groups which are male dominated. Such practices are unlawful under UK discrimination law when they involve actively discriminating against men who are better qualified to fill the positions concerned. However, it is lawful to take positive action aimed at encouraging and supporting women provided it stops short of actually discriminating in their favour. It is thus acceptable to include an equal opportunities statement in a job advertisement as a means of indicating that the organisation welcomes applications from women. Similarly employers can design and offer training courses tailored specifically for women. As long as men are not prevented from participating, such action is lawful.

Dress codes

In relation to dress codes, a tribunal will only find valid a claim of sex discrimination if the applicant or applicants can be shown to have suffered a detriment as a result of the condition being imposed. Merely treating members of the two sexes differently is not in itself sufficient to constitute unlawful indirect discrimination. For this reason it is acceptable in principle for employers to impose different dress codes on male and female staff, provided the same broad 'standard of conventionality' is applied.

It is thus lawful, as far as sex discrimination law is concerned, to insist that male employees wear business suits at work while permitting women more choice about their attire. Over the years, however, tribunals have adapted their interpretation of the term 'standards of conventionality' to reflect changing social norms. As a result sex discrimination claims have been successfully won by men who wish to retain their long hair tied in a pony-tail and women who wish to wear trousers at work.

Transsexuals

Whereas homosexuals have had great difficulty over the years in persuading the courts that they have rights under sex discrimination law, transsexuals are protected. It is therefore unlawful to discriminate against someone on the grounds that he or she is a medically defined transsexual. The rights of people undergoing gender reassignment are now specifically protected by the Sex Discrimination (Gender Reassignment) Regulations 1999.

Sexual harassment

While the area of sexual harassment is not specifically covered in the Sex

Activity 21.2

In making its judgment in *Rewcastle* v. *Safeway* (1989), a case that concerned the dismissal of a man who refused to cut his hair to a conventional male length, the tribunal made the following remark about the law on dress codes:

Whilst we naturally accept the employer's right to determine standards of appearance and dress for its employees ... we question whether a policy which is designed to mirror 'conventional' differences between the sexes can be reconciled with the underlying rationale of the sex discrimination legislation which is to challenge traditional assumptions about sexes.

To what extent do you agree with these sentiments?
Source: IRS (1993, p. 11).

Discrimination Act 1975, the courts have accepted for some years that allowing someone to be subjected to acts of harassment which have a sexual dimension amounts to unlawful sex discrimination. Although the law applies equally to men and women, the vast majority of cases are brought by women as a result of acts perpetrated by men:

> Any unfavourable treatment to which a woman is subjected that includes a significant sexual element to which a man would not be vulnerable is to be regarded as unfavourable treatment on grounds of the woman's sex and is therefore directly discriminatory within the meaning of the Act. Since such treatment will inevitably comprise a 'detriment', it is rendered unlawful by Section 6(2)(b), which stipulates that it is unlawful for an employer to discriminate against a woman by 'dismissing her, or subjecting her to any other detriment'.
>
> (IDS 1998, p. 222)

The employer's liability in harassment cases arises from the application of the doctrine of **vicarious liability**, under which employers are held responsible for the commitment of civil wrongs by employees when they are at work. The doctrine also plays an important role in health and safety law, as we will see in Chapter 31.

Sexual harassment is defined in a European Union code of practice dating from 1991. It establishes the following:

(a) that it consists of unwanted conduct of a sexual nature or based on sex, which affects the dignity of men and women at work;
(b) that sexual harassment can be physical or verbal in nature;
(c) that the conduct *either* leads to material detriment (i.e. it affects promotion, pay, access to training, etc.) *or* creates an intimidating or humiliating work environment.

In judging cases the courts focus on the reaction of the victim and do not apply any general definitions of what types of conduct do and do not amount to unlawful harassment. Hence conduct which may not offend one person in the slightest can be found to constitute sexual harassment when directed at someone else who is deeply offended.

For an employer the only valid defences relate to the notion of vicarious liability. An employer can, for example, claim ignorance of the incident of which the victim is complaining or can claim that vicarious liability does not apply because it occurred away from the workplace and outside office hours. Finally the employer can defend itself by showing that all reasonable steps were taken to prevent the harassment from occurring or continuing. In order to succeed here, the employer needs to produce evidence to show that initial complaints were promptly acted upon and that appropriate action, such as disciplining the perpetrators or moving them to other work, was taken.

Race discrimination

UK race discrimination law is governed by the Race Relations Act 1976. Under the terms of the European Union Directive on Race Discrimination, agreed in 2000, this area of law will become one of European competence at some stage before 2003. As matters stand, the principles established in the 1976 Act are very similar to those set out in the Sex Discrimination Act described above. The law applies to all workers except those recruited to work overseas or in private households. The 'direct' and 'indirect' forms of discrimination are defined in the same way as in sex discrimination law, as are the terms 'victimisation', 'positive discrimination' and 'harassment'. Moreover, the Commission for Racial Equality plays a similar facilitating role to that played by the Equal Opportunities Commission in the field of sex discrimination. Precedents from the sex discrimination arena can apply in that of race discrimination and vice versa. There is, however, no equivalent law to that contained in the Equal Pay Act operating in the field of race discrimination.

Importantly the Act extends beyond discrimination on grounds of race to embrace the notions of nationality and ethnic and national origin. It is thus as unlawful for an employer to discriminate against someone because they are French or American as it is to treat someone less favourably because of their racial origins. According to Deakin and Morris (1998, pp. 598–9), the term 'ethnicity' was defined by Lord Fraser in the case of *Mandla* v. *Lee* (1983) as applying to a distinct group within the population sharing the following essential characteristics:

- a long history of which the group is conscious as distinguishing it from other groups, and the memory of which keeps it alive;
- a cultural tradition of its own, often but not necessarily associated with religious observance;
- a common geographical origin, or descent from a small number of common ancestors;
- a common language, not necessarily peculiar to the group;
- a common literature peculiar to the group;
- a common religion different from that of neighbouring groups or from the general community surrounding it;
- being a minority or being an oppressed or a dominant group within a larger community.

According to this definition, merely practising a minority religion is an insufficient basis to constitute being of distinct ethnic origin. There also has to be a shared and long history of distinctiveness. This is why in *Dawkins* v. *Department of the Environment* (1993), Rastafarians were found not to be an ethnic group for the purposes of discrimination law.

Genuine occupational qualifications, as in sex discrimination law, permit discrimination on grounds of race at the recruitment stage for one or two kinds of job. The main grounds are authenticity and the provision of personal services to members of a particular racial community. In the case of race discrimination the defence of authenticity extends to employers of people to work in ethnic restaurants.

Most cases involving indirect discrimination under the Race Relations Act concern requirements being set for a high standard of English or for specific UK-based qualifications. As in sex discrimination law, it is necessary to be able to show objectively that these are necessary for the jobs in question. The courts will not allow employers to set conditions such as these unless it can be shown that there really is a *need* for such a condition. For example, in the case of *Hampson* v. *Department of Education and Science* (1990) a teacher was able to show that the requirement to have completed a three-year training course before being appointed to a teaching post in the UK unfairly discriminated against people of

Chinese origin who had qualified in Hong Kong. She was successful because she was able to convince the Court of Appeal that her two-year qualification followed by eight years' classroom experience made her well qualified to teach in Britain.

A fine line has to be trodden when recruiting people from overseas countries because there is a need to stay on the right side of both the Race Relations Act 1976 and the more recent Asylum and Immigration Act 1996. The former makes it unlawful to treat an overseas application unfavourably in any way, while the latter makes it a **criminal offence to employ someone who does not have the right of residence in the UK** or a valid work permit. Great care is thus called for in handling such matters.

WINDOW ON PRACTICE	A race discrimination case with important implications was brought by two women in 1996.

This case concerned the appearance at a private function of Mr Bernard Manning in the guise of a comedian. The audience consisted of 400 men who were treated to a routine consisting in large part of racially and sexually offensive jokes. Two of the waitresses employed by the hotel at the function were black. Bernard Manning noticed them and made a number of remarks directed at them during his routine.

The two women sued the hotel group which employed them on the grounds that it was vicariously liable and that they had been allowed to suffer racial harassment. The employer contested this, saying that it could not be vicariously liable for offensive remarks made by someone who was not an employee – indeed was not even a guest in the hotel and thus had no contractual relationship with it at all.

The women won their claim, successfully arguing that the hotel's management had failed to take action to prevent the harassment from occurring by removing them from the function at the earliest possible time. The employer was therefore vicariously liable and was required to pay compensation.

Source: *Burton v. De Vere Hotels* Ltd (1996).

Disability discrimination

The **Disability Discrimination Act (1995)** came into force in December 1996, since when several thousand cases have been lodged with employment tribunals. It replaced the Disabled Persons (Employment) Act 1944, which was widely criticised for being ineffective, only eight successful prosecutions having been brought during its fifty-year existence. From April 2000 the Disability Rights Commission has been in operation, with a remit in respect of discrimination against disabled people which is very similar to that of the Equal Opportunities Commission and the Commission for Racial Equality in their respective fields.

The new Act applies to all workers and to all organisations employing more than 15 people. While it shares some features in common with established legislation on sex and race discrimination, there are important differences. Of these, the most significant is the restriction of protection to direct discrimination and victimisation. There are no provisions equivalent to those on indirect discrimination in the Sex Discrimination and Race Relations Acts. The key words are as follows:

An employer discriminates against a disabled person if for a reason which relates to the disabled person's disability, he treats him less favourably than he treats or would treat others to whom that reason does not or would not apply.

(Disability Discrimination Act 1995, s. 5.1)

The Act is thus concerned with preventing an employer from discriminating directly against an individual worker or job applicant who suffers from a disability. There is no specific prohibition on the setting of requirements for use in recruitment or promotion processes which might be held to discriminate against disabled people in general. It is thus lawful to list 'good record of health' as a desirable characteristic in a person specification – that alone cannot constitute discrimination under the terms of the Act. Employers only invite tribunal claims at the point that they actually discriminate against an individual.

However, this does not mean that employers can safely use language in job advertisements which is off-putting to disabled people, because the advertisement can later be used by a rejected applicant as evidence in support of a disability discrimination claim. Newspapers and employment agencies which knowingly publish advertisements which are discriminatory may also face fines of up to £5,000 if successfully prosecuted.

The other important difference between direct discrimination on grounds of disability and that on grounds of sex or race is the existence of defences which an employer can employ. Essentially, 'less favourable treatment' is permitted if it is for a good reason. An example of this might be a typist who is required to type at a certain speed due to valid job demands. If a person with arthritis in their hands, who could only type at a much lower speed, applied for this job, they could lawfully be rejected on the grounds of their disability provided the potential employer had first explored whether any adjustment in the working environment could be made to overcome the mismatch. Discrimination is thus permitted if no 'reasonable adjustment' can be made to allow the person concerned to perform the job satisfactorily.

There are two key issues which the courts are required to rule on when determining cases brought under the Disability Discrimination Act:

1 What does and what does not constitute a disability for the purposes of the Act.
2 What is and what is not 'a reasonable adjustment' for an employer to make in order to accommodate the needs of a disabled person.

The first issue is decided with reference to the words used in the Act. These define someone as disabled if they have 'a physical or mental impairment which has a substantial and long term adverse affect on their ability to carry out normal day to day activities'. The term 'impairment' is taken by the courts to mean any kind of a loss of a key bodily function such as the ability to hear, see, walk or write. It also covers conditions involving loss of memory and incontinence. An impairment is 'substantial' if it is more than minor or trivial, while 'long term' is defined as a condition which has lasted or *might reasonably* be expected to last for 12 months or more.

The words 'normal day to day activities' have been the source of much confusion and litigation. This is because the courts have taken the phrase very much at face value. It is thus the case that someone is not disabled – and is thus not protected by the Act – if their condition stops them from climbing mountains or playing football, as these are not considered to be 'normal day to day activities'. It has to be an impairment which severely restricts someone's ability to carry out basic, commonplace tasks in the household or workplace.

However, provided the symptoms are serious in their impact, virtually all medical conditions can potentially be accepted as 'disabilities' for the purposes of the Disability Discrimination Act. This includes mental illnesses as well as those with

WINDOW ON PRACTICE

In 1997 a Mr Quinlan was dismissed from his job as an assistant working at a garden centre after seven days because he refused to carry out the heavy lifting work that formed a part of the job. He would not do this because he had had open heart surgery some ten years previously and had been told that lifting heavy weights might injure his health. He brought a claim to a tribunal under the Disability Discrimination Act arguing that it would have been reasonable for the employer to omit from his work the requirement to lift heavy weights, and that his dismissal was thus unlawful.

He lost his case on the grounds that he was not disabled under the terms of the Act. This was because lifting heavy weights was not found to constitute 'a normal day to day activity'. He could only have succeeded had his illness not allowed him to lift everyday objects. There was no consideration given to questions of reasonable adjustment, because the Disability Discrimination Act was found not to apply to Mr Quinlan in the first place.

(Quinlan v. *B&Q plc* (1997) Employment Appeals Tribunal 1386/97).

Source: L. Macdonald (1998) 'Discrimination', *Personnel Manager's Factfinder.* London: Gee Publishing.

physical symptoms. Hence the definition of disability in the Act has been found by the courts to encompass severe depression, bulimia and ME, as well as asthma, speech impairments and severe back pain. Severe facial disfigurement is also included as a relevant condition. The only exceptions are a few conditions with socially undesirable symptoms which have specifically been excluded. These include alcoholism, drug addiction, exhibitionism, kleptomania and pyromania. Hay fever is also excluded. Importantly it is irrelevant whether or not an individual has recovered from their disability. Discriminating against someone on the grounds that they have suffered from a condition in the past amounts to unlawful discrimination, provided the discrimination met the definition set out in the Act. The fact that someone can live and work normally because they are receiving treatment for their condition, for example in the form of drugs or psychiatric counselling, does not mean that they have ceased to be disabled under the terms of the Act. It is thus unlawful to discriminate against them on these grounds without an objectively justifiable reason.

The burden of proof in disability discrimination cases passes to the employer to satisfy the tribunal that no reasonable adjustments could be made to accommodate the needs of a disabled person. The courts thus assume that adjustments are possible unless the employer can show that it would be unreasonable to expect them to be made. There are no general rules here, because the courts are obliged in reaching their judgments to take account of the size and resources of the employer concerned. The large PLC is thus expected to make bigger adjustments in response to the demands of the Act than the owner of a small corner shop.

It is expected that employers consider making adjustments to the physical working environment, working arrangements and working conditions. Minor building alterations are clearly covered; so unless the employer is very small and is unable to afford to make them, it would be expected that disabled toilets and/or wheelchair ramps would be installed to accommodate a disabled person. Other examples would include changing taps to make them easier to switch on, altering lighting for people with restricted vision, and allocating specific parking spaces. However, the concept of 'reasonable adjustment' goes a great deal further, encompassing changes in all kinds of working practices. It is thus expected that employers re-organise duties, allocate ground-floor offices to wheelchair users, adjust working hours for a disabled person or allow someone to work from home if these changes would allow an individual disabled person to be employed. Of particular importance is the requirement to permit disabled people a greater amount of sick leave than other employees. Hence, as was shown in Chapter 14, it is no longer possible to dismiss a chronically ill employee on grounds of incapability, without first considering whether reasonable adjustments could be made to allow them to continue working. The courts expect to see evidence that the employer has given serious consideration to a request for adjustments and that no request is turned down without a proper investigation having first taken place.

When applicants win their cases at tribunal, there are three possible outcomes:

1 The tribunal issues a declaration affirming the complainant's rights (e.g. preventing an employer from making someone redundant).
2 The tribunal makes a recommendation (e.g. requiring a doorway to be widened to accommodate a wheelchair).
3 The tribunal makes a compensatory award.

In the case of the third outcome, there are no statutory limits on the compensation that can be paid, allowing the courts to fully recompense people for any past or estimated future losses they may have incurred.

Trade union discrimination

The freedom to join a trade union and take part in its lawful activities is generally regarded as a fundamental human right. It is included in both the European Convention on Human Rights and the founding conventions of the International Labour Organisation. Although this freedom is not couched in the language of positive rights, it is in practice difficult for a UK employer lawfully to discriminate against people simply because they have joined a union or have taken part in union activities. These rights are long established, but are now found in the Trade Union and Labour Relations (Consolidation) Act 1992. In 1990, equivalent rights were extended to people who do not wish to join a union or become involved in its activities. There are three basic rights:

(a) the right not to be dismissed for a trade union reason;
(b) the right not to suffer action short of dismissal for a trade union reason;
(c) the right not to be refused a job on trade union grounds.

The first two of these protect people who take part (or refuse to take part) 'in the activities of an independent trade union at an appropriate time'. The protection, however, only extends to employees (i.e. people working under a contract of service) and does not apply in the police and armed services. In the case of dismissals, because trade union reasons are regarded as 'automatically unfair', there is no qualifying period of service. Full rights thus apply from the first day someone is employed at a particular establishment.

In order to gain the protection of the law in this area the organisation an individual joins or becomes involved with must be one which has been listed as an independent trade union by the Certification Officer. Moreover the activities which they engage in must be authorised by the trade union concerned and must, if they take place during work time, be carried out with the consent of the employer. Industrial action is not included in the definition of 'the activities of an independent trade union at an appropriate time', but is the subject of other protective legislation.

Discrimination against prospective employees at the recruitment stage simply because they are or are not union members has been an unlawful practice since 1990. In the Employment Relations Act 1999 rights in this area were extended to cover any discrimination occurring as a result of an individual's past involvement in trade union activity. The aim was to prevent groups of employers from maintaining black-lists of individuals perceived to be union troublemakers.

Part-time workers

Discriminating against a female part-time worker has long been taken by the courts to constitute indirect sex discrimination because the vast majority of part-time workers are female. Since 2000, however, it has not been necessary for part-time workers (of either gender) to use sex discrimination law to protect themselves. The Part-time Workers (Prevention of Less Favourable Treatment) Regulations 2000 were introduced to ensure that the UK complied with the EU's Part-Time Workers Directive. They now seek to ensure that part-time workers (not just employees) are treated equally with full-time workers in all aspects of work, the key features being as follows:

1 Part-time workers who believe that they are being treated less favourably than a comparable full-time colleague can write to their employers asking for an explanation. This must be given in writing within 14 days.
2 Where the explanation given by the employer is considered unsatisfactory, the part-time worker may ask an employment tribunal to require the employer to affirm the right to equal treatment.
3 Employers are required under the regulations to review their terms and conditions and to give part-timers pro rata rights with those of comparable full-timers.
4 There is a right not to be victimised on account of enforcing rights under the Part-time Workers Regulations.

Any term or condition of employment is covered by the regulations, as is any detriment caused as a result of failure to be promoted or given access to training. It is also now unlawful to select someone for redundancy simply because they work part-time.

There are a number of problems with the new regulations, including the absence of a statutory authority to enforce the third of the above points. One of the more complex issues involves how the term 'part-time worker' should be defined, because it is used differently in different workplaces. In some organisations someone working 35 hours a week is employed on a 'part-time contract' because full-time hours are 40 per week. Elsewhere, where everyone works 35 hours, such a worker would be regarded as a full-timer. The regulations simply state that a worker is part-time if they work fewer hours in a week than are worked by recognised full-timers. This obviously poses difficulties for organisations which do not employ people to work a set number of hours a week, or for whom patterns of hours vary considerably over the course of a year. There is also a need for part-time workers who consider themselves to have been less favourably treated to name a comparator employed in a broadly similar job who is employed on a full-time basis in the same employment. Where none exists it is effectively impossible to bring a claim.

Ex-offenders

Another group who are given some measure of legal protection from discrimination at work are ex-offenders whose convictions have been 'spent'. The relevant legislation is contained in the Rehabilitation of Offenders Act 1974 which sets out after how many years different types of criminal conviction become spent and need not be acknowledged by the perpetrator. In the field of employment, protection from discrimination extends to dismissal, exclusion from a position and 'prejudicing' someone in any way in their employment. In other words, employers cannot dismiss someone, fail to recruit them or hold them back in their occupations simply because they are known or discovered to have a former conviction. Failing to disclose the conviction can also be no grounds for discrimination. Moreover, no one (the individual concerned or anyone else) is under any obligation to tell anyone else about the conviction once it has been spent. Effectively, the slate is wiped clean, allowing the ex-offender to live and work as if no conviction had been received.

The rehabilitation periods set out in the Act vary depending on the type of sentence that has been received. The tariff is as follows:

imprisonment over 30 months:	never spent
imprisonment 6 to 30 months:	ten years
less than 6 months' imprisonment:	seven years
fine or community service order:	five years
detention in a detention centre:	three years
conditional discharge:	one year
absolute discharge:	six months

The time runs from the date of the conviction, the times being cut in half for those who are under the age of 18 at this time. It is the sentence imposed that is relevant to the Act and not the sentence actually served.

Numerous jobs and occupations are excluded from the terms of the Act. Organisations which employ people to work in these positions are entitled to know about spent convictions and can lawfully discriminate against individuals on these grounds. The list includes all jobs which involve the provision of services to minors, employment in the social services, nursing homes and courts, as well as employment in the legal, medical and accountancy professions.

Summary propositions

21.1 Discrimination law is growing rapidly. The coming years will see its extension into new areas including discrimination on grounds of age, religion and political belief.

21.2 Equal pay law requires men and women to be paid the same wage for doing work which is the same or which can be shown to be of equal value unless the employer can justify a difference on grounds other than sex.

21.3 In sex and race discrimination legislation an important distinction is made between direct and indirect discrimination. The latter relates to the setting of a requirement by an employer with which more of one sex than of the other can comply.

21.4 Sexual and racial harassment claims can be brought against any employer who allows a worker to be subjected to treatment which intimidates or humiliates the victim and is sexual or racial in nature.

21.5 The Disability Discrimination Act 1995 requires employers to consider making reasonable adjustments to working conditions to accommodate the needs of a disabled person before dismissing them or failing to offer them a job.

21.6 Limited protection from discrimination is given in law to trade union members, employees who do not engage in union activity, part-time workers and ex-offenders whose convictions are spent.

References

Deakin, S. and Morris, G. (1998) *Labour Law*, 2nd edn. London: Butterworth.
Incomes Data Services (1998) *Sex Discrimination and Equal Pay*. Employment Law Handbook. London: IDS.
Industrial Relations Services (1993) 'Dress and Personal Appearance at Work', *IRS Law Bulletin* 469, pp. 2–13.
Macdonald, L. (1998) 'Discrimination', *Personnel Manager's Factfinder*. London: Gee Publishing.

Legal cases

Burton v. *De Vere Hotels Ltd* [1996] IRLR 596.
Dawkins v. *Department of the Environment* [1979] IRLR 170.
Diocese of Hallam Trustees v. *Connaughton* (1995) (EAT 1128/95).
Hampson v. *Department of Education and Science* [1990] IRLR 302.
Levez v. *T.H. Jennings (Harlow Pools) Ltd* [1999] IRLR 3.
Macarthy's Ltd v. *Smith* [1980] IRLR 209–210.
MacDonald v. *Ministry of Defence* (2000) (EAT 121/00).
Mandla et al. v. *Lee et al.* [1983] IRLR 209.
Price v. *Civil Service Commission* [1977] IRLR 291.
Quinlan v. *B&Q plc* (1997) (EAT 1386/97).
Rewcastle v. *Safeway plc* (1989) (EAT 22482/89).

General discussion topics

1 Which groups who are not currently protected would you like to see covered by anti-discrimination law? What arguments could be advanced for and against your proposition from an employer perspective?

2 How far do you think that our discrimination law is effective in achieving its aims? What could be done to make it more effective?

Chapter 5

Employee development

Stephen Gibb and David Megginson

Introduction

Issues and challenges in contemporary employee development (ED[1]) are considered here in relation to two sets of factors. First are learning issues about how the knowledge, skills and attitudes required for employment are formed and are linked to career, organisational and economic success. The main challenges raised are those involved in responding to the onset of the knowledge economy, the continuing interest in achieving 'skill revolutions', and the demands involved in managing employment 'cultures'. The theory and practice of contemporary ED, its strengths and weaknesses, are bound up with meeting each of these challenges.

The second set of factors concern the stakeholders involved in ED. The issues here are related to the contribution of individuals, employers and government as participants in ED. Challenges here include the dynamics of individual motivation to learn and participation in ED; the role of employers and training providers in supplying effective ED, and finally the challenge to government, in the form of policy development and implementation of initiatives in the promotion of ED.

The practice of ED needs to be analysed in the context of all these issues and challenges; managing effective learning through stakeholder interactions and partnership. Employers are certainly the 'hub' of the whole system, given employees'

---

[1] Many commentators seek to distinguish between training, education and development. While there are sometimes good reasons for this, for example when compiling survey data, the semantics of these distinctions can become unwieldy and intrusive. The essence of employees being 'trained', professionals being 'educated' and managers being 'developed' amounts to the same; support of learning for and at work. For this chapter the term 'Employee development' (ED) will be used to cover training at work and training for work, work-related vocational education and work-based on-job and off-job development, and what is generally thought of as soft 'development' in the employment context.

dependence upon them as suppliers of ED and the government's voluntarist approach in this aspect of HRM. A description of the different approaches to ED which can exist in employing organisations is provided in conclusion, as a focus for analysing and evaluating cases at an organisational level.

The context of employee development

The purpose of ED can be defined as developing human potential to assist organisations and individuals to achieve their objectives. The question of what exactly is meant by developing human potential needs to be considered more fully if the theory and practice of ED, and the challenges it faces, are to be properly defined. A common way of expanding upon this is to argue that in order to realise their potential in the context of employment people need to develop, in balance, their knowledge, skills and emotions/attitudes/values[2] (EVA). The capacity to learn and become competent, to be able to achieve the performance standards expected in employment, is fulfilled through integrated development of these three aspects of human potential. In this respect development in and for employment is the same as development in any other context.

The most evident form this takes is the standard organisation of learning experiences in and for employment into programmes which specify objectives in all these three aspects. The trinity of development in knowledge, skills and EVA is to be explicitly found in some form in many systems of human potential development, and is implicit in most others. Each aspect will be considered here in turn to explain what they involve and to raise key issues for evaluating contemporary ED.

The first types of objective in realising human potential in the context of employment are those relating to cognitive capacities: the development and extension of knowledge. The cognitive aspects of ED are concerned with the extent to which employees need to obtain and use information, models and theories to enable development and effective performance in jobs and their employing organisation. Bloom's taxonomy of cognitive categories (Bloom, 1956), given in Table 5.1, provides a continuum against which jobs can be measured.

---

[2] Conventionally, it is 'attitudes' which are defined as the third element of the learning trinity 'KSA'. Attitudes are defined as the positive or negative orientations people have with regard to themselves, others and the world – their likes and dislikes, conventionally studied within social psychology. Forming or changing people's attitudes is certainly a part of development in the context of employment. But this is too narrow to encompass the contemporary concerns of development in employment. Forming and developing values, people's core ideas on what is right and wrong, is a concern as well – often illustrated by organisations making their values explicit and requiring employee behaviour congruent with them in work. Supporting and using 'emotions', the psychology of people feeling 'mad, bad, sad or glad' also matters in developing effective performance. Indeed, emotional factors are often given the 'executive' role in controlling human behaviour; to shape and influence human behaviour in employment it is then possible – and, for some, necessary – to acknowledge and work with developing emotions and values, not just attitudes.

Understanding and Managing People at Work
133

Table 5.1 Bloom's cognitive categories

Type	Evidence	
Knowledge	state, list, identify	*Simple*
Comprehension	explain, give examples	
Application	demonstrate, solve, use	
Analysis	describe, break down, select	
Synthesis	combine, design, create	
Evaluation	appraise, contrast, criticise	
		Complex

Different occupations will require different types and levels of cognitive development. All human potential development in the context of employment involves knowledge; the issue is the extent to which performance depends upon knowledge, and the type of knowledge involved. Occupations can be mapped against Bloom's types, to profile where the cognitive demands are. The difference which most starkly highlights this point is the distinction made between occupations where performance greatly depends on knowledge and other cognitive capacities and areas where knowledge and cognitive capacity appear to be of little relevance and concern. With the former, knowledge-intensive development for the 'professions', such as medicine, law, engineering, teaching and social work is seen as typical, requiring several years of university-level education followed by a long period of supervised practice before becoming fully licensed. As that education progresses, the cognitive capacities required become more complex. In the case of the latter, development for relatively routine forms of programmed service provision, for example serving in a fast-food outlet or administration in a call centre, is seen as requiring little cognitive complexity and that is of the more basic kind. What is required depends only upon basic education and can be supplemented by the instruction of the employer in the course of basic training within the company.

Cognitive capacities in occupational performance also vary on a continuum of certainty – from occupations where knowledge is certain and complete to jobs where knowledge is uncertain and partial. Schön (1987) makes the distinction between what he calls 'determined practice' and 'indeterminate practice'. In the former, cognition is fixed and prescribed, and used to deal with routine circumstances. In the latter, cognition is not fixed and prescribed, it comes into operation to support creative problem-solving needed to deal with unique circumstances. This distinction is not new, but it is arguably more relevant now. In a time of new sciences, new technologies, and 'new organisations' demands on the creative use of cognition rather than its prescriptive application are greater; demands in occupations are increasingly at the complex end of Bloom's categories. The cognition involved in occupations and employment is evolving and changing fast, and it is therefore more likely to be uncertain and partial even among the most 'experienced'.

This also affects the practicalities of developing human potential in employment more than the familiar distinction between cognition-intensive and low-knowledge occupations. This is because, where knowledge is felt to be certain and complete, the most appropriate form of developmental support is clearly through the instruction and 'conditioning' of those who need the knowledge by those who currently possess the knowledge. These tend to be intermediaries – whether that mediation arises in the forms of knowledge present in books, or lectures, or the Internet. Where knowledge is uncertain and fragmented the appropriate form of learning needs to be more 'experiential'. By 'experiential' is meant a process of learning that is based on direct personal experience and reflection, undertaken in a 'community' of others who have experience of synthesis and evaluation. Only cognitive skills developed in this unmediated context, rather than knowledge gained through mediated information-processing in formal education, is of any substance and value. Such knowledge cannot be effectively codified and transmitted through systems of mediated instruction. In a sense, but not entirely, the former lends itself to being learnt as a 'science'[3], a coherent package of principles, concepts and methods; while the latter lends itself to being learnt as an 'art', requiring creativity on the part of the learner while learning.

In occupations where knowledge is becoming more certain there can be an increase in both 'science'-based pedagogy and instruction-based forms of learning. The role of Information and Communications Technologies (ICT) in supporting efficiency and effectiveness in this area of learning could be central. Where knowledge is becoming more uncertain and partial then expanding forms of experiential learning, centred on long-term learning relationships in communities of practice, may become much more important. The increase in systems of mentoring (Gibb, 1999) is one indicator of this trend in many different occupational contexts.

The fundamental issue relating to knowledge in the context of employment is the question of the extent to which cognition is forming a greater or lesser part of the development of human and organisation potential in any event, regardless of how that is categorised or learned. On the one hand there are claims for the onset of the 'knowledge economy' and the 'knowledge worker' (Tapscott, 1996); this era is supposed to be characterised by the increasing importance of 'intellectual capital' (Stewart, 1997) in many occupations and organisations. 'Knowledge management' (Davenport and Prusak, 1998) is then the latest strategic aspiration and focus for reviewing organisational effectiveness. The structure, design and culture of organisation needs to be built around managing knowledge. This suggests, in essence, that cognition is more important than ever before in employment. The implication is that the possession and use of knowledge permeates all productive activity, at all levels in an organisation, and therefore the

---

[3] The distinction between science and art as paradigms for occupational development is potentially useful and stimulating. Science is characterised by organised bodies of knowledge derived from methods which enable theories to be developed and tested. Arts are characterised by organised performances derived from methods which enable symbol systems to be developed and enjoyed. Most employment and occupations can be seen to share elements of a scientific base and an artistic base in effective performance. A recent illustration of this abstract point would be the involvement of musicians in facilitating management development (Pickard, 1999). The parallels between conducting an orchestra or playing in a jazz band are investigated to illuminate the challenges facing managers and to propose some solutions for meeting those based on musicians' experiences.

development of human potential in this respect forms a greater part of ensuring organisational effectiveness than in the past. More people need to learn more knowledge than ever before. It has been commonplace to hear of skills shortages as a potential threat to economic and business development; in the future it may be that it is cognitive deficits which cause economic and business development problems.

On the other hand there are arguments that the whole knowledge economy and knowledge worker concepts have been vastly overhyped. There is less scope for knowledge work, as information technologies enable everything from the whole systems running complex plants down to interpersonal transactions between customers and the organisation's representatives to be automated. Knowledge has migrated to computer systems, leaving people in employment to tend the computers. And when the key 'knowledge'-based institutions, particularly schools, colleges and universities, are considered there is contradictory evidence about what is happening. While education is becoming a more significant and greater part of everyone's future, there is, nevertheless, pressure for these institutions to become more concerned with helping to develop basic skills and competence. This is because the absence of basic skills among the labour force is currently the greatest problem experienced by employers, not the absence of smart 'knowledge' workers. This is a finding highlighted in, for example, employer concerns about the quality of young people's and graduate recruits' employability.

The second type of objectives in human potential development are those relating to developing psychomotor skills, through practice. The more commonplace term in use now is 'competence' rather than psychomotor skills; 'competence' being defined as the ability to do things to the standards required in employment and in practice. The difference between 'knowing how' to do something and actually being able to perform effectively is the skills or competence gap. Many people 'know how' to do many things; they can appreciate the elements of cooking and follow the recipes in cookbooks, or appreciate the principles of playing certain sports. But only some are competent enough, skilled enough, to do these well enough to produce excellent meals or compete with the best on actual playing fields.

Again there is a stark distinction between areas of human development in employment which are relatively low-skilled and areas which are highly skilled. Low-skill activities require little human potential development in the form of development through practice. These are jobs where most typical mature adults would be able to achieve a successful performance without needing much practice. For example, most people could serve behind a fast-food counter, stock shelves in a supermarket, or pack mobile phones into boxes. The main performance issue in such circumstances is usually ensuring a standard performance to set guidelines and procedures; it is about managing basic competence as conformity to procedures in the occupation.

On a bigger stage the issue of skill development raises economic development and political policy questions (Crouch, Finegold and Sako, 1999). A predominance of low-skill jobs and organisations creates a low-skill economy. This is an economy in which there are few driving forces to develop human potential in this respect. A vicious cycle then arises, where that lack of interest in human potential development means that only low-skill industries and jobs can be supported and managed, and then the preponderance of low-skill jobs and industries means that there is little demand for investing in skills development. In such conditions skills shortages are unlikely to be a problem, as the development of basic 'threshold' competence is an integral part of normal human development, and needs little in the way of additional time and investment devoted to practice. The main HR problem in these circumstances is the potential shortage of people prepared to take and stay in such low-skill jobs, and the degree of problem is contingent upon prevailing labour market conditions.

High-skill activities require significant human potential development, through substantial and continuing periods of guided practice in order to create a successful performer. This initial interest in high levels of human development for employment is further reinforced by the fact that skilled performance cannot be 'stored'; it either has to be in use and therefore constantly refreshed, or it will be lost. For example, continuing the sporting theme, professional footballers may only play once a week, but they spend all week practising. Armed forces may only encounter actual active duty irregularly, but professional armies are more effective as they constantly take part in exercises to prepare for the 'real thing'. The main performance issues in such circumstances are then ensuring a quality of 'apprenticeship' prior to licensing people to practise, and maintaining sufficient practise to keep skill levels at their peak. Such an emphasis on apprenticeship and 'Continuing Professional Development' is then one necessary hallmark of a 'true' profession. The net effect is to require sophisticated and substantial support for human development related to employment.

In high-skill economies there needs to be much investment in developing human potential through skills development. In traditional professions, such as medicine and law, skills development has long been integrated with professional development as a period of supervised practice after study and before licensing. In many modern professions, of which 'HRM' and management are two relevant examples, similar systems are being developed. Without effective foresight and planning there is great potential for skills shortages to develop and become a factor constraining economic growth. The biotechnology and software development sectors provide good contemporary examples of sectors where skill shortages throughout the range of jobs involved, not just at the top professional levels, can constrain economic development. Employers' and public policy concerns are then with 'skills revolutions'; how to attain a high-skill, high-value economy and avoid the traps of being, or becoming, a low-skill economy and having skills shortages which constrain economic and business development.

The general view is that the UK has been much in need of such a skills revolution to overcome its historically low skill levels, and to avoid skills shortages in key developing industries. Yet much has been made of the absence of even the 'basic skills' of literacy and numeracy among large parts of the labour force, needed to sustain even a low-skill economy. This situation has arisen for a variety of reasons, and many commentators look at both employers and an educational system in the UK which together have failed to manage the effective development of skills over decades. Remedying this aspect of developing human potential has been the central feature of policy development in recent times, exemplified in the development of national competence frameworks defining skills in occupations and in gearing educational systems to help develop competence.

Many of the government initiatives outlined later are responses to this central issue. Whether in any event 'skills are the answer' is, as Crouch *et al.* (1999) suggest, a claim that needs to be further debated. The logic that skills are a necessary element of future economic and social development is, they argue, fair. But skills increases in themselves are not going to be sufficient to achieve the employment and economic goals seen to be associated with these policies: job creation, high levels of employment, social inclusion, increasing living standards and equal opportunities. Critics of the use of skills revolutions as the main tool argue that there are a number of reasons for this. One is that occupations requiring truly advanced skills are still a small proportion of all jobs. Many jobs just do not require high skills, and never will. Another consideration is that the skills revolution depends on the actions of firms who have no real interest in carrying the burden for 'up-skilling' on behalf of other organisations or society in general. In this situation it is actually government that is being left to deal with the problems of development for employment; in particular to deal with the problem of unemployment. This undermines the credibility of the initiatives they develop, as they are seen as solutions to unemployment, not as integral to economic and business development and useful for employers. Finally, the necessary links between firms and employers and control of skills development is still a problem. Ideally, employers should be taking the lead, as it is their interests and experience which need to be met, but in practice it is still 'detached' government departments which have the main role. Even with the best intentions public servants cannot be a substitute for employer leadership.

The final objectives involved in developing human potential in employment are those related to developing and enhancing emotions, and values and attitudes. It is arguable that the essential difference between superior performance and ordinary, or indeed incompetent, performance is linked to emotions, attitude and values. People with emotional 'intelligence' (Goleman, 1999), 'positive' attitudes and the right values will be more effective than those lacking emotional intelligence, with negative attitudes or without the right values. Certainly, different occupations call upon some common and some particular elements of emotional intelligence, attitudes and values (Johnson and Indvik, 1999). For example, when facing difficult customers staff are meant to be equable and 'professional', rather than letting their personal feelings show. More often the crucible of the workplace as a whole can provide many spurs to interpersonal and intergroup conflict in the course of normal working life between employees, and between employers and employees.

Maintaining emotional intelligence and positive attitudes in that context of performance in a job is a perpetual challenge.

Instilling, reinforcing and leveraging emotions, values and attitudes is then an integral and inescapable part of development for employment. Pinker suggests the importance of emotions is that 'the emotions are mechanisms that set the brain's highest level goals' (1997: 373). Deliberate control of emotions is a route to managing behaviour; whether that control is personal and internal or is exerted from other sources. As far as values are concerned, Rokeach (1970) points out that many organisations explicitly identify their 'core values' with the aim of encouraging employees to behave in tune with them. These may be instrumental values, relating to the appropriate modes of conduct desired from and expected of employees in the course of their work as individuals, in groups and with customers. For example, employers will seek to enhance the ethics of amity within the workforce, often through the means of team building. There may be relationship skills involved in this, but most crucial is often the development of a team spirit, co-operation and trust between the team members. Values may also be 'terminal values', relating to the types of goals and ends which organisations wish their employees to pursue; the values which will govern their behaviour in achieving a successful performance. A concern with achieving 'quality' standards, for example, is partly based on good knowledge of systems, partly on skills developed through practice, and partly on being guided by the value of achieving quality.

The argument is that where emotions, attitudes and values are not effectively developed in an employee there is a high probability that performance standards will not be attained, even though employees may have the right knowledge and appropriate skills developed through practice. Developing human potential in the context of employment invariably raises issues about emotions, values and attitudes. These may be about harnessing and reinforcing an individual's, group's or organisation's emotions, attitudes and values in the context of jobs and work. They may be about challenging and changing the emotional intelligence, attitudes and values of individuals, groups and, on occasion, entire organisations.

Another way of thinking of this aspect of development for employment is that it is about the development of the whole person, and the development of the whole organisation. Effective development requires more than the 'digestion' of knowledge and the acquisition of skills through practice to underpin effective performance; it also depends upon the effective development of the whole person in the context of the whole organisation. There needs to be a congruence of emotions, values and attitudes with the occupational role, supported by an organisational environment which nurtures and rewards those emotions, values and attitudes. For instance, the emotions, values and attitudes which underpin performance in a caring role and organisation are not the same as those underpinning an entrepreneurial role in a profit-oriented organisation.

Sometimes, then, the development issue is about broader personal or organisational concerns. From the shelves of 'transform your life' self-help books to the most recent examples of analysing organisational values (Wickens, 1999) to catalyse change, this aspect of development for employment provides a rich seam of activity. It is most evident in, and related to, the concern with 'culture' change and culture management in the workplace that has been a high-profile concern in recent years as a focus of organisational change and development. The extent to which cultures can be controlled and changed is also open to debate. There is, however, no doubt that many organisations aspire to mould individual behaviours and the overall 'culture'.

The stakeholders: individuals, employers and government

There is, then, an agenda concerning the new and changing requirements of the knowledge economy, the old and continuing need for a skills revolution and the evergreen issues of managing behaviour and cultures in occupations and the workplace. These create the environment in which ED theory and practice has been and is evolving. Responses to this environment, in the form of actual strategies for supporting human potential development for employment, depend upon the actions of a variety of stakeholders. The primary stakeholders in ED are individuals, employers and the government. Problems or successes are not due to one set of agents alone; it is how they all interact which produces either an effective outcome or a problematic situation.

Individuals

Individual factors supporting effective ED are the levels of motivation and participation which lead employees or prospective employees themselves to seek to develop their potential in employment. Options range from opting out of the world of employment altogether, and pursuing alternative lifestyles, to consistently and extensively developing oneself with the aspiration of achieving success in employment. One career survey recently classified young people in terms of those 'getting on', those getting by and those getting nowhere (ESRC, 1999). Motivators that all these will share may include seeking greater job security through enhancement of knowledge, skills and self-development and improving personal performance for its own sake, for the pleasure of competent performance. There will be differences in people's response to seeking successful career development through enhanced knowledge, skills and self-development; seeking work enrichment, through being able to do more. The net effect is to spur active and interested participation in learning or to curtail enthusiasm for and participation in development for employment.

Developing their own potential may indeed have helped many 'getting on' individual employees or prospective employees meet these objectives in the past. Now many more employers wish to encourage their employees towards self-activated and self-directed development, to planning and managing their own development. This is a natural development of more general and focused processes of performance appraisal which are concerned with development needs. It also fits with the general trend towards employees becoming active and free agents rather than being dependent upon others to be told what to do – an aspect of the whole 'empowerment' movement and the 'new deal' in employment more generally. One difficulty with this, however, is that with the declining prospect of achieving their core goals in the organisation, such as job security or career development, the natural motivators for self-directed development may be missing for everyone; whether they are 'getting on' or 'getting by'.

There are other potential problems with relying more on self-driven potential realisation. Individuals may have misconceptions of their own potential, rating themselves incorrectly as unable to achieve some objectives when they can, or as able to achieve some objectives when they cannot. And the need to be seen as competent may lead individuals to present themselves as being competent instead of accurately assessing their own learning needs. Finally, there is the influence of the course, or ontology, of human development, and the different life-styles which accompany life stages. There are varying degrees of interest in learning and different types of concern with learning at different life stages and in different lifestyles. Individuals will be more motivated to realise their potential for employment at some stages of life than at others. Some lifestyles will emphasise the importance of development for employment more than others. Conventional ideas about the normal patterns of learning and life stages and lifestyles are being challenged, with an emphasis on lifelong learning, not just learning in youth, and a need to achieve a better 'life – work' balance (Foster, 1999) across the spectrum from those socially excluded to those who may be seen as 'workaholics'.

Employers

For employers ED is a means to an end – the end being to ensure achievement of the organisation's goals and the means being basic competence in the workforce. To achieve this employers may work in partnerships with schools, colleges and universities to develop courses that relate to the needs of businesses. They will also provide development for their own employees, through the induction of new employees, basic job training and closing any 'training gaps' identified by managers or others in reviewing the performance of staff. There may also be other organisational objectives beyond ensuring competence. These include increasing competitiveness through providing more or better ED than competitors. Employers will seek to improve product and/or service quality through more investment in ED. Continuous improvement requires continuous learning. The quality of ED provided can help by attracting the best people, by using more of their potential and productivity, and by maintaining their satisfaction as employees because they are being invested in. There can also be a concern with achieving 'culture changes' through ED interventions. Finally, there is a general concern to promote the habit of learning: keeping people 'fit' to learn. The logic and provision of many Employee Development and Assistance Programmes (EDAPs) reflects this.

Developing the potential of their workforces can help organisations meet these objectives by providing more competent, adaptable and committed employees. There are typical difficulties facing employers as they do this. One is simply a lack of resources to invest in ED, with a consequent basic failure to take up the responsibility to promote human potential development even in its most rudimentary forms, such as employee induction and health and safety training. This may be due to an assumption that development for employment has been achieved elsewhere, and the employer has no interest in incurring unnecessary further expenditure. For example, why should an employer send an employee who has become an HR manager on a long and expensive course of professional development leading to a professional qualification if they already have their own set HR systems and policies in place? Another difficulty is a narrowness of concern, seeing developing human potential only in as far as it can be 'justified' by direct and explicit benefits for the employer. This normally translates into 'hard' development for the knowledge and skills required for the specific job, to the neglect of other aspects of knowledge and skill, and the whole issue of values. The problems with analysing the costs and benefits of ED are a perennial issue, and the effect can be to preclude effective development. Lastly, there are concerns with the quality of the provision of ED provided. The quality of ED, as a service, is tied to the quality of the staff providing it. Confidence in the competence of trainers or training providers must be at the heart of the system. In many organisations this is recognised, and there is confidence in trainers who are themselves well trained in their roles, or reputable providers are used. In other circumstances bad experiences with trainers or training providers can mean that confidence in investing in ED is low.

A review of companies who have invested in ED (see Table 5.2) suggests that they gain in all key business success measures. From the employers' perspective such figures appear to suggest unambiguously that effective ED is indeed a key to business success.

Table 5.2 Learning pays: the value of learning and training to employers

	Average company	IiP accredited company	Gain
Rate of return on capital (RRC)	9.21%	16.27%	77%
Pre-tax profit margins	2.54%	6.91%	172%
Average salary	£12,590	£14,195	13%
Turnover/sales per employee	£64,912	£86,625	33%
Profit per employee	£1,815	£3,198	76%

Note: The data compare average UK companies with Investor in People (IiP)-accredited companies. The IiP standard will be explained later; in essence it is awarded to organisations which can prove that they are effectively supporting ED.

Source: National Advisory Council for Education and Training Targets 1999

Organisations will evolve systems and processes of their own to manage learning and ED to at least some extent. These will range from developing induction systems for new employees, through job-specific training, to retraining and career development. Research suggests that many companies have continued to develop and retain their own in-house training function, but a number have also been cutting back in recent years. The explanations for this decrease in internally managed ED vary from it representing straightforward cost-cutting to it representing the planned outsourcing of ED. It certainly seems that many more organisations are faced with the decision of choosing an external training provider as at least a partner, if not the major provider of ED. Much ED in organisations is managed in partnerships with others. These may be private sector providers, or public sector providers, or associated with private–public initiatives such as IiP.

The main reasons for selecting an outside provider are to obtain the best training available, and because the required training cannot be supplied in-house (The Industrial Society, 1998). Other key factors influencing the choice of provider include the availability of training facilities and the quality of the training design. A dedicated training company is likely to have broad experience in designing different courses for the various needs of different clients. An in-house training department is unlikely to have this breadth of knowledge and experience. Accreditation is also gaining importance, in part due to an environment where continuing career development and the workplace as a competitive internal labour market become more important. There are also factors which make in-house training more attractive. The two factors that seem to play a crucial role in persuading companies to develop their internal ED provisions are price and the ability to tailor a course to company needs.

So organisations develop ED strategies, deliberately and in a planned way and also as events unfold in the business; this involves developing and using some in-house provisions and also using external providers. Determining exactly which approach to ED they will invest in is still an issue, given the many different options available, and these will be considered in conclusion.

The role of government

In this area of HRM there is little substantive 'legal context',[4] in a way that parallels what is found in the legal regulation of employment through employment contracts or in specific employee relations legislation in industrial relations and areas like health and safety or managing discipline. Voluntarism still provides the main philosophy in ED in the UK – in other words, it is down to the people concerned to make decisions and develop initiatives as they see fit. Rather, the role of government is to promote the supply of ED through a number of initiatives, using a number of agencies. These agencies tend to change their name, if not their nature, with bewildering frequency. At the moment the central focus is on achieving a range of National

---

[4] One rare example would be the 1998 Teaching and Higher Education Act which amends the Employment Rights Act 1996; 16- and 17-year-old employees who have not achieved a certain standard of education/training will be entitled to reasonable paid time off during normal working hours to pursue approved qualifications. To be able to pursue learning and get an NVQ Level 2 or equivalent at least is therefore now a right for any individual. (http:www.hmso.gov.uk/acts/acts1998)

Training Targets, through the work of *Learning and Skills Councils* (LSCs) and Learning Partnerships and the initiative *Investors in People* (IiP).

From a government perspective the problems arising are ultimately about the implementation of economic and social policy. The nuts and bolts are about raising and allocating resources for ED. The balance of responsibility for paying for ED between individuals, companies, and government remains a constant concern. It seems that everyone aspires to achieve a high knowledge-based and high-skill economy, but would like to see someone else pay for it. One important aspect of this is that for the current government the challenge of dealing with groups facing social exclusion also provides a social agenda for ED, a social aspect to learning for and at work. Social exclusion includes a wide range of concerns. In the ED context it means dealing with the problems experienced by the long-term unemployed, women returners, alienated young people, and ethnic minority groups, in achieving their human potential through work and employment. In this context schools, colleges and universities, indeed education in general at all stages of life, can help drive the development of human potential to an extent. But it is often only in the context of employment, inside organisations, that many people have the opportunity to concentrate on developing their potential in the context of job experience and working with experienced practitioners.

The government's spending on training is an integral part of its broader economic and social policy. It is hard to quantify as it is bound up with its education programmes (see Table 5.3). This has become more pronounced since the Department of Education and the Department for Employment were merged in 1995/96, to form the Department for Education and Employment (DfEE). The amount being spent on training programmes in 1998/99 was £2.36 billion, excluding £951million being spent on the Welfare to Work programme. There is also some training included under the broad initiative of encouraging 'people to continue throughout their lives to develop their knowledge, skills and understanding and improve their employability in a changing labour market'.

Table 5.3 Expenditure by the Department for Education and Employment and OFSTED (£m), 1993/94–1998/99

	1993/ 94	1994/ 95	1995/ 96	e1997/ 98	†1998/ 99
Total expenditure	13 616	14 364	14 449	14 794	14 023
Expenditure on employment and training programmes of which‡:	2392	2394	2198	2496	3311
Welfare to Work	-	-	-	172	951
work-based training for young people	640	647	635	731	741
work-based training for adults	760	693	502	439	340
European Social Fund	96	108	181	270	308

Note: e – estimated, † – planned, ‡ – these are the largest single categories of expenditure – including the Welfare to Work programme OFSTED – Office for Standards in Education

Source: Department for Education and Employment Expenditure Plans 1998–99

Understanding and Managing People at Work

There are a number of national training targets (see Table 5.4), whose achievement is meant to concentrate the minds of all those involved in the provision of ED.

Table 5.4 Training targets

Targets for 11-year-olds	80% reaching standards in literacy and 75% reaching standards in numeracy
Targets for 16-year-olds	50% getting 5 higher grade GCSEs and 95% getting at least 1 GCSE
Targets for young people	85% of 19-year-olds with a level 2 qualification and 60% of 21-year-olds with a level 3 qualification
Targets for adults	50% with a level 3 qualification, 28% with a level 4 qualification, and a learning participation target (still to be set)
Targets for organisations	45% of medium and large organisations recognised as IiP, and 10 000 small organisations recognised as IiP

Note: These are the targets for England for 2002; targets for Scotland are currently being consulted upon.

Source: DfEE, 1998c

Provisions for young people in England and Wales are being reorganised into a new 'Connexions' Service (http://www.connexions.gov.uk). This will involve a host of initiatives based on eight key principles:

- raising aspirations – setting high expectations of every individual
- meeting individual need and overcoming barriers to learning
- taking account of the views of young people, individually and collectively, as the new service is developed and as it is operated locally
- inclusion – keeping young people in mainstream education and training and preventing them from moving to the margins of their community
- partnerships – agencies collaborating to achieve more for young people, parents and communities than agencies working in isolation
- community involvement and neighbourhood renewal – through involvement of community mentors and through personal advisors brokering access to local welfare, health, arts, sport and guidance networks
- extending opportunity and equality of opportunity – raising participation and achievement levels for all young people, influencing the availability, suitability and quality of provisions and raising awareness of opportunities
- evidence-based practice – ensuring that new interventions are based on rigorous research into and evaluation of 'what works'.

The emphasis is on the evolution of a broad and integrated service to give young people 'the best start in life', not just on initiatives to train them in vocational skills.

Youth training and youth credits

The problem of developing skills in young people has attracted policy attention for some considerable time. The context is one of abiding problems with youth unemployment, general disaffection with learning and training among some youth groups, and helping people cross the bridge from school to work and careers. From the government's perspective, there are clearly both economic and social concerns wrapped up in this. Youth Training and Youth Credits were launched in 1990. Under the Youth Training scheme, the DfEE guarantees the offer of a suitable training place to all 16–17-year-olds who 'are not in full-time education, are unemployed and seeking training'. Youth Training is offered via a Youth Credits system. 16- and 17-year-old school leavers (and sometimes other special groups) can use Youth Credits to buy training to N/SVQ standard from an employer or from a specialist provider of training.

Modern Apprenticeships

The 'old' system of ED, of apprenticeships managed by companies and craft unions, has been seen to have died out over time; with a decline of the industries and often organisations in which young people were apprenticed. Modern Apprenticeships were introduced in 1995. According to the DfEE, the purpose of Modern Apprenticeships is to develop technical, supervisory and craft-level skills among 16–18-year-olds. These schemes are designed to overcome the weaknesses of other attempts to improve ED for these occupations in industry, because they are industry-specific, and have been created by industry representatives in consultation with the DfEE. At the beginning of 1998, more than 150,000 young people had begun a Modern Apprenticeship, and there are now 75 Modern Apprenticeships, covering different sectors of industry and commerce.

Of all the government schemes, the Modern Apprenticeship scheme seems to be currently the most successful, attracting a rising number of entrants. However, these figures may have been inflated by some employers who have been using the scheme to train graduates, gaining a subsidy for these training costs. The government was sufficiently concerned to formally ban graduates from Modern Apprenticeship courses.

The DfEE has been considering the possibility of introducing a separate scheme for university students, whereby company-sponsored students would be able to qualify for a new type of Modern Apprenticeship scheme, where students would leave university with both a degree and a vocational qualification.

National Traineeships

National Traineeships were introduced in 1997. They offer young people who have left compulsory education a high-quality, work-based route to qualifications at intermediate level. They operate to agreed national criteria and standards set by industry and employers. In addition to specific vocational skills National Traineeships are meant to include all the key skills and components which will help young people progress in their chosen careers. National Traineeships currently cover more than 25 sectors of industry and commerce with plans for expansion into other sectors.

Work-Based Training for Adults

In 1998/1999, a new scheme called Work-Based Training for Adults was introduced to replace existing provisions. The aim of this new scheme is to help long-term unemployed adults, particularly those at risk of exclusion from the job market, to secure and sustain employment or self-employment, through an individually tailored combination of guidance, structured work experience, training and approved qualifications. The programme has some key features. It offers a combination of pre-vocational and occupational training. It provides occupational training which significantly improves skills in demand in the labour market. It provides lifelong learning facilities following Work-Based Training for Adults.

Investors in People

The aim of Investors in People (IiP) is to encourage employers to take training more seriously and improve their levels and quality of training. Employers satisfying the criteria become IiP-accredited companies. In essence, IiP provides a national 'benchmark' standard that helps employers to look at their training needs and links investment in training to the achievement of business goals. This standard is based on four principles:

- top-level commitment to develop all employees
- a regular review of the training and development of all employees
- action to train and develop individuals on recruitment and provide training throughout their employment
- evaluation of the outcome of training and development as a basis for continuous improvement.

Companies that adopt HRM practices that satisfy these four principles will be awarded IiP accreditation by Investors in People UK. By October 1998, around 10,000 firms had achieved IiP accreditation. The government provides £1.6 million to help firms achieve this accreditation. In recent times a focus upon small firms (i.e. firms employing up to 50 people) and medium-sized firms has become evident. The IiP standard, as with many other government initiatives, is currently being reviewed. Changes in the standard and the process for achieving it are expected.

This brief empirical review of IiP would suggest that an enhancement of the positive driving forces supporting employers' activities in ED and learning at work and an elimination of the negative restraining forces in order to more effectively and efficiently promote ED is still needed. That, in most accounts, would seem to involve a range of actors, from employers and their training departments, government and quasi-governmental organisations, and training providers working with individuals, groups and organisations to improve ED. Effective and efficient ED depends upon relationships and collaboration among employers, government, and training providers.

For employers these collaborations can begin with links to education, particularly the final years of secondary education, further education and Higher Education (HE), and professional development based in HE. Arguably, most centrally it involves assuring the right quantity and quality of ED in the workplace. This involves more than doing more training; it is about ED being an integral part of major business developments and company changes. This is exemplified in the UK presently by the IiP initiative. In IiP the core issues of ED, commitment to training, the planning and actions involved in training, and the need to evaluate training are seen as central business development concerns.

Improving the training market

The DfEE has a number of programmes which are aimed at encouraging individuals' investment in learning and at improving the quality and market responsiveness of training and vocational education. Current initiatives include promoting and making more accessible the benefits of lifelong learning; promoting the use of flexible learning; establishing mechanisms to achieve greater responsiveness of the further education sector to the needs of employers and promoting continuous improvement in the performance of bodies charged with supporting and delivering employee development

Welfare to Work

Welfare to Work is based on the 'New Deal' scheme for young and long-term unemployed people. Features of the scheme include helping young people, aged 18–24, who have been unemployed for more than six months to find work. It involves offering employers who take on a young unemployed person for six months a subsidy of £60 per week, providing full-time education and training for a year, and providing work in the voluntary sector or on the Environmental Task Force for up to six months. There are also a set of initiatives aimed at helping long-term unemployed people aged over 25 to find work. These include the opportunity to study while claiming the job seeker's allowance and offering a subsidy to companies which employ the long-term unemployed for six months.

National/Scottish Vocational Qualifications

National/Scottish Vocational Qualifications (N/SVQs) were launched in 1986. There are now more than 900 N/SVQs, representing different economic sectors and industries. They are divided into five ascending levels of competence:

- Level 1 – performance of routine work activities and/or achievement of a broad foundation of work competence as a basis for progression
- Level 2 – broader range of activities involving greater responsibility
- Level 3 – skilled activities involving greater responsibility
- Level 4 – complex, technical and specialised activities, including supervision and management
- Level 5 – pursuit of a senior occupation or profession, including the ability to apply a significant range of fundamental principles and techniques.

The take-up of N/SVQs varies enormously between commerce and industry sectors. Companies that have used these qualifications consistently report an improvement in product and service quality, increased staff motivation and more targeted training. Yet estimates are that only 7 per cent of employers are using N/SVQs and that only 5 per cent of the workforce have gained an N/SVQ award.

There have been other government initiatives on education and training since the election of the Labour government in 1997 to introduce what is being called 'The Learning Age' (DfEE 1997). The four main proposals are:

- a University for Industry (UFI) based on a network of local learning centres and access points to put 'learning on the High Street'
- Individual Learning Accounts (ILAs) – study and learning vouchers, with which people can buy the education and training that they need
- childcare support for those who need to take courses during the day or evening
- Learning Direct – a helpline through which people can obtain information on courses available.

As government reform of ED continues three main issues are evident: establishing the overall costs of reforms for lifelong learning; defining how much employers should contribute; and identifying what kind of learning technologies should be supported. These issues reprise the fundamental and abiding problems with all and any policy: being able clearly to identify costs and benefits among a range of options in order to structure optimum investment in people. The issue is less 'making training pay' than 'How much will it actually cost?' and 'Who pays for it?'.

During the last decade, there have also been significant changes within the framework and institutions supporting ED. To some this amounts to a revolution in training policy since 1988; to others it smacks of reorganisation in the face of uncertainty about what to do for the best when facing the challenges of improving ED. All of the UK's ED industry's major current institutional landmarks have been developed since 1988. In particular, there is continuing uncertainty about the type of system needed to ensure there is effective liaison in the development, marketing and evaluation of supply-side and demand-side initiatives. This is a common theme in the 'revolutions' – institutional and cultural – that have been heralded several times in the last two decades. How best to get everybody working together, making optimum use of limited resources, to achieve a range of stakeholder goals is a problem that has not yet been solved. This chapter can only briefly mention the main bodies involved.

At the top stands some form of national body: in England and Wales it is the National Advisory Council for Education and Training Targets (NACETT), which monitors the progress of training in relation to national targets across the range of concerns addressed above, as well as advising the DfEE on current performance and the effect of policies designed to achieve the targets. It draws its members from the Confederation of British Industry (CBI), the Trades Union Congress (TUC), the fields of education and training, and government departments. Its equivalent in Scotland was the Advisory Scottish Committee on Training Targets

(ASCETT), though, with constitutional change and a devolved parliament taking responsibility for these matters, a new institutional system is currently being developed in Scotland. A Skills Task Force advises the DfEE on the National Skills Agenda. Its purpose is to analyse and forecast skills shortages and to propose solutions. Its recommendations do affect education and training policies.

At the next level down are National Training Organisations (NTOs). The key responsibilities of the NTOs are to identify the industry sector's training needs, establish occupational standards and qualifications for their sector, provide the sector with information on training capacity, and to ensure that the sector has relevant training capacity. NTOs are larger than previous industry bodies with a similar role, covering bigger industry sectors, and are, therefore, fewer in number. In autumn 1998, there were 55, but a total of 75 are planned. They are also required particularly to look at skills requirements in their industry. The NTO National Council has devised a programme called Skills Foresight, which the NTOs are to use in order to assess skills needs. They will make use of tools like benchmarking and scenario planning, as well as local focus groups, rather than just using the old centralised forecasting of skills demands characteristic of the old systems.

Downstream there are also geographically based bodies. Until recently these were the Training and Enterprise Companies (TECs) in England and Wales and Local Enterprise Companies (LECs) in Scotland. These were set up in 1990, to improve vocational training for young people, to raise training levels in smaller businesses, and to promote local economic growth. These are being superseded by new bodies in England from 2000, and the LECs are under review, given the devolution of government in Scotland. The principles will remain; they have been run by boards of executives, made up of members from industry, local government and the training industry. This tripartite structure is likely to remain in some form, however the actual organisations evolve. They are required to work closely with the NTOs, as their responsibilities overlap. The balance between central control and local initiative will continue to be a tension in the system whatever new forms of body emerge.

The context for the evolution of ED in this aspect in the UK is continuing institutional and policy change. All these factors increase demands for more spending on ED. Whether that is forthcoming, and whether this amounts to a government-inspired institutional and cultural revolution that is preparing the UK to face the challenges of the future is still very much open to question. Whether there is enough investment, and whether it is directed at the areas of most importance to 'UK plc' are questions different stakeholders would answer quite differently.

Employers' approaches to employee development

We conclude by briefly reviewing here the practice and the theory of ED within companies. It is at the workplace where the issues involved in managing skills, knowledge and values, and the stakeholders who are concerned with ED, interact and can be evaluated. Many employers provide much ED themselves, through having and using their own trainers and training departments. Some large organisations even aspire to create their own 'universities'. It is also employers who use the substantial and strong 'private sector' concerned with ED, in the form of companies which provide training services for organisations. And it is employers who use the substantial public sector input to the development of ED, in the form of public policies and government-backed development schemes and programmes. The hub of the whole system has to be what happens within workplaces. According to an Industrial Society survey, the most common subjects that development in employment focuses upon within companies are health and safety (68 per cent), communication (61 per cent), and customer care (53 per cent)(Industrial Society 1998). Much less common are financial (14 per cent) and leadership aspects (6 per cent).

Much training is of very short duration. Surveys of employers report that a third of all training courses last less than three days (*Employment Gazette*, 1995). Of employees who received job-related training the primary clusters of activity are around very brief courses and also around longer-term, more substantial programmes.

Table 5.5 shows that two- to three-day courses remain the most popular form of training provided by external sources, suggesting that this is the form of training most in demand when organisations seek partners to provide ED. The apparent low demand for some high-profile innovative approaches, such as mentoring and even distance learning, suggests that the short course structure is consistently appealing to organisations.

Table 5.5 Training approaches used regularly for external training (% of employers citing use of these approaches), 1998

2- to 3-day courses	82
Up to 1 day courses	79
Day release	69
Residential training	63
Evening classes	55
Distance/open learning	42
Computer-based learning	24
Outdoor training	24
Coaching/mentoring	12
Video-based learning	9
Learning resource centres	6
Action learning sets	7

Source: The Industrial Society, *Training Trends*, May/June 1998

In sum, ED typically involves organisations providing one-day courses for their own employees from a menu of options, with external private providers offering two- or three- day courses, and also with organisations providing or working in partnership with accrediting institutions to offer long programmes of study and development. These are the three primary fields of development within employment: 'short and sharp' courses, extended short courses and longer programmes.

Different approaches to ED have been identified among employers. These can be classified historically, as they have changed over time in response to new demands and priorities. An example of this (Megginson, Banfield and Joy-Matthews, 1999) is to review past 'leading ideas'.

- 1964–70 Systematic approach to diagnosis of training
- 1968–75 Standardisation of training for job categories by industry. Thorough off-job basic education for skilled occupations
- 1970–75 Systematic planning of training for all categories of employee
- 1974–80 Company contribution to training for young people and long-term unemployed to meet national needs
- 1979–90 Business-orientated training directed at improving organisational effectiveness
- 1988–present Personal development with individualised plans for which each employee and their line manager take responsibility
- 1990–present Learning company development with a focus on a conscious, systemic, whole-organisation perspective
- 1998–present Knowledge management focus with knowledge workers and their intellectual properties seen as the core significant assets of the organisation

These approaches were around for some organisations before the dates suggested above as the start, and they continue in use long after their 'heyday'. Old approaches also emerge in new forms in each era. So, for example, the standardisation of training for job categories, characteristic of the systematic approach in the late 1960s, has had a rebirth with the development of the Management Charter Initiative (MCI). MCI seeks to specify management training, as does the development of National/Scottish Vocational Qualifications (N/SVQs) for other categories of employee competence.

Survey methods to find out what is being advocated by practitioners also provide a way of categorising what is involved in ED. This methodology has the advantage of being grounded in experience, but has the disadvantage of being less neat and tidy than more conceptually elegant frameworks. A complex and detailed outline of a huge range of training ideas and their development over time in the view of 633 practitioners, is spelled out in the *Developing the Developers* report (Boydell *et al.*, 1991). A more recent example of the practitioner survey (Megginson, Banfield and Joy-Matthews, 1999) surveyed very experienced developers active in the Association of Management Education and Development (AMED) and elicited a long list of 16 possible leading ideas. The surveyors asked a wider group of human resource development (HRD) practitioners to rank this long list. They calculated the proportion of respondents listing each idea as one of their top two, and the proportion listing it as one of their bottom two. Table 5.6 shows the ideas listed according to the size of the difference between these two percentages; those at the top of the list are the ideas seen as being of highest priority in the balanced view of their respondents.

Table 5.6 Leading ideas listed in order of the size of the gap between the proportion given top two priority and the proportion given bottom two priority (N=61), listed in order of size of gap.

Leading idea	% giving top 2 ranks	% giving bottom 2 ranks	% difference between top and bottom
1. Linking development to the organisation's strategy	35	5	+30
2. Focus on company or organisation learning	21	2	+19
3. Improved communication / briefing	18	0	+18
4. Linking learning to work	22	7	+15
5. Involving and participative management	15	0	+15
6. Focus on development rather than training	19	7	+12
7. Empowerment of staff	9	2	+7
8. Learners responsible for their own development	10	5	+5
9. Building balanced lives	16	16	0
10. Learning between organisations	9	10	−1

Source: Megginson, D., Banfield, P. and Joy-Matthews, J. (1999) *Human Resource Development,* (2nd edn) Kogan Page, London (p.19).

An interesting feature of this list is that it excluded from an earlier version of the survey 'accreditation and competence'. Although quite a number of the sample rated this very highly, a much larger number rated it very low. These 'low raters' were disproportionately concentrated among the more experienced of the sample of respondents.

Reviewing the historical and the survey data the dominant approaches to ED in the UK can be classified as:

- the systematic approach
- business orientation
- competencies and accreditation
- self-development
- the learning organisation
- knowledge management.

Each of these theories and approach is briefly considered here in turn.

The systematic approach

In spite of its 'antiquity' and persistent critiques, the systematic training approach maintains a remarkable hold in the world of ED. One reason for this is that many books on training, development and HRD offer it as a core 'intellectual property', organising their text around a (usually) four-stage cycle, as shown in Figure 5.1

Another reason is its simplicity in suggesting a cycle of activity which can be managed in practice, breaking down into discrete parts. A deeper question about the persistence of this approach might be, 'Why do *authors* continue to use this framework?' One reason for the continuation of this strand of thinking about ED may be that it gives a professional identity to trainers as well as to writers on

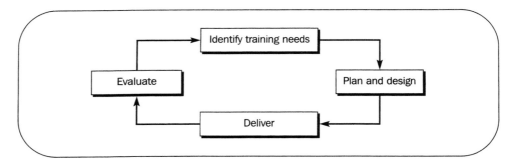

Figure 5.1

training. It provides a framework for what trainers do and enables them to describe their professional practice in a coherent way. Some of the components of this expertise are mapped in Box 5.1.

This model, however, is limited. It is a map of the 'internal content' of ED: what happens within employee development as a practical management activity; how to identify training needs, how to design and deliver training events, and how

---

BOX 5.1

The training cycle

Identify training needs
- Company and business needs
- Job and performance need
- Individual and personal need
- Self-determined needs (wants)

- Training plans and training policies
- Job analysis
- Performance appraisal
- Knowledge, skill and attitude (KSA)

Plan and design
- KSA linked to programme elements
- Learning methods linked to type of need
- Learning materials and resources
- Setting learning objectives

- On-job, at-job or off-job
- Internal or external
- Tutored or open learning resource

Deliver
- Use of range of learning methods
- Facilitation skills
- Engagement of internal providers
- Sourcing of external providers

- Instruction, coaching, mentoring
- Manage groups and teams
- A professional job role
- Being a broker of services

Evaluate
- Reactions, learning, job behaviour, organisation effects
- Feedback to learners
- Evaluating programme/strategy effectiveness

---

to evaluate them. The training cycle is also an essentially prescriptive model; it presents an ideal of what should be done, and does not reflect or describe what is actually done and the problems encountered.

Business orientation

The advent of the National Training Awards in Britain 1985 was the occasion when the business-oriented approach and theory were first formally advocated as a coherent framework, though of course many would have claimed prior to this that ED was integrated with business needs. The design of the awards required applicants to describe what had been done in terms of the four stages of the training cycle, outlined in the section on systematic training above, and they also required that the training must be preceded by identification of a business need and that the training outcome be shown to lead to a business outcome.

This approach was congruent with the spirit of the times, with businesses demanding 'bottom-line' contributions from all service functions if they were to survive deep cuts and downsizing. Arguably, the whole IiP approach, the central initiative in ED at the moment in the UK, is an incarnation of this approach.

The Institute of Personnel and Development (IPD) and Investors in People (IiP), arguably the two most notable proponents of ED in the UK, together launched a booklet called *Making Training Pay* (1997). This makes the business case for training and gives examples of how companies have benefited from training. The Confederation of British Industry also issued a survey-based report, which showed that, as well as putting more effort into training, two-thirds of employers were training their staff 'beyond the skills necessary for their jobs' (CBI, 1998).

Such reports are each small waves in a tide of change which has seen ED become a focus for effective business development and competitive success. Another survey claims to reveal that there is now a substantial attempt to link training with business objectives 'delivering human resource development in line with business objectives' (IPD, 1999: 11). This somewhat begs the question of what has been going on for the past several decades. The overemphasis in current times on having a business orientation may sometimes be seen as avoiding the specific challenges of evaluating exactly which approach is most effective and efficient and best provides value for money in different contexts.

Competencies and accreditation

An interesting 'mutation' of the business-oriented approach came when the UK government chose to put its authority behind approaches that advocated the identification of standardised competencies for occupations. The Management Charter Initiative (MCI) was one such initiative. This kind of set of competence statements specifying what it requires to 'do things well' in order to be effective in employment has, in fact, been a feature of training from the advent of systematic training. However, systematic training had offered the perspective that the particular needs of any specific group of managers (or any other group) needed to be identified. 'Universal' models of competence can thus seem to be a step back from this insight.

The government chose to put its weight behind the accreditation of individual competence because of a need to document progress towards the achievement of National Training Targets in the UK. The achievement of accredited qualifications gave the policy makers something to measure. From this emerged the whole panoply of N/SVQs. These qualifications were seen as having a number of advantages, discussed elsewhere in this chapter. A principal advantage was seen to be their portability – they could be related to other similar qualifications in other organisations and even in other EU countries.

The original work of Boyatzis (1982) on competencies had been based on finding out what behaviour led to superior performance by some individuals in a population. This work was therefore situated in particular contexts, and also provided a focus on what was required in order to 'do things better'. It was adopted by many large organisations in order to paint a vision of what was required in a major change project – and thus sought to encourage 'doing better things'; companies like BP and Boots developed such approaches. Many companies have now developed their own 'maps' of competence, though these are in essence, and often in detail, very similar.

Competencies were also proposed as providing a coherent framework for the integration of various HRM processes and initiatives. Some companies, including Commercial and General Union (see Case Study 5.1 at the end of this chapter) and Royal Bank of Scotland, had vigorous HR departments concerned with creating a set of initiatives bound together with a set of managerial behaviours which would lead to some future desirable state. Thus, selection, performance management, development and pay could all be tied down to some common framework. We have also identified cases, where having originally embraced competencies, senior HR people came to see that the model they imposed companywide did not capture the unique and crucial capabilities and contributions of a diversity of managerial roles and styles.

Self-development

This approach is grounded on two axioms:

- Any learning is a good thing as it leads to the embracing of the new and the extension of skills and capability.
- Learning which has the most potency to create these effects is that chosen and specified by the learners themselves.

The first axiom leads to the practice of employee development schemes, of which the most famous is the Ford's Employee Development and Assistance Programme (EDAP). Here a personal budget is provided to enable individuals to learn whatever they want in order to initiate or reawaken the habit of learning, and to offer a commitment on behalf of the employer to making this happen.

Recently some authorities (Hamblett and Holden, 2000) have been suggesting that employee-led development has a component that makes a difference – namely, the fact that overall control of the scheme is in the hands of the workforce or their representatives. This participation ensures effective development.

The second axiom leads to an approach to development where the learner is given central responsibility for and control over the process of identifying and meeting learning needs, and others have roles to support this development. Often personal development plans (see the CGU case study at the end of this chapter) are a part of the process, and line managers can have an important role in supporting and stimulating the consideration of development. Training functions are seen as enablers and can provide advice on the resources to deliver training or development opportunities. The experience of the authors in designing and supporting such programmes (in, for example, Texaco and ICL) is that competencies are sometimes used and found helpful in the first round of need-identification. However, they are often rejected in favour of a more individual expression of need once the learner gains confidence in expressing their own needs (Megginson and Whitaker, 1996).

The learning organisation

Ideas of organisational learning, which had been present in the literature for more than 20 years, became popular in the early 1990s with the publication of Senge (1990) in the USA and Pedler, Burgoyne and Boydell (1991) in the UK. Essentially, both advocated a systemic rather than a systematic approach to development. By this we mean that they saw that everything was connected to everything else. Simple cause and effect models (we sometimes call them 'boxes and arrows' approaches) do not capture the complex interactions between components of a system. Learning, if it is to generate new possibility for action, needs to recognise that most of our actions are grounded in basic assumptions of which we may not be aware. These assumptions limit our thinking and acting, and at the same time seal off from us the awareness that we are thus limited (Argyris and Schön, 1978).

Many trainers claim to be adopting this approach by following a recipe of prescriptions (such as Pedler *et al.*'s (1991) eleven characteristics of a learning company). Trainers do this in spite of the authors' clear advice to the contrary, and without the systemic perspective of Senge (1990). They also often lack the willingness and skill required to question basic assumptions inherent in the writing of Argyris and Schön (1978). This approach is, it would seem, much less commonly adopted than the rhetoric of its adherents would suggest.

Knowledge management

An emerging approach, which may establish itself and displace the systematic training approach, is the approach to learning via the concerns of knowledge management. Knowledge management gurus argue that knowledge held by knowledge workers creates intellectual capital which represents the intangible assets of modern organisations. These intangible assets have often far greater worth than the tangible assets of buildings and machinery. Development is therefore crucially concerned with the management and enhancement of these knowledge assets. As the field develops, there seem to be contributions from three currents of thinking. The first is the information systems (IS) perspective, which emphasises the capture, store and retrieval of knowledge. The second is the organisation learning (OL) perspective, which focuses on learning as being mediated, situated, provisional, pragmatic and contested (Easterby-Smith *et al.*, 1999). The third is a strategic perspective, which emphasises the value of intellectual capital and the worth of knowledge as embodied in patents and corporate core competencies (Davenport and Prusak, 1998). The prospect of a fusion of these perspectives is beguiling for developers, who find that conversations about learning often do not engage the attention of strategic management in the way that a hard-headed concern for tangible assets can.

Conclusion

There are a variety of approaches to achieving development in employment, with no single best way being evident in theory or practice. In a prescriptive sense, as outlined in the beginning, ED is concerned with learning for and learning at work to help individuals and organisations achieve their full potential. Individuals have development needs throughout their lives. These range from gaining basic knowledge and basic skills in education and pre-employment vocational development, through to induction and initial job-related training with an employer, and on to their lifelong performance and career development up to leaving the employer on redundancy or retirement. Employers are concerned with ensuring that their workforce is competent and that the development activities used to achieve competency are effective and efficient. This requires employers' involvement in a range of activities, from influencing and shaping government policy on education through to organising their own development activities for individuals, specific job roles and the organisation as a whole. While some issues come to more prominence in some contexts than others, there is no settled, universal and dominant prescriptive approach.

In terms of evidence for a positive evaluation of employers' activities in ED in the UK, many UK work organisations have often looked to ED as an integral part of becoming and remaining efficient and more effective. There is a long and substantial tradition of investing in ED in many UK organisations, and those which it has been quick and easy to accredit as Investors in People (IiPs) reflect that. This is simply and logically because, other things being equal, an organisation with well-developed and therefore competent employees will be more efficient and effective than an organisation with poorly developed and therefore incompetent employees.

In the light of greater challenges to be 'excellent' in order to compete successfully or to provide better-quality public services, a greater concern with ED among employers has been reinforced as a route to helping achieve these aspirations. In partnership with employers, the government has reformed the education and training system that underpins ED in the UK, to make it better fit the country's economic and social needs. The development of employees and the promotion of learning at work are now seen as a means of transforming organisations from struggling businesses or services into world-class and successful organisations. All the driving forces in the business environment push most employers towards greater levels and improved quality of ED. Evidence in the form of organisations who adopt this philosophy and succeed is plentiful; see Case Study 5.2.

However, investment in effective ED does not appear to be the norm among UK employers seeking to develop their businesses. The need for promotional initiatives like IiP, raises questions about the extent to which there is indeed a general, common-sense and logical case for transforming organisations through employers increasing their investing in ED. As exemplary employers in this respect are not the norm, either employers are ignorant of the returns to be achieved, or are led to other conclusions in reality. Perhaps the 'unambiguous' data supporting the returns on ED is discounted as unrealistic. Kellaway (2000) claims that there is

---

BOX 5.2

Chase Advanced Technologies Ltd

In 1996 Chase Advanced Technologies won a major contract to provide electronic components for fruit machines across the UK. But the contract led to problems for the company, including poor pass rates and high levels of reworking. At one point things were so bad that internal pass rates fell to 38 per cent.

An intensive training programme to tackle the immediate crisis was devised which involved 60 employees undertaking basic training in printed circuit board assembly. Quality levels began to rise, reaching 80 per cent in a few months. The company then introduced a skills training and National Vocational Qualification (NVQ) initiative and an in-house workmanship training culture, set up with support from a local college and Electronic ITEC, Bradford College's electronic training centre. A multimedia computer-based training package to support the delivery of the NVQ was also developed.

Finally the change management team began to lay the foundations for a genuine training culture. They made a commitment to the Investors in People standard and offered staff access to a nationally recognised qualification.

After 2 years of heavy losses Chase returned to profit in 1998 and the company is now a thriving organisation with a skilled and committed workforce. Managing director Eugene Martinez commented 'The training programme has led to a new spirit of enthusiasm among our staff. Having been given an opportunity to learn, many have developed a real hunger for knowledge. A working grandmother was one of the first people to gain a NVQ and has recently gained a level 3 qualification in manufacturing support. Many staff are so keen that they are even undertaking NVQ work in their own time.'

Source: DfEE Employment News, December/January 2000, p.5. Quoted in full with permission.

indeed much hype and inflation surrounding ED. As a trenchant critic of UK employers' susceptibility to management fads and fashions, she asserts that:

> Some of the dullest days I have spent in my 18 years as a wage slave have been on training courses. Training is only good if it succeeds in teaching you something useful. But most of it doesn't or doesn't do it very effectively.

(Kellaway, 2000: 81)

It seems that many employers share her views, rather than being gulled, as she supposes, by the 'nonsense' claims that ED can transform a company. A negative evaluation of employers' activities in ED in the UK would also be supported by the fact that many work organisations have failed to make ED a priority. Investment in ED in companies in the UK is consistently lower than in other countries. Employers continue either to operate inefficiently and ineffectively, or seek to become more efficient and effective by other means – the primary strategy being through deskilling work and minimising costs by actually neglecting ED. While the high-quality development of a few professionals and managers may be achieved in some companies, the limited ED that is provided by employers, and their influence on schools, colleges and universities, is of dubious quality and value. This has resulted in systematic problems in achieving even basic competence amongst the general labour force and in specific workforces, which leaves UK employers at a disadvantage. Effects range from poor health and safety standards, through poor standards of customer service and up to ineffective strategic management of the organisation as a whole. This leads to the UK being saddled with a 'low-skill, low-wage' economy. It is also badly placed to restructure and meet the demands of the knowledge economy and society.

The apparent failure of employers to support ED is compounded by governmental failures to challenge them. Government has actively handed responsibility over to employers to lead the 'skills revolutions' they seek, but employers have been found wanting. Government has thus failed to identify and resource properly the priorities and institutions needed to break free from the 'low-skill, low-wage' economy the UK is seen to have. Skills shortages cause problems not only for immediate business and service development, the main concern of employers; they can also constrain longer-term economic growth and social restructuring, a primary concern of government. As a result, UK organisations are falling further and further behind their competitors in the rest of the world. Other nations' greater governmental emphasis on investment in ED pays general economic and social dividends, while in the UK the gaps between those who are successful and those who are 'socially excluded' widen and deepen (Hutton, 1995).

The truth would seem to lie somewhere between the simplified and exaggerated negative and positive evaluations of employers' activities in ED in the UK. One estimate (Keynote, 1998) was that the total amount spent on training by the private sector in 1998 was £13.2 billion, spent on a workforce of around 21 million where around 3 million people in the year were participants in off-job training. In

BOX 5.3

Skills shortages

For 42% of employers with hard-to-fill vacancies the main reason given is not enough suitable skilled people.

Areas
- Catering occupations
- Road transport
- Miscellaneous sales and services
- Engineers and technologists
- Health and related occupations
- Health associate professionals
- Miscellaneous clerks
- Receptionists and telephonists
- Computer analysts and programmers
- Telephone sales
- Specialist managers

Effects
- Increased running costs
- Loss of quality
- Restrict business developments

Changes in skill needs
68% of employers say skills needed are increasing due to changes in processes, technology and management practices.

Skills that matter
Technical and practical skills
Computer literacy
General communication skills
Customer handling skills
Management skills
Teamworking skills
Problem-solving skills
Managing own development

Source: IRS ED Bulletin 110:*Skill Needs in Great Britain and NI 1998*

the UK the average spend is then £62 per person if all employees are considered, or £440 per person for those who actually received off-job training.[5]

The negative evaluators would be challenged by this trend, but not the basic fact. They would still wonder whether this level of activity and the development it involves are good enough. And questions about the efficiency and effectiveness of investments in ED remain in any event. The pessimist would also question where resources invested in ED are actually going. Research (DfEE: *Labour Market Trends*, 1998) shows that there is a marked bias towards younger age groups as

---

[5] There are no available estimates for similar figures on ED in the public sector.

participants in ED. This makes sense as the early career stages are when learning needs would seem most evident. But in an era where the promotion of 'lifelong learning' is important, and where organisational and job changes are so prevalent, it seems that ED needs to be – but is not yet in practice – a lifelong activity.

There are also significant variations in the occupational characteristics of ED activity (ONS, 1996). Professional employees are the most likely to receive ED, while regular training is lowest among manual workers. Again these statistics seem to reflect a 'reality' where professional jobs require more learning, and therefore attract more resources. However, many commentators argue that the provision of ED for all is a precondition of successful performance for any organisation, and in the UK it is problems with basic and intermediate ED (or vocational education and training (VET)) which present the greatest areas of need. The concentration of resources and activity among certain occupational groups may reflect an anomaly inherited from history rather than an effective allocation of resources.

There are also sector variations. Some sectors invest more in ED than others. One survey (Industrial Society, 1998) shows, for example, that off-the-job training is more widespread in the financial sector than in manufacturing. This discrepancy may reflect greater use of on-the-job ED in manufacturing rather than the financial sector, so the balance of overall investment in ED may be more equal than it first seems. It may also be the case that there are greater ED needs in the financial sector than in manufacturing; for example, due to the introduction of legislation and the demand for improved levels of competence in the selling of financial services. The pessimists' suspicion would be that ED in manufacturing is neglected because it is a low-skill, low-wage sector, thus contributing to the overall decline of that sector within the UK economy. They may also suspect that much of the investment in ED in the financial sector is of dubious value.

So learning in and for the workplace depends upon the outcome of complex interactions between individuals, employers and government. The hope is that optimum investment by each in development brings maximum gains: individuals gain attractive and useful employment, employers gain business success in high-skill industries, and governments achieve the social and economic goals they were elected to pursue. There is then a weight of expectation hanging on ED, exerted by the dependence of all these stakeholders upon it. Whether, in principle, ED can deliver on these expectations, and whether, in practice, one approach is better than another, are questions which have exercised many in HRM in recent times and which need to be pursued further.

This chapter has described and evaluated the nature of ED, what it involves and what the issues and challenges are, particularly from an employer's perspective. Seeing employers' activities as the hub of the matter is, indeed, only one way of concluding a review of ED; but it has the merit of leading on to theoretical case study analysis of workplace and employer examples, rather than to specialist theories and matters of motivation and involvement in learning, or to the evaluation of government policies and initiatives in the broader context of evaluating social and economic goals and aspirations.

From an employer's perspective the context is one of achieving their goals through creating a competent workforce. This involves them in a range of activities, from organising their own employees' development, to influencing education and development policy and taking the lead in evolving supportive national policies and systems. In all these respects the evaluation of employers' activities in ED can be positive: education is being reformed to meet the economic and social needs of the contemporary workforce, employers are investing more in ED, with gains for all; and as a result of these activities, broader social and economic goals and aspirations can be met. Changes and restructuring in companies are bringing about changes in people's tasks and responsibilities, with a subsequent need for more ED. All sectors appear to be supporting change: companies are reviewing their internal provisions, government provides new and salient frameworks which are funded and a dynamic private sector provides a range of ED options 'for all tastes and budgets'. Changes in markets, in customer requirements, and in approaches to ED are forcing providers to review their products and services, which leads to better products and services. For the government there are continuing economic, social and political gains to be made in promoting 'supply-side' policies that involve motivating employers and individuals to increase skills and employability rather than achieving economic and social aims by 'taxing and spending'.

The evaluation can also be negative: education is becoming too vocationalised and losing its fundamental purpose; insufficient investment in development in organisations is the stubborn norm; policies and institutions which are employer-led fail to deliver on longer-term economic and social goals and aspirations. The three main stakeholders arguably continue to underfund their rhetoric. Companies are still prone to limiting ED budgets; the government does not follow through on funding for its initiatives; and individuals are reluctant to pay themselves for ED. In addition, ED standards vary considerably. Internal provisions, and those offered externally by the private and public sector, are often criticised. There appear to be a significant proportion of ED programmes that are poorly planned and structured, despite decades of established advice on how to do it properly. There are continuing critiques of the success and viability of government programmes – for example, the merits of the IiP initiative. Evaluating the worth of ED, in terms of costs and benefits, has never been easy; its higher profile further exposes this, paradoxically leading to greater criticisms of ED as it grows in popularity as a business development tool. Also, current investment in ED is concentrated among the large companies, whose share of total employees is declining, and in certain employment categories and age groups.

There is then a huge demand for ED: within companies, from competent external providers, and in the form of public sector initiatives designed to support individuals and organisations. Computer-based learning is gaining popularity and may be particularly suited to some sectors which involve jobs that are heavily dependent on using IT. School, university and personal use of ICT systems is clearly growing, and this whole aspect of the design and delivery of training will be a major concern in the future. The shift towards self-managed learning offers the prospect of better focused and greater personal and professional development. New entrants to the ED market, such as computer companies and publishers, are expanding the range of courses available and offering cheaper training. Non-profit organisations are competing strongly against the commercial training companies.

Yet in companies there is a threat to training budgets and initiatives in the face of cost reduction factors and the imperatives of production/service delivery in lean organisations concerned to maintain limits to working hours. Greater use in companies of learning resource centres may increase the demand on internal company training, but may not deliver the goods without trained trainers there to facilitate. Governments are struggling to sort out the 'Who pays?' part of the equation. Getting bogged down in this, or making decisions that prove unpopular with major stakeholders, can undo all the efforts that have hitherto been made.

In many respects there is a great deal of inertia in the system. Despite promulgating and promoting the benefits of ED, it takes time and a lot of resources to establish and co-ordinate efforts which can bring real business and social benefits. Dissatisfaction with the quantity and quality of ED provided, both by the public sector and the private sector as well as within companies, can be expected to spur the further evolution of innovative approaches to ED and further restructuring of the overall system. The potential of technologies, for example, has yet to be fully realised. All this means that further, and perhaps greater, change is likely in the future. Such changes can be expected to succeed or fail according to how well they engage individuals, employers and government in partnerships as much as they will depend upon the relevance and accuracy of the substantive knowledge, skill and values identified as priorities for future human potential development.

Where that interaction involves individuals motivated to learn, able to access learning within employment and elsewhere, supported by investing employers and guided by principled economic and social policy being effectively implemented, then a synergy is possible with all benefiting. Where that interaction involves people unwilling or unable to participate in learning, compounded by employers who fail to invest in ED and there is a lack of principle or effective implementation in economic and social policy then a vicious cycle will exist, with all paying the price. These realities of providing development for employment present human, organisational and political challenges which are at the heart of HRM.

Employee development in Commercial & General Union

Stephen Gibb and David Megginson

The context

Commercial Union, a large British general insurance company, initiated a strategic change project, called Best Place to Work (BPTW), in 1996. BPTW aimed to change beliefs about working relationships and performance towards a more competitive and customer-focused set of values. Current management styles were to be challenged, structures were to become more customer-focused, and processes would be redesigned to enable more front-line decision-making. Reward systems were to become more performance-focused and awareness of the redefined brand was to be increased. A BPTW survey showed that staff wanted 'to grow and develop', and felt that opportunities were scarce. A Personal Development Planning (PDP) process was set in train to meet this aspiration, and to reinforce other aspects of the BPTW programme.

ED in the company before this point was focused upon:

- Professional insurance industry qualifications, with relatively little attention paid to N/SVQs
- IiP, which was being pursued by various parts of the business
- A tradition of attendance on residential courses at the company's training centre – Douce's Manor, in Kent.

During 1997 a relationship was established with Cranfield Business School, which delivered residential training for senior managers. During 1998 a Certificate, Diploma and MBA programme was set up with the Open University Business School for people who self-nominated and were supported by their managers.

The aims of the PDP initiative were to enable staff to:

1. Take personal responsibility for acquiring the right technical, interpersonal and business skills to do the job now, and to gain management support for this process.
2. Think ahead about their career and future possibilities – and start to chart a way forward; to see patterns in what they had done, and rethink whether they wanted them to continue or change.
3. Tune into the changes going on around them, recognise the impact of change on them and develop coping/success skills.
4. Recognise the value of developing outside of work, and gain management support for this.

The scheme had been launched and rolled out to the 8,000 staff in CU(UK) when, in February 1998, a merger was announced with another UK insurer, General Accident (GA). This merger was realised in June 1998, to form Commercial and General Union (CGU). Thereafter, attention was diverted from the PDP scheme to more pressing concerns of creating new structures and roles, and implementing a voluntary redundancy scheme.

Processes

The company's approach to the project:

- Initial research was carried out to find out what had worked elsewhere.
- Leading outside consultants were brought in to challenge thinking and assist in development of workshop design, workbooks and video.
- There was close liaison with other HR system developments, especially an emerging competency framework, IiP and a performance management system.
- Communication with stakeholders in the business was important during the development of the process.
- Champions were sought at each of the company sites, and they were trained in PDP principles and practices, and briefed in how to train managers in supporting the PDP process.
- Champions trained the managers at their site in how to support staff in preparing PDPs.
- Managers worked with their staff in supporting the development of their PDPs.
- Staff worked on developing and implementing their own PDPs.

Workbooks were produced for the workshops, outlining the process and the format for a PDP. A video was produced describing CU staff's reactions to such a process. It showed endorsement of PDPs by senior managers.

The stages in the PDP process described in the staff's 'Guide to personal development planning' were:

- Identify your 'here and now' needs – from the performance management system and from feedback from others.
- Develop for future business needs – from the competency framework, from expected role changes within BPTW, from business changes in CU, and from personal awareness of changes in business.
- Set goals based on recognising past success, get in touch with your own dream for your development, and identify an extraordinarily realistic self-image.
- Create your own plan, with prioritised needs, development goals and development actions.
- 'Do it and review it', including logging learning and learning from experience. They were given a checklist for a personal development review.

Understanding and Managing People at Work

Outcomes

All the above processes had taken place for the vast majority of CU(UK) staff before the merger with GA was confirmed. Plans had been made for embedding the scheme and ensuring its continuation over subsequent years. However, these plans were put on hold in the flurry of activity surrounding the merger.

Informal soundings of HR staff involved in supporting staff through the changes necessitated by the merger indicate that ex-CU staff may have been better equipped to make choices for themselves and for the new CGU Insurance.

It is difficult to evaluate the absolute success of the PDP programme, as it was never intended to be a discrete product, but was part of a wider (BPTW) process of change. However all three sets of workshops were very well received, and managers' workshops had an average rating of 3.25 on a scale of 1–4, where 3 = Well and 4 = Very well, in response to a range of questions asked. The staff workshops had average ratings of 3.40.

Typical comments about the workshops were:

'Interesting and well presented'

'Whilst enjoyable – a long day, lots to take in'

'Enjoyable, fun – but could have been condensed slightly'

'Facilitators assisting and guiding during activities was helpful'

'Overall a good course. Showed the importance of PDPs. Ran in a relaxed manner with plenty of activities. Plenty of motivation'

'We managers need more help in ensuring that expectations are not raised too high'

'Interesting – not as boring as I thought it would be'

'Good variety of activities and facilitator participation'

'Nice to know that CU is committed to the development of staff'

'Useful to apply in my private life'

Questions

1. Which approach to ED is this employer using?

2. Which concern seems uppermost in this example: knowledge development, skills development or EVA development?

3. In what ways does the example reflect a use of the three sectors: internal ED, adoption of public initiatives and use of external providers/partners?

4. Do the evaluation findings suggest that this ED initiative achieved the objectives the company had in mind?

5. What else might you want to evaluate to analyse the efficiency and the effectiveness of this ED initiative?

Case study 5.2

External training providers

Stephen Gibb and David Megginson

The effectiveness of ED overall depends in large part on the effectiveness of private providers. Private training providers work in a very fragmented industry, supporting a large number of training providers, which range from sole practitioners to some very large training companies. Estimates of the number of private providers vary. There appear to be around 400 principal training organisations in the UK, with many more organisations, companies, partnerships and sole practitioners which provide training. The number of value-added tax (VAT)-based enterprises listed as training providers totals 4,475 (Keynote, 1998). In addition, there are many smaller training providers who escape VAT categorisation, either because their turnover is too low or because their main business is not in training. According to the Association for Management Education and Development (AMED), there are around 10,000 independent trainers. The majority of providers fall into the categories shown below.

- **Independent, commercially run training companies** – there seem to be around 400 of these in the UK, including some long-established firms.
- **Professional/institutional bodies** – most professional bodies offer some form of training, which often complements their role as accreditation bodies. Examples include the Institute of Personnel and Development, the Chartered Institute of Marketing, and the Institute of Directors.
- **Business schools/universities** – there are over 100 training providers in this category. Business schools and universities are now heavily promoted as centres of vocational learning and training.
- **Colleges of further education** – supplying mainly vocational training.
- **Product/service companies**; for example computer companies who provide training along with hardware and software purchases.
- **Open learning providers** – there are many examples, including, of course, the Open University. The uptake of multimedia and internet systems means many open learning providers are leading the way in technological developments.
- **Sole practitioners** – many ex-company in-house trainers set themselves up as independent trainers. They may work totally independently, in collaboration with other sole practitioners, or as subcontractors of training companies.
- **Management consultancies** – some consultancies offer training, although this tends to form only a small part of their activities.

Being able to tailor a course to a company's needs is obviously of primary importance for external training providers (The Industrial Society, 1998). Training companies are increasingly offering 'tailored' courses rather than off-the-shelf options. Quality and perceived value for money are also seen to be extremely important. For an employer it is argued that price is less important (i.e. differentials between one training company and another) than the company's image and professionalism. The need for a course to be 'locally' based is no longer a consideration for most companies; the quality and subject matter are the main determinants. Even the location of local colleges and universities as external partners is less important, in view of the availability of distance learning and internet technologies. This opens up the market for the provision of ED on a global basis; providing both a threat and opportunity to private providers of ED in the UK.

The most popular choice of external partner for employers is a private sector trainer, followed by an educational institution, a professional association/institute or a non-profit making training body (Table 5.7).

Table 5.7: External training providers – percentage of organisations using each source

Type of training provider	1997	1998
Private sector trainers/providers	73	78
University/college/other FE body	56	68
Professional association/institute	45	55
Non-profit-making training body (e.g. The Industrial Society)	51	48
Equipment supplier	32	33
Training and Enterprise Council/ Local Enterprise Council	25	24
Informal employers' network/club	10	10

Note: FE – further education

Source: The Industrial Society, *Training Trends*, May/June 1998

Around a third of all training still takes place at an employer's workplace or training centre. This proportion is likely to rise as employers increase the amount of in-house training that they purchase. Further education and technical colleges are also important sites of learning, as are adult education centres and universities. Educational/academic institutions are becoming more important as sources and places of training. Figure 5.2 shows the main location of face-to-face teaching for all taught learning episodes in England and Wales during 1997 (DfEE: *Labour Market Trends*, 1998).

With only a few exceptions, private suppliers and partners are wholly UK-owned and UK-staffed. Arguably, this is because the involvement of foreign companies is problematic in the context of the specific needs of the workforce skills, knowledge and values within a nation or region. Moreover, the educational and cultural framework of each country is different, and this is reflected in training approaches and

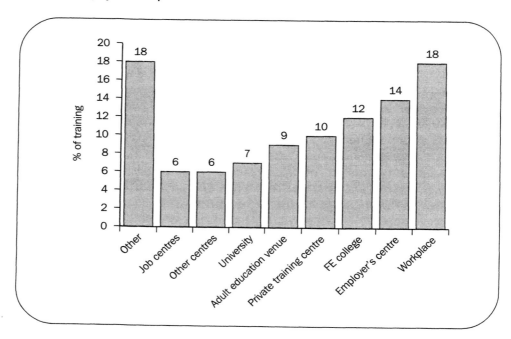

Figure 5.2 Venues for training

content. Management practice and style also vary from one country to another, as indeed does HRM practice. As a result, ED tends to be indigenous to each country. Partnerships between organisations in different parts of Europe may emerge with further Europeanisation, and harmonisation in economic and social matters.

The major exception at the moment to this national specialisation is the development of 'European managers' by some of the multinational companies. However, this type of training tends to be influenced by the corporate style emanating from the company headquarters, which, in some cases, is still culturally oriented towards one country. There is also the traditional 'North American' influence on much personal and management development. As Europe becomes more integrated, there are likely to be increased calls for some kind of mechanism by which qualifications in one country can be equated with those of another. The first step towards this is the Europass, a passport-type document which will contain details of the owner's training and the government training schemes they have been on.

Questions

1. What are the advantages and disadvantages of using external training providers?
2. What factors explain the increasing use of external training providers in the UK?
3. What factors influence an organisation's choice of external training providers?

References to Chapter 5

Argyris, C. and Schön, D. (1978) *Organizational Learning*, Reading, Mass: Addison-Wesley.

Bloom, B.S. (ed) (1956) *Taxonomy of Educational Objectives: The Classification of Educational Goals: Handbook 1, Cognitive Domain*, New York: Longman.

Boyatzis, R. (1982) *The Competent Manager*, New York: Wiley.

Boydell, T., Leary, M., Megginson, D. and Pedler, M. (1991) *Developing the Developers*, London: AMED.

Blackler, F. (1995) 'Knowledge, knowledge work and organizations', *Organization Studies*, 16(6): 1021–46.

CBI (1998) *Employment Trends*, London: CBI.

Crouch, C., Finegold, D., Sako, M. (1999) 'Are skills the answer? The political economy of skill creation in advanced industrial countries', Oxford: Oxford University Press.

Davenport, T. and Prusak, L.(1998) *Working Knowledge*, Boston, Mass: Harvard Business School.

DfEE (1995) 'Length of training courses', *Employment Gazette*, 103 (7): 37.

DfEE (1996) *Labour Force Survey*, London: DfEE.

DfEE (1998a) *The Learning Age: a New Renaissance for a New Britain*, London: DfEE.

DfEE (1998b) *Labour Market Trends*, London: DfEE.

DfEE (1998c) *National Learning Targets for England 2002*, London: DfEE.

Easterby-Smith, M., Burgoyne, J., Avaujo, L. (eds) (1999) *Organizational Learning and the Learning Organization*, London: Sage.

ESRC (1999) 'Twenty-Something in the 1990s', ESCR briefing.

Foster, J. (1999) 'Looking for balance', London: The National Work-Life Forum.

Gibb, S. (1999) 'The usefulness of theory: a case study in evaluating formal mentoring schemes', *Human Relations*, 52(8): 1055–75.

Goleman, D. (1996) *Emotional Intelligence: Why it can Matter More than IQ*, London: Bloomsbury.

Hamblett, J. and Holden, R. (2000) 'Employee-led development: another piece of left luggage?', *Personnel Review*, 29(4): 509–20.

Hutton, W. (1995) *The State We're In*, London: Jonathan Cape.

Industrial Society (1998) *Training Trends*, May/June, London: Industrial Society

IPD (1997) *Making Training Pay*, London: IPD/IiP.

IPD (1999) *Training and Development in Britain 1999*, London: IPD.

Johnson, P. and Indvik, J. (1999) 'Organizational benefits of having emotionally intelligent managers and employees', *Journal of Workplace Learning*, 11(3): 84–88

Kellaway, L. (2000) *Sense and Nonsense in the Office*, London: FT/Prentice Hall.

Keynote (1998) *Training*, Keynote marketing report.

Megginson, D., Banfield, P. and Joy-Matthews, J. (1999) *Human Resource Development*, 2nd edition, London: Kogan Page.

Megginson, D. and Whitaker, V. (1996) *Cultivating Self-development*, London: IPD.

ONS (1996) *Social Trends*, London: HMSO.

Pedler, M., Burgoyne, J. and Boydell, T. (1991) *The Learning Company*, Maidenhead: McGraw-Hill,

Pickard, J. (1999) 'Keynote speakers', *People Management*, 5(11).

Pinker, S. (1997) *How the Mind Works*, London: Penguin.

Rokeach, M. (1970) *Beliefs, Attitudes and Values: A Theory of Organisation and Change*, San Francisco: Jossey-Bass.

Schön, D. (1987) *Educating the Reflective Practitioner*, San Francisco: Jossey-Bass.

Senge, P. (1990) *The Fifth Discipline*, London: Century.

Stewart, T. (1997) *Intellectual Capital*, London: Nicholas Brealey Publishing.

Tapscott, D. (1996) *The Digital Economy: Promise and Peril in the Age of Networked Intelligence*, New York: McGraw Hill.

Wickens, P. (1999) 'Values added', *People Management*, 5(10): 33–38.

Chapter 13

THE NATURE OF
WORK GROUPS

Groups are a major feature of organisational life. The work organisation and its sub-units are made up of groups of people. Most activities of the organisation require at least some degree of co-ordination through the operation of group working. An understanding of the nature of groups is vital if the manager is to influence the behaviour of people in the work situation. The manager must be aware of the impact of groups and their effects on organisational performance.

Learning objectives

To:

➤ explain the meaning and nature of work groups and teams;

➤ distinguish between formal and informal groups;

➤ explain the main reasons for the formation of groups;

➤ examine factors which influence group cohesiveness and performance;

➤ review the characteristics of an effective work group and assess the impact of technology;

➤ analyse the nature of role relationships and role conflict;

➤ appreciate the importance of groups for effective organisational performance.

The meaning and importance of groups

Individuals seldom work in isolation from others. **Groups** are a characteristic of all social situations and almost everyone in an organisation will be a member of one or more groups. Work is a group-based activity and if the organisation is to function effectively it requires good teamwork. The working of groups and the influence they exert over their membership is an essential feature of human behaviour and of organisational performance. The manager must use groups in order to achieve a high standard of work and improve organisational effectiveness.

Definitions of a group

There are many possible ways of defining what is meant by a group. The essential feature of a group is that its members regard themselves as belonging to the group. Although there is no single, accepted definition, most people will readily understand what constitutes a group. A popular definition defines the group in psychological terms as:

> any number of people who (1) interact with one another; (2) are psychologically aware of one another; and (3) perceive themselves to be a group.[1]

Another useful way of defining a work group is a collection of people who share most, if not all, of the following characteristics:

- a definable membership;
- group consciousness;
- a sense of shared purpose;
- interdependence;
- interaction; and
- ability to act in a unitary manner.[2]

Essential feature of work organisations

Groups are an essential feature of the work pattern of any organisation. Members of a group must co-operate in order for work to be carried out, and managers themselves will work within these groups. People in groups influence each other in many ways and groups may develop their own hierarchies and leaders. Group pressures can have a major influence over the behaviour of individual members and their work performance. The activities of the group are associated with the process of leadership (discussed in Chapter 8). The style of leadership adopted by the manager has an important influence on the behaviour of members of the group.

The classical approach to organisation and management tended to ignore the importance of groups and the social factors at work. The ideas of people such as *F. W. Taylor* popularised the concept of the 'rabble hypothesis' and the assumption that people carried out their work, and could be motivated, as solitary individuals unaffected by others. The human relations approach, however, gave recognition to the work organisation as a social organisation and to the importance of the group, and group values and norms, in influencing behaviour at work.

> Human collaboration in work, in primitive and developed societies, has always depended for its perpetuation upon the evolution of a non-logical social code which regulates the relations between persons and their attitudes to one another.
> *Elton Mayo* [3]

Influences on behaviour at work

The power of group membership over individual behaviour and work performance was illustrated clearly in the famous Hawthorne experiments at the Western Electric Company in America,[4] already referred to in Chapter 3.

One experiment involved the observation of a group of 14 men working in the bank wiring room. It may be remembered that the men formed their own sub-groups or cliques, with natural leaders emerging with the consent of the members. Despite a financial incentive scheme where workers could receive more money the more work they did, the group decided on 6000 units a day as a fair level of output. This was well below the level they were capable of producing. Group pressures on individual workers were stronger than financial incentives offered by management.

Group values and norms

The group developed its own pattern of informal social relations and codes and practices ('norms') of what constituted proper group behaviour.

- **Not to be a 'rate buster'** – not to produce at too high a rate of output compared with other members or to exceed the production restriction of the group.
- **Not to be a 'chiseller'** – not to shirk production or to produce at too low a rate of output compared with other members of the group.
- **Not to be a 'squealer'** – not to say anything to the supervisor or management which might be harmful to other members of the group.
- **Not to be 'officious'** – people with authority over members of the group, for example inspectors, should not take advantage of their seniority or maintain a social distance from the group.

The group had their own system of sanctions including sarcasm, damaging completed work, hiding tools, playing tricks on the inspectors, and ostracising those members who did not conform with the **group norms**. Threats of physical violence were also made, and the group developed a system of punishing offenders by 'binging' which involved striking someone a fairly hard blow on the upper part of the arm. This process of binging also became a recognised method of controlling conflict within the group.

Another finding of the bank wiring room experiment was that the group did not follow company policy on the reporting of production figures. It was company policy that each man's output should be reported daily by the supervisor. However, the workers preferred to do their own reporting, and in order to remain in favour with the group the supervisor acquiesced to this procedure. On some days the men would actually produce more than they reported to 'build up' extra units for those days when they produced less than reported. Although actual production varied the group reported a relatively standard amount of output for each day. The men would also exchange jobs with each other even though this was contrary to management instructions.

A 'summary outline' of group norms is presented in Figure 13.1.

Socio-technical system

The systems approach to organisation and management also gave recognition to the importance of groups in influencing behaviour at work. The concept of the organisation as a socio-technical system is concerned with the interactions between the psychological and social factors, as well as structural and technical requirements. Again, it may be remembered that technological change in the coal-mining industry had brought about changes in the social groupings of the miners.[5]

New methods of working disrupted the integration of small self-selecting groups of miners who worked together as independent teams. The change had undesirable social effects and as a result the new method did not prove as economically beneficial as it should have done with the new technology. The result was a 'composite' method of working with more responsibility taken by the team as a whole. The composite method proved to be not only more rewarding socially to the miners but also more efficient economically than the previous new method of working. (The importance of autonomous work groups or teams as a feature of job design is discussed in Chapter 18.)

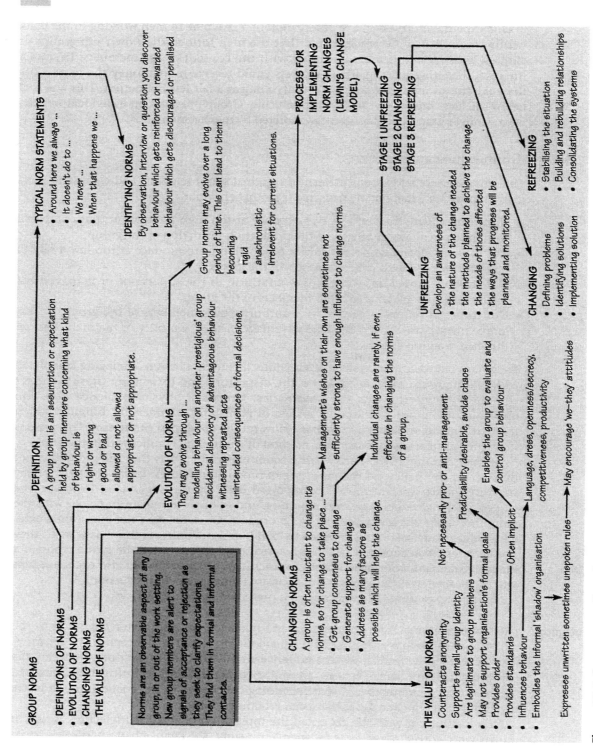

Figure 13.1 Summary outline of group norms

(Reproduced with permission of Training Learning Consultancy Ltd, Bristol.)

The importance of teamwork

How people behave and perform as members of a group is as important as their behaviour or performance as individuals. Not only must members of a group work well as a team but each group must also work well with other groups. Harmonious working relationships and good teamwork help make for a high level of staff morale and work performance. Effective teamwork is an essential element of modern management practices such as empowerment, quality circles and total quality management, and how groups manage change. Teamwork is important in any organisation but may be especially significant in service industries, such as hospitality organisations where there is a direct effect on customer satisfaction.[6]

According to ACAS (the Arbitration, Conciliation and Advisory Service), teams have been around for as long as anyone can remember and there can be few organisations that have not used the term in one sense or another. In a general sense, people talk of teamwork when they want to emphasise the virtues of co-operation and the need to make use of the various strengths of employees.

Using the term more specifically, teamworking involves a reorganisation of the way work is carried out. Teamwork can increase competitiveness by:

- improving productivity;
- improving quality and encouraging innovation;
- taking advantage of the opportunities provided by technological advances;
- improving employee motivation and commitment.[7]

An account of teamwork in a small (40-person) company is given in the Appendix to this chapter.

The general movement towards flatter structures of organisation, wider spans of control and reducing layers of middle management, together with increasing empowerment of employees, all involve greater emphasis on the importance of effective teamworking.

From a recent study of Europe's top companies, *Heller* refers to the need for new managers and new methods, and includes as a key strategy for a new breed of managers in a dramatically changed environment: 'making team-working work – the new, indispensable skill'.[8] The nature and importance of teamwork is discussed further in Chapter 14.

> All of us know in our hearts that the ideal individual for a given job cannot be found ... but if no individual can combine all the necessary qualities of a good manager, a *team* of individuals certainly can – and often does. Moreover, the whole team is unlikely to step under a bus simultaneously. This is why it is not the individual but the team that is the instrument of sustained and enduring success in management.
> *Antony Jay*[9]
>
> A successful climbing team involves using management skills essential to any organisation ... The basic planning is the foundation on which the eventual outcome will be decided. Even if it is the concept of a single person, very quickly more and more people must become involved, and this is where teamwork and leadership begin.
> *Sir Chris Bonington*[10]

Happy teams at Heineken

Included in a study of top European companies and 'making teamwork work', Heller refers to the happy teams at Heineken. As part of the cultural strength of Heineken is a realisation that: 'the best culture for an organisation is a team culture'; and that 'any large organization is a team of teams – and people who have to work together as a team must also think together as a team'.[11] Heller also lists Heineken's manifesto for 'professional team-thinking' (*see* Figure 13.2) and maintains that 'Arguing with any of these eleven points is absurd'.

1. The aim is to reach the best decision, not just a hasty conclusion or an easy consensus. The team leader always has the ultimate responsibility for the quality of the decision taken – and therefore, for the quality of the team-thinking effort that has led up to the decision.

2. To produce the best professional team-thinking, the team leader must ensure that ego-trips, petty office politics and not-invented-here rigidity are explicitly avoided. There should be competition between ideas – not between individual members of the team.

3. The team-thinking effort must first ensure that the best question to be answered is clearly and completely formulated.

4. The team-thinking process is iterative – not linear. Therefore, the question may have to be altered later and the process repeated.

5. The team leader is responsible for seeing that sufficient alternatives and their predicted consequences have been developed for evaluation by the team.

6. The team leader will thus ask 'what are our alternatives?' – and not just 'what is the answer?'

7. The team leader also recognizes that it is wiser to seek and listen to the ideas of the team before expressing his or her own ideas and preferences.

8. In any professional team-thinking effort, more ideas will have to be created than used. But any idea that is rejected will be rejected with courtesy and with a clear explanation as to why it is being rejected. To behave in this way is not naive, it is just decent and smart.

9. A risk/reward equation and a probability of success calculation will be made explicitly before any important decision is taken.

10. Once a decision is made professionally, the team must implement it professionally.

11. When you think, think. When you act, act.

Figure 13.2 Manifesto for professional team-thinking at Heineken

(Reproduced with permission from Robert Heller, *In Search of European Excellence*, HarperCollins Business © 1997, p. 231.)

Exhibit 13.1

Teamwork's own goal

FT

There are limitations to the application of teamwork methods in the workplace writes **Victoria Griffith.**

Teamwork has become a buzzword of 1990s' management theory. By grouping employees into problem-solving taskforces, say the theorists, companies will empower workers, create cross-departmental fertilisation, and level ineffective hierarchies.

Yet executives know that, in reality, teams and taskforces do not always produce the desired results. Part of the problem may lie with the way teams are organised. Members may fail to work well together for several reasons, from lack of a sense of humour to clashing goals.

Academics in the US have been studying team dynamics to try to identify problems.

Too much emphasis on harmony

Teams probably work best when there is room for disagreement. Michael Beer, a professor at Harvard Business School, says: 'Team leaders often discourage discord because they fear it will split the team.' He studied teams at Becton Dickinson, the medical equipment group, in the 1980s, and found that efforts to paper over differences sometimes led to bland recommendations by task-forces.

One working group at the company, for example, said the division's overall strategic objective was 'fortifying our quality, product cost, and market share strengths, while also transforming the industry through expanded customer knowledge and product/service innovation'. The group, says Beer, offered no organisation guidance as to which factor was more important and why.

Too much discord

Excessive tension can also destroy team effectiveness. A study published in the *Harvard Business Review* in June 1997 found that corporate team members disagreed less and were more productive when everyone had access to up-to-date information. Conflict arising from misinformation tended to escalate into interpersonal resentment.

Jean Kahwajy, a management consultant with the California-based Strategic Decision Group and an author of the *HBR* study, says: 'Nasty fights mean there will be too much politicking and wasted time.' The study recommended that team members prepare for meetings by focusing on the facts. All members should have detailed knowledge of the issues at hand and work with the same information.

An emphasis on individualism

Teams failed to deliver desired results at Apple Computer in the 1980s, says Beer, because of the emphasis the company placed early in its existence on individualism. While individual creativity served the company well in its initial phase, growth heightened the need for communication between employees.

Workers were assigned to cross-functional teams to set corporate strategy. It did not work, according to Beer, and the failure of Apple's research and development, marketing and manufacturing departments to work together undermined the corporation. 'When the dominant culture stresses the value of individual achievement and accountability, rather than collective accomplishment, team structures won't be effective,' he says.

Even companies that value collective efforts may undermine teams by basing salaries and promotion more on individual than on collective accomplishments. 'Unless the team's success is important to the employees' career, they probably won't pay much attention to it,' says Kahwajy.

A feeling of powerlessness

To work well, teams must be able to influence decisions. Jay Bourgeois, a professor at the University of Virginia's business school and co-author of the recent *HBR* article, says: 'The team that has no power ends up writing a meaningless memo. You can only do that so many times before your workers decide it's not worthwhile.' Empowerment can help convince reluctant members of the importance of a project. When Unifi, a company that guarantees fax delivery, asked employees to form a team to set out Internet strategy, initial reluctance was eventually overcome when it was made clear that the group was helping to form corporate strategy.

The failure of senior management to work well together

This creates problems because team members may walk into meetings with different priorities. 'Teams can't sort out problems that have been created at a higher level,' says Beer. 'Members can be expected to be loyal to their bosses, and if their bosses have very different priorities, there will be little common ground.'

Meeting-itis

Teams should not try to do everything together. Excessive time spent in meetings not only means wasted hours, it also means the group will be exposed to less diversity of thought. 'If everyone goes in with prepared thoughts and ideas, developed on their own, discussion will be lively, and the group will have more options,' says Kahwajy. 'If everything is done together, a couple of lead people may end up running the show.' Kahwajy warns that too much homogeneity in teams can also stifle creativity.

Seeing teams as the solution for all problems

Bourgeois says he is working with a corporation that expects its country managers – who are scattered all over the world – to work as a team. 'They have very little contact and they don't share the same goal, except in the very vague sense of serving the same corporation,' says Bourgeois. 'It's silly to see them as a team.' Moreover, there are probably some tasks that are more readily accomplished by individuals, rather than groups. 'You probably don't want to have a group decision when you're landing an aircraft at Heathrow,' he says. 'Sometimes a project is best carried out by a single person.'

The difference between groups and teams

Whereas all teams are, by definition, groups it does not necessarily follow that all groups are teams. In common usage and literature, including to some extent in this book, there is however a tendency for the terms 'groups' and 'teams' to be used interchangeably. And it is not easy to distinguish clearly between a group and a team.[12] For example, *Crainer* refers to 'teamworking' as becoming highly fashionable in recent years. It is a side effect of increasing concentration on working across functional divides and fits neatly with the trend towards empowerment. However, despite the extensive literature about teams and teamworking, the basic dynamics of teamworking often remain clouded and uncertain.

> *Teams occur when a number of people have a common goal and recognize that their personal success is dependent on the success of others. They are all interdependent. In practice, this means that in most teams people will contribute individual skills many of which will be different. It also means that the full tensions and counter-balance of human behaviour will need to be demonstrated in the team.*[13]

Belbin points out that to the extent that teamwork was becoming a fashionable term, it began to replace the more usual reference to groups and every activity was now being described as 'teamwork'. He questions whether it matters if one is talking about groups or teams and maintains that the confusion in vocabulary should be addressed if the principles of good teamwork are to be retained. Belbin suggests there are several factors that characterise the difference between groups and teams. (*See* Figure 13.3.) The best differentiator is size: groups can comprise any number of people but teams are smaller with a membership between (ideally) four to six. The quintessential feature of a small well-balanced team is that leadership is shared or rotates whereas large groups typically throw up solo leaders.[14]

(While acknowledging the work of Belbin we continue to refer to 'group' or 'team' according to the particular attention of focus and the vocabulary of the quoted authors.)

	Team	Group
Size	Limited	Medium or Large
Selection	Crucial	Immaterial
Leadership	Shared or rotating	Solo
Perception	Mutual knowledge understanding	Focus on leader
Style	Role spread co-ordination	Convergence conformism
Spirit	Dynamic interaction	Togetherness persecution of opponents

Figure 13.3 Differences between a team and a group

(Reproduced with permission from R. Meredith Belbin, *Beyond the Team*, Butterworth-Heinemann, Division of Reed Educational and Professional Publishing Ltd, © 2000.)

Formal and informal groups

Groups are formed as a consequence of the pattern of organisation structure and arrangements for the division of work, for example the grouping together of common activities into sections. Groups may result from the nature of technology employed and the way in which work is carried out, for example the bringing together of a number of people to carry out a sequence of operations on an assembly line. Groups may also develop when a number of people of the same level or status within the organisation see themselves as a group, for example departmental heads of an industrial organisation, or chief officers of a local authority.

Groups are deliberately planned and created by management as part of the formal organisation structure. However, groups will also arise from social processes and the informal organisation which was discussed in Chapter 4. The informal organisation arises from the interaction of people working within the organisation and the development of groups with their own relationships and norms of behaviour, irrespective of those defined within the formal structure. This leads to a major distinction between formal and informal groups.

Formal groups

Formal groups are created to achieve specific organisational objectives and are concerned with the **co-ordination of work activities**.

People are brought together on the basis of defined roles within the structure of the organisation. The nature of the tasks to be undertaken is a predominant feature of the formal group. Goals are identified by management, and certain rules, relationships and norms of behaviour established.

Formal groups tend to be relatively permanent, although there may be changes in actual membership. However, temporary formal groups may also be created by management, for example the use of project teams in a matrix organisation.

Formal work groups can be differentiated in a number of ways, for example on the basis of membership, the task to be performed, the nature of technology, or position within the organisation structure.

Informal groups

Within the formal structure of the organisation there will always be an informal structure. The formal structure of the organisation, and system of role relationships, rules and procedures, will be augmented by interpretation and development at the informal level. **Informal groups** are based more on personal relationships and agreement of group members than on defined role relationships. They serve to satisfy psychological and social needs not related necessarily to the tasks to be undertaken. Groups may devise ways of attempting to satisfy members' affiliation and other social motivations which are lacking in the work situation, especially in industrial organisations.

The membership of informal groups can cut across the formal structure. They may comprise individuals from different parts of the organisation and/or from different levels of the organisation, both vertically and diagonally, as well as from the same horizontal level. An informal group could also be the same as the formal group, or it might comprise a part only of the formal group. (*See* Figure 13.4.)

The members of an informal group may appoint their own leader who exercises authority by the consent of the members themselves. The informal leader may be chosen as the person who reflects the attitudes and values of the members, helps to resolve conflict, leads the group in satisfying its goals, or liaises with management or other people outside the group. The informal leader may often change according to the particular situation facing the group. Although not usually the case, it is possible for the informal leader to be the same person as the formal leader appointed officially by management.

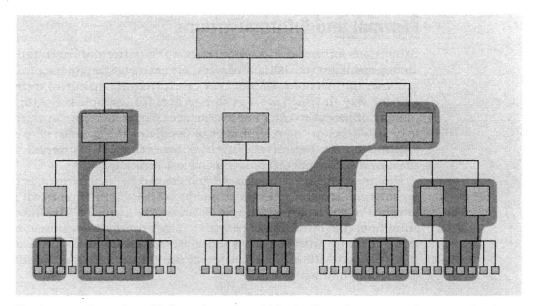

Figure 13.4 Examples of informal groups within the formal structure of an organisation

An example of informal groups

A lack of direction and clear information flow within the formal structure can give rise to uncertainty and suspicion. In the absence of specific knowledge, the grapevine takes on an important role, rumours start and the informal part of the organisation is highlighted, often with negative results. A typical example concerned an industrial organisation which was in a highly competitive market and was experiencing a drop in sales. Two top managers had suddenly lost their jobs without any explanation to members of staff and there were board meetings seemingly every other day. Although there was no specific information or statements from top management the general feeling among the staff was that whatever was about to happen it was most unlikely to be good news.

At lunchtime three junior members of staff, one female and two male, each from different departments, were having a chat. With a half smile the female member said to the others that she could well be seeing a lot more of both or at least one of them before long. She said that she had heard, unofficially, from her manager that the department was about to be awarded a very profitable order. She surmised that the other departments, which she had also heard had lost their parts of the same contracts and not had many orders recently, would have to integrate into the successful department with the possible loss of certain jobs. The other two members both believed this and talked about it within their own departments as if it were a fact. The result? Even more uncertainty throughout the organisation, increased gloom and distraction from the task. In fact, no such integration did take place, only a minor restructuring of the organisation with no direct loss of jobs other than through voluntary early retirement. However, it proved very difficult for top management to effectively quash the rumour and restore trust and morale.

Reasons for formation of groups

Individuals will form into groups, both formal and informal, for a number of different reasons relating to both work performance and social processes.

● **Certain tasks can be performed only through the combined efforts of a number of individuals working together.** The variety of experience and expertise among members of the group provides a synergetic effect which can be applied to the increasingly complex problems of modern organisations.

- **Groups may encourage collusion between members** in order to modify formal working arrangements more to their liking – for example, by sharing or rotating unpopular tasks. Group membership therefore provides the individual with opportunities for initiative and creativity.
- **Groups provide companionship and a source of mutual understanding and support from colleagues.** This can help in solving work problems, and also to mitigate against stressful or demanding working conditions.
- **Membership of the group provides the individual with a sense of belonging.** The group provides a feeling of identity, and the chance to acquire role recognition and status within the group.
- **The group provides guidelines on generally acceptable behaviour.** It helps to clarify ambiguous situations such as, for example, the extent to which official rules and regulations are expected to be adhered to in practice, the rules of the game, and what is seen as the correct actual behaviour. The informal organisation may put pressure on group members to resist demands from management on such matters as, for example, higher output or changes in working methods. Group allegiance can serve as a means of control over individual behaviour. The group may discipline individuals who contravene the norms of the group – for example, the process of 'binging' in the bank wiring room, mentioned above.
- **The group may provide protection for its membership.** Group members collaborate to protect their interests from outside pressures or threats.

Major functions of informal groups

Lysons suggests four main reasons why people form informal groups.

- **The perpetuation of the informal group 'culture'.** Culture in this context means a set of values, norms and beliefs which form a guide to group acceptance and group behaviour. Unless you broadly subscribe to the group culture, you will not belong and be an 'outsider' or 'isolate'.
- **The maintenance of a communication system.** Groups want all the information that affect their welfare, either negatively or positively. If groups are not appraised of policies and motives behind actions, they will seek to tap into formal communication channels and spread information among group members.
- **The implementation of social control.** Conformity to group culture is enforced by such techniques as ridicule, ostracism and violence. This is illustrated, for example, by the enforcement of group norms in the Bank Wiring Room discussed above.
- **The provision of interest and fun in work life.** Many jobs are monotonous and fail to hold the attention of the workers. Work may also offer few future prospects. Workers may try to compensate by interpersonal relations provided by the group and in such activities as time wasting by talking, gambling, practical joking and drinking.[15]

Expectations of group membership

Individuals have varying expectations of the benefits from group membership. Groups are a potential source of motivation and of job satisfaction, and also a major determinant of effective organisational performance. However, working in groups may mean that members spend too much time talking among themselves rather than doing. Groups may also compete against each other in a non-productive manner. It is a question of balance. It is important, therefore, that the manager understands the reasons for the formation of groups and is able to recognise likely advantageous or adverse consequences for the organisation.

Understanding and Managing People at Work

Group cohesiveness and performance

Social interaction is a natural feature of human behaviour but ensuring harmonious working relationships and effective teamwork is not an easy task. The manager's main concern is that members of a work group co-operate in order to achieve the results expected of them.

Although there are potential disadvantages of cohesive groups (discussed below) they may result in greater interaction between members, mutual help and social satisfaction, lower turnover and absenteeism, and often higher production.[16] Co-operation among members is likely to be greater in a united, cohesive group. Membership of a cohesive group can be a rewarding experience for the individual, can contribute to the promotion of morale, and aid the release of creativity and energy. Members of a high-morale group are more likely to think of themselves as a group and work together effectively. **Strong and cohesive work groups can, therefore, have beneficial effects for the organisation.**

Factors affecting cohesiveness

In order to develop the effectiveness of work groups the manager will be concerned with those factors that contribute to group cohesiveness, or that may cause frustration or disruption to the operation of the group.

The manager needs to consider, therefore, both the needs of individual members of staff, and the promotion of a high level of group identity and cohesion.

There are many factors which affect **group cohesiveness** and performance, which can be summarised under four broad headings, as shown in Figure 13.5.

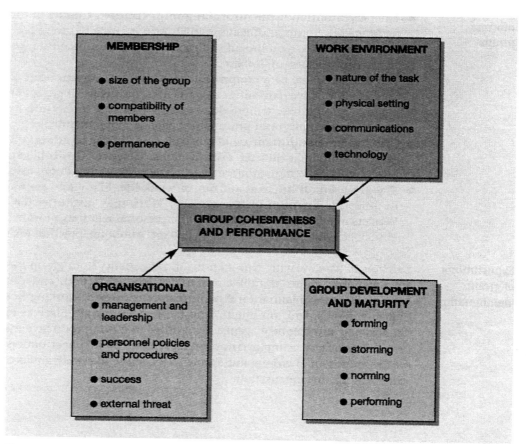

Figure 13.5 Factors contributing to group cohesiveness and performance

Membership

Size of the group

As a group increases in size, problems arise with communications and co-ordination. Large groups are more difficult to handle and require a higher level of supervision. Absenteeism also tends to be higher in larger groups. When a group becomes too large it may split into smaller units and friction may develop between the sub-groups.

It is difficult to put a precise figure on the ideal size of a work group and there are many conflicting studies and reports. Much will depend upon other variables, but it seems to be generally accepted that cohesiveness becomes more difficult to achieve when a group exceeds 10–12 members.[17] Beyond this size the group tends to split into sub-groups. A figure of between five and seven is often quoted as an apparent optimum size for full participation within the group.[18]

One particular feature of size the concept of **social loafing** and the 'Ringlemann effect' which is the tendency for individuals to expend less effort when working as a member of a group than as an individual. A German psychologist, *Ringlemann*, compared the results of individual and group performance on a rope-pulling task. Workers were asked to pull as hard as they could on a rope, performing the task first individually and then with others in groups of varying size. A meter measured the strength of each pull. Although the total amount of force did increase with the size of the work group, the effort expended by each individual member decreased with the result that the total group effort was less than the expected sum of the individual contributions.[19] Replications of the Ringlemann effect have generally been supportive of the original findings.[20]

Compatibility of the members

The more homogeneous the group in terms of such features as shared backgrounds, interests, attitudes and values of its members, the easier it is usually to promote cohesiveness. Variations in other individual differences, such as the personality or skills of members, may serve to complement each other and help make for a cohesive group. On the other hand, such differences may be the cause of disruption and conflict. Conflict can also arise in a homogeneous group where members are in competition with each other. Individual incentive payment schemes, for example, may be a source of conflict.

Permanence of group members

Group spirit and relationships take time to develop. Cohesiveness is more likely when members of a group are together for a reasonable length of time, and changes occur only slowly. A frequent turnover of members is likely to have an adverse effect on morale, and on the cohesiveness of the group.

Work environment

The nature of the task

Where workers are involved in similar work, share a common task, or face the same problems, this may assist cohesiveness. The nature of the task may serve to bring people together when it is necessary for them to communicate and interact regularly with each other in the performance of their duties – for example, members of a research and development team.

Even if members of a group normally work at different locations they may still experience a feeling of cohesiveness if the nature of the task requires frequent communication and interaction – for example, security guards patrolling separate areas who need to check with each other on a regular basis. However, where the task demands a series of relatively separate operations or discrete activities – for example, on a machine-paced assembly line – it is more difficult to develop cohesiveness. Individuals may have interactions with colleagues on either side of them but little opportunity to develop a common group feeling.

Understanding and Managing People at Work

Physical setting	Where members of a group work in the same location or in close physical proximity to each other this will generally help cohesiveness. However, this is not always the case. For example, in large open-plan offices staff often tend to segregate themselves from colleagues and create barriers by the strategic siting of such items as filing cabinets, bookcases or indoor plants. The size of the office and the number of staff in it are, of course, important considerations in this case. Isolation from other groups of workers will also tend to build cohesiveness. This often applies, for example, to a smaller number of workers on a night shift.
Communications	The more easily members can communicate freely with each other, the greater the likelihood of group cohesiveness. Communications are affected by the work environment, by the nature of the task, and by technology. For example, difficulties in communication can arise with production systems where workers are stationed continuously at a particular point with limited freedom of movement. Even when opportunities exist for interaction with colleagues, physical conditions may limit effective communication. For example, the technological layout and high level of noise with some assembly line work can limit contact between workers. Restrictions on opportunities for social interaction can hamper internal group unity.
Technology	We can see that the nature of technology and the manner in which work is carried out has an important effect on cohesiveness, and relates closely to the nature of the task, physical setting and communications. Where the nature of the work process involves a craft or skill-based 'technology' there is a higher likelihood of group cohesiveness. However, as mentioned earlier, with machine-paced assembly line work it is more difficult to develop cohesiveness. Technology also has wider implications for the operation and behaviour of groups and therefore is considered in a separate section later.

Organisational factors

Management and leadership	The activities of groups cannot be separated from management and the process of leadership. The form of management and style of leadership adopted will influence the relationship between the group and the organisation, and is a major determinant of group cohesiveness. In general terms, cohesiveness will be affected by such things as the manner in which the manager gives guidance and encouragement to the group, offers help and support, provides opportunities for participation, attempts to resolve conflicts, and gives attention to both employee relations and task problems.
Personnel policies and procedures	Harmony and cohesiveness within the group are more likely to be achieved if personnel policies and procedures are well developed, and perceived to be equitable with fair treatment for all members. Attention should be given to the effects that appraisal systems, discipline, promotion and rewards, and opportunities for personal development have on members of the group.
Success	The more successful the group, the more cohesive it is likely to be; and cohesive groups are more likely to be successful. Success is usually a strong motivational influence on the level of work performance. Success or reward as a positive motivator can be perceived by group members in a number of ways. For example, the satisfactory completion of a task through co-operative action; praise from management; a feeling of high status; achievement in competition with other groups; benefits gained, such as high wage payments from a group bonus incentive scheme.
External threat	Cohesiveness may be enhanced by members co-operating with one another when faced with a common external threat, such as changes in their method of work, or the

appointment of a new manager. Even if the threat is subsequently removed, the group may still continue to have a greater degree of cohesiveness than before the threat arose. Conflict between groups will also tend to increase the cohesiveness of each group and the boundaries of the group become drawn more clearly.

Group development and maturity

The degree of cohesiveness is affected also by the manner in which groups progress through the various stages of development and maturity. *Bass and Ryterband* identify four distinct stages in group development:

- mutual acceptance and membership;
- communication and decision-making;
- motivation and productivity; and
- control and organisation.[21]

An alternative, and more popular, model by *Tuckman* also identifies four main successive stages of group development and relationships: **forming**, **storming**, **norming** and **performing**.[22]

- **Stage 1 – forming**. The initial formation of the group and the bringing together of a number of individuals who identify, tentatively, the purpose of the group, its composition and terms of reference. At this stage consideration is given to hierarchical structure of the group, pattern of leadership, individual roles and responsibilities, and codes of conduct. There is likely to be considerable anxiety as members attempt to create an impression, to test each other, and to establish their personal identity within the group.
- **Stage 2 – storming**. As members of the group get to know each other better they will put forward their views more openly and forcefully. Disagreements will be expressed and challenges offered on the nature of the task and arrangements made in the earlier stage of development. This may lead to conflict and hostility. The storming stage is important because, if successful, there will be discussions on reforming arrangements for the working and operation of the group, and agreement on more meaningful structures and procedures.
- **Stage 3 – norming**. As conflict and hostility start to be controlled members of the group will establish guidelines and standards, and develop their own norms of acceptable behaviour. The norming stage is important in establishing the need for members to co-operate in order to plan, agree standards of performance and fulfil the purpose of the group. This co-operation and adherence to group norms can work against effective organisational performance. It may be remembered, for example, that, in the bank wiring room experiment of the Hawthorne studies, group norms imposed a restriction on the level of output of the workers.
- **Stage 4 – performing**. When the group has progressed successfully through the three earlier stages of development it will have created structure and cohesiveness to work effectively as a team. At this stage the group can concentrate on the attainment of its purpose and performance of the common task is likely to be at its most effective.

Another writer suggests that new groups go through the following stages:

- the polite stage;
- the why are we here, what are we doing stage?
- the power stage, which dominant will emerge?
- the constructive stage when sharing begins; and
- the unity stage – this often takes weeks, eating together, talking together.[23]

Understanding and Managing People at Work

Potential disadvantages of strong, cohesive groups

If the manager is to develop effective work groups then attention should be given to those factors which influence the creation of group identity and cohesiveness. However, strong and cohesive groups also present potential disadvantages for management. Cohesive groups do not necessarily produce a higher level of output. Performance varies with the extent to which the group accepts or rejects the goals of the organisation. Furthermore, with a very high level of cohesiveness and attention to social activities, there may even be a fall in output. The level of production is likely to conform to a standard acceptable as a norm by the group and may result in maintaining either a high or a restricted level of output.[24]

Individual differences in personality mean that people make a contribution to the work of the organisation in different ways and this influences the extent to which they wish to be committed to a group or team culture. For example, as *Green* points out: 'Some people find teamwork contrary to their normal style and are embarrassed; some are probably marginalised.'[25]

People also have a greater or lesser need for personal space and their own sense of individual identity.

Everyone had at least a handful of items they preferred to keep private: love letters, photographs, mementoes, a personal journal, whatever. Nothing shameful was likely to be hidden in the lockers ... The purpose of the lockers was merely to maintain a totally personal space as a way to preserve each person's necessary sense of identity in a claustrophobic and communal environment where, in time, it was easy to feel absorbed into a group identity and thereby become psychologically disassociated and quietly depressed.

Dean Koontz [26]

Once a group has become fully developed and created cohesiveness, it is more difficult for the manager successfully to change the attitudes and behaviour of the group. It is important that the manager should attempt to influence the group during the norming stage when members are establishing guidelines and standards, and their own norms of acceptable behaviour. When a group has become fully developed and established its own culture it is more difficult to change the attitudes and behaviour of its members.

Inter-group conflict

Strong, cohesive groups may develop a critical or even hostile attitude towards people outside the group or members of other groups. This can be the case, for example, when group cohesiveness is based on common status, qualifications, technical expertise or professional standing. Group cohesiveness may result in lack of co-operation with, or opposition to, non-members. As a result, resentment and inter-group conflict may arise to the detriment of the organisation as a whole.

In order to help prevent, or overcome, unconstructive inter-group conflict, the manager should attempt to stimulate a high level of communication and interaction between the groups, and to maintain harmony. Rotation of members among different groups should be encouraged.

On the other hand, inter-group rivalry may be deliberately encouraged as a means of building stronger within-group cohesiveness.[27] The idea is that a competitive element may help to promote unity within a group. However, inter-group rivalry and competition need to be carefully handled by the manager. Groups should not normally be put in a situation where they have to compete for resources, status or approval.[28]

The manager should attempt to avoid the development of 'win–lose' situations. Emphasis should be placed on overall objectives of the organisation and on superordinate goals. These are goals over and above the issues at conflict and which, if they are to be achieved, require the co-operation of the competing groups.

Characteristics of an effective work group

The characteristics of an effective work group are not always easy to isolate clearly. The underlying feature is a spirit of co-operation in which members work well together as a united team, and with harmonious and supportive relationships. This may be evidenced when members of a group exhibit:

- a belief in shared aims and objectives;
- a sense of commitment to the group;
- acceptance of group values and norms;
- a feeling of mutual trust and dependency;
- full participation by all members and decision-making by consensus;
- a free flow of information and communications;
- the open expression of feelings and disagreements;
- the resolution of conflict by the members themselves; and
- a lower level of staff turnover, absenteeism, accidents, errors and complaints.

However, as *Brooks* points out, as teams operate at the higher order of group dynamics this list is arguably more reflective of 'effective **work teams** rather than work groups and this is how it should be – these are teams not groups'.[29]

Understanding group behaviour

The effective management of work groups requires an understanding of the psychological and social influences on behaviour within organisations. *Allcorn* distinguishes between defensive and non-defensive work groups, and provides a typology based on four differing sets of culture.[30]

- Homogenised
- Institutionalised
- Autocratic

Defensive groups. They provide collective and individual defences against anxiety that results from group membership.

- Intentional

Non-defensive group. Deals with group participation in a non-defensive way. The type of group that is desirable in the workplace.

Changing the culture of a group

Attempting to change the culture of a defensive group into that of an intentional group in not easy. The intervention strategy is likely to be perceived as threatening to members of the group. Allcorn suggests that successful intervention involves the comparisons of perceptions and understandings in order to provide a thoughtful summary of the group's perceptions which is accepted by the members. This requires sensitivity to the anxiety of group members and the forces that mitigate against change. Members need to understand the actions associated with the intentional group as a basis for establishing and maintaining an intentional culture.

Allcorn reminds us that 'individual and group behaviour is highly complex, difficult to understand and even more difficult to manage'. It is important to further develop group-process skills.

The analysis of behaviour in groups, group processes and group dynamics are discussed in Chapter 14.

The effects of technology on work groups

The nature of technology and the work flow system of the organisation is a major determinant of the operation of groups, and the attitude and behaviour of their members. Low morale and a negative attitude towards management and the job are often associated with a large number of workers undertaking similar work. A number of different early studies have drawn attention to the relationship between technology and work groups.[31]

The nature of technology and the work organisation can result in a feeling of alienation, especially among manual workers. Factors which have been shown to affect alienation include the extent to which the work of the individual or the group amounts to a meaningful part of the total production process, and the satisfaction which workers gain from relationships with fellow workers and group membership.

In a study of assembly line and other factory work, *Goldthorpe* found that the technology was unfavourable for the creation of work groups.[32] However, he also found a group of workers who, although alienated, were still satisfied. Membership of a meaningful work group was not necessarily an important source of job satisfaction. The workers, all married men, aged between 21 and 46, were not interested in maintaining close relationships with fellow workers or supervisors. Their earnings were well in excess of the average manual wage at the time – they were 'affluent' workers.

Goldthorpe recognised, however, that in other situations where there is the opportunity for teamwork, the workers will have greater social expectations and the membership of work groups may be very important to them.

Technology and group behaviour

Technology is clearly a major influence on the pattern of group operation and behaviour. The work organisation may limit the opportunities for social interaction and the extent to which individuals are able to identify themselves as members of a cohesive work group. This in turn can have possible adverse effects on attitudes to work and the level of job satisfaction. In many assembly line production systems, for example, relationships between individual workers are determined by the nature of the task, the extent to which individual jobs are specified, and the time cycle of operations.

In recent years there have been attempts to remove some of the alienating aspects of mass production and assembly line work by increasing the range of tasks and responsibility allocated to small groups. These attempts include greater use of self-regulating work groups and of group technology.[33]

Group technology involves changes to the work flow system of production. With the traditional 'functional layout' of production, lines of similar machines or operations are arranged together so that components are passed back and forth until all activities are completed. However, with 'group technology' production, the work flow system is based on a grouping of workers and a range of machines. This enables work groups to perform series of successive operations using a group of machines on a family of similar components.

Impact of information technology

You may recall from our discussion in Chapter 4 that the impact of information technology demands new patterns of work organisation, and affects the formation and structure of groups. It will influence where and how people interact. Movement away from large-scale centralised organisation to smaller working units can help create an environment in which workers may relate more easily to each other. Improvements in telecommunications mean, for example, that support staff need no longer be located within the main production unit. On the other hand, modern methods of communication mean that individuals may work more on their own, from their own homes, shared offices or hotels, or work more with machines than with other people.[34]

Role relationships

In order that the organisation can achieve its goals and objectives, the work of individual members must be linked into coherent patterns of activities and relationships. This is achieved through the 'role structure' of the organisation.

A 'role' is the expected pattern of behaviours associated with members occupying a particular position within the structure of the organisation. It also describes how a person perceives their own situation.

The concept of '**role**' is important to the functioning of groups and for an understanding of group processes and behaviour. It is through role differentiation that the structure of the work group and relationships among its members are established. The development of the group entails the identification of distinct roles for each of its members. Some form of structure is necessary for teamwork and co-operation. The concept of roles helps to clarify the structure and to define the pattern of complex relationships within the group.

The formal organisational relationships (line, functional, staff or lateral) – discussed later in Chapter 15 – can be seen as forms of role relationships. These individual authority relationships determine the pattern of interaction with other roles.

The role, or roles, that the individual plays within the group is influenced by a combination of:

● **situational factors**, such as the requirements of the task, the style of leadership, position in the communication network; and
● **personal factors** such as values, attitudes, motivation, ability and personality.

The role that a person plays in one work group may be quite different from the role that person plays in other work groups. However, everyone within a group is expected to behave in a particular manner and to fulfil certain role expectations.

A person's role-set

In addition to the role relationships with members of their own group – peers, superiors, subordinates – the individual will have a number of role-related relationships with outsiders – for example, members of other work groups, trade union officials, suppliers, consumers. This is **a person's 'role-set'**. The role-set comprises the range of associations or contacts with whom the individual has meaningful interactions in connection with the performance of their role. (*See* Figure 13.6.)

Role incongruence

An important feature of role relationship is the concept of '**role incongruence**'. This arises when a member of staff is perceived as having a high and responsible position in one respect but a low standing in another respect. Difficulties with role incongruence can arise from the nature of groupings and formal relationships within the structure of the organisation. There are a number of work-related relationships, such as doctor and nurse or senior manager and personal assistant, which can give rise to a potential imbalance of authority and responsibility.

A classic account of role incongruence can be seen in *Whyte's* study of the American restaurant industry.[35] The chefs, who regarded themselves as of high status and were generally recognised as such by the staff, resented being 'told' what to do by the waiting staff who were generally regarded to be of lower status. As a result arguments broke out, disrupting performance. The conflict of status was resolved by the introduction of an ordering process by which the chefs received customers' orders without the appearance of taking instructions from the lower status waiting staff.

Difficulties with role incongruence can also arise in line-staff relationships: for instance, a relatively junior member of the personnel department informing a senior departmental manager that a certain proposed action is contrary to the policies of the organisation. Another example with staff relationships is where a person establishes him or herself in the role of 'gatekeeper' to the boss[36] – for instance, where a comparatively junior personal assistant passes on the manager's instructions to one of the manager's more senior subordinates or where the personal assistant attempts to block a more senior member of staff having access to the manager.

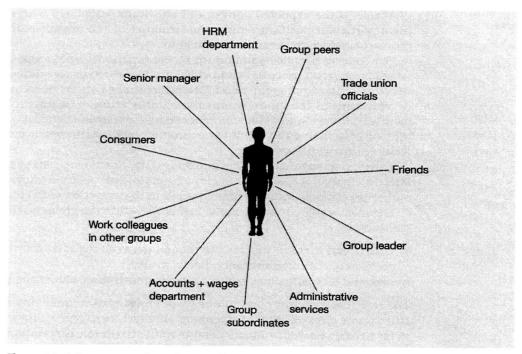

Figure 13.6 Representation of a possible role-set in the work situation

Problems over role incongruence can also lead to the possibility of role stress; this is discussed later in this chapter.

Role expectations

Many **role expectations** are **prescribed formally** and indicate what the person is expected to do and their duties and obligations. Formal role prescriptions provide guidelines for expected behaviours and may be more prevalent in a 'mechanistic' organisation. Examples are written contracts of employment, rules and regulations, standards, policy decisions, job descriptions, or directives from superiors. Formal role expectations may also be derived clearly from the nature of the task. They may, in part at least, be defined legally, for example under the Health and Safety at Work Act, or as with the obligations of a company secretary under the Companies Acts, or the responsibilities of a district auditor under the Local Government Acts.

Not all role expectations are prescribed formally, however. There will be certain patterns of behaviour which although not specified formally will none the less be expected of members. These informal role expectations may be imposed by the group itself or at least communicated to a person by other members of the group. Examples include general conduct, mutual support to co-members, attitudes towards superiors, means of communicating, dress and appearance.

Members may not always be consciously aware of these informal expectations yet they still serve as important determinants of behaviour. Under this heading could be included the concept of a psychological contract which was discussed in Chapter 2. The psychological contract implies a variety of expectations between the individual and the organisation. These expectations cover a range of rights and privileges, duties and obligations which do not form part of a formal agreement but still have an important influence on behaviour.

Some members may have the opportunity to determine their own role expectations, where, for example, formal expectations are specified loosely or only in very general terms. Opportunities for **self-established roles** are more likely in senior positions, but also occur within certain professional, technical or scientific groups, or where there is a demand for creativity or artistic flair. Such opportunities may be greater within an 'organic' organisation and will also be influenced by the style of leadership adopted – for example, where a *laissez-faire* approach is adopted.

Role conflict

The concept of role focuses attention on aspects of behaviour existing independently of an individual's personality. Patterns of behaviour result from both the role and the personality. **Role conflict** arises from inadequate or inappropriate role definition and needs to be distinguished from personality clashes. These arise from incompatibility between two or more people as individuals even though their roles may be defined clearly and understood fully.

In practice, the manner in which a person actually behaves may not be consistent with their expected pattern of behaviours. This inconsistency may be a result of role conflict. Role conflict as a generic term can include:

- role incompatibility;
- role ambiguity;
- role overload; and
- role underload.

These are all problem areas associated with the creation of role expectations. (*See* Figure 13.7.)

- **Role incompatibility** arises when a person faces a situation in which simultaneous different or contradictory expectations create inconsistency. Compliance with one set of expectations makes it difficult or impossible to comply with other expectations. The two role expectations are in conflict. A typical example concerns the person 'in the middle', such as the supervisor or section head, who faces opposing expectations from workers and from management.

   Another example might be the situation of a manager who believes in a relaxed, participative style of behaviour more in keeping with a Theory Y approach, but whose superior believes in a Theory X approach and expects the manager to adopt a more formal and directive style of behaviour.

- **Role ambiguity** occurs when there is lack of clarity as to the precise requirements of the role and the person is unsure what to do. The person's own perception of their role may differ from the expectations of others. This implies that insufficient information is available for the adequate performance of the role.

   Role ambiguity may result from a lack of formally prescribed expectations. It is likely to arise in large, diverse groups or at times of constant change. Uncertainty often relates to such matters as the method of performing tasks, the extent of the person's authority and responsibility, standards of work, and the evaluation and appraisal of performance.

- **Role overload** is when a person faces too many separate roles or too great a variety of expectations. The person is unable to meet satisfactorily all expectations and some must be neglected in order to satisfy others. This leads to a conflict of priority.

   Some writers distinguish between role overload and work overload. Role overload is seen in terms of the total role-set, and implies that the person has too many separate roles to handle. Where there are too many expectations of a single role – that is, a problem of quantity – this is work overload.[37]

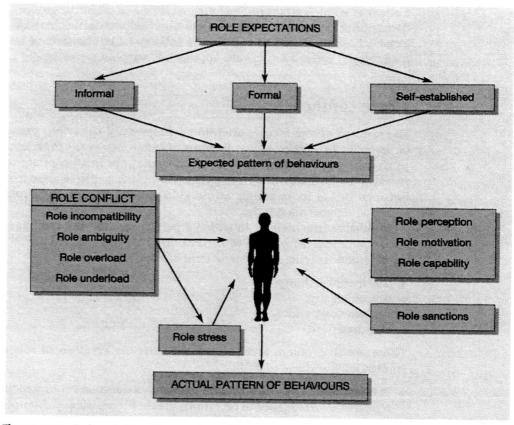

Figure 13.7 Role relationships and conflicts
(*Source*: Adapted from Miner, J. B., *Management Theory*, Macmillan (1971) p. 47.)

- **Role underload** can arise when the prescribed role expectations fall short of the person's own perception of their role. The person may feel their role is not demanding enough and that they have the capacity to undertake a larger or more varied role, or an increased number of roles. Role underload may arise, for example, when a new member of staff is first appointed, or from the initial effects of delegation.

Role conflict and matrix organisation

Problems of role conflict can often arise from the matrix form of organisation (which is discussed in Chapter 15) and, for example, from the use of flexible project teams. Where staff are assigned temporarily, and perhaps on a part-time basis, from other groups this creates a two-way flow of authority and responsibility.

Unless role differentiations are defined clearly this can result in conflicting expectations from the manager of the person's own functional grouping, and from the manager of the project team (role incompatibility). It can also lead to uncertainty about the exact requirements of the part the person is expected to play as a member of the project team (role ambiguity). The combinations of expectations from both managers may also result in role overload.

Role stress

Role conflict can result in role stress. An example of role stress can also be seen in *Whyte's* study of the American restaurant industry (referred to above under role incongruence). A number of waiting staff found the job very stressful and they cried often. One reason for this was the constant conflict between the demands of the customer to be served quickly and pressure from the chefs who were unable to produce the food in time. The waiting staff were caught between two incompatible expectations and were pulled both ways.

A survey conducted among subscribers of *Management Today* reported Britain's managers feeling burdened with increasing levels of pressure and disillusioned by diminishing control over their working lives. Many managers claimed the organisation's culture contributes to their stress and call for a change in working practices. Under considerable stress themselves managers admit to transmitting problems to their staff.[38]

Although a certain amount of stress may **arguably** be seen as a good thing, and especially at managerial level helps to bring out a high level of performance, it is also potentially very harmful. Stress is a source of tension, frustration and dissatisfaction. It can lead to difficulties in communication and interpersonal relationships and can affect morale, effectiveness at work and health.[39]

> Stress is beneficial when we feel challenged and stimulated, but negative if we feel overloaded or understimulated.
>
> Stress can be positive or negative. Some pressure can be a very good thing. The tasks and challenges we face every day can keep us motivated, give us a sense of achievement, and provide job satisfaction. Negative stress is a result of:
>
> - a mismatch between the demands made on us and our real or perceived ability to cope
> - unpleasant over or under stimulation which leads to actual or potential ill-health
> - high demand plus high constraint plus low support
>
> *Hampshire County Council*[40]

Role stress, then, is a major influence on job satisfaction and work performance. It will be discussed further in Chapter 18.

Reducing role conflict and role stress

Greater attention is now given to health problems that are classified as stress-related.[41] There is increasing evidence concerning illnesses, such as cardiovascular diseases, and social problems – for example, marriage breakdowns – which can have stress as a factor. Decreasing efficiency resulting from work stress is also extremely costly to organisations. It is important, therefore, that managers make every effort to minimise the causes of stress.[42]

There are a number of ways in which management might attempt to avoid or reduce role conflict, and the possibilities of role stress.

- Increase specification and clarity of prescribed role expectations, for example through written statements on objectives and policy, use of manuals and set procedures, introduction of appropriate rules, and detailed job descriptions. However, such measures may be resented by staff. They may restrict the opportunity for independent action and personal development, giving rise to even more role conflict.
- Improved recruitment and selection and the careful matching of abilities, motivation, interests and personalities to the demands of a particular role.
- Attention to induction and socialisation programmes, job training and retraining, staff development and career progression plans.
- Medical examinations and health screening to give early indications of potential stress-related problems.
- The creation of new roles or assimilation of existing roles. The reallocation or restructuring of tasks and responsibilities. The clarification of priorities, and the elimination or downgrading of minor roles.

- Giving advance notice and explanation of what is likely to happen, for example of an expected, additional heavy workload which must be completed urgently. Where possible and appropriate provide an opportunity for practice or experience.
- Attention to factors which may help improve group structure and group cohesiveness, and help overcome inter-group conflict.
- Change in management system and leadership style – for example, the move towards System 4 management (discussed in Chapter 7).
- Review of organisation structure, information flow and communication networks, for example members of staff being answerable to more than one superior. Bureaucratic interference and poor delegation are all common causes of work stress, whereas greater autonomy and the introduction of autonomous work groups can result in a marked reduction in stress.[43]

Other influences on behaviour

Even if there is an absence of role conflict and role stress, a person's actual behaviour may still be inconsistent with their expected pattern of behaviours. *Miner* gives three reasons that may account for this disparity.[44]

- The person does not perceive their job in the way the role prescriptions specify. This is a form of role ambiguity but may arise not because the role prescriptions themselves are unclear, but because the person misunderstands or distorts them.
- Motivation is lacking, and the person does not want to behave in the way prescribed.
- The person does not have the capabilities – knowledge, mental ability or physical skills – required to behave in the way the role prescriptions specify.

Application of sanctions

Organisations apply a number of both positive and negative sanctions as inducements for members to contribute and behave in accordance with their prescribed roles. Typical examples are: an increase in salary or wages; promotion; a sideways or downwards move in the organisation structure; the threat of dismissal.

There are also a number of less direct sanctions which may be adopted. These include: the size of office or work area; the allocation of unpopular tasks; giving opportunities for paid overtime work; level of supervision or empowerment; the amount of information given or the extent of consultation; granting or withholding privileges.

Role sanctions may also be applied through the operation of the informal organisation. Members of the group may impose their own sanctions and discipline individuals who contravene the norms of the group or expected standards of behaviour.

Synopsis

■ Groups are a major feature of human behaviour and organisational performance. Members of a group must co-operate with one another for work to be carried out. Harmonious working relationships and good teamwork help make for a high level of staff morale and work performance. Groups help shape the work pattern of organisations, and the attitudes and behaviour of members regarding their jobs. Groups develop their own values and norms of behaviour.

■ Groups are formed as a consequence of the pattern of organisation structure and arrangements for the division of work. There are two main types of groups at work, formal and informal. Formal groups are deliberately planned and created by management as part of the organisation structure, and to achieve specific organisational objectives. Informal groups are based on personal relationships and develop irrespective of the formal structure. Informal groups serve to satisfy members' psychological and social needs. Groups are formed, therefore, for a number of reasons relating to both work performance and social processes.

■ The manager's main concern is that members of a work group co-operate with one another. Factors which affect group cohesiveness can be considered under the broad headings of: membership; work environment; organisational; and group development and maturity. Membership of strong and cohesive groups can be a rewarding experience for the individual and have beneficial effects for the organisation.

■ There are, however, potential disadvantages of strong, cohesive groups and the manager should attempt to prevent unconstructive inter-group conflict. On the other hand, inter-group rivalry may be deliberately encouraged as a means of building stronger within-group cohesiveness. The effective management of work groups requires an understanding of the psychological and social influences on behaviour within organisations.

■ The characteristics of an effective work group are not always easy to isolate. The underlying feature is a spirit of co-operation in which members work well together as a united team, and with harmonious and supportive relationships. The nature of technology and the work flow system of the organisation is a major influence on the operation of groups. The impact of information technology is likely to lead to new patterns of work organisation, and affect the formation and structure of groups.

■ The concept of 'role' is important to the functioning of groups, and for an understanding of group processes and behaviour. It is through role differentiation that the structure of work groups and relationships among members is established. Role expectations may be established formally, they may be informal or they may be self-established. Inadequate or inappropriate role definition can result in role conflict including: role incompatibility, role ambiguity, role overload and role underload. Role conflict can result in role stress. It is important that the manager makes every effort to minimise role conflict and the causes of role stress.

Appendix

Teamwork in a small company

Eddie Brennan

Introduction

This is the story of a small (40-person) Dublin-based multimedia company, which we started four years ago. The main activity is producing computer courseware for a large International Company. Four of us had started the company. Our mix of backgrounds is; a journalist/marketeer; a computer systems integrator; a former company director/business consultant; and an organizational consultant in banking.

The staff numbers rose from one to ten over about four months. They were young and newly qualified, just out of third level college. This was their first job. The mix of skills were systems integrator, graphic designers and technical writers.

Difficulties

Some difficulties became apparent fairly quickly. Because the quality control function was then run by the client, the normal tension between developers and quality control was complicated by trying to keep good relations with the client. The day-to-day frustrations were exacerbated by the delays in the throughput in the client's work, which had a knock-on effect on our work.

Because of the inexperience of our young staff problems were being referred back to the Managing Director who then had to discuss the matter with the client. This was time consuming and staff morale was starting to suffer. In discussions with the client's top management it was evident that

● they were very happy with our work, and
● they were not aware that they, had problems in their own work flow.

Our cash flow was affected by the delays as payment was made on completion of specific pieces of work.

A full review with the client's top Management and Financial Controller was held on the whole work programme. They were anxious that we take on more work. When the difficulties were discussed the client agreed to pay a set amount each month, to review work progress every six months and that part of the quality control function was to be passed to us.

This immediately improved the whole relationship and helped us to concentrate on developing a longer-term strategy for the company.

Developing a strategy

When we were developing our strategy two objectives were decided early on:

- we needed to develop the business so that we were not totally dependent on the one client, while still keeping them happy;
- we wanted to maintain and to develop an innovative and creative atmosphere in the company.

To achieve the first objective we set a target of reducing the dependence on our one client by 20% per year over the next three years. We needed to build up staff numbers to allow enough 'slack' in the contract work so that there was the capacity to take on new work. Fortunately the client was encouraging us to take on more staff and promised that they could give us as much work as we could handle. We increased our staff to 15, to 20, and then to 25 over a period of 15 months.

To achieve the second objective depended on making early progress on the first. The routine production of courseware was now becoming that – just routine. Our young staff were becoming bored. To retain staff in a computer/technical environment people must feel that they are continuing to learn new processes and are being kept up to date with new technology. If they are to remain interested/satisfied/fulfilled it is important that they are challenged to think.

From the work in the early days a large library of graphics and computer routines had been built up and it was possible to incorporate these in subsequent work thus shortening the development time. This increase in productivity on the 'boring stuff' freed up staff to get at the exciting new bits.

We decided to develop autonomous teams who would be responsible for specific areas. Having read several discussions on team working over the years in QWL the profile of our small company seemed an ideal environment to implement this structure. We started a series of three-hour sessions with all of the staff. These covered subjects such as organizational development; management theory; stress management; financial management. Workshops were held on team building; customer relations; and interpersonal relationships. In all six afternoon/evening meetings were held, followed usually by a drink in the pub across the road.

What was apparent very early on was the interest and willingness of the staff to understand and to support the two strategic goals we had set ourselves. They quickly appreciated that their futures were dependent on how successful the company was in achieving them and were particularly tuned into the financial needs. (This was due to the fact that the financial controller made it very clear that if the money was not there then the new equipment was not bought – unless they preferred not to be paid that month!)

The management was surprised by the maturity, responsibility and interest that the staff took (and still take) in the health and development of the company once they were given the chance.

What is today's position?

The company is still running and now has a 60/40 split on the client dependency. Staff turnover has been very low by computer industry standards roughly 10% per year. Seven or eight of the original 10 are still working there and continue to grow with the company. What's worth noting is that the staff that do leave maintain a very good relationship with the company and many have been responsible for sending us new customers.

The salaries tend to be approximately 15% lower than industry norms, but staff feel it's 'a fun place to work' and that they have opportunities to learn new skills. They stay because of this. We have even had applications from people who have heard from friends about working conditions and want to come to work for us.

Discipline and work throughput has not been a great problem. The team structure keeps it under control largely by peer pressure, if someone on the team is not pulling their weight then their workmates let them know very quickly. Not everyone has felt comfortable with the 'flat' structure of the company and when it became apparent that they did not fit in they left. Two left for this reason.

The company earned the ISO 9000 standard within 18 months of introducing the team structure. This gave a big boost to the staff's morale. They now have an independent organisation giving them feedback on their systems. The discipline imposed by ISO 9000 has proved very useful internally – the actual mechanics of ISO 9000 has given a very clear framework for introducing new staff to the processes.

Clear project plans are developed with definite work objectives agreed with all staff. Teams are organised around specific projects like putting together a group in the film industry. Each project requires a different mix of skills so people regroup to the different projects requirements. Discussions take place on individual goals and achievements albeit in an informal way. Within this project plan work time and time keeping is very flexible. Nine to five are the normal hours but these vary for any individual at any specific time/work. It is not unusual to find groups of people working late into the night. This demands flexible security arrangements as well of course.

There is a high level of tolerance of individuals. One anecdote will help illustrate this. An individual who is particularly skilled in detecting hardware/system problems finds it very difficult to keep regular hours, yet seems to have an uncanny ability to appear when needed, day or night. His success rate in solving problems is so well appreciated, that everyone from the MD down will not have a word said against him!

What is important to staff is to feel that they are progressing in their skills. As new recruits come straight from Third-level colleges they bring with them up-to-date thinking and pass this to the 'old boys'. The 'old boys' in turn train them in on the internal skills and processes. This develops the trust needed in the team structure.

An unexpected development has been the formation of the 'social teams'. These have formed independently of the

Appendix continued

project teams and are more permanent groups. They arose around such activities as the annual 'PIX' awards. These PIX awards are internal company competitions organised to acknowledge individuals and teams for: e.g. The Most Creative Film; The Most Innovative Graphics; or The Most Original Use of Diverse Technology. Football competitions and other social activities are now organised around these teams.

What are the weaknesses?

Cash flow is still a problem. It is difficult to balance the enthusiasm to innovate with the commercial reality of 'only doing what the client is willing to pay for'.

The speed of developments in both hardware and software means that there is a constant need to invest in new processes, with the resulting training lag before they can be exploited commercially. This is a problem in such a small company as it leaves budgets very tight. There just is not sufficient spare cash to fund 'R & D' in the broadest sense.

At this stage the future will have to be amalgamation with a larger company but everyone fears that will mean a more hierarchal organization which could destroy some of the creativity and the 'fun'.

What have we learned?

- Autonomous teamwork works and saves money.
- Management needs to be self-confident, to see themselves as leaders rather than controllers.
- Teamwork saves time and allows management to concentrate on business development.
- Quality of the work improves and so does communication between different disciplines.

- It must be OK to make mistakes and OK to admit that you are in difficulties (experience is that team members willingly dig each other out – they know it could be their turn to get help next).
- Staff are very responsible and interested when treated as adults.
- It is important that staff continue to have the opportunity to learn.
- Good customer relations are developed and maintained by giving staff the ability to respond to client's requests.

It is important that the development team and the client's users get to know each other and understand each other. In many situations that we have experienced in other firms we noticed that communication between supplier and client goes through the Sales/Marketing Departments and the Head of Departments. We encourage the business analysts/developers to talk directly with the client's staff who will use the product. This has reduced misunderstanding and increased both the customer satisfaction and the developers' work. The teams have displayed a high level of creativity and innovation in their work and have developed several new processes for clients.

If we are asked 'what one thing has made the team structure a success?' The answer is that 'no one thing' works. A combination of trust, adult one-to-one relationships are vital but these must be combined with a sense of fun and achievement for everyone.

Reproduced with permission from Eddie Brennan, QWL News and Abstracts, ACAS, No. 144, Autumn 2000, pp. 8–10.

Eddie Brennan, Consultant, Uni-world Ltd. The company specialises in change management and team building by using and training the client's own staff. Contact email: brennanu@indigo.ie

---

CRITICAL REFLECTIONS

'I recognise that groups are an integral part of the work organisation but I do value my individuality and own identity, and enjoy the right of self expression.'

'That shouldn't be a problem. After all the skill of management is to make full use of people's individuality for the mutual benefit of the group as a whole.'

'Oh, I see – I think.'

What are your own views?

While teamwork may be about empowering workers, devolving responsibility, and reversing repressive workplace control structures, it can also mean intensifying attention. Instead of an individual exercising a degree of influence over their own work, they can now influence the work of others in their team through suggestion, demonstration, and exhortation. Life in teams can be stressful as individuals are subject to intense peer pressure to conform to group norms.

Wilson, F. M. Organizational Behaviour: A Critical Introduction, Oxford University Press (1999), p. 93.

How would you attempt to overcome or reduce the potentially stressful features of teamwork?

'Personal self-interest and opportunism are natural features of human behaviour and will always take preference over the demands and best interests of the group.'

Debate.

1 What is a group? Explain the importance of group values and norms, and give practical examples from within your own organisation.

2 How would you distinguish between a 'group' and a 'team'? To what extent do you believe the distinction has practical significance for managers?

3 Distinguish between formal and informal groups. What functions do groups serve in an organisation?

4 Identify different stages in group development and maturity. What other factors influence the cohesiveness of work groups? Give examples by reference to a work group to which you belong.

5 Assess the impact of technology as a determinant of group behaviour and performance. What action might be taken by management to help remove some of the alienating or stressful aspects of technology?

6 What is meant by the role structure of an organisation? Construct a diagram which shows your own role-set within a work situation. Give examples of informal role expectations to which you are, or have been, a party.

7 Explain different forms of role conflict which can result in role stress. Give an account of a work situation in which you have experienced role conflict/role stress. As manager, what action would you have taken in an attempt to rectify the situation?

8 What are the characteristics of an effective work group? As a manager, how would you attempt to develop effective group relationships and performance?

Assignment 1

Obtain, or prepare, a chart depicting the formal groupings within your organisation or a large department of the organisation.

a Using this chart, identify clearly the informal groups that exist within the formal structure.

b Discuss ways in which these informal groups aid, and/or conflict with, the work of the organisation/department.

c Explain the extent to which management recognise the influence of the informal groups.

d What conclusions do you draw from this assignment?

Assignment 2

Attempt, *preferably*, to observe a small group or project team at work; *alternatively*, recall the working of any small group of which you have recently been a member.

a (i) Explain the extent to which the group progressed through the stages of: forming; storming; norming; performing.

   (ii) Complete the following grid by giving a tick in the appropriate box to denote each contribution by individual members.

Names of group members (or reference numbers)

Forming					
Storming					
Norming					
Performing					

b (i) Give examples of the group values or norms which constituted 'proper' behaviour of group members.

(ii) Explain sanctions applied to those members who did not conform to the group norms and the apparent effectiveness of these sanctions.

c Explain the factors which influenced the cohesiveness of the group.

d Give your views, with supporting reasons, on:

(i) the apparent satisfaction derived by individuals from membership of the group; and

(ii) the effectiveness of the group as a whole.

Visit our website **www.booksites.net/mullins** for further questions, annotated weblinks, case material and internet research material.

CASE STUDY 13.1

Hovertec plc

BACKGROUND INFORMATION

Hovertec plc is a large public company which has been manufacturing civilian and military helicopters for nearly 50 years. The company is very successful in its field and during 19xx/19xx achieved total sales of over £280 million. Profits before taxation exceeded £16.5 million. Hovertec plc employs over 6000 people, most of whom work in three manufacturing plants which are situated in South-West England, Scotland and Northern Ireland.

The company has developed two main types of helicopters since the Second World War. These are the 'Falcon' range of small helicopters, which are sold to civilian operators, and the 'SX/Hawk' range of small and large military helicopters which are produced for government defence projects. Some

export orders of 'SX/Hawk' helicopters are manufactured for NATO countries and other friendly countries. The precise number and size of Ministry of Defence contracts is not published and is regarded as classified information by Hovertec plc.

Nevertheless, it is possible to gain some insight into the close relationship between the Ministry of Defence and the company from the details of the research and development (R&D) expenditure which is published in the Hovertec plc Annual Report and Accounts. During 19xx/19xx, the R&D expenditure exceeded £43 million, of which £13 million was 'raised from private venture expenditure', £2.5 million was 'funded in civilian helicopter sales prices' and £28 million was 'covered by classified research contracts'. All the research and development projects, as well as all the military and some civilian contracts, are undertaken at the largest plant in South-West England. The remaining civilian helicopter contracts are shared between the two smaller factories in Scotland and Northern Ireland.

THE MANUFACTURE OF A HELICOPTER

Without going into technical details, the manufacture of a helicopter can be divided into five interconnected processes:

1 *The power unit*, which 'drives' the helicopter like an engine drives a motor car.
2 *The helicopter loom*, which is an inter-woven collection of between 1200 and 2000 insulated copper wires and electrical cables, connecting the power unit with the various 'control' switches, dials, buttons and levers in the cockpit and passenger/crew compartment, and can be compared, in human terms, with the function of the spinal cord in linking the brain with the arms and legs, etc.
3 *The external rotor blades*, which are mounted over the cockpit and passenger/crew compartment, and also above the tail of the helicopter.
4 *The cockpit and passenger/crew compartment*, which has a different layout, services and accessories (viz. electronic weapon systems), depending on whether the helicopter is intended for civilian or military purposes.
5 *The superstructure or 'shell'*, which encases the helicopter in a similar manner to the 'bodywork' on a motor car.

Although the latest technology is used in these production and assembly processes, the manufacture of a complete helicopter is a relatively slow process, taking three weeks for a civilian unit and four weeks for the larger, more sophisticated military helicopter. The main 'bottleneck' in the process is the long time taken to assemble the helicopter loom and complete the 1200–2000 connections between the power unit and the numerous helicopter systems and services.

ASSEMBLING A HELICOPTER LOOM

Because of the complexity of the task and the high risk of error, the assembly of each helicopter loom is normally carried out by one loom technician who takes up to two weeks (ten working days) to assemble a complete loom unit. Production output is

maintained by a team of 24 loom technicians who work in two shifts of 12 technicians per shift. The loom technicians are all qualified maintenance fitters who have received extensive training from the company in loom-assembly procedures. They are the highest-paid section of the workforce after the supervisors and management, and they receive other benefits, such as membership of the company pension scheme, free BUPA medical insurance and additional holiday entitlement which is related to length of service with the company.

All of these technicians are men, aged between 36 and 50 years with between 8 and 15 years' service with the company. Many were recruited from either the Royal Navy or the Army Engineering Corps, where they received their basic training as maintenance fitters. This form of recruitment is adopted, first, because the loom technicians help to assemble both civilian and military helicopters and possible security risks have to be minimised on Ministry of Defence contracts. Second, the majority of Hovertec plc managers possess Army or Naval backgrounds and strong links are maintained with the armed services.

Perhaps the one striking difference between the working conditions at the Hovertec plc factory in South-West England and those at their previous employment in the Armed Services is that all the loom technicians belong to a trade union which is recognised by the company, although in practice the Hovertec plc management frequently circumvent the union representatives by informing the workforce directly of changes in procedures, policy, etc., using 'briefing' procedures.

AN IMPROVED HELICOPTER LOOM-ASSEMBLY METHOD

The 19xx company Corporate Plan concluded that: 'Because of the constricting squeeze on defence projects and on the finances of civilian helicopter operators, which appears likely to continue until the world recession ends and general demands picks up, future activity in the three factories will be at a lower level during the next two to three years than seemed likely a few years ago'.

A detailed cost-cutting exercise was introduced on the strength of this plan, with particular emphasis on the helicopter loom workshop. For example, all overtime working was withdrawn in September 19xx. Meanwhile, the Research and Development

Laboratories had devised a radically new method of assembling helicopter looms which, under pilot-scheme conditions, reduced the assembly time from two weeks (ten working days) to two working days. The new method had the added advantage of allowing unskilled labour to be employed and resulted in a saving of assembly costs.

Instead of one technician assembling a single loom, by following a blueprint in a painstaking way, the new method relies upon a team of five operatives working together and following a sequence of 'instructions' provided by a computer. The 1200–2000 insulated copper wires and electrical cables are previously 'colour coded' in terms of the ten main helicopter operating systems. Each operative is given responsibility for two sets of colour-coded wires and cables and is required to thread the leads of one colour through the loom, one at a time, by following a 'map' which is set out on a personal visual display unit.

The total computerised layout, which appears on a separate large screen, resembles a coloured map of the London Underground system. For example, as one operative threads each blue electrical cable through the loom, a blue light flicks on as each correct 'station' is reached. If an error is made, the appropriate light fails to appear and a buzzing alarm sounds continuously until the mistake is corrected and the correct 'route' is re-established. At the same time, the computer-directed system can also be used for the other 'colour-coded' electrical connections and the team is therefore able to assemble the loom simultaneously, without slowing down or interfering with each other's work.

Further trials conducted by the Research and Development Laboratories indicated that small groups of five female workers achieved, on average, 40 per cent higher productivity than similar teams of male operatives. The highest productivity was consistently achieved under laboratory conditions by a team of 16-to-17-year-old female school-leavers, who were permitted to choose their working partners and were also allowed to change from one 'colour code' to another whenever they became bored with one colour or started to make errors. This team was given ten-minute 'rest pauses' every hour to change 'colour codes' and was supervised by a member of the Research and Development Laboratory team, who also collected data on the group's productivity, etc.

PROPOSED CHANGES IN THE HELICOPTER LOOM WORKSHOP

Within six months, a decision was taken by the Hovertec plc senior management to transfer the new computerised system pilot-scheme to the loom workshop on a three-months' trial basis. Management informed the workforce about the proposed trials beforehand and the loom technicians accepted the proposed change after receiving a personal assurance that no redundancies would occur as a result of the trials. The company wrote to their trade union about ten days later, during the week when the trials began, to inform them of the new situation; and also pointed out that the trials would allow full-time employment to be offered to five female school-leavers, who would otherwise be out of work.

OUTCOME OF THE TRIALS

Within two weeks of the new computerised system being installed, three of the five girls in the work group handed in their notice because of continual abuse from and arguments with the loom technicians. Productivity fell far below the expected targets on every day after the first loom was completed (in four days). The cause of low productivity was invariably due to breakdowns of equipment (loss of VDU pictures was the most frequent fault) which, according to the Research and Development Department, was the direct result of vandalism. A serious argument broke out on one occasion between a loom technician and the Research and Development Supervisor, who had earlier asked the technician to leave the VDU area and return to his own work area, and the outcome was that disciplinary action had to be taken against the loom technician.

Three days later, the trade union representing the loom technicians advised the company that the men were unwilling to work alongside the girls on classified defence contracts in future. The reason given was that the girls were considered to be irresponsible and were more of a 'security risk' than the service-trained loom technicians. Management were swift to point out that none of the girls possessed any expertise in engineering or electronic systems and, in fact, three of the girls were close relatives of different loom technicians.

Output in the loom workshop fell during April and May and the company began to fall behind on outstanding defence contracts. A senior Ministry of Defence official visited the plant in South-West England to advise senior management of the

'Whitehall View' that the new computersed loom assembly trials should be suspended on all defence contract helicopters until further notice.

Tasks

a Using your knowledge of different approaches to organisation and management, comment on the Research and Development Laboratory trials carried out by Hovertec with the team of young, female workers.

b Discuss the conditions which contributed to the cohesiveness of the loom technicians as a work group.

c What factors might explain the difficulties between the group of loom technicians and the team of female workers?

d What action would you propose should be taken by the management of Hovertec?

Notes and references

1 Schein, E. H. *Organizational Psychology*, Third edition, Prentice-Hall (1988), p. 145.

2 Adair, J. *Effective Teambuilding*, Gower (1986).

3 Cited in Norton, B. 'Quick Guides to The Gurus', *Professional Manager*, November 1997, p. 21.

4 Roethlisberger, F. J. and Dickson, W. J. *Management and the Worker*, Harvard University Press (1939).

5 Trist, E. L. *et al. Organizational Choice*, Tavistock Publications (1963).

6 See, for example: Mullins, L. J. *Hospitality Management and Organisational Behaviour*, Fourth edition, Longman (2001).

7 *Teamwork: Success Through People*, Advisory Booklet, ACAS, September 1996.

8 Heller, R. *In Search of European Success*, HarperCollins Business (1997), p. xiv.

9 Jay, A. 'Nobody's Perfect – But a Team Can Be', *Observer Magazine*, 20 April 1980, pp. 26–33.

10 Bonington, Sir Chris 'Moving Mountains', *The British Journal of Administrative Management*, November/ December 1996, pp. 12–14.

11 Heller, R. *In Search of European Excellence*, HarperCollins Business (1997), p. 229.

12 See, for example: Riley, M. *Human Resource Management in the Hospitality and Tourism Industry*, Second edition, Butterworth Heinemann (1996).

13 Crainer, S. *Key Management Ideas: Thinkers that changed the management world*, Third edition, Financial Times Prentice Hall (1998), p. 237.

14 Belbin, R. M. *Beyond the Team*, Butterworth-Heinemann (2000).

15 Lysons, K. 'Organisational Analysis', *Supplement to The British Journal of Administrative Management*, no. 18, March/April 1997.

16 Argyle, M. *The Social Psychology of Work*, Second edition, Penguin (1989).

17 See, for example: Jay, A. *Corporation Man*, Penguin (1975). In an amusing historical account of the development of different forms of groups, Jay suggests that ten is the basic size of human grouping.

18 See, for example: Handy, C. B. *Understanding Organizations*, Fourth edition, Penguin (1993).

19 Kravitz, D. A. and Martin, B. 'Ringelmann Rediscovered: The Original Article', *Journal of Personality and Social Psychology*, May 1986, pp. 936–41.

20 See, for example: Karau, S. J. and Williams, K. D. 'Social Loafing: A Meta-Analysis Review and Theoretical Integration', *Journal of Personality and Social Psychology*, October 1993, pp. 681–706.

21 Bass, B. M. and Ryterband, E. C. *Organizational Psychology*, Second edition, Allyn and Bacon (1979).

22 Tuckman, B. W. 'Development Sequence in Small Groups', *Psychological Bulletin*, vol. 63, 1965, pp. 384–99.

23 Cited in Green, J. 'Are your teams and groups at work successful?', *Administrator*, December 1993, p. 12.

24 Seashore, S. E. *Group Cohesiveness in the Industrial Work Group*, Institute for Social Research, University of Michigan (1954).

25 Green, J. 'Team Building in Practice', *Chartered Secretary*, November 1997, p. 35.

26 Koontz, D. *Icebound*, BCA, by arrangement with Headline Books Ltd (1995), p. 185.

27 See, for example: Staw, B. M. 'Organizational Psychology and the Pursuit of the Happy/Productive Worker', *California Management Review*, vol. 28, no. 4, Summer 1986, pp. 40–53.

28 See, for example: Schein, E. H. *Organizational Psychology*, Third edition, Prentice-Hall (1988).

29 Brooks, I. *Organisational Behaviour: Individuals, Groups and the Organisation*, Financial Times Pitman Publishing (1999), p. 91

30 Allcorn, S. 'Understanding Groups at Work', *Personnel*, vol. 66, no. 8, August 1989, pp. 28–36.

31 See, for example: Walker, C. R. and Guest, R. H. *The Man on the Assembly Line*, Harvard University Press (1952); and Scott, W. H. *et al. Technical Change and Industrial Relations*, Liverpool University Press (1956).

32 Goldthorpe, J. H. *et al. The Affluent Worker*, Cambridge University Press (1968).

33 See, for example: Grayson, D. *Self Regulating Work Groups – An Aspect of Organisational Change*, ACAS Work Research Unit, Occasional Paper, no. 146, HMSO (July 1990).

34 See, for example: Kinsman, F. 'The Virtual Office and The Flexible Organisation', *Administrator*, April 1994, pp. 31–2; and Chowdhury, S. *Management 21c*. Financial Times Prentice Hall (2000).

35 Whyte, W. F. *Human Relations in the Restaurant Industry*, McGraw-Hill (1948).

36 See, for example: Lerner, P. M. 'Beware the Gatekeeper', *Amtrak Express*, July/August 1994, pp. 14–17.

37 See, for example: Handy, C. B. *Understanding Organizations*, Fourth edition, Penguin (1993).

38 Oliver, J. 'Losing Control', *Management Today*, June 1998, pp. 32–8.

39 See, for example: *Are Managers Under Stress? A Survey of Management Morale*, The Institute of Management (September 1996).

40 'Your Guide to Managing Stress', Central Personnel Unit, Hampshire County Council, August 1997.

41 See, for example: Gwyther, M. 'Stressed for Success', *Management Today*, January 1999, pp. 22–6.

42 See, for example, Newton, T., *Managing Stress: Emotion and Power at Work*, Sage Publications (1995).

43 Hall, K. and Savery, L. K. 'Stress Management', *Management Decision*, vol. 25, no. 6, 1987, pp. 29–35.

44 Miner, J. B. *Management Theory*, Macmillan (1971).

Chapter 14

GROUP PROCESSES AND BEHAVIOUR

If the manager is to make the most effective use of staff, then it is important to have an understanding of group processes and behaviour. It is necessary to understand the nature of group functions and roles, and factors which influence their performance and effectiveness. Attention must be given to the analysis of behaviour of individuals in group situations. The manager must be aware of the functioning and operation of work groups and teams.

Learning objectives

To:

➤ explain interactions among members of a group and membership of successful teams;

➤ detail patterns of communication networks within small work groups;

➤ examine methods of analysing behaviour of individuals in group situations;

➤ distinguish different group functions and member roles, and explain the use of frameworks of behavioural analysis;

➤ evaluate the nature of group performance and effectiveness;

➤ assess the nature and value of group dynamics;

➤ recognise the importance of understanding the functioning and operation of work groups.

Interactions among members

In order to help improve the performance of the organisation it is necessary to understand the nature of human relationships and what goes on when groups of people meet.[1] Working in a group is likely to be both a psychologically rewarding, but also a potentially demanding, experience for the individual. Group performance and the satisfaction derived by individuals are influenced by the interactions among members of the group. As an example of this, Figure 14.1 gives an unsolicited commentary from five final-year business studies degree students after completing a group-based assignment.

In order to understand the functions and processes of a group, it is necessary to understand what happens when groups of people meet; the actions and behaviour of individual members; the parts people play; the patterns of interactions and forces within the group; and influences on individual and group performance. Group processes and behaviour are discussed later in this chapter.

Membership of successful teams

In Chapter 13 we discussed the importance of teamwork for organisational effectiveness.

Organisations need workers to be more flexible, to co-operate with other workers, supervisors and managers throughout the organisation, to operate sophisticated technology and to be more adaptable. In addition, the sheer complexity of operations in industry, commerce and the services place them beyond the expertise and control of any one individual. In these circumstances some form of teamwork becomes not just desirable, but essential.[2]

If groups are to be successful and perform effectively there must be a spirit of unity and co-operation. Members of a group must work well together as a team. As *Crainer* reminds us, in most teams people will contribute individual skills many of which will

---

WHAT WE FEEL WE HAVE LEARNT FROM WORKING IN A GROUP

1 'We learnt that we had to listen to everybody's points of view and take these into consideration.'
2 'We found that we had to be prepared to make certain sacrifices and adopted a democratic decision process. However, if an individual felt very strongly about a specific point and persisted with a valid argument then this had to be included.'
3 'We often felt frustrated.'
4 'It was time-consuming and difficult to schedule meetings due to differences in timetables and preferences in working hours.'
5 'We learnt that it is good to pool resources because this increased the overall standard of the piece of work. We feel this was only because we all set high personal standards and expected these from our fellow group members. We learnt that it is possible to work in other less productive groups where individual levels of achievement may decrease.'
6 'We learnt that it is better to work in a smaller and not a larger group, as there is a tendency for individual ideas to be diluted.'
7 'Groups formed on the basis of friendship alone are not as effective as groups formed with work as the major influence. The former tend to be unproductive.'
8 'We found that it was good to get positive response, encouragement and feedback from team members. Likewise, it was demotivating to receive a negative response.'
9 'We learnt a lot about our individual personalities.'
10 'We benefited from sharing personal experiences from our industrial placements.'
11 'It is important to separate work and personal relationships.'

Figure 14.1 Unsolicited commentary from students after completing a group-based assignment

be different. However, referring to the work of *Obeng*,[3] Crainer points out that it is not enough to have a rag-bag collection of individual skills.

> *The various behaviors of the team members must mesh together in order to achieve objectives. For people to work successfully in teams, you need people to behave in certain ways. You need some people to concentrate on the task at hand (**doers**). You need some people to provide specialist knowledge (**knowers**) and some to solve problems as they arise (**solvers**). You need some people to make sure that it is going as well as it can and that the whole team is contributing fully (**checkers**). And you need some people to make sure that the team is operating as a cohesive social unit (**carers**).*[4]

Belbin's team-roles

Following years of research and empirical study, *Belbin* concludes that groups composed entirely of clever people, or of people with similar personalities, display a number of negative results and lack creativity. The most consistently successful groups comprise a range of roles undertaken by various members. The constitution of the group itself is an important variable in its success.[5]

For a fully effective group, there are eight useful types of contribution – or team-roles. Belbin describes '**team-role**' as a pattern of behaviour, characteristic of the way in which one team member interacts with another where performance serves to facilitate the progress of the team as a whole. The eight key team-roles are:

- Company Worker (CW);
- Chairman (CH);
- Shaper (SH);
- Plant (PL);
- Resource Investigator (RI);
- Monitor-Evaluator (ME);
- Team Worker (TW);
- Completer-Finisher (CF).

An explanation of these team-roles is given in Table 14.1.

The eight types of people identified are useful team members and form a comprehensive list. These are the key team-roles and the primary characters for successful teams. Creative teams require a balance of all these roles and comprise members who have characteristics complementary to one another. Belbin claims that good examples of the eight types would prove adequate for any challenge, although not all eight types are necessarily needed. Other members may be welcome for their personal qualities, for example a sense of humour, but experience suggests there is no other team-role that it would be useful to add.

Back-up team-roles and functional roles

The most consistently successful teams were 'mixed' with a balance of team-roles. The role that a person undertakes in a group is not fixed and may change according to circumstances. Individuals may have a 'back-up team-role' with which they have some affinity other than their primary team-role. If certain roles were missing members would call upon their back-up roles. Team-roles differ from what Belbin calls 'functional-roles'. These are the roles that members of a team perform in terms of the specifically technical demands placed upon them. Team members are typically chosen for functional roles on the basis of experience and not personal characteristics or aptitudes.

Belbin has developed a Self-Perception Inventory designed to provide members of a group with a simple means of assessing their best team-roles.

Table 14.1 Useful people to have in teams

Type	Symbol	Typical features	Positive qualities	Allowable weaknesses
Company worker	CW	Conservative, dutiful, predictable.	Organising ability, practical common sense, hard-working, self-discipline.	Lack of flexibility, unresponsiveness to unproven ideas.
Chairman	CH	Calm, self-confident, controlled.	A capacity for treating and welcoming all potential contributors on their merits and without prejudice. A strong sense of objectives.	No more than ordinary in terms of intellect or creative ability.
Shaper	SH	Highly strung, outgoing, dynamic.	Drive and a readiness to challenge inertia, ineffectiveness, complacency or self-deception.	Proneness to provocation, irritation and impatience.
Plant	PL	Individualistic, serious-minded, unorthodox.	Genius, imagination, intellect, knowledge.	Up in the clouds, inclined to disregard practice details or protocol.
Resource investigator	RI	Extroverted, enthusiastic, curious, communicative.	A capacity for contacting people and exploring anything new. An ability to respond to challenge.	Liable to lose interest once the initial fascination has passed.
Monitor-Evaluator	ME	Sober, unemotional, prudent.	Judgement, discretion, hard-headedness.	Lacks inspiration or the ability to motivate others.
Team worker	TW	Socially orientated, rather mild, sensitive.	An ability to respond to people and to situations, and to promote team spirit.	Indecisiveness at moments of crisis.
Completer-Finisher	CF	Painstaking, orderly, conscientious, anxious.	A capacity for follow-through. Perfectionism.	A tendency to worry about small things. A reluctance to 'let go'.

(Reprinted with permission from Belbin, R. M. *Management Teams: Why They Succeed or Fail*, The Butterworths Division of Reed Elsevier (UK) Limited/Belbin Associates (1981) p. 78.)

Revised list of team-roles

In a follow-up publication Belbin discusses the continued evolution of team-roles which now differ in a few respects from those identified in earlier research.[6] Two roles are renamed, largely for reasons of acceptability: 'Co-ordinator' replaces 'Chairman'; and 'Implementer' replaces 'Company Worker'. The most significant change is the addition of a ninth role, that of 'Specialist'. This role was added because of the significance of the importance of a given form of professional expertise in much project work and its recurring importance as an issue in a career development. A description of the evolved nine team-roles is given in Table 14.2. Strength of contribution in any one of the roles is commonly associated with particular weaknesses. These are called allowable weaknesses. Executives are seldom strong in all nine team-roles.

Table 14.2 Belbin's revised team-roles

Roles and descriptions – team-role contribution		Allowable weaknesses
Plant	Creative, imaginative, unorthodox. Solves difficult problems.	Ignores details. Too preoccupied to communicate effectively.
Resource investigator	Extrovert, enthusiastic, communicative. Explores opportunities. Develops contacts.	Over-optimistic. Loses interest once initial enthusiasm has passed.
Co-ordinator	Mature, confident, a good chairperson. Clarifies goals, promotes decision-making. Delegates well.	Can be seen as manipulative. Delegates personal work.
Shaper	Challenging, dynamic, thrives on pressure. Has the drive and courage to overcome obstacles.	Can provoke others. Hurts people's feelings.
Monitor-Evaluator	Sober, strategic and discerning. Sees all options. Judges accurately.	Lacks drive and ability to inspire others. Overly critical.
Team worker	Co-operative, mild, perceptive and diplomatic. Listens, builds, averts friction, calms the waters.	Indecisive in crunch situations. Can be easily influenced.
Implementer	Disciplined, reliable, conservative and efficient. Turns ideas into practical actions.	Somewhat inflexible. Slow to respond to new possibilities.
Completer	Painstaking, conscientious, anxious. Searches out errors and omissions. Delivers on time.	Inclined to worry unduly. Reluctant to delegate. Can be a nit-picker.
Specialist	Single-minded, self-sharing, dedicated. Provides knowledge and skills in rare supply.	Contributes on only a narrow front. Dwells on technicalities. Overlooks the 'big picture'.

(Reprinted with permission from Belbin, R. M., *Team Roles at Work*, The Butterworths Division of Reed Elsevier (UK) Limited/ Belbin Associates (1993) p. 23.)

The value of Belbin's Team-Roles Inventory

A study undertaken by *Furnham, Steel and Pendleton* had the aim of examining the psychometric properties of the Belbin Team-Role Self Perception Inventory. They believe (admittedly from relatively small samples) that there is little psychometric support for the structure of the inventories which do not give confidence in the predictive or construct validity. In a response, Belbin argues that the Inventory was a quick and useful way of intimating to readers what their own team-roles might be; and Furnham, Steele and Pendleton acknowledge that Belbin's contribution is substantial and his measure imaginative.[7]

Despite possible doubts about the value of Belbin's self-perception inventory, it remains a popular means of examining and comparing team-roles. Recall, for example, the study of the team-role preferences of local government managers (discussed in Chapter 6). In order to explore whether local government managers were distinctively different from the model of private sector management, *Arroba and Wedgwood-Oppenheim* compared samples of the two groups of managers and Belbin's eight key team-roles. There were noticeable similarities between the two groups with the noticeable exception of the marked difference between private sector managers and local government officers in the score for team workers and the team-roles they preferred to adopt. The individual characteristics of managers in the two sectors differed. The data implied that local government officers were committed to organisational objectives and dedicated to task achievement but the low score for team worker suggested the high commitment to organisational tasks was not supplemented by a concern for interpersonal processes. In local government, the drive and enthusiasm and emphasis on task were exaggerated, while attention to idea generation and productive interpersonal relationships is less marked.[8]

Constructing the perfect team

Referring to the research of Belbin, *White* refers to a team in the proper sense of the word as something about the way they work as a group that adds up to a sum greater than the individual parts – a collective spirit, a managerial alchemy that makes them such a force. If business people are happy to accept that group effort is always better than individuals working in isolation, the research of Belbin may help in constructing the perfect team. White suggests that in the end it is all about trust. The chances are that the dream team is out there, sitting opposite you or just around the corner. All you have to do is to fit them into Belbin's nine defined roles.[9]

Distribution of team roles among UK managers

Using Belbin's model, *Fisher et al.* undertook a study of the distribution of team roles among managers. Over the past 15 years many layers of management have been removed and the gap in people to lead and motivate has increasingly been filled by the creation of multitudes of teams. The participants of the study were 1441 male and 355 female managers, all with some management experience. All had completed a personality questionnaire, and were candidates short-listed for a range of management positions in both the private and public sector. The study analysed data supplied by ASE/NFER Publishing Company and results were then compared with the Belbin model. The data broadly agreed with the Belbin model. The authors conclude that as much is still unknown about teams, it is reassuring that further support has been found for the popular Belbin team-role model. There are several unresolved problems with teamworking but these might lie more with practices in staff recruitment than in team theory.[10]

Patterns of communication

The level of interaction among members of a group is influenced by the structuring of channels of communication. Laboratory research by *Bavelas*[11] and subsequent studies by other researchers such as *Leavitt*[12] have resulted in the design of a series of communication networks. These networks were based on groups of five members engaged in a number of problem-solving tasks. Members were permitted to communicate with each other by written notes only, and not everyone was always free to communicate with everyone else.

There are five main types of communication networks – Wheel, Circle, All-Channel, Y and Chains (*see* Figure 14.2).

- **The wheel**, also sometimes known as the star, is the most **centralised network**. This network is most efficient for simple tasks. Problems are solved more quickly with fewer mistakes and with fewer information flows. However, as the problems of the group become more complex and demands on the link person increase, effectiveness suffers. The link person is at the centre of the network and acts as the focus of activities and information flows, and the co-ordinator of group tasks. The central person is perceived as leader of the group and experiences a high level of satisfaction. However, for members on the periphery, the wheel is the least satisfying network.
- **The circle** is a more **decentralised network**. Overall it is less efficient. The group is unorganised, with low leadership predictability. Performance tends to be slow and erratic. However, the circle is quicker than the wheel in solving complex problems, and also copes with change or new tasks more efficiently. The circle network is

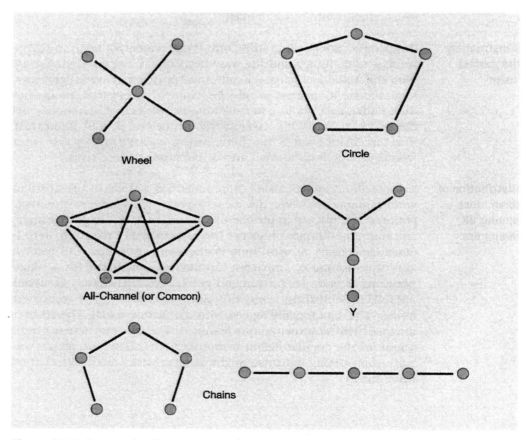

Figure 14.2 Communication networks

most satisfying for all the members. Decision-making is likely to involve some degree of participation.

- **The all-channel (or comcon) network** is a decentralised network which involves full discussion and participation. This network appears to work best where a high level of interaction is required among all members of the group in order to solve complex problems. Leadership predictability is very low. There is a fairly high level of satisfaction for members. The all-channel network may not stand up well under pressure, in which case it will either disintegrate or reform into a wheel network.
- **A 'Y' or chain network** might be appropriate for more simple problem-solving tasks, requiring little interaction among members of the group. These networks are more centralised, with information flows along a predetermined channel. Leadership predictability is high to moderate. There is a low to moderate level of satisfaction for members.

Satisfaction of group members

Findings from these studies indicate that the greater the interconnectedness of the network, the higher the general level of satisfaction of members in the group. Groups allowed to establish their own communication networks, and who did so with the minimum of links, took less time to solve their tasks. Those groups who did not minimise the number of links in their network took more time to solve the tasks.[13]

From a review of studies in communication networks, *Shaw* confirmed that simple tasks were consistently undertaken most efficiently in more centralised networks such as the wheel. More complex tasks were performed more efficiently by decentralised networks such as the circle or the all-channel.[14] (*See* Figure 14.3.) The characteristics of the different communication networks are determined by the extent of 'independence' and 'saturation'.

- **Independence** refers to the opportunities for group members to take action and to solve the problem without relying on the assistance of others.
- **Saturation** occurs when the task places an excessive information load or other demands upon a member of the network. This leads to inefficiency. The central person in a centralised network handling complex problems is more likely to experience saturation.

The individual's satisfaction with his or her position in the network relates to the degree of independence and the satisfaction of recognition and achievement needs. (See achievement motivation in Chapter 12.) A high level of dependence on other members may prevent the satisfaction of these needs, and if members of the network become frustrated they may not be so willing to share information with others. In the wheel network the central person has greater independence than the other members, but in the circle network all members have a moderate degree of dependence upon each other. Leadership is also important because this can influence the opportunity for independent action by the group members, and can also control the possibility of saturation.

Implications for the manager

Despite the obvious artificiality and limitations of these communication network studies, they do have certain implications for the manager. A knowledge of the findings may be applied to influence the patterns of communication in meetings and committees. They also provide a reasonable representation of the situations that might apply in large organisations. It will be interesting for the manager to observe the patterns of communication adopted by different groups in different situations. The manager can also note how communication networks change over time and how they relate to the performance of the group.

No one network is likely to be effective for a range of given problems. The studies draw attention to the part of the manager's job which is to ensure the most appropriate communication network for the performance of a given task. Problems which require a high level of interaction among members of the group may not be handled efficiently

Understanding and Managing People at Work

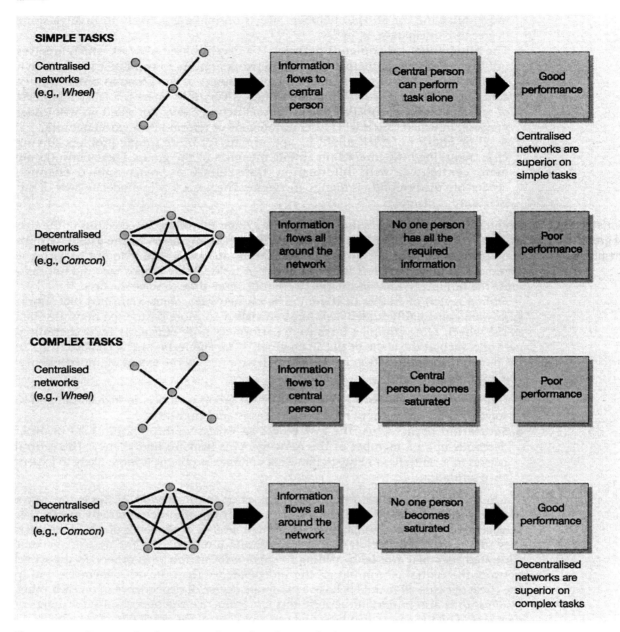

Figure 14.3 Communication networks and task complexity

(Source: Baron/Greenberg, *Behaviour in Organisations: Understanding Managing*, Third edition, Prentice-Hall Inc., Upper Saddle River, NJ.)

if there are inadequate channels of communication or sharing of information. The choice of a particular communication network may involve trade-offs between the performance of the work group and the satisfaction of its members.

Analysis of behaviour in groups

In order to understand and to influence the functioning and operation of a group, it is necessary to study patterns of interaction, and the parts played by individual members. For example, in a more recent publication *Belbin* acknowledges that:

Teamwork does not, of course, guarantee in itself good results. As in sport, there can be good teams and poor teams. And as in sport, it all depends on how the players play together.[15]

Two of the main methods of analysing the behaviour of individuals in group situations are **sociometry** and **interaction process analysis**.

Sociometry

Originally developed by *Moreno*,[16] **sociometry** is a method of indicating the feelings of acceptance or rejection among members of a group. A sociogram is a diagrammatical illustration of the pattern of interpersonal relationships derived from sociometry. The sociogram depicts the choices, preferences, likes or dislikes, and interactions between individual members of a group. It can also be used to display the structure of the group and to record the observed frequency and/or duration of contacts among members.

The basis of sociometry, however, is usually 'buddy rating' or 'peer rating'. Each member in the group is asked to nominate or to rate, privately, other members in terms of some given context or characteristic – for example, with whom they communicate, or how influential or how likeable they are. Questions may relate to either work or social activities. For example: who would you most prefer or least prefer as a workmate? Who would make a good leader of the group? With whom would you choose and not choose to go on holiday? Positive and negative choices may be recorded for each person, although sometimes positive choices only are required. The choices may be limited to a given number or they may be unlimited. Sometimes individuals may be asked to rank their choices.

Sociograms

Members' choices could be shown in tabular form. For example, Table 14.3 shows first and second choices for a group of final-year degree students. Members were asked to indicate, in confidence, those whom they would most prefer to talk to about: (i) a major work-related problem; and (ii) a difficult personal problem. Positive choices only were requested.

Table 14.3 Example of a 'tabulated' sociogram (positive choices only)

Work-related problem			Personal problem	
Second choice	First choice		First choice	Second choice
		A		///
		B	/	//
///	/	C	//	/
/		D	//	
		E	/	
		F	/	//
	/	G	//	
/////	//	H	//	
		J	/	/
	//	K		
////	///////	L		//
	/	M	/	/
		N		//
/		O	/	
14	14		14	14

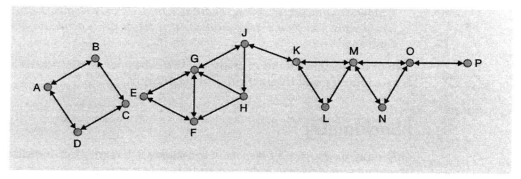

Figure 14.4 A simple illustration of a sociogram

An advantage of the diagrammatical illustration, however, is that the sociogram provides a visual description of the sociometric structure of a group. It can indicate cliques and sub-groups, compatibility, and members who are popular, isolated or who act as links. Figure 14.4 gives a simple illustration of a sociogram for a group of 15 members with single, positive choices only.

1 G and M are popular (the stars) and most often chosen by members.
2 M is the link between two overlapping cliques, KML and MNO.
3 H and P are unpopular (isolated) and chosen least by members.
4 JKMO is a chain.
5 ABCD is a sub-group and separated from the rest of the members.

It should be noted, however, that there are several methods of compiling and drawing sociograms, and a number of potential criticisms and limitations with the contribution of Moreno. Problems also arise over *how* to draw the sociogram and how to interpret the roles of individual members; 'the drawing of a sociogram is a highly arbitrary and time-consuming task'.[17] In the experience of the author less concern should be given to the concept of sociometry itself. It is better seen as a useful vehicle which, if handled sensitively, can serve to encourage meaningful discussions on patterns of social interactions, group behaviour and the perceptions of individual members towards one another.

Interaction analysis

The basic assumption behind **interaction analysis** is that behaviour in groups may be analysed from the viewpoint of its function. This approach has developed largely from the work of *Bales* on methods for the study of small groups. This aim is to provide ways of describing group process and indications of factors influencing the process.[18]

In Bales's 'Interaction Process Analysis' every act of behaviour is categorised, as it occurs, under twelve headings. These differentiate between 'task' functions and 'socio-emotional' functions. The categories apply to both verbal interaction and non-verbal interaction.

- A Socio-Emotional: Positive Reactions
   1 **Shows solidarity**, raises others' status, gives help, reward.
   2 **Shows tension release**, jokes, laughs, shows satisfaction.
   3 **Agrees**, shows passive acceptance, understands, concurs, complies.
- B Task: Attempted Answers
   4 **Gives suggestion**, direction, implying autonomy for others.
   5 **Gives opinion**, evaluation, analysis, expresses feeling, wish.
   6 **Gives orientation**, information, repeats, clarifies, confirms.

Understanding and Managing People at Work

- C **Task: Questions**
  7 **Asks for orientation**, information, repetition, confirmation.
  8 **Asks for opinion**, evaluation, analysis, expression of feeling.
  9 **Asks for suggestion**, direction, possible ways of action.
- D **Socio-Emotional: Negative Reactions**
  10 **Disagrees**, shows passive rejection, formality, withholds help.
  11 **Shows tension**, asks for help, withdraws out of field.
  12 **Shows antagonism**, deflates others' status, defends or asserts self.

In an extension of interaction process analysis, Bales gives 27 typical group roles which are based on various combinations of these original main behavioural categories.[19]

Task and maintenance functions

If the group is to be effective, then, whatever its structure or the pattern of interrelationships among members, there are two main sets of functions or processes that must be undertaken – **task functions** and **maintenance functions**.

- **Task functions** are directed towards problem-solving, the accomplishment of the tasks of the group and the achievement of its goals. Most of the task-oriented behaviour will be concerned with 'production' activities, or the exchange and evaluation of ideas and information.
- **Maintenance functions** are concerned with the emotional life of the group and directed towards building and maintaining the group as an effective working unit. Most of the maintenance-oriented behaviour will be concerned with relationships among group members, giving encouragement and support, maintaining cohesiveness and the resolution of conflict.

Task and maintenance functions may be performed either by the group leader or by members. Ultimately it is the leader's responsibility to ensure that both sets of functions are carried out and the right balance is achieved between them. The appropriate combination of task-oriented behaviour and maintenance-oriented behaviour is essential to the success and continuity of the group.

In addition to these two types of behaviour members of a group may say or do something in attempting to satisfy some personal need or goal. The display of behaviour in this way is termed **self-oriented behaviour**. This gives a classification of three main types of functional behaviour which can be exhibited by individual members of a group: **task-oriented, maintenance-oriented** and **self-oriented**.

Classification of member roles

A popular system for the classification of member roles in the study of group behaviour is that devised originally by *Benne and Sheats*.[20] The description of member roles performed in well-functioning groups is classified into three broad headings: **group task roles, group maintenance roles** and **individual roles**.

- **Group task roles.** These assume that the task of the group is to select, define and solve common problems. Any of the roles may be performed by the various members or the group leader.
- **Group building and maintenance roles.** The analysis of member functions is oriented towards activities which build group-centred attitudes, or maintain group-centred behaviour. Contributions may involve a number of roles, and members or the leader may perform each of these roles.
- **Individual roles.** These are directed towards the satisfaction of personal needs. Their purpose is not related either to group task or to the group functioning.

A 'summary outline' of individuals in groups is presented in Figure 14.5 on p. 506.

Understanding and Managing People at Work

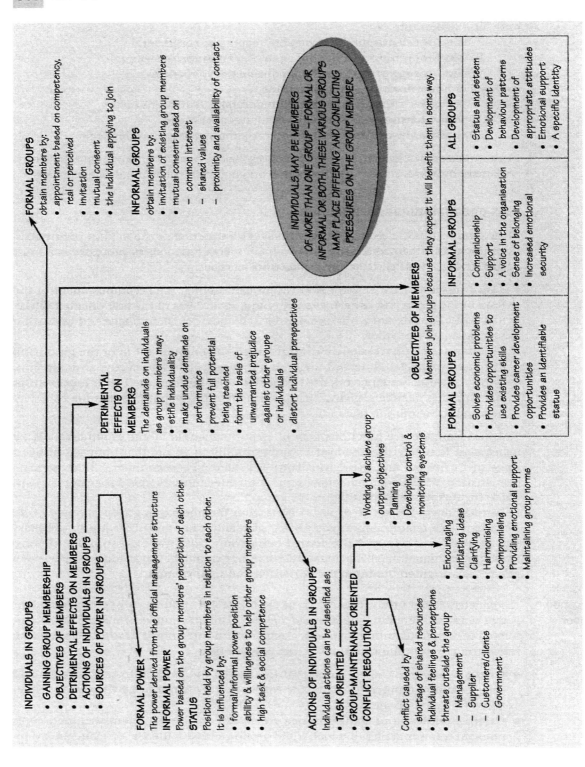

INDIVIDUALS IN GROUPS
- GAINING GROUP MEMBERSHIP
- OBJECTIVES OF MEMBERS
- DETRIMENTAL EFFECTS ON MEMBERS
- ACTIONS OF INDIVIDUALS IN GROUPS
- SOURCES OF POWER IN GROUPS

FORMAL POWER
The power derived from the official management structure
INFORMAL POWER
Power based on the group members' perception of each other
STATUS
Position held by group members in relation to each other.
It is influenced by:
- formal/informal power position
- ability & willingness to help other group members
- high task & social competence

ACTIONS OF INDIVIDUALS IN GROUPS
Individual actions can be classified as:
- TASK ORIENTED
- GROUP-MAINTENANCE ORIENTED
- CONFLICT RESOLUTION

Conflict caused by
- shortage of shared resources
- Individual feelings & perceptions
- threats outside the group
  – Management
  – Supplier
  – Customers/clients
  – Government

- Working to achieve group
  output objectives
- Planning
- Developing control &
  monitoring systems

- Encouraging
- Initiating ideas
- Clarifying
- Harmonising
- Compromising
- Providing emotional support
- Maintaining group norms

FORMAL GROUPS
obtain members by:
- appointment based on competency,
  real or perceived
- invitation
- mutual consent
- the individual applying to join

INFORMAL GROUPS
obtain members by:
- invitation of existing group members
- mutual consent based on
  – common interest
  – shared values
  – proximity and availability of contact

DETRIMENTAL EFFECTS ON MEMBERS
The demands on individuals
as group members may:
- stifle individuality
- make undue demands on
  performance
- prevent full potential
  being reached
- form the basis of
  unwarranted prejudice
  against other groups
  or individuals
- distort individual perspectives

INDIVIDUALS MAY BE MEMBERS
OF MORE THAN ONE GROUP – FORMAL OR
INFORMAL OR BOTH. THESE VARIOUS GROUPS
MAY PLACE DIFFERING AND CONFLICTING
PRESSURES ON THE GROUP MEMBER.

OBJECTIVES OF MEMBERS
Members join groups because they expect it will benefit them in some way.

FORMAL GROUPS	INFORMAL GROUPS	ALL GROUPS
• Solves economic problems	• Companionship	• Status and esteem
• Provides opportunities to use existing skills	• Support	• Development of behaviour patterns
• Provides career development opportunities	• A voice in the organisation	• Development of appropriate attitudes
• Provides an identifiable status	• Sense of belonging	• Emotional support
	• Increased emotional security	• A specific identity

Figure 14.5 Summary outline of individuals in groups
(Reproduced with permission of Training Learning Consultancy Ltd, Bristol.)

Frameworks of behavioural analysis

Several frameworks have been designed for observers to categorise patterns of verbal and non-verbal behaviour of group members. Observers chart members' behaviour on specially designed forms. These forms may be used to focus on single individuals, or used to record the total group interaction with no indication of individual behaviour.

The system of categorisation may distinguish between different behaviours in terms of the functions they are performing. The completed observation forms can be used as a basis for discussion of individual or group performance in terms of the strengths/weaknesses of different functional behaviour.

In the framework shown in Figure 14.6 there are two observation sheets, one covering six types of leader–member **task-function behaviour** and the other covering six types of leader–member **group building and maintenance function behaviour**.

TASK FUNCTIONS

1 **Initiating:** proposing tasks or goals; defining a group problem, suggesting a procedure or ideas for solving a problem.

2 **Information or opinion seeking:** requesting facts, seeking relevant information about a group concern, asking for suggestions and ideas.

3 **Information or opinion giving:** offering facts, providing relevant information about group concern; stating a belief; giving suggestions or ideas.

4 **Clarifying or elaborating:** interpreting or reflecting ideas and suggestions; clearing up confusions; indicating alternatives and issues before the group, giving examples.

5 **Summarising:** pulling together related ideas, restating suggestions after group has discussed them; offering a decision or conclusion for the group to accept or reject.

6 **Consensus testing:** sending up 'trial balloons' to see if group is nearing a conclusion; checking with group to see how much agreement has been reached.

GROUP BUILDING AND MAINTENANCE FUNCTIONS

1 **Encouraging:** being friendly, warm and responsive to others, accepting others and their contributions, regarding others by giving them an opportunity for recognition.

2 **Expressing group feelings:** sensing feeling, mood, relationships within the group, sharing one's own feelings with other members.

3 **Harmonising:** attempting to reconcile disagreements, reducing tension through 'pouring oil on troubled waters', getting people to explore their differences.

4 **Compromising:** when own idea or status is involved in a conflict, offering to compromise own position, admitting error, disciplining oneself to maintain group cohesion.

5 **Gatekeeping:** attempting to keep communication channels open, facilitating the participation of others; suggesting procedure for sharing opportunity to discuss group problems.

6 **Setting standards:** expressing standards for group to achieve, applying standards in evaluating group functioning and production.

Figure 14.6 Observation sheets for behavioural analysis

(*Source*: National Training Laboratory, Washington DC (1952).)

Understanding and Managing People at Work

Use of different frameworks

Different frameworks use a different number of categories for studying behaviour in groups. The interaction analysis method can become complex, especially if non-verbal behaviour is included. Many of the categories in different frameworks may at first sight appear to be very similar.

It is important, therefore, to keep the framework simple, and easy to understand and complete. The observer's own personality, values and attitudes can influence the categorisation of behaviour. For these reasons it is preferable to use trained observers, and wherever possible and appropriate to use more than one observer for each group. The observers can then compare the level of consistency between their categorisations. Observation sheets can be designed to suit the particular requirements of the group situation and the nature of the activity involved. An example of a reasonably simple, ten-point observation sheet used by the author is given in Figure 14.7.

Completing the observation sheet

Where appropriate, it may be helpful to note the initial seating, or standing, arrangements of the group. This will help in the identification of group members. Depending on the nature of the activity involved, it might also be possible to indicate main channels of interaction among individuals – for example, to whom eye contact, hand movements, or ideas and questions are most frequently directed. A note could also be made of changes in arrangements during, and at the end of, the activity.

Headings on the observation sheet are not necessarily exclusive. For example, leadership could be included under Taking Initiative, or under Performing Group Roles. Similarly, the role of humorist could be included under Performing Group Roles, but might also appropriately be included under the heading of Harmonising.

Observers will tend to use their own methods for completing the sheet: for example, a simple stroke or tick for each contribution and perhaps a thick stroke for a particularly significant contribution. Some observers might use some other distinguishing mark to indicate non-verbal behaviour such as body movements, smiles or eye contact. The most important point, however, is that the charting should not become too complex. The observer should feel happy with the framework and be capable of explaining the entries in a meaningful way. Where more than one observer is present there should be some degree of consistency between them.

| Group performance and effectiveness

Groups are an essential feature in the life of the organisation. For example, as *Coghlan* points out:

> *Membership of teams and groups shape an individual's perception and participation in organizational change ... Groups and teams play a key role in the process of planned organizational change. The change process typically involves teams in the organization's hierarchy responding to the change agenda and adapting to it in terms of its tasks and processes.*[21]

Individuals on teams interact extensively with one another, and with other teams in the organisation. Team-based management is used to improve communication, co-ordination and co-operation within the organisation.[22] For example, as *Green* maintains:

> *The generally perceived advantages of working in teams are the release of creativity and energy, much more interaction between people satisfying the need to belong ... Team working can improve efficiency by people planning activities together with cooperation and communication. Team members together should be able to identify many ways to improve work organisation; how information, ideas and outputs flow and how team-working can reduce costs and improve productivity.*[23]

Nature of group						
Nature of activity						
Date Name of observer(s)						

Initial arrangement of group

```
                    C  D
                 B            E
             A                F
```

Name of group members (or reference letters)

	A	B	C	D	E	F
Taking initiative – e.g. attempted leadership, seeking suggestions, offering directions						
Brainstorming – e.g. offering ideas or suggestions, however valid						
Offering positive ideas – e.g. making helpful suggestions, attempting to problem-solve						
Drawing in others – e.g. encouraging contributions, seeking ideas and opinions						
Being responsive to others – e.g. giving encouragement and support, building on ideas						
Harmonising – e.g. acting as peacemaker, calming things down, compromising						
Challenging – e.g. seeking justification, showing disagreement in constructive way						
Being obstructive – e.g. criticising, putting others down, blocking contributions						
Clarifying/summarising – e.g. linking ideas, checking progress, clarifying objectives/proposals						
Performing group roles – e.g. spokesperson, recorder, time keeper, humorist						
Other comments						

Figure 14.7 Observation sheet for behaviour in groups

Understanding and Managing People at Work

221

It is, however, difficult to draw any firm conclusions from a comparison between individual and group or team performance. An example of this can be seen from a consideration of decision-making. Certain groups, such as committees, may be concerned more specifically with decision-making, but all groups must make some decisions. Group decision-making can be costly and time-consuming, but would appear to offer a number of advantages.

- Groups can provide a pooling of resources, and can bring together a range of complementary knowledge and expertise.
- Interaction among members can have a 'snowball' effect and provoke future thoughts and ideas in the minds of others.
- Group discussion leads to the evaluation and correction of possible decisions.
- Provided full participation has been facilitated, decisions will have the acceptance of most members and they are more likely to be committed to decisions made and their implementation.

One might expect, therefore, a higher standard of decision-making to result from group discussion. However, on the one hand, there is the danger of compromise and decisions being made in line with the 'highest common view'; and, on the other hand, there is the phenomenon of the so-called risky-shift.

The risky-shift phenomenon

This suggests that instead of the group taking fewer risks and making safer or more conservative decisions, the reverse is often the case. There is a tendency for groups to make more risky decisions than would individual members of the group on their own. Studies suggest that people working in groups generally advocate more risky alternatives than if they were making an individual decision on the same problem.[24]

Presumably, this is because members do not feel the same sense of responsibility for group decisions or their outcomes. 'A decision which is everyone's is the responsibility of no one.' Other explanations offered for the **risky-shift** phenomenon include:

1 People inclined to take risks are more influential in group discussions than more conservative people.
2 Risk-taking is regarded as a desirable cultural characteristic which is more likely to be expressed in a social situation such as group working.[25]

However, groups do appear to work well in the evaluation of ideas and to be more effective than individuals for problem-solving tasks requiring a range of knowledge and expertise. From a review of the research Shaw suggests that evidence supports the view that groups produce more solutions and better solutions to problems than do individuals.[26]

'Groupthink'

The effectiveness of group behaviour and performance can be adversely affected by the idea of '**groupthink**'. From an examination of some well-known government policy-making groups, *Janis* concluded that decisions can be characterised by groupthink which he defines as: 'a deterioration of mental efficiency, reality testing, and moral judgment that results from in-group pressures'.[27] Groupthink results in the propensity for the group to just drift along. For example, Britain's do-nothing policy prior to the Second World War, and in the USA the attack on Pearl Harbor, the Bay of Pigs invasion of Cuba and the escalation of the war in Vietnam were a result of groupthink.

The idea of groupthink is not, however, limited to government policy-making groups. Janis maintains that groupthink is a generalised feature and can be apparent in any organisational situation where groups are relied upon to make important decisions.

Janis identifies a number of specific symptoms of groupthink.

1 There is an **illusion of invulnerability** with excessive optimism and risk-taking.
2 The discounting or discrediting of negative feedback which contradicts group consensus results in **rationalisation** in order to explain away any disagreeable information.
3 An unquestioned belief in the **inherent morality of the group** which leads members to be convinced of the logical correctness of what it is doing and to ignore ethical or moral consequences of decisions.
4 The group's desire to maintain consensus can lead to **negative stereotyping** of opponents or people outside the group, or to the acceptance of change.
5 There is **pressure on individual members to conform and reach consensus** so that minority or unpopular ideas may be suppressed.
6 Each member of the group may impose **self-censorship** in order to suppress their own objectives, or personal doubts or disagreements.
7 As a result of self-censorship, there is an **illusion of unanimity** with a lack of expressed dissent and a false sense of unity.
8 In the unlikely event of dissent or contrary information, this will give rise to the **emergence of 'mind guards'** who act as filters, guarding group leaders, deflecting opposition and applying pressure on deviants.

The effects of groupthink often occur in committees and working parties with a drifting along towards decisions which may be inappropriate or which are not questioned fully.[28]

Brainstorming

A **brainstorming** approach involves the group adopting a 'freewheeling' attitude and generating as many ideas as possible, the more wild or apparently far-fetched the better.[29] As an illustrative exercise a group may be asked to generate as many and varied possible uses as they can for, for example, a house brick or a car fan belt.

There are a number of basic procedures for brainstorming.

- It is based on maximum freedom of expression with a totally informal approach.
- The initial emphasis is on the quantity of ideas generated, not the quality of ideas.
- No individual ideas are criticised or rejected at this stage, however wild or fanciful they may appear.
- Members are encouraged to elaborate or build on ideas expressed by others, and to bounce suggestions off one another.
- There is no comment on or evaluation of any particular idea until all ideas have been generated.

Brainstorming is based on encouraging members to suspend judgement, the assumption that creative thinking is achieved best by encouraging the natural inclinations of group members, and the rapid production and free association of ideas. The quantity of ideas will lead to quality of ideas.

Effectiveness of brainstorming groups

One might reasonably expect that members of a brainstorming group would produce more creative problem-solving ideas than if the same members worked alone as individuals. Availability of time is an important factor. Over a longer period of time the group may produce more ideas through brainstorming than individuals could. Perhaps surprisingly, however, there appears to be doubt about the effectiveness of brainstorming groups over an individual working under the same conditions. Research findings suggest that brainstorming groups can inhibit creative thinking.

The general tenor appears to be that research studies have not substantiated claims that brainstorming groups generate more and better ideas than the same number of individuals working on their own.[30] Nevertheless, brainstorming still appears to have many advocates and is a popular activity for staff development programmes.[31] (*See* Figure 14.8.)

Despite the rather negative view of nominal group brainstorming, we should recognise the importance of innovation for successful organisational performance.[32] Any procedure which aids the process of creativity should be welcomed and there are a

---

BRAINSTORMING

Brainstorming is a problem-solving/solution-finding technique which can be used by individuals, groups or teams. Its full benefit is gained by sharing ideas and possibilities with others.

The first step is to define the problem or situation to which the group or team wants solutions or ideas. Ideally one person should act as scribe, and write up ideas on a flipchart. He or she can contribute, but should not comment on others' suggestions. Every idea should be written up, however far-fetched or silly it might seem, without challenge from others.

Everyone should be encouraged to participate.

When all possibilities have been exhausted, suggestions can be examined, clarified, amended, accepted or rejected.

It may be that several options are accepted as possible ways forward. Reverse brainstorming looks at the possibilities and then brainstorms all the *problems* associated with the ideas. This helps give an objective view of ideas or solutions.

If performed correctly, brainstorming is an excellent, non-threatening way to include all members of a team in the problem-solving/decision-making process. It has the added benefit of producing many and various ideas, some of which will be of no value, but others which may be of immediate or future benefit. Creativity is contagious, and one idea will spark off another. Often, it is one of the most apparently silly ideas that points the way to a solution.

Brainstorming:

● involves everyone;
● focuses the mind;
● encourages creativity;
● meets individual needs for team inclusion;
● encourages communication – listening, information sharing;
● maximises ideas/possible solutions to problems;
● minimises risk of overlooking elements of the problem or issue under question.

Figure 14.8 Advantages of brainstorming

Source: Susan Bishop and David Taylor, *Developing Your Staff*, Pitman Publishing/Longman Training (1994). Reproduced with permission from Pearson Education Ltd.)

number of potential positive achievements in terms of related structural techniques for stimulating innovation. These include the Delphi technique and quality circles.

The **Delphi technique** is based on multiple, anonymous inputs from individual members of the group. Ideas and suggestions are recorded by a central manager and then recirculated to other members for their feedback. The central manager collates the responses and continues the circulation process again until consensus is reached. Although a time-consuming process the Delphi technique helps to overcome the limitations of face-to-face brainstorming and symptoms of groupthink.

Quality circles are discussed in Chapter 18.

Variety of interrelated factors

Whatever the results of a comparison between individual and group performance, groups will always form part of the pattern of work organisation. It is a matter of judgement for the manager as to when, and how best, to use groups in the execution of work.

Any framework for viewing the performance and effectiveness of groups must take into account a variety of interrelated factors. These include:

● the composition, cohesiveness and maturity of the group;
● its structure, the clarification of role differentiation and channels of communication;
● patterns of interaction and group process, and attention to both task and maintenance functions;

Exhibit 14.1

Management: brainstorm in a rainstorm

Use the theatre to fire creativity writes **Arkady Ostrovsky.**

Jackets come off, ties are loosened; 20 senior business people howl, whisper and run around throwing their arms about.

Their bizarre behaviour is part of an exercise to use theatre to fuel their imagination and creativity.

One participant, Richard Hardman, international exploration director at US oil group Amerada Hess, says: 'If you want to get fit physically you go to the gym, but what do you do if your imagination needs some stretching? Theatre is very good for it.'

Four weeks of visits to theatrical events and a day's seminar and workshop took place recently during the annual London International Festival of Theatre. Events were held in association with the Global Business Network, a business strategy group, and the FT.

At one, executives took a barefoot, sensual journey through a dark labyrinth inhabited by personifications of destiny and death. At another, they were deafened by music and sprinkled with water and tickertape as they stood in a darkened warehouse watching Argentinian troupe De La Guarda's crazed, swooping musician-acrobats.

Richard Wise, chief financial officer at Coutts, the bank, says: 'You are so bound up with day-to-day imperatives that you lose the creative aspect. We tend to deal in very rationalised business structures – these performances show the benefit of brainstorming unconventional solutions.'

Performers and business people had a chance to meet after events – to the benefit of both sides, says Julia Rowntree, of the festival. 'It encourages the artist to learn more about the motives that drive the business world and, in some way, to have their say in it. For business people, it is a chance to discover what is going on outside their offices and to look at their own business from an outside perspective.'

The benefits of such exercises are notoriously difficult to measure. But, says Rick Haythornthwaite, director of Premier Oil, and a participant: 'If you test the success of this venture through the quality of thinking and the open-mindedness of the people who participate in it, back in the work place over the coming months and years, it is undoubtedly working.'

(Reproduced with permission from the Financial Times Limited, © *Financial Times* 9 July 1997.)

- the work to be undertaken and the nature of the technology;
- management system and style of leadership;
- organisational processes and procedures;
- the social system of the group and the informal organisation; and
- the environment in which the group is operating.

These are the factors that the manager must attempt to influence in order to improve the effectiveness of the group. Ultimately, however, the performance of the group will be determined very largely by the characteristics and behaviour of its members. The nature of group personality means that what works well for one group may not work well for an apparently very similar group in the organisation.

As *Wilson*, points out, for example, although teamworking, like most management ideas, is very simple, nevertheless this simplicity conceals a great challenge.

The principles of teamworking may be easily understood, but the task of installing it can be quite daunting. Introducing teamworking is not a straightforward grafting job, the simple matter of adding a new idea to those already in place. It is about making a fundamental change in the way people work. Every teamworking application is different. Each organisation, department and individual group is faced with unique problems and in some situations it is more about getting rid of old ways of doing things than injecting new ones.[33]

Ten ways to motivate your team[34]

1 Be clear about your own goals	6 Get to know individuals
2 Inform everyone of theirs	7 Incentivise everyone
3 Give the right training	8 Be tough when necessary
4 Coach and encourage	9 Give people space to grow
5 Listen to members	10 Let them get on with it

A 'summary outline' of effective work groups is presented in Figure 14.9.

Group dynamics

Interest in the study of group process and behaviour has led to the development of **group dynamics** and a range of group training methods aimed at increasing group effectiveness through improving social interaction skills.

Group dynamics is the study of interactions and forces within small face-to-face groups. It is concerned with what happens when groups of people meet.

A central feature of group dynamics is **sensitivity training**, in which members of a group direct attention to the understanding of their own behaviour and to perceiving themselves as others see them. The objectives are usually stated as:

- to increase sensitivity (the ability to perceive accurately how others react to oneself);
- diagnostic ability (the skill of assessing behavioural relationships between others and reasons for such behaviour); and
- behavioural flexibility, or action skill (the ability to relate one's behaviour to the requirements of the situation).

An account of 'problems' that have arisen with team-building exercises is given in the appendix to this chapter.

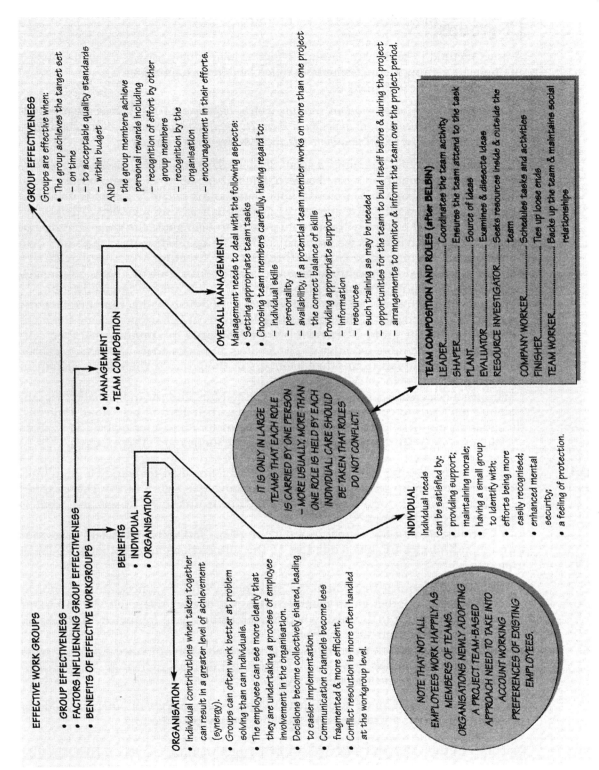

EFFECTIVE WORK GROUPS

- GROUP EFFECTIVENESS
- FACTORS INFLUENCING GROUP EFFECTIVENESS
- BENEFITS OF EFFECTIVE WORKGROUPS

ORGANISATION

- Individual contributions when taken together can result in a greater level of achievement (synergy).
- Groups can often work better at problem solving than can individuals.
- The employees can see more clearly that they are undertaking a process of employee involvement in the organisation.
- Decisions become collectively shared, leading to easier implementation.
- Communication channels become less fragmented & more efficient.
- Conflict resolution is more often handled at the workgroup level.

BENEFITS

- INDIVIDUAL
- ORGANISATION

MANAGEMENT
TEAM COMPOSITION

IT IS ONLY IN LARGE TEAMS THAT EACH ROLE IS CARRIED BY ONE PERSON – MORE USUALLY, MORE THAN ONE ROLE IS HELD BY EACH INDIVIDUAL. CARE SHOULD BE TAKEN THAT ROLES DO NOT CONFLICT.

OVERALL MANAGEMENT

Management needs to deal with the following aspects:

- Setting appropriate team tasks
- Choosing team members carefully, having regard to:
  - individual skills
  - personality
  - availability, if a potential team member works on more than one project
  - the correct balance of skills
- Providing appropriate support
  - information
  - resources
  - such training as may be needed
  - opportunities for the team to build itself before & during the project
  - arrangements to monitor & inform the team over the project period.

GROUP EFFECTIVENESS

Groups are effective when:

- The group achieves the target set
  - on time
  - to acceptable quality standards
  - within budget
  AND
- the group members achieve personal rewards including
  - recognition of effort by other group members
  - recognition by the organisation
  - encouragement in their efforts.

INDIVIDUAL

Individual needs can be satisfied by:

- providing support;
- maintaining morale;
- having a small group to identify with;
- efforts being more easily recognised;
- enhanced mental security;
- a feeling of protection.

NOTE THAT NOT ALL EMPLOYEES WORK HAPPILY AS MEMBERS OF TEAMS. ORGANISATIONS NEWLY ADOPTING A PROJECT TEAM-BASED APPROACH NEED TO TAKE INTO ACCOUNT WORKING PREFERENCES OF EXISTING EMPLOYEES.

TEAM COMPOSITION AND ROLES (after BELBIN)

LEADER................ Coordinates the team activity
SHAPER................ Ensures the team attend to the task
PLANT................ Source of ideas
EVALUATOR................ Examines & dissects ideas
RESOURCE INVESTIGATOR................ Seeks resource inside & outside the team
COMPANY WORKER................ Schedules tasks and activities
FINISHER................ Ties up loose ends
TEAM WORKER................ Backs up the team & maintains social relationships

Figure 14.9 Summary outline of effective work groups

(Reproduced with permission of Training Learning Consultancy Ltd., Bristol.)

T-groups

A usual method of sensitivity training (which is increasingly used as a generic term) is the **T-group** (training group), sometimes called laboratory training.

A T-group has been defined as:

an approach to human relations training which, broadly speaking, provides participants with an opportunity to learn more about themselves and their impact on others, and in particular to learn how to function more effectively in face-to-face situations.[35]

The original form of a T-group is a small, leaderless, unstructured, face-to-face grouping. The group normally numbers between 8 and 12 members who may be strangers to each other or who may come from the same organisation (a family group). A deliberate attempt is made to minimise any status differentials among members. There is no agenda or planned activities. Trainers are present to help guide the group, but do not usually take an active role or act as formal leader. The agenda becomes the group's own behaviour in attempting to cope with the lack of structure or planned activities. Training is intended to concentrate on process rather than content, that is on the feeling level of communication rather than the informational value of communication.

Faced with confusion and lack of direction, individuals will act in characteristic ways. With the guidance of the trainers these patterns of behaviour become the focus of attention for the group. Participants are encouraged to examine their own self-concepts and to be more receptive to the feelings and behaviours of others. Feedback received by individuals from other members of the group is the main mechanism for learning.

This feedback creates a feeling of anxiety and tension, and the individual's own self-examination leads to consideration of new values, attitudes and behaviour. Typically, the group meets for a $1\frac{1}{2}$- to-2-hour session each day for up to a fortnight. The sessions are supported by related lectures, study groups, case studies and other exercises.

The Johari window

A simple framework for looking at self-insight, which is used frequently to help individuals in the T-group process, is the 'Johari window' (see Figure 14.10). This classifies behaviour in matrix form between what is known–unknown to self and what is known–unknown to others.[36]

A central feature of the T-group is reduction of the individual's 'hidden' behaviour through self-disclosure and reduction of the 'blind' behaviour through feedback from others.

- **Hidden behaviour** is that which the individual wishes to conceal from, or not to communicate to, other group members. It is part of the private self. An important role of the group is to establish whether members conceal too much, or too little, about themselves from other members.
- **The blind area** includes mannerisms, gestures, and tone of voice, and represents behaviour of the impact of which on others the individual is unaware. This is sometimes referred to as the 'bad breath' area.

The group must establish an atmosphere of openness and trust in order that hidden and blind behaviours are reduced and the public behaviour enhanced.

Value and effectiveness of T-Groups

Reactions to the value and effectiveness of T-group training are very mixed. Specific benefits and changes in behaviour from T-group training are listed by *Mangham and Cooper* as:

- **Receiving communications:** more effort to understand, attentive listening.
- **Relational facility:** co-operative, easier to deal with.

- **Awareness of human behaviour:** more analytic of others' actions, clear perceptions of people.
- **Sensitivity to group behaviour:** more conscious of group process.
- **Sensitivity to others' feelings:** sensitivity to the needs and feelings of others.
- **Acceptance of other people:** more tolerant, considerate, patient.
- **Tolerant of new information:** willing to accept suggestions, less dogmatic.[37]

However, the experience can be very disturbing and unpleasant, at least for some members. For example, participants have described it as 'a bloodbath and a psychological nudist colony in which people are stripped bare to their attitudes'.[38] Participants are required to lay bare their inner emotions and may feel an invasion of their privacy. The unstructured situation may permit trainers to impose their own perceptions and social viewpoints on members of the group.[39]

T-group training is difficult to evaluate objectively and there is still a main problem of the extent to which training is transferred 'back home' to practical work situations. However, a number of studies do suggest that participation as a member of a T-group does increase interpersonal skills, induce change, and lead to open communications and more flexible behaviour. T-groups probably do result in a change of behaviour but it is not always clear whether such change is positive or related to improved organisational performance.[40]

T-groups now take a number of different forms. Some place emphasis on the understanding of group processes, others place more emphasis on the development of the individual's self-awareness and feelings towards the behaviour of other people. They are now used frequently as a means of attempting to improve managerial development and organisational performance.

The *Blake and Mouton* managerial grid seminars, discussed in Chapter 7, can be seen as an applied, and refined, form of T-group. A number of different training packages have been designed, often under the broad heading of interpersonal skills, which are less confrontational and less disturbing for participants. The training often involves an analysis of group members' relationships with one another and the resolution of conflict.[41]

A continuous process of improvement and innovation

The ACAS advisory booklet on teamworking concludes that even when they are in place, teams will need constant monitoring and development, if they are not to stagnate. Teamworking is not a finite project but a process of continuous improvement and innovation.

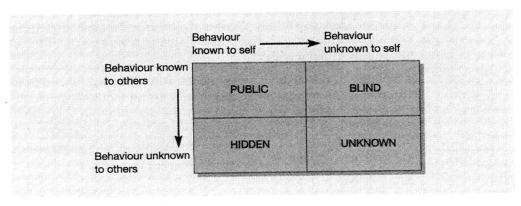

Figure 14.10 The Johari window

Understanding and Managing People at Work

The introduction of team working is a major step for an organisation to take. It is import-ant that management, trade unions and employees ensure they know how teamworking will contribute to their business strategy and that it is likely to involve a long-term transforma-tion ... The early challenge and excitement of establishing teams may fade and it is easy for organisations to accept a level of performance which is short of optimum ... In order to achieve high performance, teams require regular changes and challenges. These may include: changes to team personnel; new tasks; re-examining the contribution the team makes to the overall business aims; and ensuring that the team has regular dealings with other teams.[42]

Synopsis

■ Organisational performance and the satisfaction derived by individuals are influ-enced by the interactions among members of the group. Members of a group must work well together as a team and there must be a spirit of unity and co-operation. *Belbin* suggests key team-roles for successful groups. The level of interaction is influ-enced by the channels of communication. There are five main types of communication networks – wheel, circle, all-channel, Y and chains. Despite the artificiality, they pro-vide a reasonable representation of situations that might apply in large organisations.

■ In order to understand and to influence the functioning and operation of a group, it is necessary to study the behaviour of individual members. Two main methods are (i) sociometry, and (ii) interaction analysis. Sociometry is usually based on 'buddy rating' or 'peer rating'. It is a method of indicating feelings of acceptance and/or rejec-tion among members of a group. A sociogram gives a diagrammatical illustration of the pattern of interpersonal relationships derived from sociometry.

■ Interaction analysis is based on the assumption that behaviour in groups may be analysed from the viewpoint of its function or process. Two essential functions necessary for the success and continuity of a group are: (i) task-oriented behaviour; and (ii) maintenance-oriented behaviour. In addition, members of a group may display self-oriented behaviour. Several frameworks have been designed for observers to categorise patterns of verbal and non-verbal behaviour of group members. It is important, how-ever, that the frameworks do not become too complex.

■ Groups are an essential feature in the life of the organisation. Group decision-making would appear to offer a number of advantages, but can be adversely affected by 'groupthink' and by the 'risky-shift' phenomenon. There also appears to be some doubt about the effectiveness of brainstorming groups over an individual working under the same conditions. Viewing the performance and effectiveness of groups must take into account a variety of interrelated factors, especially the characteristics and behaviour of their members.

■ Interest in the study of group process and behaviour has led to the development of group dynamics and a range of group training methods aimed at improving social interaction skills. A usual method is the T-group, but reactions to the value and effectiveness of T-group training are mixed. A simple framework for looking at self-insight is the 'Johari window'. Effective teamwork is a process of continuous improvement and innovation.

Appendix

Barriers come down to build up team spirit

Corporate executives who regard 'team-building' exercises as a chance to let their hair down may well have paused for thought following news that a Railtrack session led to the suspension of a senior manager for allegedly drunken behaviour.

Yet the perception that corporate bonding events are a well-earned opportunity to pop a few corks endures – and catering for them is a booming business for hotels and management consultants, worth £600m a year.

Alcohol-fuelled antics at the Railtrack team-building exercise last week allegedly outraged clients and staff at the Balmer Lawn Hotel in Hampshire, and led to the suspension of Paul White, head of national contracts.

Earlier this month, Jim Hodkinson lost his job as chief executive of New Look, the fashion retailer, for groping the bottom of a female colleague during a corporate event.

But Roland Ayling, general manager of Dunston Hall hotel in Norwich, which regularly hosts company get-togethers, is not surprised. 'Of course, you get people becoming boisterous from drinking,' he says. 'That's part of the day.'

Although some events may get out of hand, once out of the office barriers come down as managers mingle with secretaries. That is why companies are happy to spend often large sums of money to help their employees get to know each other better, in the belief that it will help them work more efficiently.

'During team-building events, employees will develop a rapport which they have never had before,' says Jason Ludlow, of Events UK, which organised a team-building treasure-hunting trek in the New Forest for Railtrack managers last week.

However, not everyone agrees. Critics say few employees bring back the newly found complicity to the office. 'Nobody ever forgets where the hatchet is buried,' says one former Marks and Spencer manager, who is a veteran of many bonding sessions. The sense of common purpose developed during these exercises dissipates once it is subject to the hurlyburly of everyday life at work.'

An advertising manager adds: 'When people feel they are under pressure to bond, they stay away from these events and from one another afterwards.'

Popular team-building exercises include treasure hunting, clay pigeon shooting and sailing. Some will be tailor-made to reflect subtly a main corporate activity. For example, employees can be asked to help strangers in the street fix a tyre to test customer service skills. Some managers question the relevance of the games they have to play. The fact that I can build a raft to cross the river does not mean I can manage people properly,' says Edward Pickard who used to work at Aon Corporation, the insurance brokerage, before joining Tindall Riley.

(Reproduced with permission from the Financial Times Limited, © *Financial Times* 19 May 2000.)

CRITICAL REFLECTIONS

'I found all this discussion about group membership and building successful teams very interesting and enlightening. It certainly makes good sense to me.'

'Umm, I'm not so sure. It sounds fine in the classroom but I wonder how it works in practice for example with managing workers on a production assembly line, in a gay pub, or professionals such as doctors or lawyers?'

What are your own views?

Well-constructed and well-balanced teams have a good chance of succeeding in the modern world. But success is not ensured, however well the team functions. A common problem lies with the environment of the team. The team may be mature but the organization may not be. Hierarchies run organizations. They tolerate teams but are loath to see teams as alternatives to hierarchical decision-making.

Belbin, R. M. *Beyond the Team*, Butterworth-Heinemann (2000), p. 68.

How would you attempt to ensure the success of teams within a hierarchical organisation structure?

'Individuals will complete a task more efficiently and effectively than a group. And training in group dynamics, whilst interesting, has no practical value as a means of increasing the standard of group performance.'

Debate.

REVIEW AND
DISCUSSION
QUESTIONS

1 Discuss, with supporting practical examples, the likely advantages and disadvantages of working in a small group.

2 Contrast different types of communication networks in small groups. Give examples of a situation in which each type of network is likely to be most appropriate.

3 Assess the practical value to the manager of the analysis of group behaviour. Explain how you would go about constructing a sociogram.

4 Distinguish between: (a) group task roles; (b) group building and maintenance roles; and (c) individual roles. Give your own examples of each of these types of group member roles.

5 Suggest a framework for the categorisation of patterns of behaviour in group situations. What considerations need to be kept in mind when using such frameworks?

6 Explain what is meant by: (a) 'groupthink'; (b) the risky-shift phenomenon; and (c) brain-storming. Assess critically the likely standard of individual, compared with group, problem-solving and decision-making.

7 Explain the meaning and purpose of sensitivity training. Give your views on the practical value of group dynamics as a means of increasing the effectiveness of work groups.

8 In what ways might a manager expect to benefit from an understanding of the behaviour of people in work groups? Give practical examples relating to your own experience.

Assignment 1

Attempt, *preferably*, to observe a small group or project team at work; *alternatively*, next time you are involved in a small group discussion observe the members of your group.

a (i) Explain the nature of the **content** of the group's discussion and contrast this with the **process** of the discussion.

   (ii) Complete the grid below by giving a tick in the appropriate box to denote the behaviour of individual members in terms of:
     ● group task roles; group building and maintenance roles; individual roles.

b Explain the conclusions you draw concerning the conduct and apparent effectiveness of the group.

	Names of group members (or reference numbers)							
								Totals
Group taskroles								
Group building/maintenance roles								
Individual roles								
Totals								

Understanding and Managing People at Work

Assignment 2

MY ROLE IN THE TEAM

Purpose

To enable individual team members to consider the roles which they play within the team and identify which roles could be developed and used more to increase their effectiveness.

Method

There are twelve roles which need to be played to make most teams effective. Some team members may be able to play many roles, others only one, but most people can enhance their contribution by developing the capacity to play additional roles. Indeed, promotion prospects may depend upon it.

1 Referring to the Roles Summary Sheet below, complete the Team Role – Self Assessment sheet on page 522.

2 To refine and validate the results ask others who know you well to complete the Team Role – Colleague Assessment sheet for you.

3 Compare the results and if necessary institute a discussion to understand the reasons for colleagues perceptions of you.

4 Observe the way in which people operate who are strong in the roles in which you are weak and consider ways in which you can use your strengths to help others develop.

Team leader Forms the team Identifies strengths and weaknesses Determines contributions Monitors performance Calls meetings Provides structure Reviews team needs	**Challenger** Adopts unconventional approaches Looks afresh Challenges accepted order Provides the unexpected Ideas man Challenges complacency Provides stimulus Provides radical review	**Expert** Provides specialist expertise Acts as expert witness Provides professional viewpoint
Ambassador Develops external relationships Shows concern for external environment Sells the team Builds bridges	**Judge** Listens Evaluates Ponders Avoids arguments Avoids advocacy Promotes justice Avoids rushing Acts logically Acts pragmatically Provides balance Checks wild enthusiasm Seeks the truth	**Innovator** Uses imagination Proposes new methods Evaluates ideas Nurtures ideas Builds on others' ideas Visualizes opportunities Transforms ideas into strategies Deals with complex issues Provides vision Provides ingenuity Provides logic Helps understanding
Diplomat Promotes diplomatic solutions Has high influence Good negotiator Orientates the team Builds alliances Aids consensus Pragmatic Sees way ahead	**Conformer** Fills gaps Co-operative Helps relationships Jack of All Trades Avoids challenges to accepted order Observes Conservative	**Output pusher** Self motivated Pre-occupation with output and results 'Drives' Imposes time scales Chases progress Shows high commitment to task Intolerant Abrasive
Quality controller Checks output orientation Pre-occupation with quality Inspires higher standards Acts as team conscience Shows relationship concern	**Supporter** Builds morale Puts people at ease Ensures job satisfaction Resolves conflicts Gets to root of problem Gives advice Supports Encourages	**Reviewer** Observes Reviews performance Promotes regular review Gives feedback Acts as 'mirror' Looks for pitfalls Is process-orientated

---

TEAM ROLE – SELF ASSESSMENT SHEET

Review the twelve roles outlined on the Roles Summary Sheet and rank them according to the frequency with which you play each role.

1. _____   2. _____
3. _____   4. _____
5. _____   6. _____
7. _____   8. _____
9. _____   10. _____
11. _____   12. _____

Summary

Strong roles	Weak roles

TEAM ROLE – COLLEAGUE ASSESSMENT SHEET

Referring to the descriptions on the Roles Summary Sheet place in rank order your perception of how strongly the person plays each role.

Rank the strongest role 1 and the weakest 12.

1. _____   2. _____
3. _____   4. _____
5. _____   6. _____
7. _____   8. _____
9. _____   10. _____
11. _____   12. _____

In the space below make remarks which you feel would be helpful in:

(a) Developing weak roles.
(b) Enabling the person to play roles which you feel would be helpful to the team.

Understanding and Managing People at Work

Assignment 3

From your experience of working within a small group and/or project team at work, and as directed by your tutor, attempt to undertake **at least two** of the following tasks.

Task 1

Consider how individual members of the group fit best into the Belbin's revised nine team roles (Table 14.2, page 498).

Elaborate on both:

- their specific team-role contribution; and
- their allowable weaknesses.

_____

_____

_____

_____

_____

_____

Comment critically on the extent to which the people identified collectively help to form a balanced and comprehensive list of team-roles.

Task 2

Analyse the communication network(s) adopted by the group and level of interaction among members (Figure 14.2, page 500). Comment critically on the general level of satisfaction apparently experienced by individual group members.

_____

_____

_____

_____

_____

_____

Task 3

Classify individual member roles in terms of the amount of emphasis placed on:

- task functions;
- maintenance functions; and
- self-oriented behaviour.

_____

_____

_____

_____

_____

_____

Comment critically on the overall structure or pattern of interrelations among members of the group/team.

Task 4

Using your understanding of Sociometry, provide **in confidence** to your tutor the names of two people from your group/team with whom you would:

- most prefer to accompany you on a 'safari' type holiday;
- feel <u>least</u> uncomfortable in confiding to about a potentially embarrassing personal health or hygiene problem; and
- choose to discuss concern about progress on your course of study or at your place of work.

_____

_____

_____

_____

_____

_____

Task 5

Develop a list of critical indicators that you believe would best provide objective measures of how successfully the group/team is performing and its contribution to the overall effectiveness of the organisation.

_____

_____

_____

_____

_____

_____

Assignment 4

Working within a small group, and as directed by your tutor, adopt a brainstorming approach to providing as many possible uses as possible for:

- a 1970 edition of an American 900 page textbook on management; and
- a man or woman's leather belt

Elect a member of the group to record **all** of your responses. At the end of the allotted time delete any **obvious** duplication, total the numbers of ideas for each separate exercise, and then be prepared to share and compare with ideas and total scores from other groups.

What conclusions do you draw from this assignment?

_____

_____

_____

_____

_____

_____

Visit our website **www.booksites.net/mullins** for further questions, annotated weblinks, case material and internet research material.

Notes and references

1 See, for example: Allcorn, S. 'Understanding Groups at Work', *Personnel*, vol. 66, no. 8, August 1989, pp. 28–36.
2 *Teamwork: Success Through People*, Advisory Booklet, ACAS, September 1996, p. 12.
3 Obeng, E. *All Change*, Pitman Publishing (1994).
4 Crainer, S. *Key Management Ideas: Thinkers that changed the management world*, Third edition, Financial Times Prentice Hall (1998), p. 238.
5 Belbin, R. M. *Management Teams: Why They Succeed or Fail*, Butterworth-Heinemann (1981).
6 Belbin, R. M. *Team Roles at Work*, Butterworth-Heinemann (1993).
7 Furnham, A., Steele, H. and Pendleton, D. 'A Psychometric Assessment of the Belbin Team-Role Self-Perception Inventory', *Journal of Occupational and Organizational Psychology*, 66, 1993, pp. 245–61.
8 Arroba, T. and Wedgwood-Oppenheim, F. 'Do Senior Managers Differ in The Public and Private Sector? An Examination of Team-Role Preferences', *Journal of Managerial Psychology*, vol. 9, no. I, 1994, pp. 13–16.

9 White, J. 'Teaming with Talent', *Management Today*, September 1999, pp. 57–61.
10 Fisher, S. G., Hunter, T. A. and Macrosson, W. D. K. 'The Distribution of Belbin Team Roles among UK Managers', *Personnel Review*, vol. 29, no. 2, 2000, pp. 124–40.
11 Bavelas, A. 'A Mathematical Model for Group Structures', *Applied Anthropology*, vol. 7, 1948, pp. 19–30, and Bavelas, A. 'Communication Patterns in Task-Oriented Groups', in Lasswell, H. N. and Lerner, D. (eds) *The Policy Sciences*, Stanford University Press (1951).
12 Leavitt, H. J. 'Some Effects of Certain Communication Patterns on Group Performance', *Journal of Abnormal and Social Psychology*, vol. 46, 1951, pp. 38–50. See also: Leavitt, H. J. *Managerial Psychology*, Fourth edition, University of Chicago Press (1978).
13 Guetzkow, H. and Dill, W. R. 'Factors in the Organizational Development of Task-Oriented Groups', *Sociometry*, vol. 20, 1957, pp. 175–204.
14 Shaw, M. E. 'Communication Networks', in Berkowitz, L. (ed.) *Advances in Experimental Social Psychology*, vol. 1, Academic Press (1964).

15 Belbin, R. M. *Changing The Way We Work*, Butterworth-Heinemann (1997), p. 13.

16 Moreno, J. L. *Who Shall Survive?* Beacon House (1953). See also: Moreno, J. L. and Jennings, H. H. *The Sociometry Reader*, Free Press of Glencoe (1960).

17 Rogers, E. M. and Kincaid, D. L. *Communication Networks: Towards a New Paradigm for Research*, The Free Press (1981), p. 92.

18 Bales, R. F. 'A Set of Categories for the Analysis of Small Group Interaction', *American Sociological Review*, vol. 15, April 1950, pp. 257–63.

19 Bales, R. F. *Personality and Interpersonal Behaviour*, Holt, Rinehart and Winston (1970).

20 Benne, K. D. and Sheats, P. 'Functional Roles of Group Members', *Journal of Social Issues*, vol. 4, 1948, pp. 41–9.

21 Coghlan, D. 'Managing Organizational Change Through Teams and Groups', *Leadership & Organization Development Journal*, vol. 15, no. 2, 1994, pp. 18–23.

22 Whitfield, J. M., Anthony, W. P. and Kacmar, K. M. 'Evaluation of Team-Based Management: A Case Study', *Journal of Organizational Change Management*, vol. 8, no. 2, 1995, pp. 17–28.

23 Green, J. R. 'Team Building in Practice', *Chartered Secretary*, November 1997, pp. 34–5.

24 Kogan, N. and Wallach, M. A. 'Risk-Taking as a Function of the Situation, the Person and the Group', in Newcomb, T. M. (ed.) *New Directions in Psychology III*, Holt, Rinehart and Winston (1967).

25 For a comprehensive review of the 'risky-shift' phenomenon, see, for example: Clarke, R. D. 'Group Induced Shift Towards Risk: A Critical Appraisal', *Psychological Bulletin*, vol. 76, 1971, pp. 251–70. See also: Vecchio, R. P. *Organizational Behavior*, Third edition, Harcourt Brace and Company (1995).

26 Shaw, M. E. *Group Dynamics*, McGraw-Hill (1976).

27 Janis, J. L. *Victims of Groupthink*, Houghton Mifflin (1972) and Janis, J. L. *Groupthink*, Second edition, Houghton Mifflin (1982).

28 See, for example, Leana, C. R. 'A Partial Test of Janis' Groupthink Model: Effects of Group Cohesiveness and Leader Behavior on Defective Decision Making', *Journal of Management*, vol. 11, no. 1, 1985, pp. 5–17.

29 Osborn, A. F. *Applied Imagination Principles and Procedures of Creative Thinking*, Scribner's (1963).

30 Diehl, M. and Strobe, W. 'Productivity Loss in Brainstorming Groups: Towards the Solution of the Riddle', *Journal of Personality and Social Psychology*, vol. 53, 1987, pp. 497–509.

31 See, for example: Bishop, S. and Taylor, D. *Developing Your Staff*, Pitman Publishing/Longman Training, (1994).

32 See, for example: Waterman, R. *The Frontiers of Excellence*, Nicholas Brealey (1994).

33 Wilson, J. 'Building Teams – with Attitude', *Professional Manager*, September 1998, p. 13.

34 Browning, G. 'Brain Food: Matters for the Mind to Chew On', *Management Today*, April 2000, p. 20.

35 Cooper, C. L. and Mangham, I. L. (eds) *T-Groups: A Survey of Research*, Wiley (1971), p. v.

36 Luft, J. *Group Processes: An Introduction to Group Dynamics*, Second edition, National Press (1970). (The term 'Johari Window' was derived from a combination of the first names of the original authors, Joseph Luft and Harry Ingham.)

37 Mangham, I. and Cooper, C. L. 'The Impact of T-Groups on Managerial Behaviour', *Journal of Management Studies*, February 1969, vol. 6, no. 1, p. 57.

38 Davis, K. *Human Behavior at Work*, Fifth edition, McGraw-Hill (1977), p. 183.

39 Davis, K. and Newstrom, J. W. *Human Behavior at Work: Organizational Behavior*, Eighth edition, McGraw-Hill (1989).

40 See, for example: McKenna, E. *Business Psychology and Organisational Behaviour*, Lawrence Erlbaum (1994).

41 For an overview of experimental small group methods and training needs, see, for example: Smith, P. B. *Group Processes and Personal Change*, Harper and Row (1980). See also: Brown, R. *Group Processes: Dynamics Within and Between Groups*, Basil Blackwell (1988).

42 *Teamwork: Success Through People.* Advisory Booklet, ACAS, September 1996, pp. 46–7.

Chapter 12

THE NATURE OF WORK MOTIVATION

The relationship between the organisation and its members is influenced by what motivates them to work and the fulfilment they derive from it. The manager needs to know how best to elicit the co-operation of staff and direct their performance to achieving the goals and objectives of the organisation. The manager must understand the nature of human behaviour and how best to motivate staff so that they work willingly and effectively.

Learning objectives

To:

➤ explain the meaning and underlying concept of motivation;

➤ detail main types of needs and expectations of people at work;

➤ explain possible reactions to frustration at work;

➤ outline different approaches to work motivation;

➤ explain the nature of different theories of motivation;

➤ examine main theories of motivation and evaluate their relevance to particular work situations;

➤ appreciate the complex nature of work motivation.

The meaning of motivation

The study of **motivation** is concerned, basically, with why people behave in a certain way. The basic underlying question is 'why do people do what they do?'.[1] In general terms, motivation can be described as the direction and persistence of action. It is concerned with why people choose a particular course of action in preference to others, and why they continue with a chosen action, often over a long period, and in the face of difficulties and problems.[2]

From a review of motivation theory, *Mitchell* identifies four common characteristics which underlie the definition of motivation.[3]

● **Motivation is typified as an individual phenomenon.** Every person is unique and all the major theories of motivation allow for this uniqueness to be demonstrated in one way or another.

● **Motivation is described, usually, as intentional.** Motivation is assumed to be under the worker's control, and behaviours that are influenced by motivation, such as effort expended, are seen as choices of action.

● **Motivation is multifaceted.** The two factors of greatest importance are: (i) what gets people activated (arousal); and (ii) the force of an individual to engage in desired behaviour (direction or choice of behaviour).

● **The purpose of motivational theories is to predict behaviour.** Motivation is not the behaviour itself, and it is not performance. Motivation concerns action, and the internal and external forces which influence a person's choice of action.

On the basis of these characteristics, Mitchell defines motivation as 'the degree to which an individual wants and chooses to engage in certain specified behaviours'.

Underlying concept of motivation

The underlying concept of motivation is some driving force within individuals by which they attempt to achieve some goal in order to fulfil some need or expectation. This concept gives rise to the basic motivational model, which is illustrated in Figure 12.1.

People's behaviour is determined by what motivates them. Their performance is a product of both ability level and motivation.

$$\text{Performance} = \text{function (ability} \times \text{motivation)}$$

Kreitner et al. suggest that although motivation is a necessary contributor for job performance it is not the only one. Along with ability, motivation is also a combination of

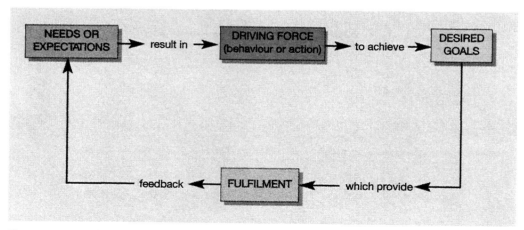

Figure 12.1 A simplified illustration of the basic motivational model

level of skill; knowledge about how to complete the task; feelings and emotions; and facilitating and inhibiting conditions not under the individual's control.[4] However, what is clearly evident is that if the manager is to improve the work of the organisation, attention must be given to the level of motivation of its members. The manager must also encourage staff to direct their efforts (their driving force) towards the successful attainment of the goals and objectives of the organisation.

> Over 22 million people are currently in employment and we cannot afford to underestimate the extent to which our economy depends on maintaining the motivation and improving the ability of the workforce. *Sir Brian Wolfson, Chairman of Investors in People UK*[5]

But what is this driving force? What are people's needs and expectations, and how do they influence behaviour and performance at work? Motivation is a complex subject, it is a very personal thing, and it is influenced by many variables. Individuals have a variety of changing, and often conflicting, needs and expectations which they attempt to satisfy in a number of different ways. For example, Green suggests over 30 ideas worthy of consideration by managers to positively influence members of their staff.[6]

Farren reminds us of the 12 human needs that been around since the beginning of recorded history: family; health and well-being; work/career; economic; learning; home/shelter; social relationships; spirituality; community; leisure; mobility; and environment/safety. 'Work and private life in the new millennium will continue to revolve around the 12 human needs.'[7]

We can consider how the various theories of motivation at work discussed later in this chapter relate to this set of human needs.

Needs and expectations at work

The various needs and expectations at work can be categorised in a number of ways – for example the simple divisions into physiological and social motives, or into intrinsic and extrinsic motivation.

Extrinsic motivation is related to 'tangible' rewards such as salary and fringe benefits, security, promotion, contract of service, the work environment and conditions of work. Such tangible rewards are often determined at the organisational level and may be largely outside the control of individual managers.

Intrinsic motivation is related to 'psychological' rewards such as the opportunity to use one's ability, a sense of challenge and achievement, receiving appreciation, positive recognition, and being treated in a caring and considerate manner. The psychological rewards are those that can usually be determined by the actions and behaviour of individual managers.[8]

Broad classification for motivation to work

Given the complex and variable nature of needs and expectations, the following is a simplistic but useful, broad three-fold classification as a starting point for reviewing the motivation to work. (*See* Figure 12.2.)

- **Economic rewards** – such as pay, fringe benefits, pension rights, material goods and security. This is an **instrumental** orientation to work and concerned with 'other things'.
- **Intrinsic satisfaction** – derived from the nature of the work itself, interest in the job, and personal growth and development. This is a **personal** orientation to work and concerned with 'oneself'.

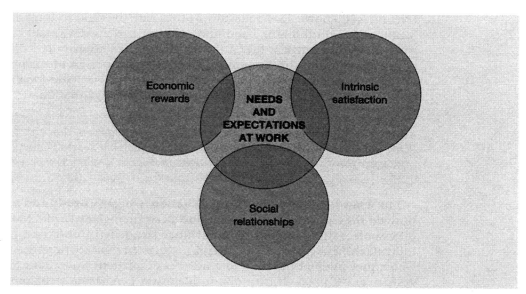

Figure 12.2 Needs and expectations of people at work

- **Social relationships** – such as friendships, group working, and the desire for affiliation, status and dependency. This is a **relational** orientation to work and concerned with 'other people'.

A person's motivation, job satisfaction and work performance will be determined by the comparative strength of these sets of needs and expectations, and the extent to which they are fulfilled. For example, some people may make a deliberate choice to forgo intrinsic satisfaction and social relationships (particularly in the short term or in the earlier years of their working life) in return for high economic rewards. Other people are happy to accept comparatively lower economic rewards in favour of a job which has high intrinsic satisfaction and/or social relationships. Intrinsic satisfaction is a personal attitude which varies according to the individual and particular circumstances. It will also vary from job to job and often between different parts of the same job. Social relationships would appear to be an important feature for many people, especially, for example, for those working in the hospitality industry where interactions with other people and the importance of supportive working relationships and good teamwork can be strong motivators at work.[9]

The psychological contract

In addition to the above categories, the motivation to work is also increasingly influenced by the changing nature of the work environment and the concept of the 'psychological contract', which was discussed in Chapter 2. The psychological contract involves a series of expectations between the individual member and the organisation. These expectations are not defined formally, and although the individual member and the organisation may not be consciously aware of the expectations, their relationship is still affected by these expectations.

Frustration-induced behaviour

If a person's motivational driving force is blocked before reaching a desired goal, there are two possible sets of outcomes: constructive behaviour or frustration. (*See* Figure 12.3.)

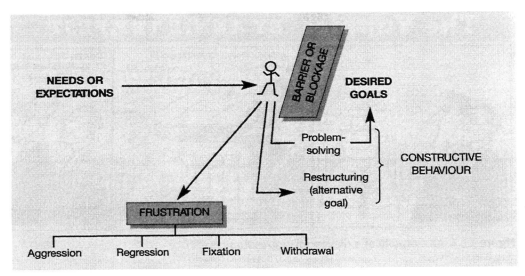

Figure 12.3 A basic model of frustration

Constructive behaviour	**Constructive behaviour** is a positive reaction to the blockage of a desired goal and can take two main forms: problem-solving or restructuring.

- **Problem-solving** is the removal of the barrier – for example, repairing a damaged machine, or by-passing an unco-operative superior.
- **Restructuring**, or compromise, is the substitution of an alternative goal, although such a goal may be of a lower order – for example, taking an additional part-time job because of failure to be promoted to a higher grading.

Note: Even if a person engages in constructive behaviour in response to a barrier or blockage it could be said that the person was 'frustrated', if only mildly or in the short term, in an attempt to satisfy a desired goal. However, the term frustration is usually interpreted as applying to **negative responses** to a barrier or blockage which prevents satisfaction of a desired goal.

Frustration (negative responses)	**Frustration** is a negative response to the blockage of a desired goal and results in a defensive form of behaviour. There are many possible reactions to frustration caused by the failure to achieve a desired goal. These can be summarised under four broad headings: aggression; regression; fixation; and withdrawal.[10] However, these categories are not mutually exclusive. Most forms of frustration-induced behaviour at work are a combination of aggression, regression and fixation.

Aggression is a physical or verbal attack on some person or object; for example, striking a supervisor, rage or abusive language, destruction of equipment or documents, malicious gossip about a superior. This form of behaviour may be directed against the person or object which is perceived as the source of frustration, that is the actual barrier or blocking agent.

However, where such direct attack cannot be made, because, for example, the source of frustration is not clear or not specific, or where the source is feared, such as a powerful superior, then aggression may be displaced towards some other person or object.

With **displaced aggression** the person may find an easier, safer person or object as a scapegoat for the outlet of frustration – for example, picking arguments with colleagues, being short-tempered with subordinates, shouting at the cleaners or kicking the waste-paper bin. (*See* Figure 12.4.) A more constructive form of displaced aggression is working off frustrated feelings through demanding physical work or sport, or perhaps by shouting/cursing when alone or in the company of an understanding colleague.

Figure 12.4 An example of a displaced aggression!

(Cartoon by Annie Tempest reproduced with the permission of Solo Syndication Limited from the *Daily Mail*, 26 February 1988. Copyright © Mail Newspapers plc.)

Regression is reverting to a childish or more primitive form of behaviour – for example, sulking, crying, tantrums, or kicking a broken machine or piece of equipment.

Fixation is persisting in a form of behaviour which has no adaptive value and continuing to repeat actions which have no positive results – for example, the inability to accept change or new ideas, repeatedly trying a machine which clearly will not work, insisting on applying for promotion even though not qualified for the job.

Withdrawal is apathy, giving up or resignation – for example, arriving at work late and leaving early, sickness and absenteeism, refusal to accept responsibility, avoiding decision-making, passing work over to colleagues, or leaving the job altogether.

Factors influencing frustration

Among the factors which determine an individual's reaction to frustration are:

- the level and potency of need (*see*, for example, Maslow's theory of motivation, discussed below);
- the degree of attachment to the desired goal;
- the strength of motivation;
- the perceived nature of the barrier or blocking agent; and
- the personality characteristics of the individual.

It is important that managers attempt to reduce potential frustration through, for example:

- effective recruitment, selection and socialisation;
- training and development;
- job design and work organisation;
- equitable personnel policies;
- recognition and rewards;
- effective communications;
- participative styles of management;
- attempting to understand the individual's perception of the situation.

Proper attention to motivation, and to the needs and expectations of people at work will help overcome boredom and frustration – induced behaviour.

Money as a motivator

Earlier writers, such as *F. W. Taylor*, believed in economic needs motivation. Workers would be motivated by obtaining the highest possible wages through working in the most efficient and productive way. Performance was limited by physiological fatigue. For Taylor, motivation was a comparatively simple issue – what the workers wanted from their employers more than anything else was high wages.[11] This approach is the **rational–economic concept of motivation.**

The ideas of F. W. Taylor and his 'rational–economic needs' concept of motivation (discussed in Chapter 3) and subsequent approaches to motivation at work have fuelled the continuing debate about financial rewards as a motivator and their influence on productivity.

Moss Kanter has observed that in many organisations 'a mountain of tradition and industrial relations practice' has built up to result in the rewards received by employees being differentiated primarily on the basis of status rather than their contribution. Often the only way individuals can increase their pay is by being promoted. This results in much time being spent by employees plotting how their present jobs may be upgraded or how otherwise they might get promotion rather than striving to improve the contribution they make in their present jobs.[12]

Where there is little pleasure in the work itself or the job offers little opportunity for career advancement, personal challenge or growth, many people may appear to be motivated primarily, if not exclusively, by money. For example, Weaver suggests that for many hourly workers in the hospitality industry, such as dishwashers, waiting or housekeeping staff, their work does not change much among different companies and there is little attachment to a particular company. For such staff, Weaver proposes a 'Theory M' programme of motivation based on direct cash rewards for above average performance. A percentage base is calculated from the average performance of workers on the staff.[13]

In a recent survey of attitudes to work involving a random sample of 1000 workers, when asked to specify the biggest problem at work the most popular response was poor pay at 18 per cent.[14] Another recent survey of human resource managers responding to *Personnel Journal* found that it is often difficult to attract, retain and motivate minimum wage workers on pay alone. The survey uncovered that 62 per cent of respondents had a problem retaining minimum wage workers strictly because of pay. Many employers must provide other incentives such as bonuses or prizes – on top of pay – to keep workers in the job.[15]

On the other hand, we frequently see pronouncements from prominent business figures that motivation is about much more than money.

> I was convinced that the success of any business depended on having the right people and motivating them properly. As I thought about this, I decided that motivation was not just about money. It was about creating an environment in which people enjoyed working. When I joined Morgan Grenfell, my aim would be to get the best out of people whether they were young or old, experienced fund managers or less experienced.
> *Nicola Horlick, formerly Managing Director, Morgan Grenfell Investment Management*[16]

The short answer appears to be: that for the vast majority of people, money is clearly important and a motivator at work **but** to what extent and **how** important depends upon their personal circumstances and the other satisfactions they derive from work. The bottom line is surely the extent to which money motivates people to work **well** and to the best of their abilities.

Motivation without money

The *Income Data Services (IDS)* draws attention to the challenges of motivation during economic circumstances of low inflation. 'Most of us have lived and worked through a unique period during which pay and prices rose continuously for decades.' IDS found that although the importance of large bonuses in motivating people could not be ignored, especially in high growth companies, there is a need to provide new forms of recognition for employees that do not depend on promotion or money. In the main employers agreed that they now face the prime challenges of: breaking with the habit of automatic annual increases in pay; shifting the focus of reward from individual performance to team success; moving from 'quantity' to 'quality'; and managing a more diverse workforce by policies which recognise different needs.[17]

Why the mystery of motivation?

An interesting, if somewhat cynical, viewpoint on approaches to motivation is put for ward by *Ritti*, who suggests that managers do act on what they know.

> *Truth to tell, we know a good deal about human motivation. And most of what we know is probably correct. Then why the mystery of motivation? The answer is simply that we don't act on what we know. Frederick Winslow Taylor put his finger squarely on the problem at the turn of the century. Taylor said that if management would only show workers how to do the job better, and then share the return of a better job with them, there would be no problem. Still, he lamented, management will never do that, for fear of driving wages up. And for the most part, he was right. So it is that the most popular schemes for raising levels of motivation all promise you can get something for nothing, a kind of motivational perpetual motion. Stress the intrinsic motivators (these don't include money, naturally), enrich the job, allow participation in decisions. In short, do everything but what Taylor recommended.*[18]

Theories of motivation

There are many competing theories which attempt to explain the nature of motivation. These theories are all at least partially true, and all help to explain the behaviour of certain people at certain times. However, **the search for a generalised theory of motivation at work appears to be in vain**. As with leadership (discussed in Chapter 8), *Handy* suggests that the search for the definitive solution to the motivation problem is another endless quest for the Holy Grail in organisation theory.[19] Nevertheless, any theory or study which aids an understanding of how best to motivate people at work must be useful.

> *All managers have a duty to motivate their teams. Motivated people take more pride in their jobs and work better. But many managers don't know how to motivate their staff.*[20]

A major determinant of behaviour is the particular situation in which individual workers find themselves. Motivation varies over time and according to circumstances. It is often most acute for younger people starting on their career, for people at mid-career positions or for those who find limited opportunities for promotion or further advancement. For employers there may be difficulties in motivating staff both in the longer term as well as in the short run.

Complexity of motivation

It is because of the complexity of motivation, and the fact that there is no ready-made solution or single answer to what motivates people to work well, that the different theories are important to the manager. They show there are many motives which influence people's behaviour and performance. Collectively, the different theories provide a framework within which to direct attention to the problem of how best to motivate staff to work willingly and effectively.

It is important to emphasise, however, that these various theories are not conclusive. They all have their critics (this is particularly true of the content theories of motivation), or have been subject to alternative findings which purport to contradict the original ideas. Many of these theories were not intended, originally, to have the significance that some writers have subsequently placed upon them. It is always easy to quote an example which appears to contradict any generalised observation on what motivates people to work. However, these different theories provide a basis for study and discussion, and for review of the most effective motivational style. (*See* Figure 12.5.)

> You don't motivate individuals. You provide them with an environment to be self-motivated. It is a personal decision, but it's management's job to provide the right environment.
> *Kathy Schofield, Director of Human Resources, HCF Bank*[21]

The manager, therefore, must judge the relevance of these different theories, how best to draw upon them, and how they might effectively be applied in particular work situations. The manager should be aware of at least the main theories of motivation.[22]

Content theories and process theories The usual approach to the study of motivation is through an understanding of internal cognitive processes – that is, what people feel and how they think. This understanding should help the manager to predict likely behaviour of staff in given situations. These different cognitive theories of motivation are usually divided into two contrasting approaches: content theories and process theories.

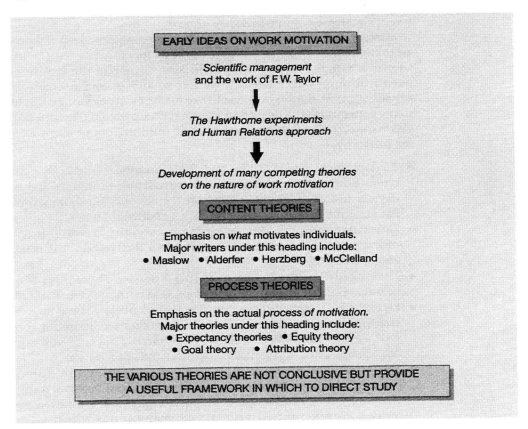

Figure 12.5 An overview of main theories of work motivation

Understanding and Managing People at Work

- **Content theories** attempt to explain those specific things which actually motivate the individual at work. These theories are concerned with identifying people's needs and their relative strengths, and the goals they pursue in order to satisfy these needs. Content theories place emphasis on the nature of needs and **what motivates**.
- **Process theories** attempt to identify the relationship among the dynamic variables which make up motivation. These theories are concerned more with how behaviour is initiated, directed and sustained. Process theories place emphasis on the **actual process of motivation**. These theories are discussed later in this chapter.

Content theories of motivation

Major content theories of motivation include:

- *Maslow's* hierarchy of needs model;
- *Alderfer's* modified need hierarchy model;
- *Herzberg's* two-factor theory; and
- *McClelland's* achievement motivation theory.

Maslow's hierarchy of needs theory

A useful starting point is the work of *Maslow*, and his theory of individual development and motivation, published originally in 1943.[23] Maslow's basic proposition is that people are wanting beings, they always want more, and what they want depends on what they already have. He suggests that human needs are arranged in a series of levels, a hierarchy of importance.

Maslow identified eight innate needs, including the need to know and understand, aesthetic needs, and the need for transcendence. However, the hierarchy is usually shown as ranging through five main levels, from, at the lowest level, physiological needs, through safety needs, love needs, and esteem needs, to the need for self-actualisation at the highest level. The **hierarchy of needs** may be shown as a series of steps, but is usually displayed in the form of a pyramid (Figure 12.6). This is an appropriate form of illustration as it implies a thinning out of needs as people progress up the hierarchy.

- **Physiological needs.** These include homeostasis (the body's automatic efforts to retain normal functioning) such as satisfaction of hunger and thirst, the need for oxygen and to maintain temperature regulation. Also sleep, sensory pleasures, activity, maternal behaviour, and arguably sexual desire.
- **Safety needs.** These include safety and security, freedom from pain or threat of physical attack, protection from danger or deprivation, the need for predictability and orderliness.
- **Love needs** (often referred to as social needs). These include affection, sense of belonging, social activities, friendships, and both the giving and receiving of love.
- **Esteem needs** (sometimes referred to as ego needs). These include both self-respect and the esteem of others. Self-respect involves the desire for confidence, strength, independence and freedom, and achievement. Esteem of others involves reputation or prestige, status, recognition, attention and appreciation.
- **Self-actualisation needs.** This is the development and realisation of one's full potential. Maslow sees this as: 'What humans can be, they must be', or 'becoming everything that one is capable of becoming'. Self-actualisation needs are not necessarily a creative urge, and may take many forms which vary widely from one individual to another.

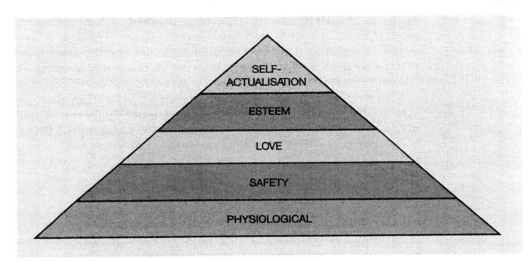

Figure 12.6 Maslow's hierarchy of needs model

Once a lower need has been satisfied, it no longer acts as a strong motivator. The needs of the next higher level in the hierarchy demand satisfaction and become the motivating influence. Only unsatisfied needs motivate a person. Thus Maslow asserts that 'a *satisfied need is no longer a motivator*'.

Not necessarily a fixed order

Although Maslow suggests that most people have these basic needs in about the order indicated, he also makes it clear that **the hierarchy is not necessarily a fixed order**. There will be a number of exceptions to the order indicated. For some people there will be a reversal of the hierarchy, for example:

- Self-esteem may seem to be more important than love to some people. This is the most common reversal of the hierarchy. It is often based on the belief that the person most loved is strong, confident or inspires respect. People seeking love try to put on a show of aggressive, confident behaviour. They are not really seeking self-esteem as an end in itself but for the sake of love needs.
- For some innately creative people the drive for creativity and self-actualisation may arise despite lack of satisfaction of more basic needs.
- Higher-level needs may be lost in some people who will continue to be satisfied at lower levels only: for example, a person who has experienced chronic unemployment.
- Some people who have been deprived of love in early childhood may experience the permanent loss of love needs.
- A need which has continued to be satisfied over a long period of time may be undervalued. For example, people who have never suffered from chronic hunger may tend to underestimate its effects, and regard food as rather an unimportant thing. Where people are dominated by a higher-level need this may assume greater importance than more basic needs.
- People with high ideals or values may become martyrs and give up everything else for the sake of their beliefs.

Maslow claims that the hierarchy is relatively universal among different cultures, but he recognises that there are differences in an individual's motivational content in a particular culture.

Degrees of satisfaction

Maslow points out that a false impression may be given that a need must be satisfied fully before a subsequent need arises. **He suggests that a more realistic description is in terms of decreasing percentages of satisfaction along levels of the hierarchy.** For example, arbitrary figures for the average person may be: satisfied 85 per cent in physiological needs; 70 per cent in safety needs; 50 per cent in love needs; 40 per cent in esteem needs; and 10 per cent in self-actualisation needs. There is a gradual emergence of a higher-level need as lower-level needs become more satisfied. The relative importance of these needs changes during the psychological development of the individual.

Maslow subsequently modified his views by noting that satisfaction of self-actualisation needs by growth-motivated individuals can actually enhance these needs rather than reduce them. Furthermore, he accepted that some higher-level needs may still emerge after long deprivation of lower-level needs, rather than only after their satisfaction.

Evaluation of Maslow's theory

Based on Maslow's theory, once lower-level needs have been satisfied (say at the physiological and safety levels) giving more of the same does not provide motivation. Individuals advance up the hierarchy as each lower-level need becomes satisfied. Therefore, to provide motivation for a change in behaviour, the manager must direct attention to the next higher level of needs (in this case, love or social needs) that seek satisfaction.

Robertson et al. commented on the possibility of testing Maslow's theory.

A proper test of Maslow's theory would involve placing individuals who are patently in need of satisfaction on all five need levels in a situation amply supplied with the means for attaining the various satisfactions and then permitting the individuals to choose at will. Such a pure test is impossible both for ethical and practical reasons. In addition, its simplicity would not reflect the important fact that behaviour in the real world is shaped by pressures and rewards which are often beyond the individual's control; choices are invariably compromises between desires and what is feasible.[24]

Applications to the work situation

However, there are a number of problems in relating Maslow's theory to the work situation. These include the following:

- People do not necessarily satisfy their needs, especially higher-level needs, just through the work situation. They satisfy them through other areas of their life as well. Therefore the manager would need to have a complete understanding of people's private and social life, not just their behaviour at work.
- There is doubt about the time which elapses between the satisfaction of a lower-level need and the emergence of a higher-level need.
- Individual differences mean that people place different values on the same need. For example, some people prefer what they might see as the comparative safety of working in a bureaucratic organisation to a more highly paid and higher status position, but with less job security, in a different organisation.
- Some rewards or outcomes at work satisfy more than one need. Higher salary or promotion, for example, can be applied to all levels of the hierarchy.
- Even for people within the same level of the hierarchy, the motivating factors will not be the same. There are many different ways in which people may seek satisfaction of, for example, their esteem needs.
- Maslow viewed satisfaction as the main motivational outcome of behaviour. But job satisfaction does not necessarily lead to improved work performance.

Maslow's theory is difficult to test empirically and has been subject to various interpretations by different writers. Reviews of the need hierarchy model suggest little clear or consistent support for the theory and raise doubts about the validity of the classification of basic human needs.[25]

However, it is important to stress that Maslow himself recognised the limitations of his theory and did not imply that it should command widespread, empirical support. He suggested only that the theory should be considered as a framework for future research and points out:

It is easier to perceive and to criticise the aspects in motivation theory than to remedy them.

A useful basis for evaluation

Although Maslow did not originally intend that the need hierarchy should necessarily be applied to the work situation, it still remains popular as a theory of motivation at work. Despite criticisms and doubts about its limitations, the theory has had a significant impact on management approaches to motivation and the design of organisations to meet individual needs. It is a convenient framework for viewing the different needs and expectations that people have, where they are in the hierarchy, and the different motivators that might be applied to people at different levels.

The work of Maslow has drawn attention to a number of different motivators and stimulated study and research. The need hierarchy model provides a useful base for the evaluation of motivation at work. For example, Steers and Porter suggest a list of general rewards and organisational factors used to satisfy different needs (*see* Table 12.1).[26]

Table 12.1 Applying Maslow's need hierarchy

Needs levels	General rewards	Organisational factors
1 Physiological	Food, water, sex, sleep	a Pay b Pleasant working conditions c Cafeteria
2 Safety	Safety, security, stability, protection	a Safe working conditions b Company benefits c Job security
3 Social	Love, affection, belongingness	a Cohesive work group b Friendly supervision c Professional associations
4 Esteem	Self-esteem, self-respect, prestige, status	a Social recognition b Job title c High status job d Feedback from the job itself
5 Self-actualisation	Growth, advancement, creativity	a Challenging job b Opportunities for creativity c Achievement in work d Advancement in the organisation

(*Source:* Steers, R.M. and Porter, L.W, *Motivation and Work Behaviour*, Fifth edition, McGraw-Hill (1991) p. 35. Reproduced with permission from The McGraw-Hill Companies Inc.)

Alderfer's modified need hierarchy model

A modified need hierarchy model has been presented by *Alderfer*.[27] This model condenses Maslow's five levels of need into only three levels based on the core needs of existence, relatedness and growth (ERG theory). (*See* Table 12.2.)

- **Existence needs** are concerned with sustaining human existence and survival, and cover physiological and safety needs of a material nature.
- **Relatedness needs** are concerned with relationships to the social environment, and cover love or belonging, affiliation, and meaningful interpersonal relationships of a safety or esteem nature.
- **Growth needs** are concerned with the development of potential, and cover self-esteem and self-actualisation.

A continuum of needs

Like Maslow, Alderfer suggests that individuals progress through the hierarchy from existence needs, to relatedness needs, to growth needs, as the lower-level needs become satisfied. However, Alderfer suggests these needs are more a continuum than hierarchical levels. More than one need may be activated at the same time. Individuals may also progress down the hierarchy. There is a frustration–regression process. For example, if an individual is continually frustrated in attempting to satisfy growth needs, relatedness needs may reassume most importance. The lower-level needs become the main focus of the individual's efforts.

Alderfer proposed a number of basic propositions relating to the three need relationships. Some of these propositions followed Maslow's theory, some were the reverse of the theory. A number of studies were undertaken to test these propositions across different samples of people in different types of organisations.

Results from the studies were mixed. For example, the proposition that the less existence needs are satisfied the more they will be desired received constant support from all six samples. However, the proposition that satisfaction of existence needs activates desire for relatedness needs was not supported in any of the six samples.

Satisfaction of needs

Unlike Maslow's theory, the results of Alderfer's work suggest that lower-level needs do not have to be satisfied before a higher-level need emerges as a motivating influence. The results, however, do support the idea that lower-level needs decrease in strength as they become satisfied.

ERG theory states that an individual is motivated to satisfy one or more basic sets of needs. Therefore if a person's needs at a particular level are blocked then attention should be focused on the satisfaction of needs at the other levels. For example, if a subordinate's growth needs are blocked because the job does not allow sufficient opportunity for personal development, then the manager should attempt to provide greater opportunities for the subordinate to satisfy existence and relatedness needs.

Table 12.2 Linking Maslow's, Alderfer's and Herzberg's theories of motivation

Maslow's hierarchy of needs	Alderfer's ERG theory	Herzberg's two-factor theory
PHYSIOLOGICAL	EXISTENCE	HYGIENE FACTORS
SAFETY		
LOVE	RELATEDNESS	
ESTEEM	GROWTH	MOTIVATORS
SELF-ACTUALISATION		

Understanding and Managing People at Work

Herzberg's two-factor theory

Herzberg's original study consisted of interviews with 203 accountants and engineers, chosen because of their growing importance in the business world, from different industries in the Pittsburgh area of America.[28] He used the critical incident method. Subjects were asked to relate times when they felt exceptionally good or exceptionally bad about their present job or any previous job. They were asked to give reasons and a description of the sequence of events giving rise to that feeling. Responses to the interviews were generally consistent, and revealed that there were two different sets of factors affecting motivation and work. **This led to the two-factor theory of motivation and job satisfaction**.

Hygiene and motivating factors

One set of factors are those which, if absent, cause dissatisfaction. These factors are related to job context, they are concerned with job environment and extrinsic to the job itself. These factors are the '**hygiene**' or '**maintenance**' **factors** ('hygiene' being used as analogous to the medical term meaning preventive and environmental). They serve to prevent dissatisfaction.

The other set of factors are those which, if present, serve to motivate the individual to superior effort and performance. These factors are related to job content of the work itself. They are the '**motivators**' **or growth factors**. The strength of these factors will affect feelings of satisfaction or no satisfaction, but not dissatisfaction (*see* Figure 12.7).

The hygiene factors can be related roughly to Maslow's lower-level needs and the motivators to Maslow's higher-level needs. (*See* Table 12.3.) Proper attention to the hygiene factors will tend to prevent dissatisfaction, but does not by itself create a positive attitude or motivation to work. It brings motivation up to a zero state. **The opposite of dissatisfaction is not satisfaction but, simply, no dissatisfaction.** To motivate workers to give of their best the manager must give proper attention to the motivators or growth factors.

Herzberg emphasises that hygiene factors are not a 'second class citizen system'. They are as important as the motivators, but for different reasons. Hygiene factors are necessary to avoid unpleasantness at work and to deny unfair treatment. 'Management should never deny people proper treatment at work.' The motivators relate to what people are allowed to do and the quality of human experience at work. They are the variables which actually motivate people.

Evaluation of Herzberg's work

The motivation–hygiene theory has extended *Maslow's* hierarchy of need theory and is more directly applicable to the work situation. Herzberg's theory suggests that if management is to provide positive motivation then attention must be given not only to hygiene factors, but also to the motivating factors. The work of Herzberg indicates that it is more likely good performance leads to job satisfaction rather than the reverse.

Since the original study the theory had been replicated many times with different types of workers, including scientists, engineers, technicians, professional workers, nurses, food handlers, assemblers, and maintenance staff. The samples have covered a number of different nationalities. Results of these studies have been largely consistent with the original findings.[29]

Herzberg's theory is, however, a source of frequent debate. There have been many other studies to test the theory. The conclusions have been mixed. Some studies provide support for the theory.[30] However, it has also been attacked by a number of writers. For example, *Vroom* claims that the two-factor theory was only one of many conclusions that could be drawn from the research.[31]

Understanding and Managing People at Work

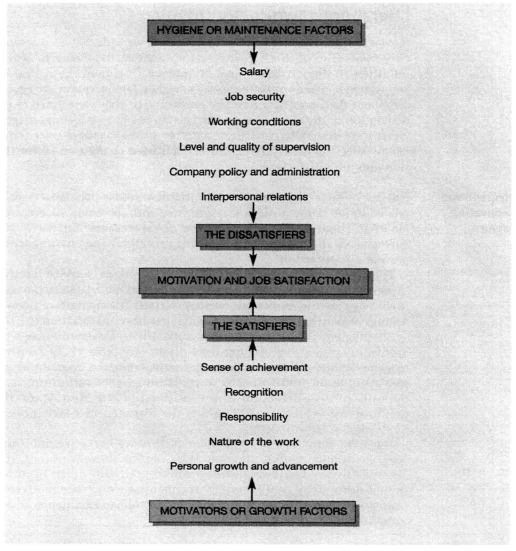

Figure 12.7 Representation of Herzberg's two-factor theory

Different interpretations interpretations

King suggests that there are at least five different theoretical interpretations of Herzberg's model which have been tested in different studies.[32] Each interpretation places a different slant on the model. This suggests doubts about the clarity of statement of the theory.

1 Do all motivators combined contribute more to satisfaction than to dissatisfaction, and all hygiene factors combined contribute more to dissatisfaction than to satisfaction?

2 Do all motivators combined contribute more to satisfaction than do all the hygiene factors combined, and all the hygiene factors combined contribute more to dissatisfaction than all motivators combined?

3 Does each motivator contribute more to satisfaction than to dissatisfaction, and each hygiene factor contribute more to dissatisfaction than to satisfaction?

4 Does each principal motivator contribute more to satisfaction than does any hygiene factor, and does each principal hygiene factor contribute more to dissatisfaction than does any motivator?

5 Is it only motivators which determine satisfaction and only hygiene factors which determine dissatisfaction?

Two general criticisms

There are two common general criticisms of Herzberg's theory. One criticism is that the theory has only limited application to 'manual' workers. The other criticism is that the theory is 'methodologically bound'.

It is often claimed that the theory applies least to people with largely unskilled jobs or whose work is uninteresting, repetitive and monotonous, and limited in scope. Yet these are the people who often present management with the biggest problem of motivation. Some workers do not seem greatly interested in the job content of their work, or with the motivators or growth factors.

However, work by *Blackburn and Mann* suggests that not all manual workers share an instrumental orientation to work. From a sample of 1000 workers in relatively low-skilled jobs, they found a variety of work orientations. These included primary concerns for outdoor work or indoor work, autonomy, intrinsic aspects, worthwhileness of the job, work colleagues, working conditions, hours of work, and promotion, as well as economic rewards.[33]

A second, general criticism concerns methodology. It is claimed that the critical incident method, and the description of events giving rise to good or bad feelings, influences the results. People are more likely to attribute satisfying incidents at work, that is the motivators, as a favourable reflection on their own performance. The dissatisfying incidents, that is the hygiene factors, are more likely to be attributed to external influences, and the efforts of other people. Descriptions from the respondents had to be interpreted by the interviewers. This gives rise to the difficulty of distinguishing clearly between the different dimensions, and to the risk of possible interviewer bias.

Continuing relevance of the theory?

More recent studies still yield mixed conclusions about the practical relevance of the two-factor theory. For example, from an examination of the relevance to industrial salespeople, *Shipley and Kiely* generally found against Herzberg. Their results:

> seriously challenge the worth of Herzberg's theory to industrial sales managers. Its application by them would result in a less than wholly motivated and at least partially dissatisfied team of salespeople.[34]

Despite such criticisms, there is still evidence of support for the continuing relevance of the theory. For example, although based on a small sample of engineers within a single company in Canada, *Phillipchuk* attempted to replicate Herzberg's study in today's environment. He concludes that Herzberg's methods still yield useful results. Respondents did not offer any new event factors from the original study although some old factors were absent. Salary and working conditions were not mentioned as a satisfier or a dissatisfier, and advancement as a satisfier did not appear. The top demotivator was company policy and the top motivator was achievement.[35]

Whatever the validity of the two-factor theory much of the criticism is with the value of hindsight, and *Herzberg* did at least attempt an empirical approach to the study of motivation at work. Furthermore, his work has drawn attention to the importance of job design in order to bring about job enrichment, self-development and self-managed learning. Herzberg has emphasised the importance of the 'quality of work life'. He advocates the restructuring of jobs to give greater emphasis to the motivating factors at work, to make jobs more interesting and to satisfy higher level needs. Job design and job enrichment are discussed in Chapter 18.

McClelland's achievement motivation theory

McClelland's work originated from investigations into the relationship between hunger needs and the extent to which imagery of food dominated thought processes. From subsequent research McClelland identified four main arousal-based, and socially developed, motives:

- the Achievement motive;
- the Power motive;
- the Affiliative motives; and
- the Avoidance motives.[36]

The first three motives correspond, roughly, to Maslow's self-actualisation, esteem and love needs.

The relative intensity of these motives varies between individuals. It also tends to vary between different occupations. Managers appear to be higher in achievement motivation than in affiliation motivation. McClelland saw the achievement need (n-Ach) as the most critical for the country's economic growth and success. The need to achieve is linked to entrepreneurial spirit and the development of available resources.

Use of projective tests Research studies by *McClelland* use a series of projective 'tests' – Thematic Apperception Test (TAT) to gauge an individual's motivation. For example, individuals are shown a number of pictures in which some activity is depicted. Respondents are asked to look briefly (10–15 seconds) at the pictures, and then to describe what they think is happening, what the people in the picture are thinking and what events have led to the situation depicted. An example of a picture used in a projective test is given in Assignment 3 at the end of this chapter. The descriptions are used as a basis for analysing the strength of the individual's motives.

People with high achievement needs

Despite the apparent subjective nature of the judgements research studies tend to support the validity of TAT as an indicator of the need for achievement.[37] McClelland has, over years of empirical research, identified four characteristics of people with a strong achievement need (n-Ach): a preference for moderate task difficulty; personal responsibility for performance; the need for feedback; and innovativeness.

- They prefer **moderate task difficulty** and goals as an achievement incentive. This provides the best opportunity of proving they can do better. If the task is too difficult or too risky, it would reduce the chances of success and of gaining need satisfaction. If the course of action is too easy or too safe, there is little challenge in accomplishing the task and little satisfaction from success.
- They prefer **personal responsibility for performance**. They like to attain success through the focus of their own abilities and efforts rather than by teamwork or chance factors outside their control. Personal satisfaction is derived from the accomplishment of the task, and recognition need not come from other people.
- They have the need for **clear and unambiguous feedback** on how well they are performing. A knowledge of results within a reasonable time is necessary for self-evaluation. Feedback enables them to determine success or failure in the accomplishment of their goals, and to derive satisfaction from their activities.
- They are **more innovative**. As they always seek moderately challenging tasks they tend always to be moving on to something a little more challenging. In seeking short cuts they are more likely to cheat. There is a constant search for variety and for information to find new ways of doing things. They are more restless and avoid routine, and also tend to travel more.

Extent of achievement motivation

The extent of achievement motivation varies between individuals. Some people think about achievement a lot more than others. Some people rate very highly in achievement motivation. They are challenged by opportunities and work hard to achieve a goal. Other people rate very low in achievement motivation. They do not care much and have little urge to achieve.

For people with a high achievement motivation, money is not an incentive but may serve as a means of giving feedback on performance. High achievers seem unlikely to remain long with an organisation that does not pay them well for good performance. Money may seem to be important to high achievers, but they value it more as symbolising successful task performance and goal achievement. For people with low achievement motivation money may serve more as a direct incentive for performance.

McClelland's research has attempted to understand the characteristics of high achievers. He suggests that n-Ach is not hereditary but results from environmental influences, and he has investigated the possibility of training people to develop a greater motivation to achieve.[38] McClelland suggests four steps in attempting to develop achievement drive:

- Striving to attain feedback on performance. Reinforcement of success serves to strengthen the desire to attain higher performance.
- Developing models of achievement by seeking to emulate people who have performed well.
- Attempting to modify their self-image and to see themselves as needing challenges and success.
- Controlling day-dreaming and thinking about themselves in more positive terms.

McClelland was concerned with economic growth in underdeveloped countries. He has designed training programmes intended to increase the achievement motivation and entrepreneurial activity of managers.

The need for power

McClelland has also suggested that as effective managers need to be successful leaders and to influence other people, they should possess a high need for power.[39] However, the effective manager also scores high on inhibition. Power is directed more towards the organisation and concern for group goals, and is exercised on behalf of other people. This is 'socialised' power. It is distinguished from 'personalised' power which is characterised by satisfaction from exercising dominance over other people, and personal aggrandisement.

Process theories of motivation

Process theories, or extrinsic theories, attempt to identify the relationships among the dynamic variables which make up motivation and the actions required to influence behaviour and actions. They provide a further contribution to our understanding of the complex nature of work motivation. Many of the process theories cannot be linked to a single writer, but major approaches and leading writers under this heading include:

- Expectancy-based models – *Vroom*, and *Porter and Lawler*
- Equity theory – *Adams*
- Goal theory – *Locke*
- Attribution theory – *Heider*, and *Kelley* (this was discussed in Chapter 11).

Expectancy theories of motivation

The underlying basis of expectancy theory is that people are influenced by the expected results of their actions. Motivation is a function of the relationship between:

(1) effort expended and perceived level of performance; and
(2) the expectation that rewards (desired outcomes) will be related to performance.

There must also be

(3) the expectation that rewards (desired outcomes) are available.

These relationships determine the strength of the 'motivational link'. (*See* Figure 12.8.)

Performance therefore depends upon the perceived expectation regarding effort expended and achieving the desired outcome. For example, the desire for promotion will result in high performance only if the person believes there is a strong expectation that this will lead to promotion. If, however, the person believes promotion to be based solely on age and length of service, there is no motivation to achieve high performance. A person's behaviour reflects a conscious choice between the comparative evaluation of alternative behaviours. **The choice of behaviour is based on the expectancy of the most favourable consequences.**

Expectancy theory is a generic theory of motivation and cannot be linked to a single individual writer. There are a number of different versions and some of the models are rather complex. More recent approaches to expectancy theory have been associated with the work of *Vroom* and of *Porter and Lawler*.

Vroom's expectancy theory

Vroom was the first person to propose an expectancy theory aimed specifically at work motivation.[40] His model is based on three key variables: **valence, instrumentality and expectancy** (VIE theory or expectancy/valence theory). The theory is founded on the idea that people prefer certain outcomes from their behaviour over others. They anticipate feelings of satisfaction should the preferred outcome be achieved.

Valence

The feeling about specific outcomes is termed **valence. This is the attractiveness of, or preference for, a particular outcome to the individual.** *Vroom* distinguishes valence from value. A person may desire an object but then gain little satisfaction from obtaining it. Alternatively, a person may strive to avoid an object but finds, subsequently, that it provides satisfaction. **Valence is the anticipated satisfaction from an outcome.** This may differ substantially from value, which is the actual satisfaction provided by an outcome.

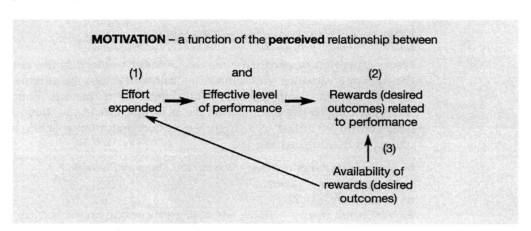

Figure 12.8 Expectancy theory: the motivational link

The valence of certain outcomes may be derived in their own right, but more usually they are derived from the other outcomes to which they are expected to lead. An obvious example is money. Some people may see money as having an intrinsic worth and derive satisfaction from the actual accumulation of wealth. Most people, however, see money in terms of the many satisfying outcomes to which it can lead.

Instrumentality The valence of outcomes derive, therefore, from their instrumentality. This leads to a distinction between first-level outcomes and second-level outcomes.

- **The first-level outcomes are performance-related.** They refer to the quantity of output or to the comparative level of performance. Some people may seek to perform well 'for its own sake' and without thought to expected consequences of their actions. Usually, however, performance outcomes acquire valence because of the expectation that they will lead to other outcomes as an anticipated source of satisfaction – second-level outcomes.
- **The second-level outcomes are need-related.** They are derived through achievement of first-level outcomes – that is, through achieving high performance. Many need-related outcomes are dependent upon actual performance rather than effort expended. People generally receive rewards for what they have achieved, rather than for effort alone or through trying hard.

On the basis of *Vroom's* expectancy theory it is possible to depict a general model of behaviour. (*See* Figure 12.9.)

The strength of the valence of an outcome is dependent upon the extent to which the outcome serves as a means to other outcomes. An outcome with a high valence is likely to be one that is perceived to be instrumental in leading to the achievement of a large number of need-related outcomes. Instrumentality is the association between first-level outcomes and second-level outcomes, measured on a range between +1.0 and –1.0. For example, if it is believed that good work performance (a first-level outcome) always results in a pay increase (a second-level outcome) instrumentality will be constant at +1.0. If the person believes a pay increase is certain to be obtained without good performance, or impossible even with it, instrumentality will be –1.0.

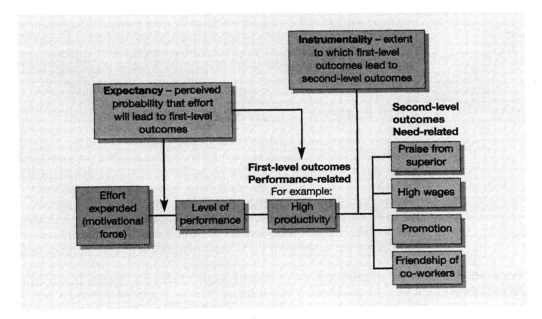

Figure 12.9 Basic model of expectancy theory

Understanding and Managing People at Work
259

Expectancy

When a person chooses between alternative behaviours which have uncertain outcomes, the choice is affected not only by the preference for a particular outcome, but also by the probability that such an outcome will be achieved. People develop a **perception** of the degree of probability that the choice of a particular action will actually lead to the desired outcome. This is **expectancy**. It is the relationship between a chosen course of action and its predicted outcome. Expectancy relates effort expended to the achievement of first-level outcomes. Its value ranges between 0, indicating zero probability that an action will be followed by the outcome, and 1, indicating certainty that an action will result in the outcome.

Motivational force

The combination of valence and expectancy determines the person's motivation for a given form of behaviour. This is the **motivational force**. The force of an action is unaffected by outcomes which have no valence, or by outcomes that are regarded as unlikely to result from a course of action. Expressed as an equation, motivation (M) is the sum of the products of the valences of all outcomes (V), times the strength of expectancies that action will result in achieving these outcomes (E). Therefore, if either, or both, valence or expectancy is zero, then motivation is zero. The choice between alternative behaviours is indicated by the highest attractiveness score.

$$M = \sum^{n} E \cdot V$$

There are likely to be a number of different outcomes expected for a given action. Therefore, the measure of $E \cdot V$ is summed across the total number of possible outcomes to arrive at a single figure indicating the attractiveness for the contemplated choice of behaviour.

Test of Vroom's model

Among the studies to test *Vroom's* model was an investigation undertaken by *Galbraith and Cummings*.[41] They studied 32 workers in a firm manufacturing heavy equipment. Productivity figures were compared with measures of job-related (second-level) outcomes such as pay, fringe benefits, promotion, style of supervision, and popularity with co-workers. The overall results suggested little significant support for the model as a whole. They did, however, indicate a marked interaction between valence and instrumentality in the case of support and consideration from supervisors, and high performance. Where workers wanted support from their supervisors, and believed this would be achieved by good performance, the workers had a high level of productivity.

The Porter and Lawler expectancy model

Vroom's expectancy/valence theory has been developed by *Porter and Lawler*.[42] Their model goes beyond motivational force and considers performance as a whole. They point out that effort expended (motivational force) does not lead directly to performance. It is mediated by individual abilities and traits, and by the person's role perceptions. They also introduce rewards as an intervening variable. Porter and Lawler see motivation, satisfaction and performance as separate variables, and attempt to explain the complex relationships among them. Their model recognises that job satisfaction is more dependent upon performance, than performance is upon satisfaction.

Explanation of relationships

These relationships are expressed diagrammatically (Figure 12.10) rather than mathematically. In contrast to the human relations approach which tended to assume that job satisfaction leads to improved performance, Porter and Lawler suggest that satisfaction is an effect rather than a cause of performance. It is performance that leads to job satisfaction.

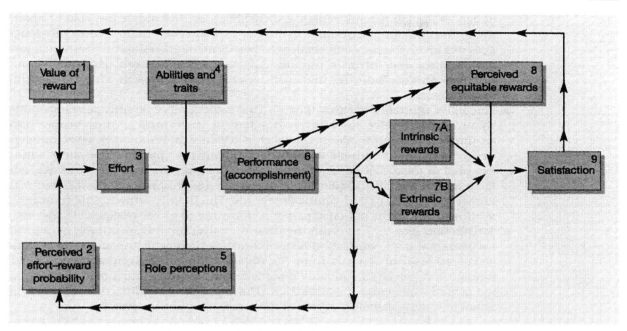

Figure 12.10 The Porter and Lawler motivation model

(*Source*: Porter, I. W. and Lawler, E. E. *Managerial Attitudes and Performance.* Copyright © Richard D. Irwin Inc. (1968) p. 165.)

- **Value of reward** (Box 1) is similar to valence in Vroom's model. People desire various outcomes (rewards) which they hope to achieve from work. The value placed on a reward depends on the strength of its desirability.
- **Perceived effort–reward probability** (Box 2) is similar to expectancy. It refers to a person's expectation that certain outcomes (rewards) are dependent upon a given amount of effort.
- **Effort** (Box 3) is how hard the person tries, the amount of energy a person exerts on a given activity. It does not relate to how successful a person is in carrying out an activity. The amount of energy exerted is dependent upon the interaction of the input variables of value of reward, and perception of the effort–reward relationship.
- **Abilities and traits** (Box 4). Porter and Lawler suggest that effort does not lead directly to performance, but is influenced by individual characteristics. Factors such as intelligence, skills, knowledge, training and personality affect the ability to perform a given activity.
- **Role perceptions** (Box 5) refer to the way in which individuals view their work and the role they should adopt. This influences the type of effort exerted. Role perceptions will influence the direction and level of action which is believed to be necessary for effective performance.
- **Performance** (Box 6) depends not only on the amount of effort exerted but also on the intervening influences of the person's abilities and traits, and their role perceptions. If the person lacks the right ability or personality, or has an inaccurate role perception of what is required, then the exertion of a large amount of energy may still result in a low level of performance, or task accomplishment.
- **Rewards** (Boxes 7A and 7B) are desirable outcomes. Intrinsic rewards derive from the individuals themselves and include a sense of achievement, a feeling of responsibility and recognition (for example Herzberg's motivators). Extrinsic rewards derive from the organisation and the actions of others, and include salary, working conditions and supervision (for example Herzberg's hygiene factors). The relationship between performance and intrinsic rewards is shown as a jagged line. This is because the extent of the relationship depends upon the nature of the job. If the

Understanding and Managing People at Work

design of the job permits variety and challenge, so that people feel able to reward themselves for good performance, there is a direct relationship. Where job design does not involve variety and challenge, there is no direct relationship between good performance and intrinsic rewards. The wavy line between performance and extrinsic rewards indicates that such rewards do not often provide a direct link to performance.

- **Perceived equitable rewards** (Box 8). This is the level of rewards people feel they should fairly receive for a given standard of performance. Most people have an implicit perception about the level of rewards they should receive commensurate with the requirements and demands of the job, and the contribution expected of them. Self-rating of performance links directly with the perceived equitable reward variable. Higher levels of self-rated performance are associated with higher levels of expected equitable rewards. The heavily arrowed line indicates a relationship from the self-rated part of performance to perceived equitable rewards.

- **Satisfaction** (Box 9). This is not the same as motivation. It is an attitude, an individual's internal state. Satisfaction is determined by both actual rewards received, and perceived level of rewards from the organisation for a given standard of performance. If perceived equitable rewards are greater than actual rewards received, the person experiences dissatisfaction. The experience of satisfaction derives from actual rewards which meet or exceed the perceived equitable rewards.

Investigations of the model

Porter and Lawler conducted an investigation of their own model. This study involved 563 questionnaires from managers in seven different industrial and government organisations. The main focus of the study was on pay as an outcome. The questionnaires obtained measures from the managers for a number of variables such as value of reward, effort–reward probability, role perceptions, perceived equitable rewards, and satisfaction. Information on the managers' effort and performance was obtained from their superiors. The results indicated that where pay is concerned, value of reward and perceived effort–reward probability do combine to influence effort.

Those managers who believed pay to be closely related to performance outcome received a higher effort and performance rating from their superiors. Those managers who perceived little relationship between pay and performance had lower ratings for effort and performance. The study by Porter and Lawler also demonstrated the interaction of effort and role perceptions to produce a high level of performance. Their study suggested, also, that the relationship between performance and satisfaction with their pay held good only for those managers whose performance was related directly to their actual pay.

A study by *Graen*, into the factors contributing to job satisfaction and performance, provided results which were generally supportive of expectancy theory.[43] A total of 169 women were engaged in part-time, temporary clerical tasks in a simulated work organisation. One group of workers received verbal recognition directly related to their prior performance. A second group received a pay increase in the hope that they would do much better. The third group received no special treatment. Questionnaires were used to obtain measures of the different variables of the theory, and details of job satisfaction and performance. In general, intrinsic rewards were found to contribute substantially more to job satisfaction and performance than did the extrinsic rewards.

Lawler's revised expectancy model

Following the original *Porter and Lawler* model, further work was undertaken by *Lawler* (*see* Figure 12.11).[44] He suggests that in deciding on the attractiveness of alternative behaviours, there are two types of expectancies to be considered: effort–performance expectancies (E $\rightarrow$ P); and performance–outcome expectancies (P $\rightarrow$ O).

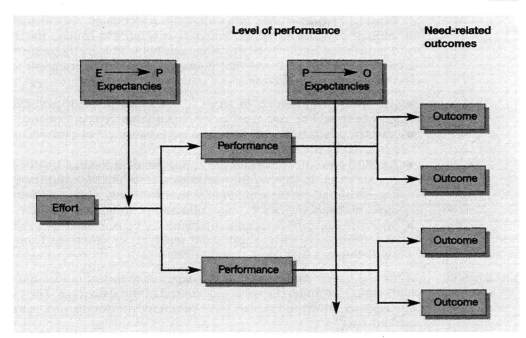

Figure 12.11 An illustration of the Lawler expectancy model

The **first expectancy (E → P)** is the person's perception of the probability that a given amount of effort will result in achieving an intended level of performance. It is measured on a scale between 0 and 1. The closer the perceived relationship between effort and performance, the higher the E → P expectancy score.

The **second expectancy (P → O)** is the person's perception of the probability that a given level of performance will actually lead to particular need-related outcomes. This is measured also on a scale between 0 and 1. The closer the perceived relationship between performance and outcome, the higher the P → O expectancy score.

Motivational force to perform

The multiplicative combination of the two types of expectancies, E → P and the sum of the products P → O, determines expectancy. The motivational force to perform (effort expended) is determined by multiplying E → P and P → O by the strength of outcome valence (V).

$$E \text{ (Effort)} = (E \to P) \times \Sigma[(P \to O) \times V]$$

The distinction between the two types of expectancies arises because they are determined by different conditions. E → P expectancy is determined in part by the person's ability and self-confidence, past experience, and the difficulty of the task. P → O expectancy is determined by the attractiveness of the outcomes and the belief about who controls the outcomes, the person him/herself or other people.

Implications for managers of expectancy theories

There are a number of different versions of expectancy theory. The main elements tend to be very similar, however, and this suggests the development of a generally accepted approach. Numerous research studies aimed at testing expectancy models appear to suggest general support for the theory,[45] but they also highlight difficulties with some of the concepts involved and with methodology. Expectancy models are not always easy to understand, or to apply. There are many variables which affect behaviour at work. A problem can arise in attempting to include a large number of variables or in identifying those variables which are most appropriate in particular situations.

Understanding and Managing People at Work

Expectancy theory does, however, draw attention to the complexities of work motivation. It provides further information in helping to explain the nature of behaviour and motivation in the work situation, and helps to identify problems in performance. Expectancy theory indicates that managers should give attention to a number of factors, including the following:

● Use rewards appropriate in terms of individual performance. Outcomes with high valence should be used as an incentive for improved performance.
● Attempt to establish clear relationships between effort–performance and rewards, as perceived by the individual.
● Establish clear procedures for the evaluation of individual levels of performance.
● Pay attention to intervening variables such as abilities and traits, role perceptions, organisational procedures, and support facilities, which, although not necessarily direct motivational factors, may still affect performance.
● Minimise undesirable outcomes which may be perceived to result from a high level of performance, such as industrial accidents or sanctions from co-workers; or to result despite a high level of performance, such as short-time working or layoffs.

Just a model   *Porter and Lawler* emphasise that the expectancy theory model applies only to behaviours which are under the voluntary control of the individual. The two general types of choices over which individuals have voluntary control of work performance in organisations are:

1 the amount of effort and energy expended; and
2 the manner in which they go about performing their work.

Porter and Lawler also emphasise that the expectancy model is just a model.

> *People rarely actually sit down and list their expected outcomes for a contemplated behaviour, estimate expectancies and valences, multiply, and add up the total unless, of course, they are asked to do so by a researcher. Yet people* do *consider the likely outcomes of their actions, do weigh and evaluate the attractiveness of various alternatives, and do use these estimates in coming to a decision about what they will do. The expectancy model provides an analytic tool for mirroring that process and for predicting its outcome, but it does not purport to reflect the actual decision-making steps taken by an individual.*[46]

The motivation of knowledge workers

Recent advantages in telecommunications and in scientific and technological knowledge have led to greater emphasis on the knowledge and expertise of staff. *Tampoe* suggests that at the core of the new industrial trend are the 'knowledge workers' – those employees who apply their theoretical and practical understanding of a specific area of knowledge to produce outcomes of a commercial, social or personal value. The performance of knowledge workers should be judged on both the cleverness of ideas and the utility and commercial value of their applied knowledge. Creativity is necessary and needs to be encouraged but should be bounded by commercial realism. This presents management with a new challenge of how to motivate the knowledge workers.[47]

Tampoe suggests that the personal motivation of knowledge workers is based on the value they place on the rewards they expect to earn at work. In addition to the individual's own motivation, the performance of knowledge workers is dependent upon four key characteristics (*see* Figure 12.12).

● task competence;
● peer and management support;
● task and role clarity; and
● corporate awareness.

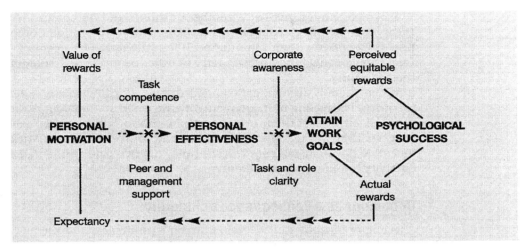

Figure 12.12 Motivating knowledge workers
(Reproduced with permission from Mahen Tampoe, 'Knowledge Workers – The New Management Challenge', *Professional Manager*, Institute of Management, November 1994, p. 13.)

The challenge to management is to ensure the effectiveness of the four key variables and to recognise the need for staff to supervise and manage themselves and the wider rewards expected by knowledge workers.

Suggestions on developing reward strategies to motivate and compensate knowledge workers are given in the Appendix to this chapter.

More creative remuneration packages

Lucas draws attention to skills shortages as one of the biggest challenges facing employers in the new millennium. In order to attract and keep talented individuals, the so-called knowledge workers, organisations cannot rely simply on a pay rise or cash bonus but have to be more creative about the way they structure remuneration packages. Individual performance-related pay is still the most widely used reward strategy, but attention is also given to employee share ownership, competence-related pay and to team reward – and also to non-cash incentives such as gift vouchers. However, Lucas points out that employees, especially high flyers, rank challenging and interesting work and freedom higher on their motivational list than money and performance-related pay. 'Research suggests that most organisations haven't recognised the need to identify and tap into their employees' personal motivators.'[48]

Equity theory of motivation

One of the major variables of satisfaction in the *Porter and Lawler* expectancy model is perceived equitable rewards. This leads to consideration of another process theory of motivation – **equity theory**. Applied to the work situation, equity theory is usually associated with the work of *Adams*.[49]

Equity theory focuses on people's feelings of how fairly they have been treated in comparison with the treatment received by others. It is based on exchange theory. People evaluate their social relationships in the same way as buying or selling an item. People expect certain outcomes in exchange for certain contributions, or inputs.

Social relationships involve an exchange process. For example, a person may expect promotion as an outcome of a high level of contribution (input) in helping to achieve an important organisational objective. People also compare their own position with that of others. They determine the perceived equity of their own position. Their feelings about the equity of the exchange are affected by the treatment they receive when compared with what happens to other people.

Most exchanges involve a number of inputs and outcomes. According to equity theory, people place a weighting on these various inputs and outcomes according to how they perceive their importance. When the ratio of a person's total outcomes to total inputs equals the *perceived* ratio of other people's total outcomes to total inputs there is **equity**.

When there is an unequal comparison of ratios the person experiences a sense of **inequity**. The feeling of inequity might arise when an individual's ratio of outcomes to inputs is either less than, or greater than, that of other people. For example, Adams suggests that workers prefer equitable pay to overpayment. Workers on piece-rate incentive payment schemes who feel they are overpaid will reduce their level of productivity in order to restore equity.

Behaviour as a consequence of inequity

A feeling of inequity causes tension, which is an unpleasant experience. The presence of inequity therefore motivates the person to remove or to reduce the level of tension and the perceived inequity. The magnitude of perceived inequity determines the level of tension. The level of tension created determines the strength of motivation. *Adams* identifies six broad types of possible behaviour as consequences of inequity (*see* Figure 12.13).

- **Changes to inputs**. A person may increase or decrease the level of his or her inputs, for example through the amount or quality of work, absenteeism, or working additional hours without pay.
- **Changes to outcomes**. A person may attempt to change outcomes such as pay, working conditions, status and recognition, without changes to inputs.
- **Cognitive distortion of inputs and outcomes**. In contrast to actual changes, people may distort, cognitively, their inputs or outcomes to achieve the same results. Adams suggests that although it is difficult for people to distort facts about

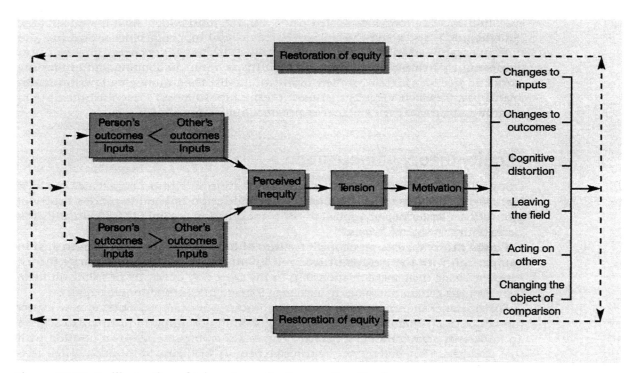

Figure 12.13 An illustration of Adams's equity theory of motivation

themselves, it is possible, within limits, to distort the utility of those facts: for example, the belief about how hard they are really working, the relevance of a particular qualification, or what they can or cannot obtain with a given level of pay.

- **Leaving the field.** A person may try to find a new situation with a more favourable balance, for example, by absenteeism, request for a transfer, resigning from a job or from the organisation altogether.
- **Acting on others.** A person may attempt to bring about changes in others, for example to lower their inputs or accept greater outcomes. Or the person may cognitively distort the inputs and outcomes of others. Alternatively, a person may try to force others to leave the field.
- **Changing the object of comparison.** This involves changing the reference group with whom comparison is made. For example, where another person with a previously similar outcome–input ratio receives greater outcomes without any apparent increase in contribution, that other person may be perceived as now belonging to a different level in the organisation structure. The comparison need not necessarily be made with people who have the same inputs and outcomes. The important thing is a similar ratio of outcomes to inputs.

Under the control of the manager

The manager may seek to remove or reduce tension and perceived inequity among staff by influencing these types of behaviour – for example, by attempting to change a person's inputs or encouraging a different object of comparison. However, there are likely to be only two courses of action under the direct control of the manager. Outcomes can be changed by, for example, increased pay, additional perks or improved working conditions; or by instigating a person leaving the field through transfer, resignation or, as an extreme measure, dismissal.

Kreitner et al. suggest at least seven practical implications of equity theory.

- It provides managers with another explanation of how beliefs and attitudes affect job performance.
- It emphasises the need for managers to pay attention to employees' **perceptions** of what is fair and equitable.
- Managers benefit by allowing employees to participate in making decisions about important work outcomes.
- Employees should be given the opportunity to appeal against decisions that affect their welfare.
- Employees are more likely to accept and support organisational change when they believe it is implemented fairly.
- Managers can promote co-operation and teamwork among group members by treating them equally.
- Employees denied justice at work are turning increasingly to arbitration and the courts.[50]

Goal theory

Another theory sometimes considered under the heading of motivation to work is goal theory, or the theory of goal-setting (*see* Figure 12.14). This theory is based mainly on the work of *Locke*.[51]

The basic premise of goal theory is that people's goals or intentions play an important part in determining behaviour. Locke accepts the importance of perceived value, as indicated in expectancy theories of motivation, and suggests that these values give rise to the experience of emotions and desires. People strive to achieve goals in order to satisfy their emotions and desires. Goals guide people's responses and actions. Goals direct work behaviour and performance, and lead to certain consequences or feedback.

Understanding and Managing People at Work

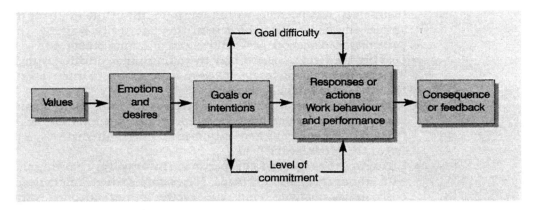

Figure 12.14 An illustration of Locke's theory of goal-setting

Goal-setting and performance

The combination of goal difficulty and the extent of the person's commitment to achieving the goal regulates the level of effort expended. People with specific quantitative goals, such as a defined level of performance, or a given deadline for completion of a task, will perform better than people with no set goal or only a vague goal such as 'do the best you can'. People who have difficult goals will perform better than people with easier goals.

A number of research studies have attempted to examine the relationship between goal-setting and performance. Although, almost inevitably, there are some contrary findings, the majority of evidence suggests strong support for the theory, and its effects on motivation.[52] Locke subsequently pointed out that 'goal-setting is more appropriately viewed as a motivational technique rather than as a formal theory of motivation'.[53] However it is viewed, the theory of goal-setting provides a useful approach to work motivation and performance.

Practical implications for the manager

Goal theory has a number of practical implications for the manager.

● Specific performance goals should systematically be identified and set in order to direct behaviour and maintain motivation.
● Goals should be set at a challenging but realistic level. Difficult goals lead to higher performance. However, if goals are set at too high a level, or are regarded as impossible to achieve, performance will suffer, especially over a longer period.
● Complete, accurate and timely feedback and knowledge of results is usually associated with high performance. Feedback provides a means of checking progress on goal attainment and forms the basis for any revision of goals.
● Goals can be determined either by a superior or by individuals themselves. Goals set by other people are more likely to be accepted when there is participation. Employee participation in the setting of goals may lead to higher performance.[54]

Much of the theory of goal-setting can be related to the system of Management by Objectives (discussed in Chapter 7). MBO is often viewed as an application of goal-setting, although MBO was devised originally before the development of goal-setting theory.

Attribution theory

A more recent approach to the study of motivation is attribution theory. Attribution is the process by which people interpret the perceived causes of behaviour. Attribution theory has been discussed in Chapter 11.

A 'summary outline' of some motivation theories and theorists is given in Figure 12.15.

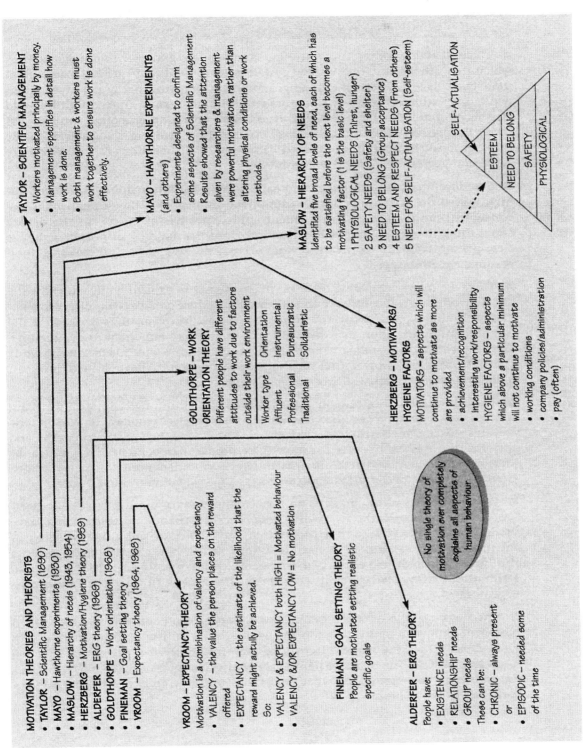

Figure 12.15 Summary of outline of motivation theories and theorists

(Reproduced with permission of Training Learning Consultancy Ltd, Bristol, England.)

Synopsis

■ The underlying concept of motivation is some driving force within individuals by which they attempt to achieve some goal in order to fulfil some need or expectation. Individuals have a variety of changing, and often competing, needs and expectations which they attempt to satisfy in a number of different ways. One useful three-fold classification of individual needs and expectations at work is economic, intrinsic and social. If a person's motivational driving force is blocked before reaching a desired goal, this can result in frustration-induced behaviour. Main reactions to frustration are aggression, regression, fixation and withdrawal.

■ The development of different approaches to organisation and management has highlighted the changing concept of motivation at work. The rational-economic concept of motivation and subsequent approaches has given rise to the debate about the influence of money as a motivator. For the majority of people money is clearly a motivator to work but to what extent and how important depends upon personal circumstances.

■ There are many competing theories which attempt to explain motivation at work. These theories are not conclusive and all have their critics or have been subject to alternative findings, particularly the content theories. However, it is because of the complexity of motivation that these different theories are important to the manager. They show that there are many motives which influence people's behaviour at work. They provide a framework within which to direct attention to the problem of how best to motivate staff to work willingly and effectively.

■ The different theories of motivation may be divided into two contrasting groups: content theories and process theories. Content theories place emphasis on what motivates and are concerned with identifying people's needs and their relative strengths, and the goals they pursue in order to satisfy these needs. Main content theories include: Maslow's hierarchy of needs model; Alderfer's modified need hierarchy model; Herzberg's two-factor theory; and McClelland's achievement motivation theory.

■ Process theories place emphasis on the actual process of motivation. These theories are concerned with the relationships among the dynamic variables which make up motivation, and with how behaviour is initiated, directed and sustained. Many of the process theories cannot be linked to a single writer, but major approaches under this heading include: expectancy-based models; equity theory; goal theory; and also attribution theory. Management faces a new challenge of how to motivate knowledge workers.

■ It is always easy to quote an example which appears to contradict any generalised observation on what motivates people to work. However, these different theories provide a basis for study and discussion, and for review of the most effective motivational style. The manager must evaluate the relevance of these different theories, and judge how best and to what extent they might be applied with advantage to particular work situations.

Understanding and Managing People at Work

Appendix

Developing reward strategies to motivate and compensate knowledge workers

Mahen Tampoe

Introduction

This is a synopsis of research-based findings on the motivation of knowledge workers and suggests that current reward strategies fail to excite the intrinsic motivational drives of this category of staff; furthermore, it suggests that in certain circumstances current reward strategies are counter-productive. It then goes on to offer a motivation and performance model which links reward strategies, organisational climates and individual competencies and to suggest actions which organisations can take to realise the promise of this model.

Knowledge workers – who are they?

Knowledge workers are those who apply their theoretical and practical understanding of an area of knowledge to produce outcomes that have commercial, social or personal value. They are likely to be drawn from a wide variety of professionally qualified and scientifically trained staff. Among them would be: doctors, scientists, computer specialists, personnel professionals, qualified accountants, managers, project managers and supervisors of knowledge workers who themselves have been promoted from being technologists to managers.

Characteristics of knowledge workers

Certain characteristics of knowledge workers differentiate them from other process dominant workers. While some of these are to do with their education and training, others are to do with the standards and expectations of their profession. Their work can also be distinguished in different ways. Namely, their work is:

- unlikely to be routine or repetitive;
- carried out to professional or quality standards and subject to these as well as the organisation's own standards of verification and approval (sometimes resulting in a conflict between work and professional standards);
- aimed at meeting operational or strategic targets derived from project objectives or established as part of a problem-solving activity;
- intrinsically motivational and provides the inner drive (as opposed to external stimulus) for creative achievement;
- continuously developing their knowledge and skill in their chosen area of expertise;
- amenable to self-management;
- not easily supervised, partly because of the specialist nature of their work and partly due to the fact that their work is not amenable to physical observation and measurement;
- less easy to procedurise and/or quantify, making it often more difficult to specify clear unambiguous performance targets;

- likely to have areas of high ambiguity, and to be susceptible to many different yet feasible solutions and outcomes.

Motivators for knowledge workers

Based on research carried out by the author, the work of other researchers and from personal experience of managing IT professionals over many years, the rewards and expectations of these knowledge workers can be summarised as a mixture of the following:

- **personal growth**, especially self-development rather than growing managerial or professional skills;
- **autonomy**, which gives them the freedom to work within the rules rather than working to rule or being allowed to define their own rules;
- **creative achievement**, where the work is commercial value rather than meeting assigned targets or being work that is intellectually stimulating but not of commercial value;
- **financial rewards**, where salary plus bonus on personal effort is valued more than salary plus bonus on group effort or purely receiving a salary and fringe benefits.

Financial rewards played a very small part in this as most of those who supported the research study were in well paid jobs and were seeking self-actualisation rewards.

The strength of preference shown for these different motivators and the findings of other researchers in this field over the last 50 years suggest that the law of diminishing returns applies very definitely to financial incentives. However, when it comes to intrinsic incentives such as personal growth, creative achievement and autonomy, the law of escalating returns seems to apply. This is most pronounced in the area of creative achievement where the more they get the more they wish to get. The expectancy theory of motivation (*Vroom, Porter and Lawler* among others) suggests that reward strategies should be designed to optimise these inherent and intrinsic motivational drivers while allowing for *Herzberg's* theory of dissatisfiers and satisfiers.

Theoretical fit

Motivational researchers and theorists who have studied the motivation of knowledge workers agree that the Expectancy Theory of motivation is the most appropriate for this category of employee. The application of expectancy theory in reward strategies does suggest a very close and intricate link between rewards, the likelihood of earning those rewards and the realisation of those rewards, if performance is delivered. Based on my research and developing on others, it is possible to

Appendix continued

hypothesise a motivation and performance model. The model suggests that the creative energy of people needs to be applied to task achievement through the application of their personal capability and the organisation's strengths, usually made up of resources, peer support, management support and finances.

Adverse effects of current reward strategies

This conflicts with current reward strategies in organisations that seem to support and reinforce hierarchies rather than lateral co-operation. In addition, they tend to reward the job rather than the individual. Usually, career progression and bonus payments (for those whose results are not measurable using hard data) depend on patronage rather than merit and there is a tendency to reward those who sustain the status quo rather than those who are innovative and entrepreneurial. Finally, most reward strategies have unfairness built into them. For example, it is easier to reward sales staff on their personal performance than scientists in research laboratories. The sense of unfairness creeps in if staff who help sales people design and develop the 'winning' solution do not share in the bonus that accompanies a successful sale. Managers often sympathise with the scientists but do nothing to change the system on the grounds that it is 'too difficult', and has historical precedence. The more hard-nosed managers usually suggest that those scientists who want bonuses should join the salesforce or stop bellyaching about their lot. This approach just does not make sense in a world hungry for innovation and the rewards that it brings.

Reward options

Staff and managers should realise that rewards are multi-faceted and usually come in bundles that combine money, achievement, personal and professional growth and self-esteem. This means that the reward options open to management are very varied, as the examples in Table 12.4 show.

Table 12.4 Reward options for knowledge workers

Financial rewards	Non-financial rewards
Salary + bonus based on gain sharing	Personal growth
Salary + profit sharing	Knowledge or professional growth
Employee ownership	Status and public or private recognition
High salary + benefits	
	Career growth
Salary and bonus on individual or team effort	Job security

What managers should do is create reward bundles (fruit bowls of choice) that more closely fit the needs of a group of employees rather than impose a blanket system on them all. For example, an individual or group could be offered a bundle which comprises salary plus profit sharing, status, personal growth. Another group or individual could be offered a different bundle comprising salary plus bonus on personal effort, career growth and professional growth. The reward bundles, drawn from a reward portfolio, are probably the fairest way to reward individual effort and contribution.

Performance measures

Inappropriate performance measures do more harm than good. In knowledge-based organisations, performance must be judged primarily by how the individual or group contributes to the **knowledge added value** of the organisation. This may take the form of specific creative outcomes, new knowledge generated or knowledge disseminated. Meeting targets and deadlines and solving critical problems, which contribute to **customer added value**, should also feature as measures.

Climate for optimising reward strategies proposed

Whatever scheme is used, it is imperative that those subject to these schemes can earn the promised rewards if they fulfil their part of the bargain. This means first of all that they can achieve the task they have been set. Among the necessary ingredients for this are:

- role and goal clarity;
- having the knowledge and skills or having the opportunity to acquire them;
- having sufficient autonomy and delegated authority to get the job done;
- having a wider understanding of what the organisation or department is trying to achieve and how the individual's work fits in with this;
- quality standards and defined deliverables;
- having a good knowledge of what is happening in the organisation as a whole and the threats and opportunities that it may experience.

However, where these conditions do not prevail and where there is strong hierarchical governance, regard strategies are wasted because the individual's skills and talents are not being tapped.

What should organisations do?

- Define and create a climate for success to match its business objectives.
- Widen opportunities for career growth by adopting multiple career streams, effective review systems, personal mentoring and strive to ensure equality of treatment for all employees.
- Reward managers on their ability to create and sustain the climate for success.

Appendix continued

- Devise fruit-bowls of reward options.
- Revise the career expectations of staff so that they value professional and technical skills development and status as highly as clambering up the management ladder.
- Reward the individual rather than the post and reward each according to his or her contribution.

- Reward staff for enhancing their own knowledge value, the collective knowledge of the organisation and contributing to the organisation's cores competence.
- Measure corporate climates and fine-tune them.
- Measure knowledge value added.
- Measure customer value added.

(Reproduced with permission of Professor Mahen Tampoe, September 1997.)

CRITICAL REFLECTIONS

'Why all this fuss about motivation? Surely, motivating people is easy – I was taught that if you are not motivated, then you are dead. And I seem to remember something about a natural hierarchy of human needs' ...

'Yes, fair enough but the real issues for management is motivating people to work to the best of their abilities and directing their efforts to the goals of the organisation – and this is certainly not always easy.'

What are your own views?

In an organization, empowerment means that each staff member is responsible for creating that organisation's culture. There aren't many motivating forces more potent than giving your staff an opportunity to exercise their idealism.

Roddick, A. *Business As Unusual: the Triumph of Anita Roddick*, Thorsons (2000), p. 70.

How would you, in practical terms, attempt to provide members of your staff with the opportunity to exercise their idealism?

'All the ideas and theories that abound about motivation at work are redundant when it comes to basic issues – money is the only thing that motivates people in the real world. For example, in a recession you can motivate employees to do anything as long as they feel their job is under threat.'

Debate.

REVIEW AND DISCUSSION QUESTIONS

1 Explain what you understand by the underlying concept of motivation. Summarise the main needs and expectations to be taken into account in considering the motivation of people at work.

2 What do you understand by frustrated-induced behaviour? Give a practical example, preferably from your own work experience, of the main forms of this behaviour.

3 Why is the study of the different theories of motivation important to the manager? Distinguish between content and process theories of motivation.

4 Critically assess the practical value of Maslow's hierarchy of needs model to improving the motivation of people at work. Give examples of the extent to which the theory could meaningfully be applied to staff in your own organisation.

5 Discuss critically the validity of the contention that the motivation for staff to work well depends on more than a high salary and good working conditions.

6 Explain your understanding of expectancy-based theories of motivation. Use a simple diagram to help explain an expectancy theory of your choice. What implications do expectancy theories of motivation have for the manager?

7 Give practical examples of situations in which each of the following theories of motivation might be appropriate: (i) achievement motivation; (ii) equity theory; (iii) goal theory.

8 Discuss how you believe managers might best develop reward strategies to motivate and compensate knowledge workers.

9 Explain fully and with supporting reasons which one theory of motivation you believe is likely to be *most* appropriate in a particular work situation of your choice.

Assignment 1

a List, as far as possible in rank order, the specific needs and expectations which are most important to you as an individual. (Do *not* include *basic* physiological needs such as to satisfy thirst or hunger, or a *minimal* standard of accommodation.)

b Explain, briefly, to what extent these needs and expectations are met currently from your present work situation; and/or to what extent you anticipate they will be met from your future career ambitions.

c Think of any work experience which you have had – even a short-term, vacation or part-time job. Briefly describe:
(i)   those aspects of the job and/or experiences which motivated you to work well; and
(ii) those which had a demotivating influence on your behaviour/actions.

d Be prepared to share your feelings and comments as part of a class discussion.

Assignment 2

MOTIVATION TO WORK PROFILE

How to complete the grid

Please complete the Motivation Grid by taking each factor in order, as follows:

Compare salary (A) with Structure (B) – cell 1. Choose which factor you value more in relation to your work and write the code for that factor in the cell. For example, if you choose a good Salary as being more important to you than Structure and guidelines, enter A in the cell. If you prefer to have well-explained procedures and clarity in your work rather than a high salary, enter B in the cell (for Structure).

Move to cell 2 – Salary (A) versus Social contact (C) – and enter your chosen letter code. Continue along the top line comparing Salary (A) with the other factors and entering the chosen letter code in each cell. Move to the second line and compare Structure (B) with each other factor.

When you have filled in all 36 cells, add up the number of entries for each letter code and enter these sub-totals into the Score Table.

If you find it very difficult to choose between two factors, you may put both letters in the cell – you will then score one half of a point for each: do not do this too often (it weakens your responses), say no more than five times.

The scores show a mirror reflection of what you felt as you filled in the Grid. These scores alter over time, as you develop in your career and as your domestic, social and physical needs change. The factors that tend to change most over time and circumstances are A, B and G.

High scores for a factor indicate a high level of need, and low scores indicate a low level of need, **relative** to other factors.

The norms obtained from 1355 managers and professionals (kept on our database) will be given to you by your tutor. If you are below the norm, you have a low need for the factor, if you are above it, you have a high need.

Motivation Grid

	Structure B	Social C	Recognition D	Achievement E	Influence F	Change G	Creativity H	Interest I
Salary A	1	2	3	4	5	6	7	8
Structure		9	10	11	12	13	14	15
Social			16	17	18	19	20	21
Recognition				22	23	24	25	26
Achievement					27	28	29	30
Influence						31	32	33
Change							34	35
Creativity								36

Motivation Grid score sheet

Please fill in the score table below. Add up the number of times you have put **A** in any cell on the Grid and enter that total in the column 'Your score' against **A**. Continue for **B, C** and the other factors until you have totalled all nine of them. Your tutor will give you the norms later.

Factor	Your score	Norm
A – Salary		
B – Structure		
C – Social contact		
D – Recognition		
E – Achievement		
F – Influence		
G – Change		
H – Creativity		
I – Interest		
Total = 36		

Assignment 3

a Write a brief description of what you think is happening to the people in the picture and what you think will happen to them in the future.

b After you have written your description compare your response with those of your colleagues.

Visit our website www.booksites.net/mullins for further questions, annotated weblinks, case material and internet research material.

CASE STUDY 12.1

Not so much a motivational pyramid, more a slippery slope

My contact with my direct line manager is limited to irregular e-malls which are purely directional and/or informative. At no point is there any attempt to either help with my staffing problems or to acknowledge that these may be stress related. It follows then that there is no form of motivation downwards from him to me, although it is taken for granted that I will be self-motivated and able to motivate my team.

In the highly competitive world of international air passenger transport, the bottom line is everything. As such, all aspects of flight operations are subject to the rigorous cost-benefit analysis known as revenue per kilometre flown. This has led to some decisions which would deeply disturb Joe Public. When he purchases an airline ticket he is taking part in a lottery – the element of chance being the availability of the flight, seat class or flight time of his choice. Joe Public feels that buying his ticket gives him this automatic right – but he should read the small print.

Price banding restrictions linked to historical marketing statistics allow airlines to estimate the number of passengers who will present themselves for a particular flight as opposed to those who will choose to exercise their flexibility muscle. For example, if 70 per cent of the plane's capacity is made up of economy seats, a condition of which is that no changes are allowed, then it can be reasonably assumed that this group will travel on the given day or not at all. Flexibility to price ratio continues up the scale until the top notch ticket is reached. The high price tag at this level promises that the airline will strive to provide the frequent flyer with all that he requires. Further, statistics indicate that having made this investment, he will almost certainly travel since, *ceteris paribus*, he has chosen to pay an inflated price to guarantee that he will reach his destination when and how he wishes.

At this stage there remains only one small percentage of passenger statistics to be correlated and here restrictions linked to price again come into play, limiting the degree of usage of the flexibility muscle to the minority of passengers travelling 'open jaw'. These people will have paid a sufficiently large supplement in order to allow themselves the luxury of being flexible in their travel arrangements. As one would expect, this market segment has been shown to be the most likely not to travel and it is this information which the airlines use in their calculations. Should, as is likely, a proportion of this user group decide to change their plans, as is their right, then the airline would be faced with the economic disaster of high revenue seats flying empty and seriously reducing the company's desired margin of revenue. In order to cover this contingency proactively, the company chooses always to overbook these seats by the calculated percentage of passengers who will probably choose not to travel.

The above organisational difficulties are not new, however the systems in which they operate have changed drastically both in the attitude to acceptable levels of passenger discomfort and in the variety and number of duties which staff are now expected to carry out. As a manager in this environment Piet Andaro faces many challenges daily, the most daunting of which is to find a way to motivate his team who know with absolute certainty that during every shift they will have irate passengers. They, the passengers, will see them as the acceptable outlet for their outrage at what they perceive as unjust/unfair treatment, not to mention downright bad service. When the expected treatment fails to materialise Joe Public is not so much outraged by the failure of the actual mechanics but that his faith and trust have been misplaced.

It is then the role of Piet and his team to achieve the unachievable – to not give the customer what he wants but to send him on his way feeling that he has received outstanding service by people who genuinely care about his needs. Most importantly to the airline, he will take with him such a positive feeling that he will happily use the airline in the future and encourage others to do so.

These problems are not eventualities – most operators working in such a fast moving environment are equipped to deal with most of these – but certainties, built into the system in order to maximise profit. Part of this drive towards even greater profits has, as with many multinationals in the 1990s, resulted in a restructuring of operations which in real terms has meant a paring down of the workforce to what senior management call optimum efficiency. In this case it also involves a flattening of the management structure to be a 'leaner fitter organisation'.

At the most extreme level, management in the organisation has been subject to great change, some enforced and some planned. Although the management structure is traditional and hierarchical, it is simultaneously attempting to achieve flatter organisation status. The motivation system therefore is roughly as follows:

1 Senior management should motivate themselves.
2 Piet should motivate himself and his team.
3 Individual members of the team should motivate themselves.
4 Sideways motivation is due to the fact that although each manager has the same title there are varying grades of responsibility and support

All those with the designation 'manager' may have the same title, but their knowledge, experience and skills levels vary dramatically. Not only do skills vary dramatically, so does motivation. To be lacking in a skill is a solvable problem, given time and the appropriate training. To be lacking in motivation is almost incurable, according to Piet. 'Although some members of management may not have perfect knowledge, built into the system is a way of finding most of what you need to know. However they would rather pick up the phone and ask me even if by doing so he is causing an already stressed customer to wait while he does so.'

A recent buzzword for organisations has been 'strategy' with each aspect of the business having its own strategy while being interdependent on all the others. Particularly highlighted and linked have been the communications minefields of customer service and human resource management. Practitioners tell us that the only way for a human resource initiative to be effective is that it must be integrated and strategic. There are arguments as to whether the human resource element should be considered first and operations based around it, or whether the operations should be put in place and then the appropriate human resource found. It is generally agreed that all human resource functions should be integrated to each other and that 'best fit' should be obtained. Often, though, this is sold to the company at all levels not as best fit but as best practice; however, once in place, as in our case study, these systems and operations are looked on as success panaceas and are never examined for their functionality. The rationale is that as they have been designed by experts at great cost then they should be left alone.

On paper the system should work, with the less able learning from the proficient, however in the real world of the service industries, people dealing with people, management demands consistency.

Failure to provide this results in frustrated staff and aggrieved passengers, leaving those at the sharp end to constantly bear the brunt of the results of this revenue versus service conundrum.

Stress-related illness has been well documented and Piet is unfortunately acquainted with this phenomenon, faced as he is with a daily stress-related absenteeism of around 25 per cent. This non-existence of one-to-one or even regular verbal contact is further exacerbated by the fact that although appraisals are built into the system, in reality they are never carried out. This means that senior management has no feedback on the operational problems and difficulties which Piet encounters and as there is no procedure in place they are never communicated. Also the question is raised of how he will be able to face the daily aggression and stress without support.

Sometimes I just feel like not going to work but the act of putting on the uniform brings about a kind of metamorphosis – I begin to look forward to the day. Each shift brings a new set of problems and with it I find new capabilities and competencies within myself. I like to be proactive wherever possible, for example if I know a flight is going to be seriously overbooked then myself and my team will have a contingency plan or plans ready for when the crisis hits. I think the secret is to treat every event as completely new; it would be very easy to become cynical as it could be said that one overbooked flight is much like another in terms of problem solving.

That is simply not the case, each flight carries a set of passengers who as individuals have unique needs and expectations. I guess you could say that my motivation comes from the satisfaction of being able to make a difference. I may not be able to materialise a seat on an aircraft which does not exist but I can try to make the situation easier by means of finding the best alternative and to compensate them any way I can.

The contrast between two managers could not be greater. Piet as a self-motivator needs no praise in order to give 120 per cent effort. He never contacts his supervisor with problems and never complains, he is seen as a reliable but uninteresting plodder. Robert, on the other hand, is only motivated by extrinsic gain. What upsets Piet and his staff is that management are starting to look on Robert as a 'high flyer', the change in attitude being so great that it is apparent to everyone: 'once he heard about the promotion on offer he became a new man'.

Everyone knows that Piet is far too conscientious, but the plus-side of this is that when his team leave for other posts then they also will be fully trained and have the same attitude to customer service as Piet, whom they all admire greatly. However when Robert moves on he will leave behind a team as demotivated as himself who will continue with the lazy could-not-care-less attitude simply because they have become used to not caring.

The summary of this dire motivational situation can be divided into four parts.

- The individual who has the correct attitude to customer service in any form, that is, someone who has a natural desire to help people, needs no outside motivation.
- The person who only sees the job as a way of getting a salary and who sees customers as numbers will constantly need outside stimulus to maintain even a mediocre performance and is in fact in the wrong job with the wrong attitude.
- Senior management who buy a 'cure all' package and then fail to check on its effects will soon discover customers leaving in droves.
- Unfortunately managers of the calibre of Piet will eventually burn out either physically or emotionally as they finally realise that no matter how hard they try they will never solve the built-in problems as well as they would like to.

I am grateful to Linda Fleming for providing this case study.

Tasks

1 Consider the probable outcomes both short and long term should the present situation continue for:
- Piet Andaro
- The Airline
- The Customer

2 Is the failure to recognise the high percentage of stress-related absenteeism deliberate on the part of the airline, i.e. would it be more costly and therefore less cost-effective to attempt to find a remedy, given that airlines traditionally have a particularly high staff turnover?

3 A new CSO is appointed after a spate of public relations disasters. The CSO investigates and decides that poor motivation is at the root of the problem. Compare the main process and content theories of motivation and discuss their suitability.

4 Many of today's fast moving industries have a very public policy that they '... don't motivate individuals ... we provide an environment for them to be self-motivated'. To what extent has the airline created this type of environment? Do you see a problem simply of poor recruitment?

5 What behavioural factors are important when attempting to find a method of motivation suitable to both Piet and Robert? Discuss whether it is possible to find one which will suit both.

Notes and references

1 See, for example: Pate, L. E., Understanding Human Behaviour', *Management Decisions*, vol. 26, no. 1, 1998, pp. 58–64.
2 Krech, D., Crutchfield, R. S. and Ballachey, E. L. *Individual in Society*, McGraw-Hill (1962).
3 Mitchell, T. R. 'Motivation: New Directions for Theory, Research, and Practice', *Academy of Management Review*, vol. 7, no. 1, January 1982, pp. 80–8.
4 Kreitner, R., Kinicki, A. and Buelens, M. *Organizational Behaviour*, First European edition, McGraw-Hill, (1999).
5 Wolfson, Sir Brian 'Train, Retain and Motivate Staff', *Management Today*, March 1998, p. 5.
6 Green, J. R. 'Has Motivation Anything to do with You', *Administrator*, October 1994, pp. 29–30.
7 Farren, C. 'Mastery: The Critical Advantage' in Chowdhury, S. *Management 21C*, Financial Times Prentice Hall (2000), p. 95.

8 See, for example: Rudolph, P. A. and Kleiner, B. H. 'The Art of Motivating Employees', *Journal of Managerial Psychology*, 4 (5), 1989, pp. i–iv.
9 For a fuller discussion, see: Mullins, L. J. *Hospitality Management and Organisational Behaviour*, Fourth edition, Longman (2001).
10 See, for example: Brown, J. A. C. *The Social Psychology of Industry*, Penguin (1954 and 1986).
11 Taylor, F. W. *Scientific Management*, Harper and Row (1947).
12 Kanter, R. M. 'The Attack on Pay', *Harvard Business Review*, March–April 1987, pp. 60–7.
13 Weaver, T. 'Theory M: Motivating with Money', *Cornell HRA Quarterly*, vol. 29, no. 3, November 1988, pp. 40–5.
14 Hudson, A., Hayes, D. and Andrew, T. *Working Lives in the 1990s*, Global Futures (1996).

15 'What You Thought: Motivating Minimum-Wage Workers', *Personnel Journal*, vol. 75, no. 3, March 1996, p. 16.

16 Vine, P. 'Women in Business', *The British Journal of Administrative Management*, November/December 1997, p. 14.

17 'IDS Focus', *Incomes Data Services Ltd*, No. 92, Winter 1999.

18 Ritti, R. R. *The Ropes to Skip and the Ropes to Know*, Fourth edition, Wiley (1994), p. 72.

19 Handy, C. B., *Understanding Organizations*, Fourth edition, Penguin (1993).

20 *Management News*, the newspaper of the British Institute of Management, No. 64, February 1990, p. 6.

21 Cited in Crainer, S. 'Re-engineering the Carrot', *Management Today*, December 1995, p. 66.

22 For a discussion on the relevance of different theories for managers, see for example: Ritchie, S. and Martin, P. *Motivation Management*, Gower (1999).

23 Maslow, A. H. 'A Theory of Human Motivation', *Psychological Review*, 50, July 1943, pp. 370–96 and Maslow, A. H. *Motivation and Personality*, Third edition, Harper and Row (1987).

24 Robertson, I. T., Smith, M. and Cooper, D. *Motivation: Strategies, Theory and Practice*, Second edition, Institute of Personnel and Development (1992), p. 21.

25 See, for example: Wahba, M. A. and Bridwell, L. G. 'Maslow Reconsidered: A Review of Research on the Need Hierarchy Theory', *Organizational Behavior and Human Performance*, vol. 1, 1976, pp. 212–40.

26 Steers, R. M. and Porter, L. W. *Motivation and Work Behaviour*, Fifth edition, McGraw-Hill (1991).

27 Alderfer, C. P. *Existence, Relatedness and Growth*, Collier Macmillan (1972).

28 Herzberg, F., Mausner, B. and Synderman, B. B. *The Motivation to Work*, Second edition, Chapman and Hall (1959).

29 Herzberg, F. *Work and the Nature of Man*, Granada Publishing Ltd (1974).

30 For examples, see: (i) Bockman, V. M. 'The Herzberg Controversy', *Personnel Psychology*, vol. 24, Summer 1971, pp. 155–89, which analyses existing evidence from a wide variety of studies; (ii) Filley, A. C., House, R. J. and Kerr, S. *Managerial Process and Organizational Behavior*, Second edition, Scott Foresman (1976). A number of different sets of interviews found a high level of validity for the theoretical prediction.

31 Vroom, V. H. *Work and Motivation*, Wiley (1964). (Also published by Krieger (1982).)

32 King, N. 'A Clarification and Evaluation of the Two-Factor Theory of Job Satisfaction', *Psychological Bulletin*, vol. 74, July 1970, pp. 18–31.

33 Blackburn, R. M. and Mann, M. *The Working Class in the Labour Market*, Macmillan (1979).

34 Shipley, D. and Kiely, J. 'Motivation and Dissatisfaction of Industrial Salespeople – How Relevant is Herzberg's Theory?', *European Journal of Marketing*, vol. 22, no. 1, March 1988, pp. 17–28.

35 Phillipchuck, J. 'An Inquiry Into the Continuing Relevance of Herzberg's Motivation Theory', *Engineering Management Journal*, vol. 8, no. 1, March 1996, pp. 15–20.

36 McClelland, D. C. *Human Motivation*, Cambridge University Press (1988).

37 See, for example: Spangler, W. D. 'Validity of Questionnaire and TAT Measures of Weed for Achievement Two Meta-Analyses', *Psychological Bulletin*, July 1992, pp. 140–54.

38 McClelland, D. C. 'Business Drive and National Achievement', *Harvard Business Review*, vol. 40, July–August 1962, pp. 99–112.

39 McClelland, D. C. and Burnham, D. H. 'Power is the Great Motivation', *Harvard Business Review*, vol. 54, March–April 1976, pp. 100–10.

40 Vroom, V. H. *Work and Motivation*, Wiley (1964). (Also published by Krieger (1982).)

41 Galbraith, J. and Cummings, L. L. 'An Empirical Investigation of the Motivational Determinants of Task Performance', *Organizational Behavior and Human Performance*, vol. 2, 1967, pp. 237–57.

42 Porter, L. W. and Lawler, E. E. *Managerial Attitudes and Performance*, Irwin (1968).

43 Graen, G. 'Instrumentality Theory of Work Motivation', *Journal of Applied Psychology Monographs*, vol. 53, no. 2, 1969, part 2.

44 Lawler, E. E. *Motivation in Work Organizations*, Brooks/Cole (1973).

45 See, for example: Eerde, van W. and Thierry, H. 'Vroom's Expectancy Models and Work-Related Criteria: A Meta-Analysis', *Journal of Applied Psychology*, October 1996, pp. 575–86.

46 Porter, L. W., Lawler, E. E. and Hackman, J. R. *Behavior in Organizations*, McGraw-Hill (1975), pp. 57–8.

47 Tampoe, M. 'Knowledge Workers – The New Management Challenge', *Professional Manager*, November 1994, pp. 12–13.

48 Lucas, E. 'Turning on the Knowledge Workers', *Professional Manager*, May 1999, pp. 10–12.

49 Adams, J. S. 'Injustice in Social Exchange', in Berkowitz, L. (ed.) *Advances in Experimental Social Psychology*, Academic Press (1965). Abridged in Steers, R. M. and Porter, L. W. *Motivation and Work Behavior*, Second edition, McGraw-Hill (1979), pp. 107–24.

50 Kreitner, R., Knicki, A. and Buelens, M. *Organisational Behaviour*, First European edition, McGraw-Hill, (1999).

51 Locke, E. A. 'Towards a Theory of Task Motivation and Incentives', *Organizational Behavior and Human Performance*, vol. 3, 1968, pp. 157–89.

52 For examples, see: (i) Latham, G. P. and Yukl, G. A. 'A Review of the Research on the Applications of Goal Setting in Organizations', *Academy of Management Journal*, vol. 18, 1975, pp. 824–45; (ii) Latham, G. P. and Locke, E. A. 'Goal Setting: A Motivational Technique that Works', *Organizational Dynamics*, Autumn 1979, pp. 28–80.

53 Locke, E. A. 'Personal Attitudes and Motivation', *Annual Review of Psychology*, vol. 26, 1975, pp. 457–80.

54 For a summary of research supporting these conclusions, see: Miner, J. B. *Theories of Organizational Behavior*, Holt, Rinehart and Winston (1980).

Chapter 8

THE NATURE OF LEADERSHIP

An essential part of management is co-ordinating the activities of people and guiding their efforts towards the goals and objectives of the organisation. This involves the process of leadership and the choice of an appropriate form of behaviour. Leadership is a central feature of organisational performance. The manager must understand the nature of leadership and factors which determine the effectiveness of the leadership relationship.

Learning objectives

To:

➤ explain the meaning and importance of leadership in work organisations;

➤ recognise the nature of managerial leadership and the exercise of leadership power and influence;

➤ detail patterns of managerial leadership and main approaches to and studies of leadership;

➤ examine leadership as an aspect of behaviour, and different styles of leadership;

➤ assess contingency theories of leadership and situational factors which determine the characteristics of leadership;

➤ explain the nature and main components of transformational leadership;

➤ evaluate the variables which determine effective managerial leadership.

The meaning of leadership

There are many ways of looking at **leadership** and many interpretations of its meaning. Leadership might be interpreted in simple terms, such as 'getting others to follow' or 'getting people to do things willingly', or interpreted more specifically, for example as 'the use of authority in decision-making'. It may be exercised as an attribute of position, or because of personal knowledge or wisdom. Leadership might be based on a function of personality, or it can be seen as a behavioural category. It may also be viewed in terms of the role of the leaders and their ability to achieve effective performance from others.

Taffinder suggests that everyone has a theory but, although we know quite a lot about management, we do not know as much about leadership.[1] Handy believes that:

> *like motivation, the search for the definitive solution to the leadership problem has proved to be another endless quest for the Holy Grail in organization theory.*[2]

According to *Crainer* there are over 400 definitions of leadership and:

> *it is a veritable minefield of misunderstanding and difference through which theorists and practitioners must tread warily.*[3]

> Nothing in business circles brings such a rush of clichés to the head as leadership, one of those humpty-dumpty words which, as Alice said, mean whatever we want them to mean ... Leadership is one of those elusive priorities, an area in which there is no absolute, no guaranteed model. So it turns out to be not only vital but also fun to talk about what makes a leader.
>
> *Sir Peter Parker*[4]

It is difficult, therefore, to generalise about leadership, but essentially it is a **relationship through which one person influences the behaviour or actions of other people**. This means that the process of leadership cannot be separated from the activities of groups and with effective teambuilding.

According to *Levine*, leaders need to focus on moving people and organisations forward by increasing the competency of staff and the co-operation of teams in order to improve the organisation.

A leader's job is to constantly challenge the bureaucracy that smothers individual enthusiasm and the desire to contribute to an organization. Leaders in the new millennium will create an environment that encourages the development of skills, learning and openness so that those on their team can participate in the deployment of financial and human resources.[5]

The importance of leadership Leadership is related to motivation, interpersonal behaviour and the process of communication.[6] Leadership is important in attempting to reduce employee dissatisfaction.[7] Good leadership also involves the effective process of delegation. The leadership relationship is not limited to leader behaviour resulting in subordinate behaviour. Leadership is a dynamic process. The leader–follower relationship is reciprocal and effective leadership is a two-way process which influences both individual and organisational performance.

Lord Sieff, for example, maintains that:

> *Leadership is vitally important at all levels within the company, from main board to the shopfloor. Leadership is the moral and intellectual ability to visualise and work for what is best for the company and its employees ... The most vital thing the leader does is to create team spirit around him and near him, not in a schoolboy sense, but in realistic terms of mature adults ... To be effective leadership has to be seen, and it is best seen in action.*[8]

Understanding and Managing People at Work

Good management leadership helps to develop teamwork and the integration of individual and group goals. It aids intrinsic motivation by emphasising the importance of the work that people do.[9]

The changing nature of work organisations, including flatter structures and recognition of the efficient use of human resources, coupled with advances in social democracy, have combined to place growing importance on leadership. The nature of management is moving away from an emphasis on getting results by the close control of the workforce and towards an environment of coaching, support and empowerment.[10]

For example, *Hooper and Potter* discuss the importance of leadership in times of change and uncertainty, and that good leaders are sensitive to the impact of the change process on people. 'Never is leadership more sought after than in times of change and uncertainty. Effective change leadership is the key to shifting people's perceptions from seeing change as a threat to seeing it as an exciting challenge.'[11]

Vecchio raises the question of whether leadership does make a difference and suggests one interesting way to learn whether leaders can have an impact is by studying the results of a change in leader. As work-unit achievements result more from the efforts of the unit's members than of one individual, and organisations have rules and policies that govern behaviour, a good argument can be made that leadership has only a modest impact on group performance. However, Vecchio also contends that: 'one has a sense that a leader, under the right circumstances, can have a powerful impact on group performance.'[12]

Leadership and management

What is the relationship between leadership and management? Sometimes management and leadership are seen as synonymous. There is, however, a difference between the two and it does not follow that every leader is a manager.

Management is more usually viewed as getting things done through other people in order to achieve stated organisational objectives. The manager may react to specific situations and be more concerned with solving short-term problems. Management is regarded as relating to people working within a structured organisation and with prescribed roles. To people outside of the organisation the manager might not necessarily be seen in a leadership role.

The emphasis of leadership is on interpersonal behaviour in a broader context. It is often associated with the willing and enthusiastic behaviour of followers. **Leadership does not necessarily take place within the hierarchical structure of the organisation**. Many people operate as leaders without their role ever being clearly established or defined. For example, *Belbin* suggests that:

> there is a clear implication that leadership is not part of the job but a quality that can be brought to a job ... The work that leadership encompasses in the context clearly is not assigned but comes about spontaneously.[13]

Differences in attitudes and relations with others

There are other differences between leadership and management. For example, *Zaleznik* explores difference in attitudes towards goals, conceptions of work, relations with others, self-perception and development.

- Managers tend to adopt impersonal or passive attitudes towards goals. Leaders adopt a more personal and active attitude towards goals.
- In order to get people to accept solutions, the manager needs continually to coordinate and balance in order to compromise conflicting values. The leader creates excitement in work and develops choices that give substance to images that excite people.

Understanding and Managing People at Work

- In their relationships with other people, managers maintain a low level of emotional involvement. Leaders have empathy with other people and give attention to what events and actions mean.
- Managers see themselves more as conservators and regulators of the existing order of affairs with which they identify, and from which they gain rewards. Leaders work in, but do not belong to, the organisation. Their sense of identity does not depend upon membership or work roles and they search out opportunities for change.[14]

The 7-S organisational framework

The differences between leadership and management have been applied by *Watson* to the 7-S organisational framework of: strategy, structure, systems, style, staff, skills and superordinate (or shared) goals. Watson suggests that whereas managers tend towards reliance on

- strategy,
- structure, and
- systems,

leaders have an inherent inclination for utilisation of the 'soft' Ss of

- style,
- staff,
- skills, and
- shared goals.

Watson also suggests, although cautiously, that 7-S management could be seen as the province of leaders. Managers will not ordinarily be capable of achieving sufficient mastery of all seven factors to attain a consistently high level of organisational performance.[15]

Fundamental differences between management and leadership

Based on experience of management approaches in both commerce and the military, *Hollingsworth* questions how many managers consider themselves first and foremost as leaders, relegating 'manager' to their job title. He argues that commercial managers need to learn from the armed forces if they wish to be viewed as leaders. Having accepted that there are some links between management and leadership, Hollingsworth lists six 'fundamental differences'.

- A manager administers – a leader innovates
- A manager maintains – a leader develops
- A manager focuses on systems and structure – a leader focuses on people
- A manager relies on control – a leader inspires trust
- A manager keeps an eye on the bottom line – a leader has an eye on the horizon
- A manager does things right – a leader does the right thing[16]

Not everyone would agree with this list. *Robinson*, for example, suggests that if the word 'manager' is replaced by 'administrator' then the lists works. However, whatever your view the list makes for a helpful basis for critical discussion on the nature of management and leadership.[17]

| Managerial leadership

Despite the differences, there is a close relationship between leadership and management in work organisations, and it is not easy to separate them as distinct activities. Many methods of management training can also be used as a means of measuring leadership style. For example, the Leadership Grid (discussed in Chapter 7) was until recently known as the Managerial Grid.

Management may arguably be viewed more in terms of planning, organising, directing and controlling the activities of subordinate staff. Leadership, however, is concerned more with attention to communicating with, motivating, encouraging and involving people.[18]

> *Management is complex, fragmented, its activities brief, opportunistic, predominantly verbal; leadership is more so. Management reacts. Leadership transforms. It makes a difference.*[19]

In Chapter 6 we discussed management as getting work done through the efforts of other people. To be an effective manager it is necessary to exercise the role of leadership. A common view is that the job of the manager requires the ability of leadership and that leadership is in effect a sub-set of management, although leadership is a special attribute which can be distinguished from other elements of management. According to *Miller et al.*, by definition there are important distinctions between the two concepts of management and leadership. 'Management involves using human, equipment and information resources to achieve various objectives. On the other hand, leadership focuses on getting things done through others. Thus you manage things (budgets, procedures, and so on), but you lead people.'[20]

Symbolic leadership

The movement away from managers relying solely on their positional power within a hierarchical structure of authority has placed greater emphasis on leadership and organisational culture, including attention to the symbols of leadership. In order to convey clearly the meaning intended, effective leadership involves managing through the skilful use of symbols – including, for example, form of communication and use of language, ceremonies, images and rituals, and physical environment.[21]

Symbolism is an important means by which managers communicate corporate intent and cultural messages. According to *Peters*, for example, in attempting to act out the vision of the organisation and to achieve their goals, managers deal in a number of different symbols.[22] *Brown* identifies the most interesting of these symbolic means as: how top executives spend their time; their use of language; their use of meetings, agendas and minutes; and their use of settings.[23]

The leadership relationship

A leader may be imposed, formally appointed or elected, chosen informally, or emerge naturally through the demands of the situation or the wishes of the group. Leadership may be attempted, successful or effective.[24]

- **Attempted leadership** is when any individual in the group attempts to exert influence over other members of the group.
- **Successful leadership** is when the influence brings about the behaviour and results that were intended by the leader.
- **Effective leadership** is when successful leadership results in functional behaviour and the achievement of group goals.

The leader may exercise authority as an attribute of position. In this case the manager is seen as a leader because of a stated position in the hierarchy. Leadership, however, is more than just adherence to a formal role prescription. It is more than eliciting mechanical behaviour which results from a superior–subordinate relationship in a hierarchical structure.

> *Remember that you can be appointed a manager but you are not a leader until your appointment is ratified in the hearts and minds of those who work for you.*[25]

A dynamic form of behaviour

Leadership is, therefore, a dynamic form of behaviour and there are a number of variables which affect the leadership relationship. Four major variables are identified by *McGregor* as:

- the characteristics of the leader;
- the attitude, needs and other personal characteristics of the followers;
- the nature of the organisation, such as its purpose, its structure, the tasks to be performed; and
- the social, economic and political environment.

McGregor concludes that 'leadership is not a property of the individual, but a complex relationship among these variables'.[26]

According to *Kouzes and Posner*, 'credibility is the foundation of leadership'. From extensive research in over 30 countries and response to the question of what people 'look for and admire in a leader, in a person whose direction they would willingly follow', people have consistently replied that they want:

> leaders who exemplify four qualities: they want them to be honest, forward-looking, inspiring and competent. In our research our respondents strongly agree that they want leaders with integrity and trustworthiness, with vision and a sense of direction, with enthusiasm and passion, and with expertise and a track record for getting things done.[27]

Sapiential authority or charisma

Leadership may be exercised on the basis of sapiential authority – that is, by wisdom, personal knowledge, reputation or expertise. A sapiential-type relationship places emphasis on a guiding and facilitating role and is often appropriate for people in creative, specialist or professional jobs where there may be particular resentment against a formal hierarchical style of managerial leadership.

Leadership may also be based on the personal qualities, or charisma, of the leader and the manner in which authority is exercised. This view of leadership gives rise to the question of 'born' or 'natural' leaders (see the discussion on the qualities or traits approach to leadership, below). Leadership may also focus on the role of the leader in terms of the relationship with followers and the adoption of a particular style of leadership.

Power and leadership influence

Within an organisation, leadership influence will be dependent upon the type of power that the leader can exercise over the followers. The exercise of power is a social process which helps to explain how different people can influence the behaviour/ actions of others. Five main sources of power upon which the influence of the leader is based have been identified by *French and Raven* as reward power, coercive power, legitimate power, referent power, and expert power.[28] We shall consider these in terms of the manager (as a leader) and subordinate relationship.

- **Reward power** is based on the subordinate's *perception* that the leader has the ability and resources to obtain rewards for those who comply with directives; for example, pay, promotion, praise, recognition, increased responsibilities, allocation and arrangement of work, granting of privileges.
- **Coercive power** is based on fear and the subordinate's *perception* that the leader has the ability to punish or to bring about undesirable outcomes for those who do not comply with directives; for example, withholding pay rises, promotion or privileges; allocation of undesirable duties or responsibilities; withdrawal of friendship or support; formal reprimands or possibly dismissal. This is in effect the opposite of reward power.
- **Legitimate power** is based on the subordinate's *perception* that the leader has a right to exercise influence because of the leader's role or position in the organisation. Legitimate power is based on authority, for example that of managers and

supervisors within the hierarchical structure of an organisation. Legitimate power is therefore 'position' power because it is based on the role of the leader in the organisation, and not on the nature of the personal relationship with others.

- **Referent power** is based on the subordinate's *identification* with the leader. The leader exercises influence because of perceived attractiveness, personal characteristics, reputation or what is called 'charisma'. For example, a particular manager may not be in a position to reward or punish certain subordinates, but may still exercise power over the subordinates because the manager commands their respect or esteem.

- **Expert power** is based on the subordinate's *perception* of the leader as someone who is competent and who has some special knowledge or expertise in a given area. Expert power is based on credibility and clear evidence of knowledge or expertise; for example, the expert knowledge of 'functional' specialists such as the personnel manager, management accountant or systems analyst. The expert power is usually limited to narrow, well-defined areas or specialisms.

Subordinates' perception of influence

It is important to note that these sources of power are based on the subordinate's *perception* of the influence of the leader, whether it is real or not. For example, if a leader has the ability to control rewards and punishments but subordinates *do not believe this*, then in effect the leader has no reward or coercive power. Similarly, if subordinates in a line department *believe* a manager in a (different) staff department has executive authority over them then even if, *de facto*, that manager has no such authority there is still a *perceived* legitimate power.

French and Raven point out that the five sources of power are interrelated and the use of one type of power (for example, coercive) may affect the ability to use another type of power (for example, referent). Furthermore, the same person may exercise different types of power, in particular circumstances and at different times.

> You have to look at leadership through the eyes of the followers and you have to live the message. What I have learned is that people become motivated when you guide them to the source of their own power and when you make heroes out of employees who personify what you want to see in the organisation.
>
> *Anita Roddick*[29]

Guidelines for building using power

According to *Yukl*, the research on power and influence is still too limited to provide clear and unequivocal guidelines for leaders on the best way to exercise their power. However, utilising terminology from *French and Raven's* taxonomy, he provides a set of guidelines on how to build and maintain power, and to use it effectively to influence attempts with peers or superiors.[30] (*See* Table 8.1.)

Table 8.1 Guidelines for building and using power

How to increase and maintain power	How to use power effectively
Legitimate power:	
● Gain more formal authority.	● Make polite, clear requests.
● Use symbols of authority.	● Explain the reasons for a request.
● Get people to acknowledge authority.	● Don't exceed your scope of authority.
● Exercise authority regularly.	● Verify authority if necessary.
● Follow proper channels in giving orders.	● Be sensitive to target concerns.
● Back up authority with reward and coercive power.	● Follow up to verify compliance.
	● Insist on compliance if appropriate.

Table 8.1 continued

How to increase and maintain power	How to use power effectively
Reward power:	
● Discover what people need and want. ● Gain more control over rewards. ● Ensure people know you control rewards. ● Don't promise more than you can deliver. ● Don't use rewards in a manipulative way. ● Avoid complex, mechanical incentives. ● Don't use rewards for personal benefit.	● Offer desirable rewards. ● Offer fair and ethical rewards. ● Explain criteria for giving rewards. ● Provide rewards as promised. ● Use rewards symbolically to reinforce desirable behaviour.
Expert power:	
● Gain more relative knowledge. ● Keep informed about technical matters. ● Develop exclusive sources of information. ● Use symbols to verify expertise. ● Demonstrate competency by solving difficult problems. ● Don't make rash, careless statements ● Don't lie or misrepresent the facts. ● Don't keep changing positions.	● Explain the reasons for a request or proposal. ● Explain why a request is important. ● Provide evidence that a proposal will be successful. ● Listen seriously to target concerns. ● Show respect for target (don't be arrogant). ● Act confident and decisive in a crisis.
Referent power:	
● Show acceptance and positive regard. ● Act supportive and helpful. ● Don't manipulate and exploit people for personal advantage. ● Defend someone's interests and back them up when appropriate. ● Keep promises. ● Make self-sacrifices to show concern. ● Use sincere forms of ingratiation.	● Use personal appeals when necessary. ● Indicate that a request is important to you. ● Don't ask for a personal favour that is excessive given the relationship. ● Provide an example of proper behaviour (role modelling).
Coercive power:	
● Identify credible penalties to deter unacceptable behaviour. ● Gain authority to use punishments. ● Don't make rash threats. ● Don't use coercion in a manipulative way. ● Use only punishments that are legitimate. ● Fit punishments to the infraction. ● Don't use coercion for personal benefit.	● Inform target of rules and penalties. ● Give ample prior warnings. ● Understand situation before punishing. ● Remain calm and helpful, not hostile. ● Encourage improvement to avoid the need for punishment. ● Ask target to suggest way to improve. ● Administer discipline in private.

(*Source: Leadership in Organizations*, Fourth edition, by Yukl, Gary. © 1998, p. 197. Prentice-Hall, inc., Upper Saddle River, NJ.)

Approaches to leadership

Due to its complex and variable nature there are many alternative ways of analysing leadership. It is helpful, therefore, to have some framework in which to consider different approaches to study of the subject.

One way is to examine managerial leadership in terms of:

● the qualities or traits approach;
● the functional or group approach, including action-centred leadership;
● leadership as a behavioural category;
● styles of leadership;
● the situational approach and contingency models; and
● transitional or transformational leadership.

(*See* Figure 8.1.)

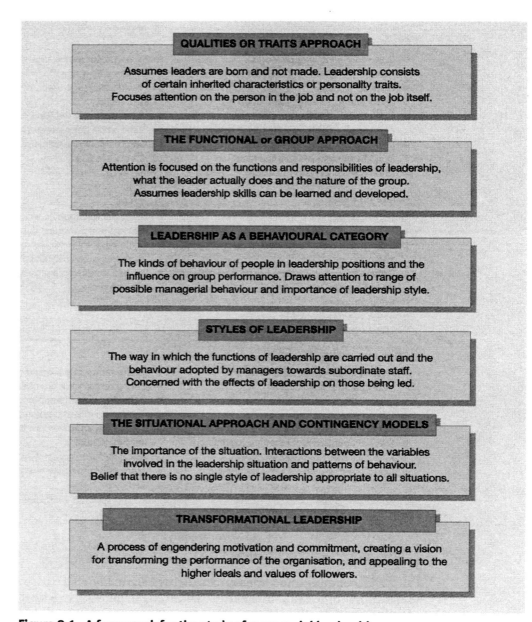

QUALITIES OR TRAITS APPROACH

Assumes leaders are born and not made. Leadership consists
of certain inherited characteristics or personality traits.
Focuses attention on the person in the job and not on the job itself.

THE FUNCTIONAL or GROUP APPROACH

Attention is focused on the functions and responsibilities of leadership,
what the leader actually does and the nature of the group.
Assumes leadership skills can be learned and developed.

LEADERSHIP AS A BEHAVIOURAL CATEGORY

The kinds of behaviour of people in leadership positions and the
influence on group performance. Draws attention to range of
possible managerial behaviour and importance of leadership style.

STYLES OF LEADERSHIP

The way in which the functions of leadership are carried out and the
behaviour adopted by managers towards subordinate staff.
Concerned with the effects of leadership on those being led.

THE SITUATIONAL APPROACH AND CONTINGENCY MODELS

The importance of the situation. Interactions between the variables
involved in the leadership situation and patterns of behaviour.
Belief that there is no single style of leadership appropriate to all situations.

TRANSFORMATIONAL LEADERSHIP

A process of engendering motivation and commitment, creating a vision
for transforming the performance of the organisation, and appealing to the
higher ideals and values of followers.

Figure 8.1   A framework for the study of managerial leadership

The qualities or traits approach

The first approach assumes that leaders are born and not made. Leadership consists of certain inherited characteristics, or personality traits, which distinguish leaders from their followers: the so-called Great Person theory of leadership. The **qualities approach** focuses attention on the man or woman in the job and not on the job itself. It suggests that attention is given to the selection of leaders rather than to training for leadership.

For example, *Drucker* (writing originally in 1955) makes the point that:

> *Leadership is of utmost importance. Indeed there is no substitute for it. But leadership cannot be created or promoted. It cannot be taught or learned.*[31]

There have been many research studies into the common traits of leadership. However, attempts at identifying common personality, or physical and mental, characteristics of different 'good' or 'successful' leaders have met with little success.[32] Investigations have identified lists of traits which tend to be overlapping, contradictary or with little correlation for most features.

It is noticeable that 'individuality' or 'originality' usually features in the list of traits. This itself suggests that there is little in common between specific personality traits of different leaders. It is perhaps possible therefore to identify general characteristics of leadership ability, such as self-confidence, initiative, intelligence and belief in one's actions, but research into this area has revealed little more than this.

Of recent interest is a series of interviews with headhunters, and senior figures in industry and the city from which *Management Today* came up with a list of Britain's most powerful women in business. A conclusion from the list is that the 'top 50 women do not fit any pattern. They wield the kind of power and influence that defies stereotypes.'[33]

Limitations of the traits approach

There are two further limitations with this approach.

- First, there is bound to be some subjective judgement in determining who is regarded as a 'good' or 'successful' leader.
- Second, the lists of possible traits tend to be very long and there is not always agreement on the most important.

Even if it were possible to identify an agreed list of more specific qualities, this would provide little explanation of the nature of leadership. It would do little to help in the development and training of future leaders. Although there is still some interest in the qualities, or traits, approach, attention has been directed more to other approaches to leadership.

The qualities or traits approach gives rise to the questions: **whether leaders are born or made**; and whether leadership is an art or a science. The important point, however, is that **these are not mutually exclusive alternatives**. Even if there are certain inborn qualities which make for a good leader, these natural talents need encouragement and development. Even if leadership is something of an art, it still requires the application of special skills and techniques.

The functional (or group) approach

This approach to leadership focuses attention not on the personality of the leader, nor on the man or woman in the job, *per se*, but on the **functions of leadership**. Leadership is always present in any group engaged in a task. The **functional approach** views leadership in terms of how the leader's behaviour affects, and is affected by, the group of followers. This approach concentrates on the nature of the group, the followers or subordinates. **It focuses on the content of leadership.**

Greater attention can be given to the successful training of leaders and to the means of improving the leaders' performance by concentrating on the functions which will lead to effective performance by the work group.

The functional approach believes that the skills of leadership can be learnt, developed and perfected. In contrast to the view of *Drucker* (referred to above), *Kotter*, for example, makes the point that successful companies do not wait for leaders to come along.

> *They actively seek out people with leadership potential and expose them to career experiences designed to develop that potential. Indeed, with careful selection, nurturing and encouragement, dozens of people can play important leadership roles in a business organization.*[34]

Principles of effective leadership

Sewell-Rutter argues that effective leadership is open to anyone with self-belief. There is no mystery, the principles of effective leadership are straightforward – and they can be acquired. He suggests that the five common characteristics all begin with 'C':[35]

- **Clarity** – of vision, of what you aspire to achieve and the values you hold dear;
- **Conviction** – and the application of inner self-belief;
- **Charisma** – creating an ethos of trust, respect and understanding to marshal and motivate your followers. Charisma can be developed;
- **Communication** – leading effective communication personally enhances respect from people;
- **Care** – recognition that results ultimately come from the combined efforts of their people.

The importance of charisma for effective leadership is emphasised by *Conger*, who also believes that many of the traits that make a successful leader can be taught, including charisma.

> *Now the big question is whether you are born with charisma or whether you can develop it. I believe you can develop elements of it. For example, you can take courses to improve your speaking skills. You can learn to stage events that send powerful messages. You can learn to think more critically about the status quo and its shortcomings. You can do more on a daily basis to motivate your team. What you simply cannot learn is how to be passionate about what you do. You have to discover that for yourself, and passion is a big part of what drives a charismatic leader. It is also what motivates and inspires those who work for the charismatic leader.*[36]

Action-centred leadership

A general theory on the functional approach is associated with the work of *John Adair* and his ideas on **action-centred leadership** which focuses on what leaders actually *do*.[37] The effectiveness of the leader is dependent upon meeting three areas of need within the work group: the need to achieve the common **task**, the need for **team maintenance**, and the **individual needs** of group members. Adair symbolises these needs by three overlapping circles (*see* Figure 8.2).

Task functions involve:

- achieving the objectives of the work group;
- defining group tasks;
- planning the work;

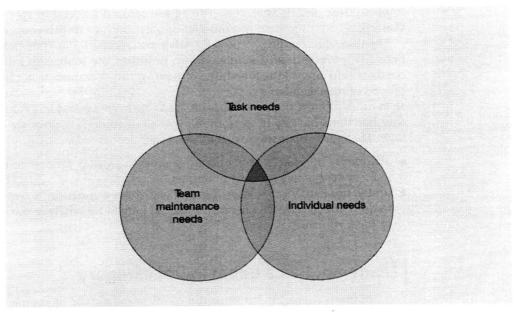

Figure 8.2 Interaction of needs within the group
(*Source:* Adair, J., *Action-Centred Leadership*, Gower Press (1979), p. 10.)

- allocation of resources;
- organisation of duties and responsibilities;
- controlling quality and checking performance;
- reviewing progress.

Team functions involve:

- maintaining morale and building team spirit;
- the cohesiveness of the group as a working unit;
- setting standards and maintaining discipline;
- systems of communication within the group;
- training the group;
- appointment of sub-leaders.

Individual functions involve:

- meeting the needs of the individual members of the group;
- attending to personal problems;
- giving praise and status;
- reconciling conflicts between group needs and needs of the individual;
- training the individual.

The action by the leader in any one area of need will affect one or both of the other areas of need. The ideal position is where complete integration of the three areas of need is achieved. In any work group the most effective leader is the person who sees that the task needs, the needs of the group and those of the individual are all adequately met. The effective leader elicits the contribution of members of the group and draws out other leadership from the group to satisfy the three interrelated areas of need.

Leadership training

Adair recognises that the qualities of leadership can be developed through regular application of practical actions associated with a particular quality. This has led to the development of a system of leadership training for helping managers to develop and improve their ability as leaders. The action-centred leadership approach to leadership training is currently used by a number of organisations in this country.

The three-circle approach used by Adair also serves to illustrate the close relationship between leadership and management. Building the team and satisfying individual needs would include leadership. Achieving the common task clearly involves the process of management.

In order to meet the three areas of need – task, group and individual – certain leadership functions have to be performed. Not all of these functions are required all of the time. Therefore, Adair suggests that the leader needs:

- **awareness** of what is going on in groups, the group process or underlying behaviour, and the actual content of discussion;
- **understanding**, that is knowing that a particular function is required; and the skill to do it effectively, which can usually be judged by whether the group responds or changes course.[38]

Leadership as a behavioural category

This approach draws attention to the kinds of behaviour of people in leadership situations. One of the most extensive research studies on behavioural categories of leadership was the *Ohio State Leadership Studies* undertaken by the Bureau of Business Research at Ohio State University. The focus was on the effects of leadership styles on group performance.

Questionnaires were designed which comprised a list of descriptive items each dealing with a specific aspect of leadership behaviour. The questionnaires were used repeatedly in different kinds of organisations and in a variety of leader–group member situations.

Consideration and structure

Results of the Ohio State studies indicated two major dimensions of leadership behaviour, labelled 'consideration' and 'initiating structure'.[39]

- **Consideration** reflects the extent to which the leader establishes trust, mutual respect and rapport with the group and shows concern, warmth, support and consideration for subordinates. This dimension is associated with two-way communication, participation and the human relations approach to leadership.
- **Structure** reflects the extent to which the leader defines and structures group interactions towards attainment of formal goals and organises group activities. This dimension is associated with efforts to achieve organisational goals.

Consideration and initiating structure can be seen as the same as maintenance function (building and maintaining the group as a working unit and relationships among group members) and task function (accomplishment of specific tasks of the groups and achievement of goals) which are discussed in Chapter 14. Consideration and initiating structure were found to be uncorrelated and independent dimensions. Leadership behaviour could, therefore, be shown on two separate axes.

Research into the effects of these four types of leadership behaviour suggest that some balance is needed between consideration and structure in order to satisfy both individual needs and organisational goals. A high consideration, high structure style appears to be generally more effective in terms of subordinate satisfaction and group performance, but the evidence is not conclusive and much seems to depend upon situational factors.

Group interaction analysis	Task functions	Maintenance functions
Ohio State leadership study	Initiating structure	Consideration
University of Michigan study	Production-centred supervision	Employee-centred supervision
McGregor, assumptions about people and work	Theory X	Theory Y
Blake and McCanse, Leadership Grid	Concern for production	Concern for people

Figure 8.3 Two major dimensions of managerial leadership

Employee-centred and production-centred supervisors

Another major research study was carried out at the *University of Michigan Institute for Social Research* at the same time as the Ohio State studies. Effective supervisors (measured along dimensions of group morale, productivity and cost reduction) appeared to display four common characteristics:

- delegation of authority and avoidance of close supervision;
- an interest and concern in their subordinates as individuals;
- participative problem-solving; and
- high standards of performance.

Likert, who has summarised the findings of the University of Michigan studies, used the terms **employee-centred** and **production-centred** supervisors.[40] These terms are similar to the dimensions of consideration and structure. The first three of these supervisory characteristics are examples of consideration. The fourth characteristic exemplifies structure.

Like consideration and structure, employee-centred and production-centred supervision need to be balanced. Likert concluded that employee-centred supervisors who get best results tend to recognise that one of their main responsibilities is production. Both the Ohio State studies and the University of Michigan studies appear to support the idea that there is no single behavioural category of leadership which is superior. There are many types of leadership behaviour and their effectiveness depends upon the variables in any given situation.

Major dimensions of managerial leadership

Despite the many types of actual leadership behaviour, we have seen that there appears to be general agreement on two major dimensions of managerial leadership. This can be extended to include the works of *McGregor* and of *Blake and McCanse*, discussed as part of managerial behaviour in Chapter 7. (*See* Figure 8.3.)

Styles of leadership

Attention to leadership as a behavioural category has drawn attention to the importance of leadership style. In the work situation it has become increasingly clear that managers can no longer rely solely on the use of their position in the hierarchical structure as a means of exercising the functions of leadership. In order to get the best results from subordinates the manager must also have regard for the need to encourage high morale, a spirit of involvement and co-operation, and a willingness to work. This gives rise to consideration of the style of leadership and provides another heading under which to analyse leadership behaviour.

Leadership style is the way in which the functions of leadership are carried out, the way in which the manager typically behaves towards members of the group.

The development of behavioural science has drawn attention to the processes of interpersonal behaviour in the work situation and to the effects of leadership on those being led. The attention given to leadership style is based on the assumption that subordinates are more likely to work effectively for managers who adopt a certain style of leadership than they will for managers who adopt alternative styles.

Broad classification of leadership style

There are many dimensions to leadership and many possible ways of describing leadership style, such as, for example, dictatorial, unitary, bureaucratic, benevolent, charismatic, consultative, participative and abdicatorial. The style of managerial leadership towards subordinate staff and the focus of power can however be classified within a broad three-fold heading.

- The **authoritarian (or autocratic) style** is where the focus of power is with the manager, and all interactions within the group move towards the manager. The manager alone exercises decision-making and authority for determining policy, procedures for achieving goals, work tasks and relationships, control of rewards or punishments.
- The **democratic style** is where the focus of power is more with the group as a whole and there is greater interaction within the group. The leadership functions are shared with members of the group and the manager is more part of a team. The group members have a greater say in decision-making, determination of policy, implementation of systems and procedures.
- A *laissez-faire* **(genuine) style** is where the manager observes that members of the group are working well on their own. The manager consciously makes a decision to pass the focus of power to members, to allow them freedom of action 'to do as they think best', and not to interfere; but is readily available if help is needed. There is often confusion over this style of leadership behaviour. The word 'genuine' is emphasised because this is to be contrasted with the manager who could not care, who deliberately keeps away from the trouble spots and does not want to get involved. The manager just lets members of the group get on with the work in hand. Members are left to face decisions which rightly belong with the manager. This is more a non-style of leadership or it could perhaps be labelled as abdication.

Solo leader and team leader

Belbin distinguishes between two broad contrasting or diverging styles of leadership in industry: the solo leader and the team leader.[41] The solo leader enjoys free range, and rules as if absolutely. The leader takes no risks with other people, adopts a directive approach, prefers specific tasks and goals, expects compliance and acts as a model for others to follow. In times of crisis or urgency the talented solo leaders have been effective in overcoming departmental barriers and obstacles, and implementing decisions quickly. However, when the solo leaders fail, they are discarded.

By contrast, the team leader declines to rule as if absolutely, and deliberately limits his or her role. The leader creates a sense of mission, expresses greater respect for and trust in subordinates, recognises the skills and strengths of others, and is more inclined to delegate. Belbin suggests that solo leadership is familiar to most people because part of crowd psychology is to seek to be led and to have faith in the leader. However, increasing uncertainty and continuous change together with societal pressure for the sharing of power has led to increasing attention to team leadership.

Attention to style of leadership

Work by such writers as *McGregor, Likert,* and *Blake and Mouton* (discussed in Chapter 7) appear to support the value of participative managerial leadership in improving organisational effectiveness. Attention to the manager's style of leadership has come about because of a greater understanding of the needs and expectations of people at work. It has also been influenced by such factors as:

- increasing business competitiveness and recognition of efficient use of human resources;
- changes in the value system of society;
- broader standards of education and training;
- advances in scientific and technical knowledge;
- changes in the nature of work organisation;
- the influence of trade unions;
- pressure for a greater social responsibility towards employees, for example through schemes of participation in decision-making and the quality of working life; and
- government legislation, for example in the areas of employment protection, and the influence of the European Union.

All of these factors have combined to create resistance against purely autocratic styles of leadership.

Exhibit 8.1

Following in your leader's footsteps

Top executives should look forward, not backwards, for inspiration writes **Richard Donkin**.

There is a fixation bordering on obsession among an increasing number of US management writers focusing on the qualities needed for corporate leadership.

The reason is that the widespread restructuring across many businesses in the west has led to a dismantling of command and control hierarchies, which have been replaced, in many cases, by semi-autonomous teams. These require different leadership qualities spread across a greater number of people at all levels of an organisation.

Arguments continue about the nature of leadership, whether it can be taught or nurtured and about what can be considered the 'right stuff'. Some consultants still draw lessons on leadership from history.

Only last month I was reading a book* that urged managers to draw inspiration from military leaders. The theory of the authors was that if it was good enough for the Marines then it was good enough for companies. It listed 14 traits and 11 principles identified by the US Marine Corps in its leadership teaching. The traits, predictably, included initiative, tact, judgment and integrity. The principles included 'knowing your Marines and looking out for their welfare' and 'keeping your personnel informed'.

There were no surprises for anyone who has read the work of John Adair, professor of leadership at Exeter University, who has comprehensively catalogued such traits in military leaders.

The problem is that military leaders do not have a good track record when transferring their skills to private enterprise, particularly modern workplaces where teams are often expected to take on increasing responsibilities.

It is encouraging, therefore, to find another author, Morgan McCall, professor of management and organisation at the University of Southern California's Marshall School of Business, arguing in his new book† that the best executives are not necessarily those who possess an identified list of traits or who have risen to the top by survival of the fittest – what he calls 'corporate Darwinism'.

The real leaders, he says, are those who learn from their experiences and who remain open to continuous learning. Learning from failures, argues Mr McCall, can prove essential for a successful career. Some executives, he writes, have been too successful for their own good. He gives several examples of top executives who lost their jobs after previously demonstrating an ability to get results.

Horst Schroeder lost his job as president of Kellogg, the breakfast cereal company, in late 1989 after just nine months. He had been a gifted and rising Kellogg executive for the previous 16 years with cross-cultural experience of running operations in Europe and in the US. But Mr Schroeder, says McCall, was an autocrat who misjudged the changing market and who could not adapt his style to endear his fellow executives. When

▶

---

the company's market share fell, there were few willing to help him.

Part of Mr Schroeder's problems, says Mr McCall, was his past success. The very qualities that contributed to his earlier success were involved in his derailment. The company and Mr Schroeder himself, he argues, should have identified the tensions at an earlier stage and resolved them. But a successful career can blind some executives to their frailties. Arrogance featured prominently in many of the high-level severances studied for the book.

How can such failures be avoided? Mr McCall belongs to a growing band of management thinkers who believe that leadership can be taught. It is notable that both his book and another forthcoming book‡ by Noel Tichy focus on the work of Roger Enrico, the chief executive of PepsiCo, the soft drinks company.

In the 18 months before Mr Enrico took up his post in early 1996, he spent several months at a house he has in the Cayman Islands. He was joined by nine executives at a time for coaching sessions during which he passed on his own experiences and discussed with them how the business could grow and how they could develop their own styles of leadership.

Part of the programme involved the executives working on projects designed to help the business grow. The result, says Mr Tichy, is that PepsiCo was left with nearly 100 better developed leaders who have not only pursued new business ideas in the company but who have also passed on what they have learnt.

Mr McCall has two caveats to such programmes. He points out that their success depends on the coaching ability of the leading executive. He also warns that senior executives should avoid using such sessions to make judgments about junior executives. These less experienced people, Mr McCall says, need to be confident to voice their anxieties without thinking they are under scrutiny.

But, as Mr Tichy's book illustrates, when a chief executive with a broad understanding of the direction the business is heading in has the ability to communi-

cate a strategy to other executives, the results can be impressive.

He cites the example of Bill Weiss, who, as chief executive of Ameritech, the US telephone company, set up an intensive leadership programme in 1991 just three years before his retirement

The scheme was designed to find future leaders and develop new strategies and values for the company. By the time Mr Weiss left, the company had been reorganised and from 1993 to 1996 it outperformed its peers, delivering a 19 per cent annual return to investors, compared with the 13.9 per cent for the Standard & Poor's Telephone Index.

There will be those who argue than not everyone in a company can be a leader but they may be missing the point. The size and scale of many multinationals today mean it is impossible to run a company alone. Today's corporate leader is more of a policymaker than a commander.

But leaders are watched closely by employees, their fellow executives and by investors. Mr Tichy says that the successful ones tend to communicate the future direction of the company using stories to outline the case for change and to explain where the company is going and how it will get there.

The debate about leadership is not going to change with the publication of this latest crop of books, but companies, particularly in western Europe where leadership programmes are thin on the ground, may take some inspiration from the way that some US company heads have sought to instill leadership into their executive teams.

*Townsend, P. L. and Gebhardt, J. E. *Five-Star Leadership: The Art and Strategy of Creating Leaders at Every Level*, John Wiley and Sons (1997).

†McCall, M. *High Flyers: Developing the Next Generation of Leaders*, Harvard Business School Press (1997).

‡Tichy, N. M. with Cohen, E. *The Leadership Engine: How Winning Companies Build Leaders at Every Level*, Harper Business (1997).

(Reproduced with permission from the Financial Times Limited, © *Financial Times* 3 September 1997.)

Continuum of leadership behaviour

One of the best known works on leadership style is that by *Tannenbaum and Schmidt* (Figure 8.4).[42] Originally written in 1958 and updated in 1973, they suggest a continuum of possible leadership behaviour available to a manager and along which various styles of leadership may be placed. The continuum presents a range of action related to the degree of authority used by the manager and to the area of freedom available to non-managers in arriving at decisions. The Tannenbaum and Schmidt continuum can be related to *McGregor's* supposition of Theory X and Theory Y. Boss-centred leadership is towards Theory X and subordinate-centred leadership is towards Theory Y.

Four main styles of leadership

Moving along the continuum, the manager may be characterised according to the degree of control that is maintained. Neither extreme of the continuum is absolute as there is always some limitation on authority and on freedom. This approach can be seen as identifying four main styles of leadership by the manager: tells, sells, consults, joins.

- **Tells.** The manager identifies a problem, chooses a decision and announces this to subordinates, expecting them to implement it without an opportunity for participation.
- **Sells.** The manager still chooses a decision but recognises the possibility of some resistance from those faced with the decision and attempts to persuade subordinates to accept it.
- **Consults.** The manager identifies the problem but does not choose a decision until the problem is presented to the group, and the manager has listened to the advice and solutions suggested by subordinates.
- **Joins.** The manager defines the problem and the limits within which the decision must be chosen and then passes to the group, with the manager as a member, the right to make decisions.

Main forces in deciding type of leadership

Tannenbaum and Schmidt suggest that there are three factors, or forces, of particular importance in deciding what types of leadership are practicable and desirable. These are: forces in the manager; forces in the subordinates; and forces in the situation.

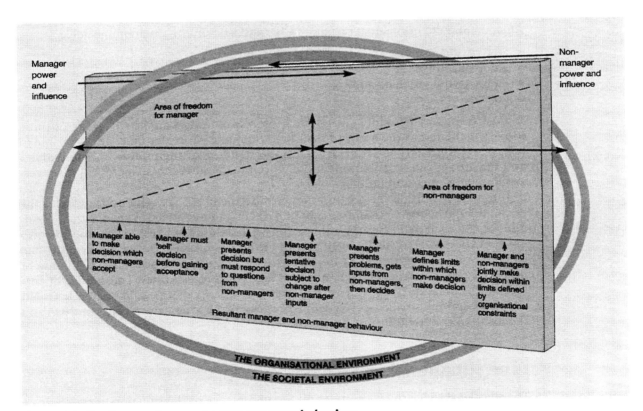

Figure 8.4 Continuum of manager- non-manager behaviour

(Reprinted by permission of the *Harvard Business Review* from 'How to Choose a Leadership Pattern' by Robert Tannenbaum and Warren H. Schmidt (May/June 1973). Copyright © 1973 by Harvard Business School Publishing Corporation.)

Understanding and Managing People at Work

1 Forces in the manager. The manager's behaviour will be influenced by their own personalities, backgrounds, knowledge and experiences. These internal forces will include:

- value systems;
- confidence in subordinates;
- leadership inclinations; and
- feelings of security in an uncertain situation.

2 Forces in the subordinate. Subordinates are influenced by many personality variables and their individual set of expectations about their relationship with the manager. Characteristics of the subordinate are:

- the strength of the needs for independence;
- the readiness to assume responsibility for decision-making;
- the degree of tolerance for ambiguity;
- interest in the problem and feelings as to its importance;
- understanding and identification with the goals of the organisation;
- necessary knowledge and experience to deal with the problem; and
- the extent of learning to expect to share in decision-making.

The greater the positive response to these characteristics, the greater freedom of action can be allowed by the manager.

3 Forces in the situation. The manager's behaviour will be influenced by the general situation and environmental pressures. Characteristics in the situation include:

- type of organisation;
- group effectiveness;
- nature of the problem; and
- pressure of time.

Tannenbaum and Schmidt conclude that successful leaders are keenly aware of those forces which are most relevant to their behaviour at a particular time. They are able to behave appropriately in terms of their understanding of themselves, the individuals and the group, the organisation, and environmental influences. Successful managers are both perceptive and flexible.

Forces lying outside the organisation are also included. Recognition is given to the possibility of the manager and/or subordinates taking initiatives to change the boundaries of the rectangle through interaction with external forces. Recognition is also given to the power available to all parties in the organisation (for example individual workers and trade unions) and to the factors which underlie decisions on the use of power by the manager. Tannenbaum and Schmidt suggest a new continuum of patterns of leadership behaviour in which the total area of freedom shared between managers and non-managers is redefined constantly by interactions between them and the forces in the environment.

The situational approach

The **situational approach** concentrates on the importance of the situation in the study of leadership. A variety of people with differing personalities and from different backgrounds have emerged as effective leaders in different situations. The person who becomes the leader of the work group is thought to be the person who knows best what to do and is seen by the group as the most suitable leader in the particular situation.

The continuum of leadership behaviour draws attention to forces in the situation as one of the main forces influencing the nature of managerial behaviour. The situational approach emphasises the situation as the dominant feature in considering the characteristics of effective leadership.

Obeying the law of the situation

It is interesting to note that the importance of the situation for managerial leadership was put forward over 50 years ago. *Mary Parker Follett* considered the way orders should be given in the manager–subordinate relationship. The problem is avoiding the two extremes of: (i) too great bossism in giving orders; and (ii) practically no orders given.

Follett's solution was what she called the 'depersonalising of orders and obeying the law of the situation'.

> *My solution is to depersonalise the giving of orders, to unite all concerned in a study of the situation, to discover the law of the situation and obey that. Until we do this I do not think we shall have the most successful business administration ... This is, ideally what should take place between any head and subordinates. One **person** should not give orders to another **person** but both should agree to take their orders from the situation. If orders are simply part of the situation, the question of someone giving and someone receiving does not come up. Both accept the orders given by the situation.*[43]

Limitations

There are, however, limitations to the situational approach. There are people who possess the appropriate knowledge and skills and appear to be the most suitable leaders in a given situation, but who do not emerge as effective leaders. Another limitation is that it does not explain fully the interpersonal behaviour or the different styles of leadership and their effect on members of the group. Finally, in the work organisation, it is not usually practicable to allow the situation continually to determine who should act as the leader.

Contingency theories of leadership

Despite the limitations of the situational approach, situational factors are important in considering the characteristics of leadership. More recent studies focus on the interactions between the variables involved in a leadership situation and patterns of leadership behaviour, and provide another general approach to the study of leadership – contingency theory. Contingency theories are based on the belief that there is no single style of leadership appropriate to all situations. Major contingency models of leadership include:

- **Favourability of leadership situation** – *Fiedler*
- **Quality and acceptance of leader's decision** – *Vroom and Yetton*, and *Vroom and Jago*
- **Path–goal theory** – *House*, and *House and Dessler*
- **Maturity of followers** – *Hersey and Blanchard*, and *Nicholls*

Fiedler's contingency model

One of the first leader–situation models was developed by *Fiedler* in his contingency theory of leadership effectiveness.[44]

Fiedler's contingency model was based on studies of a wide range of group situations, and concentrated on the relationship between leadership and organisational performance. In order to measure the attitudes of the leader, Fiedler developed a 'least preferred co-worker' (LPC) scale. This measures the rating given by leaders about the person with whom they could work least well. The questionnaire contains up to 20 items. Examples of items in the LPC scale are pleasant/unpleasant, friendly/unfriendly, helpful/frustrating, distant/close, co-operative/unco-operative, boring/interesting, self-assured/hesitant, open/guarded.

Each item is given a single ranking of between one and eight points, with eight points indicating the most favourable rating. For example:

Pleasant :   :   :   : | :   :   :   : Unpleasant
          8   7   6   5 | 4   3   2   1

The LPC score is the sum of the numerical ratings on all the items for the 'least pre-ferred co-worker'. The less critical the rating of the least preferred co-worker and the more favourably evaluated, the higher the leader's LPC score. The more critical the rating, the lower the LPC score.

The original interpretation of the LPC scale was that the leader with a high LPC score derived most satisfaction from interpersonal relationships and, when relation-ships with subordinates need to be improved, is motivated to act in a supportive, considerate manner. The leader with a low LPC score derived most satisfaction from performance of the task and achieving objectives. Establishing good relationships with subordinates is a secondary motivation. It was thought that high LPC scores would be associated with effective performance by the group. However, the interpretation of LPC has changed a number of times and there is still uncertainty about its actual meaning.

Favourability of leadership situation

Fiedler suggests that leadership behaviour is dependent upon the favourability of the leadership situation. There are three major variables which determine the favourability of the situation and which affect the leader's role and influence.

- **Leader–member relations** – the degree to which the leader is trusted and liked by group members, and their willingness to follow the leader's guidance.
- **The task structure** – the degree to which the task is clearly defined for the group and the extent to which it can be carried out by detailed instructions or standard procedures.
- **Position power** – the power of the leader by virtue of position in the organisation, and the degree to which the leader can exercise authority to influence (for example) rewards and punishments, or promotions and demotions.

From these three variables, Fiedler constructed eight combinations of group–task situations through which to relate leadership style (*see* Figure 8.5).

When the situation is

- **very favourable** (good leader–member relations, structured task, strong position power), or
- **very unfavourable** (poor leader–member relations, unstructured task, weak position power),

then a **task-oriented leader** (low LPC score) with a directive, controlling style will be more effective.

When the situation is

- **moderately favourable** and the variables are mixed,

then the leader with an interpersonal relationship orientation (high LPC score) and a **participative approach** will be more effective.

Fiedler is suggesting, therefore, that leadership style will vary as the favourability of the leadership situation varies.

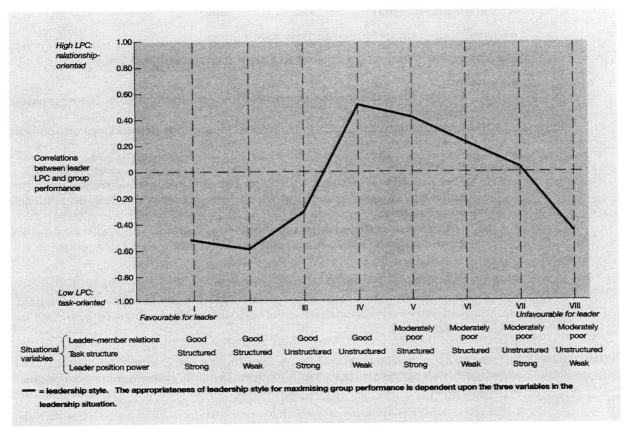

Situational variables	I	II	III	IV	V	VI	VII	VIII
Leader–member relations	Good	Good	Good	Good	Moderately poor	Moderately poor	Moderately poor	Moderately poor
Task structure	Structured	Structured	Unstructured	Unstructured	Structured	Structured	Unstructured	Unstructured
Leader position power	Strong	Weak	Strong	Weak	Strong	Weak	Strong	Weak

▬ = leadership style. The appropriateness of leadership style for maximising group performance is dependent upon the three variables in the leadership situation.

Figure 8.5 Correlations between leader's LPC scores and group effectiveness

(Adapted and reproduced with permission of the author, F. E. Fielder. *A Theory of Leadership Effectiveness*. McGraw-Hill (1967) p. 146.)

Organisational variables

Fiedler's work has been subject to much criticism[45] but it does provide a further dimension to the study of leadership. It brings into consideration the organisational variables which affect leadership effectiveness and suggests that in given situations a task-oriented, or structured, style of leadership is most appropriate. The 'best' styles of leadership will be dependent upon the variable factors in the leadership situation.

Fiedler argues that leadership effectiveness may be improved by changing the leadership situation. Position power, task structure and leader–member relations can be changed to make the situation more compatible with the characteristics of the leader. Leaders with a low LPC score could be placed in a leadership situation which is very favourable or very unfavourable. Leaders with a high LPC score could be placed in a leadership situation which is of moderate favourability.

Vroom and Yetton contingency model

Another contingency model of leadership is provided by *Vroom and Yetton*.[46] They base their analysis on two aspects of a leader's decision: its quality and its acceptance.

- **Decision quality**, or rationality, is the effect that the decision has on group performance.
- **Decision acceptance** refers to the motivation and commitment of group members in implementing the decision.

Understanding and Managing People at Work

A third consideration is

● the amount of **time required** to make the decision.

The Vroom and Yetton model suggests five main management decision styles:

● **Autocratic**
  A.I: Leader solves the problem or makes the decision alone using information available at the time.
  A.II: Leader obtains information from subordinates but then decides on solution alone.

● **Consultative**
  C.I: The problem is shared with relevant subordinates, individually. The leader then makes the decision which may or may not reflect the influence of subordinates.
  C.II: The problem is shared with subordinates as a group. The leader then makes the decision which may or may not reflect the influence of subordinates.

● **Group**
  G.II: The problem is shared with subordinates as a group. The leader acts as chairperson, rather than an advocate. Together the leader and subordinates generate and evaluate alternatives and attempt to reach group consensus on a solution.

Decision rules Vroom and Yetton suggest seven decision rules to help the manager discover the most appropriate leadership style in a given situation. The first three rules protect the **quality of decisions**.

1 Is there a quality requirement such that one solution is likely to be more rational than another?
2 Is there sufficient information to make a high-quality decision?
3 Is the problem structured?

The last four rules protect the **acceptance of decisions**.

4 Is acceptance of the decision by subordinates critical to effective implementation?
5 If you were to make the decision yourself, is it reasonably certain that it would be accepted by subordinates?
6 Do subordinates share the organisational goals to be obtained in solving the problem?
7 Is conflict among subordinates likely in preferred solutions?

These rules indicate decision styles that the manager should **avoid** in a given situation and indicate the use of others. Decision tree charts can be produced to help in the application of the rules and to relate the situation to the appropriate leadership style.

The Vroom and Jago revised decision model

In a revised version of the original model *Vroom and Jago* retain the five main decision-making styles but incorporate a larger number – 12 – of contingency variables.[47] The new model specifies that any of the five decision styles may be effective in given situations. The contingency variables relate to:

● quality requirement;
● commitment requirement;
● leader information;
● problem structure;

- commitment probability;
- goal congruence;
- subordinate conflict;
- subordinate information;
- time constraint;
- geographical dispersion;
- motivation time; and
- motivation development.

Unlike the Vroom and Yetton model which requires a definite yes/no answer, ten of these situational variables are answered on a five-point scale. For example, to the question 'How important is subordinate commitment to the decision?', the manager selects one of the following responses: no importance; low importance; average importance; high importance; critical importance.

Use of decision trees

Vroom and Jago developed four decision trees relating to a generic type of managerial problem:

- an individual-level problem with time constraints;
- an individual-level problem in which the manager wishes to develop an employee's decision-making ability;
- a group-level problem in which the manager wishes to develop employees' decision-making abilities; and
- a time-driven group problem.

The manager selects one of the trees and moves along the branches by answering the questions at each decision point. This leads to one of the five described decision-making styles.

Path–goal theory

A third contingency model of leadership is the path–goal theory, the main work on which has been undertaken by *House*,[48] and by *House and Dessler*.[49] The model is based on the belief that the individual's motivation is dependent upon expectations that increased effort to achieve an improved level of performance will be successful, and expectations that improved performance will be instrumental in obtaining positive rewards and avoiding negative outcomes. This is the 'expectancy' theory of motivation, which is discussed in Chapter 12.

Four main types of leadership behaviour

The path–goal theory of leadership suggests that the performance of subordinates is affected by the extent to which the manager satisfies their expectations. Path–goal theory holds that subordinates will see leadership behaviour as a motivating influence to the extent that it means:

- satisfaction of their needs is dependent upon effective performance; and
- the necessary direction, guidance, training and support, which would otherwise be lacking, is provided.

House identifies four main types of leadership behaviour.

- **Directive leadership** involves letting subordinates know exactly what is expected of them and giving specific directions. Subordinates are expected to follow rules and regulations. This type of behaviour is similar to 'initiating structure' in the Ohio State Leadership Studies.
- **Supportive leadership** involves a friendly and approachable manner and displaying

concern for the needs and welfare of subordinates. This type of behaviour is similar to 'consideration' in the Ohio State Leadership Studies.

- **Participative leadership** involves consulting with subordinates and the evaluation of their opinions and suggestions before the manager makes the decision.
- **Achievement-oriented leadership** involves setting challenging goals for subordinates, seeking improvement in their performance and showing confidence in subordinates' ability to perform well.

Path–goal theory suggests that the different types of behaviour can be practised by the same person at different times in varying situations. By using one of the four styles of leadership behaviour the manager attempts to influence subordinates' perceptions and motivation, and smooth the path to their goals. (*See* Figure 8.6.)

Two main situational factors

Leadership behaviour is determined by two main situational factors: the personal characteristics of subordinates; and the nature of the task.

- **The personal characteristics of subordinates** determine how they will react to the manager's behaviour and the extent to which they see such behaviour as an immediate or potential source of need satisfaction.
- **The nature of the task** relates to the extent that it is routine and structured, or non-routine and unstructured.

For example, when a task is highly structured, the goals readily apparent and subordinates are confident, then attempts to further explain the job or to give directions are likely to be viewed as unacceptable behaviour. However, when a task is highly unstructured, the nature of the goals is not clear and subordinates lack experience, then a more directive style of leadership behaviour is likely to be welcomed by subordinates.

Effective leadership behaviour is based, therefore, on both the willingness of the manager to help subordinates and the needs of subordinates for help. Leadership behaviour will be motivational to the extent that it provides necessary direction, guidance and support, helps clarify path–goal relationships and removes any obstacles which hinder attainment of goals.

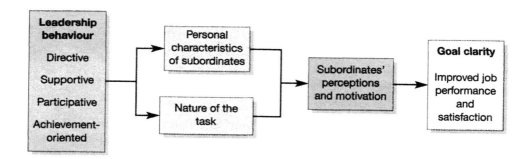

Figure 8.6 Representation of the path–goal theory of leadership

Readiness of the followers or group

A major variable in the style of leadership adopted by the manager is the nature of subordinate staff. This view is developed by *Hersey and Blanchard* who present a form of situational leadership based on the 'readiness' level of the people the leader is attempting to influence. Readiness is the extent to which followers have the ability and willingness to accomplish a specific task. It is not a personal characteristic of the individual, but how ready the individual is to perform a particular task.[50]

Readiness (R) is divided into a continuum of four levels: R1 (low), R2 and R3 (moderate), and R4 (high).

- **R1 – low follower readiness** – refers to followers who are both *unable and unwilling*, and who lack commitment and motivation; or who are *unable and insecure*.
- **R2 – low to moderate follower readiness** – refers to followers who are *unable but willing*, and who lack ability but are motivated to make an effort; or who are *unable but confident*.
- **R3 – moderate to high follower readiness** – refers to followers who are *able but unwilling*, and who have the ability to perform but are unwilling to apply their ability; or who are *able but insecure*.
- **R4 – high follower readiness** – refers to followers who are both *able and willing*, and who have the ability and commitment to perform; or who are *able and confident*.

Some people have difficulty understanding the development of followers from R1 to R2 to R3. How can one go from being insecure to confident and then become insecure again? The important thing to remember is that at the lower levels of readiness, the leader is providing the direction – the what, where, when and how. Therefore, the decisions are leader directed. At the higher levels of readiness, followers become responsible for task direction, and the decisions are follower-directed. This transition from leader-directed to self-directed may result in apprehension or insecurity. As followers move from low levels of readiness to higher levels, the combinations of task and relationship behavior appropriate to the situation begin to change.[51]

Task behaviour and relationship behaviour

For each of the four levels of maturity, the appropriate style of leadership is a combination of task behaviour and relationship behaviour.

- **Task behaviour** is the extent to which the leader provides directions for the actions of followers, sets goals for them, and defines their roles and how to undertake them.
- **Relationship behaviour** is the extent to which the leader engages in two-way communication with followers, listens to them, and provides support and encouragement.

From the combination of task behaviour and relationship behaviour derive four leadership styles (S): telling (S1), selling (S2), participating (S3) and delegating (S4). The appropriate leadership style corresponds with the readiness of the followers. (*See* Figure 8.7.)

- **S1 – telling** – emphasises high amounts of guidance (task behaviour) but limited supportive (relationship) behaviour. This style is most appropriate for *low follower readiness* (R1).
- **S2 – selling** – emphasises high amounts of both directive (task) and relationship behaviours. This style is most appropriate for *low to moderate follower readiness* (R2).
- **S3 – participating** – emphasises a high amount of two-way communication and supportive (relationship) behaviour but low amounts of guidance (task behaviour). This style is most appropriate for *moderate to high follower readiness* (R3).
- **S4 – delegating** – emphasises little direction or support with low levels of both task and relationship behaviours. This style is most appropriate for *high follower readiness* (R4).

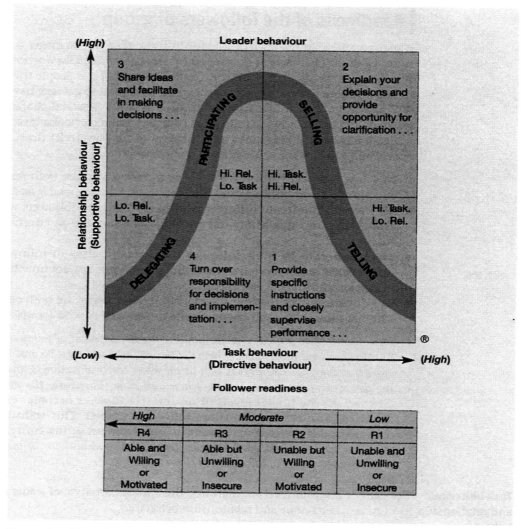

Figure 8.7 Situational leadership model

(*Source*: Hersey. P. *The Situational Leader* (1984) p. 63. Copyrighted material from Leadership Studies. Inc. Situational Leadership® is a registered trademark of the Center for Leadership Studies. Used by permission. All rights reserved.)

Development of subordinates

Hersey and Blanchard suggest that the key to using situational leadership is that any leader behaviour may be more or less effective according to the readiness of the person the leader is attempting to influence. The model draws attention to the importance of developing the ability, confidence and commitment of subordinates. The manager should help subordinates to develop in readiness to the extent that they are able and willing to go. This development should take place by adjusting leadership behaviour through the four styles of telling, selling, participating and delegating.

Transformational leadership

In recent years increasing business competitiveness and the need for the most effective use of human resources has resulted in writers on management focusing attention on how leaders revitalise or transform organisations. Based on the work of writers such as

Burns[52] this has given rise to a distinction between two fundamental forms of leadership: transactional or transformational.

- **Transactional leadership** is based on legitimate authority within the bureaucratic structure of the organisation. The emphasis is on the clarification of goals and objectives, work task and outcomes, and organisational rewards and punishments. Transactional leadership appeals to the self-interest of followers. It is based on a relationship of mutual dependence and an exchange process of: 'I will give you this, if you do that'.
- **Transformational leadership**, by contrast, is a process of engendering higher levels of motivation and commitment among followers. The emphasis is on generating a vision for the organisation and the leader's ability to appeal to higher ideals and values of followers, and creating a feeling of justice, loyalty and trust. In the organisational sense, transformational leadership is about transforming the performance or fortunes of a business.

Many writers see transformational leadership as the same thing as charismatic, visionary or inspirational leadership. For example, *Kreitner et al.* refer to charismatic leadership as transforming employees to pursue organisational goals over self-interests: 'Charismatic leaders transform followers by creating changes in their goals, values, needs, beliefs, and aspirations. They accomplish this transformation by appealing to followers' self-concepts – namely, their values and personal identity.'[53]

However, *Hunt* suggest that while charismatic leaders can have a tremendous effect on members of an organisation, there is no guarantee that this will be positive. What really matters is the nature of outputs and that the leadership mobilises power to change social systems and reform organisations.[54] Many writers believe that charisma alone is insufficient for changing the way an organisation operates.[55]

Components of transformational leadership

According to *Bass*, the transformational leader motivates followers to do more than originally expected and the extent of transformation is measured in terms of the leader's effects on followers. Applying the ideas of Burns to organisational management, Bass proposed a theory of transformational leadership which argues that the leader transforms and motivates followers by:

1 generating greater awareness of the importance of the purpose of the organisation and task outcomes;
2 inducing them to transcend their own self-interests for the sake of the organisation or team; and
3 activating their higher-level needs.[56]

Transformational leadership is comprised of four basic components:

- **idealised influence** – the charisma of the leader, and the respect and admiration of the followers;
- **inspirational motivation** – the behaviour of the leader which provides meaning and challenge to the work of the followers;
- **intellectual stimulation** – leaders who solicit new and novel approaches for the performance of work and creative problem solutions from followers; and
- **individualised consideration** – leaders who listen and give special concern to the growth and developmental needs of the followers.[57]

Yukl provides a set of guidelines for transformational leadership:

- **Articulate a clear and appealing vision** of what the organisation could accomplish or become to help guide the actions and decisions of members.

- **Explain how the vision can be attained**, and establish a clear link between the vision and a credible strategy for attaining it.
- **Act confident and optimistic**, and emphasise positive aspects of the vision rather than the obstacles and dangers.
- **Express confidence in followers** and their ability to carry out the strategy for accomplishing the vision.
- **Provide opportunities for early success** and increase the confidence of an individual or team undertaking a challenging task.
- **Celebrate successes** and maintain an awareness of continuing progress, and recognise the contribution and accomplishments of individuals.
- **Use dramatic, symbolic actions to emphasize key values** in order to reinforce the vision by actions consistent with it.
- **Lead by example** through exemplary behaviour in day-to-day interactions with subordinates: actions speak louder than words.
- **Empower people to achieve the vision** by delegating to individuals and teams authority for decisions about how to do the work.[58]

Impact on other people

Writers such as Burns and Bass identified leaders by their actions and the impact those actions have on other people. **Successful transformational leaders are usually identified in terms of providing a strong vision and sense of mission, arousing strong emotions in followers and a sense of identification with the leader.** Common examples of people referred to as transformational leaders include: Sir Winston Churchill, Sir Michael Edwardes (formerly chairman and chief executive of British Leyland); Lord Marcus Sieff (formerly chairman and chief executive of Marks & Spencer); Sir John Harvey-Jones; Anita Roddick;[59] Richard Branson; and arguably Sir Chris Bonington. Examples from America include President John F. Kennedy; Dr Martin Luther King Jr; Lee Iacocca (president of Chrysler); Mary Kay Ash (founder of Mary Kay Cosmetics (*see* Chapter 7)).[60]

'Renaissance' leaders

In his discussion of the leadership of corporate transformation, *Taffinder* refers to the importance of transformational leadership but also raises the question of whether both transactional and transformational leaders can be metamorphosed into a single 'renaissance' leader.

> *In conclusion, transformational leadership is both desirable and necessary in business today, and will increasingly become more important. Organizations must be capable of fast, radical change and those that aspire to be the best must be able to lead change rather than just follow it … Can we have Renaissance leaders? Can transactional and transformational behaviour work successfully in a single leader? Yes, without doubt and, more so, where leaders can understand the necessity and actively produce both by means of the leadership team.*[61]

Exhibit 8.2

Developing leadership in the NHS of the 21st century

The National Health Service is currently facing the challenges of the most significant change since its inception.

It was built on traditional models of leadership and beliefs that 'managers' should manage, and doctors and nurses should provide clinical care. The NHS has survived numerous structural changes in the last fifty years but none have fundamentally challenged that philosophy. Clinical leaders were encouraged to take senior roles in the leadership of their specialist clinical areas (the Director of Nursing, etc.), but the function of managing the 'business' (financial resources, human resources, strategic planning, etc.) was always perceived as being safe in the hands of the professional 'general manager'. Occurrences of clinicians moving into senior general management positions were rare and usually involved them in divesting themselves of their clinical roles.

In the 21st century it is now recognised that the NHS needs fundamental modernisation in the way it develops strategic plans, determines priorities, allocates and manages resources and manages performance and quality improvement.

The media have drawn the public's attention to quality failures, clinical negligence, and inequity in resource allocation and recruitment and retention difficulties. The Government's modernisation agenda challenges the NHS to:

- improve collaborative, integrated working across all agencies and professions in the system;
- move from a system focused around the clinical 'expert' to a consumer-centred service;
- introduce a learning culture both within professional groupings and organisations; a major shift away from the prevalent 'blame' culture;
- implement innovative approaches to the delivery of health and care.

Above all, this requires a new model of management and leadership in the NHS. The NHS needs to develop leaders who have credibility with clinicians and can inspire and motivate, an often-demoralised workforce, to own and drive continual change. The simplistic model of the past – managers plan and allocate the resource while clinicians control and spend the resource is no longer tenable.

The NHS needs to develop outward facing managers and clinicians who can lead system-wide change across the NHS.

Writers in the field of leadership have refocused. The early writers often interpreted leadership as an authority relationship, referred to as management. This is now referred to as Transactional leadership. The new model leadership is that of the Transformational leader; a process of influencing followers or staff for whom one is responsible, by inspiring them towards the 'vision' of some future state.

The ideas of the Transactional and Transformational leader are pertinent to the development of leaders in the new NHS. Many NHS organisations have encouraged and rewarded Transactional managers. These leadership qualities may have been appropriate in the NHS of the last century when managers were leading complex organisations in a more predictable and static environment. What is needed now? A group of leaders for tomorrow's NHS who share a set of common values and act as a leadership community, who can lead confidently in clinical areas, who understand how to run a patient-centred service; who deliver continuous performance improvement and who reflect the diversity of the communities they serve.* Above all what is needed are leaders who can provide strategic direction to and inspire a complex workforce in an environment that is turbulent, ever changing and difficult to predict (Transformational leaders).

To achieve the leadership community that will take the NHS successfully into the 21st century will require an integrated approach that is adequately resourced to:

- Provide education and development for the leaders of tomorrow,
- Achieve a shift in culture to develop learning organisations,
- Break down the barriers that exist between management and clinical leadership model,
- Restructure NHS organisations to place decision-making closer to patients and clinicians.

The NHS is undergoing a fundamental rethink of its traditional leadership and management models. It needs to move from a position that believes 'managers' should lead and manage, to one where 'leaders' (whether clinicians or managers) provide strategic vision and leadership, and managers support them in the implementation and operationalisation of strategic vision and plans.

* Internal Paper from Hugh Taylor, Director of Human Resources, NHS Executive, (2000)

(I am grateful to Anne Tofts, Director, *Healthskills*, for providing the above information.)

| No one best form of leadership

We have seen that there are many alternative forms of managerial leadership. It is usually claimed that a human relations, people-oriented approach is more likely to lead to job satisfaction and work performance. However, it is not always the case that democratic styles are best. There are occasions when an autocratic style of leadership is more effective. For example, we have seen from the studies by *Fiedler* that when the situation is very favourable or very unfavourable in terms of leader–member relations, task structure and position power, then a task-oriented style of leadership is most effective. Some subordinates appear to prefer a more directive, task-oriented approach and respond better to more autocratic styles of leadership. (Recall also the discussion on managerial behaviour in Chapter 7.)

Contingency models demonstrate that there are many forms of leadership. Within an organisation different individuals may fulfil the functions of leadership and there are many different styles of leadership. A potential danger with the contingency approach is that the manager may appear to lack consistency in leadership style. However, although subordinates may reasonably expect some degree of consistency from the manager in approaching the same type of problem with the same style, this is not to say that different types of problems should be approached in the same manner. Subordinates would ordinarily expect a different style of managerial leadership according to the contingencies of the situation.

Different styles at different stages of a business

Different types of leadership may also be most appropriate at different stages in the development of a business organisation. For example, *Clarke and Pratt* identify four different styles of managerial leadership required at different stages of business: champion, tank commander, housekeeper and lemon-squeezer.[62]

- **Champion.** As a new corporate venture develops into a business it needs a champion to fight for and defend the seedling business. The champion must be able to drive a small team to win orders, provide a wide range of management skills, and have the dash and energy to deal with a range of different matters.
- **Tank commander.** As the business enters its growth stage the manager must develop a strong, supportive team and have leadership qualities to be able to drive into readily exploitable parts of the market.
- **Housekeeper.** As the business runs up against boundaries erected by other growing businesses it enters the mature stage. The housekeeper has to ensure the efficient and economic management of the business. This involves skills in planning, cost control and the development of soundly based personnel policies.
- **Lemon-squeezer.** Although the mature stage might last for many years, sometimes a business goes into premature decline. At this stage the need is for the kind of leader who can extract the maximum benefit from the situation. The lemon-squeezer needs to be both tough and innovative in order, for example, to cut costs, and improve productivity and staffing levels.

Finding and fitting the manager best suited to each stage of a business is a delicate task. Clarke and Pratt suggest that most managers are one type of leader or another. Although there are exceptions, few managers are flexible enough to switch between such different leadership roles.

The right leader for the right situation

The suggestion that different types of leaders are needed at different stages of the development of a company is supported by *Rodrigues*. Organisations functioning within a dynamic environment experience three stages of change: a problem-solving stage, an implementation-of-solution stage, and a stable stage. At each of these three organisational stages a leader with different traits, abilities, and behaviour is most effective.[63]

Rodrigues suggests that organisations which exist in a dynamic environment therefore generally require three types of leaders: the innovator(s); the implementor(s); and the pacifier(s).

- **The innovator** is characterised by the need for competition, the struggle to succeed, the search for new ideas, boldness, and the belief that the environment can be controlled and manipulated. An innovator style of leadership is likely to be more effective at the problem-solving stage when an organisation needs renewing or at least some new ideas. Such a leader is best equipped to identify and 'sell' new ideas.
- **The implementor** is characterised by the need to control and influence situations, the ability to accomplish things through people, a systematic approach, and the ability to assume responsibility for decision-making. Once the innovator has sold the new ideas to the organisation, then an implementor style of leadership is likely to be most effective at the implementation stage.

- **The pacifier** is characterised by the need for a friendly atmosphere and social inter-action, the capacity to decentralise decision-making and to pacify important individuals, and the desire to base decisions on feedback from earlier decisions. When the implementor has systematically brought the organisation to the stable stage, then a pacifier style of leadership is likely to be most effective. At this stage members usually feel more competent to perform the task in hand and will accept less direction from a leader.

Effectiveness of leadership styles

Research undertaken by the consulting firm Hay/McBer, as reported by Goleman, has studied which precise leadership behaviours yield positive results. The research drew on a sample of 3871 executives worldwide and identified six, well-known different styles of leadership, each springing from different components of emotional intelligence:

- Coercive leaders – who demand immediate compliance;
- Authoritative leaders – who mobile people towards a vision;
- Affiliative leaders – who create emotional bonds and harmony;
- Democratic leaders – who build consensus through participation;
- Pacesetting leaders – who expect excellence and self-direction;
- Coaching leaders – who develop people for the future.

However, only four of these leadership styles had a positive effect. The coercive style demanded immediate compliance, lacked flexibility and motivation, and was the least effective style. The pacesetting style sets high standards of performance but leads to a drop in morale and had a largely negative impact.

Reliance on more than one style

Goleman reports that the most effective executives use a collection of distinct leader-ship styles, each in the right measure, at just the right time. Although the authoritative style of leadership can be occasionally overbearing it was found to be most effective and can motivate and inspire commitment to the goals of the organisation. The affili-ative style has potential to create harmony within teams and can be used in conjunction with the authoritative style. The democratic approach was seen as posi-tive, and encourages input from staff and helps build consensus through participation. The coaching style, although the least frequently used, can help staff identify their strengths and encourage long-term development goals. The study concludes that the most effective leaders rely on more than one leadership style, and were able to master a mixture of authoritative, democratic, affiliative and coaching styles. Leaders with the best results use most of the styles in a given week – seamlessly and in different measure – depending on the business situation.[64]

Leadership and organisational culture

Leadership is not only an essential part of the process of management, it is also an integral part of the social structure and culture of the organisation. If the manager is to be successful in dealing with people and influencing their behaviour and action this requires a leadership style which helps to foster a supportive organisational culture.

Brown, for example, believes that:

Effective leadership and workable organization design and development programmes must be based on sensitivity to, and understanding of, culture. Excellent leaders are not merely aware of their organization's basic assumptions, they also know how to take action to mould and refine them.[65]

National cultural dimensions of leadership

Another major variable influencing choice of leadership style may be national culture. For example, McGregor concluded that the social, economic and political environment affected the leadership relationship, together with the attitudes and needs of 'followers'.[66] *Tannenbaum and Schmidt* identify leaders' own value systems as factors which influence their chosen style. They also highlight subordinates' – or non-managers' – needs for independence and tolerance of ambiguity as relevant variables in the choice of style.[67] These factors vary according to the cultural context in which the leadership relationship takes place.

Stereotyping the behaviour of leaders

One should be wary of stereotyping the behaviour of leaders or subordinates, and many myths appear to have grown around notions of 'orderly' German, 'undisciplined' Italian and even 'obstructive' British workers. However, there are reasons to suggest that there may indeed be national cultural differences which are relevant to an understanding of leadership. The work of *Hofstede* has already been referred to in Chapter 2. One dimension for classifying societies, power distance, is said to influence the extent to which subordinates accept inequality, which in turn may influence the extent to which leaders wield power.[68]

Thus one might expect a more autocratic style of leadership to be characteristic of organisations in countries as diverse as France, Spain, Hong Kong and Iran which all display a high level of power distance. In contrast, countries identified as low power distance societies included Britain, Italy, the Netherlands, the Scandinavian countries and the USA. Given the inclusion of the last country within this group, it is perhaps not surprising that so many American writers advocate adopting participative styles of leadership.

Constraints of legislation

It should also be noted that, whatever their preferred style of leadership, managers operating in particular countries will be constrained by the relevant legislative measures of those societies. Within the European Union, all member countries have been bound by the provisions of the Social Charter of 1989 and the Social Charter of the 1991 Maastricht Treaty. These agreements both refer to 'workers' rights to information, consultation and participation'. It is likely, therefore, that British managers have had a significantly greater prerogative when managing people in the workplace.

In contrast, for most of the post-war period, German managers have had to work within the framework of a statutory policy of joint consultation with both works councils and worker representatives on boards of directors. *Lawrence*, for example, has described how West German personnel managers have been required to work together with employee representatives on matters relating to the recruitment, training and remuneration of staff.[69] Given this background, it is not surprising that *Hofstede* suggested that German organisations would be characterised by low power distance.

Variables affecting leadership effectiveness

Clearly, there is no one 'best' form of leadership which will result in the maintenance of morale among group members and high work performance. Three main aspects to be considered in determining the most appropriate style of leadership are: the manager, the group and the work environment.

However, there are many variables which underlie the effectiveness of leadership in work organisations. More specifically, these include the following:

- the characteristics of the manager, personality, attitudes, abilities, value system; and the personal credibility of the manager;
- the type of power of the manager and the basis of the leadership relation;
- the characteristics of the subordinates; their needs and expectations; attitudes; knowledge, confidence and experience; and their motivation and commitment;
- the relationship between the manager and the group, and among members of the group;
- the type and nature of the organisation, and different stages in the development of the organisation;
- the nature of the tasks to be achieved, the extent to which structured or routine;
- the technology, systems of communication and methods of work organisation;
- organisation structure and systems of management;
- the type of problem and the nature of the manager's decisions;
- the nature and influence of the external environment;
- the social structure and culture of the organisation;
- the influence of national culture.

Education and training in management needs to emphasise not only interpersonal skills, but also a flexibility of approach, diagnostic ability and the realisation that the most effective form of leadership behaviour is a product of the total leadership situation.

Morris, Potter and Hooper suggest that despite all the research into leadership:

something appears to be missing. Successful leaders seem to be outnumbered by unsuccessful ones.

Leadership is not a magical quality possessed by a few but is required at all levels within organisations. They see leadership selection and development as a key priority for any business. Vision, mission, beliefs and values are prerequisites for any successful initiative. These are long-term issues and so too should be leadership development:

it is lifelong and never ending, just like continuous performance improvement.[70]

Lack of confidence in abilities leaders

According to research carried out by Development Dimensions International (DDI) on the state of leadership and leadership development, the majority of staff do not have confidence in the abilities of their leaders to guide and direct the organisation in the future. Results of the research were based on contact with 52 companies, and 2360 sets of data returned from managers, non-managers and HR professionals. Of the three groups less than half (36–47 per cent) have high confidence in their leaders' ability. The DDI survey found that leaders at all levels need to develop core leadership skills: adaptability; building a successful team; communication; decision making; and building positive working relationships.

The survey also found that today's leaders are not prepared strongly for future leadership positions. It will be important to develop skills in empowering leadership, innovation, communication, visionary leadership, aligning performance for success, and strategic decision-making. The survey draws attention to the emerging global leader, and that in the future more and more leaders will need to transcend cultures and geographic boundaries. The leadership shortage is real. Organisations need to develop their leaders, or those leaders will go elsewhere. Organisations must be more serious about succession planning and developing future leaders from today's workforce.[71]

Leadership and Tomorrow's Company

In 1995 the RSA (Royal Society for the encouragement of Arts, Manufactures and Commerce) published the findings of its inquiry by a group of British business leaders into 'Tomorrow's Company – The Role of Business in a Changing World'. The inquiry, chaired by Sir Anthony Cleaver, was triggered by an urgent need to improve the sustainable competitive performance of UK companies.[72] Its conclusion was that there was no simple technical formula for success. Instead, what each company needed was an inclusive approach based on clear leadership and continuous improving relationships with customers, employees, suppliers, investors and the wider community. The Centre for Tomorrow's Company is a business-led, not-for-profit organisation, established in 1996 to inspire and enable companies to implement that agenda.

The inclusive approach to leadership

A BBC series introducing business leaders to the inclusive approach offers the following comment concerning leadership in tomorrow's company.

Every company is different. Each makes its own journey. The inclusive approach is a framework that helps with five essential steps which the company revisits from time to time as it progresses down its path of growing to become a tomorrow's company.

1 Define purpose and values
2 Review key relationships
3 Define success
4 Measure and communicate performance
5 Reward and reinforce

The inclusive approach demands clear leadership. Leadership is the crucial ingredient through which people in all the company's relationships are inspired. It takes leadership to set a direction for the company. It takes leadership to stimulate the whole organisation to understand what success looks like and how it will be achieved and measured. Leaders set the tone, by their deeds as much as by their words. They ensure that the organisation behaves in line with its purpose and values.[73]

A further discussion on Tomorrow's Company, the Excellence Model and leadership is given in Chapter 23.

Sypnosis

■ There are many ways of looking at leadership, and many interpretations of its meaning, but essentially it is a relationship through which one person influences the behaviour or actions of other people. The leader–follower relationship is reciprocal and effective leadership is a two-way process. Leadership is related to motivation, the process of communication, the activities of groups and the process of delegation. The changing nature of business organisations has placed increasing importance on leadership.

■ There is a close relationship between leadership and management, especially in work organisations. However, arguably there are differences between the two, and it does not follow that every leader is a manager. Leadership may be viewed in more general terms with emphasis on interpersonal behaviour in a broader context. Leadership is a dynamic form of behaviour and there are many variables which affect the nature of the leadership relationship.

■ Within an organisation, leadership influence will be dependent upon the type of power which the leader can exercise over other people. Leadership may be examined in terms of the qualities or traits approach; in terms of the functional or group approach; as a behavioural category; in terms of styles of leadership; through the situational approach and contingency models; and the distinction between transactional or transformational leadership.

■ Leadership style is the way in which the functions of leadership are carried out. There is a wide range of possible leadership behaviour available to the manager. Two major dimensions of leadership are consideration, concerned with relationships with the group; and structure, concerned with efforts to achieve organisational goals. Leadership style can be measured along a continuum between boss-centred (authoritarian) at one extreme and subordinate-centred (democratic) at the other extreme.

■ Contingency theories draw attention to the interactions between the variables involved in a leadership situation and patterns of leadership behaviour. The most appropriate form of leadership is dependent upon the variables in a particular leadership situation. Different contingency theories have concentrated on different situational variables. These include: favourability of the leadership situation; decision acceptance and decision quality; path–goal theory; and the 'readiness' of followers. Transformational leadership places emphasis on generating a vision for the organisation, and the leader's ability to appeal to higher ideals and values of followers.

■ It is usually claimed that democratic styles of leadership are more likely to produce effective group performance. However, there is no one 'best' style of leadership. Different types of leadership may also be needed at different stages of a business. Effective leaders use a collection of distinct styles, in the right measure, at the right time. National culture may also influence choice of leadership style. There are many variables which underlie the effectiveness of leadership in work organisations. The most effective form of leadership behaviour is a product of the total leadership situation. Leadership development should be a long-term issue for any business organisation.

CRITICAL REFLECTIONS

Despite the vast amount of writing on the subject by both academics and practising managers, it is extremely difficult to give a precise and agreed definition of leadership. Nor is there agreement on one best model or style of leadership. If leading writers cannot agree on the nature or essential characteristics of leadership, how can we ever be certain about what makes an effective leader?

What are your own views?

Confidence in identifying leadership competencies is more important than formal studies about past successes. Any discussion about competencies can easily become controversial. Many contend that the identification of competencies helps organizations to understand those qualities, characteristics, and skills that lead to outstanding performance and outcomes. Others question whether competencies can be defined at all.

Fulmer, R. M. and Goldsmith, M. 'Future Leadership Development', in Chowdhury, S. *Management 21C*, Financial Times Prentice Hall (2000), p. 176.

How would you define and identify leadership competencies?

'Organisational success depends ultimately on the qualities of its leaders. But leaders are born to be so: it is not possible to train a person to become an effective leader.'

Debate.

REVIEW AND DISCUSSION QUESTIONS

1 Explain clearly what you understand by the meaning of leadership. How would you distinguish leadership from management?

2 Discuss the main sources of power and leadership influence. Give a practical example of each of these main sources of power and influence within your own organisation.

3 Distinguish between different approaches to the study of leadership and discuss critically what you see as the relevance today of each of these approaches.

4 Explain what is meant by leadership style. What are the major dimensions of leadership behaviour? Suggest why greater attention has been given to more participative styles of leadership.

5 Assume you are a departmental manager in an organisation. Using the Tannenbaum and Schmidt continuum identify, with reasons, your preferred style of leadership. Give an example of a situation in which you might need to adopt an alternative style of leadership.

6 What do you understand by leader–situation models of leadership? Assess the practical value to the manager of: (i) Fiedler's contingency model of leadership effectiveness; and (ii) Hersey and Blanchard's model of situational leadership.

7 Discuss the main situational variables which are likely to influence the most appropriate form of managerial leadership behaviour. Detail three different work situations in which a different style of leadership is likely to be most effective.

8 Explain clearly the nature and main features of transformational leadership. Give your own examples, with supporting reasons, of people you would regard as transformational leaders.

9 If you were a consultant on leadership, what areas of needs would you include in designing a leadership training programme for managers in a large work organisation? Justify your ideas.

Assignment 1

LEAST PREFERRED CO-WORKER (LPC) SCALE

a Think of the person with whom you can work least well. This person may be someone you work with now or someone you knew in the past. The person does not have to be someone you like least.

b Describe this person as he or she appears to you by completing the scale below. Place an 'X' in one of the eight spaces according to how well the adjective fits the person. Look at the words at both ends of the line before placing your 'X'.

c There are no right or wrong answers. Work rapidly; your first answer is likely to be the best. Do not omit any items and mark each item only once.

d After you have completed the scale compare your responses with those of your colleagues.

Pleasant	:_:_:_:_:	:_:_:_:_:	Unpleasant
	8 7 6 5	4 3 2 1	
Friendly	:_:_:_:_:	:_:_:_:_:	Unfriendly
	8 7 6 5	4 3 2 1	
Rejecting	:_:_:_:_:	:_:_:_:_:	Accepting
	1 2 3 4	5 6 7 8	

Helpful	:_:_:_: 8 7 6 5	:_:_:_: 4 3 2 1	Frustrating
Unenthusiastic	:_:_:_: 1 2 3 4	:_:_:_: 5 6 7 8	Enthusiastic
Tense	:_:_:_: 1 2 3 4	:_:_:_: 5 6 7 8	Relaxed
Distant	:_:_:_: 1 2 3 4	:_:_:_: 5 6 7 8	Close
Cold	:_:_:_: 1 2 3 4	:_:_:_: 5 6 7 8	Warm
Co-operative	:_:_:_: 8 7 6 5	:_:_:_: 4 3 2 1	Unco-operative
Supportive	:_:_:_: 8 7 6 5	:_:_:_: 4 3 2 1	Hostile
Boring	:_:_:_: 1 2 3 4	:_:_:_: 5 6 7 8	Interesting
Quarrelsome	:_:_:_: 1 2 3 4	:_:_:_: 5 6 7 8	Harmonious
Self-assured	:_:_:_: 8 7 6 5	:_:_:_: 4 3 2 1	Hesitant
Efficient	:_:_:_: 8 7 6 5	:_:_:_: 4 3 2 1	Inefficient
Gloomy	:_:_:_: 1 2 3 4	:_:_:_: 5 6 7 8	Cheerful
Open	:_:_:_: 8 7 6 5	:_:_:_: 4 3 2 1	Guarded

Assignment 2

T-P LEADERSHIP QUESTIONNAIRE: AN ASSESSMENT OF STYLE

The questionnaire below describes aspects of leadership behaviour. Respond to each item according to the way you would most likely act if you were leader of a work group. Circle whether you would most likely behave in the described way always (A), frequently (F), occasionally (O), seldom (S), or never (N).

1 I would most likely act as the spokesperson of the group. **A F O S N**
2 I would encourage overtime work. **A F O S N**
3 I would allow members complete freedom in their work. **A F O S N**
4 I would encourage the use of uniform procedures. **A F O S N**
5 I would permit the members to use their own judgement in solving problems. **A F O S N**
6 I would stress being ahead of competing groups. **A F O S N**
7 I would speak as a representative of the group. **A F O S N**
8 I would needle members for greater effort. **A F O S N**
9 I would try out my ideas in the group. **A F O S N**
10 I would let the members do their work the way they think best. **A F O S N**
11 I would be working hard for a promotion. **A F O S N**
12 I would tolerate postponement and uncertainty. **A F O S N**
13 I would speak for the group if there were visitors present. **A F O S N**
14 I would keep the work moving at a rapid pace. **A F O S N**
15 I would turn the members loose on a job and let them go to it. **A F O S N**
16 I would settle conflicts when they occur in the group. **A F O S N**
17 I would get swamped by details. **A F O S N**
18 I would represent the group at outside meetings. **A F O S N**

19	I would be reluctant to allow the members any freedom of action.	A F O S N
20	I would decide what should be done and how it should be done.	A F O S N
21	I would push for increased production.	A F O S N
22	I would let some members have authority which I could keep.	A F O S N
23	Things would usually turn out as I had predicted.	A F O S N
24	I would allow the group a high degree of initiative.	A F O S N
25	I would assign group members to particular tasks.	A F O S N
26	I would be willing to make changes.	A F O S N
27	I would ask the members to work harder.	A F O S N
28	I would trust the group members to exercise good judgement.	A F O S N
29	I would schedule the work to be done.	A F O S N
30	I would refuse to explain my actions.	A F O S N
31	I would persuade others that my ideas are to their advantage.	A F O S N
32	I would permit the group to set its own pace.	A F O S N
33	I would urge the group to beat its previous record.	A F O S N
34	I would act without consulting the group.	A F O S N
35	I would ask that group members follow standard rules and regulations.	A F O S N

T _____   P _____

Scoring

a Circle the item number for items 8, 12, 17, 18, 19, 30, 34 and 35.

b Write the number 1 in front of a *circled item number* if you responded S (seldom) or N (never) to that item.

c Write a number 1 in front of *item numbers not circled* if you responded A (always) or F (frequently).

d Circle the number 1s which you have written in front of the following items: 3, 5, 8, 10, 15, 18, 19, 22, 24, 26, 28, 30, 32, 34 and 35.

e *Count the circled number 1s*. This is your score for concern for people. Record the score in the blank following the letter P at the end of the questionnaire.

f *Count the uncircled number 1s*. This is your score for concern for task. Record this number in the blank following the letter T.

After you have recorded your total scores compare your responses with those of your colleagues.

Assignment 3

a Think of:
  (i) one of the 'best' leaders, *and*
  (ii) one of the 'worst' leaders

  that you have experienced, *preferably in a work situation*.

b Identify and list those specific qualities, or lack of them, which were characteristic of *each* leader. Where possible, draw up your list under three broad headings of:
  (i) personal attributes – for example, intelligence, appearance;
  (ii) social relationships – for example, approachability, interests;
  (iii) task performance – for example, delegation, discipline.

c Give a brief description of an actual situation which illustrates the behaviour/actions of *each* leader, and the results of such behaviour/action. Keep your answer balanced. Bear in mind that even the 'best' leader is likely to have some weak points; and even the 'worst' leader some good points. Try to be as objective as possible and avoid personal bias.

d Draw up your *own* list, with brief supporting descriptions, of the main characteristics you would expect to be exhibited by a 'good' leader. Be prepared to justify your lists and descriptions in class discussion. See how your answers relate to your responses to Assignment 1 and Assignment 2 of this chapter.

Assignment 4

YOUR LEADERSHIP STYLE

a For each of the following 10 pairs of statements, divide five points between the two according to your beliefs, perceptions of yourself, or according to which of the two statements characterises you better. The five points may be divided between the A and B statements in any way you wish with the constraint that only whole positive integers may be used (i.e., you may not split 2.5 points equally between the two). Weigh your choices between the two according to the one that better characterises you or your beliefs.

1 A As leader I have a primary mission of maintaining stability. _____
  B As leader I have a primary mission of change. _____

2 A As leader I must cause events. _____
  B As leader I must facilitate events. _____ .

3 A I am concerned that my followers are rewarded equitably for their work. _____
  B I am concerned about what my followers want in life. _____

4 A My preference is to think long range: What might be. _____
  B My preference is to think short range: What is realistic. _____

5 A As a leader I spend considerable energy in managing separate but related goals. _____
  B As a leader I spend considerable energy in arousing hopes, expectations, and aspiration among my followers. _____

6 A While not in a formal classroom sense, I believe that a significant part of my leadership is that of a teacher. _____
  B I believe that a significant part of my leadership is that of a facilitator. _____

7 A As leader I must engage with followers at an equal level of morality. _____
  B As leader I must represent a higher morality. _____

8 A I enjoy stimulating followers to want to do more. _____
  B I enjoy rewarding followers for a job well done. _____

9 A Leadership should be practical. _____
  B Leadership should be inspirational. _____

10 A What power I have to influence others comes primarily from my ability to get people to identify with me and my ideas. _____
   B What power I have to influence others comes primarily from my status and position. _____

b Details of scoring and interpretation will be provided by your tutor.

Visit our website www.booksites.net/mullins for further questions, annotated weblinks, case material and internet research material.

Understanding and Managing People at Work

CASE STUDY 8.1

International practice: British Petroleum

Peter Phillips

British Petroleum (BP) is recreating itself as a radically different organisation. In 1990 the company began a fundamental change of its culture, strategy and organisation to position itself to face future challenges. As a result, the BP group now has three operating businesses and a small corporate centre (less than 200 staff). Decision making is pushed down to the lowest appropriate level. In general the company focuses on its core activities with the non-core being outsourced or bought in. There is a move towards sharing services between businesses and between regions.

For employees the changes have obviously been dramatic, BP was traditionally a cradle-to-grave organisation. Downsizing and delayering, together with the constant process of change, have had a major impact on morale. Individuals have had to learn to adjust to new ways of working and develop new understandings of career and development. In effect there is a new employment partnership between BP and its employees.

Even though BP has emerged in good financial shape, more change is seen as inevitable and the pressure to reach new and higher levels of performance is intense.

Clearly the impact on leaders in the company has been dramatic. They are pivotal in the change process but have been no less affected by the changes in BP than other staff. In addition their roles have fundamentally changed. Prior to 1990 BP managers' roles were relatively clearly defined. There were rules and procedures covering most things, a vast guide to personnel policies, and a plethora of committees. Authorities were clearly delineated and controlled.

In an organisation where all recruits were highly qualified, managers were selected on technical or professional excellence. Managers tended to solve the difficult problems and direct, check and control the work of their staff. Information was shared with those who needed to know and no further. Upward management – managing your boss – was a key skill, admitting weakness was frowned upon, the size of your empire was an indication of success, other groups were a source of competition.

These side effects of its long-established approach were offset by the fact that the company took care of its staff. There was a sense of being in an entitle-ment culture providing careers and jobs for life. With the onset of the major organisational and structural changes, the role of the company's managers became radically different. In the new cost-conscious organisation the competitive advantage was to come through the people. The leaders had to recognise and learn new skills to operate in the new world and build empowered teams to deliver the new agenda. A new set of 'OPEN' (Open Thinking, Personal Impact, Empowerment and Networking) behaviours was identified as essential for all employees in the new culture.

During 1990 and 1991, although the company as a whole arranged programmes to start and energise the change process, each leader had to help his or her team come to terms with and operate effectively in the new culture.

The primary focus at this stage in the organisation was on achieving the radical new culture. The company's performance began to deteriorate – due principally to the decline in oil price, economic recession and a high level of debt. Financial results were poor and major changes were made (including the then chairman resigning). These changes inevitably were focused on restoring the financial fortunes of the company. Costs needed to be cut, staff numbers were reduced in line with new priorities; a performance culture had to be quickly established to drive forward a leaner organisation.

The impact on morale was serious as the company's declining fortunes were debated in the media. Leaders faced the challenge of achieving tough performance targets while rebuilding morale in an atmosphere of downsizing, outsourcing and cost cutting. In the performance culture the principles of the original culture change had been reaffirmed, but how the two cultures would gel had not entirely been explained. This tension needed to be managed by the company and its leaders.

The new balance of leadership

Leaders in the new organisation must balance a number of tensions – such as between people and performance; the short and long term; sustaining current performance and growing for the future. While cost-cutting skills are important, leaders need also to be able to spot and take new business opportunities. While keeping their eyes on the performance indicators, leaders have to encourage creativity, risk taking and challenge; skills for the future must be developed while delivering this year's targets. Performance has to be maintained and morale rebuilt and new understandings of the employment relationship established – living under the constant threat of more change.

To be successful, BP has to be globally effective: its leaders have to be able to operate effectively in different cultures, to manage and relish cultural diversity. They have to be able to obtain both the benefits of localisation and those from being part of a major corporation. They need to be able to work effectively in non-BP or part-BP cultures, such as alliance and joint ventures.

Leaders have to be flexible and adaptable to translate group strategy into different local environments, build the relationships, sell the message and build and sustain performance. Strong technical and professional skills are no longer sufficient. The ability to understand and influence people inside and outside the company is critical. In such an environment, an ability to develop and maintain strong personal networks becomes essential and in international assignments tends to require longer assignments than has traditionally been the case.

On international assignments there is comparatively little support and relatively few dictates from the business centres. The leaders have considerable independence within light frameworks to deliver the performance target, but have to be aware that they, in their local environment, represent BP. Often the senior leaders in countries are representing more than one business – yet, frequently while carrying this more general responsibility they are directly accountable for one particular business. This requires a knowledge and understanding of the strategy and goals of each business and a range of contacts not easily developed when development tends to be in one of the major businesses rather than through a more general approach.

For the most senior leaders of the group their role has also changed, though clearly the need to set the strategic direction and vision for the business is still key. They need to be able to inspire others and model the desired culture. The ability to lead change becomes critical, and organisational development skills – the ability to create the organisation to deliver the agenda – are essential. They have to become coaches to their own staff to provide the appropriate level of support and challenge both to sustain current performance and to grow for the future. They have to ensure that the whole organisation is motivated and focused to reach its goals.

How leaders develop

Now, there is a premium on effective and relevant leadership development to help those who need to do so to learn new skills and prepare for the future. In the old organisation there was a miasma of development committees, a paternalistic approach to staff development and expectation of progress. The principal tool of development was job movement, usually anticipated every one to two years.

BP has long had a fast-track scheme regarded by many as a model to benchmark against. The process identified high-fliers early in their careers – often in their late twenties – and ensured focused development through key assignments towards senior positions. This process was essential, partly to ensure a pool of high calibre successors for the group, also to ensure that, given the hierarchical structure of the group, people progressed fast enough. It also reflected the norm of promoting from within and reinforced the group culture.

The changes in the group since 1990 have dramatically altered this approach to development. The flatter, smaller organisation clearly had a major impact on opportunities, and business demands now call for longer periods in jobs. Responsibility for development shifted primarily to the individual, albeit in a partnership with the line manager. Personal development plans prepared by the individual and supported by the line are a key part of the performance culture.

A major contribution to the development of senior leaders in BP has been the Leadership Competency Model. This model which describes the key leadership behaviours required by tomorrow's leaders now underpins all group leadership activities. These competencies were developed with and owned by the businesses. The model provides the linking thread in BP's leadership development framework, which openly lays out the process for developing leaders at all levels. Rather than seeking to identify high-fliers early and predict and accelerate their development to their ultimate potential, the framework breaks the leadership pool into broad bands and outlines the key development processes and experiences in each pool. Attention is focused on development within the band and acquiring the qualities required for the next level – it is accepted that individuals will move through the band at their own pace, some of course will not move into the

Understanding and Managing People at Work

next. It is generally accepted that for most individuals development will occur primarily within one business. Movement into the group sphere (or fast-track scheme) occurs when individuals have established their technical base, demonstrated strong leadership and commercial skills and have a track record of delivering performance.

Development processes have been opened up to enable individuals to form a clear development plan (and career plan). The ground rules of the general employment relationship and personal development are being clarified so that both sides understand the requirements and expectations.

The competency model is being used to profile the strengths and weaknesses of the senior leaders of the group through 360 degree feedback and assessment processes. These enable the individual and line manager with other appraisal processes, to focus on the short and long-term development needs which are critical for both personal and organisational growth.

The model also informs and interacts with the succession planning process by making individual and job matching a more objective process. It also enables the company to focus on key roles such as associate presidents (the lead individuals in each country) and to identify particular skill requirements, develop succession plans and specific training programmes, etc.

Within the leadership development framework the group attempts to align all development processes so that they are part of the same jigsaw and closely associated with company performance. Given that individuals expect to spend longer in jobs, development now has to involve a much broader range of processes. Individuals have to find ways, with line support, to grow in their existing jobs and although training (internally or externally) has a role to play, other activities such as projects, short-term job swaps, external activities, coaching and computer-based and distance learning need also to be considered.

Within the parameters of the leadership development framework and the competency model, individuality, flexibility and scope for mavericks must be retained. The purpose of the development is to identify and develop the leaders who will deliver superior performance today and in the future. The aim is to let talent develop and flourish, not to clone leaders or apply a cultural straitjacket. The models must work globally and apply to all leaders irrespective of nationality, sex, etc. The organisation needs to constantly review its models and processes in the light of strategic performance and environmental changes. This is vital for organisational renewal.

It is also accepted that competencies in themselves are not the complete picture. There are other factors involved. Personal attributes, such as moral integrity, sense of mission and will to win, are vital to really outstanding leadership. These must be monitored and developed in leaders. Accepting that these individual characteristics are important, it is essential that all managers demonstrate enthusiasm, commitment and curiosity.

Monitoring, measurement and reward are key parts of the process. They are essential to ensuring that the individual and the organisation are developing in tandem. The vital role of the leader in shaping performance and coaching becomes fundamental to the organisation's success.

The leader's role has changed and become more complex and, arguably, even more critical to the organisation's success. They must:

- ensure that high performance levels are achieved and sustained;
- handle complexity and ambiguity; enjoy leading the change process;
- ensure that the organisation, and its processes, are constantly developed to deliver the strategy and performance;
- ensure that the people within the company are motivated, developed and rewarded to produce outstanding results.

These are highly demanding tasks and skills. Developing leaders with the capacity to learn, adapt, coach, support and inspire others is a critical challenge for major companies. Meeting the challenge requires commitment, investment and creativity.

Peter Phillips is manager of Leadership Programmes at BP.

Understanding and Managing People at Work

Notes and references

1 Taffinder, P. *The New Leaders: Achieving Corporate Transformation Through Dynamic Leadership*, Kogan Page (1995).

2 Handy, C. B. *Understanding Organizations*, Fourth edition, Penguin (1993), p. 97.

3 Crainer, S. 'Have the Corporate Superheroes had their Day?', *Professional Manager*, March 1995, pp. 8–12.

4 Parker, P. 'The Shape of Leaders to Come', *Management Today*, July 1994, p. 5.

5 Levine, S. R. 'The Value-Based Edu-Leader', in Chowdhury, S. *Management 21C*, Financial Times Prentice Hall (2000), p. 90.

6 See, for example: Tack, A. *Motivational Leadership*, Gower (1984).

7 Crow, S. M. and Hartman, S. J. 'Can't Get No Satisfaction', *Leadership & Organization Development Journal*, vol. 16, no. 4, 1995, pp. 34–8.

8 Sieff, M. (Lord Sieff of Brimpton), *Management the Marks & Spencer Way*, Fontana Collins (1991), p. 133.

9 Tustin, T. 'Follow My Leader', *Management Today*, December 1989, p. 5.

10 See, for example: Gretton, I. 'Taking the Lead in Leadership', *Professional Manager*, January 1995, pp. 20–2.

11 Hooper, A. and Potter, J. 'Take it from the TOP', *People Management*, 19 August 1999, p. 46.

12 Vecchio, R. P. *Organizational Behavior: Core Concepts*, Fourth edition, Dryden Press (2000), p. 149.

13 Belbin, R. M. *Changing the Way We Work*, Butterworth-Heinemann (1997), p. 98.

14 Zaleznik, A. 'Managers and Leaders: Are They Different?' *Harvard Business Review*, May–June 1977, pp. 67–78.

15 Watson, C. M. 'Leadership, Management and the Seven Keys', *Business Horizons*, March–April 1983, pp. 8–13.

16 Hollingsworth, M. J. (Squadron Leader), 'Purpose and values', *The British Journal of Administrative Management*, January/February 1999, pp. 22–3. See also, Bennis, W. G. *On Becoming a Leader*, Addison Wesley (1989).

17 Robinson, G. 'Leadership vs Management', *The British Journal of Administrative Management*, January/February 1999, pp. 20–1.

18 See, for example: Levine, S. and Crom, M. *The Leader in You*, Simon and Schuster (1994).

19 Taffinder, P. *The New Leaders: Achieving Corporate Transformation Through Dynamic Leadership*, Kogan Page (1995), p. 37.

20 Miller, D. S., Catt, S. E. and Carlson, J. R. *Fundamentals of Management: A Framework for Excellence*, West Publishing (1996), p. 249.

21 See, for example: Sims, D., Fineman, S. and Gabriel, Y. *Organizing and Organisations*, Sage Publications (1993).

22 Peters, T. J. 'Symbols, Patterns and Settings: An Optimistic Case For Getting Things Done', *Organizational Dynamics*, Autumn 1978, pp. 3–23.

23 Brown, A. D. *Organisational Culture*, Second edition, Financial Times Pitman Publishing (1998).

24 See, for example: Bass, B. M. *Leadership, Psychology and Organizational Behaviour*, Harper & Row (1960).

25 Adair, J. *Effective Teambuilding*, Gower (1986), p. 123.

26 McGregor, D. *The Human Side of Enterprise*, Penguin (1987), p. 182.

27 Kouzes, J. M. and Posner, B. Z. 'The Janusian Leader', in Chowdhury, S. *Management 21C*, Financial Times Prentice Hall (2000), p. 18.

28 French, J. R. P. and Raven, B. 'The Bases of Social Power', in Cartwright, D. and Zander, A. F. (eds) *Group Dynamics: Research and Theory*, Third edition, Harper and Row (1968).

29 Roddick, A. *Body and Soul*, Ebury Press (1991), p. 214.

30 Yukl, G. *Leadership in Organizations*, Fourth Edition, Prentice-Hall International (1998).

31 Drucker, P. F. *The Practice of Management*, Heinemann Professional (1989), p. 156.

32 Sees for example Ghiselli, E. E. 'Management Talent', *American Psychologist*, vol. 18, October 1963, pp. 631–42.

33 Hamilton, K. 'The Women Who Move Britain', *Management Today*, March 1999, pp. 39–44.

34 Kotter, J. P. 'What Leaders Really Do', *Harvard Business Review*, May–June 1990, p. 103.

35 Sewell-Rutter, C. 'So You Want to Be a Leader?', The *British Journal of Administrative Management*, September/October 1999, pp. 8–9.

36 Conger, J. 'Charisma and How to Grow It', *Management Today*, December 1999, pp. 78–81

37 Adair, J. *Action-Centred Leadership*, Gower (1979). See also: Adair, J. *The Skills of Leadership*, Gower (1984).

38 Adair, J. *Effective Leadership*, Pan Books (1983).

39 Fleishman, E. A. 'Leadership Climate, Human Relations Training and Supervisory Behavior', in Fleishman, E. A. and Bass, A. R. *Studies in Personnel and Industrial Psychology*, Third edition, Dorsey (1974).

40 Likert, R. *New Patterns of Management*, McGraw-Hill (1961).

41 Belbin, R. M. *Team Roles at Work*, Butterworth-Heinemann (1993).

42 Tannenbaum, R. and Schmidt, W. H. 'How to Choose a Leadership Pattern', *Harvard Business Review*, May–June 1973, pp. 162–75, 178–80.

43 Follett, M. P. 'The Giving of Orders', in Metcalf, H. C. and Urwick, L. (eds) *Dynamic Administration*, Harper (1941). Reprinted in Pugh, D. S. (ed.) *Organization Theory*, Penguin (1971), pp. 154–5.

44 Fiedler, F. E. A *Theory of Leadership Effectiveness*, McGraw-Hill (1967).

45 See, for example: Filley, A. C., House, R. J. and Kerr, S. *Managerial Process and Organizational Behavior*, Second edition, Scott, Foresman (1976). They refer to the uncertainty of the interpretation of LPC and what aspects of leadership behaviour it actually represents.

46 Vroom, V. H. and Yetton, P. W. *Leadership and Decision-Making*, University of Pittsburgh Press (1973).

47 Vroom, V. H. and Jago, A. G. *The New Leadership: Managing Participation in Organizations*, Prentice-Hall (1988).

48 House, R. J. 'A Path–Goal Theory of Leadership Effectiveness', *Administrative Science Quarterly*, vol. 16, September 1971, pp. 321–38.

49 House, R. J. and Dessler, G. 'The Path–Goal Theory of Leadership', in Hunt, J. G. and Larson, L. L. (eds) *Contingency Approaches to Leadership*, Southern Illinois University Press (1974).

50 Hersey, P. and Blanchard, K. H. *Management of Organizational Behavior: Utilizing Human Resources*, Sixth edition, Prentice-Hall (1993).

51 *Ibid.*, p. 192.

52 Burns, J. M. *Leadership*, Harper & Row (1978).

53 Kreitner, R., Kinicki, A. and Buelens, M. *Organizational Behaviour*, First European edition, McGraw-Hill (1999), p. 487.

54 Hunt, J. W. *Managing People at Work*, Third edition, McGraw-Hill (1992), p. 255.

55 See, for example: Greenberg, J. and Baron, R. A. *Behavior in Organizations*, Seventh edition, Prentice-Hall (2000).

56 Bass, B. M. *Leadership and Performance Beyond Expectations*, Free Press (1985).

57 Bass, B. M. and Avolio, B. J. *Improving Organizational Performance Through Transformational Leadership*, Sage Publications (1994).

58 Yukl, G. *Leadership in Organizations*, Fourth edition, Prentice-Hall International (1998).

59 See, for example: Simms, J. 'Beauty Queen', *Marketing Business*, March 1997, pp. 48–51.

60 See, for example: Greenberg, J. and Baron, R. A. *Behavior in Organizations*, Seventh edition, Prentice-Hall (2000).

61 Taffinder, P. *The New Leaders: Achieving Corporate Transformation Through Dynamic Leadership*, Kogan Page (1995), p. 138.

62 Clarke, C. and Pratt, S. 'Leadership's Four-Part Progress', *Management Today*, March 1985, pp. 84–6.

63 Rodrigues, C. A. 'Identifying the Right Leader for the Right Situation', *Personnel*, September 1988, pp. 43–6.

64 Goleman, D. 'Leadership That Gets Results', *Harvard Business Review*, vol. 78, no. 2, March–April 2000, pp. 78–90.

65 Brown, A. 'Organisational Culture: The Key to Effective Leadership and Organizational Development', *Leadership and Organization Development Journal*, vol. 13, no. 2, 1992, pp. 3–6.

66 McGregor, D, *The Human Side of Enterprise*, Penguin (1987).

67 Tannenbaum, R. and Schmidt, W. H. 'How to Choose a Leadership Pattern', *Harvard Business Review*, May–June 1973, pp. 162–75, 178–80.

68 Hofstede, G. *Culture's Consequences: International Differences in Work-Related Values*, Sage (1981).

69 Lawrence, P. 'The Personnel Function: An Anglo-German Comparison', in Brewster, C. and Tyson, S. (eds) *International Comparisons in Human Resource Management*, Pitman (1991).

70 Morris, J., Potter, J. and Hooper, A. 'Effective Leaders at a Premium', *Professional Manager*, March 1995, pp. 26–8.

71 Bernthal, P. R., Rioux, S. M. and Wellins, R. 'The Leadership Forecast: A Benchmarking Study', *Executive Summary*, Development Dimensions International, 1999.

72 RSA, *Tomorrow's Company – The Role of Business in a Changing World* (1995), RSA.

73 BBC, *Building Tomorrow's Company, Leadership – Supporting Notes*, BBC for Business; and The Centre for Tomorrow's Company and William Tate, 1999.

CHAPTER 2

The changing world of work and the changing role of the HR professional

INTRODUCTION

The importance of the context of people resourcing has been emphasised in Chapter 1, and it is useful now to consider more broadly current changes in so far as they affect organisations, management activity and HR practitioners. The aim is to highlight some of the features of these changes whilst, in the spirit of contextuality and the exercising of informed managerial or practitioner choice, leaving it to the reader to assess the extent of the changes and the impact on their role within the current or future organisational context. This approach also seeks to recognise that whilst we are bombarded with stories of organisational turbulence and change, the state of play may be subject to exaggeration. We may live in a dynamic organisational world, but there are degrees of stability too and we need to recognise that change is evolutionary as well as revolutionary.

Changes in the world of work have implications for HR practitioners and the role and competencies expected of them in organisations, and in particular the expectation that they should demonstrably add value. Add to this the potential of e-enabled HR and it is evident that HR professionals, and line managers with responsibility for people, are experiencing change. Whether HR practitioners are entering a new era or merely contending with traditional professional adaptation is worthy of some debate. Traditionalists will underplay the rate of change and the impact on the HR profession, and conversely the plethora of excitable commentators will trespass into exaggeration – the thinking practitioner or manager will make their own informed judgements.

CHAPTER OBJECTIVES

- To highlight trends in the changing world of work.
- To provide additional contextualisation for people resourcing activities.
- To explore how these changes may be impacting on the role of HR practitioners.
- To consider the advent of e-HR and the potential this has for the restructuring of HR activities.

34

THE DRIVERS FOR CHANGE IN THE WORLD OF WORK

It would appear that the competitive environment is a major driver of change in the world of work:

> The pressures on organisations to add value, achieve sustained competitive advantage, and respond and adapt quickly and flexibly to new challenges and opportunities are relentless. The responses to these pressures have taken many forms, including new types of organisation, lean, delayered, flexible, process- or project-based, increasing reliance on information technology, and an emphasis on continuous improvement in terms of performance, quality and customer service. The quality of the human or intellectual capital possessed by organisations is seen generally as the key factor in differentiating them from their rivals and achieving superior results. The focus is on the development of business strategies to achieve longer-term goals, and the part played by human resource strategies in general, and reward strategies in particular, in supporting their achievement is now well recognised.
>
> (Armstrong and Brown, 2001)

Clearly some organisations can survive 'quite nicely thank you' on fairly traditional hierarchical structures to deliver standardised ranges of products and service, but increasingly customer orientation, product differentiation and service support require new forms of organisation. This is requiring no more than 'horses for courses' but it does draw attention to the fact that there is no guarantee that today's organisations will exist indefinitely in their present form, or indeed exist at all. Therefore there is a case for organisational strategists to recognise drivers for change and for managers to diagnose and be able to act upon the implications of these drivers, because organisational survival may depend on it. This impacts on approaches to managing people and the demands made on people managers, whether they are line managers or HR professionals. Armstrong (2000) contends that it is the context within which people are managed that is changing and HR managers have had to reposition themselves 'in the ever-changing environment of global competition, new technology, and new methods of working and organising work'. Armstrong identifies the private sector mantras as sustainable competitive advantage, added value, core competencies and strategic capability, whilst in the public sector the driving force is 'best value'.

Organisational transience, employability and the transactional psychological contract

Organisational fluidity and transience, the 'here today gone tomorrow' perspective, has impacted on feelings of job security. Whilst it may be statistically possible to prove that in many cases jobs are more secure than they have ever been, the expression of organisational and environmental uncertainty, together with the managerially projected imperative of adaptation and change, has impacted upon employee perceptions of job permanence. It has also impacted upon the mutuality of obligation between employer and employee with regard to traditional career patterns. The end of the job for life may have been subject to hyperbole, but career patterns are different and twenty-first century workers may need to engage in continuous development in order to maintain employability. This promotes a loyalty to self rather than intensifying loyalty to the organisation. Worker loyalty may have to be bought by the employer through the currency of self-development

35

opportunities. Promoting self-development is not just about offering training courses but encompasses lateral career moves, development appraisal and employer responsiveness to worker employability needs. These ideas have links to the concept of the 'war for talent' where employers compete with each other to recruit and retain valuable employees. This competition involves offering not only appropriate financial rewards but also non-financial rewards. Armstrong and Brown (2001) contend that managers should not underestimate the significance of pay as a means of attracting, retaining and providing tangible rewards to people, because it is essential to get this right since much damage can be done if it is wrong. But as a means of generating long-term commitment and motivation they argue that pay has to be regarded as only part of a whole and that it is the non-financial rewards that will ultimately make the difference. For Armstrong and Brown non-financial rewards include 'recognition, scope to achieve and exercise responsibility, opportunities for growth and development, the intrinsic motivation provided by the work itself and the quality of working life provided by the organisation'.

This refocusing of the employer–employee relationship can create the transactional psychological whereby both parties sustain the employment relationship all the time there is 'something in it for them'.

Customer aspirations and power

Although phrases like 'the customer is king' and 'delighting our customers' can be accused of being trite, there is little doubt that, amongst other things, organisations have had to become more customer-focused in order to survive and prosper in competitive environments. Excellence in customer service has always been a differentiating factor, but perhaps what is different now is that customers have had their expectations fuelled and are encouraged to feel empowered to demand quality products and good service. Customers are also more inclined to exercise their power through either the withdrawal of custom or the pursuit of compensation or restitution. Philpott (2001) sums up this customer power: 'intense competition in global and domestic markets forces businesses to keep labour costs in check and/or raise their game in terms of product quality, because empowered consumers want ever-better goods at ever-lower prices.'

This rise in customer aspirations is not only a private sector phenomenon, because citizen consumers of public services have also been encouraged, principally through public policy, to perceive themselves as fully fledged customers. It is not for this section to debate the legitimacy of the customer-driven organisation, nor to say how it should be achieved, but merely to draw attention to an issue which has implications for the world of work. Customer aspirations and power are influencing the way organisations are structured and managed and have significant implications for workers who have to contend with the increased emphasis on satisfying customer needs through being more responsive and more flexible and providing emotional labour.

The war for talent and the new paternalism

Shortage labour markets confer power to workers, as sellers of their labour, and enable a greater degree of choice to be exercised over whom to work for and on what terms.

36

This is one element of the war for talent – employers having to compete with each other to secure their human resource needs. The war for talent goes beyond this, as the name suggests, and it is argued that in order to survive in competitive product and service markets employers need to attract and retain the most talented workers. It is through securing the expertise, creativity and innovation of talented people that the organisation will prosper. In service-based and knowledge economies employees are not only the major operating cost but also the source of competitive advantage. Studies by Goleman in the USA, reported by Brown (2001), found that in low-skill work the highest performing workers contributed twice to three times as much as average workers, whilst in professional jobs top performers were capable of adding ten times as much value as their co-workers. Kets de Vries, in summing up the competition for talent (Williams, 2000), creates an interesting metaphor: 'Today's high performers are like frogs in a wheelbarrow, they can jump out at any time'. The implication is that organisations need to prevent talented employees from escaping. To extend the metaphor, this does not mean putting a lid on the wheelbarrow, it means making the wheelbarrow a sufficiently attractive place to stay. This attractiveness cannot be defined in any generic way because this rather depends on what the frogs want. Williams argues that the answer resides in talent management processes which go beyond ensuring that financial rewards are market competitive and encompasses the whole range of non-financial and environmental rewards. The work environment, depending on the type of work, might include opportunities to exercise discretion, to engage in innovative work, to have opportunities for self-development, to work with interesting people and to be able to share in success in the broadest sense. These features would be in addition to what might be considered more traditional non-financial rewards such as recognition, responsibility and being treated with respect. The role of managers in talent management is to exercise empowering leadership and deploy competencies related to coaching, mentoring and feedback.

In the war for talent the aim of the organisation is to become the employer of choice and seek to project the employer brand to the labour market. Some employers seem to be going to extraordinary lengths to retain people and this can be termed the 'new paternalism'. Examples of this include schemes for accumulating supermarket-style reward points, leisure zones at the office, 'duvet days' and concierge services. Concierge services might involve collecting dry cleaning, renewing road tax and buying birthday cards and presents (Cooper, 2000b). Chaudhuri (2000) quotes a new economy organisation as saying:

> If you want to keep staff then you have to look after them. That is why we try and create a campus atmosphere at our office. We have top quality gourmet food available and in the evenings we run cookery classes. You also get Waitrose Direct, a grocery shopping service – who wants to waste their spare time by pushing a supermarket trolley? Every morning workers are offered free fruit with breakfast.

The new paternalism and the war for talent may be fought principally in the dot.com or new economy sectors, despite the recent travails of those sectors. However, the underlying principle is that in today's world of work employers need to offer an attractive financial and non-financial rewards package, which incorporates personal choice and flexibility, if they are to compete effectively in the labour market and secure and retain the services of good people.

37

Understanding and Managing People at Work
331

We have endeavoured to draw attention, no more than that, to a number of contextual features in the changing world of work and by way of summary these are listed, with others, in Exhibit 2.1. These have been given limited treatment in this chapter principally because further changes in the world of work might render them obsolete. It is up to the informed practitioner or manager to keep up to date and be able to analyse changes in the world of work and anticipate the implications for organisations, for managers and for workers.

Exhibit 2.1   Changes in the world of work

- Job insecurity perceptions and organisational transience
- New career patterns, concern with employability and the transactional psychological contract
- New HR techniques of commitment and involvement
- The war for talent, employer branding and the new paternalism
- Globalisation and internationalisation of goods, service, finance, information and workers
- The 'new public services', best value and the Third Way
- Continuing demographic and labour market change
- Customer aspirations and power
- ICT exploitation and diffusion, including e-commerce
- Continuing corporate restructuring, take-overs and mergers

THE CHANGING ROLE OF THE HR PROFESSIONAL

In examining the changing role of the HR professional it is useful to explore the notion of 'the business partner' together with the competencies required, the pursuit of an added value contribution and the impact of e-HR which, when combined with other influences in the world of work, can result in a reconfiguration of the HR function, and may extend to the outsourcing of HR activities.

The rise of the business partner role

Armstrong (2000) is helpful in articulating the notion of the business partner:

Another concept often associated with HRM is that of the HR director as a business partner or manager. This idea is generally attributed to Ulrich (1998) but was advanced many years before by Tyson who suggested that: 'Personnel specialists as business managers integrate their activities with top management and ensure that they serve a long term strategic purpose and have the capacity to see the broad picture and to see how their role can help to achieve the company's business objectives'. In 1993 the HR director of Motorola stated that, 'I have agreed with my teams that we will be business partners in each business; we will have the understanding of what is going on to converse knowledgeably with any of the business people'.

38

Armstrong is making the point that the notion of being a business partner is not brand new, but it does appear to be receiving greater attention. In essence the philosophy of the business partner role concerns being a business manager first and a functional HR specialist second. From this perspective there is no intrinsic value in HR activities *per se*; it is in supporting business objectives that the HR specialist establishes a *raison d'être*. Clearly a prerequisite of the business partner role is to ensure that HR policies and processes are characterised by effective administration, fairness and equity, compliance with the law and effective practice, all of which requires high levels of professional competence; but, in order to add real value, it is argued, the HR business partner is expected to appreciate and understand corporate strategy, identify with the objectives of their managerial colleagues and contribute to the optimisation of people performance, and thereby organisational performance. Business results are therefore the dominant concern of the HR business partner. Within its Professional Standards the CIPD has articulated an aspirational vision of the ten competencies required of the effective HR business partner at the start of the twenty-first century. These are as follows.

Personal drive and effectiveness – The existence of a positive, 'can-do' mentality, anxious to find ways round obstacles and willing to exploit all of the available resources in order to accomplish objectives.

People management and leadership – The motivation of others, whether subordinates, colleagues, seniors or project team members, towards the achievement of shared goals, not only through the application of formal authority but also by personal role-modelling, a collaborative approach, the establishment of professional credibility and the creation of reciprocal trust.

Business understanding – Adoption of a corporate, not merely functional, perspective, including awareness of financial issues and accountabilities of business processes and operations, of 'customer' priorities, and of the necessity for cost/benefit calculations when contemplating continuous improvement or transformational change.

Professional and ethical behaviour – Possession of the professional skills and technical capabilities, specialist subject, especially legal knowledge, and the integrity in decision-making and operational activity that are required for effective achievement in the personnel and development arena.

Added-value result achievement – A desire not to concentrate solely on tasks, but rather to select meaningful accountabilities – to achieve goals which deliver added-value outcomes for the organisation, but simultaneously to comply with relevant legal and ethical obligations.

Continuing learning – Commitment to continuing improvement and change by the application of self-managed learning techniques, supplemented where appropriate by deliberate, planned exposure to external learning sources.

Analytical, intuitive and creative thinking – Application of a systematic approach to situational analysis, development of convincing, business-focused action plans, and the

39

Understanding and Managing People at Work
333

deployment of intuitive and creative thinking in order to generate innovative solutions and proactively seize opportunities.

Customer focus – Concern for the perceptions of personnel and development's customers, including the central directorate of the organisation; a willingness to solicit and act upon customer feedback as one of the foundations for performance improvement.

Strategic thinking – The capacity to create an achievable vision for the future, to foresee longer-term developments, to envisage options and their probable consequences, to select sound courses of action, to rise above the day-to-day detail, to challenge the status quo.

Communication, persuasion and interpersonal skills – The ability to transmit information to others, especially in written report form, both persuasively and cogently, display of listening, comprehension and understanding skills, plus sensitivity to the emotional, attitudinal and political aspects of corporate life.

The extent to which all of these competencies can be developed through professional education is debatable. Professional education can provide a base on which competencies can be exhibited and developed in the real world. This is, of course, no different from other professions. Hall and Torrington (1998) refer to 'the need to develop consultancy and coaching skills, political, networking and business skills, and marketing skills. We argue that these skills are most appropriately developed within the job rather than by a professional qualification, which may form the foundation for them.'

Within the business partner model, line managers and senior managers become the internal customers of the HR practitioner and the HR function, and managerial needs therefore take precedence over the needs of other stakeholders. The business partner role for HR practitioners therefore requires the adoption of a managerial ideology and the HR practitioner firmly plants his or her feet in the managerial camp, and consequently needs to demonstrate added value to the business. This tends to intensify some of the ambiguities of the HR role, because being a business partner is potentially in conflict with ideas associated with being an employee champion (as often perceived by employees) and is not entirely compatible with notions of professional status since the HR business partner's allegiance is primarily to the employing organisation rather than to the profession. The business partner role may enable the HR practitioner to jettison some of the functional activities, such as recruitment, training and discipline, through devolving them to line managers. This may create space to be a key player in performance management, quality and continuous improvement, reward strategy, organisational development and driving change, and in pursuing a place on the Board. The business partner role is frequently projected as best practice, whilst many would argue that it is best fit that counts (see also Chapter 3 for 'best practice' and 'best fit' human resource strategies). The business partner role may therefore be appropriate for the HR function within some organisations but not in others, but there is little doubt that it is becoming more pervasive. Extracts from recent job advertisements illustrate this (emphasis added):

40

HR Manager – You will work in **partnership with the business managers** to develop and implement a proactive HR function. This is a highly challenging role which will test your ability to deliver best in class HR solutions that **add value** to a demanding and **quality focused** business.

Human Resources Associate – Reporting to the HR Group Leader and **working closely with line management**, you will provide **value added support to the business.**

Human Resources Manager – You will ensure that HRM initiatives **complement the company's strategies and business plans.**

Adding value through HR practices

HR practitioners may have always known intuitively that well-managed people will work better and thereby influence the financial performance of the organisations in which they are employed, but HR practitioners are under increasing pressure to demonstrate that they add value and contribute to the bottom line. Nirvana for the HR profession must therefore be evidence of a demonstrable and causal link between people management and organisational performance. The search for proof is being pursued with energy and vigour. There is a distinction between people management by line managers and functional activity by HR specialists; as Guest and King (2001) put it, 'good people management was as much about the way front line supervisors, team leaders and middle managers engaged with their staff as it was about implementing particular HR practices'. Clearly the right balance of HR activity between the line and a specialist HR function is an additional dimension in the added-value debate, but whilst acknowledging this let us examine some of the research so far.

The CIPD, through their President Don Beattie, is convinced of a positive link: 'The business case for good people management is now proven. We have developed evidence that there is a strong correlation between people management practices and business performance' (CIPD Annual Report, 2001). Guest and Baron (2000) reported mounting evidence that it was beneficial to organisations to pursue progressive people management practices. These 18 key progressive practices are exposed in Exhibit 2.2.

The main findings from the Guest and Baron (2000) research were:

- Chief executives are waking up to the importance of good people management and most acknowledge that there is a link between HR practices and business performance. But, despite asserting that people are their greatest asset, most businesses still fail to prioritise employee issues. Only 10 per cent of chief executives agree that people are a top priority ahead of finance or marketing.

- Most businesses fail to make full use of modern HR practices. From a list of 18 key progressive HR practices, only 1 per cent of firms use more than three-quarters, 25 per cent use more than half and 20 per cent use fewer than a quarter.

- Chief executives and personnel managers both give a low rating to the performance of the HR department and the effectiveness of HR practices in their company. The areas whose performance is most highly rated are practices relating to the labour market

41

Exhibit 2.2   Key progressive people management practices

1   Realistic job previews
2   Use of psychometric tests for selection
3   Well-developed induction training
4   Provision of extensive training for experienced employees
5   Regular appraisals
6   Regular feedback on performance from many sources
7   Individual performance-related pay
8   Profit-related bonuses
9   Flexible job descriptions
10 Multi-skilling
11 Presence of work-improvement teams
12 Presence of problem-solving groups
13 Information provided on firm's business plan
14 Information provided on the firm's performance targets
15 No compulsory redundancies
16 Avoidance of voluntary redundancies
17 Commitment to single status
18 Harmonised holiday entitlement.

and employment security, with job design and financial flexibility seen as only slightly effective.

- HR managers in firms using the most key HR practices have the most positive perceptions of employee attitudes and behaviour, which are linked to higher productivity and improved financial results.

- The researchers conclude that those who embrace progressive HR practices with enthusiasm can gain a competitive advantage.

It would appear that, whilst the research is quite compelling, business leaders still remain to be convinced. The second stage of the research seeks to articulate statistical correlations between people management practices and business performance measures, and the third stage must be to examine practical applications in the workplace. Purcell *et al.* (2000) are also assertive about the link: 'The existence of a link between the way people are managed and business performance is now well established.' Guest and King (2001) agree: 'There is a link between all types of financially successful UK firms and the presence of an HR function.' Having said that, Guest and King go on to say that despite this finding, chief executives perceive line managers as the key to effective people management. This casts HR practitioners firmly in the role of supporting the line.

What do we make of this research so far? First, that the profession is even more convinced that effective HR practices and a professional HR function add value and

42

Understanding and Managing People at Work

contribute to bottom-line performance. Second, others, including senior managers, are still to be convinced. Third, we are some way from articulating the bundle of HR practices that will lift corporate performance – but the search goes on enthusiastically and there are opportunities for HR professionals to seize opportunities.

e-HR, e-enabled HR and self-service HR

e-HR is difficult to define because of a multiplicity of models depending on organisational circumstances. Clearly, for small to medium-sized businesses the potential of e-HR is constrained, whereas in multi-site, multi-national organisations (the ones we tend to hear about in relation to e-HR) the potential for exploitation of the technology is much greater. Basically e-HR is about using e-mail, the World Wide Web, the Internet and organisational intranets to facilitate and mediate HR activities, as well as providing a new learning and development medium. e-HR tends to be linked to a restructuring of HR activities and in this case it may be better to use the term e-enabled HR. e-enabled HR incorporates e-HR, self-service HR and the potential separation of HR activity into three tiers or levels.

Basic level e-enabled HR – This might incorporate the intranet provision of, first, live information on training courses, vacancies, employee benefits entitlement and the staff handbook; second, the publication of HR policies and procedures such as discipline, grievance and health and safety; and third, interactive facilities such as changes in employee details, management reporting and requests for information on staff turnover or pay rates. This self-service activity is termed disintermediation, whereby there is no personal intermediary between the information and its recipient. The benefits being sought are quick and easy access to information and a reduction in the resources required to provide it. Employers would be seeking productivity gains, reduction in HR costs in the provision of HR services, and a freeing-up of HR capacity to focus more on advisory and strategic roles. These basic-level HR transactions could alternatively be provided through a call centre supported with intranet provision.

Intermediate level e-enabled HR – With routine HR transactions, estimated by some commentators as 60 to 80 per cent of the HR load, handled in real time by e-HR, the more important HR activities are escalated to the intermediate level. This may comprise business unit level HR practitioners in the field or in a shared services centre. These HR staff are subject experts able to provide advisory and consultancy services to line managers in specialist areas such as employment law, compensation and benefits, and performance management.

Top level e-enabled HR – This level will consist of strategic business partners working with line managers to provide business solutions through people.

There are clearly similarities between these three levels and Tyson and Fell's clerk of works, estates manager and architects (*see* Chapter 1), in this case facilitated by the technology. There are implications for line managers, who by definition will have to

43

accept even more responsibility for managing their people. Goodge (2001) identifies this as a huge shift of responsibility from the HR department to line managers with 'the intelligent IT systems underpinning e-HR removing routine transactional processes from the HR function by providing line managers with the information, advice and help they once received from personnel'. There are also implications for the employees, who to a greater extent are disintermediated from HR professionals. Whilst e-HR facilitates the redefinition of HR roles and capacity, there are links also with the added-value, business orientation and strategic aspirations for the HR function introduced earlier in this chapter. Key findings from *IRS Employment Trends 721* (2001) included the following.

- The electronic revolution is well under way in the HR world, although not quite to the extent that its proponents believe.

- The systems that organisations have put in place – both internally developed and externally sourced – are generally effective in meeting their objectives, with a multitude of benefits reported.

- The majority of practitioners believe that e-HR will enable the profession to develop more of a strategic role within organisations, by reducing administrative work and improving the quality of information available to the function; and all the indications are that the use of e-HR systems will continue to grow.

- This potential for the redesign of HR services does also lend itself to the outsourcing of HR activity.

Outsourcing of HR activities

Outsourcing as a term means no more than resourcing an HR activity outside the organisation. There has always been outsourcing, prime examples being the use of recruitment agencies and training consultants. The reasons for outsourcing are generally related to cost efficiency or to the buying-in of expertise not available within the organisation. The current emphasis on the strategic role of the HR function provides another driver, and that is to outsource a range of HR activities in order to liberate the HR function to operate as a strategic business partner unencumbered with routine HR work. Whilst there are several high profile cases of this strategic rationale, such as BP Amoco, Unisys and Bank of America, other research suggests that the outsourcing of HR activities is more *ad hoc* and reactive (Pickard, 2000a, b, c). This is borne out by outsourcing trends in Europe: 'Organisations across Europe made extensive use of external providers, particularly for training and development and recruitment and selection. . . . In all countries it tended to be used opportunistically rather than as the result of deliberate strategy' (Pickard, 2000c). Hall and Torrington (1998) report that training, management development and recruitment are most likely to be outsourced, followed by outplacement, health and safety, quality initiatives and job evaluation. In this study there was less incidence of the outsourcing of reward, performance management and redundancy (*see* Assignment 7 at the end of this chapter).

44

Within the changing world of work and the hunger for economic efficiency the outsourcing of activities to bring corporate advantage has become a normal managerial pursuit. Organisations outsource cleaning, catering, security, IT support, accounting, legal advice and marketing *inter alia* – HR activity is no different. HR outsourcing is an opportunity rather than a universal solution and constitutes a part of the ongoing evaluation of the HR role and contribution to the business. In any case the in-house HR team needs to maintain professional expertise in order to manage and retain jurisdiction over external HR providers.

BRAVE NEW WORLD OR MORE OF THE SAME?

This chapter builds on some of the contextual ideas introduced in Chapter 1 by exposing changes in the world of work and the influences on the HR role within contemporary organisations. Whilst recognising that change is taking place, it is important not to become too excitable and suggest that we are entering some kind of brave new HRM world. Armstrong (2000) sums this up:

> The notion that personnel practitioners became involved in strategy formulation and implementation after HRM was invented is a travesty of the facts. Perhaps the word 'strategy' was not bandied around as much then as now but personnel specialists could not deliver effective services unless they understood the business context within which they were operating – where the business was going, what its needs were. To imply that until they travelled along the road to Damascus in the mid-1980s they were unaware of the need to innovate and think ahead is an insult to the many able personnel practitioners who were doing just that before the 1980s.

This is not meant to suggest that there is no change, but to encourage a balanced perspective. It is all a question of degree – line managers have always undertaken the management of human resources, but they may be doing more of it; the personnel practitioner has always had to have a business orientation, but perhaps it is sharper now; the personnel professional has always had to be aware of strategy, perhaps there is now a greater emphasis on this. Perhaps the personnel profession is in crisis, perhaps it is not: 'What we see is a variety of approach rather than a clear consensus about the appropriate way to organise the (personnel) function. Personnel specialists have a propensity for navel-gazing and neurosis about their role but on this occasion it seems ill founded. No doubt, however, observers will continue to tell the healthy patient that he or she is ill' (Torrington, 1998). Armstrong (2000), in concluding his analysis in 'The name has changed but has the game remained the same?', states:

> This means that practitioners must be aware of evolving business needs and how new ideas and good practice might fit those needs, however they are described. In its essentials the game has remained the same but the way it is being played has altered. Whether or not the name has changed is immaterial. New (HR) practices are developed and operated individually or 'joined up' because they meet the needs of the situation. What matters is what works.

We conclude that we may be in a new era but not a brave new world, but make up your own mind.

45

SUMMARY LEARNING POINTS

1 The world of work is changing, and whilst the rate of change may be exaggerated it is important for informed practitioners and managers to be aware of and able to react to the changes.

2 Organisational fluidity and transience coupled with exhortations to self-manage careers can result in workers giving primacy to their own employability concerns.

3 There is no doubt that customer aspirations and power are increasing and resulting in customer-driven organisations. This has significant implications for workers and for managers.

4 Employers may have to compete for good workers through offering competitive financial rewards and attractive financial rewards, and through deploying the art of talent management.

5 There are changes in the role of the HR professional encompassing business partnership, e-enabled HR, the restructuring of HR services and the potential for outsourcing HR activities. These influences should not be perceived as universal, because the role of the HR practitioner will be dependent on organisational circumstances and arguably it is 'best fit' that counts.

REFERENCES AND FURTHER READING

Armstrong, M. (2000) 'The name has changed but has the game remained the same?', *Employee Relations*, 22(6), 576–93.

Armstrong, M. and Brown, D. (2001) *New Dimensions in Pay Management*. London: CIPD.

Baron, A. and Collard, R. (1999) 'HR and the bottom line: realising our assets', *People Management*, 14 October, 30–8.

Beattie, D. (2001) *CIPD Annual Report*.

Brewster, C., Harris, H. and Sparrow, P. (2001) 'On top of the world', *People Management*, 25 October, 37–42.

Brown, D. (2001) 'Lopsided view', *People Management*, 22 November, 36–7.

Carter, M. (2000) 'e-Procurement: control shift', *People Management*, 23 November, 26–30.

Chaudhuri, A. (2000) 'Perk practice', *The Guardian: Management*, 30 August, 10–11.

CIPD (2001) *CIPD Professional Standards*. London: CIPD.

Cooper, C. (2000a) 'HR and the bottom line: in for the count', *People Management*, 12 October, 28–34.

Cooper, C. (2000b) 'Concierge services: chore competency', *People Management*, 7 December, 22–5.

Futures: the Industrial Society (2000) 'Most wanted: the quiet birth of the free worker'.

Glover, C. (2000) 'Time to show chief executives that HR makes the difference', *People Management*, 9 November, 20–1.

Glynn, C. (2000) 'Put people first on the balance sheet', *The Guardian: Management*, 16 September, 29.

46

Goodge, P. (2001) 'e-HR pure and simple', *People Management*, 8 March, 51.

Guest, D. and Baron, A. (2000) 'HR and the bottom line: piece by piece', *People Management*, 20 July, 26–31.

Guest, D. and King, Z. (2001) 'HR and the bottom line: personnel's paradox', *People Management*, 14 October, 30–8.

Hall, L. and Torrington, D. (1998) *The Human Resource Function: Dynamics of change and development*. London: FT Pitman Publishing.

Higginbottom, K. (2001) 'BP learns outsourcing lesson', *People Management*, 8 November, 8.

IPD (1994) 'People make the difference'. IPD Position Paper.

IRS Employment Trends 721 (2001) 'e-HR: personnel tomorrow', February, 6–13.

Kaplan, R. and Norton, D. (2001) 'Marked impact: business strategy', *People Management*, 25 October, 52–7.

Lecky-Thompson, R. (1997) 'Tales of the city: HR in the square mile'. *People Management*, 23 January, 22–7.

Lewis, A. (2000) 'Self-service HR: you've got to hand it to them', *People Management*, 28 September, 47.

Lewis, J. (2001) 'Out is back in: outsourcing HR's new skills', *Personnel Today*, 18 April, 24–33.

Littlefield, D. and Merrick, N. (2000) 'HR benchmarking: the realm of the peers', *People Management*, 7 December, 30–4.

Morgan, S. (2001) 'How to manage outsourcing', *People Management*, 3 May, 44–5.

People Management and Business Performance (2001) 'Performance through people: the new people management – the change agenda'. London: CIPD.

People Management and Business Performance (2001) 'The case for good people management: a summary of the research'. London: CIPD.

Philpott, J. (2001) 'The informed vote: the emerging political economy of work', *People Management*, 11 January, 42–3.

Pickard, J. (1998) 'Externally yours: outsourcing', *People Management*, 23 July, 34–7.

Pickard, J. (2000a) 'A sell-out strategy: outsourcing', *People Management*, 20 November, 32–6.

Pickard, J. (2000b) 'HR outsourcing: the truth is out there', *People Management*, 3 February, 48–50.

Pickard, J. (2000c) 'Study casts doubt on boom in outsourcing', *People Management*, 6 July, 16.

Purcell, J., Kinnie, N., Hutchison, S. and Rayton, B. (2000) 'HR and the bottom line: inside the box', *People Management*, 26 October, 30–8.

Richardson, R. and Thompson, M. (1999) *The Impact of People Management Practices on Business Performance: A review of the literature*. London: CIPD.

Schuler, R. and Jackson, S. (1999) *Strategic HRM*. Oxford: Blackwell.

Sisson, K. and Storey, J. (2000) *The Realities of HRM*. Oxford: Oxford University Press.

Sparrow, P. and Marchington, M. (1998) *HRM: The new agenda*. London: FT Pitman Publishing.

Tamkin, P., Barber, L. and Dench, S. (1997) 'From admin to strategy: the changing face of the HR function', *Institute for Employment Studies*: 332.

Thompson, M. (1998) 'HR and the bottom line: jet setters', *People Management*, 16 April, 38–41.

Torrington, D. (1998) 'Crisis and opportunity in HRM', in Sparrow, P. and Marchington, M. (eds) *HRM: The new agenda*. London: FT Pitman Publishing.

47

Turner, P. (2001) 'Professional development into the new millennium', *CIPD Professional Standards Conference*, July.

Tyler, E. (2001) 'Intranets: self service HR', *People Management*, 19 April, 51–2.

Ulrich, D. (1998) 'A new mandate for human resources', *Harvard Business Review*, January/February, 124–34.

Williams, M. (2000) 'Retention strategies: transfixed assets', *People Management*, 3 August, 29–33.

Woodruffe, C. (2000) 'Keep X on the files', *People Management*, 20 July, 53.

ASSIGNMENTS AND DISCUSSION TOPICS

1 The changing world of work: in groups, discuss the following two questions and be prepared to feed back into a whole-class discussion. First, in what way is the world of work changing compared to 10–15 years ago and what changes do you anticipate in the next decade? You can refer to Exhibit 2.1 if this is helpful. Second, what are the implications of the changing world of work for employees and for the HR professional?

2 What is meant by 'added value' and 'business partnership' in relation to the HR role? How should personnel/HR professionals respond to the demands of their internal customers, normally line management colleagues?

3 To what extent is it possible to measure the contribution of HR activities to organisational success and what measures should be used?

4 Analyse the ten CIPD competencies required by HR professionals and comment on how they can be developed. To what extent does the specific organisational role of the HR practitioner determine the mix of competencies required? Illustrate your answer with practical examples, using your own role and that of other students.

5 Consider Guest's 18 key progressive people management practices listed in Exhibit 2.2. Identify which practices are present in your workplace and discuss how effective they are.

6 Is e-enabled HR a threat or an opportunity for the HR profession? Justify your point of view with practical examples.

7 The outsourcing (or externalisation) of HR activities can be defined as the use of consultants or specialist providers to supply HR activities or services previously undertaken by the organisation's own HR specialists. It can be viewed as the HR equivalent of facilities management – the facility in this case is 'the human resource'. Using the taxonomy of HR activities below, or one of your choice, analyse a number of organisations and identify which HR activities are currently outsourced. You should make some quantitative assessment of the extent of the outsourcing of each category.

48

HR strategy development	Human resource planning
Work and job design	Recruitment
Selection	Reward strategies and systems
Job evaluation	Payroll administration
Performance management	Internal communications
Quality initiatives	Diversity initiatives
Employee relations	Health and safety
Counselling/employee assistance programmes	Training
Management development	Careers advice and planning
Redundancy and/or dismissal	Outplacement
Employment law advice	HR advisory service to line managers
Organisation development	

In relation to your findings consider the following questions. What are the reasons for the outsourcing? What are the challenges associated with outsourcing? What evidence is there for an increase in HR outsourcing in the next three years? If so, which areas do think will increase and why? Write a report and/or give a presentation on the state of play in HR outsourcing which reflects your research.

49

Chapter 7

Employee relations

Nick Bacon

Introduction

The terms 'employee relations' and, more traditionally, 'industrial relations' are used to indicate those areas of the employment relationship in which managers deal with the representatives of employees rather than managing employees directly as individuals (Edwards, 1995). Where employees seek collective representation they generally join trade unions and the reaction of managers to this potential challenge to management authority provides valuable insights into the nature of employment. As the membership of trade unions has declined over the past two decades a critical debate has developed around the nature of employment relations in non-union workplaces. The purpose of this chapter is to chart the changes in the collective regulation of labour and consider the implications of the increasing number of workers who are not represented by trade unions.

Management frames of reference and management style

The suggestion that employees may need some form of collective protection from employers provokes a strong response in many managers. Behind this response is a set of assumptions about the right to manage (frequently termed the management prerogative) and the correct power balance in the employment relationship. These assumptions held by managers are the mixture of a complex blend of experiences, predispositions, learned behaviour and prejudice. They combine to create management frames of reference (Fox, 1966, 1974) that capture the often deeply held assumptions of managers towards a labour force. Three separate frames of reference can be identified: unitarist, pluralist and radical. Each of these differ in their beliefs about the nature of organisations, the role of conflict and the task of managing employees. Managers holding a unitarist frame of reference believe the natural state of organisations is one of harmony and co-operation. All employees are thought to be in the same team, pulling together for the common goal of organisational success. The employee relations task of management is to prevent conflict arising from misunderstandings that result if they fail adequately to communicate organisational goals to employees. Any remaining conflicts are attributed to mischief created by troublemakers. A pluralist frame of reference recognises that organisations contain a variety of sectional groups who legitimately seek to express divergent interests. The resulting conflict is inevitable and the task of managers is to establish a system of structures and procedures in which conflict is institutionalised and a negotiated order is established. The radical critique of pluralism is not, strictly speaking, a frame of reference for understanding management views of the employment relationship. It draws upon Marxism and explains workplace conflict within a broader historical and social context and places a stress upon the unequal power struggle of opposing social classes.

There are no simple methods to assess the frame of reference held by managers – indeed, they usually hold a complex set of ideas rather than falling neatly into a single and possibly oversimplistic frame of reference. However, insights into management attitudes can be gained through their responses to questions about trade unions. From comparable questions posed to managers at the start of the 1980s and 1990s, Poole and Mansfield (1993) suggested the underlying pluralistic preferences of British managers were remarkably consistent. Another question posed more recently indicated that a majority of workplace managers do not have a single frame of reference. In the 1998 Workplace Employee Relations Survey (WERS 98) most managers (54 per cent) were 'neutral' about union membership, whereas 29 per cent were 'in favour' with 17 per cent 'not in favour' (Cully et al., 1999: 87). However, when managers are asked more directly whether they prefer to manage employees directly or through unions then unitarist preferences emerge. For example, 72 per cent of managers agreed with the statement 'we would rather consult directly with employees than with unions', whereas only 13 per cent disagreed (ibid.: 88). Consequently, management approaches to industrial relations are often characterised as a mixing and matching between unitarism and pluralism in the 'time-honoured' British fashion (Edwards et al., 1998). Many managers accept such a view on the grounds that it merely reflects the reality of managing employees who may at times need representation. The evidence suggests, however, that managers can deter or encourage employees from joining trade unions. In the 1998 Workplace Employee Relations Survey pro-union management attitudes were significantly associated with union presence in the workplace (Cully et al., 1998: 19).

Frames of reference are also important because they underlie the management style adopted in organisations towards the workforce. Many authors have attempted to classify management styles (Fox, 1974; Purcell and Sisson, 1983; Purcell and Ahlstrand, 1994; Storey and Bacon, 1993) and as the resulting models have become increasingly complex some now doubt the usefulness of producing yet more typologies (Kitay and Marchington, 1996). The most recent typologies attempt to highlight the interaction between HRM and industrial relations. The central question raised is the extent to which HRM and industrial relations are alternative or complementary systems for managing employees. Whether managers recognise trade unions indicates the extent to which a 'collective' approach to managing employees is preferred and it does capture a key factor in distinguishing between management approaches. In addition, the extent to which managers invest in and develop employees indicates the extent to which they stress 'individualism'. In Figure 7.1 Purcell and Ahlstrand (1994) use the dimensions of 'collectivism' and 'individualism' to identify six different management styles of employee relations.

Individualism and collectivism have recently become popular terms in employee relations. In comparison with the traditional management frames of reference – unitarism and pluralism – these concepts have 'common-sense' meanings and appear grounded in everyday management vocabularies and thinking about employee relations. Individualism in employment relations is traditionally used to denote non-unionism and/or a HRM-style investment approach to employees (Marchington and Parker, 1990; Purcell, 1987; Storey and Sisson, 1993). Correspondingly, collectivism in industrial relations in the 1970s is counterpoised

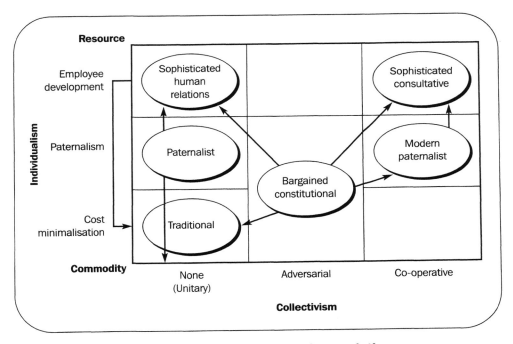

Figure 7.1 Movements in management style in employee relations

Source: Storey and Sisson, 1993, adapted from Purcell and Ahlstrand, 1994

Understanding and Managing People at Work

with individualism and HRM in the 1990s (Storey and Sisson, 1993). The 'collectivism' dimension includes a unitarist position where trade unions are not recognised, an adversarial position of conflict with unions and a co-operative position of partnership with unions. The 'individualism' dimension includes a cost minimisation approach to employees, a 'paternalist' position of care for employee welfare and an employee development scenario.

Initial studies of the adoption of HRM policies in unionised workplaces (Storey, 1992) suggested little fit between HRM and industrial relations as managers attempted to bypass industrial relations processes and deal directly with employees. This comes as no great surprise as personnel management in the UK is commonly described as pragmatic and largely opportunistic (Sisson and Marginson, 1995). In seeking the appropriate recipe for managing employees during the 1980s many managers saw an opportunity to reduce the influence of unions. This involved a secular (if disputed) shift towards unitarism as managers reasserted their prerogative over employees at work. Initially, in the 1980s this appeared in an aggressive form of 'macho-management' as senior executives, often in state-owned industries, attacked unions and the customs and practices entrenched in many workplaces (Purcell, 1982). However, most companies did not derecognise unions and commentators noted that 'the lack of clarity about how industrial relations fits with the new initiatives will sooner or later have to be addressed' (Storey and Sisson, 1993: 27). In short, the main issue on the employee relations agenda appeared to be how to combine the individual and collective approaches in a complementary fashion.

The decline of collective regulation

As employment relations transformed we appear to have witnessed 'the end of institutional industrial relations' (Purcell, 1993). The third Workplace Industrial Relations Survey (WIRS 3) in 1990 underlined the extent to which the nature of British employee relations had changed and was no longer characterised by adversarial collective bargaining at workplace level (Millward *et al.*, 1992). Recent data confirm a further decline in the collective regulation of the employment relationship in the UK. Table 7.1 illustrates this change as captured by the Workplace Industrial Relations Surveys in terms of changes to union presence (the presence of one or more union members in a workplace), union membership density (percentage of employees who are union members), union recognition for negotiating pay and conditions of employment, coverage of collective bargaining (the proportion of employees in workplaces with recognised unions covered by collective bargaining) and joint consultative committees.

As almost one half of workplaces are effectively union-free a 'representation gap' (Towers, 1997) may have developed where managers operate without any independent employee voice. Three in five workplaces have no worker representatives at all (either union or non-union representatives), and this increases to nine out of ten workplaces where unions are not present (Cully *et al.*, 1999: 95).

Table 7.1 The decline of collective regulation in the Workplace Industrial Relations Surveys (figures related to percentages of workplaces)

	1980	1984	1990	1998
Union presence	73	73	64	54
Union membership density	65	58	47	36
Union recognition	65	65	53	42
Coverage of collective bargaining	–	70	54	41
Joint consultative committees	34	34	29	29

Source: Workplace Industrial Relations Surveys, see Cully *et al.*, 1999.

The decline in union recognition during the 1980s was in part due to changes in industrial relations law. However, the number of companies which have actively sought to derecognise existing trade unions in established workplaces has remained relatively small (Claydon, 1996). Although trade unions were out of favour with the UK government there was little evidence that union members wanted trade unions to abandon their traditional roles. In a survey of almost 11,000 union members conducted by Waddington and Whitston (1997) employees revealed they continued to join unions for collective protection and to improve terms and conditions (Table 7.2).

Table 7.2 What reasons do employees give for joining unions?

Reason	%
Support if I had a problem at work	72
Improved pay and conditions	36
Because I believe in trade unions	16
Free legal advice	15
Most people at work are members	14

Source: Waddington and Whitston, 1997: 521.

A more convincing explanation for union decline during the 1980s was the changing nature of the economy, with an increase in the service sector and reductions in the number of large manufacturing plants, manual work and the public sector. The traditional habitat for the UK's system of industrial relations based on adversarial collective bargaining was disappearing (Millward *et al.*, 1992). Although the decline in trade union representation continued throughout the 1990s there is evidence that the explanation has changed as 'almost all of the change arose because workplaces that joined the WIRS population between 1990 and 1998, even controlling for their sector and employment of part-time workers, were less likely to recognise unions than similar workplaces that had dropped out of the population' (Cully *et al.*, 1999: 241).

However, when we consider the scope and depth of joint consultation and bargaining trade union influence appears lower than current levels of union recognition indicate. It is difficult to assess the extent to which managers rely upon collective agreements with trade unions in workplaces. One study comparing collective agreements at the start and end of the 1980s outlined a relative stability in procedural agreements covering how issues are handled between management and labour (Dunn and Wright, 1994). A rather different picture emerged from case studies at plant level, indicating that managers were increasingly exercising their prerogative to make important changes, particularly in working methods (Geary, 1995). The latest data from the 1998 Workplace Employee Relations Surveys indicates a deeper 'hollowing out' of collective agreements. In workplaces where union representatives are present only a 'modest' level of joint regulation occurs. No negotiations occurred over any issues in one half of the workplaces with worker representatives present (Cully *et al.*, 1999: 110). In a further 13 per cent of workplaces negotiations only occurred on non-pay issues, in 17 per cent negotiations only covered pay and in 22 per cent negotiations occurred over pay and one other issue. Managers in many workplaces appear to regard certain HR issues as 'off limits' to union representatives and do not even involve unions in providing information. In 53 per cent of workplaces with union representatives, representatives played no role at all in performance appraisals, in 52 per cent no role in recruitment, in 46 per cent no role in payment systems and in 43 per cent no role in training. This evidence suggests that in many cases trade union influence has 'withered on the vine' and where union representatives remain in place this resembles a unionised approach to industrial relations which in fact is little more than a 'hollow shell' (Hyman, 1997). Given these findings traditional debates on the most appropriate levels for collective bargaining (at the workplace, corporate or industry levels) and the balance between collective bargaining and joint consultation are giving way to the broader question of whether and on what terms trade unions are involved in any degree of joint workplace governance. The central role played by collective industrial relations has certainly declined but what types of non-union workplaces have emerged?

Non-union workplaces

According to one estimate the majority of UK workplaces had become non-union by 1995 (Cully and Woodland, 1996). In the classic account by Fox (1974) it was necessary for managers to enforce management prerogative by coercive power to justify a unitarist ideology and non-union status. Managers have often used a wide-ranging web of defences against unionisation that in their more extreme variants in the United States could combine 'sweet stuff' to make management policies more acceptable to employees, 'fear stuff' to discourage union joining and 'evil stuff' to demonise unions (Roy, 1980). A unitarist ideology can therefore include a variety of different management techniques. Returning to Figure 7.1 we can see that Purcell and Ahlstrand (1994) classify three non-union management styles in terms of whether an organisation recognises and develops individual employees. Companies adopting a 'sophisticated human relations' approach invest in staff development and use a wide range of human resource management policies to substitute for the services unions provide for members (a union substitution approach). Other non-union companies adopt a 'paternalist' approach and seek the loyalty and commitment of staff through consideration for employee welfare. Finally, some organisations maintain a 'Bleak House' strategy of cost minimisation and avoid union recruitment.

Several key commentators in the late 1980s identified the non-union sector as the most likely location for the development of HRM in the UK, foreseeing a growth in the 'sophisticated human relations' approach (Sisson, 1989). As some HRM models, but not all, are fundamentally unitarist, a non-union environment appeared well suited to the demands of developing committed and flexible employees as demonstrated by several large non-union US multinationals such as IBM, Hewlett Packard and Mars (Foulkes, 1980; Kochan *et al.*, 1986). For example, IBM had combined corporate success, a positive employee relations climate of low conflict, low labour turnover and long service, with good pay and conditions. In addition, the company provided procedures to fulfil many of the functions met by unions, including a complex array of alternative procedures (a no redundancy policy, single status, equal opportunities policies, merit pay and performance assessments), a strong emphasis on internal communications and a grievance system.

Empirical support for the apparent link between sophisticated HRM and non-unionism was also provided by several case studies in the UK outlining a union substitution approach. In the case of 'Comco' explored by Cressey *et al.* (1985) employees identified strongly with the company and enjoyed 'greater benefits' and 'less disciplinary pressure'. Most employees working at an IBM plant in the UK studied by Dickson *et al.* (1988) were positively attached to the individualistic ethos of the company and perceived little need for union protection. Scott (1994) outlined a 'golden handcuffs' approach whereby employees in a chocolate works received good terms and conditions in return for accepting a high rate of effort and strict rules. Despite this evidence, initial studies indicated that non-union companies with a sophisticated approach to managing employees may remain the exception. A study of high-tech companies in the Southeast of England where we might expect companies to reproduce the IBM non-union model uncovered little evidence of sophisticated HRM, with companies either opportunistically avoiding unions or adopting the style of 'benevolent autocracies' (McLoughlin and Gourlay, 1994). Furthermore, the assumed benefits of a 'sophisticated human relations' approach have more recently come under closer scrutiny. Blyton and Turnbull (1994) suggest that Marks and Spencer, so often held up as an exemplar non-union company, simultaneously pursued a 'union substitution' strategy in retail outlets while forcing suppliers into a cost minimisation approach. In another case study, a steel plant had widely publicised the introduction of a HRM approach and subsequently derecognised trade unions. However, employee gains proved illusory, with managerial strategy geared towards attitudinal compliance, work intensification and the suppression of any counterbalancing trade union activity (Bacon, 1999).

HRM: a union or non-union phenomenon?

The evidence from the latest UK workplace survey (WERS98) confirms the finding of the 1990 survey (WIRS3, see Sisson, 1993: 206) that sophisticated HRM practices are to be found alongside union recognition mainly in larger workplaces and those in the public sector. In short, these surveys indicate that 'an active and strong union presence is compatible with the broad suite of high commitment management practices' (Cully *et al.*, 1999: 111). Furthermore, higher union density (the proportion of employees who are trade union members) is also associated with greater joint regulation and more high commitment management (HCM) practices. Figure 7.2 indicates that of the workplaces with no recognised unions, 41 per cent had none to three HCM practices, 54 per cent four to seven HCM practices, and 5 per cent eight or more. This compares unfavourably with 25 per cent of workplaces with recognised unions reporting eight or more high commitment management practices.

However, only 4 per cent of workplaces in the workplace survey combine a majority of the workforce in unions, collective negotiations over issues and at least one half of the measured list of high commitment work practices in place. There

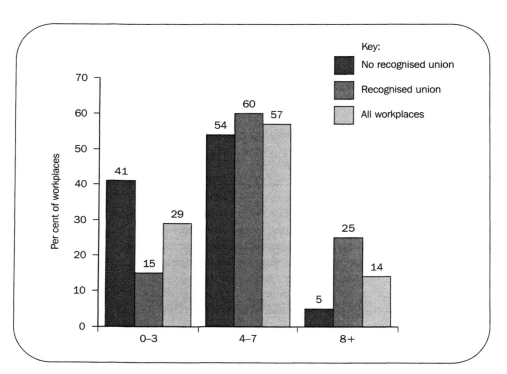

Figure 7.2 Number of high commitment management practices, by trade union recognition

Source: Cully et al., 1999

is, nevertheless, evidence from WERS98 that the combination of union recognition and HCM practices has a powerful effect on workplace performance. In the words of the WERS98 team 'workplaces with a recognised union and a majority of the HCM practices . . . did better than the average, and better than workplaces without recognition and a minority of these practices' (Cully *et al.*, 1999: 135). Sceptics of the impact of trade unions may still like to believe that adopting a wide range of HCM practices in a non-union environment may lead to even higher performance, but the fact that WERS98 could find so few such organisations casts some doubt upon this belief. In organisations where managers continue to recognise unions and are seeking to develop staff new approaches to industrial relations are developing involving 'partnership agreements'.

Partnership and the 'new unionism'

The election of 'New Labour' in 1997 has resulted in a new public policy environment. The government's Employment Relations Act 1999 and '*Fairness at Work*' programme have introduced new rights for trade unions and individual employees (Undy, 1999; Wood and Godard, 1999). In sum, this legislative programme involves a statutory route for union recognition, an extension of rights for individual employees, a national minimum wage and closer engagement with the social policies of the European Union. A central aim of this legislative programme is to 'replace the notion of conflict between employers and employees with the promotion of partnership in the longer term' (HMSO, 1998). The influence of a European approach was already felt as legislation obliged companies to establish a European works council if they employed over 1,000 employees in Europe and a minimum of 150 employees in at least two different member states. In sum, it is now commonplace to call for less destructive conflict and more co-operation to improve organisational productivity.

The issue of the balance between co-operation and conflict in union–management relations is a long-standing tension in employee relations. As the employment relationship encapsulates both shared and contrary interests the relationship between management and unions will contain elements of conflict and co-operation. As management and unions have begun to use the word 'partnership' it has become a contested term that appears inherently ambiguous and at times has no agreed meaning (Undy, 1999; Ackers and Payne, 1998). As Undy (1999: 318) has pointed out, 'What one party, or commentator, means by "partnership" is not necessarily shared by others.' As with so many terms in the area of employment relations, key pressure groups such as the TUC, the CBI and the Institute of Directors (IoDs) have sought to provide widely 'differing interpretations' of partnership (Undy, 1999: 318), defining the term for their own ends. The Institute of Personnel and Development, for example, explains that partnership 'has more to do with an approach to the relationship between employers and employees, individually and in groups, than it has to do with trade unions' (IPD, 1997: 8). Partnership can therefore be defined in both unitarist and pluralist terms. Rather unsurprisingly, the definition favoured by the TUC is pluralistic, with the stress placed on respecting union influence, whereas the IoD prefers a unitarist definition, whereby employees identify with the employer and trade unions are compliant to the wishes of management.

The Involvement and Participation Association, an independent pressure group, developed an influential definition of 'partnership' with leading companies and trade union leaders. This approach was endorsed by leading figures, including representatives from J. Sainsbury plc, the Boddington Group, the Post Office and the leaders of several trade unions (Involvement and Participation Association, 1992). This definition requires managers to declare security of employment as a key corporate objective; 'gainsharing' the results of success, and recognise the legitimacy of the employees' right to be informed, consulted and represented. In return, trade unions are required to renounce rigid job demarcations and commit to flexible working; give sympathetic consideration to the Continental model of representation of the whole workforce by means of election of representatives to new works councils, and recognise and then co-promote employee involvement methods. Case 7.2 invites you to consider the extent to which you feel companies and unions are able to sign up to a partnership agenda.

Given the lack of a general consensus on the meaning of industrial relations partnerships, it may be surprising that the term has acquired such a topical currency. A principal reason why the concept has taken hold is that it offers an industrial relations solution to the low competitiveness of much of UK industry. In this respect, partnership is no different from previous legislative changes that have sought to improve organisational performance through changes in industrial relations. Influential US literature suggests that in some companies managers may be able to forge a strategic linkage between industrial relations and HRM initiatives to create 'mutual gains enterprises' (Kochan and Osterman, 1994; Appelbaum and Batt, 1994). In such enterprises important changes are introduced in the organisation of work to enhance productivity, to the mutual benefit of employees, unions and management acting in coalition.

The signing of partnership agreements is of potential importance (IRS, 1997) although to date there is little evidence that they have become spread beyond around 40 companies. If partnerships are to become further established in UK industrial relations then managers and unions must find a workable balance between a number of key tensions beyond the above-mentioned disputes as to the meaning of the concept. The first tension is that workable partnership agreements appear to require a strategic and long-term commitment by managers to working closely with unions in the tradition of companies labelled 'sophisticated moderns' by Fox (1974). If managers are simply behaving in a short-term, contradictory or opportunistic manner then genuine industrial relations partnerships are unlikely to endure. For example, at the Royal Mail several partnership initiatives have struggled, primarily because some managers in the company are not firmly behind the partnership approach (see Bacon and Storey, 2000; Bacon and Storey, 1996).

The second tension, not unconnected to the first, is to what extent management and unions are able to commit fully to a single strategy of co-operative industrial relations. If partnerships do not secure the types of compliant trade unionism required in the CBI's definition of partnership then management commitment to such agreements may prove half-hearted. Similarly, at the same time as the TUC is supporting partnership agreements it is also pursuing an organising and campaigning approach to membership growth (Heery, 1998). It may prove difficult for unions to convince a company to sign a meaningful partnership agreement in one plant while actively recruiting union members against the wishes of the same or a similar company in another plant.

The third tension is whether partnership agreements form part of a longer-term strategy to marginalise trade unions rather than an alternative. Many observers critical of the co-operative relationships between managers and unions that are central to partnership agreements have highlighted continued employer attacks on unions (Claydon, 1989, 1996; Gall and McKay, 1994; Kelly, 1996; Smith and Morton, 1993). Although partnerships are frequently presented as a step away from attempts to derecognise trade unions this may not be the case. Evidence on this matter is not yet conclusive. Whereas one recent review of partnership agreements in six organisations reported that 'none gave serious consideration to ending recognition' (IDS, 1998: 4), a study of management attempts to restructure industrial relations in ten organisations (Bacon and Storey, 2000) revealed that derecognition had been more seriously explored. In the latter study, the new agreements signed with trade unions did not appear to reflect long-term commitments to working with trade unions nor sophisticated moves towards derecognition. Managers appeared to display unitarist preferences. However, for pragmatic reasons – for instance, the desire to maintain the trust of employees – they were willing to involve unions in joint regulation albeit within parameters managers attempted to control. In many workplaces union representatives feel they have no option but to accept management terms and union support for partnership resembles a resigned compliance. For example, in the case of United Distillers trade unions either signed the partnership agreement on offer or faced 'de facto derecognition' (Marks *et al.*, 1998: 222).

Finally, it is not yet clear whether partnership agreements will deliver greater returns for managers and trade unions. If returns are not forthcoming for either party then enthusiasm for the partnership approach may wane. Kelly (1996) has argued that, a priori, a union strategy of moderation is inferior in many respects to a militant stance. Union moderation is associated by Kelly with: eroding the willingness and capacity of union members to resist employers; inhibiting the growth of workplace union organisation; generating apathy among union members; involving union 'give' and management 'take'; resulting in attempts to drive down terms and conditions of employment and failing to genuinely represent member grievances. The key differences between militant and moderate union positions are highlighted in Case 7.3.

The extent to which Kelly is correct and neither unions nor employees will benefit from partnership agreements is an interesting question. Certainly, the number

Understanding and Managing People at Work

of partnership agreements signed between unions and management has increased, but remains low overall. There is little evidence that employers are able to offer the job security guarantees that unions seek or that trade unions are able to prevent managers unilaterally imposing changes in work organisation in order to bring managers to sign partnership agreements.

Conclusions

In this chapter we have argued that managers in the majority of workplaces no longer appear to support or utilise collective industrial relations in their employee management strategies. Sisson and Storey (2000: x) have recently restated that 'managing the employment relationship will demand both an individual and a collective perspective' in forthcoming years. However, recent evidence suggests that managers in few workplaces have sought to balance an individual and collective approach to employee management. Figure 7.3 presents a summary drawing upon the findings from WERS98 of the current pattern of employee relations. The predominant employee relations style in the British workplace is not to manage both individualism and collectivism, it is to manage neither. Considering all the

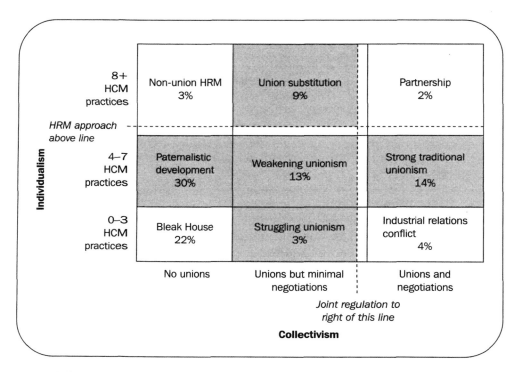

Figure 7.3 New patterns of employee relations.

workplaces which fall into the bottom left-hand quadrant of the dotted lines, approximately seven in ten (68 per cent) operate fewer than one-half of 15 high-commitment management practices and do not involve trade unions in negotiations on matters other than pay. Fifty-two per cent of workplaces in this quadrant do not recognise trade unions.

Approximately 14 per cent of workplaces could be described as pursuing a HRM approach but only 5 per cent appeared to combine individualism with either a union exclusion or partnership approach. The majority of workplaces appear to be marginalising unions, and although they remain present significant negotiations do not occur. It is tempting to classify organisations falling into the four corner boxes as having an apparently settled employee relations strategy that is unlikely to change in the near future. The numerous workplaces which fall into the 'Bleak House' classification (approximately 22 per cent) are focused upon cost reduction and will resist any attempts at unionisation. They are likely to be smaller workplaces in such sectors as wholesale and retail, hotels and restaurants. The small number of organisations which negotiate with unions but eschew developing employees ('industrial relations traditional') may be resigned to dealing with unions in the absence of a more sophisticated approach to managing employees. A few genuine examples of partnership may flourish in the current political climate but the overall number of such workplaces remains small. Companies adopting non-union HRM are likely to feel they have permanently resolved the union issue.

This leaves approximately 69 per cent of organisations (in the shaded areas of Figure 7.3) which currently operate with an opportunistic mixture of labour management policies. Organisations currently occupying these different positions face somewhat different dilemmas. Those currently using HRM policies to substitute for negotiating with unions but still recognising unions ('union substitution') may at some point in the future sign partnership deals with trade unions to share more decision-making and/or further erode union influence. Companies with 'strong traditional unionism' may further develop HR policies either to substitute for unions or develop a partnership approach. From an industrial relations perspective the most significant developments may occur within the 'weakening unionism' category. Although trade unions in these workplaces are involved in fewer negotiations managers have not developed high-commitment management practices to replace the services unions provide for members in terms of voicing collective grievances and seeking to improve terms and conditions. It would appear to be in this category of workplaces that trade unions may target recruitment to increase union density and exert greater influence. The Employment Relations Act 1999 encourages union recruitment and organising efforts as it provides a statutory recognition procedure. As so few organisations appear to have resolved the issue of managing employees through individual or collective means they are likely to face continued pressure from individual employees for increased training and more satisfying work and from employee representatives for a greater say in workplace governance.

Case study 7.1

The UK's largest private sector employers

Nick Bacon

Below is a list of the largest private sector employers in the UK taken from *Labour Research*. Which do you think:

(a) Do not recognise trade unions;
(b) Recognise and negotiate with trade unions;
(c) Recognise trade unions but only for the purposes of consultation or to represent individual employees?

Explain your decisions.

Table 7.3

Tesco	153,800	Retail – supermarkets
J Sainsbury	150,700	Retail – supermarkets
BT	125,800	Telecommunications
Lloyds-TSB	82,000	Banking and finance
Whitbread	80,000	Food and drink
Boots Co.	75,000	Retail and pharmaceuticals
Asda Group	73,700	Retail – supermarkets
Safeway Group	70,400	Retail – supermarkets
Kingfisher	69,600	Retail
Bass	67,500	Brewing and leisure
National Westminster	66,000	Banking and finance
Rentokil Initial	65,000	Business services
Barclays	60,800	Banking and finance
Granada Group	58,000	Leisure
Marks and Spencer	54,900	Retail
General Electric Co.	52,300	Electronics
HSBC Holding (Midland Bank)	50,000	Banking and finance
British Airways	47,700	Banking and finance
Allied Domecq	46,500	Food and drink
Somerfield	45,700	Retail – supermarket
Burton Group	43,700	Retail
British Steel	43,400	Steel Manufacturers
Ladbroke Group	42,000	Leisure
John Lewis Partnership	41,100	Retail – department stores
BMW – Rover Group	39,000	Motor manufacture
Scottish and Newcastle	39,000	Brewing and leisure
British Aerospace	38,500	Aerospace and engineering
MacDonald's Restaurants	36,700	Food retail
Halifax	36,000	Banking and finance
Ford	35,900	Motor manufacturing
Compass Group	35,700	Catering
Co-operative Wholesale Society	35,000	Banking, insurance, retail
OCS Group	35,000	Cleaning
Sears	32,600	Retail
Rolls Royce	31,200	Aerospace and engineering
Rank Organisation	30,300	Leisure and films
Greenhalls Group	30,100	Brewing, food, hotels
WH Smith	30,000	Retail
Royal & Sun Alliance	27,800	Insurance
Securicor Group	27,500	Security services
Wm Morrison Supermarkets	27,000	Retail – supermarkets
Unigate	27,000	Food manufacture
Lucas Varity	26,800	Engineering
BTR	26,600	Industrial conglomerate
Kwik Save Group	26,000	Retail

Understanding and Managing People at Work

The principles and practices of partnership with trade unions

Nick Bacon

As explained in Chapter 6, one option for managers and trade unions is to establish a partnership agreement. However, successful agreements depend upon a serious commitment to the principles and practices of partnership. Thinking of the last organisation you worked for, an organisation you know well or your own personal 'frame of reference', to what extent do you agree or disagree with the following statements? Your answers indicate whether organisations could be committed to a partnership agreement. *(Circle one number for each statement)*

	Agree	*Neutral*	*Disagree*
Personnel managers worry about trade unions, most other senior managers would rather they disappear.	1	2	3
Trade unions don't have a useful function in organisations.	1	2	3
All managers should share all information, however sensitive, with unions.	1	2	3
Managers can get employees to work hard without making concessions to unions.	1	2	3
Job security is a myth in today's world.	1	2	3
To attract top managers organisations have to offer extra incentives such as private health insurance that are too expensive to give to all employees.	1	2	3
Companies should train all employees to a high level even though some will leave.	1	2	3

Case study 7.3

What should trade unions do?

Nick Bacon

In Chapter 7 we outlined Kelly's (1996) argument that trade unions would benefit from a militant rather than a moderate stance. Reading through the following statements, indicate the extent to which you believe trade unions should adopt a moderate or militant stance. Explain your choices.

Trade unions should:

Union militancy		Union moderation
Make ambitious demands	*or*	Make moderate demands
Offer few concessions	*or*	Offer many concessions
Rely on members' activity	*or*	Rely on managers' good will
Rely on collective bargaining	*or*	Rely on consultation
Frequently threaten industrial action	*or*	Rarely threaten industrial action
Believe in a basic conflict of interests	*or*	Believe in a basic common interest

Employee relations at North Fire Brigade

Tom Redman and Ed Snape

Background

North Fire Brigade has a current establishment of 700 whole-time operational fire-fighters located in twelve fire stations across the region with a non-uniformed support staff of 100. In addition there are 72 part-time retained firefighters located in a further six stations. Firefighting in the UK is still virtually an exclusively male occupation when compared to the slow but steady inroads of women firefighters in some other countries. North Brigade is no different in this respect, not employing a single woman firefighter. The number of firefighters per station varies from around 30 in the smallest to over 100 in the largest. Each firefighter is a member of one of four watches (red, white, blue, and green), with each watch working for two day and two night shifts on a 42-hour week duty system. Despite the introduction of new managerial practices in the 1990s the organisation of fire fighting remains hierarchical and bureaucratised, with ten levels separating the chief officer and qualified firefighter posts.

The nature of the firefighters' job makes heavy demands in terms of personal discipline and commitment to teamwork and results in a strongly collectivist work ethic. In the words of a previous general secretary of the FBU:

> When all is said and done, at the end of it firefighting comes to this: that a small number of people will go into a darkened smoke-logged building not knowing what they are going to meet, having faith in each other, in the long run prepared to risk their lives to save the lives of other people. In the long run, no matter what transformation we effect in the Fire Service, firefighting in its final stages remains just that. And we do not forget it.

This collectivist work ethic imparts high levels of loyalty and discipline to the union. North Brigade has a union density rate of nearly 100 per cent amongst uniformed staff. The TUC-affiliated FBU is the dominant trade union for firefighters, particularly for lower grades, with the NAFO (and CACFOA) having very limited representation amongst higher-grade employees at station officer and above. Non-uniformed staff are represented by Unison. The FBU has ambitions to be an industrial union for firefighting, with its first object being 'to organise all uniformed employees'. There has been a recent history of competition between the fire service unions, with some acrimonious disputes arising over representation rights.

Collective bargaining is organised through a National Joint Council composed on the employer's side of representatives made up of various local authority bodies. However, the national bargaining system was under pressure from management initiatives to increase the range of local bargaining, in particular to reduce the scope of the National Scheme of Conditions of Service or 'Grey Book'. Here a critical report from the Audit Commission in 1995 added momentum to a move to more local bargaining. The report suggested the national framework was constraining brigade effectiveness by preventing some possible improvements in efficiency. However, the FBU see this less as a need for local flexibility and more as a simple prelude to a concerted attack on the levels of terms and conditions provided by national bargaining arrangements. Local bargaining currently occurs between four key union representatives (from a brigade committee of some 12 representatives) and the Deputy Chief Fire Officer and Assistant Chief Officers. Typical bargaining issues include changes to 'detached' duties (terms for redeploying staff between stations), the duty mix of whole-time and retained firefighters, and meal arrangements.

Cost containment

Although the fire service has probably not been on the receiving end of some of the more drastic cutbacks in public spending over the last decade, there is now considerable pressure for cost containment and 'efficiency' within the sector. According to one senior and long-serving manager:

> In the past people accepted we put out fires and that somehow was enough. Now with the general closer scrutiny we have from auditing and performance indicators and the like, it is not sufficient. We have to be much more efficient and service-minded nowadays.

Such pressures are occurring at a time of increasing demand for fire services. The FBU estimates an increase of 87 per cent in calls to the fire service between 1979 and 1998. The funding for fire services in England is calculated by the Standard Spending Assessment (SSA) formula. The majority of English County Councils, particularly rural ones, exceed their SSA allocation. North Brigade is no exception, with 1998 seeing a budget shortfall of over £2 million needed to support the current establishment and existing levels of service provision. In particular, the physical characteristics of North Brigade's geographical location, with a large concentration of heavy chemical industries, are felt to necessitate a higher level of spending than the SSA allocation.

More recently, the cost and efficiency pressures generated by 'Best Value' were occupying managerial attention. Here the brigade had set up task teams to investigate the cost reduction potential of greater collaboration with other regional brigades in areas such as the purchasing of uniforms and equipment, training, the provision of payroll services and, more controversially, the use of joint control centres. Task teams had also been set up to examine the potential for generating income by providing training courses for industry and other fire services where

North Brigade had particular expertise, for example, in relation to dealing with hazardous materials. Increasingly, the mounting pressure for cost containment and efficiency was impacting on the industrial relations climate of the industry as management attempted to reduce costs but at the same time improve service quality levels.

Industrial relations

Industrial relations in the brigade were perceived as being typical for the industry with fewer disputes occurring in North Brigade than some other more 'militant' brigades, recent protracted disputes over terms and conditions and establishment level having occurred in Merseyside, Derbyshire and, most recently, Essex. The latter three and a half-month dispute involved over 20 strikes. Following the resolution of the dispute, the Essex MP Teresa Gorman, in an open letter to Essex Fire Brigade committee, accused the FBU of 'blackmailing' and 'shroud-waving' to protect outdated practices and overgenerous terms and conditions:

> All Britain's fire services are far too overstaffed. It is one of the last of the dinosaur industries clinging to feather bedding, using shroud-waving and blackmail to prevent the modernisation of the service. The Algarve is stuffed with healthy young British males, living comfortably, their incomes supplemented by disabled pensions from the fire service. In Arizona, when the fire service was privatised, it became obvious that 80 per cent of all 'calls' could be dealt with by two men in a fast car. And the cost of the service was halved. Who will be the first council to have an open debate on privatising its fire services and let some fresh air in to the argument?

Managers at North Brigade felt the relatively dispute-free recent past could be explained by an open relationship with the union and more 'responsible' union leaders.

> We accommodate them (the union) with whatever information they want with regard to budgets. There is a standing instruction that the union can have whatever information the Brigade has. If they want information on, say, the capital or revenue budgets they can go and get it with my authority. There are no secrets here. It comes from us being able to say to the union 'We have not got the money to do this or that. There are the figures. If you can find X thousand pounds, you can have it'.

Senior management emphasised the importance of good communication with their employees, and the need for it, given a generally better-educated workforce. Employee involvement mechanisms include a brigade Intranet, newsletters, senior management visits and informal talks 'with the troops in the stations'. The latter was seen to be particularly important to counter the perceived gulf between headquarters and the stations. According to one manager, North Brigade now had 'thinking union officers rather than the table bangers of the past'. Trade union interviewees also reported that the current senior management was, to a large extent, more willing to listen to their concerns, particularly when compared to some previous senior managers, who were reluctant even to speak to other managers below a certain rank, let alone union representatives. Union–management co-operation had extended in the recent past to a joint delegation to lobby Parliament on SSA levels.

An index of the generally positive industrial relations climate of the 1990s in North Brigade was the low level of formal grievances, with few grievances reaching the 'failure to agree' stage. This was seen as a considerable achievement when set against a backcloth of cost containment, the level of organisational change and the high potential for conflict in the character of firefighting disputes. Here the nature of an emergency led to 'life or death' service results in many disputes, according to both union representatives and managers, involving some very emotional and moral arguments being thrown around. Thus, the brigade had successfully managed to reduce its establishment levels by about 10 per cent over the last eight years without any industrial action occurring. Most recently in 1998 the brigade had removed two fireboats from service and this had resulted in the loss of 15 jobs through natural wastage. Here the union officers felt they had provided 'realistic opposition' to the cuts – the original management proposal had been to lose 43 jobs through compulsory redundancy.

However, several developments were underway which had high potential for straining future management–union relationships. In particular, a number of industry-wide issues, such as the 1998 review of the national pension scheme and the move to local bargaining, were causing concern for local relationships between management and unions. The new pension proposals contained a recommendation for a two-tier scheme with considerably reduced benefits for new starters and a diminution of terms for existing staff. Equally, increasing attempts by various brigades to renegotiate and in some cases 'buy-out' 'Grey Book' conditions was a major source of instability which was seen as eventually posing considerable problems for industrial relations in North Brigade. Local issues included managerial attempts to introduce performance appraisal; appraisal-related pay, revised duty systems and a capability procedure, all of which the union had strongly resisted. Union representatives also reported increasing interest by management in the performance of individual firefighters and increased pressure on sickness levels via the introduction of formal interview panels. A key union concern here was that such pressure resulted in some employees coming to work in an unfit state and thus becoming a danger to themselves and their colleagues. Firefighters in North Brigade had also traditionally had two days' extra annual leave above the national minimum and management was being subjected to increasing pressure from the district Audit Office to reduce this.

As a result there had been a recent increase in grievance activity in disputes, with several of these reaching the 'failure to agree' stage. Here disputes varied from the cutback of hot meals on weekend shifts; a demarcation dispute (with the ambulance service) over the use of defibrillators and basic trauma life support and management's attempt to obtain a 'seamless ambulance and fire fighting service'; management attempts to get full-time staff to undertake duties traditionally carried out by retained firemen, and more flexible rostering. Union representatives reported that they were currently working very hard to hold back the members and a senior manager lamented that, given the current IR climate, a capability procedure he had been working on for two years was 'not worth the hassle of getting it out of the drawer'. According to one union representative:

> We may have been guilty of crying wolf with the members in the past. You know, always telling them that this year the management are coming for us. But now it looks like it is probably going to happen.

Thus, the industrial relations climate was generally perceived as deteriorating somewhat under the wider pressures on the industry. For example, the union representatives reported that they were becoming increasingly more sceptical of management's espoused rhetoric of seeking a 'partnership' with the union. One union representative described management's claim of having an open door policy as being 'just words' as union concerns were now more often met by 'shoulder shrugging' and 'There is no alternative' statements. Union interviewees also reported the organisational culture of the brigade changing under the creeping use of business language and new managerial 'speak'. Here the language of 'customer service' was seen as a veil for management pushing through desired organisational changes in the search for efficiency and cost cutting. Thus:

> We used to have the feel of being a big family doing a key public service. Now it very much feels like we are working for a business. (union representative)

The 'us and them' divide in the brigade was thus perceived by union representatives as increasing. For example, in relation to the meal dispute one union representative commented that 'It now seems we cannot get a meal but they can have big cars'.

Note: The amount of funding allocated to run fire services in England is calculated using a formula know as the Standard Spending Assessment. In Scotland it is the Grant Aided Expenditure, in Wales the Revenue Support Grant and in Northern Ireland a block grant for the funding of all services.

Questions

1. Management at North Brigade is very concerned that a worsening national IR environment will undermine their relatively good local IR climate. What would you advise them to do in order to protect local relationships in such conditions?

2. Many commentators have suggested that the right to strike should be removed from essential public services, such as firefighting. Do you agree with this view? What issues would be raised by such a development?

3. Fire brigades are currently under considerable pressure to increase the number of women firefighters in the service. What IR issues would be raised by the increased recruitment of women firefighters?

References to Chapter 7

Ackers, P. and Payne, J. (1998) 'British trade unions and social partnership: rhetoric, reality and strategy', *International Journal of Human Resource Management*, 9: 529–50.

Appelbaum, R. and Batt, R. (1994) *The New American Workplace*. Ithaca: ILR Press.

Bacon, N. (1999) 'Union derecognition and the new human relations: a steel industry case study', *Work, Employment and Society*, 13(1): 1–17.

Bacon, N. and Storey, J. (1996) 'Individualism and collectivism and the changing role of trade unions' in Ackers, P., Smith, C. and Smith, P. (eds) *The New Workplace and Trade Unionism*, London, Routledge, 1–40.

Bacon, N. and Storey, J. (2000) 'New employee relations strategies: towards individualism or partnership', *British Journal of Industrial Relations*, forthcoming.

Blyton, P. and Turnbull, P. (1994) *The Dynamics of Employee Relations*, London: Macmillan.

Claydon, T. (1989) 'Union de-recognition in Britain in the 1980s', *British Journal of Industrial Relations*, 27: 214–23.

Claydon, T. (1996) 'Union recognition: a re-examination', in Beardwell, I. (ed) *Contemporary Industrial Relations*, Oxford: Oxford University Press.

Cressey, P., Eldridge, J. and MacInnes, J. (1985) *Just Managing: Authority and Democracy in Industry*, Milton Keynes: Open University Press.

Cully, M. and Woodland, S. (1996) 'Trade union membership and recognition: an analysis of data from the 1995 Labour Force Survey', *Labour Market Trends*, May: 215–25 (Norwich: HMSO).

Cully, M., Woodland, S., O'Reilly, A., Dix, G., Millward, N., Bryson, A., and Forth, J. (1998) *The 1998 Workplaces Employee Relations Survey: First Findings*, London: Department of Trade and Industry.

Cully, M., Woodland, S., O'Reilly, A. and Dix, G. (1999) *Britain at Work*, London: Routledge.

Dickson, T., McLachlan, M.V., Prior, P. and Swales, K. (1988) 'Big blue and the union: IBM, individualism and trade union strategy', *Work, Employment and Society*, 2: 506–20.

Dunn, S., and Wright, M. (1994) 'Maintaining the "status quo": An analysis of the contents of British collective agreements 1979–1990', *British Journal of Industrial Relations*, 32: 23–46.

Edwards, P. (1990) 'The politics of conflict and consent', *Journal of Economic Behaviour and Organization*, 13: 41–61.

Edwards, P. (1995) 'The employment relationship', in P. Edwards (ed) *Industrial Relations*, Oxford: Blackwell, 3–26.

Edwards, P. *et al.* (1998) 'Great Britain: from partial collectivism to neo-liberalism to where?', in Ferner, A., and Hyman, R. (eds) *Changing Industrial Relations in Europe*, Oxford: Blackwell, 1–54.

Flanders, A. (1970) *Management and Unions: The Theory and Reform of Industrial Relations*, London: Faber.

Foulkes, F. K. (1980) *Personnel Policies in Large Non-union Companies*, Englewood Cliffs, NJ: Prentice Hall.

Fox, A. (1966) 'Industrial sociology and industrial relations', *Royal Commission Research Paper No. 3*, London: HMSO.

Fox, A. (1974) *Beyond Contract: Work, Power and Trust Relations*, London: Faber and Faber.

Freeman, R.B. and Medoff, J.L. (1984) *What Do Unions Do?*, New York: Basic Books.

Gall, G. and McKay, S. (1994) 'Trade union de-recognition in Britain 1988-94', *British Journal of Industrial Relations*, 32: 433–48.

Geary, J. (1995) 'Work practices: the structure of work', in P. Edwards (ed) *Industrial Relations*, Oxford: Blackwell, 368–96.

Guest, D. (1987). 'Human resource management and industrial relations', *Journal of Management Studies*, 24(5): 503–21.

Guest, D. (1989) 'Human resource management: its implications for industrial relations and trade unions', in J. Storey, (ed) *New Perspectives in Human Resource Management*, London: Routledge, 41–55.

Guest, D. (1990). 'Human resource management and the American Dream', *Journal of Management Studies*, 27(4): 378–97.

Guest, D. (1995). 'Human resource management, trade unions and industrial relations', in Storey, J. (ed) *Human Resource Management: A Critical Text*, London: Routledge, 110–41.

Guest, D. and Hoque, K. (1994) 'The good, the bad and the ugly: Employment relations in new non-union workplaces', *Human Resource Management Journal*, 5: 1–14.

Heery, E. (1996) 'The new new unionism', in Beardwell, I. (ed) *Contemporary Industrial Relations*, Oxford: Oxford University Press, 175–202.

Heery, E. (1998) 'The re-launch of the Trades Union Congress', *British Journal of Industrial Relations*, 36: 339–60.

HMSO (1998) *Fairness at Work*, White Paper.

Hyman, R. (1987) 'Strategy or structure? Capital, Labour and Control', *Work, Employment and Society*, 1(1): 25–55.

Hyman, R. (1997) 'The future of employee representation', *British Journal of Industrial Relations*, 35(3): 309–36.

IDS (1998) 'Partnership agreements', *IDS Study 656*, October.

Institute of Directors (1994) Evidence presented to the Employment Committee Enquiry, *The Future of Trade Unions*, HC 676-II, London: HMSO.

Involvement and Participation Association (1992) *Towards Industrial Partnership: A New Approach to Management Union Relations*, London: IPA.

IPD (1997) *Employment Relations into the 21st Century*, London: Institute of Personnel and Development.

IRS (1997) Partnership at work: a survey. *Employment Trends*, 645, December: 3–24.

Kelly, J. (1996) 'Union militancy and social partnership', in Ackers, P., Smith, C. and Smith, P. (eds) *The New Workplace and Trade Unionism*, London: Routledge, 41–76.

Kitay, J. and Marchington, M. (1996) 'A review and critique of workplace industrial relations typologies', *Human Relations*, 49(10): 1263–90.

Kochan, T. and Osterman, P. (1994) *The Mutual Gains Enterprise*, Cambridge, Mass: Harvard Business School Press.

Kochan, T., Katz, H. and McKersie, B. (1986) *The Transformation of American Industrial Relations*, New York: Basic Books.

Marchington, M. and Parker, P. (1990) *Changing Patterns of Employee Relations*, Hemel Hempstead: Harvester Wheatsheaf.

Marks, A., Findlay, P., Hine, J., McKinlay, A. and Thompson, P. (1998) 'The politics of partnership? Innovation in employment relations in the Scottish spirits industry', *British Journal of Industrial Relations*, 36(2): 209–26.

McLoughlin, I. and Gourlay, S. (1994) *Enterprise Without Unions: Industrial Relations in the Non-Union Firm*, Milton Keynes: Open University Press.

Millward, N., Stevens, M., Smart, D. and Hawes, W.R. (1992) *Workplace Industrial Relations in Transition*, Dartmouth: Aldershot.

Monks, J. (1998) 'Trade unions, enterprise and the future', in Sparrow, P. and Marchington, M. (eds) *Human Resource Management: The New Agenda*, London: Pitman, 171–9.

Poole, M., and Mansfield, R. (1993) 'Patterns of continuity and change in managerial attitudes and behaviour in industrial relations 1980–90', *British Journal of Industrial Relations*, 31(1): 11–36.

Purcell, J. (1982) 'Macho managers and the new industrial relations', *Employee Relations*, 4(1): 3–5.

Purcell, J. (1987) 'Mapping management styles in employee relations', *Journal of Management Studies*, 24(5): 533–48.

Purcell, J. (1991) 'The rediscovery of management prerogative: the management of labour relations in the 1980s', *Oxford Review of Economic Policy*, 7(1): 33–43.

Purcell, J. (1993) 'The end of institutional industrial relations', *Political Quarterly*, 64(1): 6–23.

Purcell, J. and Ahlstrand, B. (1994) *Human Resource Management in the Multi-Divisional Company*, Oxford: Oxford University Press.

Purcell, J. and Sisson, K. (1983) 'Strategies and practice in the management of industrial relations', in G. Bain (ed) *Industrial Relations in Britain*, Oxford: Blackwell.

Roy, D. (1980) 'Fear stuff, sweet stuff and evil stuff: management's defences against unionization in the South', in T. Nichols (ed) *Capital and Labour: A Marxist Primer*, Glasgow: Fontana, 395–415.

Scott, A. (1994) *Willing Slaves?*, Cambridge: Cambridge University Press.

Sisson, K. (1989) 'Personnel management in transition?', in Sisson, K. (ed) *Personnel Management in Britain*, Oxford: Blackwell.

Sisson, K. (1993) 'In Search of HRM', *British Journal of Industrial Relations*, 31(2): 201–10.

Sisson, K. (ed) (1994) *Personnel Management*, Oxford: Blackwell.

Sisson, K. (1995) 'Human resource management and the personnel function', in Storey, J. (ed) *Human Resource Management: A Critical Test*, London: Routledge, 87–109.

Sisson, K., and Marginson, P. (1995) 'Management: systems, structures and strategy', in Edwards, P. (ed) *Industrial Relations*, Oxford: Blackwell, 89–122.

Sisson, K., and Storey, J. (2000) *The Realities of Human Resource Management*, Buckingham: Open University Press.

Smith, P. and Morton, G. (1993) 'Union exclusion and decollectivization of industrial relations in contemporary Britain', *British Journal of Industrial Relations*, 31(1): 97–114.

Storey, J. (1992) *Developments in the Management of Human Resources*, Oxford: Blackwell.

Storey, J., and Bacon, N. (1993) 'Individualism and collectivism: into the 1990s', *International Journal of Human Resource Management*, 4(3): 665–84.

Storey, J., Bacon, N., Edmonds, J. and Wyatt, P. (1993) 'The new agenda and human resource management: a roundtable discussion with John Edmonds', *Human Resource Management Journal*, 4(1): 63–70.

Storey, J. and Sisson, K. (1993) *Managing Human Resources and Industrial Relations*, Milton Keynes: Open University Press.

Towers, B. (1997) *The Representation Gap*, Oxford: Oxford University Press.

TUC (1993) Evidence presented to the Employment Committee Enquiry, *The Future of Trade Unions*, HC 676-II, 18 October, London: HMSO.

Undy, R. (1999) 'Annual review article: New Labour's "Industrial Relations Settlement": The Third Way?', *British Journal of Industrial Relations*, 37(2): 315–36.

Waddington, J. and Whitston, C. (1997) 'Why do people join unions in a period of membership decline', *British Journal of Industrial Relations*, 35(4): 515–46.

Wood, S. (1997) *Statutory Union Recognition*, Institute of Personnel and Development, London.

Wood, S. and Godard, J. (1999) 'The statutory union recognition procedure in the Employment Relations Bill: A comparative analysis', *British Journal of Industrial Relations*, 37: 203–44.

Chapter 32 Grievance and discipline

Grievance and discipline are awkward words nowadays. They sound rather solemn and forbidding, more suitable for a nineteenth-century workhouse than a twenty-first-century business. They certainly have no place in the thinking of Britain's favourite entrepreneur, Sir Richard Branson:

> If you have the right people in place, treat them well and trust them, they will produce happy customers and the necessary profits to carry on and expand the work.
>
> (quoted in Handy 1999, p. 86)

We use them for their value as technical terms to describe the breakdown of mutual confidence between employer and employee, or between managers and managed. When someone starts work at an organisation there are mutual expectations that form the basis of the forthcoming working relationship. We explained in the opening chapter of this book how the maintenance of those mutual expectations is the central purpose of human resource management. Apart from what is written in the contract of employment, both parties will have expectations of what is to come. Employees are likely to expect, for instance, a congenial working situation with like-minded colleagues, opportunities to use existing skills and to acquire others, work that does not offend their personal value system, acceptable leadership and management from those more senior, and opportunities to grow and mature. Employers will have expectations such as willing participation in the team, conscientious and imaginative use of existing skills and an ability to acquire others, compliance with reasonable instructions without quibbles, acceptance of the authority of those placed in authority and a willingness to be flexible and accept change.

That working relationship is sometimes going to go wrong. If the employee is dissatisfied, then there is potentially a grievance. If the employer is dissatisfied, there is the potential for a disciplinary situation. The two complementary processes are intended to find ways of avoiding the ultimate sanction of the employee quitting or being dismissed, but at the same time preparing the ground for those sanctions if all else fails.

Usually, the authority to be exercised in a business is impersonalised by the use of role in order to make it more effective. If a colleague mentions to you that you have overspent your budget, your reaction might be proud bravado unless you knew that the colleague had a role such as company accountant, internal auditor or financial director. Everyone in a business has a role – most people have several – and each role confers some authority. The canteen assistant who tells you that the steak and kidney pudding is off is more believable than the managing director conveying the same message. Normally in hospitals people wearing white coats and a stethoscope are seen as being more authoritative than people in white coats without a stethoscope.

Dependence on role is not always welcome to those in managerial positions, who are fond of using phrases like, 'I know how to get the best out of people', 'I understand my chaps' and 'I have a loyal staff'. This may partly be due to their perception of their role being to persuade the reluctant and command the respect of the unwilling by the use of personal leadership qualities, and it is indisputable that some managers are more effective with some groups of staff than with others, but there is more to it than personal skill: we are predisposed to obey those who outrank us in any hierarchy.

The Milgram experiments with obedience

Obedience is the reaction expected of people by those in authority positions, who prescribe actions which, but for that authority, might not necessarily have been carried out. Stanley Milgram (1974) conducted a series of experiments to investigate obedience to authority and highlighted the significance of obedience and the power of authority in our everyday lives.

Subjects were led to believe that a study of memory and learning was being carried out which involved giving progressively more severe electric shocks to a learner who gave incorrect answers to factual questions. If the learner gave the correct answer the reward was a further question; if the answer was incorrect there was the punishment of a mild electric shock. Each shock was more severe than the previous one. The 'learner' was not actually receiving shocks, but was a member of the experimental team simulating progressively greater distress, as the shocks were supposedly made stronger. Eighteen different experiments were conducted with over 1,000 subjects, with the circumstances between experiments varying. No matter how the variables were altered the subjects showed an astonishing compliance with authority even when delivering 'shocks' of 450 volts. Up to 65 per cent of subjects continued to obey throughout the experiment in the presence of a clear authority figure and as many as 20 per cent continued to obey when the authority figure was absent.

Milgram was dismayed by his results:

> With numbing regularity good people were seen to knuckle under to the demands of authority and perform actions that were callous and severe. Men who are in everyday life responsible and decent were seduced by the trappings of authority, by the control of their perceptions, and by the uncritical acceptance of the experimenter's definition of the situation into performing harsh acts.   (1974, p. 123)

Our interest in Milgram's work is simply to demonstrate that we all have a predilection to obey instructions from authority figures, even if we do not want to. He points out that the act of entering a hierarchical system (such as any employing organisation) makes people see themselves acting as agents for carrying out the wishes of someone else, and this results in these people being in a different state, described as the agentic state. This is the opposite to the state of autonomy when individuals see themselves as acting on their own. Milgram then sets out the factors that lay the groundwork for obedience to authority.

1 **Family:** Parental regulation inculcates a respect for adult authority. Parental injunctions form the basis for moral imperatives as commands to children have a dual function. 'Don't tell lies' is a moral injunction carrying a further

implicit instruction: 'And obey me!' It is the implicit demand for obedience that remains the only consistent element across a range of explicit instructions.

2 **Institutional setting**: Children emerge from the family into an institutional system of authority: the school. Here they learn how to function in an organisation. They are regulated by teachers, but can see that the headteacher, the school governors and central government regulate the teachers themselves. Throughout this period they are in a subordinate position. When, as adults, they go to work it may be found that a certain level of dissent is allowable, but the overall situation is one in which they are to do a job prescribed by someone else.

3 **Rewards**: Compliance with authority is generally rewarded, while disobedience is frequently punished. Most significantly, promotion within the hierarchy not only rewards the individual but also ensures the continuity of the hierarchy.

4 **Perception of authority**: Authority is normatively supported: there is a shared expectation among people that certain institutions do, ordinarily, have a socially controlling figure. Also, the authority of the controlling figure is limited to the situation. The usher in a cinema wields authority, which vanishes on leaving the premises. As authority is expected it does not have to be asserted, merely presented.

5 **Entry into the authority system**: Having perceived an authority figure, an individual must then define that figure as relevant to the subject. The individual not only takes the voluntary step of deciding which authority system to join (at least in most of employment), but also defines which authority is relevant to which event. The firefighter may expect instant obedience when calling for everybody to evacuate the building, but not if asking employees to use a different accounting system.

6 **The overarching ideology**: The legitimacy of the social situation relates to a justifying ideology. Science and education formed the background to the experiments Milgram conducted and therefore provided a justification for actions carried out in their name. Most employment is in realms of activity regarded as legitimate, justified by the values and needs of society. This is vital if individuals are to provide willing obedience, as it enables them to see their behaviour as serving a desirable end.

Managers are positioned in an organisational hierarchy in such a way that others will be predisposed, as Milgram demonstrates, to follow their instructions. Managers put in place a series of frameworks to explain how they will exact obedience: they use *discipline*. Because individual employees feel their relative weakness, they seek complementary frameworks to challenge the otherwise unfettered use of managerial disciplinary power: they may join trade unions, but they will always need channels to present their *grievances*.

In later work Milgram (1992) made an important distinction between obedience and conformity, which had been studied by several experimental psychologists, most notably Asch (1951) and Abrams *et al.* (1990). Conformity and obedience both involve abandoning personal judgement as a result of external pressure. The external pressure to conform is the need to be accepted by one's peers and the resultant behaviour is to wear similar clothes, to adopt similar attitudes and adopt similar behaviour. The external pressure to obey comes from a hierarchy of which one is a member, but which certain others have more status and power than oneself.

> There are at least three important differences ... First, in conformity there is no *explicit* requirement to act in a certain way, whereas in obedience we are *ordered* or *instructed* to do something. Second, those who influence us when we conform are our *peers* (or equals) and people's behaviours become more alike because they are affected by *example*. In obedience, there is ... somebody in *higher authority* influencing behaviour. Third, conformity has to do with the psychological need for acceptance by others. Obedience, by contrast, has to do with the social power and status of an authority figure in a hierarchical situation.
>
> (Gross and McIlveen 1998, p. 508)

In this chapter we are concerned uniquely with discipline and grievance within business organisations, but it is worth pointing out that managers are the focal points for the grievances of people outside the business as well, but those grievances are called complaints. You may complain *about* poor service, shoddy workmanship or rudeness from an employee, but you complain *to* a manager.

HR managers make one of their most significant contributions to business effectiveness by the way they facilitate and administer grievance and disciplinary issues. First, they devise and negotiate the procedural framework of organisational justice on which both discipline and grievance depend. Second, they are much involved in the interviews and problem-solving discussions that eventually produce solutions to the difficulties that have been encountered. Third, they maintain the viability of the whole process which forms an integral part of their work: they monitor to make sure that grievances are not overlooked and so that any general trend can be perceived, and they oversee the disciplinary machinery to ensure that it is not being bypassed or unfairly manipulated.

Grievance and discipline handling is one of the roles in human resource management that few other people want to take over. Ambitious line managers may want to select their own staff without personnel intervention or by using the services of consultants. They may try to brush their personnel colleagues aside and deal directly with trade union officials or organise their own management development, but grievance and discipline is too hot a potato.

The requirements of the law regarding explanation of grievance handling and the legal framework to avoid unfair dismissal combine to make this an area where HR people must be both knowledgeable and effective. That combination provides a valuable platform for influencing other aspects of management. The personnel manager who is not skilled in grievance and discipline is seldom in a strong organisational position.

What do we mean by discipline?

Discipline is regulation of human activity to produce a controlled performance. It ranges from the guard's control of a rabble to the accomplishment of lone individuals producing spectacular performance through self-discipline in the control of their own talents and resources.

First, there is managerial discipline in which everything depends on the leader from start to finish. There is a group of people who are answerable to someone who directs what they should all do. Only through individual direction can that group of people produce a worthwhile performance, like the person leading the community singing in the pantomime or the person conducting an orchestra. Everything depends on the leader.

Second, there is team discipline, where the perfection of the performance derives from the mutual dependence of all, and that mutual dependence derives from a commitment by each member to the total enterprise: the failure of one would be the downfall of all. This is usually found in relatively small working groups, like a dance troupe or an autonomous working group in a factory.

Third, there is self-discipline, like that of the juggler or the skilled artisan, where a solo performer is absolutely dependent on training, expertise and self-control.

Discipline is, therefore, not only negative, producing punishment or prevention. It can also be a valuable quality for the individual who is subject to it, although the form of discipline depends not only on the individual employee but also on the task and the way it is organised. The development of self-discipline is easier in some jobs than others and many of the job redesign initiatives have been directed at providing scope for job holders to exercise self-discipline and find a degree of autonomy from managerial discipline. Figure 32.1 shows how the three forms are connected in a sequence or hierarchy, with employees finding one of three ways to achieve their contribution to organisational effectiveness. However, even the most accomplished solo performer has been dependent on others for training, and advice, and every team has its coach.

Activity 32.1   Note three examples of managerial discipline, team discipline and self-discipline from your own experience.

Figure 32.1 Three forms of discipline

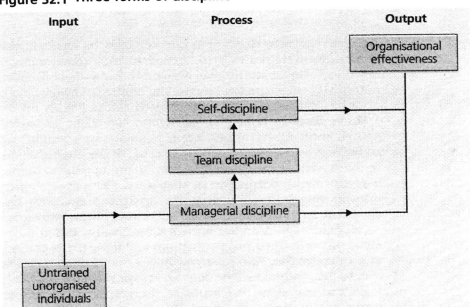

Understanding and Managing People at Work

Managers are not dealing with discipline only when they are rebuking late-comers or threatening to dismiss saboteurs. As well as dealing with the unruly and reluctant, they are developing the co-ordinated discipline of the working team, engendering that *esprit de corps* which makes the whole greater than the sum of the parts. They are training the new recruit who must not let down the rest of the team, puzzling over the reasons why A is fitting in well while B is still struggling. Managers are also providing people with the equipment to develop the self-discipline that will give them autonomy, responsibility and the capacity to maximise their powers. The independence and autonomy that self-discipline produces also produces the greatest degree of personal satisfaction – and often the largest pay packet. Furthermore the movement between the three forms represents a declining degree of managerial involvement. If you are a leader of community singing, nothing can happen without your being present and the quality of the singing depends on your performance each time. If you train jugglers, the time and effort you invest pays off a thousand times, while you sit back and watch the show.

What do we mean by grievance?

Contemporary British texts virtually ignore grievance handling, but the Americans maintain sound coverage. Mathis and Jackson (1994) have a particularly helpful review. Some years ago Pigors and Myers (1977, p. 229) provided a helpful approach to the topic by drawing a distinction between the terms dissatisfaction, complaint and grievance as follows:

- **Dissatisfaction**: Anything that disturbs an employee, whether or not the unrest is expressed in words.
- **Complaint**: A spoken or written dissatisfaction brought to the attention of the supervisor and/or shop steward.
- **Grievance**: A complaint that has been formally presented to a management representative or to a union official.

This provides us with a useful categorisation by separating out grievance as a formal, relatively drastic step, compared with commonplace grumbling. It is much more important for management to know about dissatisfaction. Although nothing is being expressed, the feeling of hurt following failure to get a pay rise or the frustration about shortage of materials can quickly influence performance.

Much dissatisfaction never turns into complaint, as something happens to make it unnecessary. Dissatisfaction evaporates with a night's sleep, after a cup of coffee with a colleague, or when the cause of the dissatisfaction is in some other way removed. The few dissatisfactions that do produce complaint are also most likely to resolve themselves at that stage. The person hearing the complaint explains things in a way that the dissatisfied employee had not previously appreciated, or takes action to get at the root of the problem.

Grievances are rare since few employees will question their superior's judgement (whatever their private opinion) and fewer still will risk being stigmatised as a troublemaker. Also, many people do not initiate grievances because they believe that nothing will be done as a result of their attempt.

HR managers have to encourage the proper use of procedures to discover sources of dissatisfaction. Managers in the middle may not reveal the complaints they are hearing, for fear of showing themselves in a poor light. Employees who feel insecure, for any reason, are not likely to risk going into procedure, yet the dissatisfaction lying beneath a repressed grievance can produce all manner of unsatisfactory work behaviours from apathy to arson. Individual dissatisfaction can lead to the loss of a potentially valuable employee; collective dissatisfaction can lead to industrial action.

There are three types of complaint that get progressively harder to handle. The first kind is factual and can be readily tested:

- 'The machine is out of order.'
- 'The stock we're getting now is not up to standard.'
- 'This adhesive won't stick.'

The second type is complaints that are based partly on subjective reactions:

- 'The work is messy.'
- 'It's too hot in here.'
- 'This job is too stressful.'

These statements include terms where the meaning is biologically or socially determined and can therefore not be understood unless the background of the complainant is known; seldom can their accuracy be objectively determined. A temperature of 18 degrees celsius may be too hot for one person but equable for another.

The third, and most difficult, type of complaint is that involving the hopes and fears of employees:

- 'The supervisor plays favourites.'
- 'The pay is not very good.'
- 'Seniority doesn't count as much as it should.'

These show the importance of determining not only what employees feel, but also why they feel as they do; not only verifying the facts ('the manifest content'), but also determining the feelings behind the facts ('the latent content'). An employee who complains of the supervisor being a bully may actually be saying something rather different. In one instance it was revealed that the root of the dissatisfaction was the employee's attitude to any authority figure, not simply the supervisor who was the subject of the complaint.

Each type of dissatisfaction is important to uncover and act upon, if action is possible. Action is usually prompt on complaints of the first type, as they are neutral: blame is placed on an inanimate object so individual culpability is not an issue. Action may be quick on complaints of the second type if the required action is straightforward – such as opening a window if it is too hot – but the problem of accuracy can produce a tendency to smooth over an issue or leave it 'to sort itself out' in time. The third type of complaint is the most difficult, and action is often avoided. Supervisors will often take complaints to be a personal criticism of their own competence, and employees will often translate the complaint into a grievance only by attaching it to a third party like a shop steward, so that the relationship between employee and supervisor is not jeopardised.

Activity 32.2 Think of an example from your own experience of dissatisfaction causing inefficiency that was not remedied because there was no complaint. Why was there no complaint?

The framework of organisational justice

The organisation requires a framework of justice to surround the employment relationship so that managers and supervisors, as well as other employees, know where they stand when dissatisfaction develops. Figure 32.2 shows a framework.

Awareness of culture and appropriateness of style

The culture of an organisation affects the behaviour of people within it, develops norms that are hard to alter and provides a pattern of conformity. If, for instance, everyone is in the habit of arriving ten minutes late, a 'new broom' manager will have a struggle to change the habit. Equally, if everyone is in the habit of arriving punctually, then a new recruit who often arrives late will come under strong social pressure to conform, without need for recourse to management action. Culture also affects the freedom and candour with which people discuss dissatisfactions with their managers without allowing them to fester.

The style of managers in handling grievances and discipline reflects their beliefs. The manager who sees discipline as being punishment, and who regards grievances as examples of subordinates getting above themselves, will behave in a relatively autocratic way, being curt in disciplinary situations and dismissive of

Figure 32.2 The framework of organisational justice

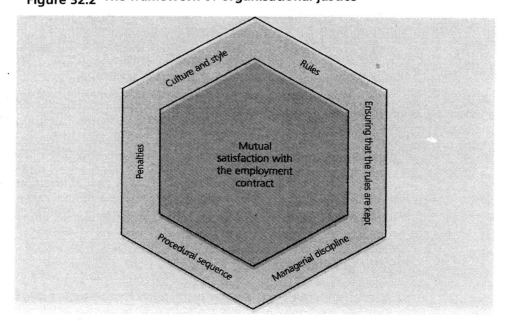

complaints. The manager who sees disciplinary problems as obstacles to achievement that do not necessarily imply incompetence or ill will by the employee will seek out the cause of the problem. That problem may then be revealed as one requiring firm, punitive action by the manager, or it may be revealed as a matter requiring management remedy of a different kind. The manager who listens out for complaints and grievances, gets to the bottom of the problems and finds solutions will run little risk of rumbling discontent from people obsessed by trivial problems.

Rules

Every workplace has rules; the difficulty is to have rules that people will honour. Some rules come from statutes, like the tachograph requirement for HGV drivers, but most are tailored to meet the particular requirements of the organisation in which they apply. For example, rules about personal cleanliness are essential in a food factory but less stringent in a garage.

Rules should be clear and readily understood; the number should be sufficient to cover all obvious and usual disciplinary matters. To ensure general compliance it is helpful if rules are jointly determined, but it is more common for management to formulate the rules and for employee representatives eventually to concur with them. Employees should have ready access to the rules through the employee handbook and notice board, and the personnel manager will always try to ensure that the rules are known as well as published.

In 1973 the Department of Employment suggested that rules fall into six categories, relating to different types of employee behaviour:

1 Negligence is failure to do the job properly and is different from incompetence because of the assumption that the employee can do the job properly, but has not.
2 Unreliability is failure to attend work as required, such as being late or absent.
3 Insubordination is refusal to obey an instruction, or deliberate disrespect to someone in a position of authority. It is not to be confused with the use of bad language. Some of the most entertaining cases in industrial tribunals have involved weighty consideration of whether or not colourful language was intended to be insubordinate.
4 Interfering with the rights of others covers a range of behaviours that are deemed socially unacceptable. Fighting is clearly identifiable, but intimidation may be more difficult to establish.
5 Theft is another clear-cut aspect of behaviour that is unacceptable when it is from another employee. Theft from the organisation should be supported by very explicit rules, as stealing company property is regarded by many offenders as one of the perks of the job. How often have you taken home a box of paper clips or a felt tip pen without any thought that you were stealing from the employer?
6 Safety offences are those aspects of behaviour that can cause a hazard.

The value of rules is to provide guidelines on what people should do, as the majority will comply. The number of people killed on the roads has declined sharply because the great majority of drivers obey the law on wearing seat belts. The date for introducing the legislation was, however, deferred twice to ensure

In a recent discussion with a group of senior managers, employees identified the following as legitimately taken at will:

paper clips, pencils, disposable pens, spiral pads, local telephone calls, plain paper, computer disks, adhesive tape, overalls and simple uniform.

Among the more problematic were:

- Redundant or shop-soiled stock. One DIY store insisted that the store manager should personally supervise the scrapping of items that were slightly damaged, to ensure that other items were not slightly damaged on purpose.
- Surplus materials. One electricity supplier had some difficulty in eradicating the practice of surplus cable and pipe being regarded as a legitimate perquisite of fitters at the end of installation jobs, as they suspected their engineers were using the surplus for private work. Twelve months later the level of material requisition had declined by 14 per cent.

that it was introduced when there would be general acceptance rather than widespread defiance of the law.

Ensuring that the rules are kept

Although the majority of car drivers wear seat belts, the majority of dog owners never had dog licences, so that legal requirement had to be repealed. It is not sufficient just to have rules; they are only effective if they are observed. How do we make sure that employees stick to the rules?

1 Information is needed so that everyone knows what the rules are and why they should be obeyed. Written particulars may suffice in an employment tribunal hearing, but most people conform to the behaviour of their colleagues, so informal methods of communication are just as important as formal statements.

2 Induction can make the rules coherent and reinforce their understanding. The rule can be explained, perhaps with examples, so that people not only know the rules but also understand why they should be obeyed.

3 Placement or relocation can avoid the risk of rules being broken, by placing a new recruit with a working team that has high standards of compliance. If there are the signs of disciplinary problems in the offing, then a quick relocation can put the problem employee in a new situation where offences are less likely.

4 Training increases awareness of the rules, improving self-confidence and self-discipline. There will be new working procedures or new equipment from time to time, and again training will reduce the risk of safety offences, negligence or unreliability.

5 Review of the rules periodically ensures that they are up to date, and also ensures that their observance is a live issue. If, for instance, there is a monthly staff council meeting, it could be appropriate to have a rules review every 12 months. The simple fact of the rules being discussed keeps up the general level of awareness of what they are.

6 Penalties make the framework of organisational justice firmer if there is an understanding of what penalties can be imposed, by whom and for what. It is

not feasible or desirable to have a fixed scale, but neither is it wise for penalties to depend on individual managerial whim. This area has been partially codified by the legislation on dismissal, but the following are some typical forms of penalty:

(a) **Rebuke:** The simple 'Don't do that' or 'Smoking is not allowed in here' or 'If you're late again, you will be in trouble' is all that is needed in most situations, as someone has forgotten one of the rules, had not realised it was to be taken seriously, or was perhaps testing the resolution of the management. Too frequently, managers are reluctant to risk defiance and tend to wait until they have a good case for more serious action rather than deploy their own, there-and-then authority. They should remember the lessons of Stanley Milgram on obedience.

(b) **Caution:** Slightly more serious and formal is the caution, which is then recorded. This is not triggering the procedure for dismissal, it is just making a note of a rule being broken and an offence being pointed out.

(c) **Warnings:** When the management begin to issue warnings, great care is required, as the development of unfair dismissal legislation has made the system of warnings an integral part of disciplinary practice which has to be followed if the employer is to succeed in defending a possible claim of unfair dismissal at tribunal. For the employer to show procedural fairness there should normally be a formal oral warning, or a written warning, specifying the nature of the offence and the likely outcome of the offence being repeated. It should also be made clear that this is the first, formal stage in the procedure. Further misconduct could then warrant a final written warning containing a statement that further repetition would lead to a penalty such as suspension or dismissal. All written warnings should be dated, signed and kept on record for an agreed period. The means of appeal against the disciplinary action should also be pointed out.

(d) **Disciplinary transfer or demotion:** This is moving the employee to less attractive work, possibly carrying a lower salary. The seriousness of this is that it is public, as the employee's colleagues know the reason. A form of disciplinary transfer is found on assembly lines, where there are some jobs that are more attractive and carry higher status than others. Rule-breakers may be 'pushed down the line' until their contempt is purged and they are able to move back up.

(e) **Suspension:** A tactic that has the benefit of being serious and avoids the disadvantage of being long lasting, like demotion. The employer has a contractual obligation to provide pay, but not to provide work, so it is easy to suspend someone from duty – with pay – either as a punishment or while an alleged offence is being investigated. If the contract of employment permits, it may also be possible to suspend the employee for a short period without pay.

(f) **Fines:** These are little used, because of contractual problems, but the most common is deduction from pay for lateness.

The important general comment about penalties is that they should be appropriate in the circumstances. Where someone is, for instance, persistently late or absent, suspension would be a strange penalty. Also penalties must be within the law. An employee cannot be demoted or transferred at managerial whim, and fines or unpaid suspension can only be imposed if the contract of employment allows such measures.

7 Procedural sequence is essential to the framework of organisational justice. It should be the clear, unvarying logic of procedure, and be well known and trusted. Procedure makes clear, for example, who does and who does not have the power to dismiss. The dissatisfied employee, who is wondering whether or not to turn a complaint into a formal grievance, knows who will hear the grievance and where an appeal could be lodged. This security of procedure, where step B always follows step A, is needed by managers as well as by employees, as it provides them with their authority as well as limiting the scope of their actions.

8 Managerial discipline. Finally, managers must preserve general respect for the justice framework by their self-discipline in how they work within it. With very good intentions some senior managers maintain an 'open door' policy with the message: 'My door is always open ... call in any time you feel I can help you.' This has many advantages and is often necessary, but it has danger for matters of discipline and grievance because it encourages people to bypass middle managers. There is also the danger that employees come to see the settlement of their grievances as being dependent on the personal goodwill of an individual rather than on the business logic or their human and employment rights.

Managers must be consistent in handling discipline and grievance issues. Whatever the rules are, they will be generally supported only as long as they deserve support. If they are enforced inconsistently they will soon lose any moral authority, depending only on the fear of penalties. Equally, the manager who handles grievances quickly and consistently will enjoy the support of a committed group of employees.

The other need for managerial discipline is to test the validity of the discipline assumption. Is it a case for disciplinary action or for some other remedy? There is little purpose in suspending someone for negligence when the real problem is lack of training. Many disciplinary problems disappear under analysis, and it is sensible to carry out the analysis before making a possibly unjustified allegation of indiscipline.

Grievance procedure

Managers, who believe that it introduces unnecessary rigidity into the working relationship, often resent the formality of the grievance procedure: 'I see my people all the time. We work side by side and they can raise with me any issue they want, at any time they want ...'. The problem is that many people will not raise issues with the immediate superior that could be regarded as contentious, in just the same way that managers frequently shirk the rebuke as a form of disciplinary penalty. Formality in procedure provides a framework within which individuals can reasonably air their grievances and avoids the likelihood of managers dodging the issue when it is difficult. It avoids the risk of inconsistent ad hoc decisions, and the employee knows at the outset that the matter will be heard and where it will be heard. The key features of grievance procedure are fairness, facilities for representation, procedural steps and promptness.

1 Fairness is needed, to be just, but also to keep the procedure viable. If employees develop the belief that the procedure is only a sham, then its value will be lost and other means will be sought to deal with grievances. Fairness is

best supported by the obvious even-handedness of the ways in which grievances are handled, but it will be greatly enhanced if the appeal stage is either to a joint body or to independent arbitration – usually by ACAS – as the management is relinquishing the chance to be judge of its own cause.

2 Representation can help the individual employee who lacks the confidence or experience to take on the management single handedly. A representative, such as a union official, has the advantage of having dealt with a range of employee problems and may be able to advise the aggrieved person whether the claim is worth pursuing. There is always the risk that the presence of the representative produces a defensive management attitude affected by a number of other issues on which the manager and union official may be at loggerheads, so the managers involved in hearing the grievance have to cast the representative in the correct role for the occasion.

3 Procedural steps should be limited to three. There is no value in having more just because there are more levels in the management hierarchy. This will only lengthen the time taken to deal with matters and will soon bring the procedure into disrepute. The reason for advocating three steps is that three types of management activity are involved in settling grievances. Having said that, it is quite common for there to be more than three steps where there is a steep hierarchy, within which there may be further, more senior, people to whom the matter could be referred. The reason for more steps has nothing to do with how to process grievances but is purely a function of the organisation structure.

The first step is the preliminary, when the grievance is lodged with the immediate superior of the person with the complaint. In the normal working week most managers will have a variety of queries from members of their departments, some of which could become grievances, depending on the manager's reaction. Mostly the manager will either satisfy the employee or the employee will decide not to pursue the matter. Sometimes, however, a person will want to take the issue further. This is the preliminary step in procedure, but it is a tangible step as the manager has the opportunity to review any decisions made that have caused the dissatisfaction, possibly enabling the dissatisfied employee to withdraw the grievance. In our experience it is rare for matters to be taken any further unless the subject of the grievance is something on which company policy is being tested.

The hearing gives the complainant the opportunity to state the grievance to a more senior manager, who is able to take a broader view of the matter than the immediate superior and who may be able both to see the issue more dispassionately and to perceive solutions that the more limited perspective of the immediate superior obscured. It is important for the management that the hearing should finalise the matter whenever possible, so that recourse to appeal is not automatic. The hearing should not be seen by the employees as no more than an irritating milestone on the way to the real decision makers. This is why procedural steps should be limited to three.

If there is an appeal, this will usually be to a designated more senior manager, and the outcome will be either a confirmation or a modification of the decision at the hearing.

4 Promptness avoids the bitterness and frustration that comes from delay. When an employee 'goes into procedure', it is like pulling the communication cord in a train. The action is not taken lightly and is in anticipation of a swift resolution.

Furthermore, the manager whose decision is being questioned will have a difficult time until the matter is resolved. The most familiar device to speed things up is to incorporate time limits between the steps, specifying that the hearing should take place no later than, say, four working days after the preliminary notice and that the appeal should be no more than five working days after the hearing. This gives time for reflection and initiative by the manager or the complainant between the stages, but does not leave time for the matter to be forgotten.

Where the organisation has a collective disputes procedure as well as one for individual grievances, there needs to be an explicit link between the two so that individual matters can be pursued with collective support if there is not a satisfactory outcome. An outline grievance procedure is in Figure 32.3.

Disciplinary procedure

Procedures for discipline are very similar to those for grievance and depend equally on fairness, promptness and representation. There are some additional features.

Figure 32.3 Outline grievance procedure

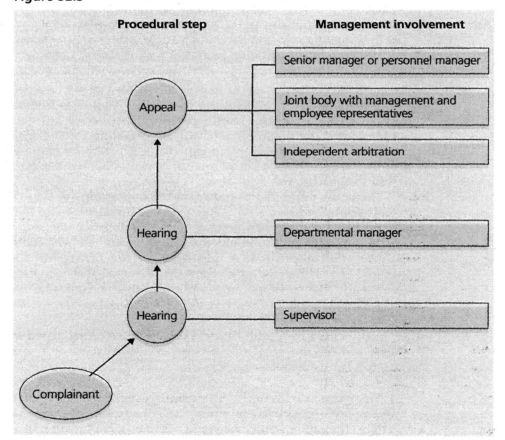

Authorisation of penalties

The law requires that managers should not normally have the power to dismiss their immediate subordinates without reference to more senior managers. Whatever penalties are to be imposed, they should only be imposed by people who have that specific authority delegated to them. Usually this means that the more serious penalties can only be imposed by more senior people, but there are many organisations where such decisions are delegated to the personnel department.

Investigation

The procedure should also ensure that disciplinary action is not taken until it has been established that an offence has been committed justifying the action. The possibility of suspension on full pay is one way of allowing time for the investigation of dubious allegations, but the stigma attached to such suspensions should not be forgotten.

Information and explanation

If disciplinary action is possible, the person to be disciplined should be told of the complaint, so that an explanation can be made, or the matter denied, before any penalties are decided. If an employee is to be penalised, then the reasons for the decision should be explained to make sure that cause and effect are appreciated. The purpose of penalties is to prevent a recurrence. An outline disciplinary procedure is in Figure 32.4.

Disputes

Procedures for the avoidance of disputes are mainly drawn up in national negotiations between employers' associations and trade unions or between single employers and unions. Disputes can arise for a wide range of reasons, but their essence is that they are collective: employees are acting in concert, and nearly always using union machinery, to persuade the management to alter a decision. Sometimes the grievance of an individual can escalate into a collective dispute if employees together feel that a matter of principle is at stake. Disciplinary penalties, especially dismissals, can also become matters for collective employee action, when the dismissal is regarded as unfair.

There are usually more steps in a procedure for collective dispute than for individual grievances, and provisions to preclude strikes, lock-outs or other forms of industrial action before procedure is exhausted.

Are grievance and discipline processes equitable?

For grievance and discipline processes to work they must command support, and they will only command support if they are seen as equitable, truly just and fair. At first it would seem that it is concern for the individual employee that is paramount, but the individual cannot be isolated from the rest of the workforce. Fairness should therefore be linked to the interests that all workers have in

Figure 32.4 Outline disciplinary procedure

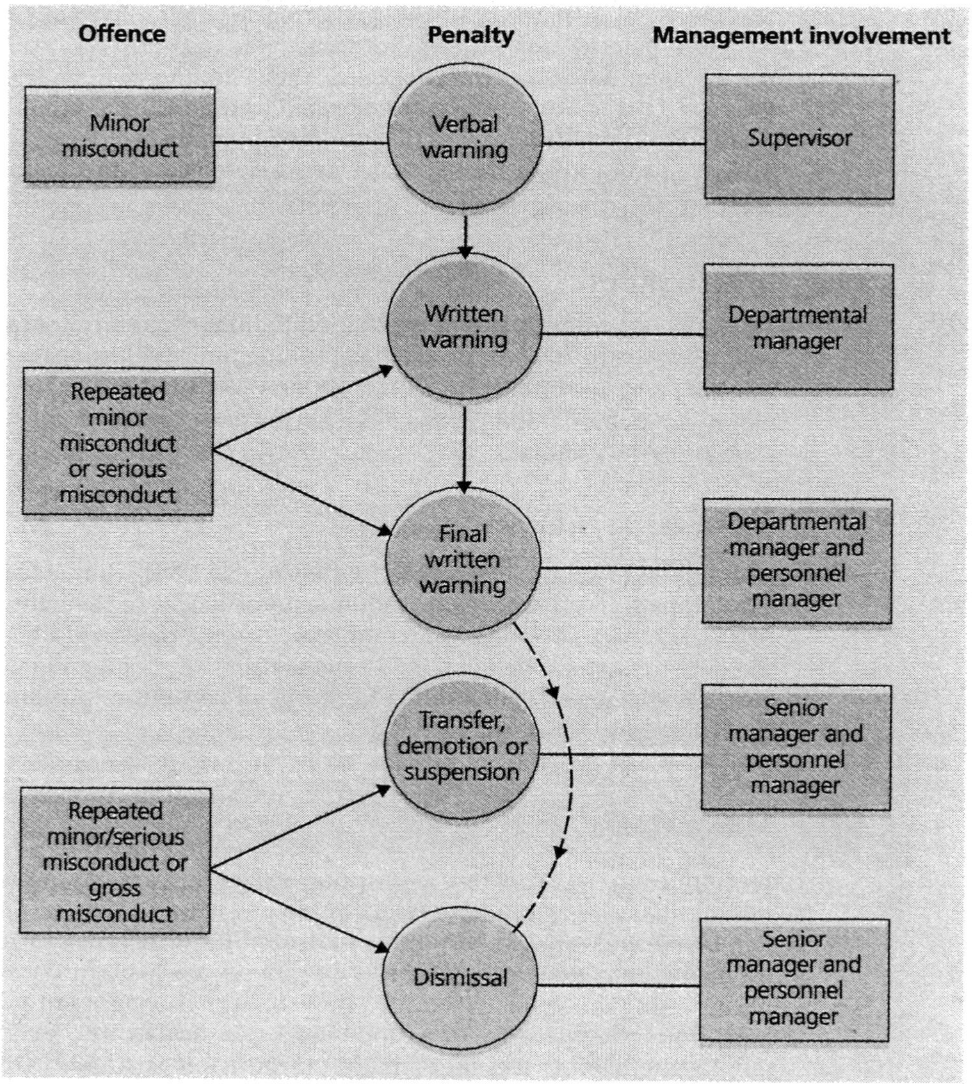

common in the business, and to the managers who must also perceive the system as equitable if they are to abide by its outcomes.

Procedures have a potential to be fair in that they are certain. The conduct of employee relations becomes less haphazard and irrational: people 'know where they stand'. The existence of a rule cannot be denied and opportunities for one party to manipulate and change a rule are reduced. Procedures also have the advantage that they can be communicated. The process of formalising a procedure that previously existed only in custom and practice clarifies the ambiguities and inconsistencies within it and compels each party to recognise the role and responsibility of the other. By providing pre-established avenues for responses to various contingencies procedures make it possible for the response to be less random and so more fair. The impersonal nature of procedures offers the possibility of removing hostility from the workplace, since an artificial social situation is created in which the ritual displays of aggression towards management are not seen as personal attacks on managers.

The achievement of equity may not match the potential. Procedures cannot, for instance, impart equity to situations that are basically unfair. Thus attempting to cope with an anomalous pay system through a grievance procedure may be alleviating symptoms rather than treating causes. It is also impossible through a grievance procedure to overcome accepted norms of inequity in a company, such as greater punctuality being required of manual employees than of white-collar employees.

A further feature of procedural equity is its degree of similarity to the judicial process. All procedures adopt certain legalistic mechanisms, like the right of individuals to be represented and to hear the case against them, but some aspects of legalism, such as burdens of proof and strict adherence to precedent, may cause the application of standard remedies rather than the consideration of individual circumstances.

There is a nice irony in the fact that equity is best achieved when procedures are not used. Procedure is there in the background and expresses principles for fair and effective management of situations. All the while the **principles** are followed and the framework for organisational justice observed, procedure is not invoked. The advantage of this is that individuals (whether employees or managers) are not named and shamed, so that matters are much easier to deal with. Only when the matter is dealt with badly does the procedural step come closer.

The existence of the procedure becomes the incentive rather than the means for action to be taken: it is not an excuse for inaction. In 1999 and 2000 there were several high profile cases of medical negligence resulting in doctors being struck off the medical register and therefore being no longer able to practise. In each case it appeared that lapses had been allowed to continue for too long before remedial action was taken.

It is accepted that some employment situations require naming and shaming first, with possible remedial action following. In most sports there is on-the-spot penalising of players for breaking the rules.

WINDOW ON PRACTICE	The 'red-hot stove' rule of discipline offers the touching of a red hot stove as an analogy for effective disciplinary action: 1 The burn is immediate. There is no question of cause and effect. 2 You had warning. If the stove was red-hot, you knew what would happen if you touched it. 3 The discipline is consistent. Everyone who touches the stove is burned. 4 The discipline is impersonal. People are burned not because of who they are, but because they touch the stove.

Activity 32.3	Think of an attempt at disciplinary action that went wrong. Which of the features of the red-hot stove rule were missing?

Notions of fairness are not 'givens' of the situation; they are socially constructed and there will never be more than a degree of consensus on what constitutes fairness. Despite this, the procedural approach can exploit standards of certainty and consistency, which are widely accepted as elements of justice. The extent to which a procedure can do this will depend on the suitability of its structure to local circumstances, the commitment of those who operate it and the way that it reconciles legalistic and bargaining elements.

Summary propositions

32.1 The authority of managers to exercise discipline in relation to others in the organisation is underpinned by a general predilection of people to obey commands from those holding higher rank in the hierarchy of which they are members.

32.2 The exercise of that discipline is limited by the procedural structures for grievance and discipline.

32.3 Grievance and discipline handling are two areas of human resource management that few other people want to take over, and provide personnel managers with some of their most significant contributions to business effectiveness.

32.4 Discipline can be understood as being managerial, team or self-discipline, and they are connected hierarchically.

32.5 Dissatisfaction, complaint and grievance is another hierarchy. Unresolved employee dissatisfaction can lead to the loss of potentially valuable employees. In extreme cases it can lead to industrial action.

32.6 Grievance and disciplinary processes both require a framework of organisational justice.

32.7 The procedural framework of disciplinary and grievance processes is one of the keys to their being equitable.

32.8 Effective management of both discipline and grievance is achieved by following the principles of the procedures without invoking them in practice.

References

Abrams, D., Wetherell, M., Cochrane, S., Hogg, M.A. and Turner, J.C. (1990) 'Knowing what to think by knowing who you are: Self categorization and norm formation', *British Journal of Social Psychology*, Vol. 29, pp. 97–119.

Asch, S.E. (1951) 'Effect of group pressure upon the modification and distortion of judgements', in H. Guetzkow (ed.), *Groups, Leadership and Men*. Pittsburgh, Penn.: Carnegie Press.

Department of Employment (1973) *In Working Order*. London: HMSO.

Gross, R. and McIlveen, R. (1998) *Psychology: A New Introduction*. London: Hodder & Stoughton.

Handy, C.B. (1999) *The New Alchemists*. London: Hutchinson.

Mathis, R.L. and Jackson, J.H. (1994) *Human Resource Management*, 7th edn. Minneapolis/St Paul: West.

Milgram, S. (1974) *Obedience to Authority*. London: Tavistock.

Milgram, S. (1992) *The Individual in a Social World*, 2nd edn. New York: Harper & Row.
Pigors, P. and Myers, C. (1977) *Personnel Administration*, 8th edn. Maidenhead: McGraw-Hill.

General discussion topics

1 Do you think Milgram's experiments would have had a different outcome if the subjects had included women as well as men?

2 What examples can individual members of the group cite of self-discipline, team discipline and managerial discipline?

3 'The trouble with grievance procedures is that they encourage people to waste a lot of time with petty grumbles. Life at work is rarely straightforward and people should just accept the rough with the smooth.'

What do you think of that opinion?

Chapter 16   Strategic aspects of performance

In our opening chapters we described the shift in emphasis away from the contract of employment towards the contract for performance. Even before the development of Taylor's Scientific Management methods a century ago, getting the most out of the workforce has always been a predominant management preoccupation, and the management literature is full of studies on the topic. Psychologists have studied motivation and leadership, ergonomists have dismantled and reconstructed every aspect of the physical environment in which people work, industrial relations specialists have pondered power relationships and reward, while sociologists discussed the design of organisations and their social structure, and operations experts have looked for ways to engineer process improvements.

In this chapter we review some major influences on our current thinking about performance. From this we explore in more detail some views on which human resource policies and practices result in high performance and then focus on understanding how this comes about. We shall conclude by briefly reviewing a range of popular strategic performance initiatives. The following three chapters look in more detail at organisational, individual and team performance.

A change in perspective: from employment to performance

The traditional human resource management approach to enhancing individual performance has centred on the assessment of past performance and the allocation of reward (Walker 1992). The secret was seen to lie in the interplay between individual skill or capacity and motivation. There has also been a pattern of thinking which set reward as separate from performance: rewards were provided in exchange for performance. This has been powerfully influenced by the industrial relations history, as trade unions have developed the process of collective bargaining and negotiation.

The prime purpose of trade unions has always been to improve the terms and working conditions of their members, although there may be other objectives in addition to this. With that objective, the union has only one thing to offer in exchange for improvements in terms and conditions, that is, some opportunity for improvement in productivity or performance. With the steadily increasing influence of unions in most industrial countries through most of the twentieth century, it was inevitable that performance improvement was something of direct interest only to management. Performance therefore became stereotyped as something of no intrinsic interest to the person doing the work.

The influence of trade unions has altered and collective bargaining does not dominate the management agenda as much as it used to. This is the most significant feature in the general change in attitudes about what we go to work for. Managements are gradually waking up to this fact and realising that there is now scope for integration in a way that was previously unrealistic. Not only is it possible to say, 'Performance is rewarded', one can now begin to say, 'Performance *is* a reward.' The long-standing motivational ideas of job enlargement, job enrichment, and so forth, become more cogent when those at work are able to look for the satisfaction of their needs not only in the job, but in their performance in it.

WINDOW ON PRACTICE

Mavis has worked in a retail store for eighteen years and has recently attended a training course in customer care.

'I always regarded the customer as some sort of enemy; we all did. In our coffee breaks we chatted away about the customer from hell, who was never satisfied, or who always put you down. Also I used to feel that I had to grin and bear it in trying to be nice to these enemies in order to earn commission.

Since the course I feel much more in control and have more self-respect. I really feel that most customers will respond positively if I approach them in the right way. It is my performance that largely affects how they behave. I actually enjoy what I am doing most of the time (and I never thought I'd say that!), because I can see myself doing a bit of good as well as selling more than I used to.'

Although it may seem like playing with words, this subtle shift of emphasis is fundamental to understanding the strategic approach to performance.

Influences on our understanding of performance

The Japanese influence

The success of Japanese companies and the decline of Western organisations has encouraged an exploration and adoption of Japanese management ideas and practices in order to improve performance. Thurley (1982) described the objectives of personnel policies in Japan as performance, motivation, flexibility and mobility. Delbridge and Turnbull (1992) described type 'J' organisations (based on Japanese thinking) as characterised by commitment, effort and company loyalty. A key theme in Japanese thinking appears to be people development and continuous improvement, or 'kaizen'.

Much of this thinking and the specific management techniques used in Japan, such as JIT (just in time), have been adopted into UK organisations, often in an uncritical way and without due regard for the cultural differences between the two nations. It is only where the initiatives are developed *and modified* for their location that they appear to succeed.

The American literature

Key writers from the American 'excellence' school, Peters and Waterman (1982), identified eight characteristics that they found to be associated with excellent companies – all American. These companies were chosen as excellent on the basis of their innovativeness and on a set of financial indicators, compared on an industry-wide basis. The characteristics they identified were:

- a bias for action – rather than an emphasis on bureaucracy or analysis;
- close to the customer – concern for customer wishes;
- autonomy and entrepreneurship – the company is split into small operational units where innovation and initiative are encouraged;
- productivity through people – employees are seen as the key resource, and the value of the employees' contribution is reinforced;
- hands-on, value-driven – strong corporate culture promoted from the top;
- stick to the knitting – pursuing the core business rather than becoming conglomerates;
- simple form, lean staff – simple organisation structure and small HQ staffing;
- simultaneous loose and tight properties – company values strongly emphasised, but within these considerable freedom and errors tolerated.

Peters and Waterman identified a shift from the importance of strategy and structural factors to style, systems, staff and skills (from the hard 's's to the soft 's's). In a follow-on book Peters and Austin (1985) identify four key factors related to excellence as concern for customers, innovation, attention to people and leadership.

Guest (1992) analyses why this excellence literature has had such an impact and identifies a range of methodological and analytical problems associated with the research, which question its validity. For example, he points out that no comparison was made with companies not considered to be excellent. We do not, therefore, know whether these principles were applied to a greater extent in excellent organisations. Hitt and Ireland (1987) go so far as to say that 'the data call into question whether these excellent principles are related to performance'. In addition, a number of the companies quoted have experienced severe problems since the research was carried out, and there remains the problem of the extent to which we can apply the results to UK organisations.

Whatever the reservations, the influence of the text on strategic thinking about performance remains profound. Even the use of the term 'excellence' means that there is a change of emphasis away from deadpan, objective terms like profitability, effectiveness, value-added and competitive advantage towards an idea that may trigger a feeling of enthusiasm and achievement. 'Try your best' becomes 'Go for it'.

More recently there has been considerable work in the USA that aims to identify HR practices which lead to high organisational performance, for example Huselid (1995) and Pfeffer (1998). The predominant method used to identify such relationships is quantitative analysis of large sets of statistical data. This type of approach is typical in research in the USA, but in the UK we tend to use a much greater mix of methods. However, the last few years have seen an increase in the use of quantitative methods in the UK, to attempt to establish the HR practices which are related to high performance, in other words to identify what are termed 'high performance work practices' in US terminology and 'high commitment work practices' in UK terminology.

HRM and the strategy literature

The HRM strategy literature provides different ways to understand the contribution of HR policies and practices to organisational performance. We noted in Chapter 3 that three distinct approaches to HR strategy can be identified. The universalist or best practice approach presupposes that certain HR policies and practices will always result in high performance, and the question is to identify exactly what these are. The contingency or fit approach suggests that different HR policies and practices will be needed to produce high performance in different firms depending on their business strategy and environment. However, it is usually considered possible to categorise different business strategies and environmental influences, and, on the basis of these, to identify the HR policies and practices that will result in high performance. Finally the resource-based view of the firm suggests that neither of these approaches is sufficient, but that every organisation and its employees should be considered as unique and that the set of HR policies and practices that will result in high performance will also be unique to that firm. From this perspective no formula can be applied, and the way that people processes contribute to organisational performance can only be understood within the context of the particular firm. These three perspectives have resulted in different investigational approaches to understanding the impact of people management on organisational performance, as will become clear in the following section.

Do people-management processes contribute to high performance?

The investigations to date have had a dual purpose, the first being to seek to establish a link between people-management practices and organisational performance. In other words, does the way that people are managed affect the bottom line? The second one follows logically from this, and is: 'If the answer to the first question is yes, then which particular policies and practices result in high performance?' Both these questions are usually investigated in parallel. A variety of different definitions of performance have been used in these studies. These range from bottom line financial performance (profitability), through productivity measures, to measurement of outcomes such as wastage, quality and labour turnover (which are sometimes referred to as internal performance outcomes). Sometimes the respondent's view of performance is used, on the basis that bottom line figures can be influenced by management accounting procedures. The studies have generally used large datasets and complex statistical analysis to determine relationships.

Much of the research has been carried out from the assumption of the universalist, or best practice approach to HR strategy. Reviewing the academic literature Richardson and Thompson (1999) come to the conclusion that the evidence indicates a positive relationship between innovative and sophisticated people-management practices and better business performance. Some researchers argue that the performance effects of HR policies and practices are multiplicative rather than additive, and this is often termed the 'bundles' approach (see, for example, MacDuffie 1995). In other words, a particular set of mutually reinforcing practices is likely to have more impact on performance than applying one or just some of these in isolation. Pfeffer (1998), for example, identifies seven critical people-management policies: emphasising employment security; recruiting the 'right' people; extensive use of self-managed teams and decentralisation; high wages solidly linked to organisational performance; high spending on training; reducing status differentials; and sharing information; and he suggests that these policies will benefit *every* organisation. In the UK the Sheffield Enterprise Programme (Patterson *et al.* 1997) has studied 100 manufacturing organisations over 10 years (1991–2001) and has used statistical techniques to identify which factors affect profitability and productivity. It has been reported that aspects of culture, supervisory support, concern for employee welfare, employee responsibility, training, job satisfaction and organisational commitment were all important variables in relation to organisational performance. It is worth noting that here variables associated with employee attitudes are included, that is, job satisfaction and commitment, in addition to the variables which comprise policies or practices. We will consider this mix in the following section. Also in the UK, Wood and de Menezes (1998) identify a bundle of HR practices which they term high-commitment management, and these comprise recruitment and selection processes geared to selecting flexible and highly committed individuals; processes which reward commitment and training by promotion and job security; and the use of direct communication and teamwork.

This avenue of work has a very optimistic flavour, suggesting that not only are people-management practices related to high organisational performance, but that we can identify the innovative and sophisticated practices that will work best in combination. On a practical level there are problems because different researchers identify different practices or 'bundles' associated with high performance (see, for example, Becker and Gerhard 1996). There have been many criticisms of this approach, partly based on the methods used – which involve, for example, the view of a single respondent as to which practices are in place, with no account taken of how the practices are implemented. A further problem is causality. It could be that profitable firms use best practice people-management methods, because they can afford to since they are profitable, rather than that such methods lead to profitability. A further issue concerns the conflict between different aspects of the bundle, along the lines of Legge's (1989) criticism of Guest's model of strategic HRM. Such contradictions are, for example, between individualism and teamwork and between a strong culture and adaptability. These contradictions can also be seen in some of the performance variables and strategic performance initiatives discussed below. Lastly, this approach ignores the business strategy of the organisation. Guest (2000) and particularly Purcell (1999) provide detailed expositions of the problems with this approach. While they recognise the value of the work they also see it as limited.

MacDuffie (1995) suggests that the best bundle is dependent on the logic of the organisation, and other researchers such as Wright and Snell (1998), have pursued the link between HR and organisational performance from the contingency, or fit, perspective. While this approach does bring the integration with business strategy to the fore, it fails to provide a more useful way forward. Attempting to model all the different factors that influence the appropriate set of HR policies and practices that lead to high performance is an extremely complex, if not impossible task. In addition to this Purcell *et al.* (2000) argue that the speed of change poses a real problem for the fit approach, and Purcell (1999) suggests that a more useful approach is to focus on the resource-based view of the firm, which is the third perspective on HR strategy that we considered in Chapter 3.

Becker and Gerhart suggest that it is more likely to be the architecture of the system, not just a group of HR practices, that results in high performance, and Purcell suggests that it is how practices are implemented and change is managed that makes the difference. The resource-based view would indicate that competencies in the implementation and management of change could form part of the basis of sustained competitive advantage. Hutchinson *et al.* (2000) term this 'idiosyncratic fit'. Part of the CIPD's major research project on investigating the link of HR to performance will involve longitudinal case studies that may shed some light on this issue.

How do HR policies and practices affect performance?

On the basis that we have sufficient evidence to claim that HR policies and practices do affect company performance (although it should be noted that some studies do not support this, for example Lahteenmaki and Storey 1998), we need to understand better the processes which link these HR practices to business performance. As Purcell *et al.* (2000) point out, 'what remains unclear is what is actually happening in successful organisations to make this connection' (p. 30). The results from one part of the CIPD study, referred to above, should help us understand how, why and where certain HR policies and practices result in high performance. Currently our interpretation focuses on the central importance of commitment in mediating the impact of HR policies and practices on business performance, and we shall consider this in more detail.

Commitment

Historically, some writers have identified commitment as resulting in higher performance. Commitment has been described as:

■ **Attitudinal commitment** – that is, loyalty and support for the organisation, strength of identification with the organisation (Porter 1985), a belief in its values and goals and a readiness to put in effort for the organisation.
■ **Behavioural commitment** – actually remaining with the company and continuing to pursue its objectives.

Walton (1985) notes that commitment is **thought** to result in better quality, lower turnover, a greater capacity for innovation and more flexible employees. In turn these are seen to enhance the ability of the organisation to achieve competitive advantage. Iles, Mabey and Robertson (1990) add that some of the outcomes of commitment have been identified as the industrial relations climate, absence levels, turnover levels and individual performance. Pfeffer (1998) and Wood and Albanese (1995) argue that commitment is a core variable, and Guest (1998, p. 42) suggests that:

> The concept of organizational commitment lies at the heart of any analysis of HRM. Indeed the whole rationale for introducing HRM policies is to increase levels of commitment so that other positive outcomes can ensue.

Hence we see the adoption of the terms 'high commitment work practices' and 'high commitment management' and their linkage with high performance. Meyer and Allen (1997) argue that there is not a great deal of **evidence** to link high commitment and high levels of organisational performance. Guest (2000) reports analyses of the Workplace Employment Relations Survey (WERS) data and the Future of Work Survey data to show some support for the model that HR practices have an impact on employee attitudes and satisfaction, which in turn

Figure 16.1 A simple model of HRM and performance

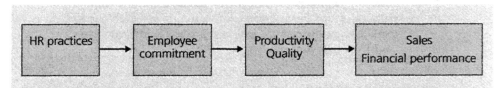

Source: D. Guest (2000) 'Human resource management, employee well-being and organizational performance'. Paper presented to the CIPD Professional Standards Conference, 11 July. Reproduced with the permission of the author.

has an impact on internal performance outcomes. He is, however, cautious about identifying causal links.

In this context Guest uses commitment as shorthand for employee attitudes and values, as shown in his model in Figure 16.1.

Some authors, however, have argued that high commitment could indeed reduce organisational performance. Cooper and Hartley (1991) suggest that commitment might decrease flexibility and inhibit creative problem solving. If commitment reduces staff turnover, this may result in fewer new ideas coming into the organisation. Staff who would like to leave the organisation but who are committed to it in other ways, for example through high pay and benefits, may stay, but may not produce high levels of performance.

As well as the debate on the value of commitment to organisational performance, there is also the debate on the extent to which commitment can be managed, and how it can be managed. Guest (1992) suggests that commitment is affected by:

■ personal characteristics;

WINDOW ON PRACTICE

Rebecca Johnson (1999) reports on performance initiatives at the Holiday Inn, Mayfair. Through a 'back to the floor' experience senior managers realised that front line staff did not have sufficient authority and autonomy to solve routine customer problems and that this was having an adverse impact on customer perceptions. A range of initiatives were thus implemented:

■ training to equip front line staff to take greater responsibility in solving customer problems;
■ new recruitment and selection strategies to help identify potential employees who are 'focused on going the extra mile', rather than those who have technical skills, which can be learned on appointment. Processes include 'auditions' to identify favourable attitudes;
■ demonstrating a genuine commitment to employees. Initiatives included attitude surveys, continued IIP recognition, a training resource centre and a network of mentors and 'buddies';
■ encouraging a sense of fun and openness;
■ a performance appraisal system which is also geared towards career development, and internal promotions where possible;
■ measuring customer feedback through a 'guest tracking system'.

Johnson reports that all these policies are paying off as profits have been increasing steadily for the last five years. She also reports the views of a recently appointed corporate sales executive who claims to have joined the organisation, partly because of the training programme, and who noted that 'the commitment is very strong'.

Source: Adapted from a case study by R. Johnson (1999) 'Case 2: Holiday Inn Mayfair', in A. Baron and R. Collard 'Realising our assets', *People Management*, 14 October.

■ experiences in job role;
■ work experiences;
■ structural factors; and
■ personnel policies.

Morris, Lydka and O'Creevy (1992/3) also identify that personnel policies have an effect on commitment. In particular they found career prospects as the most important factor in their research on graduates. This brings us to the link between commitment and the psychological contract and the role that trust and job security have on the experience of commitment.

One of the difficulties with the concept of commitment, as Singh and Vinnicombe (1998) suggest, is whether it is defined in the same way by employees and the organisation, and whether or not our general understanding of the term needs to be reviewed in the light of a different organisational environment which rarely allows for organisations to invest in the long-term careers of employees. They use a definition of commitment in their article which encompasses commitment, not only to the organisation, but to one's career.

Lastly, it is important to consider whether using commitment as a shorthand for attitudes and satisfaction is sufficient, and whether there are other important dimensions which may be lost, by focusing on commitment alone.

Major performance initiatives

We have previously considered some HR policies and practices that have been identified as related to high performance, and have noted the idea of using practices in bundles. Many of the popular performance initiatives that companies have adopted represent similar (but not the same) bundles of HR policies and practices, and we now turn to these. There are many small initiatives every day that help to improve performance, but we are concentrating here on major strategic initiatives, 'big ideas', as described by Connock (1992). A big idea with the same label may, of course, mean different things in practice in different organisatons. Mueller and Purcell (1992, p. 28) reach the heart of the issue when they say:

> It is the integration of change initiatives with other aspects of organisational life which is the key to success. It is very rare for a single initiative, however well designed to generate significant or lasting benefit.

Moving to a performance culture is an all-or-nothing change in the way the business is run. This brings us to the concern that too many initiatives in the same organisation will give conflicting messages to employees, particularly when they are introduced by different parts of the business. There may, for example, be contradictions between the messages of Total Quality Management (TQM) and those of the learning organisation type of approach. We will explore these further in Chapter 17.

Table 16.1 lists some of the major performance initiatives. They are divided according to their primary focus: organisational, individual or team. Some of them partly cover the same ground, and it would be surprising to find them in the same business at the same time.

Table 16.1 Some major performance initiatives

Organisational focus	Learning organisation
	Investors in people
	Total quality management (TQM)
	Performance culture
	Lean production
	Business Process Reengineering
	Just in Time (JIT)
	Standards: BS5750
	ISO9000
	Customer care/orientation
Individual focus	Performance management
	Performance-related pay
	Self-development/continuous development
Team focus	High-performance teams
	Cross-functional teams
	Self-regulating teams

Activity 16.1

1 Identify the main performance initiatives in your organisation.

2 What/who is the source of each initiative?

3 In what ways do they mutually support each other, and in what ways do they conflict?

Things that go wrong

The level of satisfaction with performance initiatives is typically low (Jacobs 1993; Antonioni 1994), so we close this chapter with a summary of the problems most often reported.

The process/people balance

Schemes rarely strike the right balance between a people emphasis and a process emphasis. Concentrating on being brilliant at talking to the people, getting them going and talking them down gently if they don't quite make it will not suffice if there is not a clear, disciplined process that brings in the essential features of consistency and defining sensible goals. Getting the goals and measures right is a waste of time if there is not the necessary input to changing attitudes, developing skills and winning consent.

Getting the measures right

On the basis of what gets measured gets done, it is critical that the organisation selects the most useful measure of performance for the organisaton as a whole and for the individuals within it. Single measures are unlikely to be sufficiently robust. Kaplan and Norton (1992) argue convincingly that the mix of measures which an organisation should use to assess its performance should be based around four different perspectives:

- **Financial measures** – such as sales growth, profits, cash flow and increased market share.
- **Customer measures** – that is, the customer perspective, which looks at, for example, delivery time, service quality, product quality.
- **Internal business measures** – cycle time, productivity, employee skills, labour turnover.
- **Innovation and learning perspective** – including such elements as ability to innovate and improve.

The focus must be on what is achieved: results are what count. At an individual level a focus on behaviour rather than results achieved can be unhelpful, leading to personality clashes, and misleading. Doing things in the right way is no substitute for doing the right things.

Management losing interest

A constant axiom with any initiative is the need for endorsement from senior management. With a performance initiative there is the need to go a great deal further. First, senior managers have to accept that the initiative is something in which they have to participate continuously and thoroughly. They cannot introduce it, say how important it is and then go off to find other games to play:

> studies have shown that in organisations that utilise performance management, 90 per cent of senior managers have not received performance reviews in the last two years. Clearly the problem here is that PM is not used, modelled and visibly supported at the top of the organisation. Sooner or later people at lower levels catch on and no longer feel compelled to take the time to make PM work.
>
> (Sparrow and Hiltrop 1994, p. 565)

The second aspect is indicated in that quotation. Performance initiatives will not work unless people at all levels either believe in them or are prepared to give them a try with the hope that they will be convinced by the practice.

The team/individual balance

Individuals can rarely perform entirely on their own merits; they are part of a department or team of people whose activities interact in innumerable ways. Trevor Macdonald may read the television news with a clarity and sureness that is outstanding, but it would be of little value if the lights did not work or the script contained errors. Most working people, no matter how eminent, are not solo performers to that extent. Somehow the performance initiative has to stimulate both individual and team performance, working together within the envelope of organisational objectives.

> Historically the individual has been the basis of performance management strategies. However, this may be problematic in that performance variation tends to be falsely attributed to individuals, and the enhancement of individual performance does not necessarily coincide with the enhancement of the greater unit or work system. (Waldman 1994, p. 41)

Activity 16.2 Think of situations in your own experience outside working life, where there has been a potential clash between individual performance and team performance. Examples might be:

(a) the opening batsman more concerned with his batting average than with the team winning the match;

(b) the person playing the lead in the amateur operatic society's production of *The Merry Widow* who ignores the chorus; or

(c) the local councillor more concerned with doing what is needed to earn an MBE than with supporting the collective view of the council.

How was the potential clash avoided, or not? How could it have been managed more effectively to harmonise individual and team performance?

Leaving out the development part

A key feature of managing performance is developing people so that they *can* perform. This is the feature that is most often not delivered. It is often the lack of follow-up on development needs that is the least satisfactory aspect of performance management systems.

Implementing and managing the change

If, as Purcell (1999) identifies, 'our concern should be less about the precise policy mix in the 'bundle' and more about how and when organisations manage the HR side of change', then the way that large and small performance initiatives are implemented and managed is critical. While this is well-trodden ground, there is considerable evidence of attempted changes which have failed for a wide range of reasons including: trust is low; change is seen as a management fad which will go away; change has been poorly communicated and understood; change is just a way to get us to work harder for the same money.

Getting it right

Here are four suggestions for running a successful performance initiative:

1 Develop and promulgate a clear vision for the business as a framework for individual/team goals and targets.

2 In consultation, develop and agree individual goals and targets with three characteristics: (a) what to do to achieve the target; (b) how to satisfy the customer rather than pleasing the boss; (c) targets that are precise, difficult and challenging, but attainable, *with feedback*.

3 Do not begin until you are sure of: (a) unwavering commitment from the top; (b) an approach that is driven by the line and bought into and owned by middle and first-line managers; (c) a system that is run, monitored and updated by HR specialists; (d) an agreement that every development commitment or pay commitment is honoured, or a swift, full explanation is given of why not.

4 Train all participants.

Summary propositions

16.1 Central to understanding management interest in performance is understanding the subtle change in attitudes: not only is performance rewarded, performance is also a reward.

16.2 In the UK our views of performance improvement have been influenced by the US literature, the Japanese experience and the HRM strategy literature.

16.3 There has been considerable research effort devoted to investigating the link between a bundle of people management practices and organisational performance, and some would argue that the link has been successfully demonstrated.

16.4 Much less clear are the processes by which the link is made, for example how, why and in what context? So far we see commitment as the moderating variable between HR practices and organisational performance.

16.5 Things that typically go wrong with performance initiatives are getting the people/process balance wrong, not selecting the right performance measures, management losing interest and getting the team/individual balance wrong.

16.6 Factors likely to produce success relate to a clear, understood vision, effective target setting, full management commitment, training and honouring commitments.

References

Antonioni, D. (1994) 'Improve the performance management process before discontinuing performance appraisals', *Compensation and Benefits Review*, Vol. 26, No. 2, pp. 29–37.

Becker, B. and Gerhard, B. (1996) 'The impact of human resource management on organizational progress and prospects', *Academy of Management Journal*, Vol. 39, No. 4, pp. 779–801.

Connock, S. (1992) 'The importance of big ideas to HR managers', *Personnel Managers*, June.

Cooper, J. and Hartley, J. (1991) 'Reconsidering the case for organisational commitment', *Human Resource Management Journal*, Vol. 3, Spring, pp. 18–32.

Delbridge, R. and Turnbull, P. (1992) 'Human resource maximisation: The management of labour under just-in-time manufacturing systems', in P. Blyton and P. Turnbull (eds), *Reassessing Human Resource Management*. Beverly Hills: Sage.

Guest, D. (1992) 'Right enough to be dangerously wrong; an analysis of the "In search of excellence" phenomenon', in G. Salaman *et al.* (eds), *Human Resource Strategies*. London: Sage.

Guest, D. (1998) 'Beyond HRM: Commitment and the contract culture', in P. Sparrow and M. Marchington (eds), *Human Resource Management: The New Agenda*. London: Financial Times Pitman Publishing.

Guest, D. (2000) 'Human Resource Management, employee well-being and organizational performance'. Paper presented at the CIPD Professional Standards Conference, 11 July.

Hitt, M. and Ireland, D. (1987) 'Peters and Waterman revisited; the unending quest for excellence', *Academy of Management Executive*, Vol. 1, No. 2, pp. 91–8.

Huselid, M. (1995) 'The impact of human resource management practices on turnover, productivity and corporate financial performance', *Academy of Management Journal*, Vol. 38, No. 3, pp. 635–73.

Hutchinson, S., Purcell, J. and Kinnie, N. (2000) 'Evolving high commitment management and the experience of the RAC call center', *Human Resource Management Journal*, Vol. 10, No. 1, pp. 63–78.

Iles, P., Mabey, C. and Robertson, I. (1990) 'Human resource management practices and employee commitment. Possibilities, pitfalls and paradoxes', *British Journal of Management*, Vol. 1, pp. 147–57.

Jacobs, H. (1993) 'The ratings game', *Small Business Reports*, Vol. 18, No. 10, pp. 21–2.

Johnson, R. (1999) 'Case 2: Holiday Inn Mayfair', in A. Baron and R. Collard, 'Realising our assets', *People Management*, 14 October.

Kaplan, R. and Norton, D. (1992) 'The balanced scorecard – measures that drive performance', *Harvard Business Review*, Jan.–Feb., pp. 71–9.

Lahteenmaki, S. and Storey, J. (1998) 'HRM and company performance: the use of measurement and the influence of economic cycles', *Human Resource Management Journal*, Vol. 8, No. 2, pp. 51–65.

Legge, K. (1989) 'Human resource management – a critical analysis', in J. Storey (ed.), *New Perspectives in Human Resource Management*. London: Routledge.

MacDuffie, J. (1995) 'Human resource bundles and manufacturing performance: organizational logic and flexible production systems in the world auto industry', *Industrial and Labor Relations Review*, Vol. 48, No. 2, pp. 197–221.

Meyer, J. and Allen, N. (1997) *Commitment in the workplace: theory, research and application*. London: Sage.

Morris, T., Lydka, H. and O'Creevy, M.F. (1992/3) 'A longitudinal analysis of employee commitment and human resource policies', *Human Resource Management Journal*, Vol. 3, pp. 21–38.

Mueller, F. and Purcell, J. (1992) 'The drive for higher productivity', *Personnel Management*, Vol. 24, No. 5, pp. 28–33.

Patterson, J., West, M., Lawthom, R. and Nickell, S. (1997) *The Impact of People Management Practices on Business Performance*. London: IPD.

Peters, T. and Austin, N. (1985) *A Passion for Excellence*. New York: Harper and Row.

Peters, T. and Waterman, R. (1982) *In Search of Excellence*. New York: Harper and Row.

Pfeffer, J. (1998) *The Human Equation*. Boston: Harvard Business School Press.

Plachy, R. and Plachy, S. (1993) 'Focus on results, not behaviour', *Personnel Journal*, Vol. 72, No. 3, pp. 28–33.

Porter, M. (1985) *Competitive Advantage*. New York: Free Press.

Purcell, J. (1999) 'Best practice and best fit: chimera or cul-de-sac?', *Human Resource Management Journal*, Vol. 9, No. 3, pp. 26–41.

Purcell, J., Kinnie, N., Hutchinson, S. and Rayton, B. (2000) 'Inside the box', *People Management*, 26 October.

Richardson, R. and Thompson, M. (1999) *The Impact of People Management Practices – A Review of the Literature*. London: IPD.

Singh, V. and Vinnicombe, S. (1998) 'What does commitment really mean? Views of UK and Swedish Engineering Managers', *Personnel Review*, Vol. 29, No. 2, pp. 228–54.

Sparrow, P. and Hiltrop, J.-M. (1994) *European Human Resource Management in Transition*. London: Prentice Hall.

Thurley, K. (1982) 'The Japanese model: practical reservations and surprising opportunities', *Personnel Management*, February.

Waldman, D. (1994) 'Designing performance management systems for total quality implementation', *Journal of Organisational Change Management*, Vol. 7, No. 2, pp. 31–44.

Walker, K.W. (1992) *Human Resource Strategy*. New York: McGraw-Hill.

Walton, R.E. (1985) 'From control to commitment in the workplace', *Harvard Business Review*, March/April, pp. 77–84.

Wood, S. and Albanese, M. (1995) 'Can we speak of high commitment management on the shop floor?', *Journal of Management Studies*, Vol. 32, No. 2, pp. 215–47.

Wood, S. and de Menezes, L. (1998) 'High commitment management in the UK: evidence from the Workplace Industrial Relations Survey and employers' manpower and skills practices survey', *Human Relations*, Vol. 51, No. 4, pp. 485–515.

Wright, P. and Snell, S. (1998) 'Towards a unifying framework for exploring fit and flexibility in strategic human resource management', *Academy of Management Review*, Vol. 23, No. 4, pp. 756–72.

General discussion topics

1 To what extent can the American excellence literature be applied in a UK setting?

2 Can commitment, empowerment and job flexibility be pursued together? If yes, how can this be achieved? If no, why not – what are the alternatives?

Chapter 18 Managing individual performance

The treatment of individual performance in organisations has traditionally centred on the assessment of performance and the allocation of reward. Walker (1992) notes that this is partly due to these processes being institutionalised through the use of specific systems and procedures. Performance was typically seen as the result of the interaction between individual ability and motivation.

Increasingly, organisations recognise that planning and enabling performance have a critical effect on individual performance. So, for example, clarity of performance goals and standards, appropriate resources, guidance and support from the individual's manager all become central.

In this chapter we start with the fundamental steps for managing individual performance, review performance appraisal systems, discuss the nature and use of 360-degree feedback, and then explore how performance management systems attempt to integrate both enabling and assessing individual performance.

The performance cycle

The performance cycle identifies three key aspects of effective performance, as shown in Figure 18.1. These aspects can be used as stepping stones in managing employee performance.

Planning performance

Planning performance recognises the importance of a shared view of expected performance between manager and employee. The shared view can be expressed in a variety of ways, such as a traditional job description, key accountabilities, performance standards, specific objectives or targets and essential competencies.

In most cases a combination of approaches is necessary. There is a very clear trend to use specific objectives with a timescale for completion in addition to the generic tasks, with no beginning and no end, which tend to appear on traditional job descriptions. Such objectives give individuals a much clearer idea of performance expectations and enable them to focus on the priorities when they have to make choices about what they do. There is a long history of research demonstrating how clarity of goals improves employee performance.

The critical point about a *shared* view of performance suggests that handing out a job description or list of objectives to the employee is not adequate. Performance expectations need to be understood and, where possible, to involve a contribution from the employee. For example, although key accountabilities may be fixed by the manager, they will need to be discussed. Specific

Activity 18.1	Do managers actively support employee performance in your organisation? If they do, by what means do they do this and how effective is it? If they do not, why not, and what is the impact of this?

or

Think of any organisation in which you have had some involvement:

■ How has individual performance been supported?

■ How effective was/is this?

■ How would you improve the way in which performance was/is supported?

Ongoing review

Ongoing review is an important activity for employees to carry out in order to plan their work and priorities and also to highlight to the manager well in advance if the agreed performance will not be delivered by the agreed dates. Joint employee/manager review is essential so that information is shared. For example, a manager needs to be kept up to date on employee progress, while the employee needs to be kept up to date on organisational changes that have an impact on the agreed objectives. Both need to share perceptions of how the other is doing in their role, and what they could do that would be more helpful.

These reviews are normally informal in nature, although a few notes may be taken of progress made and actions agreed. They need not be part of any formal system and therefore can take place when the job or the individuals involved demand, and not according to a pre-set schedule. The purpose of the review is to facilitate future employee performance, and provide an opportunity for the manager to confirm that the employee is 'on the right track', or redirect him or her if necessary. They thus provide a forum for employee reward in terms of recognition of progress. A 'well done' or an objective signed off as completed can enhance the motivation to perform well in the future.

Using the performance cycle

The performance cycle describes effective day-to-day management of performance. As such it was often used as the reason why no formal appraisal system was in place – 'because performance is appraised informally on a continuous basis'. In reality performance was usually managed on a *dis*continuous basis, with very little action unless there was a performance problem which needed sorting out! Even then the problem was often avoided until it had become so severe that someone would begin to talk of disciplinary procedures.

The performance cycle, as we have described above, is intended to be viewed as a positive management tool to enhance employee performance and to support whatever formal appraisal or performance management system is in place.

Appraisal systems

Appraisal systems formalise the review part of the performance cycle. They are typically designed on a central basis, usually by the HR function, and require that each line manager appraise the performance of their staff on an annual, six-monthly or even quarterly basis. Elaborate forms are often designed to be completed as a formal record of the process.

Appraisal has traditionally been seen as most applicable to those in management and supervisory positions, but increasingly clerical and secretarial staff are being included in the process. Manual staff, particularly those who are skilled or have technical duties, are also subject to appraisal, although to a lesser extent than the other groups. Long (1986) noted that there has been a substantial increase in performance reviews for non-managerial staff. It has been argued that this increase reflects the increase in individual discretion and autonomy amongst employees which makes direct monitoring more difficult (Townley 1993). Some organisations have a flexible approach whereby individuals in certain grades – for example, secretarial and clerical – can elect whether or not to be included in the appraisal system. Other organisations allow those over a certain age to opt out of the system if they so wish.

Why have an appraisal system?

The different purposes of appraisal systems frequently conflict. Appraisal can be used to improve current performance, provide feedback, increase motivation, identify training needs, identify potential, let individuals know what is expected of them, focus on career development, award salary increases and solve job problems. It can be used to set out job objectives, provide information for human resource planning and career succession, assess the effectiveness of the selection process, and as a reward or punishment in itself. Fletcher and Williams (1985) have suggested two conflicting roles of judge and helper, which the appraiser may be called upon to play, depending on the purpose of the appraisal process. If a single appraisal system was intended to improve current performance and to act as the basis for salary awards, the appraiser would be called on to play both judge and helper at the same time. This makes it difficult for the appraiser to be impartial. It is also difficult for the appraisee, who may wish to discuss job-related problems, but is very cautious about what she or he says because of not wanting to jeopardise a possible pay rise. Randell *et al.* (1984) suggest that the uses of appraisal can be divided into three broad categories, and that an appraisal system should attempt to satisfy only one of these. The categories they suggest are reward reviews, potential reviews and performance reviews. This implies that HR managers need to think more carefully about the primary purpose of their appraisal system, and make sure that procedures, training and individual expectations of the system do not conflict.

Given that there is a choice about the way the appraisal system will be used, Randell *et al.* believe that the greatest advantages will be gained by the use of performance reviews. Such reviews include appraisal of past performance, meeting objectives, identification of training needs, problems preventing better performance, and so on. This poses a great problem, particularly for the private sector, but increasingly in the public sector, where there is a predilection to link pay directly to performance. Do these organisations settle just for reward reviews and forgo the advantages of performance reviews? Do they have two different appraisal systems – one for reward and one for performance at two distinctly different times of the year? Do they forget about linking performance and pay? These are key questions in relation to performance management systems, and are discussed later in this chapter.

Activity 18.2	What are the key purposes of performance appraisal in your organisation, or any organisation with which you are familiar?
	What conflicts does this create?
	How might these conflicts be resolved?

What is appraised?

Appraisal systems can measure a variety of things. They are sometimes designed to measure personality, sometimes behaviour or performance, and sometimes achievement of goals. These areas may be measured either quantitively or qualitatively. Qualitative appraisal often involves the writing of an unstructured narrative on the general performance of the appraisee. Alternatively, some guidance may be given as to the areas on which the appraiser should comment. The problem with qualitative appraisals is that they may leave important areas unappraised, and that they are not suitable for comparison purposes. Coates (1994) argues that what is actually measured in performance appraisal is the extent to which the individual conforms to the organisation.

When the areas for appraisal are measured quantitively some form of scale is used, often comprising five categories of measurement from 'excellent', or 'always exceeds requirements' at one end to 'inadequate' at the other, with the mid-point being seen as acceptable. Scales are, however, not always constructed according to this plan. Sometimes on a five-point scale there will be four degrees of acceptable behaviour and only one that is unacceptable. Sometimes an even-numbered (usually six-point) scale is used to prevent the central tendency. There is a tendency for raters to settle on the mid-point of the scale, either through lack of knowledge of the appraisee, lack of ability to discriminate, lack of confidence or through a desire not to be too hard on appraisees. Rating other people is not an easy task, but it can be structured so that it is made as objective as possible. If performance appraisal is related to pay, then some form of final scale is normally used. A typical approach is for there to be forced distributions on this scale – so, for example, only a specified proportion of staff fall into the highest, middle and lowest categories.

Avoidance of personality measures

Much traditional appraisal was based on measures of personality traits that were felt to be important to the job. These included traits such as resourcefulness, enthusiasm, drive, application and other traits such as intelligence. One difficulty with these is that everyone defines them differently, and the traits that are used are not always mutually exclusive. Raters, therefore, are often unsure of what they are rating. Ill-defined scales like these are more susceptible to bias and prejudice. Another problem is that since the same scales are often used for many different jobs, traits that are irrelevant to an appraisee's job may still be measured. One helpful approach is to concentrate on the job rather than the person. In an attempt to do this some organisations call their annual appraisal activity the 'job appraisal review'. The requirements of the job and the way that it is performed are considered, and the interview concentrates on problems in job performance which are recognised as not always being the 'fault' of the person performing the job. Difficulties in performance may be due to departmental structure or the equipment being used, rather than the ability or motivation of the employee. Other approaches concentrate on linking ratings to behaviour and performance on the job.

Behaviourally anchored rating scales

One way of linking ratings with behaviour at work is to use behaviourally anchored rating scales (BARS). These can be produced in a large organisation by asking a sample group of raters independently to suggest examples of behaviour for each point on the scale in order to collect a wide variety of behavioural examples. These examples are then collated and returned to the sample raters without any indication of the scale point for which they were suggested. Sample raters allocate a scale point to each example, and those examples that are consistently located at the same point on the scale are selected to be used as behavioural examples for that point on the scale. Future raters then have some guidance as to the type of behaviour that would be expected at each point. BARS can be used in conjunction with personality scales, but are most helpful when used with scales that relate more clearly to work behaviour. Table 18.1 shows an example of a BARS in relation to 'relations with clients' – for the sake of clarity just one behavioural example is given at each point on the scale, whereas in a fully developed scale there may be several at each point. Another advantage of the development of BARS is that appraisers have been involved in the process and this can increase their commitment to the outcome.

Behavioural observation scales

Behavioural observation scales (BOS) provide an alternative way of linking behaviour and ratings. Fletcher and Williams (1985) comment that these scales are developed by lengthy procedures, and are similar in some ways to BARS. They indicate a number of dimensions of performance with behavioural statements for

Table 18.1 An example of a behaviourally anchored rating scale: relations with clients

Behavioural example	Points of the rating scale
Often makes telephone calls on behalf of the client to find the correct office for him/her to go to even though this is not part of the job	A
Will often spend an hour with a client in order to get to the root of a very complex problem	B
Usually remains calm when dealing with an irate client	C
If the answer to the client's problem is not immediately to hand s/he often tells them s/he has not got the information	D
Sometimes ignores clients waiting at the reception desk for up to 10 minutes even when s/he is not busy with other work	E
Regularly keeps clients waiting for 10 minutes or more and responds to their questions with comments such as 'I can't be expected to know that' and 'You're not in the right place for that'	F

each. They give the example of leadership/staff supervision as a dimension of performance, and then flesh this out with five or six behavioural statements, such as 'praises staff for doing things well' and 'passes important information to subordinates'. A five-point scale ranging from 'almost never' to 'almost always' is provided so that the appraiser can rate the extent to which each behaviour is displayed.

Meeting objectives

Another method of making appraisal more objective is to use the process to set job objectives over the coming year and, a year later, to measure the extent to which these objectives have been met. The extent to which the appraisee is involved in setting these objectives varies considerably. One of the biggest problems with appraisal on the basis of meeting objectives is that factors beyond the employee's control may make the objectives more difficult than anticipated, or even impossible. We discuss other problems with the 'meeting objectives' approach in the last section of this chapter, on performance management systems, as the process of implementing performance management invariably involves setting and meeting objectives.

Performance against job description

Some systems require the manager to appraise performance against each task specified in the job description or against each key accountability. The appraisal in this case may be in the form of narrative statements and/or a performance rating.

Performance against job competencies

When a competency profile has been identified for a particular job, it is then possible to use this in the appraisal of performance. Many appraisal systems combine competency assessment with assessment against objectives or job accountabilities.

Surveillance of actual performance

Performance appraisal need not only be centred on opinions and reactions reported back by an appraisal interview, as there are increasing opportunities for collecting primary data via various forms of electronic surveillance system. There

---

WINDOW ON PRACTICE

Dick Grote (2000), President of Grote Consulting in Dallas, reports on how the City of Irving in Texas has identified 23 competencies that are considered critical to success. For each of the competencies the designers of the appraisal system wrote dozens of examples reflecting different levels of performance in each competency – ranging from totally ineffective to excellent. Grote points out that the system took a long time to develop, but that in the long run it is much more efficient as 'all the appraiser has to do is to pick the ones that best describe how the employee behaves'.

Note: While it could be argued that much will be lost if appraisal is limited to such a reductionist approach, the use of such scales (similar to BARS and BOS) can focus and stimulate thinking and can be a *useful part* of the appraisal process.

Source: Adapted from D. Grote (2000) 'Performance Appraisal reappraised', *Harvard Business Review*, Jan.–Feb., p. 21.

Understanding and Managing People at Work

are increasing examples of how activity rates of computer operators can be recorded and analysed, and how the calls made by telephone sales staff can be overheard and analysed. Sewell and Wilkinson (1992) describe a Japanese electronics plant where the final electronic test on a piece of equipment can indicate not only faults but the individual operator responsible for them. On another level some companies test the performance of their sales staff by sending in assessors acting in the role of customer (Newton and Findlay 1996), often termed 'mystery shoppers'.

Who contributes to the appraisal process?

The direct line manager is most often the key or only source of feedback and assessment and is the most likely person to carry out the appraisal interview (see Chapter 23 for further details). The advantage of this is that the immediate supervisor usually has the most intimate knowledge of the tasks that an individual has been carrying out and how well they have been done. The annual appraisal is also the logical conclusion of ongoing management of performance that should have been taking place throughout the year between the supervisor and the appraisee. However, contributions may be made by a variety of others. For example the level of authority above the immediate manager can be involved in the appraisal process in one of two ways. First, they may be called upon to countersign the manager's appraisal of the employee in order to give a 'seal of approval' to indicate that the process has been fairly and properly carried out. Second, the manager's manager may directly carry out the appraisal. This is known as the 'grandfather' approach to appraisal. This is more likely to happen when the appraisal process is particularly concerned with making comparisons between individuals and identifying potential for promotion. It helps to overcome the problem that managers will all appraise by different standards, and minimises the possibility that appraisees will be penalised due to the fact that their manager has very high standards and is a 'hard marker'. Grandfather appraisal is often used to demonstrate fair play. Much less frequently an employee will be appraised by a member of the HR department. This may happen when there is no obvious ongoing immediate manager, for example, in a matrix organisation. This type of appraisal can be tricky to organise and much depends on the skills of the co-ordinator in the HR department.

Self-appraisal has become a familiar concept of late, and Fletcher (1993b) argues that there is little doubt that people are capable of rating themselves, but the question is, are they willing to do this? Fletcher notes that one of the most fruitful ways for individuals to rate themselves is by rating different aspects of their performance relative to other aspects, rather than relative to the performances of other people. He comments that by approaching self-appraisal in this way, individuals are more discriminating.

Self-appraisal is unlikely to be used alone, however, and individuals carry out an element of self-appraisal in some of the more traditional appraisal schemes. Self-appraisal forms part of 360-degree feedback, which we consider in the following section. Some organisations encourage individuals to prepare for the appraisal interview by filling out some form of appraisal on themselves. The differences between the individual's own appraisal and the manager's appraisal can then be a useful starting point for the appraisal interview. The difference between this and self-appraisal is that it is still the superior's appraisal that officially counts, although in the light of the subordinate's comments they might amend some of the ratings that they have given. In many schemes appraisees are asked to sign the completed appraisal form to show that they agree with its conclusions. In the event of disagreement a space is provided for details of controversial items. At the other end of the scale there are 'closed' schemes which not only eschew any form of contribution from the appraisees, but also prevent the appraisees from knowing the ratings that they have been given by their appraiser. There is a current trend to encourage employee participation in the appraisal process (see, for example, Newton and Findlay 1996).

Peers and subordinates may be invited informally by the line manager to contribute to an individual's appraisal, but again these sources are unlikely to be used alone. Although most appraisal systems focus on appraisal by the direct manager, Fisher (1994) identifies two distinct emphases – hierarchical appraisal (by the management system) and peer appraisal (which he found in some educational institutions and private professional practice firms). Redman and Snape (1992) argue that asking for this type of information from subordinates facilitates empowerment. Fletcher (1993a) comments that upward appraisal is only likely to be used as an occasional and additional activity rather than as an integral part of the appraisal process. Recent examples of upward appraisal include the Post Office (Cockburn 1993) and W.H. Smith (Fletcher 1993a). Further research by Redman and Snape (1992) revealed that only 13 per cent of their sample of 280 respondents were subject to a formal system of upward appraisal. In general their respondents (whether subject to such a system or not) found upward appraisal less acceptable than the conventional approach, and those who did receive it were reluctant to share upward appraisal data with others.

An increasingly useful source of appraisal information is from internal and external customers. This information can be collected directly by the direct manager from internal customers – for example, the training manager may collect information from a department on the support given to them by their specified training officer. Collecting information from external customers is a bit more tricky, but can be done in a positive manner, framed in terms of improving customer services, and designed to be not too time-consuming.

Activity 18.3

Almost all organisation members will have contact with a variety of internal customers. Identify your internal customers, or those of another member of staff, and design a short questionnaire to collect feedback that would be important in an appraisal situation.

What difficulties might you encounter in collecting and using this information?

Note: You can use any organisation with which you are familiar, and any role played by yourself or another person whose role you know about.

Assessment centres can be used in the appraisal of potential supervisors and managers. The advantage of assessment centres for this purpose is that ratings of potential can be assessed on the basis of factors other than current performance. It is well accepted that high performance in a current job does not mean that an individual will be a high performer if promoted to a higher level. It is also increasingly recognised that a moderate performer at one level may perform much better at a higher level. Assessment centres use tests, group exercises and interviews to appraise potential.

Effectiveness of appraisal systems

The effectiveness of appraisal systems hinges on a range of different factors and recent research by Longenecker (1997) in the USA sheds some light on this. In a large-scale survey and focus groups he found that the three most common reasons for failure of an appraisal system were: unclear performance criteria or an ineffective rating instrument (83 per cent); poor working relationships with the boss (79 per cent) and that the appraiser lacks information on the manager's actual performance (75 per cent). Other problems experienced were a lack of ongoing performance feedback (67 per cent) and a lack of focus on management development/improvement (50 per cent). Smaller numbers identified problems with the process, such as lack of appraisal skills (33 per cent) and the review process lacking structure or substance (29 per cent).

We would add that ownership of the system is also important – if it was designed and imposed by the HR function there may be little ownership of the system by line managers. Similarly, if paperwork has to be returned to the HR function the system may well be seen as a form-filling exercise for someone else's benefit and with no practical value to performance within the job. More fundamentally Egan (1995) argues that the problem with appraisal not only relates to poor design or implementation, but is rooted deeply in the basic reaction of organisational members to such a concept. Fletcher (1993a) makes the interesting comment that all systems have a shelf-life – maybe changes are required to the system to renew interest and energy. In any case, as Fletcher also notes, organisations have changed so much, and continue to do so, that it is inevitable that the nature of the appraisal process will change too (see Fletcher 1993b). There is an increasing body of critical literature addressing the role and theory of appraisal. These debates centre on the underlying reasons for appraisal (see, for example, Barlow 1989, Townley 1989, 1993; Newton and Findlay 1996) and the social construction of appraisal (see, for example, Grint 1993). This literature throws some light on the use and effectiveness of performance appraisal in organisations.

360-degree feedback

Our previous discussion of who contributes to the appraisal process, and the reasons why such a process may fail, leads us nicely into defining the nature and use of 360-degree feedback, which is a very specific term used to refer to what was previously termed multi-rater feedback.

The nature of 360-degree feedback

This approach to feedback refers to use of the whole range of sources from which feedback can be collected about any individual. Thus feedback is collected from every angle on the way that the individual carries out their job: from immediate line manager; peers; subordinates; more senior managers; internal customers; external customers; and from themselves. It is argued that this breadth of feedback provides superior feedback to feedback from the line manager's perspective only, since the latter will only be able to observe the individual in a limited range of situations. Hogetts et al. (1999) report that more than 70 per cent of United

Parcels Service employees found that feedback from multiple sources was more useful in developing self-insight than feedback from a single source. Individuals, it is argued, will find feedback from peers and subordinates compelling and more valid (see, for example, Borman 1998), and Edwards and Ewen (1996, p. 4) maintain that:

> No organizational action has more power for motivating employee behaviour change than feedback from credible work associates.

Such all-round feedback enables the individual to understand how they may be seen differently (or similarly) by different organisational groups, and how this may contrast with their own views of their strengths and weaknesses. This provides powerful information for the development of self-awareness. While 360-degree feedback may be collected using informal methods, as shown in the Window on Practice box on Humberside Tec, the term itself is a registered trade mark, and refers to a very specific method of feedback collection and analysis which was devised in the United States (see Edwards and Ewen 1996, p. 19), and they suggest that 'simplistic, informal approaches to multi-source assessment are likely to multiply rather than reduce error'. However, informal approaches to 360-degree feedback are sometimes used (as an alternative to a survey questionnaire and statistical analysis) quite successfully.

The formal process is a survey approach which involves the use of a carefully constructed questionnaire that is used with all the contributors of feedback. This questionnaire may be bought off the peg, providing a well-tested tool, or may be developed internally, providing a tool which is more precisely matched to the needs of the organisation. Whichever form is used, the essence is that it is based on behavioural competencies (for a more detailed explanation of these see Chapter 25), and their associated behaviours. Contributors will be asked to score, on a given scale, the extent to which the individual displays these behaviours.

WINDOW ON PRACTICE

Using an informal approach to 360-degree feedback at Humberside Tec

Storr (2000) reports on a 360-degree feedback process which is quite different from the survey approach. It is a process which has gradually been built up from upward appraisal for team leaders, has been piloted, and has gradually become standard. The process is owned by the appraisees, and is different because it is carried out face to face rather than using a paper system, and by all raters at the same time in a group-based approach for 90 per cent of individuals. It is a dialogue rather than a survey, and the only rule is that every individual must carry out at least one per year. The purpose of the sytem is to 'improve performance and enable people to learn and grow' (p. 38). Each group has a trained facilitator who supports both appraisers and appraisees. Different individuals have reacted differently to the approach, as might be expected: one individual said that they see it as empowerment, and many found that there was a great advantage in seeing the world from other people's point of view. Storr reports on one individual who received similar feedback from the group to that which she had received previously, from her manager, but hearing it from the six members of the group had a much stronger effect on her. Individuals often used their first experience of the process in a general way to ask the group what they should start doing, stop doing, continue doing, or do differently. Over time, however, individuals began to ask more specific questions.

Source: Summarised from F. Storr (2000) 'This is not a circular', *People Management*, 11 May, pp. 38–40.

Using a well-designed questionnaire, distributed to a sufficient number of contributors and appropriate sophisticated analysis, for example specifically designed computer packages which are set up to detect and moderate collusion and bias on behalf of the contributors, should provide reliable and valid data for the individual. The feedback is usually presented to the individual in the form of graphs, or bar charts showing comparative scores from different feedback groups, such as peers, subordinates, customers, where the average will be provided for each group, and single scores from line manager and self. In most cases the individual will have been able to choose the composition of the contributors in each group, for example which seven subordinates, out of a team of 10, will be asked to complete the feedback questionnaire. But beyond this the feedback will be anonymous as only averages for each group of contributors will be reported back, except of course for the line manager's score. The feedback will need to be interpreted by an internal or external facilitator, and done via a face-to-face meeting. It is generally recommended that the individual will need some training in the nature of the system and how to receive feedback, and the contributors will need some training on how to provide feedback. The principle behind the idea of feedback is that individuals can then use this information to change their behaviours and to improve performance, by setting and meeting development goals and an action plan.

Reported benefits include a stronger ownership of development goals, a climate of constructive feedback, improved communication over time and an organisation which is more capable of change as continuous feedback and improvement have become part of the way people work (Cook and Macauley 1997). Useful texts on designing and implementing a system include Edwards and Ewen (1996) from the US perspective and Ward (1998) from the UK perspective. A brief 'how to do it guide' is Goodge and Watts (2000).

Difficulties and dilemmas

As with all processes and systems there needs to be clarity about the purpose. Most authors distinguish between developmental uses, which they identify as fairly safe and a good way of introducing such a system, and other uses such as to determine pay awards. There seems to be an almost universal view that using these data for pay purposes is not advisable, and in the literature from the United States there is clearly a concern about the legal ramifications of doing this. Ward (1998) provides a useful framework for considering the different applications of this type of feedback, and reviews in some detail other applications such as using 360-degree feedback as part of a training course to focus attention for each individual on what they need to get out of the course. Other applications he suggests include using 360-degree feedback as an approach to team building, as a method of performance appraisal/management, for organisation development purposes and to evaluate training and development. Edwards and Ewen (1996) suggest that it can be used for nearly all HR systems, using selection, training and development, recognition and the allocation of job assignments as examples.

As well as clarity of purpose, confidentiality of raters is very important with most approaches to 360-degree feedback, and this can be difficult to maintain with a small team, as Hurley (1998) suggests. Thus raters may feel uncomfortable about being open and honest. The dangers of collusion and bias need to be eliminated, and it suggested that the appropriate software systems can achieve this,

Jacob and Flood (1995) report on how 360-degree feedback was used as part of a senior management development programme in a French agrochemicals company – Rhône-Poulenc. This approach was felt to be more accurate than an assessment centre because it collected data directly from on-the-job performance rather than from a substitute environment. The questionnaire was designed around a strategically developed competency framework – bosses, peers and subordinates took part in the process as well as the manager themselves. The identity of all contributors was anonymous, except for the immediate boss. The questionnaire took around 20 minutes to complete and was administered prior to the development programme, and at a later date after the programme. As part of the process, individual managers had to present what they had learned about themselves to others in a team setting. Despite this, Jacob and Flood state that 'most participants have suggested that they have never experienced such powerful and apparently insightful feedback about their performance'.

In the United States, where 360-degree feedback appears to have originated, Edwards and Ewen (1996) provide an example of how this process was used to improve customer satisfaction. At Chemetals when sales staff complete a client call they leave the client with a computer disk containing an assessment questionnaire. The client is asked to complete this and mail it on to another party for analysis. Analyses at July 1993, December 1993 and July 1994 demonstrate improvements on a number of aspects of customer satisfaction, particularly in communication and responsiveness. The authors maintain that there was no training, or other initiatives, in the intervening period, and while they cannot exclude some influence from other factors, it appears that the 360-degree feedback was a major cause of the improved job performance.

but they are of course expensive, as are well-validated off-the-peg systems. Follow-up is critical and if the experience of 360-degree feedback is not built on via the construction of development goals and the support and resources to fulfil these, the process may be viewed negatively and may be demotivational. London *et al.* (1997) report concerns about the way systems are implemented, and that nearly one-third of respondents they surveyed experienced negative effects. 360-degree appraisal clearly needs to be handled carefully and sensitively and in the context of an appropriate organisational climate so that it is not experienced as a threat.

Performance management systems

Performance management systems are increasingly seen as the way to manage employee performance rather than relying on appraisal alone. Bevan and Thompson (1992), for example, found that 20 per cent of the organisations they surveyed had introduced a performance management system. In 1997 Armstrong and Baron (1998a) report that 69 per cent of the organisations they surveyed said that they operated a formal process to measure manager performance. Such systems offer the advantage of being tied closely into the objectives of the organisation, and therefore the resulting performance is more likely to meet organisational needs. The systems also represent a more holistic view of performance. Performance appraisal is almost always a key part of the system, but is integrated with ensuring that employee effort is directed towards organisational priorities, that appropriate training and development is carried out to enable employee effort to be successful, and that successful performance is rewarded and reinforced. Given that there is such an emphasis on a link into the organisation's objectives it is somewhat disappointing that Bevan and Thompson found no correlation between the existence of a performance management system and organisational performance in the private sector. Similarly, Armstrong and Baron (1998a) report from their survey that no such correlation was found. They do report, however, that 77 per cent of organisations surveyed regarded their systems as effective (to some degree) – so performance management, like HR systems and processes, still remains an act of faith.

As with appraisal systems, some performance management systems are development driven and some are reward driven. A good example of a development-driven system, which does include an element of reward, is Sheard (1992) reporting on performance management at Zeneca Pharmaceuticals. Whereas in the 1992 IPD survey 85 per cent of organisations claimed to link performance management to pay, Armstrong and Baron found that only 43 per cent of survey respondents reported such a link. However, 82 per cent of the organisations that they visited had some form of performance related pay (PRP) or competency based pay, so the picture is a little confusing. What does seem to be emerging, Armstrong and Baron (1998b) suggest, is a view of performance management which centres on 'dialogue', 'shared understanding', 'agreement' and 'mutual commitment', rather than rating for pay purposes.

There are many different definitions of performance management and some have identified it as 'management by objectives' under another name. There are, however, some key differences here. Management by objectives was primarily an off-the-peg system which organisations bought in, and generally involved objectives being imposed on managers from above. Performance management tends to be tailor-made and produced in-house (that's why there are so many different versions), and there is an emphasis on mutual objective setting and on ongoing performance support and review. The term, therefore, remains ambiguous, and rightly so as it is argued that it is critical that the system adopted fits with the culture and context of the organisation (see, for example, Armstrong and Baron 1998b; Hendry *et al.* 2000).

Figure 18.2 shows a typical system, including both development and reward aspects, the main stages of which are:

Figure 18.2 Four stages of a typical performance management system

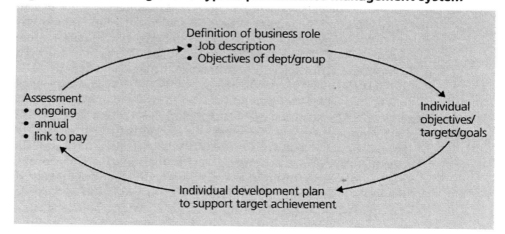

1 **A written and agreed job description, reviewed regularly.** There must be objectives for the work-group which have been cascaded down from the organisation's strategic objectives. Bevan and Thompson (1992) found that performance management organisations were more likely to have an organisational mission statement and to communicate this to employees.

2 **Individual objectives** derived from the above, which are jointly devised by appraiser and appraisee. These objectives are results rather than task oriented, are tightly defined and include measures to be assessed. The objectives are designed to stretch the individual, and offer potential development as well as meeting business needs. Many organisations use the 'SMART' acronym for describing individual objectives or targets:

■ Specific
■ Measurable
■ Appropriate
■ Relevant
■ Timed

It is clearly easier for some parts of the organisation than others to set targets. There is often a tendency for those in technical jobs, for example, computer systems development, to identify purely technical targets – reflecting heavy task emphasis – they see in their jobs. Moving staff to a different view of how their personal objectives contribute to team and organisational objectives is an important part of the performance management process. An objective for a team leader in systems development could be:

> To complete development interviews with all team members by end-July 2002.
> (written March 2002)

Clearly, the timescale for each objective will need to reflect the content of the objective and not timescales set into the performance management system. As objectives are met, managers and their staff need to have a brief review meeting to look at progress in all objectives and decide what other objectives should be added. Five or six ongoing objectives are generally sufficient for one individual to work on at any time.

3 **A development plan** devised by the manager and the individual detailing development goals and activities designed to enable the individual to meet the objectives. The emphasis here is on managerial support and coaching, very much as described in the performance support phase of managing individual performance (see the discussion of the performance cycle earlier in this chapter). Those organisations with a development-driven performance management system may well have development objectives alongside performance objectives to ensure that this part of the system is given proper attention.

4 **Assessment of objectives.** Ongoing formal reviews on a regular basis are needed. These are designed to motivate the appraisee and concentrate on developmental issues. Also, an annual assessment is needed, which affects pay received, which in turn depends on performance in achievement of objectives. Many systems still include this link with pay, but Fletcher and Williams (1992b) point to some difficulties experienced. Some organisations (both public and private) found that the merit element of pay was too small to motivate staff, and indeed was sometimes found to be insulting. Although performance management organisations were more likely to have merit or performance-related pay (Bevan and Thompson 1992), some organisations

have regretted its inclusion. Armstrong and Baron (1998a) report that staff almost universally disliked the link with pay, and one manager from one of their case study companies reported that 'the whole process is an absolute nightmare' (p. 172).

Implementation and critique of performance management

Performance management needs to be line driven rather than HR driven (see, for example, Fletcher 1993b), and therefore mechanisms need to be found to make this happen. The incorporation of line managers alongside HR managers in a working party to develop the system is clearly important. This not only ensures that the needs of the line are taken into account in the system design, but also demonstrates that the system is line led. Training in the introduction and use of the system is also ideally line led, and Fletcher and Williams (1992b) give us an excellent example of an organisation where line managers were trained as 'performance management coaches' who were involved in departmental training and support for the new system. However, some researchers have found that line managers are the weak link in the system (see, for example, Hendry *et al.* 1997).

> **WINDOW ON PRACTICE**
>
> The scheme was introduced by training a series of nominated line manager coaches from each department. They had then to take the message back to their colleagues and train them, tailoring the material to their department (Personnel/Training providing the back-up documentation). These were serving line managers who had to give up their time to do the job. Many of them were high-flyers, and they have been important opinion leaders and influencers – though they themselves had to be convinced first. Their bosses could refuse to nominate high-quality staff for this role if they wished, but they would subsequently be answerable to the Chief Executive. This approach was taken because it fits with the philosophy of performance management (i.e. high line-management participation), and because it was probably the only way to train all the departmental managers in the timescale envisaged).
>
> Source: C. Fletcher and R. Williams (1992b) *Performance Management in the UK: Organisational Experience.* London: IPM, p. 133.

Bevan and Thompson (1992) found incomplete take-up of performance management, with some aspects being adopted and not others. They noted that there was a general lack of integration of activities. This is rather unfortunate as one of the key advantages of performance management is the capacity for integration of activities concerned with the management of individual performance. This problem is still apparent. Hendry *et al.* (1997) reported the comments of Phil Wills from GrandMet, who suggests that there is still a lack of understanding of what we mean by an integrated approach to performance management, and that while alignment is critical, some organisations do not understand whether their HR processes are aligned or pulling in different directions.

It appears, not surprisingly, that performance management suffers from the same problems as traditional appraisal systems. Armstrong and Baron (1998a) report, for example, that over half the respondents to their survey feel that managers give their best ratings to people that they like (p. 202), and over half the managers surveyed felt that they had not received sufficient training in performance management processes (p. 203). They also report (1998b) that the use of ratings was consistently derided by staff and seen as subjective and inconsistent.

In terms of individual objective setting linked to organisational performance objectives, Rose (2000) reports on a range of problems. In particular he notes how SMART targets can be problematic, if they are not constantly reviewed and updated – a time-consuming process. He goes on to argue that pre-set objectives can be a constraining factor in such a rapidly changing business context, and reminds us of the trap of setting measurable targets, precisely because they are measurable and satisfy the system, rather than because they are most important to the organisation. He argues that a broader approach which assesses the employee's accomplishments as a whole and their contribution to the organisation is more helpful than concentrating on pre-set objectives. There is a further concern with SMART targets, which is that they are inevitably time constrained and have a short-term focus.

There is a very strong argument that what is most important to the organisation are developments which are complex and longer term, and hence are very difficult to pin down to short-term targets (see, for example, Hendry *et al.* 1997). Armstrong and Baron (1998b) do note that a more rounded view of performance is gradually being adopted, which involves the 'how' as well as the 'what', and inputs such as the development of competencies. There is, however, a long way to go to adequately describe performance and define what is really required for organisational success.

Summary propositions

18.1 Effective management of individual performance rests on managing the performance cycle – ongoing performance planning, support and review.

18.2 Appraisal is most often carried out by the immediate manager, but is enhanced by information from other parties.

18.3 There is a conflict in many appraisal systems in the role of the manager – as judge and as helper.

18.4 360-degree feedback is increasingly being used to provide individuals with a basis for changing behaviour and improving performance.

18.5 Performance management systems incorporate appraisal activity, but include other aspects such as a link to organisational objectives and a more holistic view of performance.

18.6 So far performance management has generally been adopted in a piecemeal way with a lack of integration between performance activities. There are, however, some good examples of carefully thought through and implemented systems.

References

Armstrong, M. and Baron, A. (1998a) *Performance Management – The New Realities*. London: IPD.

Armstrong, M. and Baron, A. (1998b) 'Out of the Tick Box', *People Management*, 23 July, pp. 38–41.

Barlow, G. (1989) 'Deficiencies and the perpetuation of power: latent functions in management appraisal', *Journal of Management Studies*, Vol. 26, No. 5, pp. 499–518.

Bevan, S. and Thompson, M. (1992) 'An overview of policy and practice', in *Personnel Management in the UK: an anaylsis of the issues*. London: IPM.

Borman, W. (1998) '360 ratings: an analysis of assumptions and a research agenda for evaluating their validity', *Human Resource Management Review*, Vol. 7, pp. 299–315.

Coates, G. (1994) 'Performance appraisal as icon: Oscar winning performance or dressing to impress?', *International Journal of Human Resource Management*, No. 1, February.

Cockburn, B. (1993) 'How I see the personnel function', *Personnel Management*, November.

Cook, S. and Macauley, S. (1997) 'How colleagues and customers can help improve team performance', *Team Performance Management*, Vol. 3, No. 1.

Edwards, M.R. and Ewen, A.J. (1996) *360 Degree Feedback*. New York: Amacom, American Management Association.

Egan, G. (1995) 'A clear path of peak performance', *People Management*, 18 May, pp. 34–7.

Fisher, C.M. (1994) 'The differences between appraisal schemes: variation and acceptability – Part 1', *Personnel Review*, Vol. 23, No. 8, pp. 33–48.

Fletcher, C. (1993a) *Appraisal: Routes to improved performance*. London: IPM.

Fletcher, C. (1993b) 'Appraisal: an idea whose time has gone?', *Personnel Management*, September.

Fletcher, C. and Williams, R. (1985) *Performance Appraisal and Career Development*. London: Hutchinson.

Fletcher, C. and Williams, R. (1992a) 'The route to performance management', *Personnel Management*, October.

Fletcher, C. and Williams, R. (1992b) *Performance Management in the UK: Organisational experience*. London: IPM.

Goodge, P. and Watts, P. (2000) 'How to manage 360° feedback', *People Management*, 17 February, pp. 50–2.

Grint, K. (1993) 'What's wrong with performance appraisals? – a critique and a suggestion', *Human Resource Management Journal*, Vol. 3, No. 3, pp. 61–77.

Grote, D. (2000) 'Performance Appraisal Reappraised', *Harvard Business Review*, Jan.–Feb., p. 21.

Hendry, C., Bradley, P. and Perkins, S. (1997) 'Missed a motivator?', *People Management*, 15 May, pp. 20–5.

Hendry, C., Woodward, S., Bradley, P. and Perkins, S. (2000) 'Performance and rewards: cleaning out the stables', *Human Resource Management Journal*, Vol. 10, No. 3, pp. 46–62.

Hogetts, R., Luthans, F. and Slocum, J. (1999) 'Strategy and HRM initiatives for the '00s: environment redefining roles and boundaries, linking competencies and resources', *Organizational Dynamics*, Autumn, p. 7.

Hurley, S. (1998) 'Application of team-based 360° feedback systems', *Team Performance Management*, Vol. 4, No. 5.

Jacob, R. and Flood, M. (1995) 'A bumper crop of insights', *People Management*, 9 February.

London, M., Smither, J. and Adsit, D. (1997) 'Accountability: the achilles heel of multisource feedback', *Group and Organizational Dynamics*, Vol. 22, No. 2, pp. 162–84.

Long, P. (1986) *Performance Appraisal Revisited*. London: IPM.

Longenecker, C. (1997) 'Why managerial performance appraisals are ineffective: causes and lessons', *Career Development International*, Vol. 2, No. 5.

Newton, T. and Findlay, P. (1996) 'Playing God? – the performance of appraisal', *Human Resource Management Journal*, Vol. 6, No. 3, pp. 42–58.

Randell, G., Packard, P. and Slater, I. (1984) *Staff Appraisal*. London: IPM.

Redman, T. and Snape, E. (1992) 'Upward and onward: can staff appraise their managers?', *Personnel Review*, Vol. 21, pp. 32–46.

Rose, M. (2000) 'Target Practice', *People Management*, 23 November, pp. 44–5.

Sewell, G. and Wilkinson, B. (1992) 'Someone to watch over me: surveillance, discipline and the just-in-time process', *Sociology*, Vol. 26, pp. 271–89.

Sheard, A. (1992) 'Learning to improve performance', *Personnel Management*, September.

Storr, F. (2000) 'This is not a circular', *People Management*, 11 May, pp. 38–40.

Townley, B. (1989) 'Selection and appraisal: reconstituting social relations', in J. Storey (ed.), *New Perspectives on Human Resource Management*. London: Routledge.

Townley, B. (1993) 'Performance appraisal and the emergence of management', *Journal of Management Studies*, Vol. 30, No. 2, pp. 27–44.

Walker, J.W. (1992) *Human Resource Strategy*. Maidenhead: McGraw-Hill.

Ward, P. (1995) 'A 360 degree turn for the better', *People Management*, 9 February.

Ward, P. (1998) *360-degree Feedback*. London: IPD.

General discussion topics

1 In what ways is the concept of performance management different from the way in which management has been traditionally practised? What are the advantages and disadvantages for employees and employers?

2 360-degree appraisal may have many advantages, but there is the argument that it can never really work because of the built-in biases, such as marking a boss well because you're due for a pay rise; marking yourself low so that you can be happily surprised by others' evaluations; marking peers down to make oneself look better.

   Discuss as many built-in biases as you can think of, and suggest how they might be tackled and whether substantive improvements could be made.

Chapter 4   Strategic aspects of organisation

Personnel managers have always been involved in the organisation of the business in their operational role. This is why there was the development phase, described in Chapter 1, of the humane bureaucrat, as businesses grew bigger and became more specialised. The interest in organisation development provided a further twist to the tale. In this part of the book we examine several aspects of personnel activities which are linked in to the organisation-as-entity and organisation-as-process. Structure and culture are largely concerned with the entity; planning, information, communication and presentation are all to do with organisaton as a process.

Strategic aspects of organisation are grounded in the simple proposition of Alfred Chandler (1962) that 'structure follows strategy'. Whatever strategy for growth a business pursued, the structure of the business followed and reflected the demands of that strategy. He was, of course, writing at a time when the idea of growth was universally accepted as an automatic objective for any business, but his analysis remains a central feature of understanding business organisations.

Chandler's three stages of business development

After examining the growth of 70 large American businesses, Chandler concluded that they all pass through three stages of development: unit, functional and multi-divisional.

Any business begins by being on a single location, with a single product and a single decision maker. It may be Rolls and Royce or Hewlett and Packard, rather than Eddie Land or Clive Sinclair but it is still a single decision-making function with two or three people working very closely together and doing almost everything. The first stage of development into the *unit firm* involves the process of vertical integration, with specialist functions being set up and other people employed as there is increasing turnover, the beginning of hierarchy and attempts to achieve some economies of scale. One further feature of this is to expand forwards or backwards in the operating chain, by acquiring other business, such as a supplier or raw materials or a retail outlet.

Evolving into a *functional organisation* introduces specialisation as departments are established to deal with different functions, such as marketing, personnel and finance. If the business expands still further and diversifies into different industries and products, there is then the final stage of turning into *a multi-divisional firm*. Chandler observed that the process of transition was usually delayed and often very dissatisfying to the original entrepreneur. His explanation for this was that the entrepreneur/founder was typically brilliant at strategy (otherwise there would not be a continuing business) but rarely interested in, or skilful at, structuring a business, especially as the structuring process put power and decision into other hands.

Chandler's thesis has been examined by a number of researchers in the period since it was first propounded. Three slight modifications are worth mentioning here, particularly in relation to the evolution of the multi-divisional form. First, Rumelt (1982) showed that the likelihood of a firm having a multi-divisional structure increased as it diversified. Miles and Snow (1984) carried out extensive studies to examine what they called 'strategic fit': the match between strategy, structure and internal management processes. They demonstrate that businesses need organisation structures and management processes that are appropriate to their strategy, or there is a likelihood that their strategy will fail. Both of these may seem unsurprising, even obvious, conclusions: their value is to confirm the enduring potency of Chandler's ideas. A more significant modification comes from Waterman and Peters (1980), who suggested that businesses could make temporary structural changes to cope with the more rapidly changing contemporary environment without abandoning their overall structure.

Having a structure that matches the strategy is thus crucial to the success of strategy, and structure (organisation-as-entity) interrelates closely with the management processes (organisation-as-process).

WINDOW ON PRACTICE

One of the most remarkable entrepreneurs and technological innovators of the 1970s was Clive Sinclair. The dramatic success of the first pocket calculator was quickly followed by the digital watch and the first home computers, ZX81 and Spectrum. An admiring prime minister gave him a knighthood and it seemed that he could do no wrong, but there was no appropriate structure to sustain the strategy. There was a shortage of management skills, especially in marketing and distribution, so there was a retreat. Sir Clive re-established his company to undertake only research and invention. Everything else was subcontracted, while the handful of people who made up Sinclair Research concentrated on the next technological breakthrough: the electric car. Technically ingenious, the product was a flop. There had been no authoritative marketing guidance to demonstrate that the product would never sell. The strategy could not succeed without the appropriate structure and management processes.

Centralisation and decentralisation

One of the popular ideas of the 1980s was the strategic business unit, which was a method of empowerment, except that it was not an individual manager being empowered, but a complete operating unit of the business. The management of a particular unit was given an agreed budget and an agreed set of targets for the forthcoming period. Thereafter they had freedom to manage themselves in whatever way they thought fit, provided that they first submitted regular reports and, second, met the targets and complied with the budget expectations.

This was a form of decentralisation, and many managers in strategic business units made the wry comment that the one thing that was not decentralised was the strategy!

What is to be decentralised and what is to remain central or drawn into the centre? Chris Hendry (1990, p. 93) makes the interesting observation that in the process of a business decentralising its operations, personnel often remains one of the last centralising forces. He attributes this to the beliefs of personnel people and Chief Executives about issues such as equity, order, consistency and control. The personnel function will relinquish these only reluctantly as they see great risks in, for instance, methods of payment being set up on different principles in separate parts of the business. What about coercive comparisons? What about equal value claims if we do not monitor closely from the centre?

The focus of this concern is changing. Control of collective bargaining and pay structures – the traditional strongholds of the Personnel Director – are being gradually abandoned and decentralised in favour of new power bases, such as group contracts, succession planning, management development and graduate recruitment (ibid., p. 99).

There is, however, a different dimension to the centralisation/decentralisation question. In writing about international companies Kobrin (1988) has demonstrated that managers have to centralise and decentralise at the same time. It does not need the international dimension to make this comment valid. Each component of the business has to have its strengths and knowledge developed and exploited to the full if it is to be effective, and this requires a greater degree of empowerment than most advocates of budget-driven strategic business units acknowledge. At the same time the individual operating unit has to maximise its contribution to group objectives, and that will inevitably lead to occasional profound conflict between unit and group objectives. The strategic role for the personnel people here is not simply to cope with the conflict when it breaks out, but somehow to develop a culture that succeeds in delivering the apparently irreconcilable requirements: enough autonomy for people to really deploy their skills, enthusiasm and commitment, but enough control for group-wide considerations

WINDOW ON PRACTICE

Henry was the Managing Director of a growing business with six operating subsidiaries. Fiona was the Financial Director, who had just joined from a rather larger company. One of the six operating subsidiaries was in difficulties and it appeared to Henry, Fiona and their Board colleagues that it would need to be closed. Fiona said she would work out the numbers over the week-end.

On Monday Fiona showed her proposals to Henry, including the cost of severance for all employed at the subsidiary, including Barry, the General Manager. She sighed and said she supposed he would like her to go down and get it done with. Henry asked if she had consulted with the Personnel Director, George. She had not, so George was asked in and a different strategy was agreed: Barry would be called up to Head Office.

Barry came, clearly having a shrewd idea of what was afoot. Henry explained the situation and said there really seemed no alternative but to close the plant, but Barry was not to worry; he would be looked after. Barry replied that the plant would only close over his dead body and that they did not know what they were talking about. Fiona produced her analysis and was closely questioned by Barry and strongly challenged on certain of her assumptions. After three hours of vigorous argument Henry called a halt by asking Barry to come back within a week with counter-proposals. Henry still felt that Fiona's analysis was correct and that the plant should close, but if Barry could produce watertight, convincing alternatives, they would be listened to. Fiona complained that her professional judgement was being doubted, but George shepherded Barry out of the room.

Five days later Barry was back with a plan that he had discussed with the General Managers of two other subsidiaries and which they said they could make work by slight variations in the way they worked together. The plan involved a drastic reduction in the workforce, but Barry's plant would remain open, targets would be met and they would be back within budget in six months' time. Now it was the turn of Henry and Fiona to question Barry closely, but eventually they agreed that his proposal was a better strategy for the group as a whole.

ultimately to prevail, when they have been tested in the furnace of unit-wide aggressive interrogation. The last part is vital.

Personnel people increasingly have as a part of their role those aspects of co-ordination that go beyond budgetary and planning controls. There are two particular suggestions.

The first is *evangelisation*, the process of winning the acceptance throughout the business of a common mission and a shared purpose. This idea of needing to win hearts and minds has been a common thread in management thinking for most of the twentieth century, and a specialised example is provided later in this chapter from the work of Hopfl (1993). It takes on particular significance in the decentralised business and it is indeed a remarkable management team that will be able to commit themselves with enthusiasm to closing down their local operation on the grounds that the business as a whole will benefit if an operation elsewhere is developed.

Co-ordination through evangelisation works through **shared belief**. The beliefs may be interpreted in different ways and may produce varied behaviours, but there is the attempt to promulgate relatively simple doctrines to which members of the organisation subscribe and through which they are energised. Some readers of this book will have learned their catechism as children, or will have studied the thirty-nine articles defining the doctrinal position of the Church of England. Although this may seem inappropriate to the business world, in the 1970s a British company, Vitafoam, was established by a man who required his senior executives to copy out his annual policy statement by hand, three times, before handing it back to him. It is now commonplace for companies to have mission statements, which come close to being unifying articles of faith.

> At the top is the mission statement, a broad goal based on the organization's planning premises, basic assumptions about the organization's purpose, its values, its distinctive competencies, and its place in the world. A mission statement is a relatively permanent part of an organization's identity and can do much to unify and motivate its members.   (Stoner and Freeman 1992, p. 188)

Evangelisation also works through **parables**. Ed Schein (1985, p. 239) identified 'stories and legends' as one of the key mechanisms for articulating and reinforcing the organisation's culture.

The company house magazine helps in circulating the good news about heroic deeds in all parts of the company network. Better are the word-of-mouth exchanges and accounts of personal experience. Evangelisation can use **apostles** – ambassadors sent out to preach the faith. These are the people – usually in senior positions – who move round the company a great deal. They know the business well and can describe one component to another, explaining company policy, justifying particular decisions and countering parochial thinking. They can also move ideas around ('In Seoul they are wondering about ... what do think?') and help in the development of individual networks ('Try getting in touch with Oscar Jennings in Pittsburgh ... he had similar problems a few weeks ago'). At times of crisis, apostles are likely to be especially busy, countering rumour and strengthening resolve. It may be important that most of the apostles come from headquarters and have personally met, and can tell stories about, the founder. Anita Roddick's Body Shop is an organisation that grew rapidly on the basis of working in a way that was markedly different from the

Understanding and Managing People at Work

conventions of the cosmetics industry that it was challenging. Its growth seemed to need people in all parts to identify closely with the vision and personality of the founder:

> The inductresses' eyes seem to light up whenever Anita's name is mentioned. We are told, in semi-joyous terms, the great tale concerning that first humble little shop in Brighton. And . . . one of our inductresses uses the phrase, 'And Anita saw what she had done, and it was good'.
> (Keily 1991, p. 3)

Co-ordination can be improved by the development and promulgation of *standards and norms*. Many companies have sought the accreditation of BS 5750, the British Standard for quality; others claim to be equal opportunity employers. Thinking companies will wish to set standards for many aspects of their operation, especially in personnel matters. The Human Resources Section at Shell Centre is charged with developing and maintaining standards relating to alcohol and drug abuse. If standards are adopted throughout a company, they become a form of co-ordination. Furthermore, it is not necessary for all of them to be developed at the centre. Decentralised standard formulation can enable different parts of the business to take a lead as a preliminary to universal adoption of the standard they have formulated: an excellent method of integration.

Planning

Just as the concept of strategy has somewhat overwhelmed the use of policy as a management instrument, it has also shaded out the use of planning. Planning had its heyday in management thinking during the 1960s, when the clever ideas of operations research were seen as a means whereby future activities could be forecast with confidence so that plans could then be made to deliver that future, 'the past is history . . . the future is planning'. The attraction of planning was that you could make the future happen instead of waiting for it to happen to you. To be a reactive manager was almost as bad as having a communicable disease.

The trouble was that the future rarely turned out as expected; some completely unforeseen event scuppered the plans. The great example was the use of Programme Evaluation Review Technique (PERT) in planning the development and production of the Polaris missile system. Sapolsky (1972, p. 246) studied its application and decided that as a planning technique it was as effective as rain dancing, and that its obvious success was due not to its technical efficiency but to the mystique of infallibility that its managers were able to promote.

As enthusiasm for change took over from a commitment to planning among managers, there was a tendency to think that all action needed to be spontaneous. Particularly in Britain, the predilection for short-term thinking received an unfortunate boost, with the concomitant difficulties of a reluctance to invest and an unwillingness to make provision – through training, for instance – to a future that might not happen. Tom Peters appeared to dismiss planning altogether, producing less than two pages devoted to the topic in a 560-page tome:

> The long-range strategic plan, of voluminous length, is less useful than before. But a strategic 'mind-set', which focuses on skill/capability building (e.g. adding value to the work force via training to prepare it to respond more flexibly and be more quality-conscious) is more important than ever.
> (Peters 1989, p. 394)

There we have another clue to the future orientation of personnel management, as we think of organisation as process rather than entity. Peters sees little scope for the strategic plan of the type beloved by the marketing specialists and the MBA graduate, but calls instead for some forward-looking, creative personnel work. This echoes the Japanese concern with the longer term. Holden (1994, p. 125) gives the example of a Japanese computer company with a development plan for all employees that takes 42 years to complete!

As will be seen in the next few chapters, personnel work requires an approach to planning that is rather more flexible and imaginative – soft as well as hard – than that of the manpower planning textbooks of the 1970s.

Information and communication

Information is a prerequisite for all decision making, and the handling of information is crucial to all personnel work: aggregated data on numbers, ages, skills, hours, rates of pay and so on and information relating to invididuals.

Communication is a varied process whereby information of the above, specific type is merged with other types of data, understanding, feeling and image to create the process whereby the organisation functions. This requires care with organisational structure, for what is an organisation chart except a statement about responsibilities, status, channels of communication and job titles? It requires an appreciation of organisational culture, an effective set of systems, procedures and drills, and it requires personal competence in members of the organisation, especially managers.

One of the main strategic aspects of communication is communicating across national and cultural boundaries, where feedback is especially important both to monitor what is happening and to develop understanding between the operations. Those in country A will inevitably have limited understanding about the situation of those in country B, to say nothing of the cultural and linguistic uncertainties that feedback can help clear up.

Recently, business expansion has frequently been by acquisition rather than simple growth of what Alfred Chandler described as the unit firm. This produces a particularly intense communications problem. Employees in the acquired company will feel a greater sense of community with each other than with those who have acquired them. They will see corporate affairs from their own standpoint and will tend to be cautious in their behaviour and suspicious in their interpretation of what they hear from their new owners. Personnel people can have a crucial part to play in managing the requisite communications and information flow.

When the expansion is by acquisition of businesses in a different country, with a different set of cultural norms, the problems are intensified. Even when initial suspicion begins to unwind, there are still difficulties. For example, there are the problems of rivalry, distorted perceptions and resource allocation.

Rivalry

Whatever is done to develop a shared sense of purpose and a common identity, companies in different countries tend to take pride in their own accomplishments and to disparage the accomplishments of other nationality groups. As long as this stimulates healthy competition, rivalry can benefit the company, but it can quickly become destructive, as occurred in one car assembly plant in Britain which constantly rejected and returned gear boxes made by a plant of the same company in a different country.

Distorted perceptions

National boundaries produce distorted ideas about the 'other' people, whose achievements are underestimated and undervalued in comparison with the achievements of your own group, which may be overestimated.

Resource allocation

Allocation of resources between competing interests is always problematical, but becomes even more difficult in international comparisons. A company in a vulnerable situation may go as far as to provide disinformation about a rival in order to win additional resources.

WINDOW ON PRACTICE

Rover Group was the largest car manufacturer in Britain and the last of the major manufacturers that could claim to be British. In view of the tradition of car manufacture, this was a point of symbolic significance. When the company developed a technical collaboration with the Japanese Honda company, there was considerable discussion and uncertainty, but the collaboration proved fruitful. At the beginning of 1994 a controlling interest in Rover Group was sold to the German company BMW. This produced a very strong reaction and anxiety that the future of the British operation would be blighted. The Honda association was also regarded as being vitiated by this move. Despite many assurances, the management had to engage in unrelenting communication and consultation for months in order to reassure company employees and to avoid uncertainties in the product and financial markets.

Brandt and Hulbert (1976) studied organisational feedback in a number of multinational companies which had their headquarters in Europe, Japan and the United States. They found that the American organisations had many more feedback reports and meetings between headquarters and subsidiaries than their European or Japanese counterparts. In contrast, Pascale (1978) found that Japanese managers in Japan used face-to-face contacts more than American managers as well as more upwards and lateral communication. Japanese managers in America used communication in the same way as Americans.

One of the few values of management jargon is that the jargon quickly becomes universally understood by the experts, no matter what their nationality. JIT, QWL, TQM are understood by managers everywhere, although NVQ and IIP are understood only by a more select audience.

Disseminating information and other messages within the organisation helps develop corporate culture and a sense of collaboration across national boundaries to integrate the business. Members of the different units in the business have to understand why a company has been acquired in Korea or Chile, even though it seems to threaten the livelihood of some parts of the parent organisation. Comprehensive communication can raise awareness of the wider market and the opportunities that are waiting to be grasped. Foulds and Mallet (1989, p. 78) suggest the following as purposes of international communication, most of which are just as relevant if one is operating within a single national boundary:

- to reinforce group culture so as to improve the speed and effectiveness of decision taking;
- to encourage information exchange in internationally related activities and prevent the 'reinvention of the wheel';
- to form the background to the succession planning activity – certain cultures demand certain types of people;
- to establish in people's minds what is expected of them by the parent company;
- to facilitate change in a way acceptable to the parent company;
- to undermine the 'not invented here' attitudes and thereby encourage changes;
- to improve the attractiveness of the company in the recruitment field – particularly where the subsidiary is small and far from base;
- to encourage small activities, which may be tomorrow's 'cream', and give such activities a perspective within the international activities.

WINDOW ON PRACTICE

The problem of communicating across linguistic boundaries is illustrated by this official translation from a government announcement in Prague:

Because Christmas Eve falls on a Thursday, the day has been designated a Saturday for work purposes. Factories will close all day, with stores open a half day only. Friday, December 25 has been designated a Sunday, with both factories and stores open all day. Monday, December 28, will be a Wednesday for work purposes. Wednesday, December 30, will be a business Friday. Saturday, January 2, will be a Sunday, and Sunday, January 3, will be a Monday.

The organisation must operate holistically. It is not the sum of its parts: the whole exists in every part, like the human body. If you are ill, a sample of your blood or the taking of your temperature is just as good an indicator to a doctor whatever part of your body it comes from. Customers have a holistic view of the organisation because they are interested in what it delivers as a product or service, not in whether the design section is more efficient than the warehouse. Managers cannot work effectively in their part of the business without understanding its simultaneous relationship to the whole. Businesses function holistically and holism is a function of constant, efficient communication, like the bloodstream and the central nervous system.

A major development in information and communication has, of course, been the arrival of personnel management information systems, discussed in Chapter 7. These enable information to be stored, located, summarised and analysed instantaneously, although one of the leading European experts on the subject feels that progress has been painfully slow:

> the development of imaginative CPISs is pathetically slow. Todays CPISs still look very much like those of 10 to 15 years ago. [They] may use a mouse to point arrows at icons, store endless amounts of data, be in technicolour and they may be networked, but the differences in value they offer ... do not represent 15 years of development.
> (Richards-Carpenter 1994, p. 63)

A strategic issue for personnel specialists is to consider how the potential of this facility can be realised more effectively.

A quite different aspect of communication for the personnel specialist is the need for propaganda or public relations.

Delegation of responsibility for aspects of personnel management by empow-

---

Understanding and Managing People at Work

ering the line manager is a theme to which there is frequent reference in this book. This empowerment goes both ways, as managers from other backgrounds bring their perspective more intrusively into what personnel specialists have liked to regard as their own preserve. The public relations approach is a clear example, with many businesses running communications with employees along similar lines to communications with customers. Often privately derided as 'hard-sell gimmicks,' these methods are not always popular in the personnel community. Perhaps the best-known of these activities was a series of commitment-raising projects in British Airways. Heather Hopfl describes the opening of a three-day workshop, 'Visioning the Future':

> This event requires a level of stage management that would not be unfamiliar to a touring rock band. ... One of the trainers stands at the door to ensure that no-one gets in early to 'spoil' the experience. Nine o'clock. The doors to the conference room are opened ... the opening music from 'Also Sprach Zarathustra' ... blasts out a triumphal welcome. ... The lights dim and the corporate logo appears before them. Three days of management development have begun.   (Hopfl 1993, p. 120)

Although this is alien to many personnel people, they soon realised that people are so used to slick presentation in all departments of their lives, that presentation of information at work needs to use contemporary techniques if it is to have impact.

Summary propositions

4.1 Organisational strategy is inextricably linked with the structure of the business; one cannot be changed without changing, or requiring change, in the other.

4.2 One common strategic initiative is to decentralise, using the strategic business unit as the locus of business activity. This requires specific measures to co-ordinate the decentralised fragments.

4.3 The international, or global, business can have considerable problems in co-ordination. Ways of dealing with them include evangelisation, the development of standards and norms and planning.

4.4 Communication in any business confirms the holistic nature of the enterprise.

References

Brandt, W.K. and Hulbert, J.M. (1976) 'Patterns of communication in the multinational company', *Journal of International Business Studies* (Spring), pp. 57–64.

Chandler, A.D. (1962) *Strategy and Structure*. Cambridge, Mass: MIT Press.

Foulds, J. and Mallet, L. (1989) 'The European and international dimension', in T. Wilkinson (ed.), *The Communications Challenge*. London: IPM.

Hendry, C. (1990) 'Corporate management of human resources under conditions of decentralisation', *British Journal of Management*, Vol. 1, No. 2, pp. 91–103.

Holden, N.J. (1994) 'International HRM with vision', in D.P. Torrington, *International Human Resource Management*. Hemel Hempstead: Prentice Hall International.

Hopfl, H. (1993) 'Culture and commitment: British Airways', in D. Gowler, K. Legge and C. Clegg (eds), *Case Studies in Organizational Behaviour*, 2nd edn. London: Paul Chapman Publishing.

Keily, D. (1991) 'Body Shop blues', *The Sunday Times*, 8 December, p. 3.

Kobrin, S.J. (1988) 'Expatriate reduction and strategic control in American multi-national corporations', *Human Resource Management*, Vol. 27, No. 1, pp. 63–75.

Miles, R.E. and Snow, C.E. (1984) 'Fit, failure and the hall of fame', *California Management Review*, Vol. 26, No. 3, pp. 10–28.

Pascale, R.T. (1978) 'Communication and decision making across cultures: Japanese and American comparisons', *Administrative Science Quarterly*, March, pp. 91–110.

Peters, T.J. (1989) *Thriving on Chaos*. London: Pan Books.

Richards-Carpenter, C. (1994) 'Why the CPIS is a Disappointment', *Personnel Management*, Vol. 26, No. 5, pp. 63–4.

Rumelt, R.P. (1982) 'Diversification strategy and profitability', *Strategic Management Journal*, Vol. 3, pp. 359–69.

Sapolsky, H. (1972) *The Polaris System Development*. Cambridge, Mass: Harvard University Press.

Schein, E.H. (1985) *Organizational Culture and Leadership*. San Francisco: Jossey-Bass.

Stoner, J.A.F. and Freeman, R.E. (1992) *Management*, 5th edn. Englewood Cliffs, NJ: Prentice Hall Inc.

Waterman, R.H. and Peters, T.J. (1980) 'Structure is not organisation', *Business Horizons*, June.

General discussion topics

1 How do you understand the ideas of evangelisation, parables, apostles and standards and norms? What are the advantages and drawbacks of using religious imagery in this context?

2 What lessons should Henry, Fiona and Barry learn from their discussions?

3 What is the difference between information and communication?